NYC ACCESS®

Orientation

Sophisticated and brutal. Exhilarating and oppressive. Earthy and aloof. A thorough description of New York City might exhaust the largest vocabulary. New York is indeed a city of dynamic contrasts, from the sleek granite high-rises of **Wall Street** and **Midtown** to the decaying old tenements of the **Bowery** and the **Bronx**, from the bohemian spirit of **Greenwich Village** to the old-money atmosphere of the **East Side**, and from the avant-garde art galleries of **SoHo** to the graffiti-covered subway stations of **Harlem**.

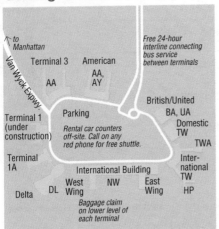

Weighted down by wall-to-wall buildings and seven million people, New York in its density may seem relentless and chaotic to first-time visitors. But it's essentially a city of small neighborhoods best explored one at a time. Don't exhaust yourself by trying to race from one end of the city to the other in the hopes of seeing "everything." Instead, make a list of must-sees in each neighborhood and enjoy all they have to offer before moving on to the next.

One of New York's chief attractions *is* the overwhelming number of places to visit. The city is home to many of the world's best restaurants, shops, and museums, as well as a glittering theater scene. But every night on the town doesn't have to include dinner at a four-star restaurant and a Broadway show to be memorable, and you don't have to spend your days splurging in the expensive shops on Fifth Avenue. Some of New York's greatest pleasures are simple and inexpensive: sitting on the front steps of the **Metropolitan Museum of Art** and watching a mime while eating a hot dog; whiling away an hour in a cafe, sipping a cappuccino as the world goes by the window; walking through **Central Park** on a clear day and gazing up at the brilliant blue sky above the tall buildings; and, when you've said and done as much as you can, waving good-bye to the **Statue of Liberty** from the window of a departing plane, humming "New York, New York."

Area code 212 unless otherwise noted.

Getting to New York City

to Manhattan

Van Wyck Expwy

Terminal 3   American
    AA   AA, AY

Free 24-hour interline connecting bus service between terminals

British/United
BA, UA

Terminal 1 (under construction)   Parking

Rental car counters off-site. Call on any red phone for free shuttle.

Domestic TW
TWA

Terminal 1A

International Building
    West Wing   NW   East Wing

Inter-national TW
HP

Delta   DL

Baggage claim on lower level of each terminal

Airports

For convenient money-saving ways to get to the following airports, call **AIR RIDE** at 800/AIR.RIDE for information on buses, trains, and vans.

John F. Kennedy International Airport (JFK)

The area's largest airport is located about 15 miles east of Manhattan in the borough of Queens and, depending on traffic, travel time can take anywhere from 45 to 90 minutes. Most transatlantic flights, as well as many domestic flights, arrive and depart from JFK. Terminals are connected by shuttle buses.

JFK Airport Information

Airport Emergency 718/656.4333
Airport Information............................718/656.4520
Airport Police 718/656.4668
Customs...718/553.1648
Dental Service 718/656.4747
Ground Transportation 800/247.7433

Immigration	718/533.1688
Lost & Found	718/244.4225
Lost or damaged baggage	See airline representatives
Medical Clinic	718/656.5344
Paging	Call individual airline
Parking Availability	718/656.5699
Traveler's Aid	718/656.4870

Rental Cars

Call for shuttles for the following companies on the red phones in any terminal:

Avis	718/244.5400
Budget	718/656.6010
Dollar	718/656.2400
Hertz	718/656.7600
National	718/632.8300

Getting to town from JFK

The best way into Manhattan by car is to take the Van Wyck Expressway to the Grand Central Parkway, which connects with the Long Island Expressway (LIE). Those going to downtown Manhattan (or to Brooklyn) should exit the LIE onto the Brooklyn-Queens Expressway (BQE). The BQE, in turn, feeds into the Williamsburg, Manhattan, and Brooklyn bridges. For Midtown destinations, continue on the LIE, which connects with the Queens-Midtown Tunnel.

Taxis from the airport can be hailed outside all major domestic and international arrival buildings. An airport employee is usually on hand if you have any questions or need assistance. A cab ride to Midtown Manhattan should cost $30 to $35, plus tunnel or bridge tolls and a tip (generally 15 percent).

Car services usually provide transportation to, but not always from, the airport. They're a good bet when you must leave for the airport during rush hour and a taxi can't be found. Rates are set in advance and are typically the same as a cab ride ($30 to $35, or $75 for a limousine). Many companies accept credit cards and offer standard as well as luxury cars and limousines. Try the following companies: **City Ride** (861.1000); **Olympic Limousine** (800/872.0044); **Tel Aviv** (505.0555); **Timely Wheels** (645.9888). Also see additional companies on page 7.

Bus service includes **Carey Transportation, Inc.** buses (718/632.0500), which depart JFK every 30 minutes from 6AM to midnight. All buses stop at Grand Central Terminal and Port Authority. Buses also depart to Queens every 30 minutes (5:30AM to 11PM) and to Brooklyn every 60 minutes (8:30AM to 8:30PM). The last departure from Grand Central to JFK is 1AM. Travel time is about an hour. **Gray Line Air Shuttle Buses** (315.3006) run from the airport to nearly 50 hotels in Manhattan every 15 minutes from 7AM to 11PM, and hourly from Manhattan to the airports. Travel time is about an hour.

Helicopter flights to and from JFK can be arranged through several companies. **New York Helicopter** (800/645.3494) offers a total of 12 10-minute shuttles, taking off from 9:50AM until 7:55PM, from the American Airlines terminal No. 3 to the E. 34th Street Heliport. Some airlines include the cost of the ride for passengers with first- or business-class tickets. Otherwise, the cost is $70 to $75. See page 7 for additional helicopter services.

La Guardia Airport (LGA)

Located closer to Manhattan in northwest Queens, La Guardia is eight miles northeast of the city, or about a 30-minute drive. Most airlines serving other American cities use the two-level main terminal. Delta Airlines shares a terminal with Northwest, and USAir has a shuttle terminal. Terminals are connected by shuttle buses.

LGA Airport Information

Airport Information	718/533.3400
Airport Police	718/533.3900
Customs	718/476.4378
Ground Transportation	800/247.7433
Lost or damaged baggage	See airline representatives in baggage-claim area
Paging	718/565.3945

Rental Cars

The following companies have desks on the lower level by baggage claim:

Avis	718/507.3600
Budget	718/639.6400
Dollar	718/779.5600
Hertz	718/478.5300
National	718/803.4101

Getting to town from La Guardia

If you're traveling to the city by car, you could take Grand Central Parkway to the Triborough Bridge, then travel south on the FDR Drive. Or, if you want to save time and the toll, get off at the Van Dam Street exit just before the Triborough Bridge, turn south on Van Dam/21st Street, and you'll meet up with the Queensborough Bridge (59th Street Bridge) going into Manhattan. If your destination is downtown (SoHo or Wall Street), take the Brooklyn-Queens Expressway to the Williamsburg Bridge, which exits at Delancey Street.

Taxis depart from in front of La Guardia's major terminals around the clock. The cost to Midtown is generally $20 to $25, plus bridge and tunnel tolls and tip (15 percent).

Car services are also available. See JFK Airport at left for more information.

Orientation

Buses include **Triborough Coach** (718/335.1000), which runs a 24-hour bus service from La Guardia's main terminal to the Jackson Heights 74th Street subway station in Queens for connections into Manhattan. The trip takes about 30 minutes. **Carey Transportation, Inc.** (718/632.0500) runs buses between La Guardia and Manhattan every 20 minutes from 6:45AM to midnight, to Queens every 30 minutes from 6:30AM to 11PM, and to Brooklyn every 60 minutes from 9:15AM to 9:15PM. **Gray Line Air Shuttle Buses** (315.3006) run from the airport to nearly 50 hotels in Manhattan every 20 minutes from 7AM to 11PM; also hourly from Manhattan to the airports. Travel time is about an hour. Limousine service may be obtained at booths within individual terminals.

Delta Water Shuttle (800/543.3779) is a high-speed boat that departs the Marine Air Terminal several times each weekday morning and early evening. Travel time is approximately 25 minutes to 34th Street and 40 minutes to Wall Street.

Newark International Airport (EWR)
Local traffic snafus are making Newark a popular choice, especially if your final destination is the West Side or downtown Manhattan. Located on Newark Bay, 16 miles southwest of Manhattan (30 minutes to an hour traveling time), it has one international and two domestic terminals, with shuttle bus connections.

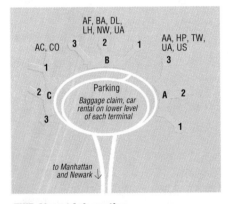

EWR Airport Information
Airport Information.............................201/961.6000
Airport Police/Lost & Found 201/961.6230
Customs...201/645.3409
Immigration......................................201/645.3239
Ground Transportation 800/247.7433
Paging.....................................Call individual airline
Parking Availability...........................201/961.4751

Rental Cars
The following are located in the baggage-claim area and are open daily from 7AM to midnight (the return lots are open for 24 hours):
Avis 800/331.1212
Budget...800/527.0700
Hertz..800/654.3131
National 800/227.7368

Getting to town from Newark International
The route to Manhattan by car is fairly straightforward. Take the New Jersey Turnpike and follow the signs to either the Holland Tunnel (downtown) or the Lincoln Tunnel (Midtown).

Taxis to Midtown cost $25 to $35. See page 3 for more information on **Car Services.**

Bus service includes **New Jersey Transit** (201/762.5100; in New Jersey, 800/772.2222), which offers 24-hour bus service every 15 to 30 minutes to Port Authority. It also offers rail service to Newark's Penn Station every 20 to 30 minutes from 6AM to 2AM. **Olympia Trails** (964.6233) runs buses from Newark to 1 World Trade Center every 30 minutes (Monday to Saturday 6:45AM to 8:45PM; Sunday, holidays 7:15AM to 8:15PM) and 41st Street at Park Avenue and 34th Street at Eighth Avenue every 20 to 30 minutes daily from 6:15AM to midnight. The ride lasts from 30 to 45 minutes. **Gray Line Air Shuttle Buses** (315.3006) run from the airport to nearly 50 hotels in Manhattan every 20 minutes from 7AM to 11PM; also hourly from Manhattan to the airports. Travel time is about an hour. **Limousine** service may be obtained at booths within individual terminals.

Airlines
Air Canada (AC) 800/776.3000
Air France (AF)...................247.0100, 800/237.2747
Air India (AI) 751.6200, 800/442.4455
Alitalia (AZ) 582.8900, 800/223.5730
American Airlines (AA).......................800/433.7300
America West (HP) 800/247.5692
British Airways (BA)...........................800/247.9297
Continental Airlines (CO).....319.9494, 800/525.0280
Delta Airlines (DL)..............239.0700, 800/221.1212
El Al Airlines (LY)...............768.9200, 800/223.6700
Finnair (AY)........................889.7070, 800/950.5000
Icelandair (FI).....................967.8888, 800/223.5500
Japan Air Lines (JL)...........838.4400, 800/525.3663
KLM Royal Dutch
   Airlines (KL).................................800/374.7747
Lufthansa (LH)............718/895.1277, 800/645.3880
Midway Airlines (JI)...........................800/446.4392
Midwest Express (YX)..718/565.3296, 800/452.2022
Northwest (NW)
   Domestic.......................................800/225.2525
   International...................................800/447.4747
Swissair (SR)..............718/995.8400, 800/221.4750
TWA (TW)
   Domestic.........................290.2121, 800/221.2000
   International....................290.2141, 800/892.4141
United Airlines (UA) 800/241.6522
USAir (US) 800/428.4322

Train and Bus Terminals
Since 1990, there has been a marked improvement in New York City's train and bus stations, thanks to an increased police presence as well as millions of dollars in renovation work.

Grand Central Terminal in the heart of Midtown Manhattan is the hub of the **Metro-North Commuter Railroad.** The New Haven, Harlem, and Hudson lines service New York State and Connecticut. For train information, call 532.4900.

Pennsylvania Station, between W. 31st and W. 33rd streets and Seventh and Eighth avenues, services all long-distance trains, including **Amtrak** (800/872.7245), **Metroliner** (800/523.8720), plus the **Long Island Railroad** (718/990.7400) and **New Jersey Transit** (201/762.5100) commuter trains.

The **Port Authority Bus Terminal,** located between W. 40th and W. 42nd streets and Eighth and Ninth avenues, is the departure and arrival point for all long-distance buses, commuter buses, and bus links to the airports. **Greyhound** has a separate ticket counter from the **Short Line** commuter line. For general information, call 564.8484.

Getting around New York City

Perhaps the most crucial element of your stay is mastering the city's transportation services and routes. The five major ways of getting around are subway, bus, taxi, car service, and foot. Of these, walking is the most highly recommended, and sometimes the quickest. Manhattan is laid out in a rather easy-to-grasp grid of north-south avenues and east/west numbered streets. Bear in mind that Fifth Avenue is the dividing line between east and west. Below Houston Street, the numbered streets end, and parts of downtown (Greenwich Village in particular) can get a little tricky, since the streets there were laid out during the time of horse-drawn carriages.

Think twice about **driving** a car to get around New York. City traffic is nightmarish, parking on the street is impossible, and parking garages are outrageously expensive. If you must arrive by car, it's best to stash it away in a parking garage and then use alternative means of transportation. Hotels sometimes offer discounted parking rates to their guests (even the most expensive hotels charge extra). Parking tickets are given without mercy, so don't park at a meter that isn't working, and be sure you understand the convoluted restrictions posted on parking signs so your car isn't towed— something that happens all too frequently.

Subways may be loud, dirty, and crowded, but they are the most efficient way to conquer longer distances within Manhattan. Actually, most of the graffiti-riddled cars have been replaced with sleeker modern cars that are air-conditioned in the summer and heated in winter.

Consult the subway map in this book (see page 10); the system is complicated and not immediately decipherable. Entrance requires the purchase of a token, which allows you to travel its length and breadth (and to make unlimited connections). Tokens are available at token booths at most stations as well as at some McDonald's restaurants and at newsstands. It's wise to purchase tokens in 10-packs if you're planning to ride often. The city recently introduced **Metrocard,** for prepaid subway access; it is available in $5 increments up to $80. By the end of 1994, it should be accepted in 70 stations. The subway system is open 24 hours, although at night it can be a lonesome wait.

Buses are a lot slower, but you have the satisfaction of seeing where you're going. A sign on the front of each bus gives its route number and final destination, and stops are clearly marked on the street, sometimes with maps showing the route served (although not every bus serves every stop). In addition to the longer-distance routes that run on the north-south avenues, there are many crosstown bus routes. (Request a transfer from the driver when you get on, so that if you're going, say, north and then west across town, you don't have to pay a second fare on the crosstown route, or vice versa.) During rush hours, buses marked "Limited" function like express subway lines and stop only at major intersections. Exact change or a bus token is required.

Taxis seem to rule the streets of New York City. In fact, there are nearly 12,000 licensed cabs—a meaningless number if you can't find one when you need one. Licensed cabs are bright yellow and signal their availability through a light on the roof. Cabs may be hailed anywhere on the street, except for crosswalks and intersections, and by law they are supposed to take you wherever you wish to go. But be forewarned—New York cab drivers are an independent bunch. The taxi rates are posted on the side of the cab, or sometimes stickered inside, and after 8PM there is a 50 cent nighttime surcharge. A cab ride in New York can be colorful, amusing, and efficient, or hellish and frustrating, depending on the traffic and the driver.

Car services and so-called **gypsy cabs** (generally owner-operated and not as strictly controlled as licensed cabs) have sprung up in town simply because yellow cabs will often not go where you wish to go—particularly to the outerboroughs or to Harlem and Washington Heights. Or you may find yourself visiting until a late hour and wish to have a car at your door rather than trying to hail one on the avenue. Car services and gypsy cabs are noted by their "livery" license plates. Car services are listed in the *Yellow Pages* and gypsy cabs can be hailed on the street—if you have to. Negotiate the fare *before* you reach your destination.

Ferries can be a good bet for crossing water. The **Staten Island Ferry** is still one of the cheapest thrills in New York City, running every 20 to 30 minutes 24 hours daily from the foot of Whitehall Street (next to Battery Park). Other ferries run between the City and New Jersey, including the **Hoboken-Battery Park City Ferry,** the **Port Imperial Ferry,** and **TNT Hydrolines.** See page 7 for phone numbers.

FYI

Climate The best months to visit New York are May, June, September, and October. July and particularly August can be oppressively hot, with high humidity and temperatures hovering in the 90s. December through February are the coldest months, with blustery winds and temperatures in the 20s and below.

Drinking The legal drinking age is 21, and many bars, restaurants, and clubs require ID. Bar hours vary (all are closed before noon on Sunday), but the legal limit for closing is 4AM. On Sunday, restaurants may not serve alcohol until noon, and liquor stores are closed, but beer, which is sold in grocery stores, may be purchased after noon.

Hours It's a good idea to call ahead to find out if a particular restaurant or shop will be open the day and time you plan to visit. Although this book provides business hours for shops, museums, galleries, and other places, keep in mind that this information may change with the seasons, the economy, or even the whim of the owner.

Money Most Citibank branches and American Express will exchange foreign currency at current market rates. Most banks won't charge a fee if the amount changed is more than $200. Traveler's checks may be purchased at most banks.

Newspapers and Periodicals There are four daily papers: the *New York Times,* the *New York Post,* the *Daily News,* and *Newsday;* and a number of weekly publications, including *New York Magazine, The New Yorker,* and *The Village Voice,* that have excellent listings and information.

Smoking It is illegal to smoke on all public transportation, in the lobbies of office buildings, in enclosed public places, in taxis, in designated areas of theaters and restaurants, and in most shops.

Street Smarts Cities attract every type of person, and that includes the worst. It is perhaps less a commentary about New York than about the times to say that you have to be alert on the street (and in buildings, the subways, etc.) and to try not to advertise helplessness, naïveté, or confusion, lest you risk attracting unsolicited assistance. Common sense dos and don'ts: Don't display your good jewelry on the subway. Don't make eye contact with people who impart a sense of danger or derangement, even though they may seem exotic to you. (View the scene from a safe distance, if you must.) Carry your purse with the clasp side against your body. Don't carry your wallet in a back pants pocket or in a way that causes it to bulge. Don't let strangers carry packages for you. If you see trouble coming, avoid it.

Telephone As of this writing, it costs 25 cents to make a local call from a pay phone. Manhattan is in the 212 area code; Brooklyn, the Bronx, Queens, and Staten Island calls require dialing 1, and then the 718 prefix.

Tipping A 15 to 20 percent gratuity is standard. In restaurants, most people simply double the sales tax. Taxi drivers are tipped 15 percent of the meter reading. Hotel bellhops and station porters expect a dollar for each bag they carry. A tip is a reward for service; if you don't get it, don't pay for it.

Visitor Information For information, brochures, maps, lists of special events, theater discount coupons, and knowledgeable help, stop by the **N.Y. Convention and Visitors Bureau** at 2 Columbus Circle (on Central Park South at Central Park West), or call 397.8200. Hours are Monday through Friday from 9AM to 5PM.

Phone Book

Area code 212 unless otherwise noted.

Emergencies

Ambulance/Fire/Police	**911**
Animal Medical Center	838.8100
Arson Hotline	718/403.1300
ASPCA	876.7700
Child Abuse and Maltreatment Reporting Center	800/342.3720
Coast Guard	668.7936
Deaf Emergency Teletypewriter (police, fire, and ambulance services)	800/342.4357
Dental	679.3966
Electrical Emergency	718/409.7100
FBI	335.2700
Lost and Found: Bus and Subway	718/330.3000
Medical	718/238.2100
NYC Taxi & Limousine Commission	302.8294
NYC Transit Authority (subway and bus information)	718/330.1234
Poison Control	764.7667 or 340.4494
State Police–New York City	374.5000

General Information

Dow Jones Report	976.4141
Municipal Art Society	935.3960
Time	976.1616
Weather	976.1212
Western Union	800/325.6000

Service

Able Messengers	687.5515
Cycle Carriers	925.9225
Kaufman Pharmacy (24 hours)	755.2266
Mid City Duplicating	687.6699
Night & Day Locksmith	722.1017
Village Copy Center	924.3456

Auto Rental

Avis	800/331.1212
Budget	800/527.0700
Dollar	800/365.5276
Hertz	800/654.3131

National 800/227.7368
Thrifty..800/367.2277

Auto Service (for members only)
AAA Highway Condition............................757.2000
AAA Road Service.....................................757.3356

Bus Service
George Washington Bridge
  Bus Station 568.5323
Greyhound..800/231.2222
New York Bus Service 718/994.5500
Port Authority Bus Terminal 564.8484

Ferry Service (to and from Manhattan)
Delta Water Shuttle..............................800/543.3779
Hoboken-Battery Park City Ferry 201/420.6307
Port Imperial (Weehawken,
  New Jersey) ....201/902.8850 or 201/902.8735
Staten Island
  (St. George, Staten Island) 806.6940
Statue of Liberty and Ellis Island 269.5755
TNT Hydrolines.....................................800/262.8743

Helicopter Service
Island Helicopter..925.8807
Jet Aviation Executive Air Fleet...........800/736.8538

New York Helicopter............................800/645.3494
Wall Street Helicopter 943.5959

Heliports
Port Authority W. 30th Street Heliport.......563.4442

Limousine Service
Carey 718/632.0500
Fugazy 661.0100
London Towncars.......................................988.9700

Rail Service
Amtrak...582.6875
Long Island Railroad 718/217.5477
Metro North...532.4900
Metropolitan Transportation Authority.......878.7000
New Jersey Transit (bus and train).....201/762.5100
  in New Jersey...................................800/772.2222
PATH Line...800/234.7284
Transit Authority.................................718/330.1234

Taxi/Car Service
All City Transportation 718/402.4747
Carmel...662.2222
Davel 645.4242
Intra-boro 344.4763
Minute Man...718/899.5600

Manhattan Address Locator

To locate avenue addresses, take the address, cancel the last figure, divide by two, then add or subtract the key number below. The answer is the nearest numbered cross street, approximately. For example, to find the cross street to 1650 Broadway, take half of 165 (roughly 83) and subtract 30 as indicated below. The answer is 53rd Street.

To find addresses on numbered cross streets, remember that numbers above Eighth Street increase east or west from Fifth Avenue, which runs north-south. Below Eighth Street, Broadway is the dividing line.

Avenues A, B, C, D ....Add 3
First Avenue ....Add 3
Second Avenue..Add 3
Third Avenue ....Add 10
Fourth Avenue ....Add 8
Fifth Avenue
  Up to 200 ....Add 13
  Up to 400 ....Add 16
  Up to 600 ....Add 18
  Up to 775 ....Add 20
  775-1286 ....Cancel last figure and subtract 18
  1286-1500..Add 45
  Above 2000 ....Add 24
Avenue of the Americas
  (Sixth Avenue)....................................Subtract 12
Seventh Avenue...Add 12
  Above 110th Street.....................................Add 20
Eighth Avenue ....Add 10
Ninth Avenue ....Add 13
10th Avenue ....Add 14
Amsterdam Avenue ....Add 60

Audubon Avenue ....Add 165
Broadway (23rd-192nd streets) ....Subtract 30
Columbus Avenue ....Add 60
Convent Avenue ....Add 127
Central Park West..........Divide house number by 10
    and add 60
Edgecombe Avenue ....Add 134
Ft. Washington Avenue.................................Add 158
Lenox Avenue...Add 110
Lexington Avenue...Add 22
Madison Avenue...Add 26
Manhattan Avenue..Add 100
Park Avenue ....Add 35
Pleasant Avenue ....Add 101
Riverside Drive
  (up to 165th Street) ....Divide house number
    by 10 and add 72
St. Nicholas Avenue ....Add 110
Wadsworth Avenue ....Add 173
West End Avenue ....Add 60
York Avenue ....Add 4

Giovanni da Verrazzano, an Italian-born navigator sailing for France, was the first European to see New York, when he discovered New York Bay in 1524. Henry Hudson, an Englishman employed by the Dutch, reached the bay and sailed up the river now bearing his name in 1609, the same year that northern New York was explored and claimed for France by Samuel de Champlain.

New York Speak

In George Orwell's *1984,* society is undermined by a language called "newspeak," sophisticated words and phrases that actually mean nothing at all.

New Yorkers have taken the opposite tack by cultivating a series of unique and simple phrases that, once understood, speak volumes. Here, then, is a simple guide to some of the more trenchant vocabulary:

Greetings and Such

Yo Could mean "Pardon me," "Watch it, you," or "Pleased to see you, my good man."

Watcha closin' doors Courtesy warning sometimes given to subway passengers by their conductor. Followed by shouts of "Yo!" when passengers are still boarding.

Cuisine

Grab a slice To purchase and consume pizza.

The Original Ray's Refers to a famed establishment on Sixth Avenue at 11th Street, whose name has since been used by dozens of imitators. See "grab a slice."

A shmear Refers to a small portion of cream cheese to be smeared upon a bagel.

A regular A cup of coffee with milk, no sugar.

A black A cup of coffee with sugar, no milk.

Wait on them Contrary to popular practice, something that waiters tell customers to do, as in "You're gonna have to wait on them fries."

Geography

The Deuce 42nd Street.

The Island Long Island. Not used to refer to Staten Island. Never, but never, used to refer to Manhattan.

Martha The lower level of the George Washington Bridge.

Uptown When used in Greenwich Village or points south, refers to the area above 14th Street.

Upstate Anywhere north of New York City, within New York State.

Over there New Jersey.

Consumerism

Bloomie's Bloomingdale's department store, as in "I saw her in Bloomie's." Not to be confused with underwear.

Boom box Portable stereo the size of a station wagon. The louder it is, the closer it must be held to the ear.

Standing on line Known everywhere else in the world as "standing in line."

Fashion victim Someone whose clothes and makeup are too trendy to wear anywhere but at a photo shoot.

East Village type The flip side of "fashion victim"; someone whose clothes and makeup are too urban funky to wear anywhere but on Avenue D.

Sample sales Sales of leftover or sample merchandise held by manufacturers in the Garment District. Although some *garmentos* like to keep the best sales a secret (more for them), they are often advertised to the public in the back of *New York Magazine* and on flyers handed out on the street or adhered to lampposts and mailboxes.

Can't afford not to buy Sales pitch. See intro.

Lotto fever An affliction that compels people to wait on line for hours for a one-in-26-million chance at wealth, although it's more likely they'll be crushed by a meteor while watching "Jeopardy" that night. Its seriousness increases as the jackpot grows.

Two-fer A theater coupon that entitles the bearer to two tickets for the price of one (plus a surcharge) to the show for which the two-fer is issued. Available next to the register at many stores; in addition, there's usually a good supply at the Convention and Visitors Bureau at Columbus Circle.

Our Fair Streets

Don't Block the Box Warning to drivers meaning "Do not drive into the intersection until there is room to cross it."

Gridlock The traffic jam that results when someone "blocks the box."

Don't Even THINK of Parking Here Courteous street sign provided by the city. Usually ignored.

Alternate parking Rules in which the side of the street one may park on is determined by the hour and day of the week.

Bridge-and-tunnel people Commuters from New Jersey and Long Island. See "Over there."

No Radio Posted on car windows as an appeal to thieves who might be tempted to break in without checking to see that the radio has been removed.

New York, Home Style

Due to unconscionable hotel expenses, many travelers have turned to bed-and-breakfast inns. A time-honored tradition in Europe, these services are becoming increasingly popular here, placing visitors in the homes of accommodating New York hosts. Beyond the attraction of saving money, most B&B guests enjoy meeting new people in the relaxed atmosphere of a home, which can make a world of difference to travelers who find the city daunting.

Here are some of the B&B services with listings in the New York area. Since B&Bs are not hotels, you must call or write well in advance of your arrival.

Abode Bed & Breakfast, Ltd. PO Box 20022, New York, NY 10028. 472.2000, 800/835.8880 (good only outside of tri-state area)

City Lights Bed & Breakfast PO Box 20355, Cherokee Station, New York, NY 10028. 737.7049; fax 535.2755

New World Bed & Breakfast 150 Fifth Avenue, Suite 711, New York, NY 10011. 675.5600, 800/443.3800; fax 675.6366

Urban Ventures, Inc. PO Box 426, New York, NY 10024. 594.5650; fax 947.9320

How to Read this Guide

NEW YORK CITYACCESS® is arranged so you can see at a glance where you are and what is around you. The numbers next to the entries in the following chapters correspond to the numbers on the maps. The text is color-coded according to the kind of place described:

Restaurants/Clubs: Red   **Hotels:** Blue

Shops/ 📍 Outdoors: Green   **Sights/Culture:** Black

Rating the Restaurants and Hotels

The restaurant star ratings take into account the quality, service, atmosphere, and uniqueness of the restaurant. An expensive restaurant doesn't necessarily ensure an enjoyable evening; however, a small, relatively unknown spot could have good food, professional service, and a lovely atmosphere. Therefore, on a purely subjective basis, stars are used to judge the overall dining value (see the star ratings above right). Keep in mind that chefs and owners often change, which sometimes drastically affects the quality of a restaurant. The ratings in this guidebook are based on information available at press time.

The price ratings, as categorized above at right, apply to restaurants and hotels. These figures describe general price-range relationships among other res-taurants and hotels in the area. The restaurant price ratings are based on the average cost of an entrée for one person, excluding tax and tip. Hotel price ratings reflect the base price of a standard room for two people for one night during the peak season.

Restaurants

★	Good	
★★	Very Good	
★★★	Excellent	
★★★★	An Extraordinary Experience	
$	The Price Is Right	(less than $10)
$$	Reasonable	($10-$15)
$$$	Expensive	($15-$20)
$$$$	Big Bucks	($20 and up)

Hotels

$	The Price Is Right	(less than $100)
$$	Reasonable	($100-$150)
$$$	Expensive	($150-$250)
$$$$	Big Bucks	($250 and up)

Map Key

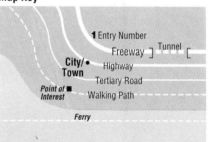

Walter Cronkite
Newscaster Emeritus, CBS Evening News

Museum of Broadcasting.

South Street Seaport Museum.

Staten Island Ferry. Best $1 ride in the city. Magnificent view of Lower Manhattan.

Cable ride from Manhattan to **Roosevelt Island.** Exciting view of the East River.

Ellis Island. Where freedom began for many Americans.

Brooklyn Botanic Garden. Where bonsai and horticultural beauty abound.

Gracie Mansion.

Clarke's Bar. A saloon at the corner of 55th Street and Third Avenue in the best tradition of the old New York City saloons before they tore down the el.

Zabar's, the deli supreme. However, almost any deli in New York should be visited for its smells and sights.

City Hall. A magnificent example of Federal architecture.

The **John Finley Walk** along the East River near **Gracie Square,** where you can watch the ships coming down the river.

Edward Kosner
Editor and Publisher, *New York Magazine*

Lunch in the **Grill Room** of the **Four Seasons.**

Chili and a bacon-cheeseburger in the back room of **P.J. Clarke's.**

The **Carousel** in **Central Park.**

The **Cloisters.**

The **Century Association Clubhouse.**

Café des Artistes.

The gallery with the fountain at **The Frick Collection.**

Fifth Avenue from 12th Street to Washington Square.

The promenade at **Battery Park City.**

Le Cirque at lunch.

The view of Midtown Manhattan from the riverside in Long Island City.

The **Metropolitan Opera** in top form.

The **Oak Bar** at the Plaza at dusk on a winter evening.

Madison Square Garden when the Knicks are hot.

"New York is a city of dreams."

                                    Isaac Bashevis Singer

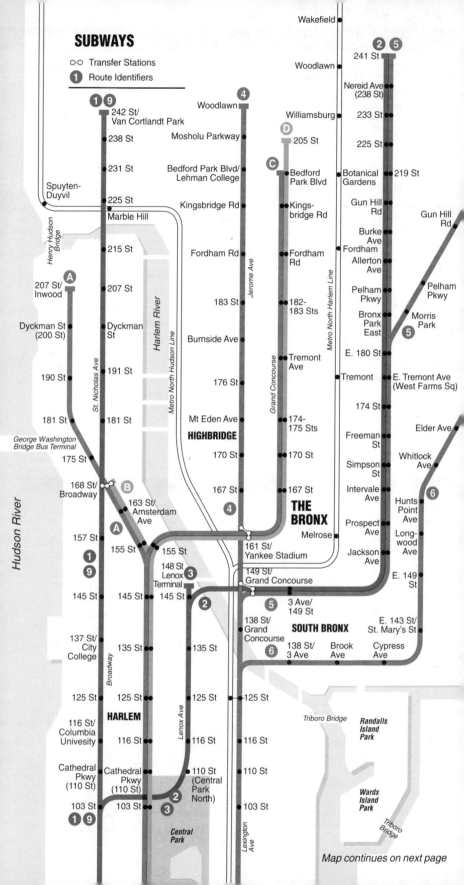

SUBWAYS

- ○—○ Transfer Stations
- ❶ Route Identifiers

② ⑤ 241 St
Wakefield
Woodlawn
Nereid Ave (238 St)
233 St
Williamsburg
225 St
Ⓓ 205 St
219 St
Ⓒ Bedford Park Blvd
Botanical Gardens
Gun Hill Rd
Kingsbridge Rd
Gun Hill Rd
Burke Ave
Fordham
Allerton Ave
Pelham Pkwy
Bronx Park East
Morris Park
⑤

① ⑨ 242 St/ Van Cortlandt Park
238 St
231 St
225 St
Marble Hill
215 St
207 St
Dyckman St
191 St
181 St

Spuyten-Duyvil

Henry Hudson Bridge

Ⓐ 207 St/ Inwood
Dyckman St (200 St)
190 St
181 St

George Washington Bridge Bus Terminal

175 St
168 St/ Broadway **Ⓑ**
163 St/ Amsterdam Ave **Ⓐ**
157 St
155 St
①
⑨
148 St Lenox Terminal

145 St
145 St
145 St

137 St/ City College
135 St
135 St

Harlem River
Metro North Hudson Line
St. Nicholas Ave
Broadway

Hudson River

④ Woodlawn
Mosholu Parkway
Bedford Park Blvd/ Lehman College
Kingsbridge Rd
Fordham Rd
183 St
Burnside Ave
176 St
Mt Eden Ave
HIGHBRIDGE
170 St
167 St
④

Jerome Ave

Ⓓ 205 St
Bedford Park Blvd
Kingsbridge Rd
Fordham Rd
182-183 Sts
Tremont Ave
174-175 Sts
170 St
167 St
THE BRONX
Melrose

Grand Concourse
Metro North Harlem Line

161 St/ Yankee Stadium
149 St/ Grand Concourse
⑤ 3 Ave/ 149 St

E. 180 St
Tremont
E. Tremont Ave (West Farms Sq)
174 St
Freeman St
Simpson St
Intervale Ave
Prospect Ave
Jackson Ave
E. 149 St

Elder Ave
Whitlock Ave
Hunts Point Ave **⑥**
Long-wood Ave
E. 143 St/ St. Mary's St

138 St/ Grand Concourse
⑥
138 St/ 3 Ave
Brook Ave
Cypress Ave
SOUTH BRONX

② 145 St
③ 145 St

155 St

149 St/ Grand Concourse

135 St

Lenox Ave

125 St
125 St
125 St
125 St

HARLEM

116 St/ Columbia Univesity
116 St
116 St
116 St

Cathedral Pkwy (110 St)
Cathedral Pkwy (110 St)
110 St (Central Park North)
110 St

103 St
103 St
103 St
103 St
① ⑨
②
③

Lexington Ave

Central Park

Triboro Bridge
Randalls Island Park

Wards Island Park

Triboro Bridge

Map continues on next page

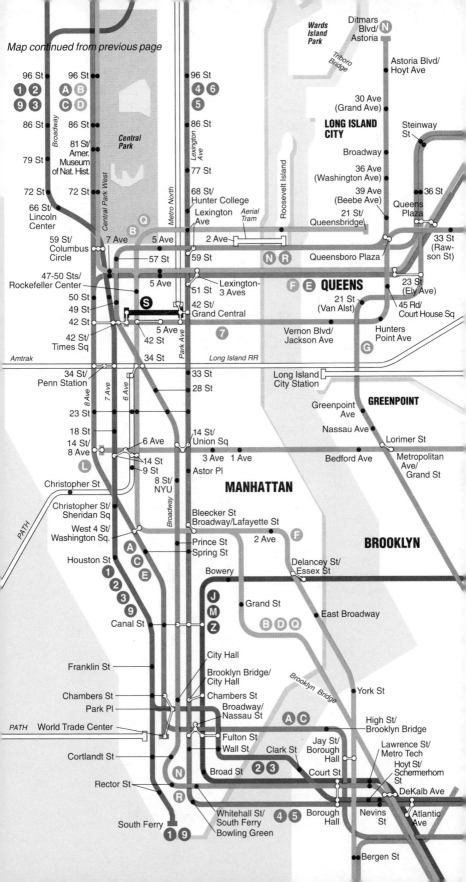

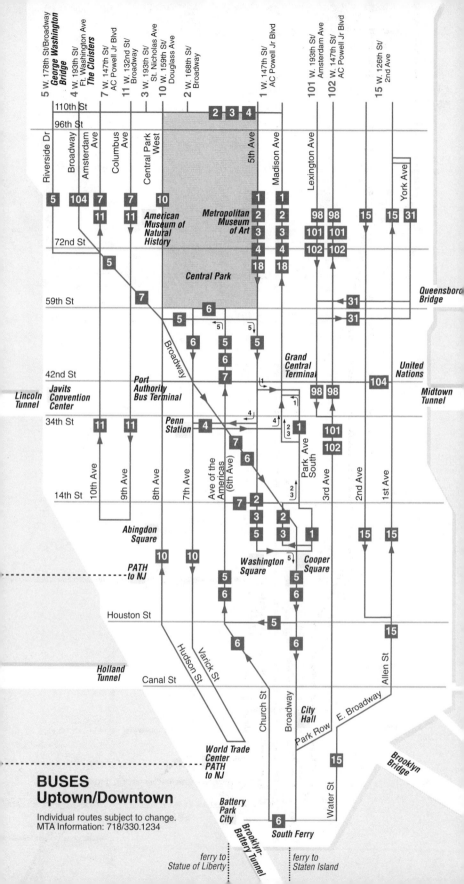

BUSES
Uptown/Downtown

Individual routes subject to change.
MTA Information: 718/330.1234

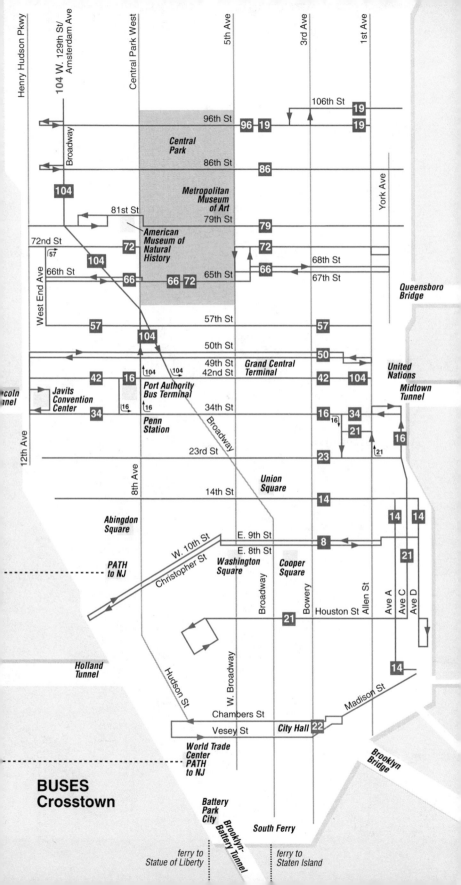

**BUSES
Crosstown**

Lower Manhattan

It all began on Lower Manhattan island, bounded by **Chambers Street** and the **East** and **Hudson rivers.** Here, at the confluence of these majestic waterways, the earliest explorers—**Giovanni da Verrazano, Esteban Gómez,** and **Henry Hudson**—first touched land. And it was here, in 1625, that the Dutch set up **Fort Amsterdam** to protect the southern perimeter of their settlement, called "Nieuw Amsterdam." The skyscrapers and canyons of today's **Financial District** stand where the tiny Dutch settlement, which later became the prime residential enclave of post-Revolutionary New York, once flourished.

The narrow alleys of the Financial District are a reminder of the scale of colonial America. But, except for a few fragments of old foundations, not a single building erected during the 40 years of Dutch rule remains. When the British Army withdrew in 1783 after seven years of occupation, the village of New York—which covered 10 blocks north from what is now Battery Park—lay almost totally in ruins. But once New York City pulled itself together and began to push north, the city grew swiftly. Two blocks of low-rise commercial buildings from this early surge of development have survived: the **Fraunces Tavern** block and **Schermerhorn Row.**

When **City Hall**—the one still in use today—was being built in 1811 on the northernmost fringe of town, the north side of the building was covered with common brownstone, instead of marble, because no one ever expected the building to be seen from that side. But by 1820, New York City had expanded another 10 to 15 blocks, and by 1850 the limits had pushed two miles north to 14th Street. A fire, in 1835, leveled most of Lower Manhattan, but even that didn't halt the expansion of what had become the leading commercial center and port in the new country after the War of 1812. Pearl Street was on the original shoreline of the East River, but landfill added Water Street, then Front Street, and finally South Street, where by the 1820s a thick forest of masts congested the port. The **South Street Seaport Museum** evokes that maritime era. By 1812, lawyers, insurance companies, merchants, and financiers were crowding out families in what quickly became the Financial District, whose symbolic and geographic center was the intersection of Broad and Wall streets (named for the wooden wall that served as the northern fortification of "Nieuw Amsterdam"). The construction of the **Merchants' Exchange** in 1836 speeded up the area's transition to a commercial district.

Today, you can visit the current commodities and stock exchanges, but in the limestone-and-glass caverns of Wall Street, only a few of the old public buildings remain: **Federal Hall**, the former **U.S. Custom House** on Bowling Green, the famous **Trinity Church** (an 1846 incarnation, several times removed from the original), and the less well known but earlier **St. Paul's Chapel.** A 20th-century masterpiece worth going out of your way to look at is the **Woolworth Building.**

Whitehall is architecturally reminiscent of Dutch governor **Peter Stuyve- sant's** mansion (renamed by his English replacement), which was on nearby Whitehall Street. **Bowling Green**, a cattle market in Dutch days, and then a green for bowling and recreation at the center of a desirable residential area, is now an egg-shaped park at the foot of Broadway with its 1771 fence still intact. And the **Civic Center**—the cluster of old and new government buildings, some handsome, some horrendous, just north of the Financial District—has become the western boundary of Chinatown.

Created by landfill, the present **Battery Park** offers cooling breezes, welcome greenery, and a panoramic view of **New York Harbor.** It's the jumping-off spot for the ferries to **Liberty Island, Ellis Island,** and **Staten Island,** the best sightseeing buy for close-ups of the Statue of Liberty and the New York City skyline. The observation deck at the **World Trade Center** can't be beat for an aerial perspective of Manhattan Island and its surroundings. Nearby, two massive developments, residential and commercial **Battery Park City** and the **World Financial Center,** symbolize Lower Manhattan's emergence as the new epicenter of downtown activity.

1 **Ellis Island National Monument** On 1 January 1892, when a boat carrying 148 steerage passengers from the SS *Nevada* pulled into the new pier at Ellis Island, **Annie Moore,** a 15-year-old Irish girl became the first immigrant to set foot on the island. More than 16 million souls followed in her footsteps before the island was closed in 1932. In 1907, its peak year, 1,285,349 people were admitted. The original station burned to the ground in 1897, and the Ellis Island National Monument was erected by **Boring & Tilton** in 1898. The present complex of buildings was already decaying during the World War II years when German aliens were imprisoned there. When it finally closed in 1954, vandals moved in and did their best to destroy what was left. In 1990, after eight years of restoration (at a cost of $156 million,

with much of the funding spearheaded by **Lee Iacocca**), the main building opened as a museum. The fate of the other 32 buildings is undetermined, although plans to turn the hospital (where immigrants with contagious diseases were held) into an international conference center have been discussed.

On Ellis Island:

Ellis Island Museum of Immigration
Visitors can now follow the footsteps of their ancestors upon arrival in America: from the **Baggage Room,** where they dropped off what were often all of their worldly belongings, to the **Registry Room,** where they underwent 60-second medical and 30-question legal examinations, and on to the **Staircase of Separation,** which led to the ferryboats that transported the immigrants who were granted

admittance (98 percent of those who arrived here) to either Manhattan or New Jersey, where they would then catch trains to points farther west. Also on view are exhibitions tracing the immigration experience: **Treasures from Home** contains personal property brought here by immigrants; the **American Immigrant Wall of Honor** is inscribed with the names of more than 420,000 American immigrants who were commemorated by their descendants through a donation to the Statue of Liberty-Ellis Island Foundation (call 883.1986 for more information). Another wall is in the making to accommodate the overwhelming response. In the **Oral History Studio** visitors are given the opportunity to listen to immigrants reminisce about their experiences here. ♦ Free. Daily 9:30AM-3PM. Closed some holidays. 363.3200. Statue of Liberty Ferry from Castle Clinton in Battery Park: fee (combination ticket to the Statue of Liberty available). Daily 9AM-3PM. 269.5755

1 Statue of Liberty National Monument

Officially named *Liberty Enlightening the World,* the figure alone (supported by a steel skeleton engineered by **Gustave Eiffel**) is 151 feet high, not counting the pedestal, which adds another 89 feet. It is a full 30 feet taller than the Colossus of Rhodes, one of the Seven Wonders of the Ancient World. French sculptor **Frederic Auguste Bartholdi's** original idea was to place a statue of a peasant woman holding the Lamp of Progress to Asia at the entrance to the Suez Canal—an idea that was rejected by the sultan of Egypt. When Bartholdi came to the New World from France looking for a site for Liberty, he traveled up and down the Eastern Seaboard and as far west as Salt Lake City, but he never for a moment seriously considered any place but **Bedloe's Island,** which he saw as his ship sailed into New York Harbor. It was finally placed on its pedestal, designed by **Richard Morris Hunt,** in 1886.

Bartholdi situated her carefully. As a ship rounds the Narrows between Brooklyn and Staten Island, she appears on portside, striding forward in a gesture of welcome. Then, as it passes directly in front of her, she is suddenly erect and saluting. It is an optical illusion, but one of the most impressive in the world.

The island, which was renamed **Liberty Island** in 1956, was used as a quarantine station in the early 18th century, and after 1811 was the site of **Fort Wood,** which is the star-shaped structure that forms the pedestal's base. In the years between, it was a popular place for hanging pirates.

Since the statue's restoration (completed in 1986), climbing the spiral staircase to its crown is easier than it had been for a hundred years, but there are still 171 steps to climb after the 10-story elevator ride. The view is worth it, but the panorama on the ground is impressive, too, as is the outlook from the promenade around the top of the pedestal, just under Miss Liberty's feet. The line to go up to the crown can be quite long in the summer; you may be turned away if you arrive after 2PM, so plan to visit in the morning. ♦ Fee for ferry service from Castle Clinton in Battery Park, daily 9AM-3PM; frequency varies by season. 269.5755

Within the Statue of Liberty:

The Statue of Liberty Museum

Chronicles the panorama of immigration beginning with the arrival of the Dutch. The museum also contains exhibitions on the statue itself, including the torch, which was re-created and replaced during the 1986 restoration. ♦ Free. Daily 9AM-5PM. 363.3200

R.O. BLECHMAN

2 Battery Park The Dutch began rearranging the terrain the moment **Peter Minuit** bought Manhattan from the Native Americans in 1626. When they dug their canals and leveled the hills, they dumped the dirt and rocks into the bay. Over the next 300 years or so, more than 21 acres were added to the tip of the island, creating the green buffer between the harbor and the dark canyons of the Financial District. The park takes its name from a line of cannons that once overlooked the harbor. Despite its bellicose moniker, it has always been a place for those **Herman Melville** described as "men fixed in ocean reveries." ♦ Southern tip of Manhattan

Within Battery Park:

Staten Island Ferry This trip provides an excellent visual orientation to New York City. The ferry leaves from the southern tip of Manhattan, weaves through harbor traffic— from tug to sailboat, yacht to cruise ship— and travels past the Statue of Liberty and Ellis Island to the northeast edge of Staten Island, then back again. En route, passengers have a glorious view of the city's celebrated skyline. The price, although recently doubled to 50 cents, is still one of the best bargains around. No cars are allowed. ♦ Fee. Daily 24 hours. South St at State St. 718/390.5253

Verrazano Monument During the celebration of the Hudson-Fulton Festival, an extravaganza marking the 300th anniversary of **Henry Hudson's** trip up the river, New York's Italian-Americans placed this heroic group by **Ettore Ximenes** at the edge of the harbor in 1909. It commemorates their countryman, who got here first. It should be noted that the female figure representing Discovery is trampling a book labeled *History*.

Castle Clinton National Monument
Castle Clinton was originally called West Battery, a defense post housing 28 cannons within eight-foot-thick walls. It faced Castle William on Governors Island, and the pair were fortified to block the harbor from enemy attack. **John McComb, Jr.,** designed the original building in 1811, which fell into disuse when no enemy appeared. As an entertainment emporium called **Castle Garden,** the structure was redesigned and the main hall was used for the American premiere of singer **Jenny Lind,** presented by showman **P.T. Barnum.** For several years, it was the **Emigrant Landing Depot,** processing more than seven million immigrants before giving up that role to Ellis Island. In one of its final incarnations—1896 to 1941—the building housed the **New York Aquarium** (now at Coney Island in Brooklyn). Finally, as need for repairs became apparent and its historical importance was realized, the building was designated a National Landmark and renovations were begun. It has been restored as a fort and also serves as an information

center and a ticket office for the **Statue of Liberty Ferry,** which leaves Battery Park daily on the hour (more often during the summer). ♦ Daily 8:30AM-5PM. State St at West St. 344.7220

Battery Park Control House One of two surviving ornate entrances to the original IRT Subway (the other is at 72nd Street and Broadway), the term "control house" was coined by engineers who designed them to control crowds coming and going in two directions at once. This one was built in 1905 and was designed by **Heins & LaFarge.** ♦ State St at Battery Pl

3 Church of Our Lady of the Rosary This pair of Georgian town houses, originally designed in 1800 by **John McComb, Jr.,** was restored in 1965 as a shrine church dedicated to **St. Elizabeth Ann Seton,** the first American-born saint, who lived here in 1801. The exteriors were faithfully returned to their original condition, providing a small reminder of the character of this entire neighborhood at the beginning of the 19th century. ♦ Daily 6:30AM-6PM. 7 and 8 State St (at Water St). 269.6805

3 New York Unearthed In the fall of 1990, a permanent archaeological display (administered by the **South Street Museum**) opened in an annex behind 17 State Street. Visitors enter at street level, where they view 10 dioramas, created by graphic designer **Milton Glaser,** that hold such items as medicine vials, crucibles, cannon balls, and bottles, all excavated on or near this site. On the lower level, museumgoers may board the **Unearthing New York Systems Elevator,** which takes them on a simulated dig, four centuries back into New York history. ♦ Call for schedule. Closed Saturday and Sunday. 17 State St (at Water St). 669.9416

4 Peter Minuit Plaza The small park honors the man who bought Manhattan from the Native Americans for a small price. The flagpole is a memorial to the first Jewish settlers, who arrived in 1654. They had been expelled from Portugal to a Dutch colony at Recife in Brazil, but were driven from there in a Portuguese conquest. On the way back to Holland, their ship was attacked by pirates, and the survivors were taken to the nearest Dutch colony, Nieuw Amsterdam, where they were allowed to stay. ♦ South St at State St

5 Battery Maritime Building The sheet-metal-and-steel facade of this Beaux Arts ferry terminal has been painted green to simulate copper. Before the Brooklyn Bridge was built, there were 17 ferry lines between Lower Manhattan and Brooklyn. One of them operated out of this terminal, designed by **Walker & Gillette** in 1906, until 1938. Today, it houses the small fleet of white ferries that serves Governors Island. ♦ 11 South St (at Whitehall St)

6 Governors Island When the Dutch arrived here in 1624, they established their first toehold on what they called "Nut Island." The British established their own governor here even before the Dutch governor surrendered Nieuw Amsterdam to them in 1665. Among the other historic landmarks on the island, in addition to the British **Governor's Mansion,** is the 1840 **Admiral's House,** the home of the commanding general of the army garrison stationed here from 1790 until 1966. Governors Island is now the headquarters of the U.S. Coast Guard, which has overall responsibility for all the waterways in the country east of the Continental Divide.

The island is an idyllic place with sweeping lawns and fine old houses on traffic-free roads, a few hundred yards from the tip of Manhattan. But, alas, as a government reservation, it is closed to the public except for one day a year, usually in May or June, when they polish up the brass and welcome visitors for the annual open house. ♦ For further information, call the Support Center New York, Special Services. 668.3402

7 Fraunces Tavern This Georgian brick building (illustrated above), built in 1719, became the tavern of **Samuel Fraunces** in 1763, and was made famous when **George Washington** said farewell to his officers here on 4 December 1783. Washington returned six years later to old City Hall, five blocks away, to take the oath of office as the first president of the new nation. The building was refurbished in 1927 in the spirit and style of the period rather than as an accurate restoration. ♦ 54 Pearl St (at Broad St)

Within Fraunces Tavern:

Fraunces Tavern Restaurant ★$$$
Wood-burning fireplaces, a warm colonial atmosphere, and an all-American menu make this one of the better spots for downtown dining. ♦ American ♦ Breakfast, lunch, and dinner. Closed Saturday and Sunday. Reservations recommended. 269.0144

Fraunces Tavern Museum Permanent and changing exhibitions of decorative arts, period rooms, paintings, and prints and manuscripts from 18th- and 19th-century America are on display. ♦ Admission. M-F 10AM-4:45PM; Sa noon-4PM. 425.1778

8 United States Custom House This 1907 building by **Cass Gilbert** has been called one of the finest examples of the Beaux Arts style in New York City, and it is instantly apparent why. The granite facade is surprisingly delicate, despite an ornate frieze and Ionic columns with Corinthian capitals along the face. Four monuments, representing Africa, Asia, Europe, and America, are **Daniel Chester French** and **Adolph Weinman's** contribution to the magnificence that, despite the building's name and purpose, is somehow very un-American in style. **Reginald Marsh** painted the murals in the wonderful oval rotunda. In 1994, the **National Museum of the American Indian** will open a permanent exhibition space here. ♦ Broadway at Bowling Green. 962.8800

In primeval Manhattan a 60-foot-deep spring-fed pond, which the Dutch named *Der Kolck* (Rippling Water), covered the area from present-day Duane to White, and Baxter to Lafayette streets. For many years it was the city's best source of drinking water. A fountain at one end became the source of the city's first bottled water in the 1780s. In 1791, after slaughterhouses and tanneries managed to pollute the pond, the city decided to fill it in, a project that took 10 years. The landfill provided a site for New York's first outdoor circus in 1811 but eventually became the poor people's Coney Island, attracting what Mayor Philip Hone called "unbreeched little tatterdemalions" and other outcasts of society. At the nearby intersection of Baxter and Worth streets was the infamous Five Points, considered the worst slum New York has ever produced. For a 15-year period the former Coulter's Brewery on the present site of the New York County Courthouse is said to have averaged 15 murders each and every night. Reformers eventually managed to cool it down, but there are New Yorkers alive today who remember when it wasn't safe to come near this neighborhood. When the New York-born gangster Al Capone was led off to prison on tax evasion charges in the 1930s, he said, "I shoulda never left Five Points."

Restaurants/Clubs: Red		**Hotels:** Blue
Shops/ ♥ Outdoors: Green		**Sights/Culture:** Black

9 Bowling Green In 1734, a group of citizens leased the space facing the Custom House as a bowling green for an annual rent of one peppercorn. In the process it became the city's first park. In 1729, the park was embellished with an equestrian statue of England's **King George III,** which was demolished by a crowd that assembled here to listen to a reading of the Declaration of Independence on 9 July 1776. The statue was melted down to make bullets that, according to some contemporary accounts, were responsible for the killing of 400 British soldiers during the war that followed. ◆ Broadway at Battery Pl

At Bowling Green:

The Charging Bull In response to the stock-market crash of 1987, **Arturo DiModica** sculpted this 3.5-ton bronze bull—an emblem of the business community—to attest to the "vitality, energy, and life of the American people in adversity." It was recently put on the selling block; since the city is not allowed to buy works of art, the sculpture is looking for a patron.

10 Whitehall Building A 1930s real-estate guide said that the tenants of this 1903 building, which at the time included the **Internal Revenue Service, Quaker Oats,** and the **Bon Ami Cleanser Co.,** had "an intimate relationship with the landlord," and no one ever moved out. There has been some turnover since the guide was written, but tenants are still (understandably) reluctant to give up what may be the best of all harbor views. Originally designed by **Henry J. Hardenbergh,** the rear section was designed by **Clinton & Russell** in 1910. ◆ 17 Battery Pl (between West and Washington Sts)

William Marcy "Boss" Tweed began his political career in 1848 as the organizer of the Americus Volunteer Fire Company, whose unusually large fire engine was painted with the head of a tiger. The fire company was associated with Tammany Hall (the Democratic political machine), and it was an easy step from one to the other. By 1853 Tweed had become a congressman; by 1867 he was powerful enough to overthrow Reform mayor Fernando Wood and put his own man, George Opdyke, in charge at City Hall. In 1868, he became Grand Sachem of Tammany Hall, which gave him backroom control over the state as well as the city. Attacks by cartoonist Thomas Nast in *Harper's Weekly* led to his downfall in 1873. He was convicted, but jumped bail and slipped away to Spain, where he was captured by police who recognized him from the Nast cartoons. He died in prison three years later.

11 Downtown Athletic Club The arched ground-floor arcade and the window treatment of this Moorish-influenced Art Deco masterpiece, designed by **Starrett & Van Vleck** in 1926, are perfection itself, and the interior by **Barnett-Phillips** is even better. The rooms are reminiscent of a 1920s ocean liner. In addition to an enclosed roof garden, the building originally contained a miniature golf course. Off-limits to women until 1978, the club now boasts a coed, cross-cultural membership. ◆ 19 West St (at Morris St). 425.7000

12 Brooklyn-Battery Tunnel In the early 1930s, builder **Robert Moses** announced that he was going to construct a bridge between Lower Manhattan and Brooklyn to connect his Long Island parkway system with his West Side Highway, which reached a dead end at Battery Park. Preservationists were appalled, and even **Eleanor Roosevelt** got into the act when she wrote: "Isn't there room for some consideration of the preservation of one of the few beautiful spots that still remain to us on an overcrowded island?" City officials, noting that the city would lose $29 million a year in real-estate taxes, also opposed it. The battle raged until 1939, when **President Roosevelt** stepped in and denied federal funds for the project. The bridge became a tunnel, and Battery Park was saved. But Moses got his revenge by keeping most of the park enclosed behind a construction fence for more than four years, even though there was no construction going on behind it. When the tunnel, engineered by **Ole Singstad** in 1949, finally opened, it carried more than 15 million cars in its first year. ◆ From West St (between Morris and Rector Sts), Manhattan to Hamilton Ave, Brooklyn

13 26 Broadway This graceful giant, which was first built in 1885 and altered in 1922 by **Carrère & Hastings,** curves to follow the street line. The most important business address in the world for a half century, this was where **John D. Rockefeller** said that he had revolutionized the way of doing business "to save ourselves from wasteful conditions and eliminate individualism." There is no denying he accomplished his goal, and at the same time built one of the world's greatest fortunes behind these walls—the headquarters of **Standard Oil.** When the Supreme Court dissolved the trust in 1911, the building became home to **Socony Mobil,** one of the new companies that rose from the ashes. ◆ At Bowling Green

14 India House Richard J. Carman built this beautiful brownstone as headquarters for the **Hanover Bank** in 1854. At other times it was used as the **New York Cotton Exchange** and the main office of **W.R. Grace and Co.** It is now a private club. ◆ 1 Hanover Sq (between Pearl and Stone Sts)

15 Hanover Square Named for the English royal family of the **Georges,** this was once a small London-style park at the center of a residential neighborhood. Homeowners included **Captain William Kidd,** who was considered a solid citizen in New York but something quite different by the British; they hanged him for piracy in 1701. Captain Kidd has gone down in popular history as the most bloodthirsty of pirates, and even today people poke around beaches along the coast in hopes of finding the fabulous treasure he supposedly buried. The square was also the home of New York's first newspaper, the *New-York Daily Gazette,* established in 1725. **George E. Bissell's** statue of **Abraham de Peyster,** a one-time mayor of the city, was moved here from Bowling Green. ◆ Between Stone and Pearl Sts

16 United States Assay Office Built in 1930 and designed by **James A. Wetmore,** this is a division of the United States Mint for refining gold and silver bullion and melting down old coins. It is also a storehouse that contains about 55 million troy ounces of gold, worth more than $2 billion at the official government price. ◆ Old Slip (between Front and Water Sts)

17 HRC Tennis Nonmembers are allowed to reserve tennis courts 24 hours in advance, but should be prepared to pay high rates for the privilege, especially during the peak hours—after 5PM during the week. ◆ Piers 13 and 14 (off Wall and South Sts). 422.9300

18 Sloppy Louie's ★$$$ Before the renaissance of South Street Seaport forced Louie to clean up his act and raise his prices, this was a no-nonsense restaurant catering to the people who worked in the area's markets. The quality is still good enough for the most demanding fishmonger; it's just more genteel. ◆ Seafood ◆ Lunch and early dinner. 92 South St (between Fulton and John Sts). Reservations recommended for six or more. 509.9694

New York's first subway (one car, seating 22 passengers) was fueled by a blast of air from a huge steam-driven fan, which would suck the car back when it reached the end of the line. It traveled 10 miles an hour and ran under Broadway from Warren to Murray streets, a distance of 312 feet. It was conceived and constructed in 1870 by Alfred Ely Beach, a publisher and the inventor of the typewriter.

19 South Street Seaport In the days of sailing ships, most of the port's activities were along this stretch of the East River, which has been re-created as a museum of ships. With the coming of steamships, the deeper piers on the Hudson River took away the traffic, and the East River piers went into decline. In 1967, a group of preservation-minded citizens banded together to buy some of the rundown waterfront buildings and began acquiring a collection of historic ships. Twelve years later commercial interests moved in and provided funds to restore the old buildings and add some new ones. The result of the restoration, thanks to the ingenuity of architects **Ben** and **Jane Thompson,** is a mix of old and new made to look old. In many ways more a shopping center than a historic site, it has nonetheless revitalized a derelict neighborhood, transforming it into one of New York's most fascinating enclaves. It is especially active after 5PM, when young Wall Streeters drift by for an after-work drink in surroundings dramatically different from their high-tech offices. The streets within the Seaport are paved with stones often called Belgian blocks. Before the days of asphalt, most of the city's streets were made of these stones, which arrived here as ballast in the holds of tall-masted sailing ships. ◆ Daily 10AM-5PM. Water St to East River (between Dover and Fletcher Sts). 669.9400

Within South Street Seaport:

Titanic Memorial Lighthouse This structure originally overlooked the harbor from the Seamen's Church Institute on Water Street at Cuyler's Alley. It is a memorial to the 1,500 who died when the White Star Line's *Titanic* struck an iceberg in 1912. It was moved here in 1976 to mark the entrance to the Seaport. The black ball suspended above it was a time signal that was dropped from the top of the pole each day at noon, giving everyone in the neighborhood a reliable means of synchronizing his or her watch. ◆ Fulton St at Water St

Brookstone The ultimate hardware store, Brookstone displays one of each tool or gadget in stock like an objet d'art next to a card describing its virtues. Each is the best in its class. You pick up a clipboard when you enter and write down your order as you go. At the end, it is delivered via a dumbwaiter from the loft above. ◆ M-Sa 10AM-9PM; Su 11AM-6:30PM. 18 Fulton St (between Front and Water Sts). 344.8108

Museum Gallery Changing exhibitions covering America's nautical heritage are housed in a former warehouse built in 1868. The **Melville Research Library** upstairs is open by appointment only. ♦ Admission. Daily 10AM-5PM. 213 Water St (at Fulton St). 669.9420

Abercrombie & Fitch Sports clothing has kept this chain in business since 1892. ♦ M-Sa 10AM-9PM; Su noon-7PM. 199 Water St (at Fulton St). 809.9000

Strand Bookstore The downtown branch of New York's landmark bookstore stocks a large selection of new books at huge discounts, plus remainders and review copies. ♦ M-Sa 10AM-9PM; Su 10AM-8PM. 159 John St (at Front St). 809.0875

The Chandlery New York's best source for fiction and nonfiction on ships of all kinds and the waters they sail also has rare prints and ship models and otherwise hard-to-find books on New York City and its history. ♦ M-Sa 10AM-6PM; Su 11AM-6PM. 209 Water St (at Fulton St). 669.9453

Fulton Market This is a reconstruction (pictured above) of an 1882 structure that once housed a fresh produce and meat market. The items sold there were brought over from Long Island farms on the *Fulton Ferry*, which connected Fulton Street in Manhattan with Fulton Street in Brooklyn. The new building houses shops and restaurants, including many stalls selling fresh food in imitation of the old market. ♦ Daily 7AM-7PM. 11 Fulton St (between South and Front Sts). 608.2920

The Ships Visiting ships make Piers 15, 16, and 17 an always changing experience, but the Seaport's permanent collection includes two tall ships: *Peking,* a steel-hulled, four-masted bark built in 1911, and *Wavertree,* a full-rigged iron ship built in 1885. They are open to the public every day from 10AM to 5PM, as is *Ambrose,* the steel lightship that was anchored at the entrance to the harbor from 1908 until 1963, when she was replaced by a permanent tower. Boarding tickets, available on Pier 16 and at the Visitors Center at Fulton and Water streets, allow admission to all exhibition galleries and daily changing events. Other ships in the South Street Seaport fleet include the working tugboat *W.O. Decker* and the schooner *Lettie G. Howard. Pioneer,* a former cargo schooner, makes daytime and twilight sails in the harbor. Hours vary according to season. Reservations can be made within 14 days of a sail;

unreserved tickets are sold each day starting at 10AM at Pier 16 (669.9400). Special exhibitions are scattered throughout the Seaport; there are also special holiday events. Two separate walking tours guide you to them. ♦ Daily 10AM-5PM. East River (between South and Fulton Sts). 669.9400

JAN HIRD PORKORNY, ARCHITECTS & PLANNERS

Schermerhorn Row A row of Federal-style warehouses and counting houses (shown above) built by **Peter Schermerhorn** in 1812 have been restored. At various times in their history, the buildings were used as stores, taverns, rooming houses, and hotels. Greek Revival cast-iron storefronts were added later when the *Fulton Ferry* brought more stylish customers into the area. The upper floors are the least altered from the original, but the mansard roof at the western end was added in 1868 when 2 Fulton Street was the Fulton Ferry Hotel. The ground floor currently houses a variety of interesting shops, including **The Nature Company, The Body Shop,** and **The Sharper Image.** ♦ Between Fulton and South Sts

Seaport Line Harbor Cruises The sidewheeler *Andrew Fletcher* takes 90-minute cruises from March to December on Saturday and Sunday at 1PM, 3PM, and 5PM, and in the warmer months it takes longer music cruises with live entertainment on Saturday night. ♦ Tickets available at Pier 16. 233.4800

Pier 17 The stepped plaza overlooking the East River is the best part of this festive pier, which contains shops and restaurants in several varieties and price ranges. The Brooklyn Bridge frames the ever-changing view of the waterborne traffic, and in spite of the crowds, it is one of the city's more relaxing experiences. ♦ South St (between Fulton and Beekman Sts)

20 Fulton Fish Market The present 1907 home of this venerable institution, established here in 1821, was called the **Tin Building** by old salts who remembered the wooden building it replaced. The market was originally located here to serve fishing boats, but today the catch arrives in refrigerated trucks. Daytime visitors find it a quiet place, but it is frantic between midnight and 8AM. Early risers can watch the activity wind down by taking guided tours at 6AM on the first and third Thursday of each month from April to October; reservations are required. ♦ Daily 10AM-6PM. South St at Fulton St. Tour information 669.9416

21 Brooklyn Bridge This milestone in civil engineering, built from 1869 to 1883 and designed by **John A. Roebling** and **Washington Roebling,** is an aesthetic masterpiece as well as a structural one. The Brooklyn Bridge gets its dynamic tension from the massive strength of its great stone pylons and Gothic arches contrasted with the intricate web of its woven suspension cables. In 1855, John Roebling's proposal for a bridge across the East River was met with derision, but far-sighted residents of Brooklyn (still a separate city) pushed the idea after the Civil War. The Roebling family's fate was inextricably tied up with that of the bridge.

John died as the result of an accident on a Brooklyn wharf before work on the bridge began, but his son, Washington, carried on, even when he got the bends during construction and became partially paralyzed for the rest of his life. The Brooklyn Bridge was the first to use steel cables. For 20 years it was the world's longest suspension bridge; for many more its span was the longest. The subject of many poems, paintings, paeans of praise, and bad jokes, the bridge still gives a special lift to the bicyclists, walkers, and marathoners who cross it. ♦ From Park Row, Manhattan to Cadman Pl, Brooklyn

Verrazano-Narrows Bridge
Completed 1964; total length 6,690'; center span 4,260'; maximum clearance above water 228'.

Brooklyn Bridge
Completed 1883; total length 3,455'6"; center span 1,595'6"; maximum clearance above water 133'.

Manhattan Bridge
Completed 1909; total length 2,920'; center span 1,470'; maximum clearance above water 135'.

Williamsburg Bridge
Completed 1903; total length 2,793'6"; center span 1,600'; maximum clearance above water 135'.

Queensboro Bridge
Completed 1909; total length 3,724'; major span 1,182'; maximum clearance above water 135'.

George Washington Bridge
Completed 1931; total length 4,760'; center span 3,500'; maximum clearance above water 212'.

San Francisco's Golden Gate Bridge
Completed 1936; total length 6,460'; center span 4,199'; maximum clearance above water 222'.

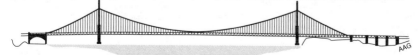

22 Bridge Cafe ★$$ It can't be just the cachet of dining in a City Hall hangout that draws customers from all over town to this Franco-Italo-American bistro set in such an out-of-the-way place. The brick-walled bar/dining room, noisy and friendly, has a certain simple waterfront charm. The food is good but not worth a cab ride. Stop in only if you're already in the neighborhood. ♦ International ♦ Lunch and dinner; dinner only on Saturday; brunch also on Sunday. 279 Water St (at Dover St). Reservations recommended. 227.3344

23 127 John Street A huge electric display clock designed by **Corchia-de Harak Associates,** in addition to the nearby colorful steel patio furniture, adds a touch of whimsy to the Water Street streetscape. ♦ View from Water St (between Fulton and John Sts)

24 Wall Street Plaza This 1973 white-aluminum-and-glass structure by **I.M. Pei & Associates** richly deserved the award presented by the American Institute of Architects for its classical purity, rather rare in the new buildings in this area. The 1974 sculpture in its plaza, by **Yu Yu Yang,** consists of a stainless-steel slab with an opening that faces a polished disk. It is a memorial to the Cunard liner *Queen Elizabeth,* whose history is outlined on a nearby plaque. ♦ 88 Pine St (between Water and Front Sts)

25 Seaport Suites Hotel $$$ This suites-only hotel is just a two-minute walk from Wall Street and in the heart of the historical district that harks back to New York's early days. Suites come in four sizes, from an oversize double room to a miniature apartment that can sleep four people. All have fully equipped kitchens and many have a separate living room for business meetings or just plain lounging. ♦ 129 Front St (at Wall St). 742.0003, 800/777.8483; fax 742.0124

On 16 December 1835, fire engulfed Lower Manhattan, scorching everything south of Wall Street and east of Broadway. More than 650 buildings were burned. The conflagration took nearly 20 hours to bring under control; final loss of property was some $20 million.

"Going down Wall Street you pass what looks like an alley called New Street. The street is hardly new. The name was bestowed in 1647 because the street was the first in this part of town laid out by the new English government."

Joyce Gold,
From Windmills to the World Trade Center

26 74 Wall Street The nautical decoration around the arched entrance of this solid-looking 1926 building by **Benjamin Wistar Morris** is a reminder that it was built for the **Seamen's Bank for Savings,** the second-oldest savings bank in the city. It was chartered in 1829 as a financial haven for sailors, who usually arrived in the port with their pockets full of back pay accumulated while they were out at sea. The official address of the property was 76 Wall Street, but before it was changed, superstitious seamen refused to leave their money there because the numbers added up to 13. ♦ At Pearl St

27 55 Wall Street One of the first buildings in the area after the Great Fire of 1835 leveled 700 structures between Wall and South streets, Coenties Slip, and Broad Street, this building was designed by **Isaiah Rogers** in 1836. It was built as a three-story trading hall for the **Merchants' Exchange,** and later became the Custom House. In 1907, its height was doubled when it was remodeled and expanded by **McKim, Mead & White,** and it became the headquarters of **First National City Bank,** which still maintains an impressive-looking branch here under its new name, **Citibank.** ♦ Between William and Hanover Sts

28 Bank of New York The bank has occupied several buildings on this site since its founding by **Alexander Hamilton** in 1784. **Commodore Vanderbilt** used one of them as his banking headquarters. The present Georgian building was built in 1927 and designed by **Benjamin Wistar Morris,** and is easily one of the most attractive in the area, with tall, arched windows and a broken pediment framing a handsome galleon lantern. ♦ 48 Wall St (at William St). 495.1784

29 40 Wall Street The tower was built in 1929, the same time as the Chrysler Building uptown, and was secretly designed by **H. Craig Severance** and **Yasuo Matsui** to be two feet higher, which would have made it the tallest in the world. (But the Chrysler's builders outfoxed the bankers with a secret plan of their own. They pushed a 123-foot stainless-steel spire through a hole in their roof.) This was the headquarters of the **Bank of the Manhattan Company,** which eventually merged with **Chase National Bank.** The **Manhattan Co.** was founded in 1799 by **Aaron Burr,** who was blocked by political rivals when he tried to charter a bank. Instead he received legislative permission to establish a water company. In the charter's fine print, he was granted the power to loan money to property owners who wanted to connect their buildings to his wooden water mains. Before he had dug up too many streets, Burr abandoned the water business and became what he had always wanted to be: a banker. ♦ Between William and Nassau Sts

Restaurants/Clubs: Red   **Hotels:** Blue
Shops/ 🌿 Outdoors: Green   **Sights/Culture:** Black

Past Perfect: The New York City Landmarks Preservation Commission

When the noble, Roman-style **Pennsylvania Train Station** fell victim to the wrecker's ball in 1965, public outrage was not enough to stay its death sentence. In its place rose a modern construction of glass and steel that sorely lacked the elegance and historic significance of its predecessor. Penn Station was but one of the city's magnificent old buildings razed in the name of modernism.

To halt the further destruction and demolition of New York's past, the **New York City Landmarks Preservation Commission** was formed by **Mayor F. Wagner** on 19 April 1965. In October of that year, the Commission designated its first landmark, the former **Astor Library** on Lafayette Street in the East Village. Built as the first free public library in the 1850s, today it houses **Joseph Papp's Public Theater,** birthplace of *Hair* and *A Chorus Line.*

Nearing its 30th anniversary, the Commission now protects over 20,000 of New York City's one million buildings. More than 1,000 of these are interspersed one by one throughout the five boroughs; the balance are found clustered within 60 historic districts. The landmarks range from little-known structures in out-of-the-way corners of the city to modest 17th-century houses and graveyards. The roster includes **Grand Central Station, Carnegie Hall,** the **Empire State Building,** the interior of the elegant **Four Seasons** restaurant, and the nostalgic **Cyclone** roller coaster and **Wonder Wheel** rides that once made **Coney Island** America's favorite urban playground.

Although one of New York City's smallest agencies, the Commission is nevertheless the largest municipal preservation agency in the United States. Consisting of 11 commissioners appointed by the mayor for three-year terms (of these, only the chairman receives a salary) and a full-time staff, the agency is responsible for designating city landmarks and historic districts and regulating changes to already designated buildings. The owner of a protected landmark—be it another city agency, a federal government agency, an individual, or a business—must obtain the permission of the Commission before it can alter, reconstruct, or demolish a landmark's exterior or, in some cases,

interior features. The Commission itself has very few funds for grants or "brick and mortar" expenses, so the owner is usually the party who absorbs the cost of approved restorations and alterations; the Commission's role is to judge whether they are appropriate.

New York was settled and developed over the centuries by builders from many countries. The mosaic of architectural styles is a source of pride for the city's eight million residents. These landmarks serve as a reminder of the city's history and give it the cachet that tourists have come to expect.

In November 1993, the Commission moved to a landmark building near South Street Seaport. Its headquarters, in an Italian Renaissance Revival structure designed in 1909 by **Hunt & Hunt,** stands on the site of the first official marketplace in 17th-century New Amsterdam. The current building served as Manhattan's first police precinct until 1973, then stood vacant for 20 years.

The Commission's research library is open by appointment only to visiting or local historians, architects, and architecture buffs. The Commission also operates Brooklyn's **Architectural Salvage Warehouse** (see page 293), which sells architectural and decorative elements rescued from historic buildings before they were demolished: fireplace mantels, lighting fixtures, doors, and wrought-iron gratings are purchased and recycled back into the homes of New Yorkers. The Commission is located at 100 Old Slip. Call 487.6800 for more information.

Recommended reading:

Guide to New York City Landmarks, The New York City Landmarks Preservation Commission, by **Andrew S. Dolkart** (Preservation Press; 1992)

The Landmarks of New York and *The Landmarks of New York II,* by **Barbaralee Diamonstein** (Harry Abrams; 1988 and 1993)

29 30 Wall Street When this structure was built as the **United States Assay Office** in 1921 by architects **York & Sawyer,** the facade of its predecessor, the **Bank of the United States,** designed in 1826 by **Martin E. Thompson,** was dismantled and eventually reconstructed in the American Wing of the **Metropolitan Museum of Art.** Additions were made in 1955 by the firm of **Halsey, McCormack & Helmer.** ♦ Between William and Nassau Sts

Wall Street's first financier was probably Frederick Phillipse, whose house was at the northern end of New Amsterdam. Indian wampum, made from Long Island clam shells, was the legal tender of the colony, and in 1665, Phillipse bought several barrels of it, creating an artificial shortage. Anyone who needed any wampum to settle debts and continue in business had to buy it from Phillipse, at his rates.

29 Federal Hall National Memorial This Americanization of the Parthenon is one of New York City's finest examples of Greek Revival architecture and a fitting National Landmark. At the front of the building, which was designed in 1842 by **Town & Davis, John Quincy Adams Ward's** statue of **George Washington** marks the spot where the Revolutionary War general became the country's first president. A building on this site served as the United States governmental seat in the days when New York City was the nation's capital. Doric columns climbing 32 feet high span the building's face. Enter for a self-guided tour of the interior of the building, which was designed by **John Frazee** and **Samuel Thompson,** as well as exhibitions organized by both the **Historic Hudson Valley** and the **Museum of the American Constitutional Government.** ♦ M-F 9AM-5PM. 15 Pine St or 26 Wall St (at Nassau St). 264.8711

30 Morgan Guaranty Trust Company If ever a single man epitomized the American capitalist, **J.P. Morgan** (1837-1913) was that man. His son, **John Pierpont Morgan, Jr.,** took control of the empire in 1913, the year this building was built by **Trowbridge & Livingston,** and, like his father, was apparently not without enemies. On 16 September 1920, at the height of the lunch hour, a carriage parked on Wall Street suddenly exploded, killing 33 people, as well as the horse, and injuring 400. The marble walls of the building still have scars from the disaster. No reason was ever determined, and the owner of the carriage was never found. ♦ 23 Wall St (at Broad St)

The World Trade Center has more than a half-million square feet of glass.

On 7 August 1974, circus performer Philipe Petit took a 45-minute walk on a 131-foot steel cable running between the North and South Towers of the World Trade Center. When asked why, he explained: "When I see three oranges, I have to juggle, and if I see two towers, I have to walk." In July 1975, Owen Quinn, a skydiver and dock builder, dove from the 110th floor of the North Tower. At about the 60th floor, after he had gained enough momentum, he opened his parachute. The entire trip took two minutes. On 27 May 1977, mountain climber George Willig scaled the South Tower in a three-and-a-half-hour climb. "I thought I'd like to try it," he said.

"I should have been born in New York, I should have been born in the Village, that's where I belong."

John Lennon

31 New York Stock Exchange The NYSE's giant portico, colonnade, and sculptures express austerity and security— key design goals in 1903 when this building (pictured above) was designed by **George B. Post** and when the upper section was designed in 1923 by **Trowbridge & Livingston.** The solemn facade masks the leading-edge technology that drives the exchange today. That technology, integrated with the judgment and skills of the trading floor's professionals, provides investors with the broadest, most open, and most liquid equities market in the world. Before entering the gallery that overlooks the trading floor, visitors go through an exhibition area that includes visual presentations and frequent lectures on the history and workings of the institution. A multilingual, pre-recorded explanation of what's happening three floors below is provided from a glass-enclosed gallery overlooking the floor. The tickets for tours are dispensed at 20 Broad Street; try to arrive before noon as there are a limited number. ♦ Free. Visitors Gallery M-F 9:15AM-3:45PM. Tours M-F 9:15AM-3PM. 20 Broad St (at Wall St), third floor. 656.5168

32 Bankers Trust Building The pyramid on top of this 31-story tower, built in 1912 by **Trowbridge & Livingston,** became the corporate symbol of **Bankers Trust** and remained its logo even after the bank moved its main headquarters up to 280 Park Avenue in 1963. ♦ 16 Wall St (at Nassau St)

Within the Bankers Trust Building:

La Tour D'Or ★$$$ The dramatic restaurant in the 31st-floor space that was once a pied-à-terre for **J.P. Morgan** has views that extend in every direction, but the best is from the comfortable bar that overlooks the harbor and the Statue of Liberty. ♦ French ♦ Lunch. Closed Saturday and Sunday. Reservations recommended. 233.2780

33 Irving Trust Company Building/The Bank of New York Ralph Walker's only skyscraper was built in 1932 on what was called the most expensive piece of real estate in the world in the 1930s. He said his design was one of superimposed rhythms, a steel frame draped outside with rippling curtains of stone. The gold, red, and orange Art Deco mosaics created by **Hildreth Meière** in the banking room off Wall Street make a visit rewarding even if you are not a depositor.
♦ 1 Wall St (at Broadway)

34 Waldenbooks The Lower Manhattan branch of the national chain is spacious, and many of its departments are separated by alcoves. Especially strong in business, the bookstore also offers wide selections in cooking, history, and sports, with many remainder and sale books. ♦ M-F 8AM-6PM. 57 Broadway (at Exchange Pl). 269.1139

35 Trinity Church This historic architectural and religious monument has a strong square tower punctuated by an exclamation point spire, and the good fortune to stand at the head of Wall Street. The shaded grassy cemetery—a welcome open space in this neighborhood—offers a noontime haven for office workers. The cemetery came first, and such notables as **Alexander Hamilton, William Bradford,** and **Robert Fulton** are buried here (marked by placards that are especially helpful when gravestone inscriptions have worn away). This is the third Trinity Church on this site. The original was built in 1698, paid for by taxation of all citizens, regardless of religion, because the Church of England was the official religion of the colony. It burned in 1776. The second was demolished in 1839.

The present Trinity was designed in 1846 by **Richard Upjohn; Richard Morris Hunt's** brass doors were added later. The **Chapel of All Saints,** designed by **Thomas Hash,** was built in 1913; and the **Bishop Manning Memorial Wing** by **Adams & Woodbridge** in 1965. In 1992, work was completed on a time-consuming effort to restore the building to its original appearance. Workers steamed away a layer of paraffin that was mistakenly applied to the building in the 1920s to keep it from crumbling; beneath the paraffin were layers of coal dust and pollutants that had made this building blacker than many other historic buildings. The result, rosy sandstone as Upjohn had intended, was quite a surprise to the thousands of Wall Streeters who, every day for years, had been walking past what they believed to be a very dark building.
♦ Services: M-F 8AM, noon; Sa 9AM, noon; Su 9AM, 11:15AM. Museum: free; M-F 9-11:45AM, 1-3:45PM; Sa 10AM-3:45PM; Su 1-3:45PM. Broadway at Wall St. 602.0800

36 American Stock Exchange The building was known until 1953 as the Curb Exchange because before 1921 brokers stood at the corner of Wall and Broad streets and communicated with one another through hand gestures. The present building was designed in 1930 by **Starrett & Van Vleck.**
♦ 86 Trinity Pl (between Thames and Rector Sts). 306.1000

36 Syms Located in the heart of the Financial District, this famous discount house is primarily for men and women with conservative tastes. Sizes range from lean and trim to 46 portly, at discounts of 30 to 50 percent. Unlike most other discount stores, Syms leaves the original labels on the stock, and each price tag shows both the nationally advertised price and Syms' price. Selections include double-breasted and single-breasted suits in conservative pinstripes, herring-bones, and Harris tweeds, double-pleated slacks, jeans, and all the accessories to go with them. But the greatest strength is the shirt department, which takes up nearly the entire second floor. You can't beat the selection or the prices—everything from Viyella and pure cotton to cotton/poly for the drip-dry set. Finally, on the third and fourth floors are the women's departments, which feature designer suits, dresses, separates, and coats. ♦ M-W 9AM-6:30PM; Th-F 9AM-8PM; Sa 10AM-6:30PM; Su noon-5:30PM. 42 Trinity Pl (at Rector St). 797.1199

When the first burials took place in St. Paul's and Trinity churchyards, they provided employment for gentlemen licensed by the city as Inviters to Funerals. Dressed in somber black, with long black streamers attached to their stovepipe hats, they marched in pairs from house to house extolling the virtues of the recently deceased. As they walked through the streets, one tolled a bell and the other pounded the pavement with a long black pole. They served as masters of ceremonies at the funeral itself, and their fee was determined by the turnout. At the gravesite the 12 pallbearers were given souvenir spoons engraved with figures of the 12 apostles, which were usually so badly cast they were known as monkey spoons. Female relatives were given a mourning brooch or ring, which had a compartment containing strands of the deceased's hair. (If they were burying a bald man, it was the hair of his nearest male relative.) Spoons, brooches, and rings were all sold by the Inviters, who also earned a fee for supervising the party that followed every funeral. The quality of the wine served was a tribute in itself, and many people stored away the best they could afford to be used at their own funerals. When a person became mortally ill, a different pair of licensed professionals, known as Comforters of the Sick, were hired by relatives to spend as many hours as were needed reading Scriptures, singing hymns, and otherwise preparing the doomed soul for an easy entry into Heaven.

37 Bank of Tokyo Trust Alterations that took place in 1975 by **Kajima International** modernized **Bruce Price's** 1895 building. The eight Greek ladies by **J. Massey Rhind** still guard the building from their perch on the third floor. Look further up and you'll find more of them on an even higher level. ◆ 100 Broadway (at Pine St). 766.3400

38 Trinity and U.S. Realty Buildings The Trinity Building by **Francis H. Kimball** replaced **Richard Upjohn's** five-story 1840 building of the same name, which was the first office building in the city. After the present Gothic structure was built in 1906, its developers, U.S. Realty Company, acquired a similar 50-foot plot next door and constructed an identical 21-story building for their own use, with a shared service core along Thames Street. Fantastic creatures sporting lions' heads and eagles' wings watch as you approach the entrance to the Trinity Building. ◆ 111 and 115 Broadway (at Cedar Sts)

39 Equitable Building The massive structure is noteworthy not for any particular stylistic qualities but for its size, which changed the history of building in New York. This 40-story block contains 1.2 million square feet of office space on a site of slightly less than one acre. The public outcry when it was completed in 1915 by **Ernest R. Graham** caused the creation of the 1916 zoning laws, the first ever in the country, to ensure a minimum of light and air on city streets in the future. ◆ 120 Broadway (between Pine and Cedar Sts)

40 Marine Midland Bank One of Lower Manhattan's more successful modern-style steel-and-glass high-rises, this one was designed by **Skidmore, Owings & Merrill** in 1967. The sleek black building has an appropriateness of scale, largely due to a spandrel design that helps it fit into its older, more ornate surroundings. A vermilion cube by sculptor **Isamu Noguchi** enlivens the plaza. ◆ 140 Broadway (at Liberty St)

41 Chase Manhattan Bank Built as a catalyst to revitalize the aging Wall Street area in 1960, the bank's aluminum-and-glass face rises an impressive 813 feet, and it is still a fittingly imposing base for the Rockefeller banking empire. The designers, **Skidmore, Owings & Merrill,** gave the tower a trend-setting feature—its large plaza, home to *A Group of Four Trees* by **Jean Dubuffet** and a sunken sculpture garden by **Isamu Noguchi.** ◆ 1 Chase Manhattan Pl (near Nassau St)

42 Louise Nevelson Plaza The small triangular park with large steel sculptures created by the late Louise Nevelson is a popular lunch spot. ◆ Bounded by Maiden Ln and Liberty and William Sts

43 Federal Reserve Bank of New York This is the banker's bank, where the nations of the world maintain the balance of trade by the storage and exchange of gold, which is housed on five underground floors. The riches inside the building are represented on the outside in the best Renaissance style, with **Samuel Yellin's** finely detailed ironwork adding to the serene beauty of the limestone-and-sandstone facade (designed by **York & Sawyer** in 1924). Free tours of the gold vaults are available weekdays on a limited basis. Reservations are required at least one week in advance. ◆ 33 Liberty St (between William and Nassau Sts). 720.6130

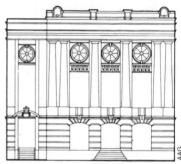

44 Chamber of Commerce of the State of New York Designed by **James B. Baker** in 1901, this ornate Beaux Arts edifice (shown above) is ponderous from its heavy stone base to its massive top, with Ionic columns adding to its almost predatory look. ◆ 65 Liberty St (at Liberty Pl)

45 McDonald's $ You'll know that this is not the typical home of the golden arches as soon as the tuxedo-clad doorman welcomes you and leads you to the glass-and-wood dining room, where a classical pianist is serenading diners. The food is standard McDonald's fare, except espresso and cappuccino are served from silver trays and pastries come from **Dumas,** an Upper East Side bakery. Worried about the market? A Dow Jones ticker tape looms above. ◆ Fast food ◆ Breakfast, lunch, and dinner. 160 Broadway (near Maiden Ln). 385.2063

46 Century 21 This is a larger version of the Brooklyn discount department store, with three bustling floors of top-quality housewares, clothing, toys, and electronics, popular labels intact. Even Wall Street loves a bargain. ◆ M-F 7:45AM-7PM; Sa 10AM-6:30PM. 22 Cortlandt St (between Broadway and Church St). 227.9092

More than 1,200 people were killed in riots near Tudor City in 1863, caused when the rich newcomers to the area were permitted to buy draft exemptions that the poor could not afford.

Restaurants/Clubs: Red   Hotels: Blue
Shops/ ◆ Outdoors: Green   Sights/Culture: Black

47 Battery Park City When this eclectic complex of 14,000 rental apartments and condominiums is finally complete, it will support a population larger than that of Bozeman, Montana (the residential population will be approximately 25,000). The total development cost of this 92-acre landfill site (at right) adjacent to the Financial District is estimated at $4 billion, including the privately financed $1.5 billion World Financial Center. The master plan—devised in 1979 by **Cooper, Eckstut Associates**—divides the blocks into parcels, with individual developers for each one, thus avoiding a superblock appearance. About 30 percent of the site is open parkland with parks linked by the 1.2-mile landscaped waterfront. **The Esplanade** (designed by landscape architects **Stanton Eckstut** between Liberty and West Thames streets; Eckstut, **Susan Child Associates,** and artist **Mary Miss** at the South Cove; and **Carr, Lynch, Hack & Sandell** between North Cove Yacht Harbor and Chambers Street), which extends the entire length of the site, provides a perfect place to relax and watch the river traffic. Access for the disabled has been incorporated into the overall design.

The first completed section was **Gateway Plaza** (1982), a trio of 34-story towers and three six-story buildings that provide 1,712 residential units. The structures, designed by **Jack Brown** and **Irving Gershorn,** were begun before the current master plan was established.

The architects who worked on **Rector Place** (1988), the second phase of residential construction, included **Charles Moore, James Stewart Polshek, Gruzen, Ulrich Franzen, Conklin Rossant, Mitchell Giurgola,** and **Davis, Brody & Associates.** Developed under the master plan, this nine-acre plot contains 2,200 apartments grouped around one-acre **Rector Park,** designed by landscape architects **Innocente & Webel.**

The third phase, **Battery Place** (scheduled for completion near the year 2000), consists of 2,800 residential units on nine parcels located between Rector Place and Pier A. The architects involved in the initial three buildings are **The Ehrenkrantz Group & Eckstut, Gruzen Samton Steinglass,** and **James Stewart Polshek & Partners.** The southern end of this area will include the **Museum of Jewish Heritage,** a hotel, the largest residential building in this complex, and **South Gardens,** a three-acre park designed by architects **Machado & Silvetti** and landscape architect **Hanna Olin.** ♦ Pier A (between Battery Park and Chambers St)

To summon help, a subway motorman will blast his horn in a pattern of *long-short, long-short.*

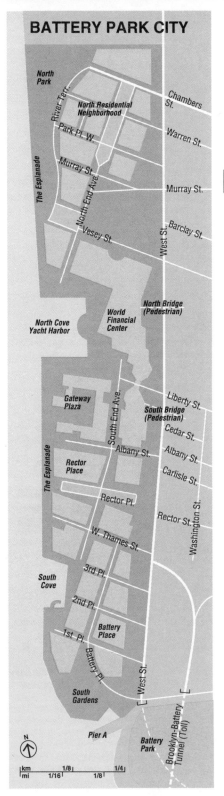

BATTERY PARK CITY

North Park

North Residential Neighborhood

Chambers St.

River Terr.

Park Pl. W.

Warren St.

The Esplanade

Murray St.

North End Ave.

Murray St.

Vesey St.

Barclay St.

West St.

North Bridge (Pedestrian)

World Financial Center

North Cove Yacht Harbor

Liberty St.

Gateway Plaza

South End Ave.

South Bridge (Pedestrian)

Cedar St.

The Esplanade

Rector Place

Albany St.

Albany St.

Carlisle St.

Rector Pl.

Washington St.

W. Thames St.

Rector St.

3rd Pl.

South Cove

2nd Pl.

1st Pl.

Battery Place

Battery Pl.

West St.

South Gardens

Pier A

Battery Park

Brooklyn-Battery Tunnel (Toll)

N

km   1/8   1/4
mi   1/16   1/8

48 World Financial Center More than eight million square feet of office, retail, and recreational space have been created on landfill produced by the construction of the World Trade Center across West Street. Designed by **Cesar Pelli & Associates** and built in 1981, the WFC includes four 33- to 50-story office towers, two nine-story buildings designated as gatehouses, a four-acre plaza, and a glass **Winter Garden,** whose most dramatic feature is 16 palm trees (the only ones of this size in the city), each a uniform 45 feet high. Tenants include **Bally of Switzerland, Caswell-Massey, Godiva Chocolatier, Manufacturers Hanover Trust, Rizzoli International Bookstore,** and **Plus One Fitness Clinic.** The **Courtyard,** a two-level outdoor piazza, houses four international restaurants and cafes. The **World Financial Center Plaza** is a stellar example of public space design: three and a half beautifully landscaped acres of parkland on the Hudson River with twin soft reflecting pools. The WFC presents an ongoing series of music, dance, and theater events as well as visual arts installations, and is world headquarters for such companies as **American Express, Merrill Lynch,** and **Dow Jones.** ♦ Daily 7AM-1AM. West St (between Vesey and Liberty Sts)

Within the World Financial Center:

Hudson River Club ★★★$$$$ The menu specializes in food from the Hudson River Valley: trout, shad roe, and smokehouse products, as well as regional wines. The clublike setting, with its plush banquette seating and armchairs, has a breathtaking view of North Cove Harbor Marina and the Statue of Liberty. Three dining rooms accommodate 190 people; there are also private dining areas that seat from 10 to 200. ♦ American ♦ Lunch and dinner; dinner only on Saturday. 4 WFC, upper level. Jacket and reservations required. 786.1500

Le Pactole ★★$$$$ This 10,000-square-foot restaurant features the talents of French chef **Alain Quirin.** For the adventurous, a *tournabroche*—a spit-roasting machine from France—is used to prepare grilled game birds, lamb, and whole pineapples roasted with honey. Within the restaurant is a lounge area, where lighter fare is served, and separate banquet facilities for business clients, with such amenities as telex and fax machines, and audio and video facilities. On weekends, there is dancing in a private dining room. A gourmet shop delivers meals to offices and homes in the Wall Street area. Gigantic windows overlook the Hudson. ♦ French ♦ Lunch and dinner. Closed Saturday. 2 WFC, second level. Reservations recommended. 945.9444

Pipeline ★$$ Designed by **Sam Lopata** to look like an oil refinery, this vast space seats 120 indoors and 150 more outside. The interior features brightly colored pipes, catwalks, ladders, and a great video/jukebox system. Chef **Gonzalo Figueroa** creates such dishes as corn chowder, and penne with tuna and white-bean salad; for dessert the chocolate truffle cake and bread pudding are musts. Also featured are Battery Park Picnic Baskets, which are special lunch and dinner take-out boxes. ♦ American ♦ Lunch and dinner. WFC, ground floor. Reservations recommended. 945.2755

Au Mandarin $$ The authentic Mandarin menu is popular at lunch. ♦ Mandarin ♦ Lunch and dinner. Winter Garden, ground floor. 385.0313

Donald Sacks ★$$ Good potpies, salads, and grilled sandwiches are served at this outpost of SoHo's famed take-out shop. Relax in the elegant mahogany-and-marble room while enjoying the river view. ♦ American ♦ Lunch and dinner; early dinner on Saturday and Sunday. 2 WFC, courtyard. Lunch reservations recommended. 619.4600

Barneys New York Architect **Peter Marino** designed the 10,000-square-foot men's store overlooking the Hudson. Keeping its Wall Street clientele firmly in mind, Barneys features fine collections of sportswear, outerwear, furnishings, formalwear, shoes, and a special shirt collection from **Truzzi.** During Special Designer Weeks, when different designers are featured, the store makes made-to-measure clothing available at the ready-to-wear cost. ♦ M-Th 10AM-9PM; F 10AM-8PM; Sa 10AM-7PM; Su noon-6PM. 2 WFC, upper level. 945.1600. Also at: Seventh Ave (at W. 17th St). 929.9000; 660 Madison Ave (at E. 61st St). 826.8900

Mark Cross A full range of signature luggage, billfolds, handbags, desk sets, and jewelry boxes are carried in this quality accessory store. ♦ M-F 11AM-5:30PM; Sa 11AM-5PM. 2 WFC, upper level. 945.1411. Also at: 645 Fifth Ave. 421.3000

Tahari Tahari's full line of sophisticated clothing for women, including scarves, jewelry, and handbags, is stocked here. The shop also contains antiques from Ellie Tahari's collection. ♦ M-F 10AM-6:30PM; Sa 11AM-6PM; Su noon-5PM. 2 WFC, upper level. 945.2450. Also at: 802 Madison Ave. 535.1515

Downtown Sound The music store stocks lots of CDs—which you can listen to on the headphones that hang from the wall—and fast, computer-aided service, plus audio equipment and accessories. ♦ M-F 10AM-6PM; Su noon-5PM. 4 WFC, lobby. 587.0093

Restaurants/Clubs: Red	**Hotels:** Blue
Shops/ 🌳 Outdoors: Green	**Sights/Culture:** Black

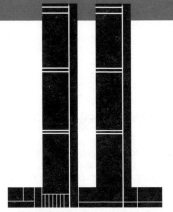

49 World Trade Center The World Trade Center consists of seven buildings—two towers (see above), four low plaza buildings, and the 22-story **Vista Hotel**—which form a semicircle around a five-acre plaza. All buildings are connected at ground level by the concourse, a vast shopping mall and pedestrian walkaround filled with 60 shops, banks, and concourse restaurants and gathering places. Designed by **Minoru Yamasaki & Associates** and **Emery Roth & Sons** and built from 1962 to 1977, the monolithic twin towers are, at 110 stories, the highest and most prominently sited of any buildings in the city, rising as an architectural gateway to Lower Manhattan. The World Trade Center offers 9.5 million square feet of office space, and is home to more than 1,200 trading firms and organizations. Some 50,000 people work in the complex, and 80,000 more visit daily. Almost 2,000 cars can park in the underground garages, and it is a major station for city subway and PATH lines. On 26 February 1993, a bomb was detonated in the parking garage of 1 World Trade Center, killing six people and injuring many. Due to the massive explosion, parts of the building and all of the restaurants that are listed here as within the WTC were still closed at press time. Damage is scheduled to be repaired by 1994-95, but the reopening dates of the restaurants are still unknown. Call ahead before you make plans. ♦ Church St (between Liberty and Vesey Sts). 435.4170

Within the World Trade Center:

The Observation Deck Floor-to-ceiling windows at the top of 2 WTC, the more southerly of the twin towers, are marked with unobtrusive diagrams to explain what you are seeing. The walls behind you on all four sides of the building display the history of world trade. The view from the deck has been called the best in the world, but if you want a better one, take the escalator up to the rooftop promenade. Another thrill: take the quarter-mile, 58-second elevator ride from the mezzanine level of 2 WTC to the 107th floor. Tickets are sold on the mezzanine level of 2 WTC. Fortunately, this attraction is open, despite the bombing. ♦ Admission. Daily 9:30AM-9:30PM; call for holiday schedule. 435.7377

The Restaurant at Windows on the World ★★$$$$ **Warren Platner** designed this spectacular terraced restaurant at the top of 1 WTC so that every table has an unobstructed view to the south and east. The menu changes frequently, and traditional international selections are augmented by such sophisticated original creations as fricassee of lobster with spinach and cucumbers or sautéed venison with juniper berries, wild mushrooms, and galette potatoes. The wine list, which offers more than 600 choices, is excellent. At press time, this location was still closed for repairs. Call 435.4170 to find out when it will reopen. ♦ Continental ♦ Jacket, tie, and reservations required. 938.1100

The Hors d'Oeuvrerie at Windows on the World ★★$$ As the name suggests, this is the place to sip a cocktail, snack on a wide assortment of delicacies, listen to piano music from 4:30PM, dance from 7:30PM until 1AM, and marvel at the views to the south and west. At press time, this location was still closed for repairs. Call 435.4170 to find out when it will reopen. ♦ International ♦ Cover. Jacket required. Reservations recommended for Sunday brunch. 938.1100

Cellar in the Sky ★★★★$$$$ The small 40-seat area at Windows on the World has no windows, but the wonderful dining experience more than makes up for it. A seven-course prix fixe dinner, with appropriate wines, is served here each evening. The menu, which changes biweekly, includes such heavenly entrées as steamed salmon with tomato-and-champagne sauce or lobster surrounded by pasta topped with pesto. The service is attentive and background music is provided by a classical guitarist. At press time, this location was still closed for repairs. Call 435.4170 to find out when it will reopen. ♦ Continental ♦ One seating at 7:30PM. Jacket, tie, and reservations required. 938.1100

Classic Books A wide selection of nonfiction, fiction, travel, and business titles is in stock, plus several tables of remainders. ♦ M-F 7:30AM-7PM; Sa 10AM-5PM; Su noon-6PM. 133 WTC, concourse. 466.0668

Benjamin Book & Co. Given the location, it's no wonder this bookseller specializes in business and computer titles. An interesting and helpful array of travel books are for sale, too, as well as a full range of fact and fiction. ♦ M-F 7AM-6PM; Sa 10AM-4:30PM. 408 WTC, concourse. 432.1103

Subway Stations IRT, BMT, and IND lines all stop here. See page 5 for more information.

Path Stations The Port Authority-operated PATH (Port Authority Trans-Hudson) rapid rail transit line, serving Hoboken, Newark, Jersey City, and Harrison, New Jersey, has its downtown terminus here. ♦ PATH Sq, lowest level. 800/234.7284

TKTS Half-price day-of-performance tickets are available for evening performances of Broadway and Off-Broadway shows. Wednesday, Saturday, and Sunday matinee tickets are sold from 11AM to closing the day before the performance. ♦ M-F 11AM-5:30PM; Sa 11AM-3:30PM. 2 WTC, mezzanine. 768.1818. Also at: Broadway (at 47th St)

Commodities Exchange Four exchanges trade in gold, silver, coffee, cotton, and other commodities in a frenzied setting, somewhat like an auction. Watch the activity from a glass-enclosed balcony overlooking the trading floor. ♦ M-F 9:30AM-3PM. 4 WTC, ninth floor. 938.2018

Austin J. Tobin Plaza The five-acre space between the towers is graced with a fountain that surrounds a 25-foot bronze construction by **Fritz Koenig.** The granite pyramid at the entrance is by **Masyuki Nagare,** and the stainless-steel abstract sculpture is by **James Rosati.** Also note the **Alexander Calder** stabile just outside on Church Street. Other sculpture is often temporarily displayed on the windy plaza, which is frequently used as a setting for concerts and other events. Other works of art commissioned for the World Trade Center include **Louise Nevelson's** *Sky-Gate New York* on the mezzanine of 1 WTC, and a three-ton tapestry by **Joan Miró,** which hangs in the mezzanine of 2 WTC.

New York Vista Hotel $$$$ This sleek yet welcoming Hilton International with views of the Hudson River from the highest floors, designed in 1981 by **Skidmore, Owings & Merrill,** is packed during the week with businesspeople who want proximity to Wall Street and the World Trade Center, and, on weekends, with visitors who want to be near the sights and charms of old New York. Free weekend shuttle buses uptown make it a pleasure to venture out of the neighborhood, too. A fitness center provides a free indoor swimming pool, jogging track, sauna, and exercise rooms (fee for racquetball and massage). The business center offers secretarial services, personal computers, and cellular phones. An added tariff buys a room or suite on one of the Executive floors, with access to a special lounge for complimentary cocktails, breakfast, and other perks. The adjacent concourse of the World Trade Center is a bazaar of stores and restaurants. There's a comfortable spot in the lobby for express breakfast or lunch, and the **Tall Ships Bar** (drinks, piano music, hearty potpies, and sandwiches) becomes a jammed singles bar after work. At press time, the hotel was temporarily closed for repairs incurred from the bombing, but it's due to reopen in fall of 1994. ♦ 3 WTC. 938.9100, 800/445.8667

Within the New York Vista Hotel:

American Harvest ★★$$$ The chef's brave attempt at translating American regional dishes into fine restaurant fare is often quite successful. Appetizers, vegetables, and desserts are notably delectable, and the American wine list is good. The surroundings are plush and elegant, the service polite and eager. There's complimentary parking, too. At press time, the restaurant was still closed for repairs. Call 435.4170 to find out when it will reopen. ♦ American ♦ Plaza Level. Jacket required. 938.9100

Greenhouse Bar and Restaurant
★★★$$$ The skylight roof allows an unusual view of the World Trade Center twin towers soaring above and lets the sun stream through to the beautifully planted gardenlike room set with rattan chairs. Good salad plates, omelets, unusual sandwiches, moderately priced main courses, unique breads, and tempting desserts make it one of the best informal hotel restaurants. The wine bar, with tastes by the glass served at the table by a knowledgeable sommelier, is an added attraction. The restaurant is excellent for breakfast, lunch, and snacks. At press time, it was still closed for repairs. Call 435.4170 to find out when it will reopen. ♦ American ♦ Plaza Level. 938.9100

50 **The Millenium** $$$$ Fifty-five stories high, the sleek Millenium has overlooked downtown New York since being built in the shadow of the World Trade Center in 1992. It offers 561 elegant guest rooms and suites, an indoor pool and health center, an executive business center, and other amenities. The hotel's restaurants are the formal **Taliesin** and the casual **Grill.** ♦ 55 Church St (between Fulton and Dey Sts). 693.2001, 800/835.2220; fax 571.2316

51 **195 Broadway** There are more columns on the facade of this building, designed in 1917 by **William Welles Bosworth** as headquarters for the **American Telephone & Telegraph Company,** than on any other building in the world, with even more inside (the lobby is like an ancient Athenian temple). The ornamental panels over the Broadway entrance, as well as the bronze seals on the lobby floor and the other interior decorative elements are by **Paul Manship,** whose best-known work in New York is the *Prometheus* fountain in Rockefeller Plaza. ♦ Between Dey and Fulton Sts

52 **St. Paul's Chapel** Built in 1766 by **Thomas McBean,** this is Manhattan's only remaining pre-Revolutionary War church, surviving 1776's Great Fire. St. Paul's is not only a rare Georgian architectural gem but is also important historically. Said to be the most impressive church in the colony when built, its grandeur loses nothing in the shadow of that neighboring temple of commerce, the World Trade Center. It's humbling to remember that in 1750 this site was a wheat field; the cemetery once extended to the Hudson River; and **George Washington** came here to pray after his swearing-in as the country's first president. McBean's plan for St. Paul's was much influenced by **St. Martin-in-the-Fields** in London, designed by his teacher, **James Gibb.** The interior, lit by Waterford crystal chandeliers, is one of the city's best. Come here for the concerts of classical and church music Monday and Thursday at 12:10PM (donation requested), or for services Sunday at 8AM. ♦ Broadway (between Vesey and Fulton Sts). 602.0800

53 New York County Lawyers' Association Among the beautiful rooms in this structure designed in 1930 by **Cass Gilbert** is a second-floor assembly hall that is an exact copy of the main room of Philadelphia's **Independence Hall.** ♦ 14 Vesey St (between Church St and Broadway)

54 Woolworth Building One of the city's most dramatic skyscrapers was designed by **Cass Gilbert** in 1913 as the headquarters of **Frank Woolworth's** chain of five-and-dime stores. The building is a Gothic celebration inside and out, with picturesque details enhancing the forceful massing and graceful vertical thrust, which culminates in a perfectly composed crown. Inside, the lobby features a soaring glass mosaic ceiling and marble walls awash with more Gothic detail. An added surprise are the caricature bas-reliefs, including one of Gilbert himself with a model of the building and another of Frank Woolworth counting nickels and dimes. The Woolworths were so pleased with Gilbert's work that they paid for it in cash ($1.5 million) and maintain an office here. Worth a visit. ♦ 233 Broadway (between Barclay St and Park Pl)

55 City Hall Surprisingly, New York City is still doing business (with a little help from the nearby Municipal Building) in the same building that was its headquarters in 1811 when the building was completed. This elegant scaled-down palace by **Mangin and McComb,** a winning entry in a design competition, successfully combines the Federal style with French Renaissance details. The central hall has a sweeping twin-spiral marble staircase under a splendid dome, making it the perfect setting for public functions and grand entrances. Kings, poets, and astronauts have been received here. Upstairs, the grand **City Council Chamber** (also used by the Board of Estimate) and the **Governor's Room,** now a portrait gallery with paintings by **Sully, Trumbull, Inman,** and

others, are worth a visit. There are always exhibitions with historical or artistic themes. Interiors were restored and refurbished between 1902 and 1920, and the exterior was restored and repaired by **Shreve, Lamb & Harmon** in 1959. What is known today as **City Hall Park** has always been the city's village green or town common; equally grand in scale, the park sets off the mass of City Hall. ♦ M-F 9AM-5PM. City Hall Park (between Broadway and Park Row)

56 Pace University Originally founded as an accounting school, Pace now offers courses in the arts and sciences as well as business, education, and nursing. The welded copper sculpture on the facade, by **Henri Nachemia,** represents *The Brotherhood of Man.* The building itself was designed by **Eggers & Higgins** in 1970. ♦ Nassau St (between Frankfort and Spruce Sts)

57 New York City Courthouse The building was known as the **Tweed Courthouse** because Tammany Hall chieftain **William Marcy Tweed** escalated its cost to 52 times the appropriated amount, most of which went into his own bank account. Because of the scandal, the building became a symbol of graft and has always been something of a municipal stepchild. Recent attempts to restore it have been halfhearted, but it has been saved from destruction. The original building, designed by **John Kellum** and constructed in 1872, had a grand staircase in front, which was removed in 1955 to make room for the widening of Chambers Street. The result is a blank space that ruins the facade. ♦ 52 Chambers St (between Broadway and Centre St)

58 Ellen's Cafe and Bake Shop ★$ Ellen Hart Sturm, a former Miss Subway beauty queen, runs this bustling upscale cafe and bakery across from City Hall. The walls are lined with photos of former Miss Subways (Ellen sponsors yearly reunions for these beauties). Try the Mayor's Special (toasted Thomas' English Muffin halves layered with tuna salad and tomato slices, topped with melted cheese). Be sure to save room for Ellen's pecan pie. ♦ American ♦ Breakfast, lunch, and early dinner. Closed Sunday. 270 Broadway (at Chambers St). 962.1257. Also: Ellen's Stardust, 1377 Sixth Ave. 307.7575

59 Ecco ★$$$ The restaurant has none of the downtown funkiness you'd expect in this neighborhood. Carved mahogany, beveled mirrors, and the two-story-high tin ceiling provide a clubby, 19th-century atmosphere. The waiters bustle through the mixed crowd of Wall Streeters and art dealers. Stick with pasta and dessert. ♦ Italian ♦ Lunch and dinner. Closed Sunday. 124 Chambers St (between W. Broadway and Church St). Reservations required. 227.7074

60 Stuyvesant High School This is a new location, built in 1991 by **Alexander Cooper & Partners,** for one of the most prestigious and progressive public high schools in the country. Since the difficult-to-earn **Westinghouse** scholarships were first awarded, Stuyvesant students have routinely finished the competition among the top 10 from all over the U.S. Graduates include Nobel laureates **Joshua Lederberg** and **Raoul Hoffman.** ♦ 345 Chambers St (off West St)

61 Surrogate's Court Monumental sculptures, including a pair by **Philip Martiny** at the entrance—one representing Britannia (an English soldier and a maiden), the other America (a Native American and a Pilgrim)—along with an array of cherubs, eagles, festoons, ship prows, and shields, let you know something important is going on here. The French Empire facade, reminiscent of the Paris Opera, is only the beginning. The interior has a mosaic ceiling by **William de Leftwich Dodge,** marble walls and floors, and allegorical reliefs. The huge double stairway is yet another touch borrowed from the Opera. Intended to be the last resting place of important city records, the building, which was designed in 1911 by **John R. Thomas** and **Horgan & Slattery,** also serves as the Surrogate's Court. Over the years this became its primary function, as the need grew for more space to probate wills and administer guardianships and trusts. ♦ 31 Chambers St (at Centre St)

McKIM, MEAD & WHITE

62 Municipal Building McKim, Mead & White created this neoclassical skyscraper (illustrated above) in 1914 to house city government offices. The building straddles a city street and coexists quite happily with neighboring, smaller City Hall without upstaging it. The almost baroque confection is topped with a fanciful cluster of colonnaded towers capped by **Adolph Weinman's** gilded statue. ♦ 1 Centre St (at Chambers St)

63 Police Plaza At three full acres, this is the largest public plaza in New York. On the south side is a prison window from the 1763 **Rhinelander Sugar Warehouse,** which was on this site until 1895. (The original building was used by the British to house American prisoners of war during the Revolution.) The five interlocking oxidized-steel disks, a 1974 creation by **Bernard Rosenthal,** represent the five boroughs of the city. Just beyond, an eight-foot waterfall marks the entrance to a multilevel parking garage under the plaza, which was designed in 1973 by **M. Paul Friedberg.** ♦ Chambers St (pedestrian mall between Municipal Building and Police Headquarters)

64 St. Andrew's Church The Roman Catholic church was established here in 1842 to minister to the needs of Irish immigrants. Its mission has changed along with the neighborhood. In the late 18th century, it offered a 2:30AM Mass for night workers from nearby newspaper offices, and later became the first to offer a noon Mass for businesspeople. The present church was designed by **Maginnis & Walsh** and **Robert J. Reiley** in 1939. ♦ 20 Cardinal Hayes Pl (at Duane St/St. Andrews Pl). 962.3972

65 United States Courthouse Here's another Lower Manhattan structure trying to be a temple. This civic building, designed in 1936 by **Cass Gilbert** and **Cass Gilbert, Jr.,** presents a traditional, stately image with rows of Corinthian columns as a base for a tower crowned with a gold pyramid. ♦ 40 Centre St (at Foley Square)

66 New York County Courthouse A National Landmark, this hexagon-shaped building, designed by **Guy Lowell** in 1926, won a 1912 competition. The Roman style of the building—particularly the Corinthian portico—works much better here than at the neighboring U.S. Courthouse. ♦ 60 Centre St (at Pearl St)

67 Jacob K. Javits Federal Building The smaller building on the left houses the U.S. Customs Court, and the taller one with the strange windows is filled with government offices. Both buildings were designed by **Alfred Easton Poor** and **Kahn & Jacobs** in 1967. ♦ 26 Federal Plaza (between Duane and Worth Sts)

During the peak years of immigration on Ellis Island, the record of languages spoken by an official interpreter was 15. One interpreter was Fiorello La Guardia, who would later become the famous—and possibly the most beloved—mayor of New York City, responsible for cleaning up the corruption of Tammany Hall. He worked at Ellis Island for an annual salary of $1,200 from 1907 to 1910. He was the first mayor to serve an until-then unprecedented three terms, from 1935 to 1945.

Studio Shoo-Ins: How to Get TV Tickets

New York is headquarters for a variety of major TV shows that the public can attend without charge. Although most tickets must be obtained in advance, many programs offer standby seats (policies vary, so call ahead). Lines for standby seats often form hours in advance, particularly when well-known guests are booked. The following addresses for written ticket requests do not always reflect the location of the studio or the place where standby tickets are distributed. Audience members must be 18 or older. Request tickets by postcard unless otherwise indicated, and specify which show you want to see and the number of seats. Asking for a certain day or week is discouraged. But if you will only be visiting New York for a short time and you send in your request a few months in advance, most studios will try to accommodate you, usually permitting two to four tickets per postcard. Even if you don't stipulate a specific date, it can take a few months to receive tickets for the more popular shows.

Donahue (NBC)
NBC, 30 Rockefeller Plaza
New York, NY 10112
212/664.3056

Tapings are Monday through Thursday at 4PM, with an additional taping Thursday at 1PM. There is a two- to four-month wait, and you can request tickets for up to six people. Limited standby seats are available (for tapings on the same day) at 2:30PM at the main hall information desk at 30 Rockefeller Plaza.

Geraldo (CBS)
CBS Television, 524 W. 57th Street
New York, NY 10019
212/265.1283

Tapings take place Tuesday through Thursday at 1PM and 3PM. For ticket requests for up to 10 people, call the above number or send a letter with a stamped, self-addressed envelope; expect a one-month wait. Standby tickets are sometimes available at 530 W. 57th Street, one hour before taping.

Late Night with Conan O'Brian (NBC)
NBC, 30 Rockefeller Plaza
New York, NY 10112
212/644.3056

David Letterman's successor accepts postcards requesting no more than two tickets and will not accommodate specific dates. The show is taped Monday to Friday at 5:30PM; a limited number of standby tickets (one per person) are distributed at 9AM in NBC's main lobby; entry isn't guaranteed.

The Late Show with David Letterman (CBS)
"The Late Show" Tickets, 1697 Broadway
New York, NY 10019
212/975.2476

"The Late Show," taped Monday through Friday at 5:30PM, is one of the hottest tickets in town—expect a three- to four-month wait. One hundred standby tickets are distributed weekdays at noon, though the line forms as early as 9AM. Two tickets are allotted for each postcard.

Live with Regis and Kathie Lee (ABC)
"Live" Tickets
Ansonia Station
P.O. Box 777
New York, NY 10023
212/456.3537

This talk show broadcasts Monday through Friday at 9AM. Request up to four tickets per postcard, but be prepared to wait—about eight to 10 months. Standby tickets are available after ticket-holders are seated each weekday; the line usually starts forming around 7:30AM at the studio, 7 Lincoln Square (at W. 67th Street and Columbus Avenue).

NBC Studio Tours
30 Rockefeller Plaza
New York, NY 10112
212/664.4000

Tours leave every 15 minutes from 9:30AM to 4:30PM daily. Tours cost $8 and the areas of the studios visited vary due to broadcasting schedules.

The Rush Limbaugh Show (Independent)
Unitel Studios, 515 W. 57th Street
New York, NY 10019
212/397.7367

The show is taped Monday to Thursday at 5:30PM. Tickets can only be requested by phone: call Monday to Thursday from 10AM to 1PM. There is usually a three-month wait, although tickets from last-minute cancellations are often available by phone.

Sally Jessy Raphael (NBC)
"Sally Jessy Raphael" Tickets
P.O. Box 1400
Radio City Station
New York, NY 10101
212/582.1722

Tapings are scheduled Monday through Thursday at 11AM. Each request can yield up to six tickets, with a usual two- to three-month wait. For standby, show up at 10AM at the studio at 515 W. 57th Street.

Saturday Night Live (NBC)
"Saturday Night Live" Tickets
NBC, 30 Rockefeller Plaza
New York, NY 10112
212/664.3056

A ticket lottery is held each year at the end of August; only postcards (two tickets each) sent in August will be accepted. Since the majority of each audience fills up with network associates, advertisers, and their families and friends, few seats make it to the lottery. Winners are seated on Saturday at 8PM for a dress rehearsal and 11:30PM for the live taping. On Saturday morning, 50 standby tickets for each of these seatings are distributed at 9:15AM at NBC at the 49th Street entrance of Rockefeller Plaza. One person is admitted per ticket, although holding a ticket does not guarantee admission. Fans have been known to camp out overnight for tickets when a popular host is scheduled.

Chinatown/Lower East Side/ Little Italy

In New York's early days, the swampy territory just northeast of City Hall was considered worthless. But as waves of immigrants began arriving in the middle of the 18th century, the former marshes became valuable to the real-estate developers who packed the newcomers into crowded tenements. The distinct ethnic flavors of Chinatown, the Lower East Side, and Little Italy were established as each immigrant group settled the area roughly bounded by the **East River** and **Lafayette, Chambers,** and **Houston streets.**

Nearly every part of New York has metamorphosed several times during the last two centuries. But in this area, it's mainly the populace—rather than architecture—that has changed. During the 1860s, thousands of Germans arrived, forcing the long-settled Irish farther uptown. Between 1881 and 1910, 1.5 million Jews fled Romania, Hungary, and Russia, creating the largest Jewish settlement in the world on Manhattan's Lower East Side. Italians, Greeks, Poles, and Turks were among the other settlers. The neighborhood continues to be a first stop for newly arrived immigrants—today's predominantly Hispanic population fills streets that carry the legacy of the Jews they replaced.

The southwestern portion of this area is a magnet for Chinese immigrants, who began arriving from San Francisco during the 1870s. Since immigration laws were changed in the mid-1960s, the neighborhood has welcomed more of them than ever. Once covering three square blocks and now 40 square blocks and growing, the area's more than 150,000 Chinese residents make Chinatown the largest Chinese community outside of Asia. The need for more living space has caused new arrivals to cross Canal Street into the enclave traditionally reserved for immigrants from Naples and Sicily. The result is that the neighborhood called Little Italy is now filled with hundreds of sweatshops and other businesses identified by Chinese ideograms. (Distressed about this

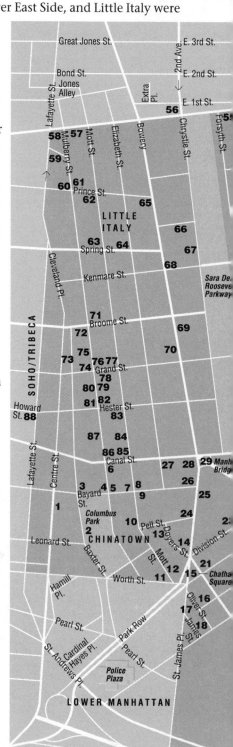

situation, Italian community leaders have requested that signs along Mulberry Street be posted only in Roman letters.)

Chinatown is a neighborhood that thrives on street life. Except for pagoda telephone booths, don't expect quaintness. What you will find is a warren of shops selling exotic vegetables and bargain-basement Chinese clothing and housewares, along with Formica- and vinyl-filled restaurants, many of which prepare wondrous dishes. (When he retired as food critic for the *New York Times*, **John Canaday** identified his favorite New York restaurant as

Chinatown.) The largest crowds appear on **Chinese New Year**, in January or February, when a parade snakes through the streets and revelers toss firecrackers and throng the restaurants.

The Lower East Side is roughly the area below Houston Street, from the Bowery to the East River. During the 1880s and 1890s, immigrants from Eastern Europe flooded into the airless redbrick tenements. At the turn of the century, this was the world's largest Jewish settlement, a slum that later became a center of culture and community (documented by, among others, critic **Irving Howe** in his 1976 study "World of Our Fathers") that spawned many writers, businessmen, and intellectuals. Most of the upwardly mobile Jewish immigrants left as quickly as possible; now the Lower East Side is home to Chinese, Puerto Ricans, and African-Americans. Although many synagogues remain empty, the old crowd comes back for a steak at **Sammy's Famous Roumanian Jewish Steakhouse** or to shop. **Orchard Street** is still discount heaven for everything from fabrics to designer dresses. In observation of the Sabbath, most nonreligious sites on the Lower East Side are closed Friday afternoon and all day Saturday.

Mulberry Street is the main drag of Little Italy (bounded by Canal, Lafayette, and Houston streets and the Bowery), a bustling residential area filled with neighborhood stores and old Italian social clubs. Former residents and visitors come for the food—to buy salamis, cheeses, and pasta, dine in one of the plentiful restaurants, or linger over an espresso and pastry in a *caffè*. The area was settled mainly between 1880 and 1924 by immigrant families, many of whom have moved on. But they always come back—especially for the **Feast of San Gennaro**, a week-long religious celebration held each September that is famous for its eating, drinking, and merrymaking.

1 Criminal Courts Building Called the "Tombs" after its Egyptian Revival ancestor across the street, this giant ziggurat is the third Manhattan jail, the last built before prisoners were housed at Riker's Island. Designed by **Harvey Wiley Corbett** in 1939, it is an elegant Art Moderne structure (you'll recognize Corbett's hand in Rockefeller Center). In its day, the Tombs' 835-cell jail was considered a standard for penal reform: each cell housed only one prisoner. ♦ 100 Centre St (between Leonard and White Sts)

2 Columbus Park The only real open space in Chinatown provides a setting for ball-playing and outdoor entertainment, and is a staging area for the dragon dancers during Chinese New Year. It replaces **Mulberry Bend,** once a red-light district and part of the 19th-century slum neighborhood known as **Five Points.** ♦ Bounded by Worth and Bayard Sts, and Mulberry and Baxter Sts

3 Thailand Restaurant ★$$ Some of the best and cheapest Thai food around is served here, at one of Chinatown's few Thai restaurants. ♦ Thai ♦ Lunch and dinner. 106 Bayard St (at Baxter St). 349.3132

4 Saigon House Restaurant ★★$ The decor could use some help, but the food is authentic Vietnamese. Appetizers and soups are best: crisp spring rolls, shrimp with sugar cane, cold shrimp-and-pork roll, seafood and chicken soups with lemongrass. One of the city's rare Vietnamese restaurants, it's a favorite among lawyers and judges who work at the nearby courthouses. ♦ Vietnamese ♦ Lunch and dinner. 89-91 Bayard St (at Mulberry St). 732.8988

5 Chinatown History Museum Chinatown is a place, but it is also a symbol of the cultural richness and complexity of Chinese-American history. Begin a visit to this 40-square-block neighborhood by exploring this small museum founded in 1980, or join one of their organized walking tours. The museum now houses the nation's largest research collection of oral histories, photographs, and artifacts relating to the Chinese-American experience. ♦ Nominal admission. M-F, Su noon-5PM. 70 Mulberry St (at Bayard St). 619.4785

6 Kamman Food Products, Inc. Even if you're not buying, drop in to see the astonishing selection of fresh vegetables, dried fish of all kinds, herbs, teas, noodles and, in the basement, kitchenware. The take-out barbecued ducks and chickens are delicious. ♦ Daily 9AM-9PM. 200 Canal St (at Mulberry St). 571.0330

Restaurants/Clubs: Red	**Hotels:** Blue
Shops/ ♣ Outdoors: Green	**Sights/Culture:** Black

7 Bo Ky Restaurant ★$ The specialty of this popular restaurant, owned by Chiu Chow people from Vietnam, is the big bowls of steaming hot rice noodles topped with shrimp, fish, shrimp balls, or sliced roast duck. ♦ Vietnamese ♦ Breakfast, lunch, and dinner. 80 Bayard St (at Mott St). No credit cards. 406.2292

8 Tai Hong Lau ★$$ Inexpensive, authentic Cantonese cooking is served. Try the winter melon treasure, a curved piece of white melon atop a mixture of mushrooms, roast duck, chicken, pork, and shrimp, surrounded by broccoli florets. ♦ Cantonese ♦ Breakfast, lunch, and dinner. 70 Mott St (between Canal and Bayard Sts). 219.1431

8 Eastern States Buddhist Temple of America, Inc. The sparkling gold mountain of Buddhas in the window beckons you into this temple with more than a hundred statues of Buddhas and other religious articles in the back. For a song, you can either pick up a fortune (not in a cookie) or buy a bottle of Mazola oil to offer at the elaborate shrine. Neighborhood worshipers come here to pay respects and light incense. ♦ 64B Mott St (between Canal and Bayard Sts). 966.4753

8 Wonton Garden ★$ This is a fine place for the many varieties of Cantonese noodle dishes, especially wonton noodles in chicken broth with roast pork and various Chinese vegetables. ♦ Cantonese ♦ Breakfast, lunch, and dinner. 52-56 Mott St (at Bayard St). No credit cards. 966.4886

9 New Lin Heong ★$ The greasy-spoon restaurant—heavy on the oyster sauce and sweet-and-sour—is popular because of the low prices, generally good-humored staff, and heaping plates of delicious *chow fun*. Also try the big batter-dipped fried fantail shrimp. Expect long lines but fast turnover on weekends. ♦ Cantonese ♦ Breakfast, lunch, dinner, and late-night meals. 69 Bayard St (at Mott St). No credit cards. 962.8195

10 Lung Fong Bakery Although most of these beautiful sweets are an acquired taste, this is the best bakery in Chinatown. The unadventurous should try the huge, meltingly good almond and walnut cookies. ♦ Daily 8AM-9PM. 41 Mott St (at Pell St). 233.7447

11 Hunan Garden ★★$ Spicy Hunan specialties and Cantonese fare highlight this friendly restaurant with a large and interesting menu. Gather several friends together and call ahead for the special Chinese banquet. ♦ Hunan/Cantonese ♦ Lunch and dinner. 1 Mott St (at Worth St). 732.7270

12 Chinatown Fair The usual (pinball machines and the latest video games) and the unusual (a live chicken that challenges you to a game of tic-tac-toe) can be found in this amusement arcade. ♦ 8 Mott St (between Park Row and Pell St). No phone

12 20 Mott Street ★★$$ This is as close to the Hong Kong dining experience as you'll find in New York. Ask for the baked conch stuffed in its own shell. The dim sum is among the best in the neighborhood. ♦ Cantonese ♦ Breakfast, lunch, and dinner. Between Park Row and Pell St. 964.0380

12 Peking Duck House ★★$$ The main reason to dine here is the Peking duck, enough for six as an appetizer. The laboriously crisped duck is carved tableside in home style (with the flesh clinging to the skin) rather than the usual banquet style (skin only). It is served with the traditional accompaniments: thin pancakes in which to roll the duck, slivered cucumbers, and a scallion brush to swab the duck with *hoisin* sauce. Order some steamed pork dumplings to munch before the duck arrives. ♦ Peking/Szechuan ♦ Lunch and dinner. 22 Mott St (between Park Row and Pell St). 227.1810

13 Doyers Street The narrow little street with a wishbone-shaped curve was once known as "Bloody Angle." Opium dealers who thrived in the area during the last century lured their competitors here, where they could be ambushed beyond the blind turn. ♦ Pell St near Bowery

13 Nam Wah Tea Parlor ★$ The oldest and most colorful Hong Kong dim sum parlor provides funky fun, but the food is not as good as at other restaurants in the area. ♦ Dim sum ♦ Breakfast, lunch, and early dinner. 13 Doyers St (between Pell St and Bowery). No credit cards. 962.6047

13 Viet-Nam ★★$ With patience and perhaps a few wrong turns, you'll be glad you sought this place out. The flashing sign signals you're in the right place and, after the descent down the steep stairs, you'll have some of the best and most authentic Vietnamese food in the city. What they save on the decor, they put into the food—the menu lists some one hundred items. Start with any of the perfectly done egg rolls, then try the chicken with lemongrass. ♦ Vietnamese ♦ Lunch and dinner. 11 Doyers St (between Pell St and Bowery). 693.0725

Each John Doe burial in Potter's Field (on the Long Island Sound) costs New York City $300.

14 Edward Mooney House Originally built in 1789, the oldest Federal-style house in Manhattan was modified in 1971 to become a busy branch of the New York Off-Track Betting Corp., which has since moved on to larger quarters. ♦ 18 Bowery (at Doyers St)

15 Chatham Square The monument in the center of the square is the **Kim Lau Memorial**, designed by **Poy G. Lee** in 1962 and dedicated to Chinese-American war dead. ♦ Bowery (between E. Broadway and Park Row)

16 Mariners' Temple Designed in 1842 by **Minard Lafever**, this is a brownstone Greek temple, originally called the **Oliver Street Church**, which served sailors based at the nearby East River piers. It is now a Baptist church serving a widely varied community. ♦ 12 Oliver St (at Henry St)

17 First Shearith Israel Cemetery Near Chatham Square, which it once covered, this is the surviving fragment of the **Congregation Shearith Israel's** first burial ground (there are two more), the oldest Jewish cemetery in Manhattan. The most ancient gravestone is dated 1683. Shearith Israel, founded by early Portuguese and Spanish settlers in 1654, is now located uptown at a synagogue on Central Park West. ♦ 55 St. James Pl (between Oliver and James Sts)

18 St. James Roman Catholic Church The Greek Revival-style Roman Catholic church built in 1837 is an interesting neighbor to the nearby Mariners' Temple; both were designed by **Minard Lafever.** ♦ 32 James St (between St. James Pl and Madison St)

19 William Clark House Originally built in 1824, this house—and especially the entrance—would appear to epitomize all the elegance of the Federal style. But there is a twist: it is one of the very few known to have four floors (two or three were preferred). ♦ 51 Market St (between Monroe and Madison Sts)

20 Nice Restaurant ★★★$$ One of Chinatown's better Cantonese restaurants serves excellent barbecued duck, a selection of very good dim sum, and a cold dessert of melon and tapioca. ♦ Cantonese ♦ Breakfast, lunch, and dinner. 35 E. Broadway (between Catherine and Market Sts). 406.9510

21 Golden Unicorn ★★★$$ Larger and more elegant than the typical Chinatown storefront kitchen-cum-restaurant, Golden Unicorn feels like a real restaurant, done up in sleek black and peach with lots of mirrors and even a napkin folded in your glass. It is popular with families who come to sample the amazing array of daytime dim sum, so be sure to arrive early. Dinner is equally good, and interestingly enough, the nonspicy dishes are better than the hot ones. Start with tasty fried dumplings, then move on to egg foo yung. ♦ Cantonese ♦ Breakfast, lunch, and dinner. 18 E. Broadway (at Catherine St), second floor. 941.0911

22 Triple 8 Palace Restaurant ★★★$$$ Ignore the awful decor—this is one of the best (and largest) restaurants in Chinatown. Excellent appetizers include steamed dumplings, fresh oyster pancakes, moist and tender soy chicken and abalone, and vegetable soups. Hordes of workers stop by at lunch for the best dim sum around, but it's crowded on weekends as well. ♦ Hong Kong ♦ Breakfast, lunch, and dinner. 59 Division St (under Manhattan Bridge), top floor. 941.8886

22 Canton ★★$$$ Have the owner, **Eileen,** order for you at this restaurant that's popular with uptowners. ♦ Cantonese ♦ Lunch and dinner. Closed Monday and Tuesday. 45 Division St (at Manhattan Bridge). No credit cards. 226.4441

23 Great Shanghai ★★$ Though it's been here forever, Great Shanghai owes its modern pink and gray and neon decor to a recent remodeling. But the food is pure Chinatown. Skip the appetizers and share as many main dishes as there are in your party. You won't be disappointed if you don't restrict yourself to one item. ♦ Shanghai ♦ Lunch and dinner. 27 Division St (between Manhattan Bridge and Bowery). 966.7663

24 Noodle Town ★$ One of the best noodle houses for curried Singapore-style noodles, Noodle Town serves panfried Cantonese noodles with different meats and the thick rice porridge called *congee*. ♦ Cantonese ♦ Breakfast, lunch, dinner, and late-night meals. 28½ Bowery (at Pell St). 349.0923

25 Confucius Plaza Designed in 1976 by **Horowitz & Chun** and at odds with its smaller 19th-century neighbors, this huge, chunky building solves a pressing need for more living space. It also houses a public school whose population is almost entirely first- and second-generation Chinese. ♦ Bowery (between Division St and Manhattan Bridge)

26 First Taste ★★★$$ Probably the best Hong Kong cuisine in Chinatown is served in this charming newer restaurant where the staff speaks English and is more than willing to explain each dish. Start with the broiled eel shish kebab or cold jellyfish topped with baby squid or chicken or beef consommé. The less adventurous might try the soft, silky bean curd steamed with fresh scallops or crisp salt-baked chicken with spicy ginger sauce. Hot red-bean soup or lotus seeds in a cool broth with rock sugar are great for dessert. ♦ Hong Kong ♦ Lunch and dinner. 53 Bayard St (between Bowery and Elizabeth St). 962.1818

27 Oriental Town Seafood ★★$$ Don't be surprised when they seat strangers at your table just to make sure the restaurant is filled to the gills, which it always is. But the seafood is so good that you won't mind feeling like a sardine. ♦ Cantonese/Seafood ♦ Breakfast, lunch, and dinner. 14 Elizabeth St (between Canal and Bayard Sts). 619.0085

27 Lin's Sister Associates Corp. Herbs, vitamins, and various traditional medicines are carried in this Chinese drugstore. If you're feeling poorly, stop in for a detailed consultation and prescription from an herbalist, who might recommend a tea, capsules, or a poultice. ♦ Daily 10AM-6:30PM. 18A Elizabeth St (between Canal and Bayard Sts). 962.5417

27 King Fung ★★$$ Recently renovated, King Fung is a combination of every Chinese restaurant you've ever been to: the decor is replete with lanterns, lions on pedestals, fan-shaped windows, and dragons. Everything is done with care—including tablecloths and full sets of utensils—and the food is excellent and beautifully presented. ♦ Cantonese ♦ Breakfast, lunch, and dinner. 20 Elizabeth St (at Canal St). Credit cards at dinner only. 964.5256

28 Silver Palace ★★$$ This bustling dining room is best for dim sum. Regulars get preference when the line gets long, which it regularly does on Sunday. Point to what you want off the carts rolling by, and keep eating. Bills are totaled by the record of empty plates. ♦ Cantonese ♦ Breakfast, lunch, and dinner. 50 Bowery (between Bayard and Canal Sts). Credit cards Sunday and at dinner only. 964.1204

28 Phoenix Garden ★★$$ One of the best and most sophisticated Cantonese restaurants in Chinatown, Phoenix Garden makes no culinary concessions to Western tastes and, unlike most restaurants in this part of town, has maintained its high quality for many years. Prices are—justifiably—slightly more uptown than in the rest of the neighborhood. In 1993, a fire forced this restaurant to close. It's scheduled to reopen in 1994; call before you go. ♦ Cantonese ♦ 46 Bowery (between Bayard and Canal Sts). 233.6017

28 Hee Seung Fung (HSF) ★$$ Long lines are common because these folks are unusually welcoming to Westerners. It's less risky than usual to order dim sum here, as the restaurant offers a photographic guide to the 75 available varieties. You can't go wrong with the *harkow* (steamed shrimp dumpling). A full menu is offered at dinner. ♦ Dim sum ♦ Breakfast, lunch, and dinner. 46 Bowery (between Bayard and Canal Sts). No credit cards. 374.1319

29 Manhattan Bridge The elaborate approach to the bridge from Canal Street is a shadow of its former self, but the quality still shows. Originally known as the **Court of Honor,** the bridge—a 1905 work by **Gustav Lindenthal**— was designed so that vehicles would pass under a triumphal arch designed by **Carrère & Hastings.** Brooklyn-bound streetcars were forced to go around the arch, and the subway was hidden underneath it. The **Daniel Chester French** sculptures (representing Manhattan and Brooklyn) that flanked the arch were moved to the front of the Brooklyn Museum in 1963. ♦ From Canal St at Bowery, Manhattan to Tillary St at Flatbush Ave, Brooklyn

30 Eldridge Street Synagogue The congregation of **K'hal Adath Jeshurun Anshe Lubz** built this as the first Orthodox synagogue in the area during a time when other congregations were transforming Christian churches for their own use. Constructed in grand scale in 1887 by **Herter Bros.,** the main sanctuary was an opulent room with brass chandeliers and an ark imported from Italy. The building fell into disrepair over the years—although the congregation has never missed a Sabbath—and is currently being restored to its original splendor. It is now operating as a center for the celebration of American Jewish history. Comedian **Eddie Cantor** spent his boyhood in a building across the street (he answered to the name **Edward Iskowitz** back then). ♦ 12 Eldridge St (between Forsyth and Canal Sts). 219.0888

31 Harry Zarin Co. Fabric Warehouse Decorator fabrics at super prices are sold— everything from opulent silk brocades to mattress ticking. ♦ Daily 9AM-5:30PM. 72 Allen St (at Grand St). 226.3492

31 Fishkin Women's sportswear by **Adrienne Vittadini** and **Liz Claiborne,** sweaters by **Pringle,** handsome boots and shoes by **Via Spiga** and **Nickels,** and silk and cashmere are sold at a 20-percent discount. ♦ M-Th 10AM-5PM; F 10AM-4PM; Su 9:30AM-4:30PM. 314 Grand St (at Allen St). 226.6538

32 Leslie's Originals Fashionable footwear at a 30-percent discount is sold here. Women's shoes include bare sandals, espadrilles, pumps, and quality-leather shoes and boots, depending on the season. The men's stock includes loafers, wingtips, and sport shoes. ♦ M-W 9:30AM-6PM; Th 9:30AM-7PM; F 9:30AM-4:30PM; Su 9AM-6PM. 319 Grand St (between Allen and Orchard Sts). 431.9196

33 A.W. Kaufman Luxurious lingerie from a variety of designers, including **Christian Dior, Mary McFadden,** and **Lejaby,** are packed into this narrow shop along with imports from Belgium and Switzerland. ♦ M-Th 10:30AM-5PM; F 10:30AM-2:30PM; Su 10AM-5PM. 73 Orchard St (at Grand St). 226.1629

34 Sunray Yarn Co. Inc. This shop stocks a full array of yarns, including **Paton, Lion Brand, Bernat,** and **Missoni,** plus their own brand, which they sell to the designers on Seventh Avenue. ♦ M-Th, Su 10AM-5PM. 349 Grand St (at Essex St). 475.9655

35 Guss Pickle Products The oldest purveyor of pickles in New York is still the best. You can get a kosher dill sour enough to make your face pucker. The sauerkraut and pickled peppers and tomatoes are terrific as well. The merchandise is displayed in the shop and on the sidewalk in brine-filled barrels. ♦ M-Th, Su 9AM-6PM; F 9AM-3PM. 35 Essex St (between Grand and Hester Sts). 254.4477

36 Seward Park Two blocks of tenement buildings were removed in 1900 to make way for this three-acre breathing space (named for **William H. Seward,** governor of New York, a U.S. senator, and Lincoln's secretary of state). In its early days, the park was a gathering place for immigrants looking for daily work. The southern and western edges are the site of a regular Sunday flea market, during which elderly people sell *tchotchkes* (knickknacks). The prices are good, and the bargaining is entertaining in itself. ♦ Canal St (between E. Broadway and Essex St)

37 Educational Alliance Built in 1891 by **Arnold Brunner,** this is the United States' first settlement house, founded in 1889 by so-called "uptown Jews," who felt an obligation to help fellow Jews in the downtown ghetto and to stem possible anti-Semitism. It held classes to Americanize youngsters, provided exercise and bathing facilities, and gave assistance to women whose husbands had deserted them, which was common among immigrant families. Among the young people the Alliance served was **Arthur Murray,** who learned how to dance here. ♦ 197 E. Broadway (at Jefferson St)

38 Ritualarium In 1904, the former **Arnold Toynbee Hall** of the **Young Men's Benevolent Association** was converted to a *mikvah,* a ritual bath for Orthodox Jewish women, who are required to attend in preparation for marriage and on a monthly basis after that. Because the Scriptures command that the water be pure, rainwater is collected in cisterns. Tours are given by appointment. Call **Mrs. Bormiko** at 674.5318 for information. ♦ 313 E. Broadway (at Grand St). 475.8514

39 Abrons Arts Center This performing- and visual-arts complex, built by **Prentice & Chan, Ohlhausen** in 1975, is part of the **Henry Street Settlement,** a social service agency that has operated on the Lower East Side since 1893. Among its programs are arts workshops, professional performances, and exhibitions—all meant to help participants develop a form of self-expression through the arts and an appreciation of the cultural diversity of New York City. The Center contains three theaters: the **Recital Hall,** the **Experimental Theater,** and the **Harry DeJur Playhouse.** ♦ 466 Grand St (between Pitt and Willett Sts). 598.0400

40 Bialystoker Synagogue Built in 1826 as the **Willett Street Methodist Episcopal Church,** it was purchased by the Congregation Anshei Bialystok in 1905 and is the oldest structure housing a synagogue in New York. ♦ 7 Willett St (between Grand St and Williamsburg Bridge). 475.0165

41 Williamsburg Bridge Built in 1903 by **Leffert L. Buck,** this is the second bridge to span the East River. Its construction changed Williamsburg in Brooklyn from a resort area to a new home for immigrants from the Lower East Side. The bridge is unusual in that there are no cables on the land side of the steel towers, robbing it of some of the soaring grace of a full suspension span. ♦ From Delancey St at Clinton St, Manhattan to Washington Plaza, Brooklyn

42 Ratner's ★$$ Its glory days far behind, this New York institution is now more a cultural than a gustatorial experience. All the standard Jewish dairy dishes are listed, but few are worth the inevitable heartburn. It's best to soak in the *Yiddishkayt* over a bowl of soup, a plate of panfried cheese or potato blintzes, or the deep-fried *pirogen.* ♦ Jewish dairy ♦ Breakfast, lunch, and dinner; breakfast and lunch only on Friday; dinner only on Saturday. 138 Delancey St (between Norfolk and Suffolk Sts). 677.5588

43 Streit's Matzoth Company This is the only Manhattan producer of the unleavened bread used during Passover. Watch the huge sheets of matzo as they pass by the windows on conveyor belts. ♦ 150 Rivington St (at Suffolk St). 475.7000

44 Schapiro's House of Kosher and Sacramental Wines Tour the only still-operating winery in the city on Sunday from 11AM to 4PM, or during the week by appointment. ♦ Nominal fee. 126 Rivington St (between Norfolk and Essex Sts). 674.4404

Restaurants/Clubs: Red	**Hotels:** Blue
Shops/ 🌳 Outdoors: Green	**Sights/Culture:** Black

45 Economy Candy Company People with a longing for old-fashioned penny candy will find it in this store that has been selling candy of all kinds, as well as dried fruits, nuts, coffees, teas, and other delicacies, since 1937. Though the prices are good, a penny won't go very far. When you stop in, ask for the mail-order catalog. ♦ M-F 8:30AM-6PM; Sa 10AM-5PM; Su 8AM-6PM. 108 Rivington St (between Essex and Ludlow Sts). 254.1832

46 Orchard Street The old pushcarts are gone, but bargain hunters still flock to Orchard Street, a seething indoor-outdoor bazaar of discount dresses, coats, shoes, linens, fabrics, and accessories. More than 300 stores line Orchard and surrounding streets from Houston to Canal streets on the Lower East Side. On Sunday, many of the streets are closed to traffic, and the latest from **Ralph Lauren** to **Christian Dior** is hawked from the sidewalks. This kind of shopping is not for the faint of heart, but if you go prepared for the rough and tumble of bartering and remember that not all stores take credit cards or have gracious salespeople, you can turn up some jewels among the schlock—and have fun, too. Go weekdays if you can. Sunday is insane, and many stores are closed on Saturday. ♦ Between Canal and Houston Sts

47 Beckenstein The enormous and excellent collection of fabrics, including men's shirting of pure cotton, cashmere, mohair, and silk charmeuse is discounted 15 percent. Women's and home furnishing fabrics are also available. ♦ M-F, Su 9AM-5:30PM. 130 Orchard St (between Rivington and Delancey Sts). 475.4887. Also at: 125 Orchard St. 475.7575

48 Lower East Side Tenement Museum This small, fascinating museum is visited predominantly by the curious descendants of immigrants who fled to the U.S. at the end of the 19th and beginning of the 20th centuries. The grim reality of the appalling hardships they faced are palpable here, re-created in an abandoned tenement. More than 300,000 Russians, escaping brutal pogroms, were crammed into a single square mile in living conditions that can only be understood after a visit here. The museum offers changing exhibits usually relating to immigrant history and organizes two-hour Sunday walking tours through this and nearby ethnic neighborhoods filled with history. ♦ Nominal admission. Tu-F 11AM-5PM; Su 10AM-5PM. 97 Orchard St (between Broome and Delancey Sts). 431.0233

49 Fine & Klein An extensive collection of high-end handbags, briefcases, and accessories includes the latest from **Carlos Falchi, Enny and Lisette** (sometimes **Valentino** and **Givenchy,** too). You'll find good discounts and gracious service at this Orchard Street institution. Upstairs, at **Lea's,** enjoy a 30-percent discount on women's clothing from such designers as **Albert Nippon** and **Louis Feraud.** ♦ M-F, Su 9AM-5PM. 119 Orchard St (between Rivington and Delancey Sts). 674.6720

50 Giselle Sportswear Better American sportswear for women, including warm, woolly alpaca jackets and soft leather jackets and pants are sold at 25 percent off. ♦ M-Th, Su 9AM-6PM; F 9AM-3PM. 143 Orchard St (between Delancey and Rivington Sts). 673.1900

50 Anna Z High-fashion European clothing for women includes designs by **Bill Kaiserman** and **Malisy Gilbert Basson** at 20 percent off retail. ♦ M-F, Su 10AM-6PM. 143½ Orchard St (at Rivington St). 533.1361

50 Tobaldi European high-fashion men's clothes are discounted 20 percent. Merchandise includes tweed jackets, leather jackets, pure cotton shirts, silk ties, and bikini underwear. ♦ M-Th, Su 9:30AM-6PM; F 9:30AM-2:30PM. 83 Rivington St (at Orchard St). 260.4330

51 Congregation Adath Jeshurun of Jassy Synagogue This 1903 building was also the home of the First Warsaw Congregation. Now abandoned, it still projects a rich and distinctive image with its collage of architectural styles. ♦ 58-60 Rivington St (between Allen and Eldridge Sts)

52 The Hat/El Sombrero $ You won't find the best Mexican food here, but it's a real neighborhood hangout. Try nachos *traditionales* and a margarita, and soak in the local color. ♦ Mexican ♦ Breakfast, lunch, and dinner. 108 Stanton St (at Ludlow St). No credit cards. 254.4188

52 The Ludlow Street Cafe $ Live music starts around 10PM nightly at this relaxed, upbeat cafe. Go on Monday for **Beat Rodeo,** a lively country-rock band whose members love to keep the audience happy, especially the would-be rock 'n' rollers who join in from time to time. ♦ Cafe ♦ Dinner; lunch also on Saturday and Sunday. 165 Ludlow St (between E. Houston and Stanton Sts). 353.0536

52 Max Fish A jukebox keeps the beat at this bright (vibrant paintings cover white walls), popular (the crowd spills onto the sidewalk) club, filled with the young and attractive who stop in for pinball, billiards, and cheap beer. ♦ Ludlow St (between E. Houston and Stanton Sts). No phone

53 Katz's Delicatessen ★$ Have a look (the "Send a salami to your boy in the Army" sign is a World War II relic), take a ticket when you come in, then pick up some sausages or a warm brisket on rye at this famous old delicatessen that's worth a visit. This is also the site of the memorable deli scene in the 1989 film *When Harry Met Sally.* You can be waited on at the tables or order at the counter. ◆ Deli ◆ Breakfast, lunch, and dinner. 205 E. Houston St (at Ludlow St). No credit cards. 254.2246

54 Russ & Daughters This is a shopping mecca for serious connoisseurs of lox and bagels and cream cheese, not to mention smoked Nova Scotia salmon, golden smoked whitefish, unctuous sable carp, tart-crisp herring, salads, dried fruits, nuts, and other foods that many native New Yorkers call appetizing. ◆ M-W 9AM-6PM; Th-Sa 9AM-7PM; Su 8AM-6PM. 179 E. Houston St (between Orchard and Allen Sts). 475.4880

55 Yonah Schimmel ★$ Legendary knishes are served in this dumpy old storefront. It's also known for clabbered milk (yogurt) and borscht, the same Jewish specialties they've been dishing up since the turn of the century. ◆ Snacks ◆ M-Th, Su 9AM-5PM; F 9AM-4PM. 137 E. Houston St (at Forsyth). 477.2858

56 Irreplaceable Artifacts of North America Lighting fixtures, architectural antiques, garden ornaments, stained-glass windows, and other interesting junk from Europe, Canada, South America, and the United States is sold here. ◆ M-F 10AM-6PM; Sa-Su 11AM-5PM. 14 Second Ave (at Houston St). 780.9700

57 Knitting Factory An impressive weekly roster of performances—everything from jazz to poetry readings to the latest performance art—are held in this vital two-level venue. ◆ Cover. Shows daily; call for the schedule. 47 E. Houston St (between Mott and Mulberry Sts). 219.3055

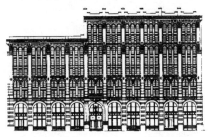

58 Puck Building The Romanesque Revival building (pictured above) reflects the influence of the Chicago School in its bold and vibrant use of brickwork. It was once the home of the humor magazine *Puck,* whose spirit remains in the two larger-than-life statues perched on third-floor ledges at the northeast corners. The interior of this great building, constructed in 1885 to the designs of **Albert Wagner,** has been renovated as commercial condominiums for art galleries, workshops, and design offices. The Puck's opulent rooms are also rented out for weddings and other celebrations. ◆ 295-309 Lafayette St (at E. Houston St)

59 Urban Archaeology Owner **Gil Shapiro** has moved his seemingly infinite collection of architectural ornaments, display cases, lighting fixtures, and much, much more into the immense quarters of a four-story former candy factory. Interior designer **Judith Stockman** revamped all 50,000 square feet, a process that included sandblasting candy off the walls. Two lovely skylit areas show off cast-iron furniture, garden accessories, and vintage motorcycles. The stock is sold wholesale and retail. ◆ M-F 7AM-6PM; Sa 10AM-4PM. 285 Lafayette St (between E. Houston and Prince Sts). 431.6969

60 Do Kham Clothing, jewelry, and accessories from Tibet and the Himalayas, some designed by the amiable store owner, **Phlegye Kelden,** a former Tibetan monk, are sold here. Check out his chic fake- and genuine-fur hats. ◆ M-Sa 10AM-7:30PM; Su 10AM-8:30PM. 51 Prince St (between Lafayette and Mulberry Sts). 966.2404

61 Old St. Patrick's Cathedral When the new cathedral at Fifth Avenue and 50th Street was consecrated in 1879, this became a Roman Catholic parish church serving a predominantly Irish neighborhood. Originally built by **Joseph Mangin** in 1815, it was New York's first Gothic Revival building. The church was restored in 1868 by **Henry Englebert** after its historic facade was badly altered in an 1866 fire. ◆ 264 Mulberry St (between E. Houston and Prince Sts)

62 Old St. Patrick's Convent and Girls' School Built in 1826, the beautiful Federal doorway framed with Corinthian columns makes this unusually large Federal-style building a treasure. ◆ 32 Prince St (at Mott St)

63 D & G Bakery For more than three decades this has been a landmark bakery in the Little Italy neighborhood. Come early for the breads baked fresh daily in a 100-year-old coal-fired brick oven in a nearby basement. D & G Bakery is known for its heavenly prosciutto loaf studded with strips of meat and other breads with cheese, olives, herbs, or drizzled with olive oil. ◆ Daily 8AM-2PM. 45 Spring St (between Mott and Mulberry Sts). 226.6688

64 Just Shades As the name implies, nothing but lampshades is sold in this store. In stock are shades of string, parchment, silk, and burlap; others can be custom-ordered. ◆ M-Tu, Th-Su 9:30AM-4PM. 21 Spring St (between Mott and Elizabeth Sts). 966.2757

65 Connecticut Muffin Co. A friendly staff serves up fresh-baked goods at this shop. Try a banana-nut muffin or cheddar-cheese scone. ◆ M-F 7AM-3PM; Sa-Su 8AM-3PM. 10 Prince St (between Elizabeth St and Bowery). 925.9773

New York City boasts 2,700 traffic signals.

66 Off SoHo Suites $ The 38 suites are large and tastefully furnished, and the prices are rock bottom. What's the snag? This isn't exactly Park Avenue and the least expensive suites sometimes share a bath and kitchen. But this is one of the very few recommended in this area east of SoHo (hence the name), with easy access to all mass transit. Most suites have color TV, marble bathtubs, air-conditioning, a gourmet eat-in kitchen, and access to a fitness center. ♦ 11 Rivington St (between Chrystie St and Bowery). 979.9808, 800/633.7646; fax 979.9801

67 Sammy's Famous Roumanian Jewish Steakhouse ★★$$$ Sammy's is the best Jewish restaurant in the city, but it's not kosher. The room is low-down and tacky, and the so-called entertainment—an electric piano and a comic who thinks he's **Henny Youngman**—is so bad it's good. If you're unfamiliar with the cuisine, order almost everything the waitress tells you to, but in only half the quantity she recommends. Among these are likely to be chopped liver (yes, you do want the works to put on it: chicken cracklings and shredded black radishes with onion, laced with chicken fat), *kishke,* and unborn eggs. And those are just the appetizers. For a main course, Romanian tenderloin steak, a rib steak, a fried breaded veal chop, or boiled beef with mushroom-barley gravy will do fine. Mashed potatoes with fried onions, and *kasha varnishkes* (buckwheat groats with bowtie macaroni) are musts on the side. Portions are large, the food is authentically heavy (even without liberal pourings from the pitcher of chicken fat on the table), and the bill mounts up quickly. Try an egg cream, the classic New York *digestif.* Management supplies a container of milk, a bottle of Fox's U-Bet chocolate syrup, and the seltzer. You mix: syrup, about a quarter of a glass of milk to taste, and seltzer to fill. Stir well for a nice foam. You'll definitely want to try this place—once. ♦ Eastern European/Jewish ♦ Entertainment nightly. Dinner. 157 Chrystie St (between Delancey and Rivington Sts). Reservations required. 673.0330

68 Mazer Store Equipment Co. Craig Claiborne, Mimi Sheraton, Lauren Bacall, and Stockard Channing buy their Garland restaurant-style stoves here. Mazer not only discounts the stove, which now comes with porcelainized oven walls, back, and roof, but arranges for the oven to be installed and burners to be adjusted. Service is what distinguishes this store from others of its kind. ♦ M-F 8:30AM-4:30PM. 207 Bowery (at Kenmare St). 674.3450

69 New York Gas Lighting Company This lighting store, one of the best in the neighborhood, takes its name from its authentic open-flame gaslights. It also offers an array of handsome fixtures including opalescent chandeliers from the Czech Republic, lamps made from antique ginger jars, and the Hunter wood ceiling fan. ♦ M-F 9AM-5PM; Sa-Su 10:30AM-5PM. 145 Bowery (between Broome and Grand Sts). 226.2840

70 Bowery Savings Bank The 1894 building designed by **McKim, Mead & White** is a double treat. Outside, the Roman columns attached to a Renaissance facade are somehow apropos on the edge of Little Italy. Inside, take a look at the opulent detailing. ♦ 130 Bowery (between Grand and Broome Sts)

71 Road to Mandalay ★★$$ In typical New York fashion, you'll find this cozy Asian restaurant in the middle of Little Italy. All the food is good, but the noodle dishes are particularly special. ♦ Thai/Burmese ♦ Dinner; lunch also on Saturday and Sunday. 380 Broome St (between Mott and Mulberry Sts). 226.4218

72 Caffè Roma ★★$ Knowledgeable New Yorkers favor this lovely old-world bakery and coffeehouse over the slicker Ferrara. No redecorating was necessary to make this place look authentic. It just is. ♦ Bakery/Cafe ♦ Breakfast, lunch, and dinner. 385 Broome St (at Mulberry St). No credit cards. 226.8413

72 Grotta Azzurra ★$$$ The kitsch of dining in an ersatz blue cave may appeal to some, though the food may not appeal to many. Chicken cacciatore is a safe bet, but avoid the seafood. Still, the portions are ample, you don't need a reservation, and it's fun. ♦ Neapolitan ♦ Lunch and dinner. 387 Broome St (at Mulberry St). No credit cards. 226.9283

73 The Police Building A commanding presence with an imposing dome as a symbol of authority, this 1909 building by **Hoppin & Koen** was the main headquarters of the **New York City Police Department** for nearly 65 years. The new copper dome was crafted by French artisans brought here to restore the Statue of Liberty's copper flame, and the 1988 restoration was the work of **Ehrenkranz Group & Eckstut.** The interior, by **dePolo/Dunbar,** has been converted into 55 cooperative apartments. ♦ 240 Centre St (between Grand and Broome Sts)

74 Italian Food Center A one-stop shopping emporium for Italophile foodies, this family-run corner store is stocked with domestic and imported Italian foodstuffs, including more than a dozen kinds of breads baked daily on the premises and a vast array of Italian cold cuts. The park bench outside is usually occupied by afternoon strollers who've stopped in for any of the take-out goodies for which the **De Mattia** family has been rightfully known for more than 20 years. Try the "New York Special" hero sandwich or any of the fresh pizzas, focaccias, bruschettas, or temptingly displayed spinach or sausage rolls. ♦ Italian/Takeout ♦ Daily 8AM-7PM. 186 Grand St (at Mulberry St). 925.2954

75 Benito I and Benito II ★$$ The original owners of this pair of small trattorias sold out and moved off to LA. The restaurants are no longer related, but the tradition lingers on, and either one is a good choice for a hearty low-cost Italian meal. ♦ Neapolitan ♦ Benito I: lunch and dinner. 174 Mulberry St (between Broome and Grand Sts). 226.9171. Benito II: lunch and dinner. 163 Mulberry St (between Broome and Grand Sts). No credit cards. 226.9012

76 Alleva Dairy You can almost breathe the agelessness of tradition when you walk into this old-fashioned cheese store. In the same family for more than 100 years, there's always a proud Alleva on hand to tend to the regular customers who come from all over the city for the mozzarella (fresh and smoked) made daily (which constitutes a good part of the 4,000 pounds of cheeses made here each week). After 90 years of selling just cheese, the Allevas added a selection of dried pastas, an excellent fresh tomato sauce packaged to go, and smoked and cured meats. ♦ Daily 8:30AM-6PM. 188 Grand St (at Mulberry St). 226.7990

77 Piemonte Ravioli Company The same family has been churning out freshly made pasta from generations-old recipes since 1920 in this small, old-fashioned store that gives no hint of its important role as one of America's major suppliers. The refrigerator and counter are always stocked with dozens of types, colors, shapes, and fillings. The filled pastas, such as ravioli and cannelloni, are favorites. Try the plump ravioli stuffed with cheese, spinach, or porcini mushrooms. ♦ Tu-Sa 8:30AM-6PM; Su 8AM-3PM. 190 Grand St (between Mott and Mulberry Sts). 226.0475

"Something's always happening here. If you're bored in New York, it's your own fault."

Myrna Loy

77 Pearl River Chinese Products Any Sinophile's passion for clothing and housewares can be satisfied in this store. Pearl River carries cotton T-shirts, silk jackets, pillowcases, sheets, and bedspreads in pastel pinks, blues, and yellows embroidered with flowers and animals. For Chinese cooking, an easy-to-use wok with a wooden handle is another find. ♦ Daily 10AM-8PM. 200 Grand St (at Mott St). 966.1010

78 Ferrara $ This is a slick emporium with an extensive take-out department featuring a wide variety of Italian pastries, cookies, and candies. The espresso bar is one of the city's more popular places for cappuccino and the like. In nice weather the bar extends out onto the sidewalk, where a counter dispenses Italian gelati. ♦ Bakery/Cafe ♦ Breakfast, lunch, and dinner. 195 Grand St (between Mulberry and Mott Sts). 226.6150

78 E. Rossi & Co. An old-fashioned, crowded, family-run store, it sells bocce balls, pasta machines, T-shirts, Italian greeting cards, cookbooks in both Italian and English, religious statuary, and big buttons that read "Kiss me, I'm Italian." ♦ M-F 9:30AM-6PM; Sa 10AM-7PM; Su 10AM-5PM. 191 Grand St (at Mulberry St). 966.6640

70 Angelo's of Mulberry Street ★$$$ An old Little Italy standby that might be a bit too touristy, Angelo's churns out consistently decent food. ♦ Southern Italian ♦ Lunch and dinner. 146 Mulberry St (between Grand and Hester Sts). 966.1277

80 Ristorante Taormina ★$$$ With its blond wood and peach furnishings, exposed brick walls, large windows, and graceful tall plants, this attractive restaurant would be more at home farther uptown than in Little Italy. Begin a delightful dining experience with the excellent stuffed artichokes. Any of the veal entrées are quite good, as are most of the items on the menu. ♦ Neapolitan ♦ Lunch and dinner. 147 Mulberry St (between Grand and Hester Sts). 219.1007

81 S.P.Q.R. $$ Though the multilevel room is grand and gorgeous, the kitchen is often troubled. Stick to the simple items and you'll eat decently. ♦ Italian ♦ Lunch and dinner. 133 Mulberry St (between Grand and Hester Sts). 925.3120

Restaurants/Clubs: Red **Hotels:** Blue
Shops/ 🌂 Outdoors: Green **Sights/Culture:** Black

81 Umberto's Clam House $$$ Umberto's is a landmark because a famed underworld figure was assassinated here, but the seafood is probably better at Vincent's. ♦ Clam bar ♦ Lunch, dinner, and late-night meals. 129 Mulberry St (at Hester St). 431.7545

82 Forzano Italian Imports Inc. If you want a souvenir from Little Italy, this is the place. The speakers pipe Italian music onto the street, and inside you'll find a large selection of Italian records and tapes—plus just about everything else, including espresso-makers in every shape, size, and price, a variety of meat grinders, and such kitschy fare as T-shirts proclaiming your Italian heritage and devil horns to keep bad luck away. ♦ M-Th 10AM-10:30PM; F-Sa 10AM-midnight. 128 Mulberry St (at Hester St). 925.2525

82 Caffè Napoli ★$ You'll feel like you're at a sidewalk cafe even when you're sitting inside. Take a cue from the locals, who come here for dessert rather than going to the more famous Ferrara. If you can't decide which of the marvelous-looking pastries to get, you can't go wrong with a cannoli. ♦ Cafe ♦ Lunch, dinner, and late-night meals. 191 Hester St (at Mulberry St). No credit cards. 226.8705

82 Restaurant Puglia ★$ Generous portions of spaghetti with parmigiana specialties highlight the food served at long tables that patrons share in the European style at this rambling restaurant. The young crowd sings along with the waiters to the live music. ♦ Southern Italian ♦ Lunch, dinner, and late-night meals. Closed Monday. 189 Hester St (between Mulberry and Mott Sts). No credit cards. 966.6006

83 Vincent's Clam Bar ★$ Choose the fresh seafood with a choice of hot, medium, or mild tomato sauce at this city institution. Hot is for serious masochists, of which there appear to be many. An expanded menu offers a variety of meat entrées, chicken, salads, coffee, and dessert. ♦ Seafood ♦ Lunch, dinner, and late-night meals. 119 Mott St (at Hester St). 226.8133

83 Pho Bânc Restaurant ★$ If you need a break from the plethora of Italian restaurants, come here for authentic Vietnamese cooking with excellent whole shrimp summer rolls. A plate of exotic lettuces and an array of sauces accompany the meal. ♦ Vietnamese ♦ Lunch and dinner. 117 Mott St (between Hester and Canal Sts). 966.3797. Also at: 3 Pike St (soup only). 233.3947; 6 Chatham Sq. 587.0870

84 Wong Kee ★$ The good, fresh food at low prices will make you wonder how they stay in business. Try the boiled skinless chicken breast, roast duck, scrambled eggs with pork, wonton, cabbage soup, glazed pork, or any of the wide rice noodles. You're probably better off if you skip the chef's suggestions.

♦ Cantonese ♦ Lunch and dinner. 113 Mott St (between Hester and Canal Sts). No credit cards. 226.9018

84 Chao Chow ★$ Come here for what is perhaps the best *lo soi* duck in New York; it's cooked in a rich sauce of cinnamon, eight-star anise, and nutmeg. ♦ Northern Chinese ♦ Breakfast, lunch, and dinner. 111 Mott St (between Hester and Canal Sts). No credit cards. 226.2590

85 Oriental Pearl ★$$ Suggested from the extensive menu at this large, dull-looking restaurant are the Peking spare ribs and the steamed flounder or shrimp with walnuts. This is one of the few restaurants where you can order stewed and roasted geese. ♦ Cantonese ♦ Breakfast, lunch, and dinner. 103 Mott St (at Canal St). 219.8388

86 Luna ★$$ Almost 100 years old, this restaurant feels more like an oversize kitchen than a touristy spot. The hallway that leads to the dining room gives you a full view of the bustling kitchen. Despite, or perhaps because of, the haphazard mix of tables and booths, propped-up photographs, and occasionally gruff service, the experience is authentic—and filling. ♦ Southern Italian ♦ Lunch, dinner, and late-night meals. 112 Mulberry St (between Hester and Canal Sts). No credit cards. 226.8657

87 Lo Spuntino ★★$ Small, narrow, and tiled in white, Lo Spuntino is not as flashy as the rest of the cafes on Mulberry Street. The hand-painted sign and the gorgeous desserts in the window let you know you are in the right place. An assortment of mousses is always available (pumpkin, pear, white-chocolate almond), as well as standard Italian pastry fare—cannoli, eclairs, etc. ♦ Cafe ♦ Breakfast, lunch, and dinner. 117 Mulberry St (between Hester and Canal Sts). Unlisted phone

87 Il Cortile ★$$$ The lines to get in may be too long, the rooms may be too noisy, and the waiters too harried, but the food is fresh and cooked well and the room is beautifully decorated. ♦ Northern Italian ♦ Lunch and dinner; late-night meals also on Friday and Saturday. 125 Mulberry St (between Hester and Canal Sts). 226.6060

88 Holiday Inn Downtown $$ The only hotel in Chinatown has very little Oriental detail in either the public areas or 220 guest rooms to distinguish it from any other contemporary hotel in Manhattan. Its Hong Kong-style restaurant, **Pacifica**, is very good, but with the plethora of less expensive and often more authentic restaurants within blocks of the hotel, it would be a shame to eat in. ♦ 138 Lafayette St (at Howard St). 966.8898; fax 966.3933

SoHo/TriBeCa

The name SoHo was coined to define the district South of Houston Street, not to honor the neighborhood in London. Combined with the wedge-shaped territory known as TriBeCa (city departmentese for **Triangle Below Canal** Street), it includes the area bounded by **Houston**, **Lafayette**, and **Chambers streets** and the **Hudson River.**

In spite of soaring prices in SoHo, relatively little is neat and prettied-up. White-on-white galleries and chic buildings occupy grimy streets where 19th-century cobblestones show through the ravaged asphalt. The area was occupied by Native Americans during the 17th century (that's who the wall of Wall Street was supposedly protecting the early settlers from, although, in fact, it was the British they were more concerned about), then by farms and estates spread between old New York and the outlying suburb of Greenwich Village. In the early part of the 19th century, the land was bought to build houses on (the oldest one still standing, at 107 Spring Street, dates from 1806), and from the 1840s to 1860s it was the center of the city, boasting the major department store **Lord & Taylor,** on Grand Street, as well as the city's principal hotel, **The American House,** at Spring Street and West Broadway.

Industry followed, setting up business in prefabricated cast-iron buildings fashioned to look literally like temples of commerce. By the 1960s, light industry had moved on to new areas, and **Robert Moses,** the city's master builder, viewed SoHo as a wasteland of useless industrial buildings that he wanted to level and replace with the Lower Manhattan Expressway. When that plan was abandoned in the mid-1960s, artists looking for large, cheap studio space discovered SoHo. Avant-garde galleries, one-of-a-kind boutiques, and nouvelle cuisine restaurants followed close behind. Today, SoHo continues to hold its own as an alternative to the art world of Madison Avenue or 57th Street. The neighborhood is saturated with an artistic mix of original ideas and junk, sheer exuberance and exhibitionism. Keep in mind that many of the shops, restaurants, and galleries don't open until 11AM or noon and are closed on Monday and during the month of August.

TriBeCa, unlike SoHo, retains much of the bohemian quality that once characterized the entire complex of cast-iron architecture between Houston and Chambers streets before it went upscale. Because this neighborhood overlaps the City Hall area, with its enormous daytime working population, it has been more successful in resisting the tide of fad enterprise. Greek coffee shops, shoe repairs, pet shops, and appliance and camera stores enliven commercial streets little changed since the 1930s. Art and commerce have, of course, transformed TriBeCa to a certain degree, but they have not overwhelmed it. With easy access to Chinatown and Lower Manhattan, it remains a unique, artistic, and ethnic New York neighborhood.

1 Washington Market Park Progress has reduced the former Washington Market to this little park. In its day the market extended up along the river from Fulton Street into this neighborhood. Even Washington Street, which once formed its spine, is now just a two-block-long thoroughfare between Murray and Chambers streets. The old market was essentially a wholesale produce exchange (now centered at Hunt's Point in the Bronx), but it was also a distribution point for the imported foods that are being rediscovered in gourmet shops. Many New York households stocked their larders with goods from the market. The park that remains is one of Manhattan's better play areas for young children. It is clean, safe, and, from a kid's point of view, great fun.
♦ Chambers St (at Greenwich St)

2 Tommy Tang's ★★$$ Local restaurant critics have given high marks to the Thai cuisine served here. A correspondent for the *Bangkok Post* called Tommy Tang the best Thai chef in America. The staff will guide you through the intricacies of the menu. ♦ Thai ♦ Lunch and dinner; dinner only on Saturday. Closed Sunday. 323 Greenwich St (between Reade and Duane Sts). 334.9190

Restaurants/Clubs: Red **Hotels:** Blue
Shops/🌳 Outdoors: Green **Sights/Culture:** Black

3 P.S. 234 Too bad all schools aren't as well designed (some of the architectural elements seem to come straight out of a child's imagination) or as nicely sited as this one built in 1988 by architect **Richard Dattner.** Be sure to study the fanciful fence by artist **Donna Dennis** that encloses the schoolyard. ♦ 300 Greenwich St (between Warren and Chambers Sts). 233.6034

4 Cheese of All Nations If you can't find a particular type of cheese among the more than 1,000 varieties from around the world in this shop, chances are it's not imported to the U.S. Shelves full of various packaged crackers for the 50 cheese spreads made on the premises are also sold. Manhattanites come from all corners of the island for their favorite specialties. ♦ M-F 8AM-6PM. 153 Chambers St (between Greenwich St and W. Broadway). 732.0752

5 Bouley ★★★★$$$$ Chef/owner **David Bouley's** outstanding French menu includes such excellent dishes as a pastiche of three salads (hot goose foie gras, grilled shrimp, wild mushrooms); roasted Maine lobster served in its own consommé with crisp asparagus, winter mint, and fresh black truffles; and sautéed Maine sea scallops with potato crusts. The handsome Provençal interior was designed by Bouley and architect **Kevin White.** Good first-time choices are the prix fixe luncheon and dinner menus. Some say a table at Bouley is the best to be had in Manhattan. ♦ French ♦ Lunch and dinner; dinner only on Saturday. Closed Sunday. 165 Duane St (between Greenwich and Hudson Sts). Jacket and tie required. Reservations required weeks in advance. 608.3852

6 Duane Park Cafe ★★$$$ You'll let out a sigh of relief the moment you set foot inside this comfortable restaurant that's pretty as well as quiet. Once seated, you'll discover the menu, a creative mix of **K-Paul's, Hubert's,** and **Marcella Hazan** (the two head chefs have logged time with each of the above). Menu standouts include sweetbreads accompanied by wild mushrooms and polenta, grilled tuna with olive paste, and a gorgeous pear hazelnut tart. ♦ Continental ♦ Lunch and dinner; dinner only on Saturday. Closed Sunday. 157 Duane St (between W. Broadway and Hudson St). Reservations required. 732.5555

7 The Odeon ★★$$$ If you're looking for a place to sit and schmooze over a late-night drink, consider The Odeon. When it first opened, this neon-lit room was the hottest spot downtown—to the art community what Le Cirque is to international cafe society. The pretensions of the kitchen and the sometimes uppity staff turn off serious diners, though trend-spotters search here for the occasional celebrity. ♦ American/French ♦ Lunch, dinner, and late-night meals. 145 W. Broadway (at Thomas St). Reservations recommended. 233.0507

8 Delphi $ Greek cooking served in large portions at incredibly low prices makes this bustling taverna particularly appropriate for families. The daily special is usually very fresh broiled fish. ♦ Greek ♦ Lunch and dinner. 109 W. Broadway (at Reade St). 227.6322

9 Anbar Shoe Steal Discontinued shoe styles are sold at amazing savings. Sacha London, Charles Jourdan, and Nickels labels have been discovered here among the hodgepodge of not-so-beautiful shoes. ♦ M-F 8:30AM-6PM; Sa 11AM-5PM. 60 Reade St (between Church St and Broadway). 964.4017

ROſEMARIEſ

10 Rosemarie's ★★$$$ With the legendary Bouley just down the block, this downtown niche of Manhattan plays host to some of the city's best eateries. Rosemarie's is something of a hidden treasure, known by few but revered by those who have joined its roster of devotees. Warm and romantic, with an excellent Northern Italian menu (osso buco is a house specialty), this intimate spot should be high on your list if you're looking for a wonderful culinary experience with a reasonable-for-Manhattan tab. ♦ Northern Italian ♦ Lunch and dinner; dinner only on Saturday. Closed Sunday. 145 Duane St (between W. Broadway and Church St). Reservations recommended. 285.2610

11 American Telephone & Telegraph Long Lines Building Designed by **John Carl Warnecke & Associates** and built in 1974, this almost windowless (except for the high, squared portholes) edifice houses electronic wizardry for communications. Texturized pink Swedish granite contrasts with vertical stripes of a beige granite used for decoration. ♦ Church St (between Thomas and Worth Sts)

12 The Clocktower Gallery This nonprofit sibling of **P.S. 1 Museum,** the exhibition space in Long Island City, is situated in the high-ceilinged tower room of a former office building. The institute is dedicated to supporting new and experimental projects and artists working in areas not covered by established museums. Built in 1870 by **Griffith Thomas** and expanded in 1890 by **McKim, Mead & White,** it is sponsored by the Institute for Contemporary Art. ♦ Suggested contribution. W-Sa noon-6PM. 108 Leonard St (between Broadway and Lafayette St). 233.1096

13 Aux Delices des Bois Stop in for your own supply of the same mushrooms that the chefs at **China Grill** and **21** will be cooking with tonight; shiitake, crimini, portobello, enoki, chanterelle, and lobster are among the varieties that **Amy** and **Thierry Farge** import from all over the world. ♦ M-F 9AM-7PM; call ahead for Saturday hours. 4 Leonard St (between W. Broadway and Hudson St). 334.1230

14 The Sporting Club ★$$ Up to nine different events are beamed in by satellite onto screens in every corner of the room in this sports fanatic's dream. The main event is shown on three 10x10 foot screens above the bar. A glance at the patented electronic scoreboard will tell you the status of every pro and college game being played that day. The menu is made up of appropriately named dishes—try the George Steinbrenner. ♦ Continental ♦ Lunch, dinner, and late-night meals; brunch also on Saturday and Sunday. 99 Hudson St (between Franklin and Leonard Sts). Reservations required for major sporting events. 219.0900

15 Nautical Chart Supply Co. This supplier to the big shipping companies now makes its nautical wares available to the general public, including everything from a laminated card explaining basic knots and how to tie them to sailing directions to Scotland, the *Modern Marine Engineers Manual,* and marine barometers. ♦ M-F 9AM-5PM. 90 Hudson St (at Harrison St). 925.8849

Chanterelle

16 Chanterelle ★★★★$$$$ Young chef **David Waltuck,** acclaimed as a fresh, unspoiled genius, attracted fashionable uptown crowds to the dining room he and his wife, **Karen,** established on Grand Street. Now the crowds flock to this pretty space designed by **Bill Katz,** where little has changed but the address. The food is original, artfully presented, and always delicious. The seafood sausages are justifiably renowned. Alas, they don't serve breakfast anymore. ♦ French ♦ Lunch and dinner. Closed Monday and Sunday. 2 Harrison St (at Hudson St). Reservations required. 966.6960

16 New York Mercantile Exchange Built in 1884, this is another headquarters, like the one at 628 Broadway, for the big dealers in dairy and poultry products. The main offices used to be uptown, but this great old building, closer to the actual markets, is where the action was at the turn of the century. ♦ 6 Harrison St (at Hudson St)

The first slaves brought from Africa arrived in New York in 1625. The practice grew, and the first slave market was established at the foot of Wall Street in 1711; it was not until 1827 that slavery was abolished in New York.

17 Just Kidding The cotton children's clothing, some of which is made downstairs in the basement or by artists in the neighborhood, is wonderful, but owner **Margaret Owen's** most effective marketing tool may be the play area in the back: little ones beg to stay longer. ♦ M-Sa 11AM-7PM; Su noon-6PM. 22 Harrison St (between Greenwich and Hudson Sts). 219.0035

18 Puffy's Tavern Retaining the atmosphere of a speakeasy, which it was during Prohibition, this pre-TriBeCa bar pulls you in from the street to have a beer, hang out, and listen to the jukebox with the after-work crowd and neighborhood regulars. ♦ M 4PM-4AM; Tu-Su noon-4AM. 81 Hudson St (at Harrison St). No credit cards. 766.9159

19 A.L. Bazzini Company The largest dried fruit and nut suppliers in the city for more than a hundred years has shelves filled with exotic condiments and spices to the right as you enter. Upstairs you'll find the aromatic dry-roasted peanuts plus a full array of gourmet treats, including great coffee beans. Order a cappuccino to go on your way out. ♦ M-F 8AM-7PM; Sa 9AM-6PM. 339 Greenwich St (at Jay St). 334.1280

20 Independence Plaza Built in 1975 by architects **Oppenheimer, Brady & Vogelstein** and **John Pruyn,** this 40-floor middle-income housing project is a little off the beaten path and has great views of the river. ♦ Greenwich St (between Duane and N. Moore Sts)

21 Harrison Street Row Originally built in 1828 and restored in 1975 by **Oppenheimer, Brady & Vogelstein,** this row of impeccably restored Federal houses acts as an antidote to the massive apartment houses above it. ♦ 37-41 Harrison St (at Greenwich St)

22 Tribeca Grill ★★$$$ **Drew Nieterent,** owner of **Montrachet,** one of the city's best restaurants, has teamed up with several partners, including **Robert De Niro** to open this loftlike restaurant in the former Martinson Coffee Building. The first-rate bistro fare includes rare seared tuna with sesame noodles, arugula salad with *bocconcini* and basil oil, and pan-seared snapper with warm vinaigrette. Desserts are a must, especially the chocolate cake. Sketches and paintings by De Niro's late father, **Robert,** adorn the walls. The mahogany bar is the original bar from Maxwell's Plum. De Niro has converted the warehouse into a film production center. ♦ American ♦ Lunch and dinner; dinner only on Saturday; brunch also on Sunday. 375 Greenwich St (at Franklin St). 941.3900

23 Riverrun Cafe ★$$ One of the first restaurants in TriBeCa, it's a neighborhood staple for decent food and a comfortable place to sit, eat, and talk without feeling hassled. The colorful map outside will help you find your way to your next downtown destination. ♦ Continental ♦ Lunch and dinner; brunch also on Saturday and Sunday. 176 Franklin St (between Hudson and Greenwich Sts). 966.3894

24 Commodities This is a natural foods supermarket with a large stock of organic and otherwise healthy comestibles, as well as bodycare products, cookbooks, and health food for your pet. An extensive variety of flour, rice, cereal, beans, and pasta is sold in bulk from rows of wooden bins. ♦ Daily 10AM-8PM. 117 Hudson St (at N. Moore St). 334.8330

25 Franklin Street Potters Watch potters create in this working studio and gallery, formerly a cheese store. All of the wares are lead-free and microwave- and dishwasher-safe. ♦ M-F 10AM-6PM; call ahead for Saturday and Sunday hours. 151 Franklin St (between Hudson and Varick Sts). 431.7631

26 Walkers $$ This place is run by the people who own **The Ear Inn.** Have a drink with police officers from the First Precinct finishing up their shifts or chat with the other friendly folk over free, after-five munchies. ♦ American ♦ Lunch, dinner, and late-night meals. 16 N. Moore St (at Varick St). 941.0142

27 White Street An eclectic range of styles reflects the history of the TriBeCa cast-iron district. There are more attractive streets nearby, but none more typical. Contrast the authentic Federal details of No. 2, which was originally built as a liquor store in 1809; the artful stonework of No. 10, which was designed by **Henry Fernbach** in 1869; and the mansard roofline of No. 17. The upper stories of Nos. 8 and 10 are shorter than the lower floors—a favorite Renaissance Revival device that makes the buildings appear taller. ♦ Between W. Broadway and Church St

27 SoHo Photo Gallery Here you'll find the oldest and largest cooperative gallery for photographers in the United States. ♦ Tu 7-9PM; F-Su 1-6PM. 15 White St (between W. Broadway and Church St). 226.8571

27 Montrachet ★★★$$$$ The setting is very stylish (**Spanier & Dennis** created the interior) and the food very good in this very French establishment. Chef **Debra Ponzek** produces wonderfully imaginative contemporary fare that fans say is among the best in the area. Montrachet is also respected for its extensive and well-chosen wine list. Depending on who you are or who the staff thinks you are not, the service can be somewhat haughty. ♦ French ♦ Dinner; lunch also on Friday. Closed Sunday. 239 W.

Broadway (at White St). Reservations recommended. 219.2777

28 Artists Space One of the most original and certainly one of the most successful of the alternative space galleries, this perennial springboard for new talent maintains a file of about 3,500 artists from New York State and New Jersey, which is used by collectors, curators, and architects in search of an artist who falls into a specific category: conceptual, feminist, under 35, etc. ♦ Tu-Sa noon-7PM. 223 W. Broadway (between Franklin and White Sts). 226.3970

28 El Teddy's ★★$$$ Inside the three-story building topped with a life-size replica of the Statue of Liberty's crown are old-fashioned booths, vintage 1940s wallpaper, and a neon fish tank, among other eclectic touches. The cuisine is basic Mexican fare. The margaritas are some of the best in town. ♦ Mexican ♦ Lunch and dinner; dinner and late-night meals only on Saturday and Sunday. 219 W. Broadway (between White and Franklin Sts). 941.7070

28 two eleven ★$$$ A longtime artists' hangout, this one isn't bohemian in the slightest. On the contrary, it's exactly what you'd expect a TriBeCa restaurant to be. High ceilings and fans, greenery, subdued colors, and interesting music add to the hushed, intense atmosphere. The outdoor cafe is quite popular in the warmer months. ♦ American ♦ Lunch, dinner, and late-night meals. 211 W. Broadway (at Franklin St). 925.7202

29 Franklin Furnace Call it an alternative art space or an experimental outpost, but this is the country's largest public collection of published art works: books, periodicals, postcards, pamphlets, and cassette tapes. It also presents temporary installations using text and image. Performances by artists are held from February to April and September to December. ♦ Free. Tu-Sa noon-6PM. 112 Franklin St (between W. Broadway and Church St). 925.4671

30 Let There Be Neon Founded by **Rudi Stern,** one of America's foremost neon artists, this gallery features clocks, chairs, windows, signs, stage sets, and interiors, all in neon. ♦ M-F 8:30AM-5:30PM. 38 White St (between Broadway and Church St). 226.4883

31 Arqua ★★$$$ A typical late-1980s chic New York City restaurant, Arqua has a cavernous room, deafening acoustics, minimalist decor, and beautiful people. The food is good and is most enjoyable at lunchtime, when you can actually hear your companion. ♦ Italian ♦ Lunch and dinner; dinner only on Saturday. 281 Church St (at White St). Reservations recommended. 334.1888

Restaurants/Clubs: Red	**Hotels:** Blue
Shops/ 🌳 Outdoors: Green	**Sights/Culture:** Black

32 Barocco ★★$$$ No one seems to care that they are practically sitting on the laps of their neighbors in this sparse but lively trattoria; the diners are too content knowing that they are among the chicest and most with-it of the downtown crowd. To satisfy your palate as well as your ego, have the delicious *fettunta* (garlic bread) with any of the excellent homemade pastas. Portions are extremely generous. ◆ Italian ◆ Lunch and dinner; dinner only on Saturday and Sunday. 301 Church St (at Walker St). Reservations recommended. 431.1445

33 Thai House Cafe ★$ Though it's small, unassuming, and generic-looking, if you can stand the Muzak, you'll enjoy excellent authentic Thai food and friendly, helpful service. ◆ Thai ◆ Lunch and dinner. Closed Sunday. 151 Hudson St (at Hubert St). No credit cards. 334.1085

34 Jan Weiss Gallery Weiss, a quantitative investment analyst-turned-art collector, shows the work of contemporary American, Australian, and European artists. ◆ Th-Sa noon-6PM and by appointment. 68 Laight St (at Greenwich St). 925.7313

Capsouto Frères

35 Capsouto Frères ★★$$$ Owners of one of the first trendsetting TriBeCa restaurants to attract a citywide clientele, the *frères* (brothers) are almost always on hand to make their guests welcome. Drop in at the bar for a mid-afternoon cup of espresso, or linger over a long dinner. The menu reflects French and American styles, and there are always some interesting surprises and good desserts. ◆ French ◆ Lunch and dinner; brunch also on Saturday and Sunday; dinner only on Monday. 451 Washington St (at Watts St). Reservations recommended. 966.4900

36 Holland Tunnel Built in 1927, the Holland was the world's first underwater tunnel for vehicles, dipping nearly a hundred feet below the surface of the Hudson River. The tunnel is about 29 feet wide with a 12-foot ceiling. Its north tube is 8,558 feet long, and its south tube stretches 8,371 feet. One of the major problems of the tunnel's construction was ventilation: 42 huge fans at each end provided the solution. **Clifford M. Holland** was the engineer who masterminded this building marvel, and the feat secured his name in New York—and American—history. ◆ From Canal St, Manhattan to 12th St, Jersey City

37 Nosmo King ★★$$$ In this out-of-the-way, oddly comfortable place, you can indulge in the pleasures of denial and gratification simultaneously: wade into the excesses of gourmet cuisine featuring local, organic, and free-range ingredients, including poultry, seafood, produce, and game. Exotic mushrooms, seared tuna, and dairyless desserts are available—and delicious. But there's no butter, no meat, and no smoking. Ask for a booth. ◆ American ◆ Lunch and dinner. 54 Varick St (at Canal St). 966.1239

38 Triplet's Roumanian Restaurant ★$$$ Don't be misled by the decidedly un-Romanian decor; the food is as authentic as it gets this side of the Danube. And as you may have guessed, it's owned and run by identical triplets (brothers) with a fascinating history— they were separated at birth and reunited at age 19. On weekend nights, you'll feel like a tagalong at cousin Sophie's wedding. Stuffed cabbage and professional egg creams made at your table are among the highlights. ◆ Eastern European ◆ Dinner; private parties only on Tuesday and Wednesday. Closed Monday. 11-17 Grand St (at Sixth Ave). Reservations required. 925.9303

39 Moondance Diner ★$ A real diner with gussied-up diner food, this spot jives with the creative atmosphere of the neighborhood. Soups, burgers, and sandwiches are best bets. Barbecued chicken is moist, tender, and wonderfully sloppy. The coffee, tinged with cinnamon, is served as it should be—in a pitcher. The wine prices are good and the breakfasts great. ◆ American ◆ Breakfast, lunch, and dinner; open 24 hours on Friday and Saturday. 80 Sixth Ave (at Grand St). No credit cards. 226.1191

40 Ronald Feldman Fine Arts Inc. The gallery's eclectic and challenging stable includes American, European, and Russian artists. ◆ Tu-Sa 10AM-6PM; Monday by appointment. 31 Mercer St (between Canal and Grand Sts). 226.3232

41 Industrial Plastic Supply Co. Plastic of every description and color fills this sprawling space, and they'll cut any of it to any size without charge. Look for resins and rubber for mold-making, picture frames, mirrors, decorative accessories, and lots of things you never knew could be made of plastic. ◆ M-F 9AM-5:30PM; Sa 9AM-4:30PM. 309 Canal St (between Broadway and Mercer St). 226.2010

42 Pearl River Mart This Chinese department store stocks Chinese imports, including groceries and a good selection of kimonos. It's a good place to wander around; you almost always come away with something. ◆ Daily 10AM-8PM. 277 Canal St (at Broadway), second and third floors. 431.4770

43 443 Broadway In a neighborhood of iron buildings pretending to be stone, this five-story building, designed by **Griffith Thomas** in 1860, is the real thing, and it's a real beauty, once you get past the altered ground floor. The building next door, at No. 447, built at the same time, is also stone, but its storefront is iron, right out of **Daniel Badger's** catalog. ◆ Between Howard and Grand Sts

44 Amsterdam's ★$$ This always-jumping two-tier restaurant includes a long bar along one side and open rotisseries on the other. Best bets are the chicken and seafood. ◆ American ◆ Lunch and dinner. 454 Broadway (at Grand St). Reservations recommended. 925.6166. Also at: 428 Amsterdam Ave. 874.1377

45 L'Ecole ★★$$$ **Jacques Pepin,** author and cooking school director, is Dean of Special Programs at the **French Culinary Institute,** whose students run this restaurant in a building designed by **John Correja** and constructed in 1880. Some good dishes can be had here; particularly recommended are the regional dinners that they prepare from time to time. Like all student-operated restaurants, however, it sometimes has its off days. ◆ French ◆ Lunch and dinner. 462 Broadway (at Grand St). 219.8890

46 478 Broadway Of all the cast-iron buildings in New York, the magazine *Architectural Record* hailed this one, built in 1874 and designed by **Richard Morris Hunt,** as the "most serious attempt to utilize the almost unlimited strength of the material." ◆ Between Grand and Broome Sts

Within 478 Broadway:

Pure Mädderlake This is an eclectic, spirited shop with three personalities: a florist specializing in fresh flowers that grow in English gardens; a home furnishings boutique stocked with antique furniture and a wide variety of tabletop items, including an exclusive line of crystal from Vienna; and a professional photography studio in the back. ◆ M 9AM-3PM; Tu-F 9AM-6PM; call ahead for Saturday and Sunday hours. 941.7770

47 486 Broadway Built in 1883 by **Lamb & Rich,** this titanic former home of the Mechanics Bank combines Romanesque and Moorish elements in brick, stone, and terracotta. Look up at the mansard roof with its projecting windows and small cupolas. ◆ At Broome St

48 Haughwout Building Famous as the building that contained New York's first elevator (a reminder of which is a little rusting sign over the door just to the left of the main entrance), this cast-iron Italian palazzo was designed by **John Gaynor** and built in 1857. The store is now the **SoHo Mill Outlet,** and the building is in a sinful state of disrepair. In better days it was **E.V. Haughwout's** cut glass and silver store. ◆ 490 Broadway (at Broome St)

49 Canal Jean Co. The original home of surplus chic has much more than just jeans. Shop here for the SoHo look without flattening your wallet. ◆ M-Th 11AM-7PM; F-Sa 10AM-8PM. 504 Broadway (between Broome and Spring Sts). 226.1130

50 521-523 Broadway Nothing but this section remains of the luxurious **St. Nicholas Hotel,** which was built in 1854 and once extended along Broadway, Mercer, and Spring streets. Its original frontage on the three streets was 750 feet. Inside, the rugs, tapestries, crystal chandeliers, and beveled mirrors made it a tourist attraction even among visitors who couldn't afford to stay there. The hotel's dining rooms accommodated 600, and there was usually a line outside. The bridal suite, filled with satin, lace, rich rosewood, and crystal, was said to have been designed to intimidate newlyweds, but it attracted them by the score, and for 30 years was considered the best place to begin a happy marriage. **Long Island Fabrics,** on the ground floor of No. 521, stocks a good selection of African prints (925.4488). ◆ Between Broome and Spring Sts

50 495 Broadway Proof that hope springs eternal: this handsome brick-and-stone structure with fine iron panels, designed by **Alfred Zucker** in 1893, replaced an 1860 cast-iron building at almost the same time the district began heading for its decline. ◆ Between Broome and Spring Sts

51 SoHo Antiques Fair and Flea Market This weekend flea market takes advantage of those who've made brunch or lunch, gallery hopping, and window shopping in SoHo part of their weekend. It's not half as big as the Annex Antiques Fair and Flea Market, but you might uncover a real find from dealers who prefer the smaller scale of this corner parking lot. ◆ Free. Sa-Su 9AM-5PM. Broadway at Grand St. 682.2000

Before 1929, the site now occupied by La Guardia Airport was an amusement park.

52 Yohji Yamamoto Themes of recent collections by this talented Japanese designer have included turn-of-the-century Eastern Europe and haute couture with an asymmetrical twist. The prices are high, but the shop is worth a visit even if only to see the iron, rolled-steel, and bronze fixtures designed in London by **Antony Donaldson.** ♦ M-Sa 11AM-7PM. 103 Grand St (at Mercer St). 966.9066

53 Niall Smith Antiques This is a popular haunt for designers and collectors from all over the world in search of neoclassical European furniture dating from the late 18th and early 19th centuries. ♦ M-Sa noon-6PM. 96 Grand St (between Greene and Mercer Sts). 941.7354

54 Greene Street These five cobblestoned blocks are in the heart of the **SoHo Cast-Iron Historic District** (designated in 1973), an area taken over by textile manufacturing and other light industry after the retail and entertainment center of the city moved north in the mid-19th century. The 50 cast-iron buildings still intact on Greene Street were built between 1869 and 1895. Functionally, cast iron anticipated modern steel-frame building techniques, but decoratively, it was used to imitate styles and manners of traditional masonry construction. Designers particularly loved ornate Renaissance and neoclassical motifs, which they altered with a free and fantastical hand. The two outstanding buildings on this street—both in excellent condition—are by **J.F. Duckworth:** Nos. 28-30 (1872), a magnificently mansarded representative of the Second Empire style with leafless Corinthian columns, and Nos. 72-76 (1873), also Corinthian, but here treated in an Italianate manner with a pedimented porch and porticoes all the way up the projecting center bays. The building was built for the **Gardner Colby Company,** whose initials appear on the pilasters. Also noteworthy are the arched lintels and columns, with their egg-and-dart motifs, of Nos. 114-120, designed in 1882 as a branch of a department store; the Ionic capitals turned sideways at Nos. 132-134, 136, and 138 (1885); and all of the extraordinarily ornate No. 31 (1876). Of course, all here is not necessarily iron. Several masonry buildings of the same period sport decorative ironwork—Nos. 42-44 and 84-86, for example—and one is, well, paint. The brick side wall on the corner is graced by **Richard Haas'** trompe l'oeil mural (1975) that mimics the cast-iron facade of the building. Many interior spaces remain intact as well. Perhaps the easiest to visit, and ones that best demonstrate the expansive qualities of a loft space, are galleries such as No. 142.
♦ Between Canal and W. Houston Sts

55 The Drawing Center This elegant space, designed by **James Stewart Polshek** in 1986, is an important nonprofit exhibition space for unaffiliated artists, as well as exceptional scholarly shows of works on paper from historical and contemporary periods. ♦ Tu, Th-F 10AM-6PM; W 10AM-8PM; Sa 11AM-6PM. 35 Wooster St (between Grand and Broome Sts). 219.2166

55 Performing Garage This space is home to **The Wooster Group,** one of America's oldest experimental theater companies, founded in 1967 by director **Richard Schechner.** Under the direction of **Elizabeth LeCompte,** it redefines traditional notions of story line, thematic content, and performance structure. ♦ 33 Wooster St (between Grand and Broome Sts). 966.3651

56 La Jumelle ★★$$$ La Jumelle means "the twin"—and this twin's twin is **Lucky Strike,** just two doors down. Both are charmingly frumpy bars-cum-restaurants with their bistro menus written on blackboards. The clientele is young, trendy Upper West Side on a trip to SoHo. ♦ French ♦ Dinner and late-night meals. 55 Grand St (between Wooster St and W. Broadway). Reservations recommended. 941.9651

56 Lucky Strike ★★$$ At this very popular late-night SoHo hangout, the food is good, if nondescript—except for the french fries, which are excellent. This place is airy, comfortable, and unpretentious. ♦ French ♦ Lunch, dinner, and late-night meals; brunch also on Saturday and Sunday. 59 Grand St (between Wooster St and W. Broadway). 941.0479

57 Jour et Nuit ★★$$ With all those beautiful people streaming in, concentrating on the food at this popular bistro is difficult but really worth the effort. Try the foie gras on toast with fig confit, and tuna tartar. ♦ French ♦ Lunch and dinner; brunch also on Saturday and Sunday. 337 W. Broadway (at Grand St). Reservations required. 925.5971

58 West Broadway ★★$$ Talented chef **Ralph Pagano** creates hearty New American fare. While the tasty food and SoHo location are magnets, the space itself can be noisy, though the bar area is fine for drinking and gazing. Sunday brunch features a jazz band, and current artwork is exhibited. ♦ American ♦ Lunch and dinner; dinner only on Saturday; brunch also on Sunday. Closed Monday. 349 W. Broadway (between Grand and Broome Sts). Reservations required. 226.5885

Prior to a regentrification in the 1970s, TriBeCa was a bypassed eyesore of abandoned warehouses and cast-iron hulls. In an area of just over 200 acres, local meatpackers have moved over to make room for the area's new community of some 8,000 TriBeCans—actors, lawyers, and young professionals with an average income of $55,000. The median cost of a condominium loft is $450,000.

59 Felix ★$$$ Another player in the see-and-be-seen intersection of Grand Street and W. Broadway—SoHo's answer to the Left Bank—Felix, like **Lucky Strike, Jour et Nuit,** and **La Jumelle,** also attracts a cross section of models and downtown hipsters for its simple bistro fare and outdoor cafe people-watching. ♦ French ♦ Lunch and dinner. 340 W. Broadway (at Grand St). 431.0021

60 Manhattan Brewing Co. $$ Once a Con Edison power station, this massive building is now a restaurant and the fourth largest microbrewery in the country. Call for brewery tour information. ♦ International ♦ Lunch and dinner; late-night meals also on Friday and Saturday. 42 Thompson St (at Broome St). Reservations recommended for dinner Friday and Saturday. 925.1515

61 Alison on Dominick Street ★★★$$$ Regulars (and there are many) are the only ones who don't have a hard time finding this restaurant offering some of the best dining in SoHo, overseen by gracious owner **Alison Price.** Even stoics after a hard day at the Stock Exchange warm to the candlelit dining room and predictably good French Mediterranean kitchen headed by **Tom Valenti.** ♦ French Country ♦ Dinner. 38 Dominick St (between Varick and Hudson Sts). Reservations recommended. 727.1188

62 Bell Caffe $ The neighborhood artists who hang out here want to keep it a secret. The table you're sitting at, as well as most everything else, was probably saved from destruction when co-owner **Kurt** found it on the street. The food is okay (homemade breads, soups, vegetable pies), but the scene is more the point. There's live music every night but never a cover. ♦ Cafe ♦ Lunch, dinner, and late-night meals. 310 Spring St (between Greenwich and Hudson Sts). 334.2355

Until the late 1700s the western area of what is today called TriBeCa was owned by Trinity Church (Broadway and Wall Street). Its most prominent parishioners, most probably those with the most generous wallets, had streets named after them: (John) Chambers, (James) Duane, and (Joseph) Reade.

---

63 Castillo Cultural Center This progressive, independent cultural center encompasses a performance space, gallery, publishing house, photo lab, and video lab. One notable performance included a live hair montage—three-dimensional environments created on top of peoples' heads. ♦ M-Sa 10AM-10PM; Su noon-6PM. 500 Greenwich St (between Spring and Canal Sts). 941.5800

64 The Ear Inn ★$ Built in 1817, this place is now a designated Landmark of the City of New York. You can easily picture the seafaring rowdies who once frequented this dark and dusty bar and restaurant. There are poetry readings on weekends, and regulars say it has the best jukebox in town. The Ear Inn is off the beaten path (the original shoreline of the river used to be only five feet away from the entrance), but worth it. ♦ American ♦ Lunch, dinner, and late-night meals; brunch also on Sunday. 326 Spring St (between Washington and Greenwich Sts). 226.9060

65 New York City Fire Museum The Fire Department's own collection of apparatus and memorabilia dating back to colonial times is combined here with that of the **Home Insurance Co.** This is the largest exhibition of its kind in the country, and if you have youngsters in tow they won't complain a bit about the long walk west when they discover this is the destination. ♦ Voluntary contribution. Tu-Sa 10AM-4PM. 278 Spring St (between Varick and Hudson Sts). 691.1303

66 Ceramica Classic Italian patterns appear on imported linens, mosaics, and earthenware—the Rafaelesco, a dragon pattern Rafael used on many of his frames, is particularly beautiful. Everything is handmade for the store. ♦ Tu-Sa 11:30AM-7PM; Su 11:30AM-6PM. 59 Thompson St (between Broome and Spring Sts). 941.1307

66 Classic Toys Put together your own private army, create a miniature zoo, or mount a wee Wild West show from this imaginative collection. Collectors and commercial photographers, as well as local children, shop here for tin soldiers and matchbox cars, circus sets, and stuffed dinosaurs. ♦ W-Su noon-6:30PM. 69 Thompson St (between Broome and Spring Sts). 941.9129

66 0 To 60s Jewelry, furnishings, folk art, and unusual objects from 1900 through 1960 are showcased in this store. ♦ M-Sa noon-7PM. 75 Thompson St (between Broome and Spring Sts). 925.0932

67 Il Bisonte These fine handcrafted leather handbags, portfolios, luggage, and accessories come straight from Florence. ♦ M, Su noon-6PM; Tu-Sa noon-6:30PM. 72 Thompson St (between Broome and Spring Sts). 966.8773. Also at: 22 E. 65th St. 717.4771

Restaurants/Clubs: Red   Hotels: Blue
Shops/ 🌱 Outdoors: Green   Sights/Culture: Black

68 Think Big If you can find a use for a six-foot-long pencil or a wristwatch too big for King Kong, more power to you. This famous store has a whole line of outsize items that will make you feel like a Lilliputian. ♦ M-Sa 11AM-7PM; Su noon-6PM. 390 W. Broadway (between Broome and Spring Sts). 925.7300

68 Barolo ★★$$$ Italian food with excellent pasta and broiled fresh fish is served in this enormous restaurant, probably the largest in SoHo. Go and see the nine magnificent matching cherry trees in the garden (this is where the action is anyway). Those in-the-know go elsewhere for dessert. ♦ Italian ♦ Lunch and dinner; late-night meals on Friday and Saturday. 398 W. Broadway (between Spring and Broome Sts). Reservations recommended. 226.1102

69 O.K. Harris Works of Art A SoHo landmark for 20 years, this gallery is a record-setter, with more than 60 artists represented and an average of 50 exhibitions each year in its 11,000-square-foot spread. **Ivan Karp,** an early champion of Pop Art, is the gallery's founder and chief point man. ♦ Tu-Sa 10AM-6PM. 383 W. Broadway (between Broome and Spring Sts). 431.3600

69 Portico Owner **Steven Werther** travels far and wide to find craftspeople who meet his meticulous standards of construction. Among the pieces that have made the grade are handmade reproductions of Shaker furniture, Argentine antiques, and dishes and glassware from Italy. In the middle of the store—it stretches all the way to Wooster Street—is a pleasant cafe setting where you can sit and relax with a cappuccino or a cup of tea (try one from the United Society of Shakers in Maine). ♦ M-Sa 11AM-7PM; Su noon-6:30PM. 379 W. Broadway (between Broome and Spring Sts). 941.7800

69 Gemini GEL at Joni Weyl New and vintage prints from the venerable L.A. workshop, including editions by **Ellsworth Kelly, Roy Lichtenstein,** and **Robert Rauschenberg,** are on view. ♦ Tu-Sa 10:30AM-5:30PM. 375 W. Broadway (between Broome and Spring Sts), second floor. 219.1446

69 Betsy Senior Contemporary Prints Senior maintains a select inventory of prints from small American publishers, as well as new editions by rising stars. ♦ By appointment. 375 W. Broadway (between Broome and Spring Sts), second floor. 941.0960

69 SoHo Emporium This frightening gaggle of some 40 independent boutiques sells everything from furs and jewelry to crafts and crystal. Should you be in need of advice—a way out, perhaps—there is even a fortune-teller. ♦ M-F noon-8PM; Sa-Su 11AM-8PM. 375 W. Broadway (between Broome and Spring Sts). 966.6091

70 Kenn's Broome Street Bar $ This 1825 building was altered in 1868 to become a boardinghouse and a saloon. The hamburgers served here today come on pita bread. There are other trendy touches, but your grandfather would still recognize the bar, which hasn't changed much in all these years. ♦ American ♦ Lunch, dinner, and late-night meals. 363 W. Broadway (at Broome St). 925.2086

70 The Cupping Room Cafe ★★$$$ Waffles with berries, giant muffins (the whole wheat is addictive), bagels with fixings, and a choice of terrific coffees and teas draw a fiercely loyal crowd. ♦ Continental ♦ Breakfast, lunch, and dinner; late-night meals also Tuesday through Saturday. 359 W. Broadway (at Broome St). Dinner reservations recommended. 925.2898

71 Sura Kayla Dried, silk, and fresh flowers; candles; antique and vintage knickknacks; custom-made furniture (pine dining and end tables with white birch legs, for example); and gift ideas galore fill this store. They also do party planning. ♦ By appointment only. 484 Broome St (at Wooster St). 941.8757, 627.9000

71 59 Wooster Street Originally a warehouse, this six-story building, designed by **Alfred Zucker** in 1890, dominates the corner where it stands. Its mass is relieved by arched, iron-rimmed windows on its Broome Street facade, and by highly sculptural reliefs scattered over its surface. The seemingly random play between the rough-hewn masonry, smooth brickwork, and crenolated roofline (look hard and you'll see hand-size human faces way up top) somehow pulls the building together and gives it an oddly noble presence. It's best seen from the south side of Broome Street. ♦ At Broome St

Within 59 Wooster Street:

Brooke Alexander In luxurious quarters designed by the English architect **Max Gordon, Carolyn** and **Brooke Alexander** feature painting and sculpture by some of the most vigorous talents, including **Jane Dickson, Yvonne Jacquette,** and **Tom Otterness.** ♦ Tu-Sa 10AM-6PM. Second floor. 925.4338

David N. Dinkins assumed the city's highest office in 1990 as the city's first black mayor.

72 Printed Matter Bookstore at Dia This nonprofit art center specializes in books made by artists, which means the artist has been directly involved with the conceptualization, design, and production of the work. The average price per book is $10 to $15—choose among 5,000 titles by 2,500 artists—making them one of very few bargains in the art world. ♦ Tu-Sa 10AM-6PM. 77 Wooster St (between Broome and Spring Sts). 925.0325

73 Brooke Alexander Editions Longtime champions of the graphic image, **Brooke** and **Carolyn Alexander** have opened a roomy, light-filled space that every print maven dreams about. Featured are American prints since 1960 by such contemporary masters as **Johns, Lichtenstein,** and **Judd,** as well as a selective inventory of works by younger artists and distinctive Europeans. ♦ Tu-Sa 10AM-6PM. 476 Broome St (between Greene and Wooster Sts), fourth floor. 925.2070

74 SoHo 20 Gallery The gallery is a coop-erative of women artists with group and individual shows. ♦ Tu-Sa noon-6PM. 469 Broome St (at Greene St). 226.4167

75 Craft Caravan, Inc. Traditional African handicrafts are the draw, and some interesting household items are in a display case up front—Beauty Pageant talc powder and Elephant Powder laundry detergent, for instance. ♦ Tu-F 10AM-6PM; Sa-Su 11AM-6PM. 63 Greene St (between Broome and Spring Sts). 431.6669

75 Heller Gallery One of the most important representatives of the modern glass movement, this always interesting gallery usually has two solo shows and a monthly overview. ♦ Tu-Sa 11AM-6PM; Su noon-5PM. 71 Greene St (between Broome and Spring Sts). 966.5948

75 5&10-No Exaggeration $$ The antiques in this vintage 1940s jazz club are all for sale. The food is okay, but people come for the entertainment. ♦ Mexican/American ♦ Dinner and late-night meals; hours vary according to the event, so call ahead. 77 Greene St (between Broome and Spring Sts). Reservations required. 925.7414

76 The Second Coming Home furnishings, furniture, apparel, and jewelry that was fashionable in the 1940s and 1950s fill this shop. Among the selections are overstuffed Art Deco furniture, dresses in black rayon and velvet, and printed fabrics. The building, one of four on the street designed by **Isaac Duckworth** in 1873, was called the "King of Greene Street" ("The Queen" is 28 Greene Street). This one is a masterpiece of French Second Empire in cast iron. ♦ M-Sa noon-7PM; Su 1-6PM. 72 Greene St (between Broome and Spring Sts). 431.4424

76 Luna D'Oro Jewelry, handicrafts, and furnishings from South and Central America are carried in this shop. ♦ Daily 11AM-6PM. 66 Greene St (between Broome and Spring Sts). 925.8225

77 Marianne Novobatzky Here you'll find women's clothing designed by Novobatzky for urban living with an attention to detail rarely found in today's high-speed world. If you don't find the perfect fit or color in her ready-to-wear collection, a new garment will be custom-stitched for you in her workshop downstairs. All of the display pieces in the shop were sculpted by artist **John Ittner.** ♦ M-F noon-7PM; Sa noon-6PM. 65 Mercer St (at Broome St). 431.4120

77 Friends of Figurative Sculpture Bronze sculptures of the human figure in a variety of sizes are featured in this friendly gallery. ♦ By appointment only. 53 Mercer St (between Grand and Broome Sts). 226.4850

78 Michael Carey American Arts & Crafts Come here for a good selection of pottery, lighting, and furniture by **Gustave Stickley** (1858-1942) and other period designers. ♦ Tu-Sa 11AM-6PM or by appointment. 77 Mercer St (between Broome and Spring Sts). 226.3710

78 The Enchanted Forest This bewitching shop looks like a miniature set for a fantasy adventure. Beasts, books, and handmade toys are part of the celebration. ♦ M-Sa 11AM-7PM; Su noon-6PM. 85 Mercer St (between Broome and Spring Sts). 925.6677

78 Leekan Designs The always exotic window invites you in to peruse. Among the offerings are antique jade and porcelain, wood carvings, silk rugs, embroidered hangings, wedding baskets, and inexpensive folk art and other treasures imported from China and Southeast Asia. ♦ M-W, F 11AM-6PM; Th, Sa 11AM-7PM; Su noon-6PM. 93 Mercer St (between Broome and Spring Sts). 226.7226

79 Spring Street Natural ★★$$ Any one of the several varieties of fresh fish is a winning choice here. The light-filled interior is strewn with plants. ♦ American ♦ Lunch and dinner; brunch also on Saturday and Sunday; late-night meals on Friday and Saturday. 62 Spring St (at Lafayette St). 966.0290

80 New York Open Center Each year the Center offers hundreds of workshops, courses, lectures, and performances that explore spiritual and social issues, psychology, the arts—in short, all aspects of traditional and contemporary world culture. Check out the bookstore for the latest literature on all the above. ♦ Bookstore: M-F 11:30AM-10PM; Sa 11AM-9PM; Su 11AM-7PM. 83 Spring St (between Broadway and Crosby St). 219.2527

81 P.P.O.W. The adventuresome young partners, **Penny Pilkington** and **Wendy Olsoff** (hence the name), pride themselves on their preference for individuals over trends. They show **David Wojnarowicz** and **Erika Rothenberg** as well as installation work (built environments) by **TODT**. ♦ Tu-Sa 10AM-6PM. 532 Broadway (between Spring and Prince Sts), third floor. 941.8642

82 101 Spring Street Designed by **N. Whyte** in 1871, this building displays a sensitive approach to the use of cast iron as complex ornament. The ground floor is completely unchanged. ♦ At Mercer St

83 Betina Riedel Chic and comfy women's clothes are sold in the designer's store. ♦ M-Sa 11AM-7PM; Su noon-6PM. 113 Spring St (between Mercer and Greene Sts). 226.2350

84 Jacques Carcanagues Jewelry, textiles, furniture, sculpture, and ritual objects from around the world are sold. ♦ Daily 11:30AM-7PM. 106 Spring St (between Mercer and Greene Sts). 925.8110

85 Jay Gorney Art This gallery is a trendy venue for contemporary painting and sculpture, with a more than ample dose of late-1980s marketing savvy. ♦ Tu-Sa 10AM-6PM. 100 Greene St (between Spring and Prince Sts). 966.4480

85 110 Greene Street The sign says this is The SoHo Building, but long before anyone ever thought of calling this neighborhood SoHo, it was an annex of the **Charles Broadway Rouss Department Store** that thrived over on Broadway. It was designed by **William J. Dilthy** and built in 1908. ♦ Between Spring and Prince Sts

85 Wolfman-Gold & Good Company Very expensive tableware and home accessories are sold in this boutique. ♦ M-W, F-Sa 11AM-6PM; Th 11AM-6PM; Su noon-5PM. 116 Greene St (between Spring and Prince Sts). 431.1888

85 Buffalo Chips Bootery After 17 years on their feet as hairdressers, **Ron Tassely** and **Paul Greyshock** turned their passion for cowboy boots (and their desire to find a comfortable pair) into a business. Working with the Ammons and Stallion boot companies, they designed a fashionable line of podiatrist-approved cowboy boots with steel-reinforced arches and low, tapered heels for proper support. If you can't find a pair that you like among the 50 or so on display, they'll be glad to do a custom design. They also sell artwork and jewelry by Southwestern artists. ♦ M-Sa 11AM-7PM; Su noon-6PM. 116 Greene St (between Spring and Prince Sts). 274.0651

86 Kelley and Ping ★★$ After two successful years at their popular Thai restaurant **Kin Khao** two blocks away, **Brad Kelley** and **Lee Ping** opened this gastronomic venture in 1993. You can watch the Thai chef at work in the open kitchen, enjoy a simple, savory meal of duck soup or noodles prepared in many ways (plus delicious dumplings and scallion pancakes, and other Asian treats), then buy the ingredients to prepare your own feast at home—all at unbeatable prices. ♦ Pan Asian ♦ Lunch and dinner. 127 Greene St (between Spring and Prince Sts). 228.1212

87 SoHo Kitchen and Bar ★$$ Pizzas and fries, another theatrical interior by owner **Tony Goldman** (dramatic lighting, immense canvases, black ceiling), and Manhattan's longest wine list (96 wines, 14 champagnes) are highlights. Oenophiles shouldn't miss the "flights of wines"—a heady experience in which four to eight wines within a specific category are sampled in two-and-a-half-ounce increments. ♦ American ♦ Lunch and dinner; late-night meals on Friday and Saturday. 103 Greene St (between Spring and Prince Sts). 925.1866

87 Barbara Gladstone Gallery Gladstone's elegant two-tiered space allows her to mount dual exhibitions from an ever-increasing stable of European and American artists. **Vito Acconci, Anish Kapoor, Rosemarie Trockel,** and **Genny Holzer** are part of her distinguished roster. ♦ Tu-Sa 10AM-6PM. 99 Greene St (between Spring and Prince Sts). 431.3334

87 Zona One of the very best reasons to visit SoHo, **Louis Sagar's** high-ceilinged, wonderfully airy space is as much a gallery as a store: **Paolo Soleri's** bells, garden tools, furniture of the Southwest, terracotta, and other well-designed housewares from the Great American Desert (and all over the world) are displayed with great care and imagination—qualities every store should aim for. It's worth buying something just to get it gift-wrapped. ♦ M-W, F-Sa 11:30AM-6:30PM; Th 11:30AM-7PM; Su noon-6PM. 97 Greene St (between Spring and Prince Sts). 925.6750

The worst blackout prior to New York's 1977 25-hour power failure was in 1965, when the city was without electrical power for 13 hours.

87 Jekyll & Hyde The fine fabrics and quality tailoring of the outstanding men's suits and belts will bring out the best in you. In fact, you'll probably like the transformation. ♦ M-W 11AM-6:30PM; Th 11AM-7PM; F-Sa noon-7PM; Su noon-6:30PM. 93 Greene St (between Spring and Prince Sts). 966.8503

88 Platypus All sorts of housewares, from designer kettles and flatware (**Alessi, Michael Graves, Aldo Rossi**) to wicker furniture and antiques (18th- and 19th-century pine armoires, cupboards, cribs) are available. Stop in for Godiva chocolates as well. ♦ M, Su noon-6PM; Tu-Sa 11AM-6PM. 126 Spring St (at Greene St). 219.3919

88 Penny Whistle Toys The downtown branch of this refreshing toy store has new and old-fashioned board games, indoor gyms, costumes, and rattles for infants—all lovingly assembled by owner **Meredith Brokaw,** wife of the well-known TV anchor. ♦ M-Sa 11AM-7PM; Su 11:30AM-6PM. 132 Spring St (between Greene and Wooster Sts). 925.2088. Also at: 1283 Madison Ave. 369.3868; 448 Columbus Ave. 873.9090

88 Peter Roberts Antiques Peter Roberts is a specialist in American Arts and Crafts furniture and accessories. ♦ M-Sa 11AM-7PM; Su noon-6PM. 134 Spring St (between Greene and Wooster Sts), ground floor. 226.4777

88 Jaap Rietman Just one flight up, this is an unsurpassed source for the best books and periodicals on art, architecture, and photography. The staff is knowledgeable and the atmosphere conducive to browsing—it's actually encouraged. It's a cozy retreat on rainy days. ♦ M-F 9:30AM-6PM; Sa 10:30AM-6PM. 134 Spring St (between Greene and Wooster Sts), second floor. 966.7044

88 Laurence Miller Gallery Works by photography greats **Lee Friedlander** and **Helen Levitt** hang in this gallery beside those of younger shutterbugs, all chosen with Miller's customary discretion. ♦ Tu-F 10AM-6PM; Sa 11AM-6PM. 138 Spring St (between Greene and Wooster Sts), third floor. 226.1220

New York is the only major city in the country that has an official residence for its mayor (Gracie Mansion).

89 Manhattan Bistro ★$$ The best choices here are the homey French specialties—slow-cooked stews and small steaks with sensational skinny fries. Relax with a glass of wine and indulge in the sport of people-watching. ♦ French ♦ Breakfast, lunch, dinner, and late-night meals. 129 Spring St (between Greene and Wooster Sts). Dinner reservations required. 966.3459

89 The Grass Roots Garden **Larry Nathanson** is the green thumb behind this cornucopia of plants. ♦ Tu-Sa 9AM-6PM; Su noon-6PM. 131 Spring St (between Greene and Wooster Sts). 226.2662

90 Boom ★★$$$ This is a hot SoHo spot for "world cuisine." Innovative creations range from Sengalese mafta, a peanut-based vegetarian dish, to avocado blinis with lobster, Ossetra caviar, and crème fraîche. The candlelit setting is eclectic yet romantic. Boom is great for people-watching at the bar. ♦ Eclectic ♦ Lunch and dinner; brunch also on Saturday and Sunday; late-night meals also on Thursday, Friday, and Saturday. 152 Spring St (between W. Broadway and Wooster St). 431.3663

91 Tennessee Mountain ★$$ The smells (which waft down Spring Street) are better than the food—ribs, fried chicken, and vegetarian chili—but the frozen margaritas will put you in the proper mood. ♦ American ♦ Lunch and dinner; brunch also on Saturday and Sunday. 143 Spring St (at Wooster St). Reservations recommended. 431.3993

91 Putumayo Each season owner **Dan Storper** and his team, inspired by the traditional styles of a foreign country, design a new collection of these moderately priced casual clothes. Interior designer **Susan Brynner** redecorates the shop in the same spirit, making each visit, if not a shopping spree, an interesting experience. Recent inspiration has come from Scandinavia, Greece, Morocco, and India. ♦ M-Sa 11AM-7PM; Su noon-6PM. 147 Spring St (between Wooster St and W. Broadway). 966.4458

91 Morgane Le Fay The window at this women's clothing boutique is always austere and monochromatic. Featured inside is the clothing of **Liliana Ordas**—flowing dresses, coats, capes, and skirts in a wide range of wool flannels, wool crepes, jerseys, and velvets. ♦ M-Sa 11AM-8PM; Su 11AM-7PM. 151 Spring St (between Wooster St and W. Broadway). 925.0144

91 The Irish Secret The traditional and innovative fashions by contemporary Irish designers include beautifully tailored dresses in silk, linen, cotton, or wool. ♦ Daily 11AM-7PM. 155 Spring St (between Wooster St and W. Broadway). 334.6711

91 Kin Khao ★★$$ The trendiest place around for Thai food, this dark, cavelike spot offers such tasty dishes as excellent *phad thai,* crispy duck, and wonderful dumplings. For refreshment, try the Cosmopolitan—fresh lime juice, cranberry juice, Absolut Citron, and Grand Marnier in a chilled martini glass. ♦ Thai ♦ Dinner. 171 Spring St (at W. Broadway). 966.3939

92 Tootsi Plohound You would probably never guess that a store with a name like this sells unusual and well-made men's and women's shoes. ♦ M-Sa 11:30AM-7:30PM; Su noon-7PM. 413 W. Broadway (between Spring and Prince Sts). 925.8931

92 415 West Broadway There are eight galleries in this impressive six-story building with a simple cast-iron storefront. ♦ Between Spring and Prince Sts

Within 415 West Broadway:

Maxwell Davidson Gallery This seasoned dealer, formerly on upper Madison, hosts a variety of artists, with an emphasis on Realism. ♦ Tu-Sa 10AM-6PM. Fifth floor. 925.5300

Witkin Gallery The focus is on vintage and contemporary photography by such artists as **Evelyn Hofer, George Tice,** and **Jerry N. Uelsmann.** Also available are new, rare, and out-of-print books on photography. ♦ Tu-Sa 11AM-6PM. Fourth floor. 925.5510

92 Mary Boone A much publicized upstart in the early 1980s heyday of neo-Expressionism, Boone has settled into the establishment with a solid roster of American and mid-career European artists. **Eric Fischl, David Salle,** and **Julian Schnabel** (who has since moved on to the Pace Gallery) are among her successes. ♦ Tu-Sa 10AM-6PM. 417 W. Broadway (between Spring and Prince Sts). 431.1818

92 Beau Brummel **Ralph Lauren** began his career designing ties for Beau Brummel. Today, most of the men's clothing and accessories sold here are by European designers. ♦ M-Sa 11AM-8PM; Su noon-7PM. 421 W. Broadway (between Spring and Prince Sts). 219.2666

92 Nancy Hoffman Gallery Hoffman's generous space is the backdrop for easygoing paintings and works on paper by such Realists as **Joseph Raffael** and **Peter Plagens,** as well as oils on canvas by **Rafael Ferrer** and others. ♦ Tu-Sa 10AM-6PM. 429 W. Broadway (between Spring and Prince Sts). 966.6676

92 Dapy Exotic high-tech gifts and gadgets as well as smaller, less expensive toys like dancing Coke cans are sold. ♦ Daily 11AM-8PM. 431 W. Broadway (between Spring and Prince Sts). 925.5082

93 Joovay Fine cotton and silk lingerie, sleepwear, and a good selection of toiletries are featured in this boutique. ♦ Daily noon-7PM. 436 W. Broadway (between Spring and Prince Sts). 431.6386

93 Vuccria ★$$ SoHo art folk come here for Sicilian home cooking and warm, friendly service. On a good night, the chicken with sausage and mushrooms and the penne with eggplant are excellent, as is the angel-hair pasta with seafood. Ask for a seat along the north wall. ♦ Italian ♦ Lunch and dinner; brunch also on Saturday and Sunday. 422 W. Broadway (between Spring and Prince Sts). Reservations recommended. 941.5811

93 420 West Broadway Two of SoHo's most prestigious galleries, **Leo Castelli** and **Sonnabend,** as well as several others are housed in this heavy-hitter building. ♦ Between Spring and Prince Sts

Within 420 West Broadway:

Charles Cowles Gallery Contemporary painting joins sculpture and ceramics by a wide-ranging stable that includes many West Coast artists. ♦ Tu-Sa 10AM-6PM. Fifth floor. 925.3500

Germans van Eck This ambitious Dutch-born dealer boasts a healthy mix of eccentric American and European painters and sculptors. ♦ Tu-Sa 10AM-6PM. Ground floor. 219.0717

Hirschl & Adler Modern American and European paintings, drawings, prints, and sculpture from the mid-1950s through the present are displayed in this gallery. ♦ Tu-Sa 10AM-6PM. Fourth floor. 966.6211

Leo Castelli Gallery A must-see on anyone's SoHo circuit, Castelli's extraordinary gallery features a veritable Who's Who of Abstract Expressionist and Pop artists, many of whom have shown with Castelli since the early 1960s. **Jasper Johns, Ellsworth Kelly,** and **Ed Ruscha** are but a few of the gallery regulars. ♦ Tu-Sa 10AM-6PM. Second floor. 431.5160

Sonnabend Gallery Ileana Sonnabend's celebrated and highly respected eye has drawn in such Americans as **Robert Morris,** who shares the floor with an ever-growing list of distinguished Europeans, including **Jannis Kounellis, Gilbert & George,** and **Anne** and **Patrick Poirier.** ♦ Tu-Sa 10AM-6PM. Third floor. 966.6160

Restaurants/Clubs: Red   **Hotels:** Blue
Shops/ 🌳 Outdoors: Green   **Sights/Culture:** Black

94 Paracelso A moderately priced source for women's clothes in natural fibers, Paracelso's styles—many from India—are casual and loose-fitting. ♦ Daily 1-7PM. 414 W. Broadway (between Spring and Prince Sts). 966.4232

94 Harriet Love This is the shop that originally made antique clothes fashionable, and it's still one of the best in the business. (The owner is the author of *Harriet Love's Guide to Vintage Chic.*) Many of the clothes— all in mint condition— date from the 1940s and 1950s, and a few go back even further. Harriet Love also stocks vintage jewelry, alligator- and crocodile-skin bags, and brand-new clothing with a vintage feel. ♦ Tu-Su 11:30AM-7PM. 412 W. Broadway (between Spring and Prince Sts). 966.2280

95 Ad Hoc Softwares Owners **Julia McFarlane** and **Judith Auchincloss** scour the marketplace for a wide range of bed and bath items, including unbleached, chemical-free linen and cotton sheets from Austria and West Germany, Italian and French waffle towels, and high-quality blankets from Europe. Also stocked are a broad selection of French and English bodycare products, and small gift items. ♦ M-Sa 11AM-7PM; Su noon-6PM. 410 W. Broadway (at Spring St). 925.2652

95 Spring Street Books In addition to a top-notch selection of books, this store features a good selection of newspapers, foreign magazines, and remainders. The late hours are a boon to last-minute gift shoppers. ♦ M-Th 10AM-11PM; F 10AM-midnight; Sa 10AM-1AM; Su 11AM-10PM. 169 Spring St (between W. Broadway and Thompson St). 219.3033

96 Berrys ★$$ A convivial bistro that has become established as an in-place for Sunday brunches, Berrys is noisy, dark (it has a certain Victorian appeal), and crowded, but cozy and friendly as well. The food is well-prepared and the menu imaginative. ♦ American ♦ Lunch and dinner; brunch also on Saturday and Sunday. 180 Spring St (at Thompson St). Reservations recommended; required for Sunday brunch. 226.4394

97 Bébé Thompson These designer clothes for children include imported handmade cotton and wool outfits that will still be in style long after they have been outgrown. ♦ Daily noon-7PM. 98 Thompson St (between Spring and Prince Sts). 925.1122

97 Anvers Belgian designer **Anne Kegels'** sober designs suit busy women who need versatile clothing that can be dressed up or down for the occasion. ♦ Daily noon-7PM. 110 Thompson St (between Spring and Prince Sts). 219.1308

97 Peter Hermann Hermann provides the finest handbags, belts, and luggage in the world, mostly from Europe. ♦ M-Sa noon-7PM; Su noon-6:30PM. 118 Thompson St (between Spring and Prince Sts). 966.9050

98 Spring Street Garden The always charming window displays show off just some of the exotica within—unusual varieties of tulips (the French parrot tulip is stupendous), miniature roses, and all sorts of dried flowers. Delivery within Manhattan is available. ♦ Tu-Sa 11:30AM-7PM. 186½ Spring St (between Thompson and Sullivan Sts). 966.2015

99 Mezzogiorno ★★$$$ **Roberto Magris** designed this airy restaurant, which, during the warmer months, opens out onto the sidewalk. Coal-oven pizzas and carpaccio—shaved raw beef with your choice of accompaniments—are the highlights, though you can't go wrong with pasta. ♦ Italian ♦ Lunch, dinner, and late-night meals. 195 Spring St (between Thompson and Sullivan Sts). No credit cards. 334.2112

99 Nick & Eddie ★★$$ Locals meet in the late afternoon in this old-fashioned neighborhood restaurant; uptowners, in search of the "SoHo experience," arrive later. The dependable American menu includes marinated salmon on grilled sourdough bread, fresh salads, steaks, french fries served in paper cones, and juicy hamburgers. ♦ American ♦ Lunch and dinner; brunch also on Saturday and Sunday. 203 Spring St (at Sullivan St). Reservations recommended. 219.9090

100 Cafe ★★$$$ Sit on the lovely terrace on the Sixth Avenue side or at cafe tables for lunch on Spring Street. If you're in the mood for elegance, head inside to the dining room decorated with medieval religious antiques. ♦ Cafe/French ♦ Lunch and dinner; brunch also on Saturday and Sunday. 210 Spring St (at Sixth Ave). Reservations recommended. 274.0505

101 Le Erbe All-natural herbal products from Italy for the face, body, and hair are sold in this intimate shop. A variety of beauty services are available by appointment. ♦ Tu-Sa 11AM-7PM. 196 Prince St (at Sullivan St). 966.1445

101 Raoul's ★★$$$ The fare at this reliable, forever-popular bistro is as French as you can get in SoHo: foie gras, steak au poivre, rare breast of duck. A maître d' with personality, attentive service, and an always interesting crowd make Raoul's a great choice. ◆ French ◆ Dinner; late-night meals on Friday and Saturday. 180 Prince St (between Thompson and Sullivan Sts). Reservations recommended. 966.3518

101 Hans Koch Ltd. Fine belts and handbags are featured in this shop. If nothing suits your fancy, Mr. Koch will whip up something that will. ◆ M-Th, Su noon-8PM; F-Sa 11AM-9PM. 174 Prince St (between Thompson and Sullivan Sts). 226.5385

102 Omen ★★$$$ First-timers to this quiet, attractive restaurant that has cultivated a loyal following should try *omen*—Japanese noodles served with a variety of toppings and flavorings—a perfect introduction to the extensive menu. ◆ Japanese ◆ Dinner. Closed Monday. 113 Thompson St (between Spring and Prince Sts). Reservations recommended. 925.8923

102 Sacco Shoes You won't be disappointed with the selection of classically avant-garde women's footwear and bags. If you're hankering for ankle-high boots, this is the place. ◆ M-F 11AM-8PM; Sa 11AM-7PM; Su noon-7PM. 111 Thompson St (between Spring and Prince Sts). 925.8010

102 Peter Fox Shoes All Peter Fox designs, inspired by Victorian and medieval styles, are handmade (except for the stitching of the sole to the leather) in Italy. Check next door for the full line of wedding styles; bridal customers have included supermodel **Paulina Porizkova** and model-turned-actress **Phoebe Cates**. ◆ M-Sa 11AM-7PM; Su noon-6PM. 105 Thompson St (between Spring and Prince Sts). 431.6359

103 Milady ★$ This neighborhood bar underwent a face-lift of sorts not too long ago. They changed the name and the decor, but the clientele is basically the same—local types who come for a beer and conversation. Simple entrées include great burgers and salads. ◆ American ◆ Lunch and dinner. 162 Prince St (at Thompson St). 226.9340

103 Vesuvio's Bakery A SoHo landmark, this charming storefront has been selling chewy loaves of bread, breadsticks, and the most addictive pepper biscuits since 1928. If you want to catch up on neighborhood goings-on, speak to owner **Anthony Dapolito**: he's one of SoHo's genuinely concerned citizens. ◆ M-Sa 7AM-7PM. 160 Prince St (between W. Broadway and Thompson St). 925.8248

104 101 Wooster Street The law firm of **Dolgenos Newman & Cronin** maintains this contemporary art exhibition right in their workspace. With the assistance of a professional curator, they show art that might not make it into a commerical gallery due to lack of marketability. Exhibitions that focus on socially relevant issues, such as the UN Decade for Women, are featured. ◆ Sa-Su noon-6PM. 101 Wooster St (between Spring and Prince Sts). 925.2800

105 Detour The accent is on femininity in this collection of mostly European clothing. Detour also sells men's clothing at 425 W. Broadway and recently opened a women's store at 472 W. Broadway. ◆ Daily 11AM-8PM. 114 Wooster St (between Spring and Prince Sts). 219.8183

105 Comme des Garçons Japanese couturier **Rei Kawakubo** designs fashion-forward clothes under the Comme des Garçons label. She also designed this stark showroom to function as a dramatic setting for her exotic line—a truly minimalist experience. ◆ M-Sa 11AM-7PM; Su noon-6:30PM. 116 Wooster St (between Spring and Prince Sts). 219.0661

105 T&K French Antiques Among the direct imports from France are copper bathtubs, ornate bird cages, and fine antique furniture. ◆ Tu-F 11AM-6:30PM; Sa noon-6PM; Su 1-5PM. 120 Wooster St (between Spring and Prince Sts). 219.2472

106 130 Prince Street Designed in 1989 by **Lee Manners & Associates,** this new "PoMo" building is home to English jewelry designer **Stuart Moore's** shop of sophisticated *bijoux,* plus eight art galleries—**Louver, Lohring Augustine, Perry Rubenstein, Christine Burgin, Andrea Rosen, Petersberg, Victoria Munroe,** and **Tony Shafrazi**—each of which commissioned its own architect to design the space according to its specifications. ◆ At Wooster St

Within 130 Prince Street:

Louver Gallery This gallery displays contemporary painting and sculpture from **Peter Shelton, David Nash, Tony Bevam,** and **Pieter Laurens Mol,** among others. ◆ Tu-Sa 10AM-6PM. Second floor. 925.9205

Stuart Moore Visit this jewelry shop if you are in the market for exceptionally well-made (expensive) jewelry in 18K gold or platinum. Custom work is the specialty, and the mark-up on gemstones exceeding $6,000 in cost is only 20 percent—a bargain, if you can afford it. ◆ Tu-Sa noon-6:30PM; Su noon-4:30PM. Ground floor. 941.1023

106 Reinstein/Ross This is a shop devoted entirely to the exquisite jewelry created by **Susan Reinstein,** namely, multicolored sapphires and 22K gold, often alloyed in subtle colors, most of which she has developed herself. ◆ Tu-Sa 11:30AM-6:30PM; Su noon-6PM. 122 Prince St (between Greene and Wooster Sts). 226.4513. Also at: 29 E. 73rd St. 772.1901

agnès b.

106 agnès b. Classics for men, women, and children—such as V-necked sweaters and cotton T-shirts—are made modern by this French designer. How does she do it? She takes the sweater and makes the V neck lower and sexier, and stripes the T-shirts in fresh colors like baby blue and maroon. The children's line is sold uptown in her shop at 1063 Madison Avenue. ♦ M-Sa 11AM-7PM; Su noon-6PM. 116-118 Prince St (between Greene and Wooster Sts). 925.4649

107 David Beitzel Gallery Beitzel's eye is broad-ranging, and he tends to favor emerging artists who work in highly individual idioms. ♦ Tu-Sa 10AM-6PM. 102 Prince St (at Greene St). 219.2863

107 Annina Nosei Gallery This gallery is a champion of contemporary American and international artists (who come from as far away as Argentina and Zaire). ♦ Tu-Sa 10AM-6PM. 100 Prince St (between Mercer and Greene Sts). 431.9253

107 Fanelli Cafe ★$ A holdover from the district's days as a neighborhood of factories, this cafe is still a good choice for those in search of a terrific hamburger and fries, and a favorite among factory workers as well as arty newcomers. The service could be a little more genteel, but the place doesn't invite kid gloves. Be sure to admire the beautiful glass door. ♦ American ♦ Lunch, dinner, and late-night meals. 94 Prince St (at Mercer St). No credit cards. 226.9412

108 A Photographer's Place The shop buys and sells photographic books, antiques, and prints. ♦ M-Sa 11AM-8PM; Su noon-6PM. 133 Mercer St (between Spring and Prince Sts). 431.9358

109 Zoë ★★$$$ The cuisine keeps getting better at this restaurant, where the crowd is as uptown as it is downtown. Don't pass up the sweet corn with crabmeat dumplings soup or the grilled salmon with Moroccan spices. ♦ Contemporary American ♦ Lunch and dinner; brunch also on Saturday and Sunday. Closed Monday. 90 Prince St (between Broadway and Mercer Sts). Reservations recommended. 966.6722

"If I live in New York, it is because I choose to live here. It is the city of total intensity, the city of the moment."

Diana Vreeland

110 Little Singer Building In a letter to the *Sun* in 1904 when he designed this 12-story building for the **Singer Sewing Machine Co.**, **Ernest Flagg** said, "I believe tall buildings will shortly become unsafe. As an architect, I will never have anything to do with buildings of this kind." A year later he began work on the big Singer Building, a 41-story, 612-foot tower on Broadway at John Street, which was demolished in 1967, leaving this as a monument to what was lost. ♦ 561-563 Broadway (between Spring and Prince Sts)

111 560 Broadway This is a fine old structure remodeled to house several distinguished galleries. ♦ At Prince St

Within 560 Broadway:

Dean & DeLuca The ultimate and original high-tech grocery is housed here in a block-long, 9,700-square-foot space. Wonderful kitchenware, cookbooks, and all you would ever want to eat from the world's gastronomic centers are displayed with extraordinary panache. Added bonuses: a coffee/espresso bar, a butcher, a fishmonger, and a full range of take-out dishes. This is one of the must-see places for anyone passionate about food. ♦ M-Sa 8AM-8PM; Su 9AM-7PM. Ground floor. 431.8350

Max Protetch Gallery The primary commercial outlet in New York for drawings by such distinguished architects as **Louis I. Kahn, Frank Lloyd Wright, Michael Graves, Aldo Rossi,** and **Rem Koolhaas,** Protetch also exhibits painting, ceramics, and sculpture. It's well worth a visit to his spacious quarters. ♦ Tu-Sa 10AM-6PM. Second floor. 966.5454

Salvatore Ala Off the beaten track but always worth a look, this gallery shows American, British, and European artists, with an emphasis on sculpture. ♦ Tu-Sa 10AM-6PM. Third floor. 941.1990

111 Duggal Downtown Professional photographers in the neighborhood come to this extension of the W. 20th Street branch for their film and processing needs. It's a huge space with a continually changing photography exhibition along the right-hand wall and windows through which you can watch the technicians work. ♦ M-F 7:30AM-9PM; Sa 10AM-6PM. 560 Broadway (between Spring and Prince Sts). 941.7000. Also at: 9 W. 20th St. 924.7777

111 Zero This is a showroom for Zero, the Italian high-tech modular display system. ♦ By appointment only. 560 Broadway (at Prince St). 925.3615

Restaurants/Clubs: Red   Hotels: Blue
Shops/ ♥ Outdoors: Green   **Sights/Culture: Black**

112 Savoy ★★$$$ Run by chef **Peter Hoffman** and his wife, pastry chef **Suzan Rosenfeld,** Savoy's eclectic menu follows the seasons' whims, but don't leave without having a slice of chocolate hazelnut ganache torte. ♦ Continental ♦ Lunch and dinner; dinner only on Sunday. 70 Prince St (at Crosby St). Reservations recommended for dinner. 219.8570

113 280 Modern Decorative arts are this gallery's draw, with an emphasis on designer furniture from the 1920s to the 1960s. There is also a good selection of original works by the late **Piero Fornasetti** and new pieces from his son's company in Milan. ♦ M-Sa 11AM-7PM; call ahead for Sunday hours. 280 Lafayette St (between E. Houston and Prince Sts). 941.5825

113 Secondhand Rose Antiques dealer **Suzanne Lipshutz** (a.k.a. Secondhand Rose) fills 5,000 square feet with treasures from the late 1800s to the 1970s. Her impressive stock ranges from custom-made leather furniture to antique wallpaper and linoleum. ♦ M-F 10AM-6PM; by appointment only Saturday and Sunday. 270 Lafayette St (at Prince St). 431.7673

114 Barbara Flynn Gallery A spirit of invention pervades this gallery, formerly the Art Galaxy. Artists represented include the technological wizards **Kristin Jones** and **Andrew Ginzel.** ♦ Tu-F 10AM-5PM; Sa 11AM-6PM. 113 Crosby St (between Prince and E. Houston Sts). 966.0426

115 568-578 Broadway A boon for art lovers is the proliferation of gallery clusters in fine old Broadway buildings, making life easy for the browser, rain or shine. This dual-entry structure now houses so many galleries that it has been dubbed "The Mall" by art world locals. ♦ Between Prince and E. Houston Sts

Within 568-578 Broadway:

Crown Point Press This is the New York gallery for San Francisco's preeminent etching workshop. ♦ Tu-F 9:30AM-5:30PM; Sa 10AM-6PM. 568 Broadway, first floor. 226.5476

Castelli Graphics Prints, drawings, and photographs by many of the artists represented by Leo Castelli Gallery (**Roy Lichtenstein** and **Jasper Johns,** for example) can be viewed, as well as artists from their own stable, such as **Robert Cumming.** ♦ Tu-Sa 10AM-6PM. 578 Broadway, third floor. 941.9855

Curt Marcus Gallery Contemporary American and European artists in all mediums are exhibited here. ♦ Tu-Sa 10AM-6PM. 578 Broadway, 10th floor. 226.3200

115 Academy of American Poets For more than half a century this little-known academy has been the city's—and the nation's— headquarters for American poets. It sponsors an annual grant of $10,000 to assist American poets at all stages of their careers, and organizes a Poetry Reading Series at points around the city to further public interest and recognition. Since the Academy's beginning in 1934, these events have featured such literary lights as Manhattan-born **Walt Whitman.** Call or write for a reading schedule. ♦ M-F 9:30AM-5:30PM. 584 Broadway (between Prince and E. Houston Sts), suite 1208. 274.0343

115 Stark Gallery Current works by contemporary American and European artists are exhibited at this gallery, which features avant-garde abstractionists. ♦ Tu-Sa 10AM-6PM. 594 Broadway (between Prince and E. Houston Sts). 925.4484

115 Alternative Museum Two spacious galleries house a museum founded and operated by artists for unrecognized artists. Poetry readings and concerts—folk, jazz, traditional—take place, with the emphasis on the international and unusual. ♦ Free. Tu-Sa 11AM-6PM. 594 Broadway (between Prince and W. Houston Sts). 966.4444

116 The Cockpit Re-creations of the vintage goatskin and horsehair jackets preferred by daring young men in their flying machines are available here along with what The Cockpit calls "current issue." Everything to do with flying—from B-17 flight bags and shorts made from Flying Tigers briefing maps to books, watches, patches, gloves, and boots— is here. If the selection overwhelms you, ask for their mail order catalog. ♦ M-Sa 11AM-7PM; Su 12:30-6PM. 595 Broadway (between Prince and W. Houston Sts). 925.5455, 800/354.5514

116 Museum for African Art This vibrant museum is one of only two in the country specializing in sub-Saharan art (the other is part of the Smithsonian). Painted wooden masks, life-size carved figures, vivid textiles, and architectural sculptures all contribute to the complex and interesting rotating exhibits mounted by founder/director **Susan Vogel.** Behind an 1860s cast-iron facade, **Maya Lin**

designed the striking galleries, which opened in 1993. (As the **Center for African Art,** the museum was on E. 68th Street for a decade before moving to these expanded quarters.) ♦ Donation requested. W-Th, Su 11AM-6PM; F-Sa 11AM-8PM. 593 Broadway (between W. Houston and Prince Sts). 966.1313

TheNewMuseum
OF CONTEMPORARY ART

116 The New Museum of Contemporary Art Founder/director **Marcia Tucker** is the force behind this unique institution. She not only shows artists who have trouble getting a foot in the museum establishment's door, but shows all aspects of their work. As many as three or four shows are mounted at one time, often including videos and installations. The changing storefront installations are one of lower Broadway's great attractions. ♦ Donation requested. W-Th, Su noon-6PM; F-Sa noon-8PM. 583 Broadway (between Prince and W. Houston Sts). 219.1222

117 Guggenheim Museum SoHo Further enhancing this area's status as a mecca for contemporary art lovers is the new downtown branch of the Guggenheim, one of the world's preeminent collections of modern and contemporary art. Within a landmark 19th-century loft building, architect **Arata Isozaki** designed the 30,000 square feet of galleries, which opened in 1992. The six-story brick structure, with its cast-iron storefronts and detailed cornice, was designed in 1881 by **Thomas Stent** for **John Jacob Astor III,** and in its early days housed garment manufacturers and stores. Inside, the flexible and modern exhibit spaces retain the original cast-iron columns. The **Guggenheim Museum Store** is definitely worth a visit. ♦ Donation requested. M, W, Su 11AM-6PM; Th-Sa 11AM-8PM. Store hours: M-W, Su 11AM-6PM; Th-Sa 11AM-8PM. 575 Broadway (at Prince St). 423.3878

118 Tansuya Corporation The Japanese word *tansu* means cabinet, and you can have one custom-made and lacquered here. They also build modern and traditional Japanese-style furniture, trays, and lacquered boxes; each piece an original. ♦ Tu-Sa 10AM-6PM; Sunday by appointment only. 159 Mercer St (between Prince and W. Houston Sts). 966.1782

118 Distant Origin A clone of the incomparable Zona around the corner on Wooster Street, this shop stocks an impressive selection of Southwestern paintings, pillows, pottery, and furniture. ♦ Tu-Sa 11AM-6PM; Su noon-5PM. 153 Mercer St (between Prince and W. Houston Sts). 941.0025

118 After the Rain The sister store of **The Enchanted Forest,** this is a grown-up's fantasy of kaleidoscopes, art glass, tapestries, and handmade jewelry. ♦ M-Sa 11AM-7PM; Su noon-6PM. 149 Mercer St (between Prince and W. Houston Sts). 431.1045

119 Jerry's ★$$ This is a bustling lunch spot for SoHo's working population, especially the gallery crowd (Jerry used to own the frame shop down the street). Fresh salads, sandwiches, and daily soups are served. The dinnertime tempo is considerably slower. ♦ American ♦ Breakfast, lunch, and dinner; brunch also on Saturday; brunch only on Sunday. 101 Prince St (between Mercer and Greene Sts). 966.9464

119 Edward Thorp Gallery Thorp's affinity for landscape painting with a twist is clear in the work of artist **April Gornik.** He also represents **Deborah Butterfield,** who sculpts horses out of found objects. Large group shows are frequent. The gallery is located above the Prince Street post office. ♦ Tu-Sa 10AM-6PM. 103 Prince St (between Mercer and Greene Sts). 431.6880

120 Phyllis Kind Gallery An eclectic collection of contemporary paintings and "outsider" art by American and international artists is shown. ♦ Tu-Sa 10AM-6PM. 136 Greene St (between Prince and W. Houston Sts). 925.1200

120 John Weber A longtime art world fixture, Weber has supplemented his distinguished roster of minimal and conceptual artists, including **Sol LeWitt** and the estate of **Robert Smithson,** with some bright new—and offbeat—talent. ♦ Tu-Sa 10AM-6PM. 142 Greene St (between Prince and W. Houston Sts), third floor. 966.6115

120 Sperone Westwater The New York home to many of Italy's most innovative artists, including **Mario Merz,** "the three C's" (**Sandro Chia, Francesco Clemente, Enzo Cucchi**), and **Susan Kothenberg,** this gallery also boasts an impressive roster of other European and American talents. ♦ Tu-Sa 10AM-6PM. 142 Greene St (between Prince and W. Houston Sts), second floor. 431.3685. Also at: 121 Greene St

One man's junk is another man's treasure, and you can find outstanding examples of both along Canal Street between Broadway and Sixth Avenue. The selections range from used clothing to seemingly useless pieces of electronic equipment, plumbing supplies, and other assorted gadgets and hardware. It costs nothing to look at, and very little to buy the endlessly fascinating things you see here. The street was originally a wide drainage ditch carrying polluted water from the Collect Pond (eventually filled to become the Foley Square area) over to the Hudson River. Citizen complaints about the stench and the mosquito problem led to the filling of the ditch—which the city preferred to call a canal—in 1820.

New York City in Fact . . .

Art and Architecture

AIA Guide to New York City by **Norval White** and **Elliot Willensky** (1988, Harcourt Brace Jovanovich)

The Building of Manhattan by **Donald Mackay** (1987, Harper & Row)

The City Observed: New York. A Guide to the Architecture of Manhattan by **Paul Goldberger** (1979, Random House)

The City That Never Was: 200 Years of Fantastic and Fascinating Plans That Might Have Changed the Face of NYC by **Rebecca Reed Shanor** (1988, Viking Press)

The Columbia Historical Portrait of New York by **John A. Kouwenhoven** (1972, Harper & Row)

The Landmarks of New York by **Barbaralee Diamonstein** (1988, Harry N. Abrams); Vol. 2 (1993, Harry N. Abrams)

Lost New York: Pictorial Record of Vanished NYC by **Nathan Silver** (1982, American Legacy Press)

Manhattan Architecture by **Richard Berenholtz** and **Donald Martin Reynolds** (1988, Prentice Hall Press)

New York Architecture 1970-1990 by **Heinrich Klotz** (1989, Rizzoli)

New York Observed: Artists and Writers Look at the City, 1650 to the Present, edited by **Barbara Cohen, Seymour Chwast,** and **Steven Heller** (1988, Harry N. Abrams)

Nightmares in the Sky by **Stephen King** and **f-stop Fitzgerald** (1988, Viking Penguin Inc.)

On Broadway: A Journey Uptown Over Time by **David W. Dunlap** (1990, Rizzoli)

Guidebooks

The Best Guided Walking Tours of NYC by **Leslie Gourse** (1989, The Globe Pequot Press)

Ethnic New York: A Complete Guide to the Many Faces and Cultures of New York by **Mark Leeds** (1991, Passport Books)

From Trout Stream to Bohemia: A Walking Guide to Greenwich Village History by **Joyce Gold** (1988, Old Warren Press)

From Windmills to the World Trade Center: A Walking Guide to Lower Manhattan History by **Joyce Gold** (1988, Old Warren Press)

Literary Neighborhoods of New York by **Marcia Leisner** (1989, Starrhill Press)

Manhattan's Outdoor Sculpture by **Margot Gayle** and **Michele Cohen** (1988, Prentice Hall Press)

New York, A Guide to the Metropolis: Walking Tours of Architecture and History by **Gerard R. Wolfe** (1988, McGraw-Hill)

New York City Yesterday & Today: 30 Timeless Walking Adventures by **Judith H. Browning** (1990, Corsair Publications)

Permanent New Yorkers: A Biographical Guide to the Cemeteries by **Judi Culbertson** and **Tom Randall** (1987, Chelsea Green Publishers)

The Streets Where They Lived: A Walking Guide to the Residences of Famous New Yorkers by **Stephen W. Plumb** (1989, Marlor Press)

Other

Movie Lover's Guide to New York by **Richard Alleman** (1988, Harper & Row)

The New York Theatre Sourcebook by **Chuck Lawliss** (1981, Simon & Schuster)

The Street Book—An Encyclopedia of Manhattan's Street Names and Their Origins by **Henry Moscow** (1978, Fordham University Press)

Under the Sidewalks of New York: The Story of the World's Great Subway Station by **Brian J. Cudahy** (1988, The Stephen Greene Press/Pelham Books)

You Must Remember This: An Oral History of Manhattan from the 1890s to World War II by **Jeff Kisseloff** (1989, Harcourt Brace Jovanovich)

Zagat New York Restaurant Survey (1994, Zagat)

. . . and Fiction

The Age of Innocence by **Edith Wharton,** originally published 1920 (1968, Charles Scribner's Sons)

Catcher in the Rye by **J.D. Salinger,** originally published 1951 (1964, Bantam Books)

Diedrick Knickerbocker's History of New York by **Washington Irving,** originally published 1840 (1981, Sleepy Hollow)

Fourth Street East: A Novel of How it Was by **Jerome Weidman** (1970, Pinnacle Books)

The House of Mirth by **Edith Wharton** (1905, Charles Scribner's Sons)

This Side of Paradise by **F. Scott Fitzgerald** (1920, Charles Scribner's Sons)

Time and Again by **Jack Finney** (1970, Simon & Schuster)

A Tree Grows in Brooklyn by **Betty Smith,** originally published 1943 (1968, Harper & Row)

Washington Square by **Henry James,** originally published 1880 (1990, New American Library)

Children's Books

The Cricket in Times Square by **George Selden** (1960, Farrar, Straus & Giroux)

Eloise by **Kay Thompson** (1955, Simon & Schuster)

From the Mixed up Files of Mrs. Basil E. Frankweiler by **E.L. Konigsburg** (1967, Atheneum Children's)

Harriet the Spy by **Louise Fitzhugh** (1964, Harper & Row Junior Books)

The Little Red Lighthouse and the Great Gray Bridge by **Hildegarde H. Swift** (1942, Harcourt Brace Jovanovich)

Stuart Little by **E.B. White** (1945, Harper & Row Junior Books)

Edna St. Vincent Millay gained her middle name by virtue of being born in St. Vincent's Hospital.

120 The Pace Gallery The downtown branch of the blue-chip gallery is located in a vast space that provides a dramatic backdrop for large-scale paintings and sculpture. ♦ Tu-Sa 10AM-6PM. 142 Greene St (between Prince and W. Houston Sts), ground floor. 431.9224

120 Barbara Toll Fine Arts This gallery's adventuresome point of view always warrants a visit. All mediums, including large installation works by Scottish artist **David Mach,** are exhibited. ♦ Tu-Sa 10AM-6PM. 146 Greene St (between Prince and W. Houston Sts). 431.1788

120 Metro Pictures Along with an odd, somewhat dated assortment of painters and photographers, this gallery is home to the many-guised self-portraitist **Cindy Sherman,** one of the 1980's true originals. ♦ Tu-Sa 10AM-6PM. 150 Greene St (between Prince and W. Houston Sts). 925.8335

121 Back Pages Antiques An impressive collection of classic Wurlitzer jukeboxes, working slot machines, Coca-Cola vending machines, Seeburg nickelodeons, pool tables, and advertising signs is available here. Everything has been lovingly restored; even the mooseheads seem to have a new lease on life. If you need to furnish a party room, look no further. ♦ M-Sa 9AM-6PM; call ahead for Sunday hours. 125 Greene St (between Prince and W. Houston Sts). 460.5998

122 Whole Foods A full selection of everything you need for a sound body and soul is available here: vitamins, grains, fresh fish, organic vegetables, kosher chicken and turkeys, cosmetics, and an impressive assortment of books to tell you what you should be doing with all these things. ♦ M-F 8AM-10PM; Sa-Su 9AM-10PM. 117 Prince St (between Greene and Wooster Sts). 673.5388

122 Dean & DeLuca Cafe An airy, white-brick space provides a refreshing backdrop for a peaceful breakfast, lunch, or snack at this cafe run by the gourmet food emporium at Broadway and Prince. It's a good place to come on Sunday morning to read the paper (thoughtfully provided by D&D) and sip cappuccino. ♦ M-Th 8AM-8PM; F-Sa 8AM-9PM; Su 9AM-8PM. 121 Prince St (between Wooster and Greene Sts). 254.8776

122 Prince Street Bar & Restaurant ★$ The faithful clientele come as much for the lively bar scene as for the fairly standard burgers, salads, and sandwiches. ♦ American ♦ Lunch and dinner; brunch also on Sunday. 125 Prince St (at Wooster St). 228.8130

123 Paula Cooper Gallery A SoHo pioneer nearly two decades ago, Cooper has built a stable of remarkable winners, including **Jennifer Bartlett, Jonathan Borofsky, Elizabeth Murray,** and **Joel Shapiro.** ♦ Tu-Sa 10AM-6PM. 155 Wooster St (between Prince and W. Houston Sts). 674.0766. Also at: 149 Wooster St

123 147 Wooster Street Designed in 1876 by **Jarvis Morgan Slade,** the arched storefront decorated with bands of fleur-de-lis and other floral motifs is all hand-carved in marble. Only the cornice is iron. ♦ Between Prince and W. Houston Sts

123 Dia Center for the Arts "The New York Earth Room," a permanent installation by conceptual artist **Walter da Maria,** has become a SoHo fixture. ♦ W-Sa noon-6PM. 141 Wooster St (between Prince and W. Houston Sts). 473.8072

124 Susan P. Meisel Decorative Arts Twentieth-century decorative arts, including hand-painted English pottery created by **Clarice Cliff** between 1928 and 1938, 1950s Mexican sterling silver jewelry, and vintage watches are exhibited. ♦ Tu-Sa 10AM-6PM. 133 Prince St (between Wooster St and W. Broadway). 254.0137

124 Louis K. Meisel Meisel championed the photo-realists back in the 1970s and has stuck to his convictions despite the art world's ever-changing tides. ♦ Tu-Sa 10AM-6PM. 141 Prince St (between Wooster St and W. Broadway). 677.1340

125 SoHo Wine & Spirits Welcome to what may very well be the most civilized, not to mention best-stocked, small wine store in town. But there is no wine snobbery in this well-organized, well-designed outlet, which also carries the world's great spirits, including the city's most extensive choice of single-malt Scotch whiskys. ♦ M-Sa 10AM-8PM. 461 W. Broadway (between Prince and W. Houston Sts). 777.4332

A Manhattan Special is not an express bus from Brooklyn. And it has nothing to do with the subways. But it's been a part of New York City since 1885. Described as "the world's most delicious coffee soda," the Manhattan Special is a hand-brewed concoction of freshly roasted coffee beans and 100 percent granulated sugar (practically unheard of in the beverage industry today). The result is a lusty espresso coffee soda that's well worth sampling, a special New York taste treat. (It also comes sugar- and caffeine-free.)

Restaurants/Clubs: Red | Hotels: Blue
Shops/ 🌱 Outdoors: Green | Sights/Culture: Black

125 Yoshi The latest fashions from an international set of young designers, including **Faycolamor** from France, **Gemmakahng** from New York, and Englishman **Jasper Conran,** are featured in this store. To top it off is a particularly wonderful selection of *chapeaux.* ♦ Daily 11AM-8PM. 461 W. Broadway (between Prince and W. Houston Sts). 979.0569

125 I Tre Merli ★★$$$ The exposed brick walls give this Italian restaurant and wine bar a quiet charm. Though the service can be inattentive, the food—especially the raw artichoke salad—is quite good. During the summer, the tables spill out onto W. Broadway. ♦ Italian ♦ Lunch, dinner, and late-night meals; brunch also on Saturday and Sunday. 463 W. Broadway (between Prince and W. Houston Sts). Reservations recommended. 254.8699

126 Amici Miei ★★$$$ Pasta dominates the menu at this fashionable SoHo staple. Check the upstairs and downstairs rooms in back for more private dining. ♦ Northern Italian ♦ Lunch and dinner; brunch also on Saturday and Sunday. 475 W. Broadway (at W. Houston St). 533.1933

127 Can ★$$$ Stylish presentations of French-Vietnamese fare are served at this restaurant. The eccentric owner, **Eleanor,** is as charmingly offbeat as the modern decor and innovative cuisine. ♦ French/Vietnamese ♦ Lunch and dinner. 482 W. Broadway (at W. Houston St). Reservations recommended for dinner. 533.6333

127 If Boutique You can buy designer clothes by **Thierry Mugler, Jean Paul Gaultier, Romeo Gigli,** and **Moschino,** and terrific belts, shoes, and jewelry at this shop. Best feature: the sales here are real sales. ♦ M-Sa noon-7:30PM; Su noon-7PM. 474 W. Broadway (at W. Houston St). 533.8660

127 Rizzoli Bookstore of SoHo Stop in to peruse one of the best selections of fine art books, foreign magazines, and music recordings in the city. ♦ M-Th 11AM-11PM; F-Sa 11AM-midnight; Su noon-8PM. 454 W. Broadway (between Prince and W. Houston Sts). 674.1677. Also at: 250 Vesey St. 385.1400; 31 W. 57th St. 759.2424

127 Claiborne Gallery Leslie Cozart specializes in Mexican furniture, mostly from the 19th century, plus a line of iron furniture designed by her father, **Omer Claiborne.** ♦ Tu-F 11AM-7PM; Sa noon-7PM; Su noon-6PM. 452 W. Broadway (between W. Houston and Prince Sts). 475.3072

128 Untitled This tiny wedge of a store sells all sorts of art and photography postcards, wrapping and note papers, calendars, and a small selection of books and periodicals. ♦ M-W 10AM-8PM; Th-Sa 10AM-10PM; Su 11AM-7PM. 159 Prince St (between W. Broadway and Thompson St). 982.2088. Also at: 680 Broadway. 254.1360

129 Betsey Johnson For more than two decades, Johnson's fashion statements have been providing the youthful with a statement of their own. ♦ M-W, F-Sa 11AM-7PM; Th 11AM-8PM; Su noon-7PM. 130 Thompson St (between Prince and W. Houston Sts). 420.0169. Also at: 251 E. 60th St. 319.7699; 1060 Madison Ave. 734.1257; 248 Columbus Ave. 362.3364

129 Eileen Lane Antiques Scandinavian, Biedermeier, and Art Deco furniture and lighting are the specialty of this antique shop. ♦ Daily 11AM-7PM. 150 Thompson St (between Prince and W. Houston Sts). 475.2988

130 Arturo's Pizzeria ★$$ Is this crowd the overflow from nearby John's Pizzeria, or would these pizzaphiles patronize this joint even if they *could* get into John's? Check out both and see; John's and Arturo's provide quintessential Village pizza experiences, with brick ovens that turn out the city's best thin-crust pies. If you want live jazz, come to Arturo's. ♦ Pizzeria ♦ Lunch, dinner, and late-night meals. 106 W. Houston St (at Thompson St). 677.3820

131 Belgis Freidel Gallery Rare posters and turn-of-the-century prints, including the work of **Henri de Toulouse-Lautrec** and **Pierre Bonnard,** are exhibited. ♦ Tu-Su noon-6PM. 131 Thompson St (between Prince and W. Houston Sts). 475.0248

131 Opal White Edwardian and Victorian clothing, including a wide selection of antique wedding dresses, are for sale at this shop. ♦ By appointment only. 131 Thompson St (between Prince and W. Houston Sts). 677.8215

132 Elephant & Castle $ One of the best hamburgers in town can be had for a modest price, along with omelets and a hefty bowl of hot Indian pudding with Häagen-Dazs vanilla ice cream. ♦ American ♦ Breakfast, lunch, and dinner; brunch also on Saturday and Sunday; late-night meals also on Friday and Saturday. 183 Prince St (between Thompson and Sullivan Sts). 260.3600

133 Depression Modern Owner **Michael Smith** likes to redecorate his shop, and does so every Saturday with the Moderne furniture of the 1930s and 1940s that he spends the rest of the week restoring to its original perfect condition. ♦ W-Sa noon-7PM; Su noon-6PM. 150 Sullivan St (between Prince and W. Houston Sts). 982.5699

133 Joe's Dairy Only about three storefronts remain that give an indication of the old Italian-American enclave along Thompson and Sullivan streets. Joe's Dairy, with its checkered tile floor and sweating glass cases, is one of them. Parmigiana-Reggiano is hewn from fragrant wheels, and sweet ricotta is drawn from moist, cool places. A few times a week intense acrid smoke pours from its basement door—mozzarella *afumicato* is being made. ♦ Tu-Sa 7:30AM-6PM; call ahead for weekend hours. 156 Sullivan St (between Prince and W. Houston Sts). 677.8780

134 Frontiere ★$$$ The name of this romantic SoHo place refers to the French and Italian border—the region of influence on this cuisine. Old-fashioned stone walls, a fireplace, and intimate lighting add up to an inviting experience. ♦ Southern French/Northern Italian ♦ Lunch and dinner. 199 Prince St (between Sullivan and MacDougal Sts). Reservations recommended for dinner. 387.0898

Provence

135 Provence ★★★$$$ **Michel** and **Patricia Jean's** Provençale bistro has a lot going for it: a creamy and potent fish soup, a heady onion tart, roasted chicken in garlic, perfectly charred crème brûlée, a trendy crowd, and, of course, French waiters. When it's warm, the garden is lovely for lunch or an early dinner. ♦ French ♦ Lunch and dinner. 38 MacDougal St (at Prince St). Reservations required. 475.7500

136 Souen Downtown ★$ This pretty, airy Japanese-style room serves ultra-healthy food, including soba noodles and vegetable specialties. ♦ Macrobiotic ♦ Lunch and dinner; brunch also on Saturday and Sunday. 210 Sixth Ave (at Prince St). 807.7421. Also at: 28 E. 13th St. 627.7150

137 Brother's Bar-B-Q ★$ Best described as a funky dive and loved for its down-home Southern grub, Brother's is the next best choice if Harlem's well-known (more expensive, and somewhat more authentic) Sylvia's is too far out of your way. Come for the heaping portions of tangy ribs, barbecued chicken smoked over hickory wood for 10 hours, and hefty side orders of mashed potatoes, collard greens, and corn bread. Monday is All-You-Can-Eat BBQ Night. ♦ Barbecue ♦ Lunch and dinner; late-night meals also on Friday and Saturday. 228 W. Houston St (between Sixth Ave and Varick St). 727.2775

138 S.O.B.'s Sounds of Brazil ★★$$ Specializing in Bahian and Brazilian food, this casual restaurant becomes a late-evening showcase for salsa, samba, reggae, and whatever else is currently being imported from the Caribbean, South America, and Africa. The *caipirinha*, a sweet and sour Brazilian cocktail, keeps them coming back. ♦ Brazilian ♦ Cover. Lunch, dinner, and late-night meals. Closed Sunday. 204 Varick St (at W. Houston St). Dinner reservations required. 243.4940

139 375 Hudson Street Say the word "advertising" and Madison Avenue naturally comes to mind. But many advertising agencies have recently relocated downtown, including **Saatchi & Saatchi,** the world's largest advertising agency holding company, which occupies this building. Most of its neighbors are printing companies. ♦ At W. Houston St

Only a few areas remain to remind us of the once predominant Federal-style brick row house. The four-block Charlton-King-Vandam Historic District (1828-34) (bounded by Sixth Avenue and Houston, Varick, and Vandam streets) was developed primarily by John Jacob Astor. It has the city's largest concentration of these old homes and was designated a National Landmark in 1966. There is a fine example of the period in the unbroken row on the north side of Vandam Street. A larger row along Charlton's north side includes the noteworthy Nos. 37 and 39, along with four Greek Revival replacements. King Street mixes Federal with a potpourri of later styles. At the corner of King and MacDougal streets is one of the few 19th-century storefronts left in the city.

The New York City Council passed a bill requiring photographic records be made of any building about to be razed. Photos become part of the municipal archives. Councilman Harry Stein, sponsor of the bill, said his only regret was that no one had thought of the idea 150 years before.

Bests

Gerry Frank
Author, *Where to Find It, Buy It, Eat It in New York*

Taking in an afternoon game at **Yankee** or **Shea stadiums** on a warm summer day.

Looking out over the **East River** at the Manhattan skyline from **Lighthouse Park** on **Roosevelt Island**.

Buying a classy new suit at **Gorsart**.

Visiting the **Museum of Immigration** on Ellis Island.

Taking a ride on one of the 388 elevators in **Rockefeller Center** (preferably to the top).

Sitting on one of the 7,674 benches in **Central Park** on a glorious spring day.

Wandering through the **Frick Collection**.

Looking down one of the open grates that expose 238 miles of subway tracks below the city streets.

Watching magazine moguls lunch at **44**.

Visiting the Romanesque/Byzantine-style **St. Bartholomew's Church**.

Gawking at the Fabergé eggs at the **Forbes Magazine Galleries**.

Sampling Martine's chocolates at **Bloomingdale's**.

Enjoying a leisurely and luxurious weekend at the new **Four Seasons Hotel**.

Taking in the farmer's market on Monday, Wednesday, Friday, and Saturday at **Union Square**.

Tuning in to **Joan Hamburg** for great consumer advice (WOR-710 AM radio—weekdays from 10AM to noon).

Sipping an espresso or cappuccino in **Little Italy**.

Visiting **75½ Bedford Street**, site of the city's narrowest house.

Watching a favorite episode of a favorite TV show at the **Museum of Television and Radio**.

Getting up as early as 4AM to witness the activity at the **Fulton Fish Market**.

Losing yourself in a frozen hot chocolate at **Serendipity 3**.

Visiting the **Federal Hall National Memorial** (26 Wall Street), where George Washington took oath as the first U.S. president.

Relaxing in the **Ford Foundation's** garden atrium.

Taking the kids to see **The Cloisters**.

Taking a **Circle Line** cruise.

Visiting the **United Nations**.

Taking a boat trip on the lake in Central Park on a summer day (**Loeb Boathouse**).

Touring backstage at the **Metropolitan Opera**.

Taking a bargain ride on the **Staten Island Ferry**.

Riding through **Central Park** in a hansom cab.

Gallery hopping in **SoHo** on a Saturday afternoon.

Dancing at the **Rainbow Room**.

Attending the flea market and antiques sale on Sunday at Sixth Avenue and 26th Street.

Exploring the towering beauty of the **Cathedral Church of St. John the Divine**.

Watching the lights on the **Statue of Liberty** while walking along the promenade at Battery Park.

Enjoying happy hour at **Molly Bloom's**.

Enjoying the Easter flower show at **Macy's**.

Securing a bargain ticket for a Broadway matinee at the **TKTS** booth in Times Square.

Watching the **Rockettes** at **Radio City Music Hall**.

Getting into a political discussion with a cab driver.

Browsing the **"New York Is Book Country"** book fair on Fifth Avenue in September.

Getting pampered at **Elizabeth Arden**.

Having one of the finest French dinners anywhere at **La Reserve**.

Visiting Theodore Roosevelt's birthplace and George Washington's headquarters (1785 Jumal Terrace).

Taking home fresh fruit and vegetables from **Grace's Marketplace**.

Henry Wolf
Photographer

Taking a cab up **Park Avenue** at 2AM, making 15 blocks on one light, easy.

Jim McMullen's—a lively, congenial place to eat and look at models, politicians, yuppies, and Wall Streeters and taste good, reasonable food. Chicken potpie, mashed potatoes, and chocolate brownies.

Weyhe Bookstore—slightly dusty, slow help, but wonderful art books, often rare, out-of-print volumes. Nothing like it in New York.

Robert A.M. Stern
Architect

W. 67th Street between Central Park West and Columbus Avenue. Elegant studio buildings, containing dramatic double-height rooms, that make the block in some ways more like Paris than Paris.

The **Sheep's Meadow** in Central Park. New York's great front lawn, framed by the fantastic mountain range of Midtown's skyscrapers.

The **Promenade** along Brooklyn Heights. A brilliant urban sleight of hand, overwhelming the sight and sound of the Brooklyn-Queens Expressway with breathtaking views of the harbor and Lower Manhattan.

The soaring lobby of the main branch of the **Brooklyn Public Library**, where classicism and modernism join forces to form a grand public space.

As the crowds gather for an evening of theater, the main plaza at **Lincoln Center** becomes an outdoor stage.

Greenwich Village

Radical and old guard, grand and glitzy, authentic and ersatz. Greenwich Village is anything but a homogeneous neighborhood. Bounded by the **Hudson River, Broadway,** and **Houston** and **14th streets,** the birthplace of the bohemian spirit is home to students of **New York University,** actors in Off-Broadway theaters, jazz musicians, and an assortment of other residents who work uptown. The Village arouses fanatical loyalty in its residents, who fight among themselves about social and political issues of the day, but also fight to maintain the human scale and history of this neighborhood.

Greenwich Village's eccentric personality starts with the layout. In the 1790s, the area's country estates were sold off in lots or subdivided and developed by large landholders. Weavers, sailmakers, and craftspeople moved into rows of modest homes along streets that followed the boundaries of the old estates

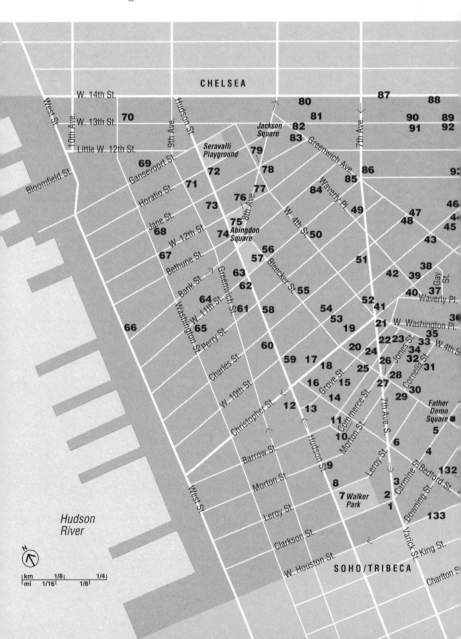

and travelers' paths. Later, when a grid was established for new streets in Manhattan, it was too late to change the Village's crazy maze of thoroughfares.

New Yorkers fleeing epidemics of smallpox, yellow fever, and cholera that ravaged New York in the 1790s and early 1800s settled in Greenwich Village, which was far removed from the congested city center. Hastily built houses and hotels arose to accommodate the newcomers. Bank Street is named for Wall Street banks that opened here along with other commercial ventures during the severe epidemic of 1822.

In the 1830s, prominent families began to build town houses at **Washington Square**, which had become a public park in 1828. New York society took over Fifth Avenue and the side streets from University Place to Sixth Avenue. But the fashionable Washington Square elite soon gravitated to **Gramercy Park**, **Madison Square**, and upper Fifth Avenue, so that by the late 1850s the

Village had turned into a quiet backwater of middle-class, old-line Anglo-Dutch families. Warehouses and industrial plants proliferated along the Hudson River, and commercial development began to the east and north. But the Village always retained its residential character. In the 1880s and 1890s, Irish and Chinese immigrants moved in, while Italians populated the tenements built south of Washington Square.

Houses from all periods coexist in the Village, but only one of the many brownstones that once lined Fifth Avenue from Washington Square to Central Park in what was called "Two Miles of Millionaires" survives. One of the first brownstone mansions designed in the Italianate style, it was built in 1853 at 47 Fifth Avenue for **Irad Hawley**, president of the Pennsylvania Coal Company. The **Salmagundi Club**, the city's oldest club for art and artists (founded in 1870), moved into the brownstone in 1917, and opens its doors for exhibitions from time to time.

As the high rollers moved out, their large houses were divided into flats and studios and their stables into homes. The cheap rents appealed to such writers as **Edgar Allan Poe**, **Horace Greeley**, **Walt Whitman**, **Mark Twain**, and **Edna St. Vincent Millay**, who at one time occupied the narrowest house in the city—just nine and a half feet wide—at 75$\frac{1}{2}$ Bedford Street. Such artists as **Albert Bierstadt, Frederic Edwin Church, John Frederick Kensett,** and **John La Farge** of the Hudson River School; Impressionists **Ernest Lawson** and **Robert Henri;** and painters **William James Glackens, John French Sloan,** and **Edward Hopper** of the early 20th-century Ashcan School moved to Greenwich Village, which established itself as the seat of bohemia in the United States before World War I.

After the war, Greenwich Village continued to be a magnet for those looking for sexual freedom, radicalism, and revolt in politics and the arts. **Upton Sinclair** founded the **Liberal Club** on MacDougal Street; the **Washington Square Players** (later renamed the **Theater Guild**) organized in 1917; and the following year, the **Provincetown Players**, the company that gave **Eugene O'Neill** his first chance, opened in the Village (the company still puts on plays at the **Provincetown Playhouse** on MacDougal Street).

Sharing the Village's streets with bohemians in the 1930s were families who had been here for generations, white-collar workers, and Irish and Italian blue-collar workers. After World War II, the Beat Generation and hippies discovered the Village, as did entrepreneurs and developers. Although residents have fought hard to keep the community the way it was, apartment houses and high-rises have made inroads. Some of the development, such as **Westbeth**, a Bell Telephone Laboratories building recycled as housing for artists, has been architecturally sensitive. One of the Village's largest landowners, **Sailors' Snug Harbor**, however, has been criticized for some of the decisions it has made for its 21 acres of leased land near Washington Square. In 1801, **Captain Robert Richard Randall** deeded the land and a small cash gift for the purpose of establishing a home for retired seamen, now in North Carolina, which is financed by the returns on the Greenwich Village holdings. **Trinity Parish**, the other large landowner with deeds from the same period, is usually given high marks for helping to maintain the ambience of the Village.

Today, every style of 18th- and 19th-century architecture, culture, and history intermingle in Greenwich Village, from the gracious classical houses on the north side of Washington Square, where writers **Henry James** and **Edith Wharton** lived, to converted stables in MacDougal Alley behind them, where in the 1900s sculptors **Jo Davidson** and **Gertrude Vanderbilt Whitney** and actor **Richard Bennett** occupied houses. **Judson Memorial**, a square-towered church designed in the Romanesque style by **McKim, Mead & White**, is as well-known for its experimental theater productions as for its historical or architectural value. New York University now has colleges and schools at its Washington Square campus. **The New School for Social Research**, America's first university for adults, is still championing social causes and offering a dazzling variety of night-school courses. In 1970, the New School and **Parsons School of Design** formed a partnership that broadened the excellent curriculum of both schools.

History is everywhere—in such bars as the **Minetta Tavern** on MacDougal Street, filled with photos and memorabilia from earlier days, and the **Cedar Tavern** on University Place, where Abstract Expressionists **Jackson Pollock, Franz Kline,** and **Larry Rivers** used to hang out. At the **Gansevoort Market**, the city's wholesale meat market, you can imagine what the area was like when **Herman Melville** worked as a customs inspector for 19 years at what was then the **Gansevoort Dock**.

1 Raoul's on Varick ★★$$$ The artful setting of this restaurant shows off the *très* fashionable diners, as if the trompe l'oeil ceiling and the Issey Miyake suits were designed in tandem. The menu doesn't sway from this theme—the creative combinations are exciting and satisfying, starting with the complimentary quiche or sashimi. The wine list is surprisingly reasonable. ♦ French ♦ Lunch and dinner; dinner only on Saturday. Closed Sunday. 225 Varick St (between W. Houston and Clarkson Sts). Reservations recommended. 929.1630

2 Carmine Street Public Pools Don't be confused by the name: these indoor and outdoor public pools aren't actually located on Carmine Street anymore, thanks to a zoning law that created Clarkson Street out of the west half of Carmine. Nonmembers are permitted to swim in the outdoor pool only. Call for hours, and bring along a padlock. ♦ Clarkson St (at Seventh Ave South). 242.5228

3 Cafe Español $$ Spanish cuisine served in an authentic Catalan atmosphere at reasonable prices is welcome in an area that is resisting pretentiousness less and less. ♦ Spanish ♦ Lunch and dinner. 63 Carmine St (at Seventh Ave South). 675.3312

4 Cent' Anni ★$$$ At times this seems like one of the best informal Italian restaurants in town, and at one time it was, but it can be disappointing. The menu features an extraordinary minestrone, a few outstanding pasta dishes, and a huge Tuscan-style porterhouse steak. ♦ Italian ♦ Lunch and dinner. 50 Carmine St (between Bleecker and Bedford Sts). Reservations recommended. 989.9494

4 46 Carmine Street **Jackson Pollock** lived in an apartment in this building between 1932 and 1933 while studying at the Art Students League. ♦ Between Bleecker and Bedford Sts

5 House of Oldies Here is an incredible collection of rare and out-of-circulation rock 'n' roll and R&B LPs, including 10,000 rock 'n' roll 78s and over a million 45s. Additional stock is sent up from the basement via a dumbwaiter. ♦ M-Sa 11AM-7PM. 35 Carmine St (between Sixth and Seventh Aves South). 243.0500

5 Village Flute & Sax Shop **Doctor Rich** repairs woodwind instruments for some of the best in the business. You can take lessons here, buy or sell a musical instrument, or just drop by and see a genuine craftsman at work. ♦ M-F 10AM-5PM; Sa 11AM-2PM. 35 Carmine St (between Sixth and Seventh Aves South). 243.1276

5 Church of Our Lady of Pompeii The gilded marble interior of this 1927 church designed by **Matthew Del Gaudio** convinces you this structure might have been picked up intact from the hills of Italy. The illusion goes further than that—some services are conducted in Italian. The square across the street is named for **Father Antonio Demo,** who served this parish from 1901 until 1936. ♦ 25 Carmine St (between Sixth and Seventh Aves South)

6 Mary's ★$$$ Few vestiges of the old Greenwich Village remain, but Mary's certainly qualifies—except that the attitude and the prices have more of a modern edge. The rooms are still charming, especially the upstairs salon, which is worth the wait. And the food—Mary's does wonders with chicken—harkens back to Mama's kitchen. The side-street location is a bit of a hunt. ♦ Italian ♦ Lunch and dinner. 42 Bedford St (at Seventh Ave South). Reservations required. 243.9755

7 New York Public Library, Hudson Park Branch The original 1905 building by **Carrère & Hastings,** who also designed the main branch up on Fifth Avenue, was expanded in 1935 at about the same time the **Carmine Street Public Pools** was added behind it. The library's **Early Childhood Resource and Information Center,** a facility for small children and their parents, is located here. ♦ M-Tu, F 1-6PM; W 10AM-6PM; Th 1-8PM. 66 Leroy St (between Seventh Ave South and Hudson St). 243.6876

8 Anglers & Writers ★$$ Literary Paris of the 1930s is recaptured in this cozy, unpretentious cafe/tearoom owned by mother-and-son team **Charlotte** and **Craig Bero.** Mismatched English and Austrian china, turn-of-the-century American country furniture, and shelves of books—with an emphasis on **Hemingway, Fitzgerald,** and fly-fishing—create an ideal atmosphere for writing in a journal, reading (or writing) a novel, reminiscing with friends, or gazing out the large picture windows, which overlook James J. Walker Park and the Hudson River. ♦ M-F 9AM-midnight; Sa-Su 9AM-10PM. 420 Hudson St (at St. Luke's Pl). 675.0810

9 Village Atelier ★$$$ The farmhouse setting is an appropriate backdrop for the Midwestern American food served here. The roast chicken stuffed with apples, prunes, sausage, and wild rice is outstanding, as are the freshwater fish dishes. ♦ American ♦ Lunch and dinner; dinner only on Saturday. Closed Sunday. 436 Hudson St (at Morton St). Reservations required. 989.1363

In the 1790s, 22,000 victims of yellow fever were buried in Washington Square Park. In 1824, a huge celebration was held when 20 highwaymen were hanged from an elm in the park's northwest corner.

Restaurants/Clubs: Red	Hotels: Blue
Shops/ 🌳 Outdoors: Green	Sights/Culture: Black

10 75½ Bedford Street Built in 1873, this nine-and-a-half-foot-wide building is thought to be the narrowest in the city, and was the last New York City residence of **Edna St. Vincent Millay** and her husband, **Eugen Boissevain.** No. 77 next door, built in 1800, is the oldest house in the Village. ♦ At Commerce St

10 Cherry Lane Theater Built as a brewery in 1846, this building was converted to a 184-seat theater (founded by **Edna St. Vincent Millay**) for avant-garde productions in 1924. *Godspell* had its world premiere here. ♦ 38 Commerce St (between Bedford and Barrow Sts). 989.2020

10 The Grange Hall ★$$ If noise is not a problem, check out the raucous scene at this West Village restaurant (site of the former **Blue Mill**), which offers farm-fresh food at reasonable prices. A large array of vegetables and grain preparations are available in appetizer sizes for those who like a variety of healthy tastes. ♦ American ♦ Lunch and dinner; dinner only on Monday; brunch also on Saturday and Sunday. 50 Commerce St (between Bedford and Barrow Sts). 924.5246

11 39 and 41 Commerce Street This well-preserved pair of mansard-roofed houses with a central garden dates to 1831. An apocryphal but oft-repeated tale is that they were built by a sea captain for his two unmarried daughters, who were not on speaking terms. ♦ Between Bedford and Barrow Sts

12 St. Luke-in-the-Fields James N. Wells designed this simple Federal-style building in 1822. Restored after a 1981 fire, it still has the feeling of a country church. **St. Luke's School,** one of the city's most highly respected Episcopal parochial schools, was established in 1945. The thrift store next door is a tad more expensive than you'd expect, but it's well stocked. ♦ 487 Hudson St (between Barrow and Christopher Sts)

13 Grove Court Between 10 and 12 Grove Street, at the middle of what some consider to be the most authentic group of Federal-style houses in America, you can find one of the most charming and private enclaves in Manhattan. These six brick-fronted buildings were built in 1854 as houses for working men when the court was known as "Mixed Ale Alley." ♦ Between Bedford and Hudson Sts

14 Chumleys $$ A speakeasy during the 1920s (the anonymous building has the advantage of a back exit to Barrow Street), it still doesn't have a sign. Villagers who want to make a real impression enter through the back door. It's a cozy, convivial place with working fireplaces and wooden benches deeply carved with customers' initials. The food isn't terrific, but it's a great place to stop for a drink. ♦ American ♦ Dinner. 86 Bedford St (between Barrow and Grove Sts). 675.4449

15 Pink Teacup $$ Longtime regulars of what was once downtown's only soul food shack have been disappointed that the Teacup pulled up stakes and moved to a slicker location around the corner from its original site on Bleecker Street. It's still the only soul food restaurant in the Village, and if you like smothered pork chops, collard greens, black-eyed peas, and smooth banana pudding, they now come as gentrified as the hamburgers and pizzas in other places. ♦ Southern ♦ Lunch, dinner, and late-night meals. 42 Grove St (between Bleecker and Bedford Sts). No credit cards. 807.6755

chez michallet

16 Chez Michallet ★$$$ This charming and intimate French-style bistro is always packed with a neighborhood crowd. Especially good are the steak and french fries. ♦ French ♦ Dinner. 90 Bedford St (at Grove St). Reservations recommended. 242.8309

16 Twin Peaks In 1925, **Clifford Reed Daily** transformed this very conventional 1830 residence into a fairy-tale fantasy as a reaction against the mediocrity of Village architecture. Pseudo-Tudor details trim the stucco facing, and an unorthodox flap acts as a front cornice (there's an attic room behind it). It's not great architecture, but it *is* great fun. ♦ 102 Bedford St (between Grove and Christopher Sts)

17 Lucille Lortel Theatre Formerly the **Theatre De Lys,** this 299-seat house was a major boost to Off Broadway in the 1950s, when a revival of the Brecht-Weill classic *The Threepenny Opera* was staged here. It was later renamed for its distinguished owner, **Lucille Lortel,** who produced *Brecht on Brecht* and **John Dos Passos'** *USA.* More recently, it was home to the hugely successful *Steel Magnolias* during its two-and-a-half-year run. ♦ 121 Christopher St (between Bleecker and Hudson Sts). 924.2817

17 McNulty's Tea and Coffee Company This place has sold exotic coffees (from China, Sumatra, Indonesia) and teas (more than 250 varieties) since 1895; the experience shows. ♦ Tu-Sa 10AM-9PM; Su 1-7PM. 109 Christopher St (between Bleecker and Hudson Sts). 242.5351

18 Pot Belly Stove Restaurant $ If you feel like having a hamburger, an omelet, or a salad at 3AM, this is one of the better places to satisfy the urge. ♦ American ♦ Lunch, dinner, and late-night meals. 94 Christopher St (between Bleecker and Bedford Sts). No credit cards. 242.8036

19 Fat Cat Billiards There are pool tables, and lots of them, in this popular hangout for the college-age (and under) crowd. Pizza and hot dogs are available from the kitchen (soda, too, but no hard stuff). It's open until the wee hours. ◆ M-Th, Su 2PM-2AM; F-Sa 2PM-4AM. 75 Christopher St (between Seventh Ave South and Bleecker St). 675.6076

20 Grove Street Cafe ★$$$ This place is easy to fall in love with—the quaint, softly lit room is conveniently located near all the Village theaters. The mostly very good nouvelle cuisine is priced more fairly than at places of a similar ilk. Service is better, too. The BYO wine policy helps keep the tab in line. ◆ Continental ◆ Dinner. 53 Grove St (between Bleecker St and Seventh Ave South). Reservations recommended. 924.8299

20 Fukuda ★$$$$ An outstanding sushi bar is the highlight of this small restaurant. ◆ Japanese ◆ Dinner. Closed Monday. 61 Grove St (between Seventh Ave South and Bleecker St). Reservations recommended. 242.3699

21 Christopher Park Until the Parks Department put a sign near the entrance, everyone thought this was Sheridan Square. The confusion began when the IRT Sheridan Square subway stop was opened in 1918, and was compounded when **Joseph Pollia's** statue of the Civil War general was placed here (possibly by mistake) in 1936. ◆ Seventh Ave South (between Grove and Christopher Sts)

21 Sheridan Square Because Christopher Park is closer to the Sheridan Square subway stop, which is around the corner, Sheridan Square is at the same time one of the best-known and hardest-to-find spots in all of Greenwich Village. The community garden in the center yielded rare archaeological treasures when it was created in the early 1980s. It was the only spot in Manhattan that hadn't been disturbed since Indians lived here. ◆ W. Fourth St (between Washington Pl and Seventh Ave South)

21 The Ridiculous Theatrical Company The late, great **Charles Ludlam** felt that farce, parody, and travesty were essential ingredients for comic drama. They still are—Ludlam's virtuosic company continues the tradition with such delights as a severely adapted *A Tale of Two Cities*. ◆ 1 Sheridan Sq (W. Fourth St at Seventh Ave South). 691.2271

In 1942, distressed by commercial publishers' lack of interest in her work, Anaïs Nin borrowed $175 and, with a friend, rented a loft at 144 MacDougal Street, purchased a used printing press, and went on to print three of her books. In 1944, in search of more professional surroundings, she moved to a larger space at 17 E. 13th Street.

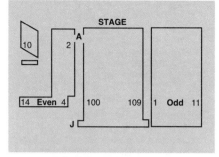

22 Circle Repertory Company The old **Sheridan Square Playhouse** has been the home of the **Circle Repertory Company** since it was founded by **Marshall W. Mason** in 1974. A permanent company of artists (which has included **Judd Hirsch** and **William Hurt**) performs new American drama, including the works of **Lanford Wilson, Edward J. Moore,** and **Jules Feiffer.** ◆ 99 Seventh Ave South (between Barrow and Grove Sts). 924.7100

23 One If By Land, Two If By Sea ★★$$$$ There is no sign outside this charming restaurant, but don't give up. Once you've found it, you'll never forget it. A large bar and a working fireplace are just inside the door. The two-level interior is romantically candlelit, and the food (beef Wellington is the thing here) is beautifully prepared. ◆ Continental ◆ Dinner. 17 Barrow St (between W. Fourth St and Seventh Ave South). Reservations required. 228.0822

24 Sweet Basil The giants of the jazz world perform here regularly. Most people come to listen to music and have a drink, but Sweet Basil also offers food, including good salads and stir-fry dishes. ◆ Cover. Shows nightly at 9PM and 11PM. 88 Seventh Ave South (between Bleecker and Grove Sts). 242.1785

24 Actor's Playhouse This has been one of the high spots on the Off-Broadway theater scene since it raised its first curtain in 1940. Productions have included *10% Review* and *The Good and Faithful Servant.* ◆ 100 Seventh Ave South (between Bleecker and Grove Sts). 691.6226

25 The Manhattan Chili Company ★$ When you're in the mood for a good bowl of chili, go no farther. It comes in a wide range of spices, and there's even vegetarian chili for those watching their cholesterol levels. If you're with someone who's not a chili fan, there are plenty of other Southern fixin's to keep them happy. The Dos Equis beer is, fortunately, inexpensive—you'll need more than one to wash down the Texas Chain Gang chili (classification: "hot hot"). In warm weather there's garden seating. ◆ Tex-Mex ◆ Lunch, dinner, and late-night meals. 302 Bleecker St (off Seventh Ave South). 206.7163

26 Ottomanelli's Meat Market If you're a long way from home, you're probably not in the market for fresh game or a fine veal roast. But there aren't many butcher shops like this one anymore. Drop in to see what you're missing. ◆ M-F 8AM-6:30PM; Sa 7AM-6PM. 285 Bleecker St (between Jones St and Seventh Ave South). 675.4217

27 John's Pizzeria ★★$ Some years ago **Woody Allen** wrote in *The New Yorker* that John's, a New York City institution, makes the best coal-oven pizza in town. Even if you have to wait in line to find out for yourself—and you will—you'll agree it was worth it. ◆ Italian ◆ Lunch and dinner. 278 Bleecker St (between Morton St and Seventh Ave South). 243.1680

27 Aphrodisia Scoop your choice from among the 800 herbs and spices into a small paper bag and label with the name and price. They also have a good selection of books for healthy living. ◆ M-Sa 11AM-7PM; Su noon-5:30PM. 264 Bleecker St (at Seventh Ave South). 989.6440

28 Cucina Stagionale $ The menu is basic Italian with a twist (try the eggplant manicotti), and the price is right. There's almost always a line of people happily waiting to get in, bottles of wine in hand. ◆ Italian ◆ Lunch and dinner. 275 Bleecker St (between Jones and Cornelia Sts). No credit cards. 924.2707

29 Trattoria Pesce Pasta ★$$ Just opened and already a place apart from the neighborhood's heavy-on-the-garlic Italian contenders, this small restaurant serves great dinners in a warm and gracious atmosphere. Start with *pasta e fagioli,* a broth rich with beans, vegetables, and macaroni. The fish specialties change according to the offerings of the daily market, but look for an excellent *zuppa di pesce,* an Italian bouillabaisse, or the mixed seafood grill. ◆ Italian ◆ Lunch, dinner, and late-night meals. 262 Bleecker St (at Cornelia St). 645.2993

30 A. Zito & Sons Bakery The bread's crunchy crust and delicate inside texture lures such devoted customers as **Frank Sinatra.** Pick out your own loaf, fresh from the oven. ◆ M-Sa 6AM-6PM; Su 6AM-1PM. 259 Bleecker St (between Sixth Ave and Cornelia St). 929.6139

30 Murray's Cheese Store The competitive prices of the large assortment of cheeses—of which 90 percent are imported—and superior service will keep you coming back. Now in larger quarters, it also offers groceries, salads, meats, delicacies—a self-styled "mini-Balducci's." ◆ M-Sa 8:30AM-7:30PM; Su 9AM-5PM. 257 Bleecker St (between Sixth and Seventh Aves South). 243.3289

31 Home ★★$$ In a cozy spot best described as urban farmhouse, this new breed of neighborhood restaurant infuses a contemporary flair into classic and nostalgic American cooking. Heartwarming entrées such as peppered shoulder steak and cumin-crusted pork chops are as memorable as the signature homemade ketchup, onion rings, and must-have chocolate pudding. You *can* go home again. ◆ American ◆ Breakfast, lunch, and dinner; brunch, lunch, and dinner on Saturday and Sunday. 20 Cornelia St (between W. Fourth and Bleecker Sts). 243.9579

32 The Cornelia Street Café $$ Here's a charming spot on a neat little Village side street. The food's okay but a little pricey considering its neighborhood appeal. ◆ Cafe/Bistro ◆ Lunch and dinner. 29 Cornelia St (between Bleecker and W. Fourth Sts). 989.9318

33 The Bagel ★$ This tiny restaurant and deli is known for its Village Breakfast—strawberry pancakes—as well as the standard deli fare. The Bagel also makes a great sandwich; try the pastrami or corned beef. ◆ American ◆ Breakfast, lunch, and dinner. 170 W. Fourth St (at Cornelia St). No credit cards. 255.0106

34 Caffè Vivaldi ★$ This old-world Village favorite always pleases with its relaxed and cozy atmosphere that's a throwback to earlier times. Is this Manhattan or turn-of-the-century Vienna, with dramatic arias playing in the background and the smell and sound of the espresso machine and a crackling fireplace? Head here on a cold winter's day with your significant other for a light lunch or sweets. ◆ Cafe ◆ Daily 11AM-1AM. 32 Jones St (between Bleecker and W. Fourth Sts). 929.9384

35 Pink Pussycat Boutique Take a peek at the incredible selection of erotic paraphernalia, even if you're too embarrassed to buy anything. ◆ M-F 10AM-2AM; Sa-Su 10AM-3AM. 167 W. Fourth St (between Sixth and Seventh Aves South). 243.0077

36 St. Joseph's Church The oldest Roman Catholic church building in Manhattan, this Greek Revival temple was built in 1834 by **John Doran.** It has a gallery inside as well as delicate crystal chandeliers and a gilded

---

Restaurants/Clubs: Red   **Hotels:** Blue

Shops/ 🌳 Outdoors: Green   **Sights/Culture:** Black

sanctuary that contrasts with the simplicity of the Greek Revival exterior. The outside wall on Washington Place is made of Manhattan schist, which underlies the whole island. ♦ 371 Sixth Ave (at W. Washington Pl)

37 Gus' Place ★$$ Casual, gracious Gus' Place specializes in Mediterranean—predominantly Greek—cuisine. The appetizers alone are enough to send you away satiated and mighty happy. But then you'll miss Gus' specialty, lamb shank, and that would be a shame. ♦ Mediterranean/Greek ♦ Dinner and late-night meals; brunch and lunch also on Saturday and Sunday. Closed Monday. 149 Waverly Pl (near Sixth Ave). 645.8511

37 Gay Street Thought to be named after a family who lived here in the mid- to late-18th century, the block contains a well-preserved group of Greek Revival houses on the east side and Federal row houses on the west. No. 14 is the location of the basement apartment that was the setting for **Ruth McKenney's** play *My Sister Eileen*, which later was made into the musical *Wonderful Town*. ♦ Waverly Pl to Christopher St

38 Oscar Wilde Memorial Bookshop This small shop offers a tasteful selection of books on gay and lesbian subject matter, including literary classics, legal guides, sociology, and periodicals. ♦ Daily 11:30AM-7:30PM. 15 Christopher St (at Gay St). 255.8097

39 LainaJane Galleria Silk and cotton lingerie, kimonos, PJs, and his-and-her boxer shorts are all reasonably priced. ♦ M, Su noon-8PM; Tu-F 11AM-8PM. 35 Christopher St (at Waverly Pl). 727.7032

40 158 Waverly Place In 1948, while playing the role of Billie Dawn in *Born Yesterday*, **Judy Holliday** and her husband, **David Oppenheim,** moved into a large apartment on the seventh floor of this building. They lived here until 1952, when they moved into the Dakota. ♦ Between Gay and Christopher Sts

40 Pierre's ★$$$ The bistro's cozy atmosphere is enhanced by a wandering accordian player. Try the salmon puff pastries (delicate morsels stuffed with spinach), and for dessert, the *tarte tatin* (apple pie baked with a caramel sauce and served with homemade whipped cream). The steak *pommes frites* are good as well. ♦ French ♦ Lunch and dinner. 170 Waverly Pl (at Christopher St). Reservations required. No credit cards. 929.7194

40 Northern Dispensary This basic brick, Georgian-vernacular, triangular building was built by **Henry Bayard** and **John C. Tucker** in 1831. According to records, **Edgar Allan Poe** was treated here for a head cold in 1837. ♦ 165 Waverly Pl (between Grove and Christopher Sts). 242.5511

41 Lion's Head $$ Local journalists, writers, and community politicians consider this a major hangout. The bar is the main thing, but the food is perfectly acceptable. ♦ American ♦ Lunch, dinner, and late-night meals. 59 Christopher St (at Seventh Ave South). 929.0670

42 Three Lives & Company This shop carries a wonderful selection (particularly fiction and specialty books) and hosts occasional Thursday night readings. The owners are knowledgeable and helpful. ♦ Daily 1-7PM; extended hours in winter. 154 W. 10th St (between Sixth and Seventh Aves South). 741.2069

43 Crystal Gardens This shop for the spiritually inclined offers quartz, minerals, medicine jewelry, seminars, consultations, and an interesting newsletter written by co-owner **Connie Barrett.** ♦ Daily noon-8PM. 21 Greenwich Ave (between Christopher and W. 10th Sts). 727.0692

44 New York Public Library, Jefferson Market Branch **Frederick Clark Withers** and **Calvert Vaux** modeled this 1877 structure, built on the site of the old **Jefferson Market** and originally used as the **Third Judicial District Courthouse,** after **Mad King Ludwig II** of Bavaria's castle Neuschwanstein. It is the epitome of Victorian Gothic, with steeply sloping roofs, gables, pinnacles, sets of variously shaped arched windows, and stone carvings all set off by a rather unusual clock tower that served as a fire lookout. After the occupants moved out in 1945, the building sat idle until citizens pressured the city government to find a new user and the public library agreed to move in. **Giorgio Cavaglieri** handled the 1967 remodeling. ♦ M 10AM-6PM; Tu, Th 1-6PM; W 1-8PM; Sa 10AM-5PM. 425 Sixth Ave (at W. 10th St). 243.4334

45 Balducci's In Greenwich Village, Balducci's is the ne plus ultra grocer. From humble beginnings many years ago as a produce stand across the street from its present site, this family-run store has become one of the most grand and best-stocked specialty shops in New York City. Not only is there still gorgeous produce, but they also offer first-rate cheese, fish, cold cut, take-out, and bakery departments. The shelves hold packaged products from all over the world but concentrate on delicacies from Italy and France. ♦ Daily 7AM-8:30PM. 424 Sixth Ave (at W. Ninth St). 673.2600

46 Jefferson Market One of just about everything you might want can be found here, and the meats and fish are especially fine. The staff is extremely helpful; longtime customers are treated with neighborly respect. ◆ M-Sa 8AM-9PM. 455 Sixth Ave (at W. 10th St). 675.2277

46 Patchin Place Like **Milligan Place** around the corner on Sixth Avenue, this cluster of small houses constructed in 1848 by **Aaron D. Patchin** was built as rooming houses for waiters and other personnel from the now-departed **Brevoort Hotel** over on Fifth Avenue. It became famous in the 1920s as the home of poet **e.e. cummings,** among others. ◆ W. 10th St (between Sixth and Greenwich Aves)

47 Gran Caffé Degli Artisti ★$ Don't choose a window seat; instead, ask for a table in the back, where it's dark, cozy, candlelit, and filled with funky antique furnishings. Skip the Italian entrées and go directly to the iced mochaccino and one of the decadent pastries or cakes. ◆ Cafe ◆ Lunch, dinner, and late-night meals. 46 Greenwich Ave (between W. 10th and W. 11th Sts). 645.4431

48 El Charro Español $$$ Though not authentic Mexican, or even Tex-Mex, the food is fresh, tasty, and abundant at this casual spot. ◆ Tex-Mex ◆ Lunch and dinner. 4 Charles St (at Greenwich Ave). Reservations recommended Friday through Sunday. 242.9547

49 Village Vanguard This world-famous basement jazz club also features Dixieland, blues, avant-garde, and folk music. Pop singers, comedians, and poets have appeared. ◆ Cover. Shows M-Th, Su 9:30PM and 11:30PM; F-Sa 9:30PM, 11:30PM, and 1AM. 178 Seventh Ave South (at Perry St). Reservations recommended. 255.4037

50 Patisserie J. Lanciani ★$ Magnificent cakes, tarts, brownies, and croissants are served in this pretty storefront cafe. ◆ Cafe ◆ M, Su 8AM-10PM; Tu-Th 8AM-11PM; F-Sa 8AM-midnight. 271 W. Fourth St (between Perry and W. 11th Sts). 929.0739, 477.2788

51 Pleasure Chest Not as froofy-looking as the Pink Pussycat, this erotic emporium is for folks into more serious pleasures. ◆ M, Th-Su noon-10PM; Tu-W noon-9PM. 156 Seventh Ave South (at Charles St). 242.2158. Also at: 302 E. 52nd St. 371.4465

52 Riviera Cafe $$ People-watching is the best thing on the menu here, which includes such standards as burgers and salads. Sip some wine and watch most of Greenwich Village pass by your table. Choose indoor or outdoor dining or the sports bar. ◆ American ◆ Lunch, dinner, and late-night meals. 225 W. Fourth St (between Christopher St and Seventh Ave South). 242.8732

53 Very Special Flowers You won't find the usual mums, gladioli, or carnations here. Instead VSF concentrates on complicated topiary, dried-flower arrangements, and exotic bouquets made from flowers flown in daily from Holland and France. ◆ M-Sa 10AM-5PM. 204 W. 10th St (between Bleecker St and Seventh Ave South). 206.7236

54 La Metairie ★★$$$$ A white picket fence and hand-painted duck sign welcome you to this minuscule French restaurant. Start with foie gras or carpaccio. The filet mignon and grilled fish are both excellent. ◆ French ◆ Dinner. 189 W. 10th (between Bleecker St and Seventh Ave South). Reservations required. 989.0343

55 Pierre Deux Stop here for Provençal furniture, china, clothing, fabrics, and accessories. ◆ M-F 10AM-6PM; Sa 10AM-5PM. 367 Bleecker St (at Charles St). 243.7740. Also at: 870 Madison Ave. 570.9343

56 Cottonwood Cafe $$ In the heart of the West Village, this low-down Texan joint serves crisp-breaded chicken-fried steak with sides of fabulously lumpy mashed potatoes, cornmeal-dipped fried okra, and the obligatory cream gravy—it's enough to make the roughest ranchero coo with pleasure. The hefty beef ribs are the most authentic mesquite-smoked, Texas-style barbecued ribs in town. After 10PM, something called "original Texas" music—C&W with an overlay of Village artiness—is performed in the back room. The neighborhood crowd downs great nonclassic margaritas and Lone Star beer. ◆ Southern ◆ Lunch and dinner. 415 Bleecker St (between W. 11th and Bank Sts). 924.6271

56 Bird Jungle Pick up a parrot or a mynah bird or any one of a dozen varieties of feathered friends. The window action can be a bit frightening at times. ◆ M-F 12:30-6:30PM; Sa 11AM-6:30PM; Su 11AM-5:30PM. 401 Bleecker St (at W. 11th St). 242.1757

57 Biography Bookshop As the name implies, this bookstore has the best selection of biographies anywhere. Feel free to browse. ◆ M-F noon-8PM; Sa noon-10PM; Su noon-6PM. 400 Bleecker St (at W. 11th St). 807.8655

58 Different Light Books Probably the best bookstore of its kind in the city, this is an excellent place to find literature on a wide variety of gay- and lesbian-related topics and issues. ◆ M-Th, Su 11AM-10PM; F-Sa 11AM-11PM. 548 Hudson St (between Charles and Perry Sts). 989.4850

The residents of Greenwich Village named Waverly Place after Sir Walter Scott's novel *Waverly* to honor him the year after his death.

59 Lucy Anna Folk Art & Antique Quilts

When **Karen Taber's** grandmothers—Lucy and Anna—handed down their quilts to their granddaughter, they planted a seed of interest that has blossomed into this attractive shop filled with antique quilts (lots of pastels) as well as new items—such as stuffed animals—made out of quilt scraps. ♦ Tu-Sa noon-7PM; Su noon-5PM. 502 Hudson St (between Christopher and W. 10th Sts). 645.9463

60 Taylor's This snug gourmet takeout is run by **Spartan** and **Cindi Taylor.** The onion-poppy hot dog buns—with Pommery mustard mixed into the dough—give you a good reason to eat hot dogs, and the triple-fudge brownies will throw off your calorie count for the week. ♦ Takeout ♦ Daily 6AM-9PM. 523 Hudson St (between W. 10th and Charles Sts). 645.8200

60 Mesa Verde ★$ Tasty beef, shrimp, and chicken fajitas and specialty burritos highlight the menu here, site of the former Upstairs at the Downstairs. ♦ Southwestern ♦ Lunch and dinner. 531 Hudson St (between Charles and W. 10th St). Reservations recommended. 206.7093

60 Sazerac House ★★$$ Better-than-average gumbo, jambalaya, and other New Orleans fare is served. Brunch is the way to go here. Eggs are transformed into a delicious concoction called "Eggs Sazerac"—scrambled eggs with Canadian bacon and scallions. This is the oldest structure on the street (1826) and was once part of a farm. ♦ Cajun/Creole ♦ Lunch and dinner. 533 Hudson St (at Charles St). Reservations recommended. 989.0313

61 Caribe ★$ Yet another island motif restaurant/bar: Jamaican food and music in a junglelike setting. The food is pretty good (try the jerk chicken or pork), and the atmosphere, call it West Indian/West Village, is funky and fun. ♦ West Indian ♦ Lunch and dinner. 117 Perry St (at Greenwich St). 255.9191

62 Fishs Eddy This shop specializes in collecting and selling odd and interesting bits of glassware and porcelain, such as old dishes from railroad cars and remnants from extinct social clubs. ♦ M-Sa 10AM-8PM; Su 11AM-7PM. 551 Hudson St (between Perry and W. 11th Sts). 627.3956. Also at: 889 Broadway. 420.9020

62 White Horse Tavern Among the folks who have frequented this famous bar was the poet **Dylan Thomas,** who, in a particularly depressive funk, literally drank himself to death in the corner. His supposed last words: "I've had 19 straight whiskeys. I believe that's the record." The french fries are okay and the burgers are good. ♦ M-Th, Su 11AM-2AM; F-Sa 11AM-4AM. 567 Hudson St (at W. 11th St). 243.9260

63 Harlequin ★$$$ Paella is the house specialty in this rather elegant Spanish restaurant, but if Spanish food is your favorite, you might feel underwhelmed. ♦ Spanish ♦ Dinner. 569 Hudson St (at W. 11th St). 255.4950

64 Burgundy Wine Company The finest wines of Burgundy and the Rhone are the specialty of this shop. Ask for a mail-order catalog, an informative brochure filled with vignettes about wine merchant **Al Hotchkin's** travels through the vineyards plus his thoughts on the wines he discovers. ♦ Tu-Sa 10AM-7PM. 323 W. 11th St (between Greenwich and Washington Sts). 691.9092

65 The Black Sheep ★★$$ Welcome to every tourist's idea of a Village restaurant—brick walls, bad paintings, comfortable, and dark. The six-course dinner with limited choices is a good value, and the wine list is excellent. ♦ French ♦ Dinner and late-night meals. 342 W. 11th St (at Washington St). Reservations recommended. 242.1010

66 Westbeth In its years as **Bell Telephone Laboratories,** this was where the transistor was invented and the first TV pictures were transmitted. When Bell Labs moved to the suburbs in 1965, **Richard Meier Associates** renovated the 1900 **Cyrus Eidlitz**-designed building and turned it into housing exclusively for artists, the **Westbeth Theater** complex, and the studios of the **Merce Cunningham Dance Company.** ♦ 463 West St (at Bank St)

67 Tortilla Flats $ Cheap Tex-Mex eats and wild times are served in this popular West Village dive. ♦ Tex-Mex ♦ Lunch, dinner, and late-night meals. 767 Washington St (at W. 12th St). 243.1053

68 Kelter/Malce This store has beautiful antique quilts from the early 1800s, as well as a good selection of Amish and patchwork quilts, Beacon and Pendleton blankets, Navajo weavings, folk art, and antique Christmas ornaments. ♦ M-Sa by appointment. 74 Jane St (between Greenwich and Washington Sts). 989.6760

69 Restaurant Florent ★★$$ A meat market diner-turned-hip bistro, this is a welcome late-night spot for those seeking a complete meal, not something off the snack menu. The meat entrées are, of course, the specialties of the house (try the *boudin noir* appetizer if you're the red-blooded type), but the fish dishes are also fine. After midnight you can order from the all-night breakfast menu. Part of the attraction of this attractive establishment is the involvement of **Tibor Kalman's M & Co., A Design Group,** which was responsible for the graphic design and, to some extent, the layout of the restaurant itself. ♦ Continental ♦ Daily 24 hours. 69 Gansevoort St (between Greenwich and Washington Sts). 989.5779

70 Gansevoort Market The city's wholesale meat district is housed in this collection of old brick buildings. The action intensifies in the early morning hours before the sun comes up, when people from restaurants all over New York converge to find the best meat to offer you for dinner. ♦ Gansevoort and W. 14th Sts (between Ninth Ave and the Hudson River)

71 El Faro ★$$ The rich and fragrant paella is a standout in this casual Spanish restaurant. ♦ Spanish ♦ Lunch and dinner. 823 Greenwich St (at Horatio St). 929.8210

72 Myers of Keswick If you're an Anglophile you'll have fun perusing this English grocery and its selection of typical Brit eats: Oxo, Bovril, Marmite, Lucozade, Smarties, and fresh pork pies and bangers. They also stock Kensington teapots and mugs and circular tea bags. ♦ M-F 10AM-7PM; Sa 10AM-6PM; Su noon-5PM. 634 Hudson St (between Jane and Horatio Sts). 691.4194

73 Peanut Butter & Jane This children's clothing store stocks more than 200 brands, from basics to one-of-a-kinds by local artists, as well as toys and accessories. ♦ M-Sa 10:30AM-7:30PM; Su noon-5PM. 617 Hudson St (between W. 12th and Jane Sts). 620.7952

74 La Ripaille ★★$$$ Set in what looks like a French farmhouse, La Ripaille's provincial dishes are never less than good—and sometimes quite good—but it's a mite pricey for what it is. ♦ French ♦ Dinner. Closed Sunday. 605 Hudson St (between Bethune and W. 12th Sts). Reservations recommended. 255.4406

75 Abingdon Square The square is named for **Charlotte Warren,** wife of the **Earl of Abingdon** and daughter of **Sir Peter Warren,** whose estate once covered this area. The statue at the uptown entrance, placed here in 1921, is a memorial to the American dead of World War I. ♦ Eighth Ave (between W. 12th and Hudson Sts)

76 Foul Play Books of Mystery & Suspense This specialty shop with black walls and red neon has a wide selection of mystery, espionage, suspense, and true crime books in both hardcover and paperback. Do a little detective work of your own and see if you can find the hidden door in the rear of the store. ♦ M-Sa 11AM-9:45PM; Su noon-5PM. 13 Eighth Ave (at W. 12th St). 675.5115. Also at: 1465-B Second Ave. 517.3222

77 Casa di Pré ★$$ It's often overlooked, but this place serves honest, homey food cooked with a light hand. ♦ Italian ♦ Lunch and dinner. 283 W. 12th St (at W. Fourth St). Reservations recommended for three or more. 243.7073

78 Corner Bistro ★$ If strolling around the Village has whetted your appetite for a fat, juicy burger, this neighborhood standby is the place to go. You'll have plenty of time to check out the locals in this dark, cozy pub—the aloof service is usually extremely slow. ♦ American ♦ Lunch, dinner, and late-night meals. 331 W. Fourth St (between W. 12th and Jane Sts). No credit cards. 242.9502

79 Jane Street Seafood Cafe ★$$$ Fresh and simple seafood dishes—and some surprisingly well-executed complex ones—don't completely compensate for the nonchalant service and high prices. ♦ Seafood ♦ Dinner. 31 Eighth Ave (at Jane St). 243.9237

80 Nell's The doormen are less choosy these days, now that the club is less in vogue. But you might still spy hip literary types and the occasional celeb lounging on one of the cushy couches. The club's main claim to fame among younger patrons is that its owner, Nell, costarred in *The Rocky Horror Picture Show.* ♦ Cover. M-Tu, Su 10PM-3AM; W-Sa 10PM-4AM. 246 W. 14th St (between Seventh and Eighth Aves). 675.1567

80 Jerry Ohlinger's Movie Material Store The collection includes innumerable posters and thousands of stills in both color and black-and-white, including some 10,000 from Disney films alone. ♦ Daily 1-7:45PM. 242 W. 14th St (between Seventh and Eighth Aves). 989.0869

· FOURTEEN ·

80 Fourteen ★★$$$ This bistro is a reminder of the days a century ago when the neighborhood included New York's largest French community. The quality of the food and the attentive service would make a Parisian feel right at home. The restaurant has a devoted following of admirers who yearn for simple, classic French dishes that are dependably good. ♦ French ♦ Lunch and dinner; dinner only on Saturday and Sunday. 240 W. 14th St (between Seventh and Eighth Aves). Reservations recommended. 206.7006. Also at: 323 E. 79th St. 535.1414

81 Integral Yoga Institute All aspects of yoga teaching are presented: meditation, breathing, relaxation, diet and nutrition, stress management, Hatha for pregnant women, video classes, chanting. The institute's store next door sells all kinds of macrobiotic essentials as well as natural cosmetics and remedies. Vitamins, minerals, herbs, and homeopathic remedies are for sale across the street at the **Natural Apothecary** (No. 234). ♦ M-F 10AM-8:30PM; Sa 9AM-5PM. 227 W. 13th St (between Seventh and Eighth Aves). 929.0586

82 Cafe de Bruxelles ★$$$ A sophisticated bar scene is the best attraction at this lovely spot, which has also made a name for itself as the only Belgian restaurant downtown. Rich *waterzooi,* a Belgian bouillabaisse, is the ticket. ♦ French/Belgian ♦ Lunch and dinner. Closed Monday. 118 Greenwich Ave (at W. 13th St). Reservations recommended. 206.1830

83 Bennie's Burritos ★$ You'll understand why it gets so rowdy here after sipping one of Bennie's high-octane margaritas and eating any one of his 12-inch-long burritos with a tempting choice of fillings at bargain prices. This is the Village's *numero uno* cheap tortilla joint, so expect a line. ♦ Tex-Mex ♦ Lunch, dinner, and late-night meals; brunch also on Saturday and Sunday. 93 Greenwich Ave (between W. 12th and W. 13th Sts). No credit cards. 727.0584. Also at: 93 Ave A (at Sixth St). 254.2054

84 Ye Waverly Inn $$ Longtime Villagers don't seem to care that the quality of the food has declined somewhat. They still like the authentic Early American charm and low prices. ♦ American ♦ Dinner; lunch also on Saturday and Sunday. 16 Bank St (at Waverly Pl). 929.4377

85 Chez Brigitte ★$$ Homey, simple, inexpensive French food is cooked by a friendly Frenchwoman. Counter service only. ♦ French ♦ Lunch and dinner. 77 Greenwich Ave (at W. 11th St). No credit cards. 929.6736

86 St. Vincent's Hospital Built in 1979 by **Ferrez & Taylor,** the modern monstrosity that is the hospital's main building is proof that not every Village community protest is successful. But St. Vincent's has been serving the community well in every other way since it was founded by the **Sisters of Charity** in 1849. It has become the largest Catholic hospital in the United States. St. Vincent's has a Doctor Directory and a physician referral service (790.1111). ♦ Seventh Ave South (between W. 11th and W. 12th Sts). 790.7000

87 West 14th Street Best known as a magnet for bargain-hunters, this street is also home to a number of noteworthy loft buildings. Walk on the north side of the street and look across at Nos. 138-146 (1899), an ostentatious confection that drew on the 1893 Chicago World's Fair for its inspiration; and Nos. 154-160 (1913), **Herman Lee Meader's** colorful glass and tile design that is literally grounded in Art Nouveau and aspiring to Art Deco. ♦ From Sixth to Seventh Aves

88 Salvation Army Centennial Memorial Temple This 1930 building by **Voorhees, Gmelin & Walker** is one of the best Art Deco extravaganzas around, with an overblown entrance and unrestrained interiors that capture the exuberance and color of the era. The building houses the executive offices and programs of the Salvation Army. ♦ 120 W. 14th St (between Sixth and Seventh Aves)

89 Cafe Loup ★★$$$ This cozy, comfortable standby for simple French cooking has an informal, friendly atmosphere and is always packed with interesting Village habitués. ♦ French ♦ Lunch and dinner. 105 W. 13th St (between Sixth and Seventh Aves). Reservations recommended. 255.4746

90 New Deal ★$$$ Lions and tigers and bears, oh my! Newly relocated to more roomy surroundings, New Deal specializes in exotic wild game—like rattlesnake. For the faint of stomach, there's a selection of more traditional meat options. ♦ American/Eclectic ♦ Dinner; lunch also on Sunday. 133 W. 13th St (between Sixth and Seventh Aves). Reservations recommended. 741.3663

90 Village Community Church This abandoned gem is thought by architectural historians to be the best Greek Revival church in the city. The original design, dating to 1846, is attributed to **Samuel Thompson** and based on the Theseum in Athens. But the materials are the antithesis of the Doric model: the six huge columns and the pediment are of wood, and the walls are brick and stucco. ♦ 143 W. 13th St (between Sixth and Seventh Aves South)

91 Zinno ★★$$$ This sleek ground-floor town house bar and restaurant offers chamber jazz and good pasta. ♦ Italian ♦ Lunch and dinner. Closed Sunday. 126 W. 13th St (between Sixth and Seventh Aves). 924.5182

92 Lora ★★$$ Chef-owner **Lora Zarubin,** onetime San Francisco caterer to the stars, created this intimate bistro, which draws the fashion, photography, and art crowds. Zarubin continues to refine her eclectic California cuisine. Sip champagne at the bar or share dessert and coffee in the Parisian-style cafe in front. ◆ Regional American ◆ Lunch and dinner. Closed Sunday. 104 W. 13th (between Sixth and Seventh Aves). Reservations recommended. 675.5655

93 Famous Ray's Pizza ★$ Though a number of imposters have tried to claim title to the name "Famous Ray the Pizza King," this Village institution is the only real heir to the throne, serving more than 2,000 loyal customers a day. Expect a line for delicious pizza that's never anything less then fresh out of the oven. Ray's "Famous Slice" has *all* the toppings, but purists opt for the traditional red (tomato sauce), white (mozzarella), and green (basil and parsley). ◆ Pizzeria ◆ Lunch, dinner, and late-night meals. 465 Sixth Ave (at W. 11th St). No credit cards. 243.2253

94 Butterfield House The 1962 edifice by **Mayer, Whittlesey & Glass** is an unusually sensitive apartment block. The fine seven-story, bay-windowed section on 12th Street is an in-scale counterpoint to a series of row houses. Beyond an interior courtyard, the wing on 13th Street is taller, adapting to the stronger, larger scale of that block. ◆ 37 W. 12th St (between Fifth and Sixth Aves)

95 Kate's Paperie All sorts of *papier* is found here, from gift wraps and marbleized papers to printmaking and handmade papers, paper quilts by **Carolyn Cole, Noguchi** paper lamps, and Samurai-inspired dolls constructed with different textures of handmade grass papers. In addition, you'll find a nice selection of journals, photo albums, and pens, and printing and engraving services. ◆ M-F 10AM-7PM; Sa 10AM-6PM. 8 W. 13th St (between Fifth and Sixth Aves). 633.0570

96 East West Books This is an excellent source for books on Eastern philosophy, religion, cooking, medicine, and New Age lifestyles. ◆ M-Sa 10AM-7:20PM; Su 11AM-6:20PM. 78 Fifth Ave (between W. 13th and W. 14th Sts). 243.5994

97 Parsons School of Design Parsons holds a unique place in American education. Here, art and industry were for the first time firmly linked on a large institutional level, even before **Gropius** and the **Bauhaus** school. Founded as the Chase School in 1896 by painter/art teacher **William Merritt Chase**, the institution was spurred to its current high position in the world of art and design education by the leadership of **Frank Alvah Parsons.** Parsons arrived in 1907 and as the school's president implemented his vision of art and directly influenced both industry and everyday life. Under his direction the school changed its name to the New York School of Fine and Applied Arts and added programs such as interior architecture and design, fashion design and illustration, and advertising art. In 1940, the name was changed to honor President Parsons. In 1970, Parsons School again took an innovative step in art education, joining with the **New School for Social Research** to broaden the scope of both institutions. Parsons moved to a site within the New School campus near Washington Square in Greenwich Village. Here, nearly 7,000 full- and part-time students can utilize the city's vast cultural and professional resources. The Parsons staff is made up primarily of professionals working in New York's vibrant art and design industry. In 1977, the school added a Garment District extension, the **David Schwartz Fashion Center,** at 40th Street and Seventh Avenue. Work by Parsons students is shown from March through June at the exhibition center at 2 W. 13th Street and 66 Fifth Avenue. ◆ 66 Fifth Ave (between W. 12th and W. 13th Sts). 229.8930

97 Forbes Building The heart of the Forbes publishing empire is located in this 1925 **Carrère & Hastings** building. What's best here is the **Forbes Magazine Galleries** on the main floor. The collection includes more than 500 toy boats, displayed along with Art Deco fittings from the liner *Normandie* and models of the late **Malcolm Forbes'** private yachts. There is a collection of 12,000 toy soldiers and 250 trophies awarded for every accomplishment from raising Leghorn chickens to surviving a working lifetime in the corporate battlefields. American history is represented in a collection of **Presidential Papers,** historical documents, and model rooms. But the best part, for many, is a display of 12 **Fabergé** Easter eggs, the world's largest private collection of these priceless objects created for the czars of Russia. Admission is limited to 900 tickets a day and is reserved for group tours and advance reservations on Thursday. ◆ Free. Tu-W, F-Sa 10AM-4PM (hours subject to change). 62 Fifth Ave (at W. 12th St). 206.5548

98 First Presbyterian Church Joseph C. Wells modeled this fine Gothic Revival church with an imposing tower after **Magdalen College** at Oxford. The south transept, an 1893 addition by **McKim, Mead & White,** includes an outdoor pulpit overlooking the inviting garden. The **Church House,** which adjoins the church on the uptown side, was designed in 1960 by **Edgar Tafel** to perfectly match the 1846 building. A three-year restoration of all the wood, stained glass, and masonry was completed in the spring of 1991. ◆ 48 Fifth Ave (between W. 11th and W. 12th Sts)

99 Gotham Bar and Grill ★★★$$$$ Although it seemed destined to fail shortly after opening in 1984, chef **Alfred Portale** changed the fate of this breathtaking restaurant with his culinary talents. Now one of the most consistently successful venues in the neighborhood, this palatial postmodern setting (winner of the 1984 Restaurant and Hotel Design Award) makes you feel important for just being here. Start with one of the inventive pastas to tantalize your palate before the main course. The kitchen doesn't falter in the basics either— the rack of lamb will truly melt in your mouth. The service *can* be haughty but is always completely professional. ♦ Continental ♦ Dinner. 12 E. 12th St (between University Pl and Fifth Ave). Reservations required. 620.4020

100 Asti $$$ Opera is sung while you eat routine Southern Italian standards. Go for the fun, not the food. ♦ Italian ♦ Lunch and dinner. Closed Monday. 13 E. 12th St (between University Pl and Fifth Ave). 741.9105

101 Bowlmor Lanes The New Amsterdam Dutch introduced bowling to America, but their legacy seems to be unappreciated in Manhattan, where there are only a handful of places to play the game. This one includes a bar and grill and a pro shop. ♦ M-Th, Su 10AM-1AM; F-Sa 10AM-4AM. 110 University Pl (between E. 12th and E. 13th Sts). 255.8188

101 Japonica ★★$$$ Brown rice sushi and spectacular specialty rolls, along with friendly service, draw diners from all over the city to this neighborhood Japanese restaurant. The hot food is sublime as well— try the grilled bluefin tuna or sizzling vegetables. For those who dislike raw fish, there's even cooked sushi. One complaint: long waits for a table. ♦ Japanese ♦ Lunch and dinner. 100 University Pl (at E. 12th St). 243.7752

102 Forbidden Planet This is the city's headquarters for science fiction, horror, and fantasy books, comics, and related merchandise. ♦ M-Sa 10AM-7PM; Su noon-7PM. 821 Broadway (at E. 12th St). 473.1576

Restaurants/Clubs: Red   Hotels: Blue
Shops/ 🌳 Outdoors: Green   Sights/Culture: Black

103 The Cast Iron Building Designed by **John Kellum** in 1868, this building was converted from the **James McCreery Dry Goods Store** into apartments by **Stephen B. Jacobs** in 1973. In a city known for outstanding cast-iron structures, this is a most representative example, sporting layers of Corinthian columns topped by arches. Unfortunately, the uppermost story added later is an insensitive mismatch. ♦ 67 E. 11th St (at Broadway)

CEDAR

104 Cedar Tavern $ Now just a dark bar, this barnlike restaurant and bar was a hangout for Abstract Expressionist artists in the 1950s. Among the regulars were **Jackson Pollock, Roy Lichtenstein,** and **Larry Rivers.** ♦ American ♦ Lunch, dinner, and late-night meals. 82 University Pl (between E. 11th and E. 12th Sts). 929.9089

104 Bradley's ★$$ Some of the most famous musicians in the progressive jazz world might show up to play a set in this Village hangout, which is a favorite of writers from the nearby *Village Voice* and serves simple good cooking. ♦ American ♦ Lunch, dinner, and late-night meals. 70 University Pl (between E. 11th and E. 12th Sts). 228.6440

105 Il Cantinori ★★$$$ Country antiques from Italy set the stage for an authentic Tuscan meal. For a starter, try the assortment of grilled vegetables, then move on to the *tonno alla pesto,* a grilled tuna steak sliced and served with pesto vinaigrette and diced tomatoes. And for dessert? Apple tart, gelati of all kinds, *tiramisù,* and double-layer chocolate cake. ♦ Italian ♦ Lunch and dinner. 32 E. 10th St (between University Pl and Broadway). 673.6044

106 Knickerbocker Bar & Grill ★$$$ Fascinating 19th-century artifacts and posters fill this casual neo-Village bar and restaurant. The classy menu offers good steakhouse fare, along with grilled fish and pasta dishes, in a subdued atmosphere. Live jazz, often featuring name performers, is the draw. Chef **Peter Fiori,** formerly of Bouley, has given a lift to the menu. ♦ American ♦ Lunch, dinner, and late-night meals. 33 University Pl (at E. Ninth St). Reservations recommended. 228.8490

107 Rose Cafe ★★$$$ Specialties include grilled salmon, crisp potato pancakes with crème fraîche and caviar, and oven-roasted chicken with mushroom tarragon sauce and garlic mashed potatoes. ♦ American/Bistro ♦ Lunch and dinner. 24 Fifth Ave (at W. Ninth St). 260.4118

108 Marylou's ★★$$$ Skip the appetizers and soups and go directly to the generous main courses, particularly the perfectly broiled fish, of which there are usually at least a half-dozen fresh choices. In fact, given the graceful, traditional appointments in the several dining rooms—pleasant wood-framed paintings, fireplaces, library walls—the friendly service, and fair prices, this is the best seafood restaurant in the Village, and one of the top in town. ♦ Seafood ♦ Dinner and late-night meals. 21 W. Ninth St (between Fifth and Sixth Aves). Reservations recommended. 533.0012

109 Eighth Street Since the 1960s the stretch of Eighth Street between Sixth Avenue and Broadway has been the shopping district for suburban raffish types who want that Village look, whatever that may be. The selection of stores—mostly shoes and accessories—has spilled over to Broadway, where secondhand reigns. ♦ Between Broadway and Sixth Ave

110 MacDougal Alley Like **Washington Mews,** this is a street of converted stables, with the advantage of trees but the same disadvantage of parked cars. No. 7, on the north side, was built in 1899 as a studio for a stained-glass artisan. No. 17 1/2 was converted to a home for **Gertrude Vanderbilt Whitney,** founder of the **Whitney Museum,** in 1934. No. 19, on the south side, was built in 1901 as an automobile stable, and the 1854 stable that is No. 21 was reconstructed in 1920 by architect **Raymond Hood.** ♦ Off MacDougal St (between Washington Sq North and W. Eighth St)

111 New York Studio School of Drawing, Painting & Sculpture The **Whitney Museum** was established here in 1931. Tradition was already evident on the block, which was the heart of the Village art scene at the time. It began with the conversion of a stable at 4 W. Eighth Street by **John Taylor Johnston** as a gallery for his private art collection. His friends were so impressed that they got together and founded the **Metropolitan Museum of Art** in 1870. ♦ 8 W. Eighth St (between Fifth and Sixth Aves)

112 One Fifth Avenue ★★★$$$ Jerry Kretchmer and chef **Alfred Portale** of Gotham Bar and Grill have teamed up again with this mostly seafood place. If they're available, don't miss Diver scallops with sea urchin sauce, and wild striped bass Provençale. **Cafe One Fifth** has just opened in the front room. Both eateries share the same staff, chef, and telephone number, but the cafe's menu leans toward seafood with Thai and Southwest touches. ♦ American ♦ Lunch and dinner. At Eighth St. 529.1515

113 Patricia Field Trendsetting fashions are Field's forte, great for those who live by their own dress code. Unless you work in a most uncorporate job or as a bartender in an after-hours club, you probably won't get a chance to wear most of what's for sale here. Still, the music's great and the clientele colorful, and

it's fun to see the latest in New York's alternative cutting-edge fashions and accessories, including outrageous wigs and makeup. Most people stop in just for the experience. ♦ M-Sa noon-8PM; Su 1-7PM. 10 E. Eighth St (between Fifth Ave and University Pl). 254.1699

114 Washington Mews Some of these charming little buildings behind the town houses on Washington Square North were originally stables built in the early 1900s. But those on the south side of the alley, more uniform because they were all stuccoed at the same time, date from the '30s. Most are now used by NYU. Their size and quaintness contribute to the small-scale, congenial atmosphere of the neighborhood. ♦ Washington Sq North to E. Eighth St (between University Pl and Fifth Ave)

115 Washington Square North At one time there were 28 of these exemplary Greek Revival row houses—home to the cream of New York society when they were built in 1831, and later the center of an artistic community. The first six constructed, Nos. 21 to 26, by **Martin E. Thompson,** remain intact. Nos. 7 to 13 were gutted in the late 1930s, and the facades alone are left, fronts for an apartment complex now owned by NYU. Of those demolished, No. 1 was at one time or another the home of **Edith Wharton, William Dean Howells,** and **Henry James,** who set his novel *Washington Square* at No. 18, his grandmother's house; No. 3 was where **John Dos Passos** wrote *Manhattan Transfer;* and No. 8 was once the official residence of the mayor. To the west of Fifth Avenue, the mock Federal wing of the apartment tower at 2 Fifth Avenue was a compromise by the builder, **Samuel Rudin,** in response to vociferous community objection to the original plan, which had the tower directly on the square. ♦ Between University Pl and MacDougal St

116 Washington Square Hotel $$ In 1961, this was called the **Hotel Earle** and was the first New York residence of **Bob Dylan,** who played bars and coffeehouses in the neighborhood. Today, its modest accommodations are popular with dollar-conscious graduate students and young Europeans. All 180 rooms have been recently renovated; ask for one overlooking Washington Square. There is no restaurant, porters, or room service, but the location is perfect if you plan to spend a lot of time in the Village. ♦ 103 Waverly Pl (at Washington Sq West). 777.9515; fax 979.8373

117 Washington Square Village life centers around this square, which is the largest public space south of 14th Street. Joggers, children, punks, and grandes dames provide the local color; flea markets and fairs occupy the grounds on weekends. The area was a marsh, a potter's field, a venue for public hangings, and a military parade ground before it was claimed as a public park in 1828. Elaborate, fashionable houses soon appeared around it, and NYU appropriated the east side in the late 1830s. The **Memorial Arch,** designed by **Stanford White** of **McKim, Mead & White,** was originally a wooden monument built in 1889 for the centennial celebration of **George Washington's** inauguration. It became so well liked that private funds were raised to rebuild it permanently in stone. The sculpture of Washington on the west pier was created by **Alexander Stirling Calder,** father of the late **Alexander Calder.** By the 1950s the park had seriously decayed. The city transit authority was using the arch as a bus turnaround, and there was a proposal to run Fifth Avenue underneath it. Popular outrage blocked the tunnel, put a halt to the buses, and gave momentum to the movement to redesign the park—a community effort that was realized in the 1960s. The park has become haven to a variety of street types—performers, wanderers, and drug-dealers—but the local community has made a concerted effort to keep the park safe. Weekend afternoons in warm weather still bring out a wild mix. ♦ Bounded by W. Fourth St, Waverly Pl, University Pl, and MacDougal St

118 Grey Art Gallery An offbeat art gallery in a renovated building, it offers changing high-quality art and photography shows. The backdrop for exhibitions is a grid of white-painted Doric columns. ♦ Tu, Th-F 11AM-6:30PM; W 11AM-8:30PM; Sa 11AM-5PM. 33 Washington Pl (at Washington Sq East). 998.6780

119 Caffè Pane e Cioccolato ★$ Here is lighter fare for the après-park tour. The pasta and salads are surprisingly good, and the cappuccino is excellent. ♦ Cafe ♦ Lunch, dinner, and late-night meals. 10 Waverly Pl (at Mercer St). 473.3944

120 Antique Boutique The city's largest used-clothing store, the Antique Boutique boasts more than 30,000 pieces, including leather motorcycle jackets, men's oversize cashmere coats, and gabardine shirts. It's not unusual to see some of New York's top designers shopping here for ideas they'll take home in their minds if not in a shopping bag. ♦ M-Sa 10AM-10PM; Su 11AM-8PM. 712-714 Broadway (between W. Fourth St and Washington Pl). 460.8830

121 Bottom Line Cabaret A small cabaret-style nightclub with a superlative sound system, Bottom Line was the model for Boston's **Paradise** and LA's **Roxy.** Best known as the launching pad for **Bruce Springsteen** and **Patti Smith,** among others, its days as an industry showcase are long gone. But the club still continues a remarkably consistent booking policy, which includes jazz groups,

comedy, drama, and assorted special presentations. The place is comfortable, clean, and efficient. A bar menu is available. Call for changing show schedules. ♦ Cover, minimum. 15 E. Fourth St (at Mercer St). 228.7880

122 New York University (NYU) More than 15,000 full-time students study at the Washington Square campus of New York's largest private university, comprised of 14 schools, including the **Tisch School of the Arts** and the highly regarded **NYU School of Business and Public Administration.** The campus extends beyond the classroom and dormitory buildings and into the converted lofts and Greek Revival row houses common in Greenwich Village. When the old University Heights campus was sold to the **City University of New York** in 1973, NYU's focus shifted here. Architects **Philip Johnson** and **Richard Foster** were commissioned to make a master plan that would unify the disjointed collection of buildings and enable the campus to handle the increased activity. Their plan called for rebuilding some of the older structures, refacing the existing ones with red sandstone, and establishing design guidelines for future construction. Only three buildings were refaced before the plan was abandoned. ♦ 50 W. Fourth St. 998.4636

Within New York University:

Elmer Holmes Bobst Library Designed by **Johnson** and **Foster** to be the focal point of the university, this stolid-looking cube is 150 feet high and clad in Longmeadow redstone (in the tradition of Washington Square), with a 12-story interior atrium around which the stacks and reading rooms are organized. Chevronlike stairways with gold anodized aluminum railings give scale to the atrium, and the design of the black, gray, and white marble floor, influenced by Palladio's piazza for Venice's San Giorgio Maggiore, adds to the decorative interior detailing that is the antithesis of the austere exterior. ♦ Washington Sq South at La Guardia Pl. 998.2505

123 Judson Memorial Baptist Church This Romanesque church, erected in 1892 by **McKim, Mead & White,** was built as a bridge between the poor to the south of the square and the rich above it, and has always had a full program of social activities. The best part is inside, where you can appreciate the fine stained-glass windows by **John LaFarge.** The church was named for **Adinoram D. Judson,** the first Baptist missionary to Burma. **Judson Hall** and the bell tower above it are now NYU dormitories. ♦ 55 Washington Sq South (between Thompson and Sullivan Sts). 477.0351

124 Hagop Kevorkian Center for Near Eastern Studies Designed in 1972 by **Philip Johnson** and **Richard Foster,** this huge granite building fits snugly into its corner site and is highlighted by an interesting array of angled corner windows. Peer through the double-glass doors on the Sullivan Street entrance to see decorative elements taken from an 18th-century Damascene house. ♦ 50 Washington Sq South (at Sullivan St). 998.8877

125 Vegetarian Paradise 2 ★$ Vegetarian versions of iron steak and Peking duck are made out of bean curd, taro root, etc. There's not a speck of meat in this restaurant. ♦ Vegetarian/Chinese ♦ Lunch and dinner. 144 W. Fourth St (between MacDougal St and Sixth Ave). 260.7130

126 La Lanterna di Vittorio ★★$ Although the least known of the Village's coffeehouses, it's well worth a visit. There's no sidewalk seating, but you can sit as long as you like at the marble tables inside. Order a cup of concentrated espresso or frothy cappuccino and a "Mount St. Helens," a peak of crisp bitter chocolate concealing stripes of chocolate mousse and sweetened coconut—an adult Mounds bar. ♦ Cafe ♦ Daily 10AM-3AM. 129 MacDougal St (at W. Third St). 529.5945

126 Blue Note Jazz Club Top jazz artists perform here nightly at 9PM and 11:30PM (and sometimes again at 1AM) and on weekends for a jazz brunch and matinee at 1PM and 3:30PM. A reasonably priced Continental menu is available. **Grover Washington Jr., Modern Jazz Quartet,** and **Oscar Peterson** all make appearances. ♦ Varying cover, minimum. 131 W. Third St (between MacDougal St and Sixth Ave). Reservations recommended. 475.8592

127 Bleecker Bob's Golden Oldies Despite its name, don't look for Bob's unofficial music hall-of-fame store for hard-to-find vintage albums and old 45s directly *on* Bleecker Street. The selection is voluminous, grouped according to genre (there's everything except classical and opera) and not artist, but the knowledgeable staff knows the location of every last recording and late-night browsing is an encouraged Village tradition. You might be browsing elbow-to-elbow with old rock stars themselves. ♦ M-Th, Su noon-1AM; F-Sa noon-3AM. 118 W. Third St (between MacDougal St and Sixth Ave). 475.9677

127 Caffè Reggio ★$ Built around 1785, this fabulously dingy and dark room was the first cafe in America. You may recognize it from *The Godfather II* and *Serpico.* ♦ Cafe ♦ Daily 9AM-3AM. 119 MacDougal St (at W. Third St). No credit cards. 475.9557

127 Players Theatre When the **Shakespeare Wright Company** first opened this 248-seat theater in 1959, they mainly performed works by the Bard. Today, they rent out the space for a variety of performance venues: music, drama, comedy, one-person shows. ♦ 115 MacDougal St (at W. Third St). 254.5076

127 Minetta Tavern ★$$ The caricatures and murals behind the old oak bar and elsewhere in this Italian restaurant will take you back to the Village of the 1930s. ♦ Italian ♦ Lunch and dinner. 113 MacDougal St (at Minetta Ln). 475.3850

128 La Bohème ★$$ Specialties from Provence enliven the menu of this homey bistro tucked away on tiny Minetta Lane, across from the **Waverly Cinema.** In warmer months the room opens onto a charming, quiet street, a rare situation in noisy Manhattan. Wood-oven pizza is a favored item. ♦ French ♦ Dinner; lunch also on Sunday. 24 Minetta Ln (at Sixth Ave). 473.6447

128 Minetta Lane Theatre This newer Off-Broadway theater presents revues as well as new plays in a more comfortable setting than many. Seats 378. ♦ 18 Minetta Ln (between Minetta St and Sixth Ave). 420.8000

128 1 Minetta Street **DeWitt Wallace** and his wife, **Lila Acheson,** published the first issue of the *Reader's Digest* from a basement apartment in 1922. ♦ At Sixth Ave

129 Speakeasy Of the city's three surviving traditional folk music venues (along with Bitter End and Bottom Line), this one still maintains the "informal" atmosphere. Today, all types of musicians and performers take the stage. It has frequent open mike/cabaret nights. ♦ 107 MacDougal St (between Bleecker St and Minetta Ln). 674.7346

130 Porto Rico Opened in 1907, this old-time coffee bean store is actually one of the Village's younger arrivals. But the regular Saturday morning line of caffeinoholics implies it might be the uncontested favorite. ♦ M-Sa 9AM-9PM; Su noon-7PM. 201 Bleecker St (between Sixth Ave and MacDougal St). 477.5421

131 Caffè Dante ★★$ You will hear Italian, or some dialect, spoken here, but the strong coffee and the let-them-sit-as-long-as-they-want attitude is really what makes it seem so authentic. If you're not counting calories, treat yourself to the cheesecake. ♦ Cafe ♦ Daily 10AM-2AM. 79 MacDougal St (between W. Houston and Bleecker Sts). No credit cards. 982.5275

131 Joe's ★★$ Though the clean, modern rooms belie its age, for more than four decades Joe's has been one of the neighborhood's better choices for zesty Italian cooking. ♦ Italian ♦ Dinner. Closed Tuesday. 79 MacDougal St (between W. Houston and Bleecker Sts). 473.8834

132 Da Silvano ★$$$ An uneven, too-pricey, but quite interesting menu draws heavily on the central Italian kitchen. The elegantly rustic rooms bring in a handsome, affluent clientele. The service is correct, and the wine list well chosen. ♦ Italian ♦ Lunch and dinner. 260 Sixth Ave (between W. Houston and Bleecker Sts). Reservations recommended. 982.0090

133 Film Forum Forced to leave its Watts Street location, the Film Forum moved here in September 1990. The intriguing new space was designed by **Stephen Tilly** and **Jay Hibbs.** The agenda is the same: independent American and foreign films and retrospectives (the work of **Samuel Arkoff** and **Preston Sturges**, for example). ♦ 209 W. Houston St (between Varick St and Sixth Ave). 627.2035

134 Chez Jacqueline ★$$$ Order carefully and you can get a tasty meal in this popular bistro. Kidneys in cognac, cream, and mustard sauce, and roasts of the day are safe main courses. The garlic-laden *brandade* (warm salt cod puree) is a good starter. Skip dessert. ♦ French ♦ Lunch and dinner. 72 MacDougal St (at W. Houston St). Reservations required. 505.0727

134 Aggie's ★★$ Though it looks like an LA diner the attitude is pure New York and the food is hearty home-cooking no matter where you're from. ♦ American ♦ Breakfast, lunch, and dinner; lunch only on Sunday. 146 W. Houston St (at MacDougal St). No credit cards. 673.8994

134 Raffetto's Fresh pasta is made daily (you can see the alchemy going on next door) and cut into a variety of widths before your eyes. Also made fresh are ravioli and tortellini, and imported Italian products to create your own first-rate dishes. There's none better in Manhattan. ♦ Tu-F 9AM-6:30PM; Sa 8AM-6PM. 144 W. Houston St (between Sullivan and MacDougal Sts). 777.1261

135 MacDougal-Sullivan Gardens Historic District These 24 houses date from 1844 to 1850. To attract middle-class professionals, **William Sloane Coffin** (heir to the **W.J. Sloane** furniture fortune) modernized them in 1920 and combined their gardens to make a midblock private park. ♦ Sullivan and MacDougal Sts (between W. Houston and Bleecker Sts)

On a Clear Day You Can See . . . Manhattan!

When the streets get a little too littered, the air a bit too smoggy, and the crowds just too intense, remember that everything looks better from a distance—and New York City's no exception. Unlike the aging actress whose left profile is better than her right, the Big Apple shines every which way, especially from the following vantage points:

Cadman Plaza ♦ At Furnam St, downtown Brooklyn

Circle Line ♦ Pier 83, W. 42nd St at the Hudson River. 563.3200

Columbia Heights ♦ Pineapple St, Brooklyn Heights

Empire State Building Observatories ♦ Fifth Ave at W. 34th St. 736.3100

Fort Tryon Park and the Cloisters ♦ Washington Heights

Liberty State Park ♦ South of the Holland Tunnel, New Jersey

Promenade ♦ Brooklyn Heights

The Rainbow Room Restaurant ♦ 30 Rockefeller Plaza. 632.5000

River Cafe ♦ 1 Water St, Brooklyn Heights. 718/522.5200

Riverside Church ♦ W. 120th St at Riverside Dr. 222.5900

Roosevelt Island Tramway Station ♦ Second Ave at E. 59th St. 832.4543

Staten Island Ferry ♦ Leaves from Battery Park. 806.6940

Statue of Liberty ♦ Liberty Island. 363.3200

The Terrace ♦ 400 W. 119th St at Morningside Dr. 666.9490

Top of the Sixes Restaurant ♦ 666 Fifth Ave, 39th floor. 757.6662

Triborough Bridge ♦ Above Wards Island

Windows on the World Restaurant ♦ 1 World Trade Center, 107th floor. 938.1111

World Trade Center Observation Deck ♦ 2 World Trade Center, 107th floor. 466.7377

It is rumored that during World War II a man secretly lived within the Washington Square Memorial Arch for seven months and was discovered when he hung his wash out to dry.

136 Sullivan Street Playhouse This 153-seat theater has long been home to the longest-running production in American history, *The Fantasticks,* which opened in May 1960. In honor of this feat, Sullivan Street along this block has been dubbed "Fantasticks' Lane" by the city. ◆ 181 Sullivan St (between W. Houston and Bleecker Sts). 674.3838

137 Le Figaro Café $ It's not the Beat hangout it once was, and there are no more underground shows downstairs. Now it's a high-volume beanery serving the weekend blitz on Bleecker Street. It's a little softer on Sunday, but still a teen dream. ◆ Cafe/Bistro ◆ M-Th 10AM-2AM; F-Sa 9AM-4AM; Sa 9AM-2AM. 184 Bleecker St (at MacDougal St). No credit cards. 677.1100

138 Caffè Borgia ★$ This old-world coffeehouse is authentic right up to the smoke-faded mural. It's a perfect place to sip a cappuccino and spend an afternoon with a good book. ◆ Cafe ◆ M-Th, Su 10:30AM-2AM; F 10:30AM-4AM; Sa 10:30AM-5AM. 185 Bleecker St (at MacDougal St). 674.9589. Also: Caffè Borgia II, 161 Prince St. 677.1850

139 Collector's Stadium Once upon a time if you wanted baseball cards, you had to take a rubbery piece of gum along with them. They're collector's items now, and serious collectors come here. ◆ Daily 11AM-7PM. 214 Sullivan St (between Bleecker and W. Third Sts). 353.1531

140 Il Mulino ★★★$$$$ Behind the most unassuming facade is the best Italian restaurant in the Village; only the wait at dinnertime—even with reservations—brings it down a notch. Try it at lunch if you're impatient. Once seated, you'll be treated to crispy fried zucchini. Order any of the pastas, seafood (salmon sometimes comes with porcini mushrooms), and the house red. If you're still in the running after all that, go for the sinfully rich chocolate mousse (this wicked concoction is turned out daily), or if that seems too much, try a poached pear topped with fresh cream. ◆ Italian ◆ Lunch and dinner; dinner only on Saturday. Closed Sunday. 86 W. Third St (between Thompson and Sullivan Sts). Reservations required. 673.3783

141 Nostalgia and All That Jazz Here's an impressive selection of vintage records with an emphasis on jazz, as well as one of New York's best selections of early radio programs and film soundtracks. ◆ Daily 1:30-9PM. 217 Thompson St (between Bleecker and W. Third Sts). 420.1940

142 Village Chess Shop You can play chess from noon to midnight with another expert like yourself, or buy unique chess sets made from materials ranging from nuts and bolts to ivory and onyx. ◆ Daily noon-midnight. 230 Thompson St (between Bleecker and W. Third Sts). 475.9580

142 Grand Ticino ★★$$ Down a few steps from the street, this dark little Italian restaurant will satisfy your romantic notions of an evening out in Greenwich Village—forest-green walls and burnished wood, muted wall sconces, linen tablecloths, waiters who are Italian and really do this for a career . . . aaahhh. And the cuisine won't disappoint either, though it's not the best in the area. Yes, it's the place featured in *Moonstruck.* ◆ Italian ◆ Lunch and dinner. 228 Thompson St (between Bleecker and W. Third Sts). 777.5922

142 El Rincon de España ★$$ This is good Spanish fare if you stick to seafood. A best bet is paella, of which there are several versions. ◆ Spanish ◆ Lunch and dinner. 226 Thompson St (between Bleecker and W. Third Sts). 260.4950

142 Stella Dallas The shop is a good source for reasonably priced men's and women's retro rags from the 1930s to 1950s, collected by a fashion stylist and a clothing designer. ◆ Daily 1-9PM. 218 Thompson St (between Bleecker and W. Third Sts). 674.0447

142 Il Ponte Vecchio ★★$$ This is one of the better neighborhood Italian restaurants. If the *agnoletti* (pasta stuffed with cheese or meat) is not on the menu, request it. ◆ Italian ◆ Lunch and dinner. 206 Thompson St (between Bleecker and W. Third Sts). Reservations recommended. 228.7701

143 Science Fiction Shop Although New York's sci-fi fans may miss the otherworldly atmosphere of the old shop on Eighth Avenue, they're still hooked on the excellent stock of new, out-of-print, and used books and periodicals sold here. ◆ M-Sa 11AM-7PM; Su noon-6PM. 163 Bleecker St (between Thompson and Sullivan Sts). 473.3010

144 Village Gate/Top of the Gate Once a commercial laundry, this vital establishment is run by owner **Art D'Lugoff.** Famous productions include *MacBird* and *Jacques Brel is Alive and Well and Living In Paris.* The intimate upstairs cabaret often has performance revues or comedy shows. Call for show schedules. No cover is charged at the street-level cafe. ◆ Cover, minimum. 160 Bleecker St (at Thompson St). 475.5120

Restaurants/Clubs: Red   **Hotels:** Blue
Shops/ ◉ Outdoors: Green   **Sights/Culture:** Black

145 Tommy's Red Caddy ★★$$ Here's good Mexican food at good prices. This friendly place has one of the best lunch specials in town, and there's never a wait. ♦ Tex-Mex ♦ Lunch, dinner, and late-night meals. 92 W. Houston St (at La Guardia Pl). 777.0300

145 Time Landscape An environmental sculpture of a precolonial forest demonstrates what the area looked like in the 15th century. To gain access, call 431.9563. ♦ W. Houston St (at W. Broadway)

146 Bitter End This small room has served as a springboard for numerous musical careers but now features mostly once-famous folkies and/or young hopefuls performing rock, folk, country, and occasionally comedy. ♦ Cover, minimum. Daily 7:30PM-4AM. 147 Bleecker St (between La Guardia Pl and Thompson St). 673.7030

146 Peculier Pub More than 250 brands of beer from 35 countries are served here to students from almost as many American colleges. ♦ M-Th, Su 4PM-2AM; F 4PM-4AM; Sa 2PM-4AM. 145 Bleecker St (between Thompson St and La Guardia Pl). 353.1327

147 Ennio & Michael ★★$$$ Welcome to a large, well-run, smartly designed, and happily busy trattoria. The hearty food has a bit more refinement than is usually found in such places. Everything from antipasto to pasta is first-rate, and better cannoli cannot be found. ♦ Italian ♦ Lunch and dinner. 539 La Guardia Pl (at Bleecker St). 677.8577

148 University Village This 1966 high-rise housing complex is noteworthy in a city where high-rises are the norm, thanks to **I.M. Pei & Partners'** deft handling of scale, a result of the well-articulated facade. The concrete framing and recessed glass clearly define each apartment unit and provide a straightforward, unadorned exterior pattern. Because of a pinwheel apartment plan, the inner corridors are short and apartments are unusually spacious. Two towers are owned by NYU, the third is a co-op. A 36-foot-high sculpture in the plaza between the towers is an enlargement of a cubist piece by **Picasso.** Pei & Partners used the same exterior treatment in the **Kip's Bay** housing project (Second Avenue at W. 30th Street). ♦ 100 and 110 Bleecker St (at La Guardia Pl); 505 La Guardia Pl (at Bleecker St)

149 Cable Building This 1894 **McKim, Mead & White** building was once the headquarters and powerhouse of the Broadway Cable Traction Company, which operated streetcars propelled by underground cables in the 19th century. ♦ 611 Broadway (at W. Houston St)

Within the Cable Building:

Angelika Film Center Big commerical hits as well as a selection of independent and foreign films are shown in this six-screen cinema. The cafe, a good spot for reading the paper or writing in a journal, serves snacks until midnight. ♦ 995.2000

Bests

Barbara Kirshenblatt-Gimblett
Folklorist, Tisch School of the Arts, NYU

Fresh-smoked mozzarella, still warm and milky, from **Joe's Latticini** on Thompson Street.

Silvery glints in **Lower East Side** skies as pigeon flyers exercise their birds.

The elusive aroma of vanilla, rotten eggs, almonds, turpentine, and old shoes exuded by durian in **Chinatown** as the thick prickly skin splits and exposes the coveted creamy fruit.

Reading Yiddish books salvaged from Hitler's Europe at the **YIVO Institute for Jewish Research.**

Thirty varieties of local apples at the **Union Square Greenmarket** in late September.

Spotting fuzzy dice, palm crosses (during the Easter season), air freshener, magnetic saints, lucky charms, and other dashboard ornaments in parked cars.

Thanking André Soltner after lunch at **Lutèce.**

Statue of Puck on the **Puck Building,** built in 1885.

Rummaging through old prints at **Pageant Book and Print Shop.**

Rustic Korean stews and incendiary homemade pickles at **Woo Chon Restaurant** (5 W. 36th St).

Marks of the hand on the city—chalk lines on the asphalt for skelly and hopscotch, painted signs for shoe repair and fish shops, barber poles.

Walking Tour C of **Greenwich Village** in the *AIA Guide to New York City* on an autumn evening.

Kasuri (indigo ikat) pants and jackets at **Kimono House** on Thompson Street.

Any performance by the **Wooster Group.**

Speed chess, backgammon, and shoe shines on 42nd Street, outside the **New York Public Library.**

Edna Lewis' crab cakes at **Gage & Tollner.**

New York is the only American city to house an American embassy, the United States Mission, located across the street from the United Nations.

East Village

The East Village is counterculture central, where spiked hair and nose rings are as common as fur coats on Madison Avenue. In this neighborhood bounded by **Broadway**, the **East River**, and **Houston** and **14th streets**, many of the galleries, boutiques, clubs, and restaurants represent the cutting edge of what's *next* in downtown.

Believe it or not, the East Village was once the grandest part of Greenwich Village. **Governor Peter Stuyvesant's** estate originally covered the area from the present Fourth Avenue to the East River and from Fifth to 17th streets. He was buried beneath his chapel, now the site of **St. Mark's-in-the-Bowery Church** (built in 1799), known as much for its ministry to the disadvantaged and far-out religious services as for its historical significance. In the 1830s, the houses of the **Astors, Vanderbilts,** and **Delanos** lined Lafayette Street from Great Jones Street to Astor Place. Almost nothing is left from those times except the **Old Merchants' House** on Fourth Street near Lafayette Street and

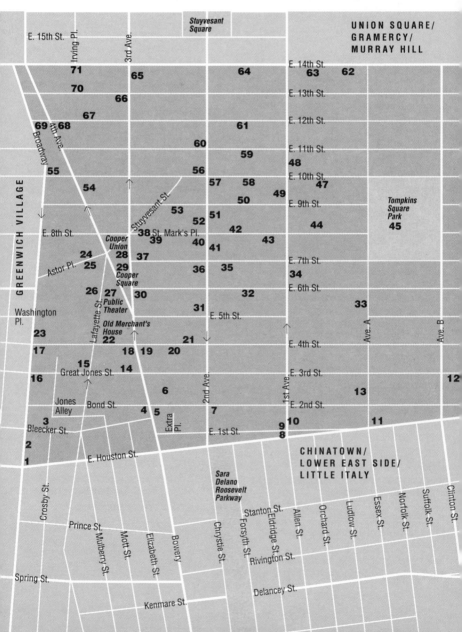

the remaining homes of **Colonnade Row** (also known as **LaGrange Terrace**), where **John Jacob Astor** and **Warren Delano, FDR's** grandfather, lived.

Astor Place was once the scene of the **Vauxhall Gardens**, where people went in the summer to enjoy music and theater. It was replaced by the popular **Astor Place Opera House**, which is remembered chiefly for the 1849 riot between rival claques (hands hired to applaud a certain performer or act) of the British actor **William Macready**, in which 34 people were killed (or 22, depending on which account you read) before the militia brought the crowd under control. Astor Place was named for the first John Jacob Astor, who arrived from Germany in 1789 at the age of 21 with $25. Before his death at the age of 85, he had made a fortune in fur trading and Manhattan real estate.

The **Astor Library**, built with a bequest from John Jacob Astor, is now the home base of the **New York Shakespeare Festival** at the **Public Theater**, a multimedia, multistage enterprise, where something exciting is always on the boards or on the screen. Other architectural survivors from the 1850s are the Italianate **Cooper Union**, the country's first coeducational college and the first open to all races and creeds; and **McSorley's Old Ale House**, where everyone who counts has had a glass of the special dark ale since it opened in the mid-19th century. **John Sloan** did a painting of it, and **Brendan Behan** hung out in a corner near the potbellied stove.

Little India, the stretch of Sixth Street between First and Second avenues, contains at least 20 Indian restaurants, with another half-dozen spilling over onto the avenues. The area got its name in 1968, when five brothers arrived here from India and found that they liked everything about New York except the distance they had to travel to find a good Indian meal. One of them solved the problem by opening his own restaurant, and before long his brothers got into the business as well; others soon followed. (The largest Indian community is out in Queens, where the most recent immigrants have settled; the second largest occupies the stretch of Lexington Avenue in the mid-20s.)

Near Astor Place at Cooper Square (Third Avenue) and Seventh Street is **Little Ukraine**—a world of Byzantine churches with onion domes, shops with Slavic music and painted eggs, and restaurants serving piroshki and stuffed cabbage

1 Louisiana Community Bar and Grill ★$$
Formerly **K-Paul's,** this is the place where you can get Cajun cuisine from chefs trained by **Paul Prudhomme** and listen to blues, jazz, and zydeco musicians. ♦ Cajun ♦ Lunch and dinner. 622 Broadway (at E. Houston St). Reservations recommended. 460.9633

2 Center for Book Arts The Center offers a gallery and teaching and work space for hand-producing and publishing books, including hand bookbinding, papermaking, and letterpress printing. ♦ Gallery M-F 10AM-6PM; Sa 10AM-4PM. 626 Broadway (between E. Houston and Bleecker Sts), fifth floor. 460.9768

2 New York Mercantile Exchange Herman J. Schwartzmann designed this cast-iron jungle with bamboo stems, lilies, and roses complemented with Oriental motifs in 1882. The Exchange, obviously no longer here, was once headquarters for all the big butter-and-egg men and wholesale dealers in coffee, tea, and spices. The ground floor is currently occupied by **Urban Outfitters,** clothier to many a university student. ♦ M-Sa 10AM-10PM; Su noon-8PM. 628 Broadway (between E. Houston and Bleecker Sts). 475.0009

3 Bayard Condict Building The one and only **Louis Sullivan** building in New York is hidden among the industrial high-rises on Bleecker Street. The Bayard (formerly the **Condict Building**) was an anachronism even when it was completed in 1898, when the Renaissance Revival style that followed the 1893 Chicago World's Fair turned popular taste away from the elegant, quintessentially American designs of Sullivan and the Chicago School. The intricate cornice filigree and soaring vertical lines of the terracotta-clad steel piers are Sullivan trademarks; the six angels at the roofline were applied under client duress. ♦ 65 Bleecker St (at Crosby St)

4 Bouwerie Lane Theatre In 1874, when the lower end of the Bowery was a theater district, **Henry Engelbert** built this fanciful cast-iron building as a bank. Today, it is the home of the **Jean Cocteau Repertory,** an unusual company of resident actors that often performs several works in the same week. Its presentations are usually classical plays or plays by writers better known for other literary endeavors. ♦ 330 Bowery (at Bond St). 677.0060

5 CBGB and OMFUG Long after everyone has forgotten what the initials of this Bowery dive stand for (Country, Bluegrass, Blues, and Other Music for Uplifting Gourmandisers), they will remember it as the birthplace of punk rock. A long, dark bar illuminated by neon beer signs, it still plays host to an array of groups under a wide banner of styles. Uptowners used to go slumming here; now it attracts the suburban hard-core crowd and the nostalgic, but it still boasts one of the best rock PA systems in town. ♦ Cover. Daily 8PM-3AM. 315 Bowery (at Bleecker St). 982.4052

6 New York Marble Cemetery Located on the inside portion of the block (enter from an alley on Second Street), this early 1800s cemetery was one of the first built in the city and is one of the very few left in Manhattan. The burial vaults are underground, and the names of those interred are carved into marble tablets set into a perimeter wall that surrounds a small grassy area. Down the block (52-74 E. Second Street) is the **New York City Marble Cemetery,** started in 1831 along the same nonsectarian lines but with aboveground vaults and handsome headstones. Genealogists can trace New York's early first families—the **Scribners, Varicks, Beekmans, Van Zandts, Hoyts,** and one branch of the **Roosevelts**—from tombstone information. Burial here is restricted to the descendants of the original vault owners, but no one has applied since 1917. ♦ Bounded by E. Second and E. Third Sts (between Second Ave and Bowery)

7 Anthology Film Archives Located in the **Second Avenue Courthouse** building, the Archives is a center for the preservation and exhibition of film and video works. Only students, scholars, museums, and universities have access to the Archives' library, but the daily screenings are open to all. Call for the schedule. ♦ 32 Second Ave (at E. Second St). 477.2714

8 Style Swami Colorful women's and men's African clothing designed by **Alpana Bawa** is showcased in this shop, along with home furnishings. ♦ M, W-Su noon-7PM. 70 E. First St (between First and Second Aves). 254.1249

City Lore

8 City Lore In a gentrified brownstone just off First Avenue, a group of serious folklorists explore New York cultural traditions through photo and tape archives, oral histories, discussion groups, music and film festivals, and concerts. ♦ M-F 9:30AM-6:30PM; call for an appointment. 72 E. First St (between First and Second Aves). 529.1955

9 Boca Chica ★$ Wild *musica latina* on weekends makes this funky East Village club a must for night owls. Other days of the week are only slightly calmer, with rivers of exotic Brazilian drinks keeping customers in jovial spirits and a good South American menu that can get as hot as the salsa music. ♦ South American ♦ Dinner; brunch, lunch, and dinner on Sunday. 13 First Ave (at E. First St). 473.0108

10 ARKA This general store for the Ukrainian community stocks tapes, records, books and newspapers, embroidery threads and fabrics, egg decorating kits, and more. ♦ M-Sa 10AM-6PM; Su 10AM-3PM. 26 First Ave (between E. First and E. Second Sts). 473.3550

11 The Spiral A live-music club with a circular theme (you'll know you're almost there when you spot the neon curlicue above the entrance), this place prefers the offbeat (a jazz-infused funk band is cool) to the more conventional rock- and blues-type bands. ♦ Cover. Call for show times. 244 E. Houston St (at Ave A). 353.1740

12 Nuyorican Poet's Cafe $ By the time this forum for young Puerto Rican poets in the 1970s closed in 1982, one of the founding members, the late **Miguelo Pinero,** had achieved international acclaim as a playwright. Back in business in 1990, the place is packed with poets and an eclectic audience. ♦ Cafe ♦ Cover. W-Sa 8PM-closing. 236 E. Third St (between Aves B and C). 505.8183

13 Two Boots ★$ Louisiana cuisine with a remote Italian twist is the specialty of this skylit East Village original. Try the shrimp *Mosca* (skillet-baked on a bed of spicy Cajun breadcrumbs) or shrimp pizza. If you can't make it in to admire the counterculture memorabilia embedded in the see-through plastic bar or to play the Cajun-flavored jukebox, you can still order the pizza for home delivery from **Two Boots to Go** across the street (505.5450). ♦ Cajun ♦ Lunch and dinner. Closed Monday. 37 Ave A (between E. Second and E. Third Sts). 505.2276

14 Great Jones Cafe ★$ Blackened fish and other decent, reasonably priced eats are served in a loud and lively roadside bar atmosphere. ♦ Cajun ♦ Dinner. 54 Great Jones St (between Bowery and Lafayette St). No credit cards. 674.9304

14 Engine Company 33 Ernest Flagg and W.B. Chambers, the architects of the U.S. Naval Academy and Scribner's Bookstore, designed this 1898 home for Engine Company 33. The company was formed in 1865, the same year the professional fire department replaced volunteer companies. ♦ 44 Great Jones St (between Bowery and Lafayette St). 570.4233

15 376-380 Lafayette Street This richly ornamented yet somewhat uncomfortable warehouse is most notable because it was designed by **Henry J. Hardenbergh** in 1888, several years after he designed the **Dakota** apartments up on W. 72nd Street. ♦ At Great Jones St

15 Time Cafe ★$$ Healthy foods—including great salads and breads—are emphasized in this popular American eatery. Time feeds the trendy crowds from breakfast until late at night. Within the cafe itself is a Moroccan club called **Fez,** which offers jazz, poetry readings, and cushy couches. ♦ American ♦ Breakfast, lunch, dinner, and late-night meals. 380 Lafayette St (at Great Jones St). Reservations recommended. 533.7000

16 Acme Bar & Grill ★$$ Here is carbo-loading at its finest—Cajun-style chicken, jambalaya, gumbo, and the best mashed potatoes with cream gravy. A ledge along one entire wall is lined with every conceivable kind of hot sauce, if you dare. And there's a music room (separate cover charge) downstairs. ♦ Southern ♦ Lunch and dinner. 9 Great Jones St (between Lafayette St and Broadway). 420.1934

17 Tower Records The ultimate store for the listener comprises a main building on Broadway and E. Fourth Street for pop, jazz, R&B, dance, and more; a classical annex next door (on Lafayette Street); and video and electronic annexes in between. If they don't have it, chances are it's going to be tough to find. ♦ Daily 9AM-midnight. 692 Broadway (at E. Fourth St). 505.1500. Also at: 1961 Broadway. 799.2500

18 Marion's Continental Restaurant and Lounge ★$$ Marion's was the place to be in the 1960s, when senators, presidents, and movie stars were regulars. It closed in the early 1970s because the glamorous proprietor, **Marion Nagy,** wanted to spend more time with her family. In 1990, Marion's son and a business partner reopened the landmark with much of its signature decor intact: the corner banquette reserved for **John** and **Jackie Kennedy,** the tropical fish tank, the tile bar, and the walls adorned with clown paintings, **Utrillo** reproductions, and signed photographs of **Clark Gable** and **Frank Sinatra.** Vodka Gibsons (Marion's drink), old-fashioneds, and Manhattans are inexpensive. The quality of the food is not uniformly dependable, although the Caesar salad and the lamb shank with lentils are both good. ♦ Continental ♦ Dinner. 354 Bowery (between E. Fourth and Great Jones Sts). No credit cards. 475.7621

19 Phebes Place During the 1960s this was a popular hangout among Off-Broadway playwrights **Sam Shepard, Robert Patrick,** and **Leonard Melfi.** Today, it continues to attract the East Village arts crowd as well as a lot of police officers. Cheap pitchers of domestic beer pull in the college students. ♦ M-F 4PM-4AM; Sa 5PM-4AM. 361 Bowery (at E. Fourth St). 473.9008

Restaurants/Clubs: Red   Hotels: Blue
Shops/ 🌳 Outdoors: Green   **Sights/Culture: Black**

20 La Mama E.T.C. First called **Cafe La Mama,** this theater has been in the vanguard of the Off-Broadway movement since 1962. Under the direction of **Ellen Stewart,** it has been instrumental in presenting both American and international experimental theater artists to this country. Stewart nurtured playwrights **Sam Shepard, Lanford Wilson, Ed Bullins, Tom Eyen, Israel Horovitz,** and **Elizabeth Swados,** among others. Directors **Tom O'Horgan, Marshall Mason, Wilford Leach, Andrei Serban,** and **Peter Brook** have helped to stage many extraordinary productions here. ♦ 74A E. Fourth St (between Second and Third Aves). 475.7710. Also at: The Annex, 66 E. Fourth St. 473.8745

21 Cucina di Pesce ★$$ A more reasonably priced good seafood restaurant—with Italian overtones—would be hard to find in Manhattan. To accommodate the crowds, an annex called **Frutti di Mare** has been opened across the street (No. 28) and serves lunch and dinner. Both are on the same block as the **La Mama** theater complex. ♦ Italian ♦ Dinner. 87 E. Fourth St (between Second Ave and Bowery). No credit cards. 260.6800

22 Old Merchants' House This outstanding example of an 1830s Greek Revival town house remains intact with interiors and furnishings just the way they were when wealthy merchant **Seabury Tredwell** and his family lived here, thanks to Tredwell's daughter, **Gertrude.** Having fallen in love with an unacceptable suitor whom she was forbidden to wed, Gertude chose not to marry at all and, after her father's death, resolved to maintain the family home just as her father would have liked. Paintings, furniture, china, and books give an insight into their tasteful and conservative style. The hours that the house is open to the public may be expanded. Call for more information. ♦ Admission. Groups of more than 20 by appointment Monday through Friday; individuals Sunday 1-4PM. Closed August. 29 E. Fourth St (between Bowery and Lafayette St). 777.1089

23 Bayamo ★$$ The menu seems a little gimmicky, but the food is consistently good. In fact, Bayamo is one of the better eateries on the lower Broadway strip. The inventive appetizers include fried or grilled chicken wings and fried wontons. Happy hours and late nights get a little crowded, and sometimes the mob is six-deep at the bar, clamoring for silly drinks. If that's not your speed, maybe lunch or early evening on the balcony is best. Note painter **Nadia Rodin's** wonderful party scene on the wall just as you enter. ♦ Cuban/Chinese ♦ Lunch and dinner; late-night meals also on Friday and Saturday. 704 Broadway (between Washington Pl and E. Fourth St). 475.5151

23 Shakespeare & Co. Though not related to its Paris namesake, this bookstore is a favorite among New Yorkers. ♦ M-Th, Su 10AM-11PM; F-Sa 10AM-midnight. 716 Broadway (between Washington Pl and E. Fourth St). 529.1330. Also at: 2259 Broadway. 580.7800

24 Cooper Square Books At 6,000 square feet, this is one of the largest independent bookstores in the city, with good philosophy, literature, travel, and children's sections. ♦ M-Th 9AM-11PM; F 9AM-midnight; Sa 10AM-midnight; Su 10AM-10PM. 21 Astor Pl (between Broadway and Lafayette St). 533.2595

25 Astor Place Hairstylists Considering all there is to do in New York, it may seem strange that watching haircuts has become a spectator sport on Astor Place, but look at the pictures in the window and on the walls and you'll understand why. The prices are extremely low, too. One of the signs in the window says they also do regular haircuts, but don't count on it. ♦ M-Sa 8AM-8PM; Su 9AM-6PM. 2 Astor Pl (between Fourth Ave and Broadway). 475.9854

25 Astor Wines and Spirits The selection is large, with generally good prices, but the staff is sometimes less than thoroughly knowledgeable. ♦ M-Sa 9AM-9PM. 12 Astor Pl (at Lafayette St). 674.7500

26 Astor Place Theatre Across the street from the more artistically ambitious **Public Theater,** this 299-seat Off-Broadway venue has long runs (*The Foreigner*) and interesting musicals (*Tent Meeting, Middle of Nowhere*) that click with the theater crowd. ♦ 434 Lafayette St (between Astor Pl and E. Fourth St). 254.4370

26 Colonnade Row The city's business and social leaders—the **Astors, Vanderbilts, Delanos**—once occupied the homes on Colonnade Row, also known as **LaGrange Terrace.** Only four of the nine built in 1833 by **Seth Greer** remain. The streetfront Corinthian colonnade was used to give the row a sense of unity and solidity. Despite designation as a New York City Landmark, these unique and historic structures have fallen into disrepair. ♦ 428-434 Lafayette St (between Astor Pl and E. Fourth St)

Inside the doorway of the Public Theater are two white rectangular columns. "May Peace Prevail on Earth" is written on each in Japanese and English. The columns were sent to the late Joseph Papp by the Society of Prayer for World Peace, an organization that does not aim to convert lost souls, but is dedicated to planting as many peace poles as possible.

26 Indochine ★★$$ The trendy French/Vietnamese food is consistently good (though not as good as either a true French or Vietnamese bistro). The softly lit tropical-themed room is lovely, and the people-watching lovelier still. ♦ French/Vietnamese ♦ Dinner. 430 Lafayette St (between Astor Pl and E. Fourth St). Reservations recommended. 505.5111

27 Public Theater The landmark home of the **New York Shakespeare Festival (NYSF)** has six theaters. The Romanesque Revival buildings were designed for **John Jacob Astor** by **Alexander Saeltzer** (south wing, 1853), **Griffin Thomas** (center, 1859), and **Thomas Stent** (north wing, 1881) as New York City's first free library and served as the **Hebrew Immigrant Aid Sheltering Society.** These structures were on the verge of being demolished in the mid-1960s, when that dynamic man of the theater **Joseph Papp** came to the rescue with the NYSF and architect **Giorgio Cavaglieri.** Today, the NYSF not only manages to continually mount superb presentations but always seems to find the money needed to avert financial crises. The list of extraordinary shows that originated here and went on to Broadway includes *Hair* by **Gerome Ragni** and **James Rado**, *That Championship Season* by **Jason Miller**, **Michael Bennett's** *A Chorus Line* (which won three Pulitzers), **David Rabe's** *Sticks and Bones*, **Caryl Churchill's** *Serious Money*, and **Rupert Holmes'** *The Mystery of Edwin Drood*. About 25 theatrical productions are mounted each year; the lively **Festival Latino** is a regular summer event. Film viewings were introduced in 1981.

Cavaglieri—who also renovated the **Jefferson Market Courthouse**—did an admirable job salvaging much of the interior: many of the theater spaces are impressive, and the entrance and lobby still include the original Corinthian colonnade. **Quiktix,** half-price tickets for performances from Tuesday to Sunday, are available two hours before curtain. ♦ Theaters: Newman (seats 299); Anspacher (seats 299); Martinson (seats 1,650); LuEster (seats 135); Susan Stein Shiva (seats 100); Little Theater (seats 90). 425 Lafayette St (between E. Fourth St and Astor Pl). 598.7150

28 Cooper Union
Founded by multimillionaire **Peter Cooper** in 1859, this is a full-tuition-scholarship private college (shown at right). The inventor and industrialist, so brilliant with problems of application in the country's young

NICHOLAS OHOTIN

iron and rail industries, spent his entire life ashamed that he'd never learned to spell or read, and the opening of Cooper Union was his attempt to help underprivileged young men and women get the education they deserved but couldn't afford. Cooper Union was the first coeducational college, the first open to all races and creeds, and the first to offer free adult education courses, many at night, to accommodate those working in the daytime. Architect **Frederick A. Petersen** used the rails Cooper produced in his ironworks in the college's construction (a grid of T-shaped rails was used to transmit loads to the walls). This building is considered by some to be the oldest extant building in America framed with steel beams, and was declared a National Landmark in 1962. Two other breakthroughs in the building were the use of an elevator and the placing of vents under each of the 900 seats in the **Great Hall** auditorium—in the basement—through which fresh air was pumped. The Great Hall has, since the school's founding, been the scene of open expression on crucial issues of the day, from suffrage to civil rights. **Abraham Lincoln** delivered one of his most eloquent speeches here shortly before he was nominated as a presidential candidate. Both the NAACP and the American Red Cross were started in the building. Cooper Union still sponsors provocative lectures and many other events under its **Great Hall Programs,** which are open to the public. When architect **John Hejduk** gutted and renovated the building in 1974, he provided pristine classrooms, offices, and exhibition space—all with a high-modern Corbusian vocabulary. **Augustus Saint-Gaudens, Adolph A. Weinman,** and **Leo Friedlander** were graduates of the art school. More recent alumni include **Milton Glaser, Alex Katz,** and **Seymour Chwast.** ♦ 7 E. Seventh St (at Fourth Ave). 353.4195

29 Cooper Square The statue of **Peter Cooper** seated in this triangular park is by **Augustus Saint-Gaudens,** a former Cooper Union student. Its base is by **Stanford White,** who spent his boyhood in this neighborhood. Cooper was a self-made man who used the profits from a small grocery store to buy a glue factory up on 34th Street. He then invented a way to make better glue and became the biggest manufacturer in the country. Cooper invested the profits from that enterprise in Manhattan real estate and branched out to Baltimore, where he made a fortune selling land. When iron ore was found on his property, he went into business making rails for the expanding railroads. He also went into partnership with **Cyrus Field** to develop the transatlantic telegraph cable, and with **Samuel F.B. Morse** to perfect his telegraph. Cooper was inventive himself, and as a boy created an automatic fly swatter and a self-rocking cradle. ♦ E. Seventh St (at Fourth Ave)

30 Manhattan Fruitier Owner **Jehv Gold** puts together stupendous baskets filled with exotic seasonal fruits from all over the world. No matter what your needs are, he can supply the appropriate arrangement. Delivery in and around Manhattan is available. ♦ M-F 9AM-5PM. 210 E. Sixth St (between Second and Third Aves). 260.2280

31 Sugar Reef ★$$ A colorful decor, an Island menu, and an active bar scene attract an interesting crowd. Trends come and go, but Sugar Reef seems to have found its niche, thanks to the consistently good food. Chicken and shrimp dishes are particularly tasty, and the mood music is always right. ♦ West Indian ♦ Dinner. 93 Second Ave (between E. Fifth and E. Sixth Sts). 477.8427

32 Back From Guatemala The best merchandise from Central and South America and Asia, including scarves, exotic ethnic clothing, and various crafts are featured in this appealing shop. For a twist on the same theme, visit **Chrysalis** up the block at 340 E. Sixth Street (533.8252). Run by the same people, it focuses on contemporary ethnic jewelry, accessories, stationery, and gift items. ♦ M 1-10PM; Tu-Sa noon-10:30PM; Su 2-10:30PM. 306 E. Sixth St (between First and Second Aves). 260.7010

32 Passage to India ★★$ With more than 20 restaurants, competition is heavy on this block in Little India, but this small spot is among the best. The freshly baked breads and tandoori specials are highlights. ♦ Indian ♦ Lunch, dinner, and late-night meals. 308 E. Sixth St (between First and Second Aves). 529.5770

32 Mitali ★★$$ This is generally considered to be the most popular Indian restaurant on the block, and justifiably so. ♦ Indian ♦ Lunch and dinner. 334 E. Sixth St (between First and Second Aves). Reservations recommended. 533.2508. Also at: 296 Bleecker St. 989.1367

33 Ci Vediamo ★$ The kitsch murals of gondolas and crooning strains of "Moon River" almost make you forget this is the East Village. The pastas range from good to excellent, especially when you remember they're a third the price they'd be on uptown Madison Avenue. Try the lusty tomato-based *fettuccine alla siciliana* with eggplant and mozzarella, and save room for the classic Italian ricotta cheesecake. *Ci Vediamo* means "see you later," and they probably will. ♦ Italian ♦ Dinner and late-night meals. 85 Ave A (between E. Fifth and E. Sixth Sts). No credit cards. 995.5300

34 Miracle Grill ★$$ Grilled chicken on skewers with papaya-tomatillo salsa, New York steak with *chipotle* (smoked jalapeño pepper) butter, and vanilla-bean flan are just a few of the inventive specialties served at this tiny and casual restaurant. ♦ Southwestern ♦ Dinner. 12 First Ave (between E. Sixth and E. Seventh Sts). 254.2353

35 Caffè della Pace ★$ This warm and unpretentious little cafe, a few steps up from the street, has good cappuccino and great *tiramisù* (literal translation—"pick-me-up"), which is too rich to describe. ♦ Cafe ♦ Lunch, dinner, and late-night meals. 48 E. Seventh St (between First and Second Aves). No credit cards. 529.8024

36 Kiev ★★$ A better buy, not to mention better borscht, would be hard to find. This is one of the best low-down restaurants in town. The constant traffic sometimes makes it difficult to get a table, but the food and prices are wonderful. The fried cheese blintzes, fried or boiled cheese or potato *pirogen,* fried veal cutlets, and all of the soups are very satisfying. ♦ Russian ♦ Daily 24 hours. 117 Second Ave (at E. Seventh St). No credit cards. 674.4040

37 St. George's Ukrainian Catholic Church An old-world cathedral with modern touches, this 1977 church by **Apollinaire Osadea** is the anchor of a Ukrainian neighborhood of more than 1,500 people. ♦ 33 E. Seventh St (at Cooper Sq)

37 The Fragrance Shoppe Owner **Michael DeMeo,** formerly a city fireman, and his congenial staff love to get to know their customers and share their knowledge of fragrance and bodycare products. They'll introduce you to the store's own line, which includes facial and skincare products, body oils, and shampoos; help you develop a signature scent using a selection of more than a hundred essential perfume oils; and show you the products they import from other companies, including Mason Pearson brushes from England. ♦ M-Sa noon-8PM; Su 1-7PM. 21 E. Seventh St (at Cooper Sq). 254.8950

37 McSorley's Old Ale House Not so long ago, this saloon, which has been here since 1854, had a men-only policy, and it was among the first targets of the women's liberation movement in 1970. The current clientele, which includes women, is mostly college students, but except for that, McSorley's hasn't changed much since it was a gathering place for crusty old Irishmen who slept in Bowery hotels and spent all their waking hours here. ♦ Daily 10AM-1AM. 15 E. Seventh St (at Cooper Sq). No credit cards. 473.9148

37 Surma This Ukrainian shop has Slavic cards, books, videos, and records, plus egg-decorating kits and honey. ♦ M-Sa 11AM-6PM. 11 E. Seventh St (at Cooper Sq). 477.0729

38 St. Mark's Place In the 1960s, this extension of Eighth Street from the Bowery to Tompkins Square Park was the East Coast capital of hippiedom. The sidewalks were crowded with flower children and the smell of marijuana was everywhere. Among the shared interests of the street's denizens was the famous rock club **The Electric Circus,** which was in a former Polish social club at No. 23. Then, in the 1970s, the street became the punk boardwalk, and multicolored Mohawks filled the air. The street is quieter these days—witness the corner of Second Avenue, where the old **St. Mark's Cinema** has been converted into co-op apartments and retail stores have been taken over by **The Gap**—but the street's far from dead. ♦ Ave A to Third Ave

Book Nooks

New York City is a book lover's paradise. Just take a look at the eight-plus pages of bookstore listings in the *Yellow Pages.* Following are some of the favorites. (Many of these are described in *New York City ACCESS.* Check the index for page numbers.)

Art and Architecture

Asia Society ♦ 725 Park Ave. 288.6400

Hacker Art Books ♦ 45 W. 57th St. 688.7600

Morton Books ♦ 989 Third Ave. 421.9025

Rizzoli ♦ 31 W. 57th St. 759.2424

Untitled ♦ 159 Prince St. 982.2088

Urban Center Books ♦ 457 Madison Ave (within Villard Houses). 935.3595

Foreign Language

Kinokuniya Bookstore (Japanese) ♦ 10 W. 49th St. 765.1461

Lectorum Publications (Spanish) ♦ 137 W. 14th St. 929.2833

Librarie de France ♦ 610 Fifth Ave. 581.8810

Libreria Hispanica ♦ 115 Fifth Ave. 673.7400

Vanni (Italian) ♦ 30 W. 12th St. 675.6336

General Interest

Books & Co. ♦ 939 Madison Ave. 737.1450

Burlington Bookshop ♦ 1082 Madison Ave. 288.7420

Coliseum Books ♦ 1771 Broadway. 757.8381

Endicott Booksellers ♦ 450 Columbus Ave. 787.6300

Gotham Book Mart and Gallery ♦ 41 W. 47th St. 719.4448

Madison Avenue Bookshop ♦ 833 Madison Ave. 535.6130

St. Mark's Books ♦ 12 St. Mark's Pl. 260.7853

Shakespeare & Co. ♦ 716 Broadway. 529.1330; 2259 Broadway. 580.7800

Tower Books ♦ 383 Lafayette St. 228.5100

Secondhand and Out-of-Print

Academy Books and Records ♦ 10 W. 18th St. 242.4848

Argosy Bookstore ♦ 116 E. 59th St. 753.4455

Gotham Book Mart and Gallery ♦ 41 W. 47th St. 719.4448

Gryphon Bookshop ♦ 2246 Broadway. 362.0706

Strand Bookstore ♦ 828 Broadway. 473.1452

Specialty

Applause Theater Books (performing arts) ♦ 211 W. 71st St. 496.7511

Biography Bookstore (biographies) ♦ 400 Bleecker St. 807.8655

Books of Wonder (children's) ♦ 132 Seventh Ave South. 989.3270; 464 Hudson St. 645.8006

The Drama Bookshop (dramatic arts) ♦ 723 Seventh Ave South. 944.0595

East West Books (Eastern philosophy and holistic health) ♦ 78 Fifth Ave. 243.5994; 568 Columbus Ave. 787.7552

Forbidden Planet (science fiction and comics) ♦ 227 E. 59th St. 751.4386; 821 Broadway. 473.1576

Joseph Patelson Music House (classical music) ♦ 160 W. 56th St. 582.5840

Judith's Room (feminist) ♦ 681 Washington St. 727.7330

Kitchen Arts & Letters (food and wine; cookbooks) ♦ 1435 Lexington Ave. 876.5550

Liberation Bookshop (African-American History; African History) ♦ 421 Lenox Ave. 281.4615

Murder Ink (mysteries) ♦ 2486 Broadway. 362.8905

Mysterious Bookshop (mysteries) ♦ 129 W. 56th St. 765.0900

New York Bound Bookshop (New York) ♦ 50 Rockefeller Plaza. 245.8503

Oscar Wilde Memorial Bookshop (gay and lesbian) ♦ 15 Christopher St. 255.8097

Paraclete (theology) ♦ 146 E. 74th St. 535.4050

A Photographer's Place (photography) ♦ 133 Mercer St. 431.9358

Revolution Books (revolutionary) ♦ 13 E. 16th St. 691.3345

Three Lives & Company (literature) ♦ 154 W. 10th St. 741.2069

Traveller's Bookstore (travel) ♦ 22 W. 52nd St. 664.0995

39 St. Mark's Bookshop This popular bookstore is a good source for journals on African culture, feminist issues, socialism, and cultural theory. ♦ Daily 11AM-11:30PM. 12 St. Mark's Pl (between Second and Third Aves). 260.7853

39 St. Mark's Sounds A true music-lover's store, it doesn't have the conveyor-belt feeling of **Tower Records,** and they sell and trade used records in excellent condition. ♦ Daily 11AM-11:30PM. 20 St. Mark's Pl (between Second and Third Aves). 677.3444

39 Dojo ★$ The menu combines Oriental flavors and healthy food (try the chicken sukiyaki salad or the incredibly inexpensive soy burger with tahini sauce). For warm-weather dining, choose the outdoor porch, which is great for people-watching, though not so swell when panhandlers and car exhaust mingle at your table. ♦ Oriental/Health food ♦ Lunch, dinner, and late-night meals. 24 St. Mark's Pl (between Second and Third Aves). No credit cards. 674.9821

39 Khyber Pass ★$$ A former judge of the Supreme Court in Afghanistan runs this authentic Afghan restaurant. Sit back on a throw pillow and enjoy stuffed ravioli with lamb, tender, moist lamb kebabs, fresh salads with yogurt dressing and, for dessert, rice pudding topped with pistachios. ♦ Afghan ♦ Lunch, dinner, and late-night meals. 34 St. Mark's Pl (between Second and Third Aves). 473.0989

40 Gem Spa Smoke Shop Take a break from browsing at this old-style newsstand that sells just about every relevant paper and periodical, and slide up to the counter for a luscious egg cream, the quintessential New York drink. Nowadays they're served up by the current owners, who are East Indian. ♦ Daily 24 hours. 131 Second Ave (at St. Mark's Pl)

40 B&H Dairy and Vegetarian Cuisine Restaurant ★$ No one is still around from the days when B&H stood for **Bergson and Heller** and the clientele was the cast and crew of the Yiddish theater productions along Second Avenue, not even the classic countermen who used to patrol the place. But then again, neither are the junkies who used to fall asleep in their Yankee bean soup. The restaurant has been refurbished several times (the vegetarian offerings are quite recent), but thank goodness they haven't messed with the challah recipe. The French toast is heavenly. ♦ Vegetarian ♦ Breakfast, lunch, and dinner. 127 Second Ave (between E. Seventh St and St. Mark's Pl). 505.8065

41 Orpheum Theatre This refurbished theater has been around since 1908, when it was the scene of many Yiddish theater hits. *Little Mary Sunshine* had a long run here. In recent years, it's hosted such winners as *Little Shop of Horrors* and comedienne **Sandra Bernhard's** one-woman show. ♦ 126 Second Ave (between E. Seventh and E. Eighth Sts). 477.2477

42 Cafe Orlin $ Neighborhood regulars congregate here for good coffee and desserts. During the warmer months, choose an outside table and watch the parade. ♦ Cafe ♦ Daily 9AM-2AM. 41 St. Mark's Pl (between First and Second Aves). 777.1447

42 The Holiday Cocktail Lounge This funky old bar is frequented by everyone from skinheads to ladies with crocheted vests and platinum-blond wigs. The amazingly low-priced drinks (for New York, anyway) are the main draw. ♦ Daily noon-1AM. 75 St. Mark's Pl (between First and Second Aves). 777.9637

43 Theater 80 St. Mark's If nostalgic classics like *The Philadelphia Story* and *Bringing Up Baby* just don't make it on TV, come here. Serious film students as well as those longing for a taste of Old Hollywood frequent this tiny revival house, one of the last surviving in Manhattan and an East Village institution. Check the computer printout posted in the front window or call for the schedule. ♦ 80 St. Mark's Pl (between First and Second Aves). 254.7400

44 Mogador ★$$ Moroccan cuisine is prepared here without fanfare. Lamb, beef, and *merguez* (sausage) kebabs, couscous, and a selection of appetizers are brought around to your table on an enormous tray. Go all the way and top off your meal with Turkish coffee—as delicious as it is muddy. ♦ Moroccan/Middle Eastern ♦ Lunch, dinner, and late-night meals. 101 St. Mark's Pl (between Ave A and First Ave). No credit cards. 677.2226

45 Tompkins Square Park The original plan for this 16-acre park called for extending it all the way east to the river. It was to be a farmers' market, and part of the plan was to cut a canal through the middle to give easy access to Long Island farmers. But the land became a parade ground instead in the 1830s. In 1874, it was the site of America's first labor demonstration, when a carpenters' union clashed with club-wielding police. Among the injured was **Samuel Gompers,** who later became president of the **American Federation of Labor.** The little Greek temple near the center covers a drinking fountain placed there by a temperance organization in 1891. The park gained its modern-day notoriety during hippiedom, when it served as the grounds for "love-ins" and "be-ins," and more recently when it was the site of a violent confrontation over real-estate speculation in the area and efforts to enforce a nighttime curfew. ♦ Bounded by E. Seventh and E. 10th Sts, and Aves A and B

Restaurants/Clubs: Red   **Hotels:** Blue
Shops/ ♣ Outdoors: Green   **Sights/Culture:** Black

46 Jacob Riis Houses Plaza The large number of people who actually use this park is a tribute to **M. Paul Friedberg's** careful and creative 1966 plan. Both adults and children find it a pleasant alternative to the streets, with its amphitheater, clever playground furniture, and plenty of room in which to roam. ♦ Bounded by E. Sixth and E. 10th Sts, FDR Dr, and Ave D

RUSSIAN &TURKISH
BATHS

47 Russian & Turkish Baths The last remaining bathhouse in a neighborhood that once was full of them still gets its steam heat the old-fashioned way: enormous boulders are heated up in the sub-basement and when they're red-hot, water is thrown on them, releasing what the owners claim is true, penetrating wet heat—not mere steam heat. And if you've never had a *platza* rub, try it. Softened oak branches are tied together in the old Russian style to form a natural loofalike scrub, soapy and tingly and very refreshing. There's also a Turkish bath (sauna). Upstairs are cots if you're overwhelmed, and a small food and drink bar. ♦ Daily 9AM-10PM (coed: M-Tu, F-Sa; women: W; men: Th, Su). 268 E. 10th St (between Ave A and First Ave). 473.8806

48 DeRobertis Pastry Shop ★$ If you can get past the display counters filled with traffic-stopping cheesecakes, pies, cakes, and *biscotti,* you'll find a wonderfully tiled coffeehouse that hasn't changed a bit since they began making frothy cappuccino here back in 1904. ♦ Cafe/Bakery ♦ Tu-Th 9AM-11PM; F-Sa 9AM-midnight. 176 First Ave (between E. 10th and E. 11th Sts). 674.7137

49 Theater for the New City Now located in what used to be an indoor market, this offbeat, roots-in-the-1960s troupe has managed to keep its old ambience and point of view. The productions are hit and miss. Each of the four theaters seats between 60 and 100. ♦ 155 First Ave (between E. Ninth and E. 10th Sts). 254.1109

50 Enchantments Local and visiting witches stop here regularly for the tools of their craft: herbs, oils, tarot cards, caldrons, and ceremonial knives (used to cut air and create a sacred space), plus jewelry, books, and calendars. ♦ M-Sa noon-9PM; Su 1-8PM. 341 E. Ninth St (between First and Second Aves). 228.4394

51 Veselka ★$ An amazing array of Eastern European specialties—*pirogen,* kielbasas, blintzes, stuffed cabbage—are turned out at bargain-basement prices in this bare-bones yet cozy establishment. ♦ Polish ♦ Daily 24 hours. 144 Second Ave (at E. Ninth St). 228.9682

51 Ukrainian ★$ Within the **Ukrainian National Home,** this place serves such wonderful Ukrainian specialties as *pirogen,* blintzes, and stuffed cabbage. The combination platter gives a sampling of all three. ♦ Ukrainian ♦ Lunch and dinner. 140 Second Ave (between St. Mark's Pl and E. Ninth St). 529.5024

52 Ottendorfer Library Anna Ottendorfer, founder of the German-language newspaper *New York Staats Zeitun,* founded this terracotta beauty, which was built by **William Schickel** in 1884. Before becoming a branch of the New York Public Library, it was the **Freie Bibliothek und Lesehalle,** a German-language library and reading room. ♦ M, W, F 1-6PM; Tu 1-7PM; Th 10AM-6PM. 135 Second Ave (between St. Mark's Pl and E. Ninth St). 674.0947

53 Cloisters Cafe ★$$ Gigantic salads and inventive entrées are served in a stained-glass-filled environment. In good weather, the restaurant's garden is the most inviting spot in the neighborhood. ♦ American ♦ Lunch, dinner, and late-night meals. 238 E. Ninth St (between Second and Third Aves). No credit cards. 777.9128

53 Cafe Tabac ★★$$ This is a hangout for wannabes and those they want to be—**Madonna, Keith Richards, Naomi Campbell, Calvin Klein.** The East Village eatery's menu has evolved from bistro to continental American, but food takes a back seat to celebrity and model watching. Be forewarned—upstairs is unofficially reserved for regulars and big names. The downstairs dining room and bar are generally noisy and crowded. ♦ American ♦ Dinner and late-night meals. 232 E. Ninth St (between Second and Third Aves). 674.7072

54 Briscola ★★$$$ This neighborhood find serves authentic Sicilian specials such as whole wheat pasta with eggplant and aged sheep cheese, pasta Consardi, and swordfish carpaccio. ♦ Sicilian ♦ Dinner. Closed Sunday. 65 Fourth Ave (between E. Ninth and E. 10th Sts). 254.1940

Each of the 11,787 licensed yellow cabs in New York City (a number frozen since 1937) pays a medallion fee of $140,000. Unlike London cabbies, who undergo a rigorous two-year program (while managing to retain their politeness), New York City drivers sign up for an obligatory 40-hour training course. When possible, give the cross street when telling the driver your destination.

By 1643, 18 languages were spoken in New York City. More than 75 are spoken today.

55 Grace Church The fascinating spire atop this white marble church is sited at a bend of Broadway, providing a focal point for any southern approach. **James Renwick, Jr.,** won the right to design the Episcopal church in a competition. He worked with an unfettered Puginesque vocabulary to produce a Gothic Revival structure in 1846 that many consider to be the city's best. **Heins & LaFarge** designed an enlargement for the chancel in 1900. Renwick's rectory, next door at 804 Broadway, is another marvel—a restrained foil for the more fanciful church. ♦ 800 Broadway (at E. 10th St)

56 St. Mark's-in-the-Bowery Church Erected in 1799 on the site of a garden chapel on **Peter Stuyvesant's** estate, St. Mark's has always been held in high regard as a neighborhood church, and the late-Georgian style encourages this congenial attitude. As the membership grew, a Greek Revival steeple designed by **Ithiel Towne** was added in 1828 to give the church a more urban image, and a cast-iron Italianate portico was added to the entrance in 1854. This mélange does not mesh successfully, but it does reflect the parishioners' concerns during the church's early history. A fire nearly destroyed the building in 1978. Architect **Herman Hassinger** took charge of the restoration, which included rebuilding the steeple according to the original design. The interior was gutted and redesigned in a simple and straightforward manner, typical of the pre- and post-Revolutionary War period. The stained-glass windows on the ground floor, newly designed by Hassinger, use themes similar to the original windows. The churchyard where Peter and six generations of Stuyvesants are buried has been covered with cobblestones and is now used as a play yard. St. Mark's is also home to the **Poetry Project, Inc.** (674.0910), **Danspace** (674.8112), and **Ontological Theatre** (533.4650). ♦ Second Ave (at E. 10th St). 674.6377

57 Second Avenue Deli ★$$ The deli is very famous, very popular, and very good—for certain Jewish specialties. Try the superb chopped liver—passed out on bits of rye bread to the waiting crowds when lines get long on weekends—stuffed breast of veal, Romanian tenderloin steak, boiled beef, stuffed derma, or kasha *varnishkas*. Ask to be seated in the **Molly Picon** room, with its wealth of Yiddish theater memorabilia. ♦ Jewish ♦ Breakfast, lunch, dinner, and late-night meals. 156 Second Ave (at E. 10th St). 677.0606

In February 1989, 18,900 potholes were created in New York's streets, considerably fewer than in February of 1988, when the city reported 33,000.

58 10th Street Lounge A severe metal facade and forbidding steel doors give way to this popular neighborhood watering hole. The interior is warmed up with votive candles, a hodgepodge of overstuffed couches, and, for a curious touch of academia, school desks used as tables. ♦ Daily 4PM-4AM. 212 E. 10th St (between First and Second Aves). 473.5252

59 Veniero's Pasticceria ★$ Mirrors, gold, chandeliers—hey, it's only a bakery and cafe. Let your eyes feast not on the fixtures but on the *biscotti*, the creamy pastries, the golden cheesecakes. These are the true bounty of Veniero's, which also supplies many of New York's Italian cafes with its baked goods. There's also a seating area, where cappuccino goes well with a *sfogliatelle*. ♦ Cafe/Bakery ♦ M-Th, Su 8AM-midnight; F-Sa 8AM-1AM. 342 E. 11th St (between First and Second Aves). No credit cards. 674.7264

60 Iso ★$$ Drop by this favorite destination in the East Village for creative Japanese food. Quarters are cramped, but the staff and customers make do in an upbeat atmosphere with fresh flowers and **Keith Haring** artwork. Sushi-with-a-twist is the specialty, but cooked selections are given the same attention. ♦ Japanese ♦ Dinner and late-night meals. 175 Second Ave (at E. 11th St). 777.0361

61 Angelica's Kitchen ★$ A place like this could only exist in the East Village. The seasonal macrobiotic menu (no dairy products, and don't even look for the presence of sugar) changes with the solstice and equinox and guarantees some delicious vegetarian specialties made with organically grown ingredients, such as the lentil/walnut pâté. A Zen-like setting complements the mood and provides a tranquil backdrop for a colorful, mixed-bag clientele. Angelica is an herb believed to bring good luck. ♦ Organic/Vegetarian ♦ Lunch and dinner. 300 E. 12th St (between First and Second Aves). 228.2909

61 John's of Twelfth Street ★$$ Remember those little Italian restaurants lit by dripping candles stuck in wine bottles that used to turn up in the movies? John's could have been the model for all of them. It's one of the city's oldest and was once a favorite of **Arturo Toscanini.** The menu is traditional, the special salad outstanding. ♦ Italian ♦ Dinner. 302 E. 12th St (between First and Second Aves). Reservations recommended. No credit cards. 475.9531

62 Pedro Paramo ★$ The authenticity and peso-friendly menu of this restaurant with Mexican owners may fool you into believing you're south of the border—or maybe it's the ever-flowing Mexican beer and excellent margaritas. Start off a traditional Mexican meal with some of the city's best guacamole, and take it from there. ♦ Mexican ♦ Lunch and dinner. 430 E. 14th St (between First Ave and Ave A). 475.4581

63 Immaculate Conception Church Now a Roman Catholic church, this 1894 building designed by **Barney & Chapman** was originally an Episcopal mission of Grace Church, which included a hospital and social service facilities arranged in a cloisterlike setting punctuated by the elaborate tower. ♦ 414 E. 14th St (between Ave A and First Ave)

64 Las Mañanitas ★$$ The bill of fare in this restaurant in the basement floor of an old town house includes all the Tex-Mex standards along with margaritas famous throughout the neighborhood. The food is complemented by live music on Friday. ♦ Mexican ♦ Lunch and dinner. 322 E. 14th St (between First and Second Aves). 475.2558

65 Kiehl's Since 1851 Located at the historical **Peter Stuyvesant Pear Tree Corner,** this vintage establishment produces handmade cosmetics and 118 essences (including four kinds of patchouli oil), using natural ingredients and extracts according to centuries-old formulations. The white-coated staff is extremely helpful and generous with samples. Kiehl's also displays an impressive collection of new and vintage motorcycles. All in all, it's an East Village *must.* ♦ M-F 10AM-6:30PM; Sa 10AM-6PM. 109 Third Ave (between E. 13th and E. 14th Sts). 475.3400

66 CSC Repertory Classic dramas are performed here with a contemporary twist—"recontextualized," as they say. ♦ 136 E. 13th St (at Third Ave). 677.4210

67 Footlight Records Collectors of vintage LPs rejoice! Here is the world's largest selection of film soundtracks and original Broadway cast albums as well as top vocalists (**Sinatra, Crosby, Merman**), jazz greats (**Django Reinhardt, Bix Beiderbecke**), and out-of-print records of all sorts. In most cases, you may listen before buying. ♦ M-F 11AM-7PM; Sa 10AM-6PM; Su noon-5PM. 113 E. 12th St (between Third and Fourth Aves). 533.1572

68 Utrecht Art & Drafting Supplies This major manufacturer of professional art and drafting supplies offers excellent prices. Mail-order catalogs are available at the store or by calling 800/223.9132. ♦ M-Sa 9AM-6PM. 111 Fourth Ave (between E. 11th and E. 12th Sts). 777.5353

69 Strand Bookstore The largest used bookstore in New York has a fanatical following hooked on its thousands of review copies of new books, its hundreds of coffee-table books, and its tables full of mass-market and trade paperbacks, all sold at a generous discount. Antiquarian books are here, too. If you have to get lost somewhere in New York, this is the best possible place. ♦ M-Sa 9:30AM-9:30PM; Su 11AM-9:30PM. 828 Broadway (at E. 12th St). 473.1452. Also at: 159 John St. 809.0875

70 Dullsville The owners of this shop travel to flea markets all over the country to accumulate an odd assortment of goods, including **Russell Wright** dinnerware and the largest selection of Bakelite jewelry in New York City. ♦ M-Sa 11:30AM-7PM. 143 E. 13th St (between Third and Fourth Aves). 505.2505

71 Palladium Partners **Steve Rubell** and **Ian Schrager** (of **Studio 54** and **Morgan's** fame) had a great idea—to convert the old Academy of Music into a dance palace. In 1985, they hired **Arata Isozaki** and **Eiko Ishioko** to revamp the interior and commissioned artists like **Francesco Clemente** and **Keith Haring** to do their thing in individual rooms and spaces. The clientele is mostly out-of-towners and the very young. Immense banks of video monitors pulsate over the vast dance floor. ♦ Cover F-Sa 10PM-4:30AM. 126 E. 14th St (between Third and Fourth Aves). 473.7171

Bests

Patricia Jean
Restaurant Owner, Provence

The Frick Collection. Because it feels grand and special, and I can never walk by without going in.

The **Union Square Greenmarket,** where the city and country really meet. Because it's really seasonal produce from the region. Because you can't beat the bread from **Boiceville** or the tomatoes from Long Island (no, not New Jersey).

Horseback riding in **Central Park,** ice-skating at **Rockefeller Center,** and looking up at the buildings around and feeling a sense of solitude.

Florent for onion soup and tripe at two in the morning. As close as you get to Paris without losing New York.

The food stores, especially **Dean & DeLuca** and **Jefferson Market.**

SoHo's streets before the stores and galleries open. It has the best neighborhood feeling in all New York, and it all changes after noon.

Dinner at the **River Café** at sunset because there's not a more beautiful and edifying view around!

Saturday afternoon gallery-hopping.

The flowers everywhere, but especially at the market on 28th Street.

The feeling that anything is possible (it comes and goes, but I've only felt this in New York).

Three Lives Company Bookstore—the best bookstore ambience in New York; owned and operated by people, not corporate entities.

Union Square/ Gramercy/ Murray Hill

Both Union Square, formerly known as **Stuyvesant**, and Murray Hill were named for farms, while Gramercy inherited its name from an early 19th-century housing development that lured the rich by offering them access to their own private park.

Together these three neighborhoods cover **14th** to **39th** streets, from **Sixth Avenue** to the **East River**. In recent years, publishers, ad agencies, photography studios, and other companies running from high uptown rents have moved into these areas, which have been residential for the most part since the commercial center of the city moved north in the 19th century. Almost none have tampered with the building exteriors, except to restore them. The area exudes a newfound energy, and the new residents gravitate to a host of fashionable eateries and cafes recently opened to accommodate them.

Gramercy Park, the centerpiece of the Gramercy area, was established in the 1830s by lawyer and landowner **Samuel Ruggles.** To make one of his tracts more valuable, he sacrificed 42 potential building lots to create a

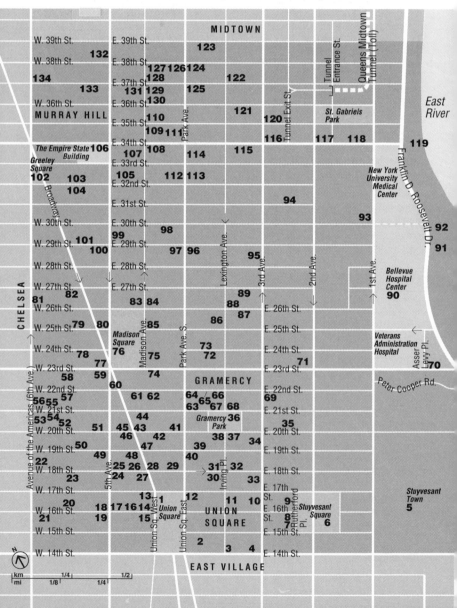

London-style park. Then he set aside more land for a wide avenue north of the park (which he named Lexington, for the Revolutionary War battle) and for Irving Place south of it (which he named for his friend **Washington Irving**, who created "Father Knickerbocker," one of the symbols of New York).

The land that Ruggles owned was once part of a huge estate that belonged to **Peter Stuyvesant**, the last governor-general of New Netherlands, who retired there after the British took over. His original 1651 deed noted a valley created by a creek called *Crommessie,* a combination of two Dutch words meaning "crooked little knife" (for the shape of a nearby brook). The name was eventually altered to Gramercy to fall more easily off English-speaking tongues.

Stuyvesant's name lives on in the neighborhood east of Gramercy, and in another London-style park that straddles Second Avenue. After the Stuyvesant family sold part of their estate to the Delanceys in 1746, it was developed into a working farm known as **Rose Hill.** It is a quiet residential area today, but through the beginning of the 20th century the notorious **Gas House Gang** ruled the neighborhood, averaging an estimated 30 holdups every night on E. 18th Street alone.

The original Gas Housers' territory included another residential neighborhood, Murray Hill, which extends north from 34th to 39th streets, and east from Sixth Avenue. The gang took its name from factories along the East River that produced gas to illuminate the city in the 18th century. The stretch between 23rd and 34th streets is often called **Kips Bay**, after a farm established by **Jacobus Kip** in 1655.

By the end of the 19th century, when **J. Pierpont Morgan** moved to Kips Bay, a gentlemen's agreement had been established restricting the streets of Murray Hill to private houses. Until the invasion of high-rise hotels and apartments in the 1920s, it was a neighborhood of elegant mansions, many of which still stand.

Today, where gas storage tanks once sprouted east of **Stuyvesant Square**, thousands of people occupy middle-class apartments in the **Stuyvesant Town** and **Peter Cooper Village** rental complexes (both built in the late 1940s and attacked for being grim, functional, and without ornamentation), and in **Waterside** (high-rises built in 1974 on the East River between E. 25th and E. 30th streets). Visible from FDR Drive is **Bellevue Hospital Center**, which originated as a six-bed infirmary on the site of the present City Hall in a building that it shared with a poorhouse and a jail.

---

1 Union Square In 1811, when the city fathers decreed that all of Manhattan's streets should follow a rigid grid pattern, Broadway was already in place, cutting an angle from southeast to northwest. Rather than change it, they turned it to the city's advantage by creating squares wherever Broadway crossed a north-south avenue. What may have inspired them was this existing square, which grew up around the meeting point of Broadway, the post road to Albany, and Boston Post Road, which later became Third Avenue. In the years before the Civil War, it was the heart of a fashionable residential neighborhood, surrounded by prestigious stores and theaters. When fashion moved uptown, the square became a center for labor demonstrations and rallies. It was landscaped and altered in 1936, when it was also raised a few feet above ground level to allow for the subway station under it. The pavilion at the north end, sometimes used for summer concerts, was added at the same time. The redesign also forced Broadway to make a left turn at E. 17th Street and share its right-of-way with Park Avenue South before getting back on course at E. 14th Street. The landscapers came back almost 50 years later to begin a multiphase renovation (phase one began in 1984) to transform the area once again. (The park had become a gloomy hangout for drug pushers and derelicts.) Among their accomplishments to date is the replacement of the magnificent **Independence Flagstaff** at the center of the park, originally donated by **Tammany Hall.** The face-lift also includes new Art Deco-style subway kiosks, which flank the equestrian statue of **George Washington,** the masterpiece of sculptor **John Quincy Adams Ward,** which was placed there in 1856. Ward's collaborator was **Henry Kirke Brown,** who was responsible for the figure of **Abraham Lincoln** at the other end of the park. Nearby is a representation of the **Marquis de Lafayette,** created in 1876 by **Frederic Auguste Bartholdi,** who gave us the Statue of Liberty 10 years later. ◆ Bounded by E. 14th and E. 17th Sts (between Park Ave South and University Pl)

1 Union Square Greenmarket In 1976, as part of the effort to transform Union Square, the **Manhattan Planning Office of the New York City Planning Department** urged the **Council on the Environment** to start a greenmarket in what was then a parking lot. (A similar market was then already in full swing at E. 59th Street and Second Avenue.) After a slow start—due to the community's skepticism regarding the previous, unsuccessful attempts to clean up the longtime illicit activities within the park—the turnaround came in 1984, when the **Parks Department** rebuilt the park itself and the **New York City Department of Transportation** rebuilt the public place just north of it. As many as 60 regional farmers and food producers participate in Manhattan's 27 greenmarkets, of which this is the largest and most interesting. Baked goods, fish, cheese, eggs, honey, and plants are sold, in addition to a huge variety of fruits and vegetables. Some locals make a beeline for the fresh flowers, and at Christmastime, the freshest trees, wreaths, and garlands can be found here. All perishables must be sold within 24 hours of harvesting. ◆ M, W, F-Sa 8AM-6PM. E. 17th St at Broadway. 788.7900

2 Zeckendorf Plaza There are more than 670 cooperative apartments in this 1987 building by **Davis, Brody & Associates.** Four illuminated pyramids sit atop the sprawling complex. Life here is self-contained, with such amenities as a health club and shopping facilities. At 108 E. 15th is the 225-seat **Gertrude and Irving Dimson Theater,** the permanent home of the **Vineyard Theater Company.** The development is often cited as a key to the gentrification of the Union Square neighborhood. ◆ Bounded by E. 14th and E. 15th Sts, and Irving Pl and Union Sq East. 826.2900

3 Consolidated Edison Building This massive structure (shown above), completed in 1929 by **Henry J. Hardenbergh,** has its critics, but everyone loves its clock tower built in 1926 by **Warren & Wetmore.** It is softly lit at night, as it should be, considering that its owner is the electric company. The building, which fills nearly the whole block, replaced two structures that each had an impact on the city. **Tammany Hall,** which controlled City Hall for more than 100 years, was headquartered here in a large but unassuming brick building that had a spacious auditorium for public meetings, and a smaller one that became a profit center as **Tony Pastor's Music Hall,** which, in 1881, became the birthplace of American vaudeville. It was next door to a jewel box of a building known as the **Academy of Music,** the predecessor of the Metropolitan Opera, which in its decline became the scene of anti-Tammany rallies. In its heyday, it was the anchor for a string of the city's best restaurants, hotels, and theaters. ◆ 4 Irving Pl (at E. 14th St). 460.4600

4 Con Edison Energy Museum The age of electricity, brought to New York in 1882 by **Thomas Edison,** is chronicled with exhibitions, artifacts, and imaginative displays that extend from the present into the future. A representation of today's New York at night is reached through a long passageway that is a tour of underground New York, complete with a passing subway. ◆ Free. Tu-Sa 10AM-4PM. 145 E. 14th St (between Third Ave and Irving Pl). 460.6244

Restaurants/Clubs: Red
Shops/ 🌳 **Outdoors:** Green
Hotels: Blue
Sights/Culture: Black

5 Stuyvesant Town There are 8,755 moderately priced rental apartments in this complex, which looks forbidding from the street (when it was built in 1947, **Lewis Mumford** called it "police state architecture"). The roadways within the complex are virtually free of cars. The tenants, many of whom are senior citizens and young families, live a carefree existence, thanks to good security and careful maintenance provided by the landlord, the Metropolitan Life Insurance Company. In the blocks between E. 20th and E. 23rd streets, the development is known as **Peter Cooper Village,** an upscale version of Stuyvesant Town, with larger apartments and higher rents. Peter Cooper people are also allowed air conditioners, forbidden below E. 20th Street by the landlord, due to insufficient wiring. ♦ Bounded by E. 14th and E. 20th Sts (between FDR Dr and First Ave)

6 Stuyvesant Square Created in 1836 at the edge of the **Gas House District** (one of the city's poorest neighborhoods), this four-acre oasis, donated to the city by the Stuyvesant family, was the dividing line between rich and poor. In the center of the western half is a 1936 sculpture of **Peter Stuyvesant** by **Gertrude Vanderbilt Whitney,** founder of the Whitney Museum. ♦ Bounded by E. 15th and E. 17th Sts (at Second Ave)

7 Friends' Meeting House The simple, two-story Greek Revival structure, built in 1860 by **Charles T. Bunting,** reflects the peaceful nature of the **Society of Friends,** which holds meetings here. ♦ 221 E. 15th St (at Rutherford Pl). 777.8866

8 216 East 16th Street Part of a row of striking Italianate houses built in the early 1850s, this is still a joy to behold. The lower stories are brownstone, but brick is used on the upper floors, which, along with its wonderful windows, makes it unusual. ♦ At Rutherford Pl

9 St. George's Episcopal Church It's easy to believe that this solid brownstone, vaguely Romanesque church was where financier **J.P. Morgan** attended services. Dating from 1846, it was the design of **Otto Blesch** and **Leopold Eidlitz.** ♦ E. 16th St at Rutherford Pl. 475.1216

9 St. George's Chapel Built in 1911 by **Matthew Lansing Emery** and **Henry George Emery,** this Romanesque companion sits in the shadow of the massive church—most certainly one of New York's overlooked treasures. ♦ Rutherford Pl (north of the church)

10 Tien Fu ★★$ A full range of Chinese specialties is presented in this busy neighborhood restaurant. ♦ Chinese ♦ Lunch and dinner. 180 Third Ave (between E. 16th and E. 17th Sts). 505.2000

11 Washington Irving High School Originally a girls' technical high school, Washington Irving's curriculum expanded to include a full range of subjects when it moved here from Lafayette Street in 1912. The huge bust of Irving at the E. 17th Street corner was created in 1885 by **Friedrich Baer.** ♦ 40 Irving Pl (between E. 16th and E. 17th Sts)

12 Guardian Life Insurance Company In 1911, when this building was designed, there was a new architectural movement away from flat-topped buildings with cornices, which were beginning to get boring for many corporate clients. **D'Oench & Yost** responded by producing a four-story mansard roof for the top of this lavish tower. Not satisfied that it was unusual enough to become their signature, the insurance company added a huge electric sign. However, it worked against them. Their name was **Germania Life,** which set them apart as pariahs when World War I broke out. They solved the problem by changing their name. The 1961 extension behind it, adding little more than space, was designed by **Skidmore, Owings & Merrill.** ♦ 201 Park Ave South (at E. 17th St)

THE CITY BAKERY

13 The City Bakery ★★$ Fresh ingredients from the Greenmarket just half a block away are turned into tasty dishes at this bakery/cafe. Such hearty soups as lentil or potato with cumin served with warm focaccia are made on the premises each morning, as is the heavenly range of sweets for which City Bakery is well known. Their tart-as-art follows the fruits of the season. Another much larger City Bakery opened in Midtown in late 1993. ♦ American ♦ Breakfast, lunch, and early dinner. Closed Sunday. 22 E. 17th St (between Fifth Ave and Broadway). 366.1414. Also at: Sony Plaza, 550 Madison Ave (between E. 55th and E. 56th Sts). 833.8020

14 Union Square Cafe ★★★★$$$ Owner **Danny Meyer** is one of the brightest and most innovative among the new generation of restaurateurs. His young staff is welcoming, and the service is cordial yet professional. Food festivals, featuring produce from the **Union Square Greenmarket,** add to the Continental liveliness of this popular, attractive cafe. You can't go wrong with the generous tuna steak. ♦ American ♦ Lunch and dinner; dinner only on Sunday. 21 E. 16th St (between Union Sq West and Fifth Ave). 243.4020

15 Coffee Shop ★$ Cutting-edge kids spill year-round into the sidewalk cafe of this slick diner with a Brazilian flair. The clubby back room, with its fish tank and TV, is a fun hideaway. ♦ Eclectic ♦ Breakfast, lunch, dinner, and late-night. 29 Union Sq West (at E. 16th St). 243.7969

15 Richard Stoddard Performing Arts Books Here you'll find mostly out-of-print books plus ephemera relating to the performing arts—playbills, autographs, and periodicals. ♦ M-Tu, Th-Sa 11AM-6PM. 18 E. 16th St (between Union Sq West and Fifth Ave), room 305. 645.9576

16 Revolution Books Before you start your revolution, stop here for inspiration from the masters of the art. The books cover a range of political science topics, with an emphasis on the radical. ♦ M-Sa 10AM-7PM; Su noon-5PM. 13 E. 16th St (between Union Sq West and Fifth Ave). 691.3345

16 Steak Frites ★$$ Steak and fries are the meat and potatoes at this Union Square spot. It's dimly lit and romantic, but service can be spotty. ♦ French bistro ♦ Lunch and dinner. 9 E. 16th St (between Union Sq West and Fifth Ave). Reservations required. 463.7101

17 B. Shackman & Co. The original sign, which may have been placed here when the store opened in 1898, says Shackman specializes in favors and novelties. Its old-fashioned toys, Victorian cards, books, and, yes, favors, make this a favorite stop for anyone with an ounce of nostalgia. ♦ M-F 9AM-5PM; Sa 10AM-4PM. 85 Fifth Ave (at E. 16th St). 989.5162

18 Emporio Armani If Emporio, rather than Giorgio, precedes Armani, it means that the merchandise (which includes men's and women's clothing, accessories, bath products, and leather luggage) goes for about 50 percent less than Armani's signature collections. Check around for some Armani wit: wood sculptures of a bra, panties, a suitcase, and ties; the eagle-shaped air-conditioning unit on the ceiling; and another eagle—this one with an antique manhole cover for an eye—worked into the hundred-year-old chestnut floor. ♦ M-Sa 11AM-7PM; Su 1-6PM. 110 Fifth Ave (at W. 16th St). 727.3240

19 Paul Smith Rock stars and Wall Street bankers have been found here shopping for classic clothing with a twist. This is the eccentric Englishman's only U.S. outlet—he has 45 stores in Japan and seven in London—for his handsomely made suits, sports jackets and slacks, plus occasionally wacky play clothes. ♦ M-W, F-Su 11AM-7PM; Th 11AM-8PM. 108 Fifth Ave (at W. 16th St). 627.9770

19 Joan & David This is one of two Manhattan boutiques (the other is at 816 Madison Avenue) for the exclusive lines of shoes, clothing, and accessories by wife-and-husband team **Joan** and **David Helpern.** The high-tech interior is the work of London designer **Eva Jiricna.** The staff is very friendly. ♦ M-Sa 11AM-7PM; Su 1-6PM. 104 Fifth Ave (between W. 15th and W. 16th Sts). 627.1780

19 Mesa Grill ★★$$ Despite the spacious setting and high ceilings, the incredible noise level here eliminates any chance of dinner chit-chat. Still, this upscale, hip Southwestern restaurant packs them in. Chef/owner **Bobby Flay's** original menu makes an art form of quesadillas and tostadas, and the barbecued ribs garner rave reviews. ♦ Southwestern ♦ Lunch and dinner. 102 Fifth Ave (between W. 15th and W. 16th Sts). 807.7400

20 17 West 16th Street In 1916, **Margaret Sanger** established America's first birth control clinic on Amboy Street in the Brownsville section of Brooklyn. In 1923, she moved to this unusual 1846 Greek Revival house, which was the headquarters for her Birth Control Clinical Research Bureau for the next 50 years. ♦ Between Fifth and Sixth Aves

21 St. Francis Xavier Church This baroque Roman Catholic monument to the Jesuit missionary would be right at home in his native Spain. The interior is the sort of thing American tourists go out of their way to see in Europe. ♦ 30 W. 16th St (between Fifth and Sixth Aves). 736.8500

22 Siegel-Cooper & Company Originally **Siegel-Cooper Dry Goods Store,** this garish white brick and terracotta retail temple (fashioned by **DeLemos & Cordes,** under the influence of the Chicago World's Fair of 1893) lived up to its slogan "The Big Store—A City In Itself" with 15½ acres of space, 17 elevators, a tropical garden, and a smaller version of **Daniel Chester French's** monument *The Republic,* which had graced the Fair. (The fountain at the base of the statue became a favorite rendezvous for New Yorkers, who used to say, "Meet me at the fountain.") The store was located in the fashionable shopping district called "Ladies' Mile," but when **Macy's** and **B. Altman** moved uptown, the store sold its inventory to Gimbels and the statue to Forest Lawn Cemetery in Los Angeles. The building was converted into a military hospital during World War I, and in recent years it has served as construction space for television scenery and home to garment manufacturing firms. ♦ Sixth Ave at W. 18th St

23 Prix Fixe ★★$$ Because chef **Terrance Brennan** shops prudently—bargains at the **Fulton Fish Market,** for example—he is able to turn out elegant cuisine at cut-rate prices. Order from a number of prix fixe dinners or à la carte. Especially good are the salmon tournedos in a horseradish crust, and grilled chicken with basil mashed potatoes. ♦ American ♦ Lunch and dinner; dinner only on Saturday. Closed Sunday. 18 W. 18th St (between Fifth and Sixth Aves). 675.6777

23 Book-Friends Cafe $ This old-fashioned salon features books from the Victorian, Edwardian, Belle Epoque, and Bloomsbury eras in a cafe where you can discuss them. Go for afternoon tea or one of the *Conversations,* during which experts speak about things like Kiki's Paris, New York Literary Neighborhoods, and Sylvia Beach and the Expatriates. ♦ American ♦ Lunch and dinner; lunch and early dinner on Saturday and Sunday. 16 W. 18th St (between Fifth and Sixth Aves). 255.7407

23 Academy Books and Records You'll find a good selection of out-of-print, used, and rare books and records as well as used CDs. ♦ M-Sa 9:30AM-9PM; Su 11AM-7PM. 10 W. 18th St (between Fifth and Sixth Aves). 242.4848

24 Barnes & Noble Bookstore Originally a purveyor of textbooks with branches at most major local colleges, this store has branched out all over town in recent years. There are two here, the main store on the southeast corner and the **Sale Annex** across the street. You can still buy and sell textbooks, but the selection of books and records beyond that is almost overwhelming, at prices that are surprisingly low. Those in the know head for an overlooked part of the annex—the corner in the back of the ground floor that sells used books, many of which are real treasures at affordable prices. ♦ M-F 9:30AM-7:45PM; Sa 9:30AM-6:15PM; Su 11AM-5:45PM. 105 Fifth Ave (at E. 18th St). 807.0099

25 Daffy's Imagine three floors of designer clothes for every age group at incredible discount prices. ♦ M-Sa 10AM-9PM; Su 11AM-6PM. 111 Fifth Ave (at E. 18th St). 529.4477. Also at: 335 Madison Ave. 557.4422

26 America ★$$$ This was once the ultimate trendy restaurant. And though the luster has ever so slightly dimmed, it is still a great draw for the young crowd. Everything about it is big. It has 350 seats, and about as many things on the menu. But it isn't the food you come here for—it's the huge bar, where standing room is three-deep. Almost everyone drinks Rolling Rock beer or large, sweet, powerful drinks with names like "Woo-Woo" and "Russian Quaaludes." The appeal is the unrelenting noise and the sense of belonging that comes from elbowing through the mobs of people. The regulars love it, and so do out-of-town groupies. ♦ American ♦ Lunch and dinner. 9 E. 18th St (between Broadway and Fifth Ave). 505.2110

27 Paragon This gigantic sporting goods store has an extensive sportswear collection. Its sales often have spectacular bargains. ♦ M-F 10AM-8PM; Sa 10AM-7PM; Su 10AM-6PM. 867 Broadway (at E. 18th St). 255.8036

28 MacIntyre Building This 1892 **R.H. Robertson** Romanesque office building has obviously seen better days, but it hasn't lost its pride. You can tell by the way those beasts at the corners are sticking their tongues out at you. ♦ 874 Broadway (at E. 18th St)

29 Old Town Bar ★$ Judging from the popularity of this century-old tavern, it's bound to be around another hundred years. Sit in the time-worn wooden booths and order an excellent burger (served with fried onions on an English muffin) or the famous chicken wings, a mountainous portion of crisp fries, and the perfect mug of draft beer. ♦ American ♦ Lunch, dinner, and late-night meals. 45 E. 18th St (between Broadway and Park Ave South). 529.6732

30 Sal Anthony's $$ This casual restaurant overlooks the street through a huge bay window above an outdoor cafe. The management claims that the space was once an apartment rented by **O. Henry,** which is not very likely, although the writer did live in the neighborhood and would have been pleased to work in such pleasant surroundings. ♦ Italian ♦ Lunch and dinner. 55 Irving Pl (between E. 17th and E. 18th Sts). Reservations required. 982.9030

31 Paul and Jimmy's ★$$$ Hearty food served in an old-world manner is the mainstay of this classic restaurant. ♦ Italian ♦ Lunch and dinner. 123 E. 18th St (between Irving Pl and Park Ave South). Reservations required. 475.9540

31 Fresh Art All the requisites for an old-fashioned English garden—flowers, plants, planters, and furniture—are available in this charming basement-level shop. ♦ M-F 9AM-6PM; Sa noon-5PM. 71 Irving Pl (between E. 18th and E. 19th Sts). 995.5044

31 Friend of a Farmer ★$$ Country cooking and on-the-premises baking take you back to your grandma's kitchen. If you bring her along, she'll undoubtedly ask for the recipe for the daily special. The Long Island duckling and Cajun-style chicken are always good. ♦ American ♦ Breakfast, lunch, and dinner. 77 Irving Pl (between E. 18th and E. 19th Sts). 477.2188

31 Choshi ★$$ The fresh and well-prepared sushi and sashimi here are great buys at lunch. Choose between indoor and outdoor dining. ♦ Japanese ♦ Lunch and dinner. 77 Irving Pl (between E. 18th and E. 19th Sts). 420.1419

32 Pete's Tavern ★$$ There are several saloons in New York that claim to be the oldest in town, and this is one of them. Pete's also claims that **O. Henry** did some of his writing here in a corner booth. If the bar was as busy then as it is now, his powers of concentration must have been incredible. The menu, which runs from Italian specialties to hamburgers, isn't unusual, but the setting is unusually comfortable, and the sidewalk cafe is among the city's best. ♦ Italian/American ♦ Lunch and dinner. 129 E. 18th St (at Irving Pl). 473.7676

33 Fat Tuesday's $$ The name refers to both the restaurant upstairs and the club downstairs. Built in 1894, when this was a German neighborhood, it was originally called **Scheffel Hall** and housed a drinking and singing society. As **Joe King's** rathskeller in the years after World War I, it became a place for college students from all over the country to drink and sing, and a generation of them regularly lined up around the block for the pleasure. There are traces of them left in carved initials in the woodwork inside, but it has been modernized into a run-of-the-mill hangout for the quiche-and-salad set. The basement room under the old rathskeller features top names from the jazz world, including frequent Monday night visits by **Les Paul,** the man who invented the new sounds. ♦ American ♦ Lunch and dinner; late-night also on Friday and Saturday. Shows: M-Th, Su 8PM, 10PM; F-Sa 8PM, 10PM, midnight. 190 Third Ave (between E. 17th and E. 18th Sts). 533.7900; basement 533.7902

34 Chez Faina This inviting shop features couture lingerie and boudoir accessories, as well as unusual matching gifts for mothers and their infants. ♦ M-Sa 11AM-7PM. 228 Third Ave (between E. 19th and E. 20th Sts). 254.1922

35 Police Academy and Museum In spite of what you may have seen in the movies, this academy takes its job very seriously. The building has a swimming pool and a gymnasium, as well as a museum that shows how the city's police officers came to be called New York's finest, with displays that help you understand what they've been through to earn the title. Visitors are welcome, but call first since they close when meetings are scheduled. ♦ Free. M-F 9AM-2PM. 235 E. 20th St (between Second and Third Aves). 477.9753

36 Gramercy Park/Gramercy Park Historic District Established by **Samuel Ruggles** in 1831, this former marshland became the model of a London square ringed by proper 19th-century neoclassical town houses. It is the sole surviving "private park" in New York City—only surrounding residents have a key to get in—but the perimeter is well worth a stroll. Many notables have lived in this neighborhood, including **James Harper,** the mayor of New York City in 1844, and **Samuel**

J. Tilden, governor of New York State (1874–86), who was an unsuccessful presidential candidate; his home is now the **National Arts Club.** The statue in the park is of actor **Edwin Booth,** who lived at number 16 Gramercy Park South until he had the building remodeled by **Stanford White** in 1888 for **The Players Club.** Numbers 34 and 36 on the east side are among the city's earliest apartment buildings, designed in 1883 by **George DaConha** and in 1905 by **James Riles,** respectively. Note the magnificent ironwork on Nos. 3 and 4 Gramercy Park West, attributed to **Alexander Jackson Davis,** one of the city's more individualistic and energetic architects. The Gramercy Park Historic District extends in an irregular area out from the park, including all of the west and south frontages and part of the east, the park itself, and Irving Place almost to E. 19th Street on the west side and to E. 18th Street on the east, as well as parts of E. 20th and E. 21st streets west of the park. Of particular interest is the beautiful block between Irving Place and Third Avenue on E. 19th Street (remodeled as a group by **Frederick J. Sterner**). ♦ Between E. 20th and E. 21st Sts (at Lexington Ave)

37 The Brotherhood Synagogue This austere brownstone cube was designed in 1859 by **King & Kellum** as a Friends' meeting house, and was remodeled in 1975 by **James Stewart Polshek** as a synagogue. ♦ 28 Gramercy Park South (between Third Ave and Irving Pl)

38 National Arts Club Built in 1845 by **Calvert Vaux,** this building has housed the National Arts Club since 1906, but its colorful history began when politician **Samuel J. Tilden,** who gained fame by destroying the **Tweed Ring,** used the coup to become governor of New York. To protect himself in the topsy-turvy days of early unions and political machinery, Tilden installed steel doors at the front of this Victorian Gothic home and had a tunnel dug to E. 19th Street as an escape route. ♦ 15 Gramercy Park South (at Irving Pl)

38 The Hampden-Booth Theatre Library In 1888, founder **Edwin Booth** charged **The Players Club** with the task of creating "a library relating to the history of the American stage and the preservation of pictures, bills of the play, photographs, and curiosities." Small group tours and use of the library, which includes four major collections (from **Edwin Booth, Walter Hampden,** the **Union Square Theatre,** and **William Henderson**), are granted by appointment only. ♦ 16 Gramercy Park South (at Irving Pl). 228.7610

39 Silverado ★★$$ This is the latest venture from Wolfgang Puck protégé **Richard Krause.** Chef-owner Krause has retained his Californian roots with seared tuna and mango relish, and potato pancakes with crème fraîche and caviar. But he"s added a southwestern flair with adobe and pastel decor and dishes like chile-rubbed chicken. To avoid the yuppie crush in back, choose the more peaceful bar up front. ♦ American ♦ Lunch and dinner. 99 E. 19th St (between Park Ave South and Irving Pl). 505.5500

40 Canastel's ★$$$ This popular restaurant features old-world specialties in a 1980s setting. ♦ Northern Italian ♦ Lunch and dinner; late-night meals also on Friday and Saturday. 229 Park Ave South (at E. 19th St). 677.9622

41 Positano ★★$$$ Another of the vaguely Italian restaurants that serve the fashionable and fashion-conscious crowd, Positano is filled to capacity every night. (Even the street outside is bumper-to-bumper with waiting limos.) The best elements are the tasteful decoration (**Croxton Associates**) and the logo (**Milton Glaser**). ♦ Italian ♦ Lunch and dinner. Closed Sunday. 250 Park Ave South (at E. 20th St). 777.6211

42 DARTS Unlimited Dart enthusiasts have been coming here for 24 years for their professional English darts (300 types), flights (more than 1,000 kinds), and the best-quality boards. Novices should request a copy of the *Rules and Regulations of the United States Darting Association for English Darts.* ♦ Tu-F noon-5:30PM; Sa 11AM-4PM. 30 E. 20th St (between Broadway and Park Ave South). 533.8684

42 Theodore Roosevelt Birthplace Teddy Roosevelt was born here in 1858 and lived in a house on the site until he was a teenager. The original house was destroyed in 1916, but was faithfully reconstructed seven years later by **Theodate Pope Riddle** as a memorial to the 26th president. The **National Historic Site** incorporates 26 E. 20th Street, once the home of Roosevelt's uncle. The restoration contains five rooms of period furniture and an extensive collection of memorabilia, including teddy bears. ♦ Nominal admission; seniors, children free. W-Su 9AM-5PM. 28 E. 20th St (between Park Ave South and Broadway). 260.1616

43 Goelet Building Chicago architects developed steel-framed office buildings with highly ornamental exteriors, and in the 1880s, firms such as **McKim, Mead & White** began developing their own variations on the theme, which they called "New York Style." This is a prime example. ♦ 900 Broadway (at E. 20th St)

44 Luxe ★★$$$ **River Cafe** alumnus **Rick Laakonen** brings his stylish, New American cooking to the burgeoning **Flatiron District.** The room is lush, but the service is inconsistent. ♦ French/American ♦ Dinner. 24 E. 21st St (between Park Ave South and Broadway). 674.7900

45 901 Broadway Originally **Lord & Taylor Dry Goods Store,** this 1869 **James H. Giles** building displays a romantic cast-iron facade with echoes of Renaissance castle architecture as a monument to the glories of this formerly fashionable shopping neighborhood before Lord & Taylor moved uptown along with its neighbors **W&J Sloane** and **Arnold Constable.** Industrial tenants have occupied it ever since, and the remodeled mundane ground floor has no connection with the fanciful upper ones. ♦ At E. 20th St

46 Saint Laurie Limited This 1869 building by **James H. Giles** was originally part of the **Lord & Taylor** emporium and has been restored for a manufacturer of quality men's and women's suits. An on-site museum  demonstrates how clothing is produced, with a tour of the workrooms and exhibitions of changing styles. Custom tailoring is also available at low prices. ♦ M-W, F-Sa 10AM-6:30PM; Th 10AM-8PM; Su noon-5PM. 897 Broadway (between E. 19th and E. 20th Sts). 473.0100

47 ABC Carpet The original owner of this 1882 building was **W&J Sloane,** which moved uptown and became one of the city's leading furniture dealers. It specialized in carpets and rugs when it was here, and the tradition is continued by one of Sloane's former competitors, ABC, founded in 1897 and one of New York's lowest-priced sources of fine carpets of every description; in this building you will find wall-to-wall carpeting, remnants, and tile. Across the street, at number 881, are six floors of merchandise, including antique and reproduction rugs and furniture, plus bed, bath, linen, and lighting departments. ♦ M, Th 10AM-8PM; Tu-W, F 10AM-7PM; Sa 10AM-6PM; Su 11AM-6PM. 888 Broadway (at E. 19th St). 473.3000

48 Arnold Constable Dry Goods Store Building A glorious two-story mansard roof tops this skillful marriage of Empire and Italianate styles, designed by **Griffith Thomas** in 1877. Note the rare combination of marble and cast iron in the facade—the city's first use of cast-iron construction for retail space. ♦ 881-887 Broadway (at E. 19th St)

Restaurants/Clubs: Red   **Hotels:** Blue
Shops/ 🌳 Outdoors: Green   **Sights/Culture:** Black

49 News Bar ★$ A magnet for the artistic crowd from the nearby ad agencies, architectural firms, and photography studios, this sleek espresso bar/newsstand was designed in a handsome minimalist style by its owner, a caffeinophile architect. Fresh pastries and great sandwiches are just an excuse to order any of the espressos, cappuccinos, or steamed milks. Pull up a chair at the countertop facing the window and immerse yourself in one of the 400 art, politics, and fashion magazines and newspapers for sale. ♦ Cafe ♦ Breakfast, lunch, and early dinner. 2 W. 19th St (between Fifth and Sixth Aves). 255.3996

50 Magickal Child Tucked away in the deep shade cast by high loft buildings, this is a perfect setting for a store specializing in swords, daggers, candlesticks, and other supplies for your explorations into the occult. A free-mail-order catalog is available. ♦ M-Sa 11AM-8PM; Su noon-8PM. 35 W. 19th St (between Fifth and Sixth Aves). 242.7182

51 Caffe Bondi ★★$$ What began as a small neighborhood cafe and pasticceria has expanded to include a full-blown restaurant with an outdoor patio. The bright, tiled decor, friendly and efficient staff, and delicious entrées and desserts make this a great place for breakfast or a snack, and a lovely setting for lunch or dinner. Try any of the simple pastas or Sicilian specialties, based on the owners' Mediterranean roots. ♦ Italian ♦ Breakfast, lunch, and dinner. 7 W. 20th St (between Fifth and Sixth Aves). 691.8136

52 Periyali ★★★$$$ The friendly staff is justly proud of the traditional Greek menu. Giant white beans with garlic sauce, charcoal-grilled octopus, *all* the phyllo pastries, and fresh whole fish are just a few good options. For dessert there's baklava, of course, and something wonderful called *diples* (thin strips of dough, deep-fried and dipped in honey). White stucco walls, wooden floor, and soft Greek music complete the experience. ♦ Greek ♦ Lunch and dinner; dinner only on Saturday. Closed Sunday. 35 W. 20th St (between Fifth and Sixth Aves). Reservations recommended. 463.7890

53 Limelight Discotheque In better days, the **Church of the Holy Communion,** designed in 1846 by **Richard Upjohn,** had **John Jacob Astor** and **Cornelius Vanderbilt** among its parishioners. When the neighborhood died, the church died with it and, to add insult to injury, became a dance club in 1982. ♦ Tu-Su 10PM-4AM. 660 Sixth Ave (between W. 20th and W. 21st Sts). 807.7850

54 Chelsea Billiards Pool sharks rejoice! This state-of-the-art pool hall is the largest in the city: 45 Brunswick Gold Crown pool tables and six tournament-size snooker tables. Call for information about the pool school. ♦ Daily 24 hours. 54 W. 21st St (between Fifth and Sixth Aves). 989.0096

55 Cal's ★★$$ Still underappreciated and relatively unknown, Cal's offers a unique menu, a great bar, and a big, roomy setting. Stroll around the gentrified **Flatiron District** after your meal. ♦ American ♦ Lunch and dinner; dinner only on Saturday and Sunday. 55 W. 21st St (between Fifth and Sixth Aves). Reservations recommended. 929.0740

56 Lox Around the Clock ★$ Few are the places that can satisfy a burning desire for good deli food at 3AM. It may not be the Carnegie Delicatessen, but Lox Around the Clock's pastrami is mighty popular with the hungry after-club set. Often crowded and noisy with monitors playing MTV and music videos till the wee hours, it offers a good, basic, full-scale deli menu with okay lox. ♦ Delicatessen ♦ Daily 7AM-5AM. 676 Sixth Ave (at W. 21st St). 691.3535

57 The Chocolate Gallery You'll find a full range of supplies for cake bakers and candy makers, including the complete line from Wilton. Professionals frequently stop in. ♦ M-W, F-Sa 10AM-6PM; Th 10AM-7PM. 34 W. 22nd St (between Fifth and Sixth Aves). 675.2253

57 Lola ★$$$ Simply decorated yet appealing, this restaurant serves authentic spiced and curried foods of the islands along with more familiar Italian fare. Management encourages grazing/tasting of several appetizers. Don't bypass the "Lolita," an intoxicating frozen combination of brandy, triple sec, and lemon juice. ♦ West Indian/Caribbean ♦ Lunch and dinner. 30 W. 22nd St (between Fifth and Sixth Aves). Reservations required. 675.6700

58 Stern's Dry Goods Store This restoration of **Henry Fernbach's** 1878 building is possibly the most sensitive of any cast-iron building in New York. ♦ 32-36 W. 23rd St (between Fifth and Sixth Aves)

59 Western Union Building A reflection of the city's Dutch origins, this building was created by **Henry J. Hardenbergh** in 1884, the same year as his **Dakota** apartment house overlooking Central Park. ♦ 186 Fifth Ave (at W. 23rd St)

Restaurants/Clubs: Red   **Hotels:** Blue
Shops/ 🍵 Outdoors: Green   **Sights/Culture:** Black

60 Flatiron Building In 1902, when **David H. Burnham** (of Chicago World's Fair fame) filled the triangular site where Broadway crosses Fifth Avenue in a most reasonable but unconventional manner—with a triangular building—he raised many eyebrows and made history. This limestone-clad Renaissance palazzo was one of the city's first skyscrapers, at 285 feet high, and it is one of Burnham's best. At the juncture between traditionalism and modernism, the structure, with its articulated base and strong cornice, looks like an ocean liner in a column's clothing. Built as the **Fuller Building,** people soon dubbed it the Flatiron for its shape, once they stopped calling it Burnham's Folly. ◆ 175 Fifth Ave (between E. 22nd and E. 23rd Sts)

Within the Flatiron Building:

Scuba Network Fins, masks, snorkels, and everything else you need to dive are here, including lessons that can lead to certification in as little as two weeks (if you have the time and the extra cash to pay for the rush service); it usually takes five weeks. ◆ M-Tu, Th 11AM-8PM; W, F 11AM-7PM; Sa 11AM-6PM; Su noon-4PM. 228.2080

61 Rascals ★$$ Serving a simple but all-encompassing menu ranging from hamburgers to swordfish, this large restaurant also features dancing every night. ◆ American ◆ Dinner and late-night. Closed Monday and Sunday. 12 E. 22nd St (between Park Ave South and Broadway). 420.1777

62 Chefs, Cuisiniers Club ★★$$$ Backed by big wigs from **Aureole,** the **Water Club,** and **Andiamo,** this watering hole for local chefs—a place where they can unwind and enjoy a good meal after their workday is over—opened in the fall of 1990. The C.C. Club serves what the management calls Progressive American cuisine—it changes according to what is fresh and available on the market—and is open to the public. ◆ American ◆ Lunch and dinner; dinner only on Saturday. Closed Sunday. 36 E. 22nd St (between Park Ave South and Broadway). Reservations recommended. 228.4399

63 Calvary Church This Protestant Episcopal church, designed in 1846 by **James Renwick,**

Jr., the architect of **St. Patrick's Cathedral,** once had steeples, but Renwick himself had them removed in 1860 because, some critics said, they embarrassed him. If the exterior was less than perfect, the architect more than made up for it with the nave, which is exquisite. The Sunday-school building on the uptown side, also a Renwick design, was added in 1867. ◆ 273 Park Ave South (at E. 21st St). 975.0170

64 Protestant Welfare Agencies Building Designed in 1894 by **Robert W. Gibson** and **Edward J.N. Stent,** this was originally the home of the Episcopal Church's missionary society. The sculpture over the entrance represents **St. Augustine** preaching to the barbarians in Britain, and the first Anglican bishop in the New World, **Samuel Seabury,** bringing Christianity to the native Americans. ◆ 281 Park Ave South (at E. 22nd St)

65 Umeda Learn to detect the subtleties of sake at this elegant bar. Fortunately for novices, the menu offers a detailed explanation—origin, flavor, degree of dryness or sweetness—of more than 20 varieties of the rice wine. ◆ M-Sa 6-11PM. 102 E. 22nd St (between Park Ave South and Lexington Ave). 505.1550

66 Russell Sage Foundation Building The foundation that set out to dispense $63 million for good works in 1906 did much of its own good work in this 1912 building by **Grosvenor Atterbury** before selling the building to Catholic Charities, which in turn sold it for development as apartments. ◆ 4 Lexington Ave (at E. 22nd St). 750.6000

67 Gramercy Park Hotel $$ This 1927 edifice by **Thompson & Churchill** was **Stanford White's** last home and is a favorite of European travelers who fancy the relaxed old-world style and sensible prices. The choice rooms face the park (guests have access), which is ringed with historical landmarks and turn-of-the-century brownstones. Rooms vary in quality, so ask to see a few if you're not satisfied with yours. ◆ 2 Lexington Ave (at E. 21st St). 475.4320, 800/221.4083; fax 505.0535

68 1 Lexington Avenue The introduction of elevators and changed zoning laws allowed for bigger and better buildings, among them this 1910 apartment house by **Herbert Lucas.** It replaced a mansion owned by **Cyrus W. Field,** who is remembered for connecting Europe and America by an underocean telegraph cable. The iron fence, designed by **Stanford White,** is all that is left of the original house. ◆ At E. 21st St

69 Rolf's Restaurant ★$$ Believe it or not, New York was once famous for its German restaurants. This is one of the very few still operating. It isn't a cavernous beer hall, but its walls and ceilings are covered with enough art, stained glass, and carved wood to fill one.

113

And the menu is just as good. Try the veal shank, shell steak, or excellent potato pancakes. ♦ German ♦ Lunch and dinner. 281 Third Ave (at E. 22nd St). 473.8718

70 Public Baths, City of New York In 1906, right-thinking architects **Arnold W. Brunner** and **William Martin Aiken** finally used the overappropriated style of the Romans in its original manner—for baths (like Caracalla, or those of Diocletian). This pompous formal structure is now a public swimming pool. ♦ E. 23rd St (at Asser Levy Pl, formerly Ave A)

71 School of Visual Arts Working professionals teach more than 5,500 students the fundamentals of illustration, photography, video, film, animation, and other visual arts in buildings scattered throughout the neighborhood. Frequent exhibitions in the main building on E. 23rd Street are free to the public. The luminary faculty includes **Milton Glaser, Eileen Hedy-Schultz, Ed Benguiat,** and **Sal DeVito.** ♦ 209 E. 23rd St (between Second and Third Aves). 679.7350

72 Samuel Weiser's Bookstore This interesting shop deals in new and used esoteric and metaphysical materials, including tarot cards, audio and video tapes, and crystals. ♦ M-W 9AM-6PM; Th-F 10AM-7PM; Sa 9:30AM-5PM; Su noon-5PM. 132 E. 24th St (between Lexington Ave and Park Ave South). 777.6363

73 Miller's Harness Company The flagship store of the world's largest supplier of riding apparel and equipment has everything from derbies to chaps to videotapes on horsemanship. ♦ M-W, F-Sa 10AM-6PM; Th 10AM-7PM. 117 E. 24th St (between Lexington Ave and Park Ave South). 673.1400

74 Live Bait $$ It's hard to tell who's better looking here, the staff or those who frequent this noisy hangout. They really pack them in after work, so be prepared to feel like a sardine as you down an oyster from a shot glass or a Rolling Rock straight from the bottle. The decor is like that of a fishing shack, and although a sign above the bar says, "If you want home cooking, stay home," the cuisine is strictly Carolina homestyle. ♦ Southeastern U.S. ♦ Lunch, dinner, and late-night. 14 E. 23rd St (at Madison Ave). Reservations recommended. 353.2400

75 Metropolitan Life Insurance Company Originally, the 700-foot marble tower (adjacent to the main building) was decorated with 200 carved lions' heads, ornamental columns, and a copper roof. But its four-sided clock, which at 26 1/2 feet is 4 1/2 feet taller than Big Ben, hasn't changed since 1909, when the tower was built. The north building, across E. Fourth Street, was designed in 1932 by **Harvey Wiley Corbett** and **E. Everett Waid** and is surprisingly light for all its limestone mass. Note the sculpted quality of the polygonal setbacks, the vaulted entrances at each of the four corners, and the Italian marble lobby. This block was the site of the **Madison Square Presbyterian Church.** Completed by **Stanford White** in 1906, it was his last, and many say his finest, building. ♦ 1 Madison Ave (between E. 23rd and E. 25th Sts)

76 Madison Square Although this seems a quiet alcove in the midst of madness, imagine what it *was*—a swampy hunting ground, then a paupers' graveyard. The square dates from 1847, when it was a parade ground and only a small part of a proposed park that was laid out in the **Randell Plan** of 1811—the plan that created the city's grid street pattern. Like other squares in this part of town, it was the focus of a fashionable residential district that flourished in pre-Civil War days. After the war, the fancy **Fifth Avenue Hotel,** the **Madison Square Theater,** and the second home of **Madison Square Garden** all faced the square. This incarnation of the Garden will always be remembered because **Stanford White,** who designed the building, was shot and killed in its roof garden by **Harry Thaw,** the jealous husband who thought White was paying too much attention to his wife, **Evelyn Nesbit.** Today, the square is ringed by heavy-duty public and commercial buildings, but manages to retain its air of quiet imperturbability. Stroll through and observe the statuary: *Chester A. Arthur* by **George Bissel,** 1898; *Admiral David Farragut* by **Augustus Saint-Gaudens,** 1880; *William H. Seward* by **Randolph Rogers,** 1876. Or find one of the private benches hidden along the square's fence. ♦ Bounded by E. 23rd and E. 26th Sts (between Madison and Fifth Aves)

77 200 Fifth Avenue This is the center of America's wholesale toy business, which extends into several nearby buildings. Its 15 floors are a dreamland for children, who, alas, are not allowed to browse. But the lobby is open to the public and not to be missed. ♦ (At W. 23rd St)

78 Follonico ★★$$$ Veteran chef **Alan Tardi,** formerly of **Le Madri,** is now cooking in his own place. Exposed brick, wood paneling, an open kitchen, and a wood-burning oven give this Tuscan place a traditional, old-world warmth. The vegetable plate and pastas are highly recommended. ♦ Italian ♦ Lunch and dinner; dinner only on Friday and Saturday. Closed Sunday. 6 W. 24th St (between Fifth and Sixth Aves). Reservations recommended. 691.6359

79 Serbian Orthodox Cathedral of St. Sava Built in 1855 by **Richard Upjohn** for Trinity Church, this chapel became a cathedral of the **Eastern Orthodox** faith in 1943. The beautiful altar and reredos inside are by **Frederick Clarke Withers.** The parish house was designed in 1860 by **Jacob Wrey Mould.** ◆ 15 W. 25th St (between Broadway and Sixth Ave). 242.9240

80 Worth Monument This richly ornamented obelisk in a plot separating Broadway and Fifth Avenue marks the grave of **Major General William Jenkins Worth,** for whom the street in Lower Manhattan and the city of Fort Worth, Texas, were named. After fighting the Seminoles in Florida, he went on to become a hero of the Mexican War in 1846. The monument was designed in 1857 by **James C. Batterson.** ◆ W. 25th St at Fifth Ave

81 Annex Antiques Fair and Flea Market This is the city's original, largest, and most popular weekly antiques and flea market (though GreenFlea is creating some serious competition uptown). Treasures can be found amid the eclectic and fascinating trash year-round, as hundreds of vendors congregate in this parking lot in the middle of the Flower District. You'll find everything from Tiffany silver to bentwood chairs and '50s collectibles. A newer indoor annex with an entrance at 122 W. 26th Street follows the same hours. ◆ Nominal admission. Sa-Su 9AM-5PM. W. 26th St at Sixth Ave. 243.5343

82 Ohashi Institute Founder **Wataru Ohashi** believes it's our reaction to stress that causes physical, mental, and emotional problems. With this in mind, he has developed a technique based on traditional shiatsu massage. After a session with the master himself, or with one of his superbly trained disciples, you'll feel both energized and at peace. ◆ M-F 9:30AM-6PM; Sa 9:30AM-4PM. 12 W. 27th St (between Sixth Ave and Broadway), ninth floor. 684.4190

83 50 Madison Avenue This perfectly harmonious adaptation of a Renaissance palace by **Renwick, Aspinwall & Owen** was constructed in 1896 as a home for the American Society for the Prevention of Cruelty to Animals. ◆ At E. 26th St

84 New York Life Insurance Company This 1928 Gothic masterpiece was designed by **Cass Gilbert,** the architect of the **Woolworth Building** and New York's **Federal Courthouse.** The square tower topped by a gilded pyramid—a style Gilbert called "American Perpendicular"—is dramatically lighted at night. Its lobby is a panorama of detail, from polychromed coffered ceilings to bronze elevator doors, and ornate grilles over the subway entrances. ◆ 45-55 Madison Ave (between E. 26th and E. 27th Sts)

85 Appellate Division of the Supreme Court of the State of New York Here, in the busiest appellate court in the world, nine justices hear most appeals in civil and criminal cases arising in New York and surrounding counties. With few exceptions, their decisions are final. The building, designed by **James Brown Lord**—murals, statuary, and all—was finished in 1900 at $5,000 under budget, with a final price tag of just under $644,000. It is one of the city's treasures. Stop in and be impressed. The building is open to the public Monday through Friday, from 9AM to 5PM, with access to the courtroom when the court is not sitting. ◆ E. 25th St at Madison Ave. 340.0400

86 69th Regiment Armory Designed in 1905 by **Hunt & Hunt,** this is where the infamous *Armory Show* introduced modern art to New York in 1913—the most famous work in the show was **Marcel Duchamp's** *Nude Descending a Staircase.* Note the gun bays overlooking Lexington Avenue, and the expression on the Lexington Avenue facade of the barrel-vaulted Drill Hall behind it. ◆ 68 Lexington Ave (between E. 25th and E. 26th Sts). 889.7249

87 La Colombe D'Or ★★$$$ This small bistro is always busy, and with good reason. The food is well prepared, the service efficient, the prices affordable. ◆ French Provençal ◆ Lunch and dinner; dinner only on Saturday and Sunday. 134 E. 26th St (between Third and Lexington Aves). Reservations recommended. 689.0666

88 Sido ★$$ Here you'll find one of the best spots for Middle Eastern dishes. The menu lists all the standard fare and much that is unusual, including a very minty tabbouleh salad and a spectacular dish of ground lamb baked in sesame sauce. The room is clean but unattractively kitsched up. In the evening, tables are often filled with expatriate Middle Easterners, and on Sunday, with their whole families. Try the house wine. Four kinds of halvah—plain, pistachio, almond, and marble—are sold in the grocery store next door. ◆ Middle Eastern ◆ Lunch and dinner. 81 Lexington Ave (at E. 26th St). Reservations recommended. 686.2031

89 Per Bacco ★$$$ This well-established neighborhood restaurant has an extensive menu, friendly service, and a relaxing setting. ◆ Italian ◆ Lunch and dinner; dinner only on Saturday. Closed Sunday. 140 E. 27th St (between Third and Lexington Aves). 532.8699

90 Bellevue Hospital Center Established in 1736, this municipal hospital cares for some 80,000 emergency cases per year. Its services are available to anyone, with no restrictions, including ability to pay. Bellevue was a pioneer in providing ambulance service, in performing appendectomies and Caesarean sections, and in developing heart catheterization and microsurgery. It is not, as is often believed, solely a psychiatric hospital. The principal building was designed in 1939 by the prestigious architectural firm **McKim, Mead & White** and underwent subsequent additions in 1939. ◆ 462 First Ave (at E. 27th St). 561.4141

91 Waterside There are 1,600 apartments in these brown towers built by **Davis, Brody & Associates** in 1974 on a platform over the East River. They are a world apart, reached by a footbridge across FDR Drive at E. 25th Street, or by the riverfront esplanade to the north. The river views here are spectacular. The complex overlooks a wide bay, the scene of Macy's annual Fourth of July fireworks display. ◆ E. 25th to E. 30th Sts (between East River and FDR Dr)

92 The Water Club ★★★$$$ This glass-enclosed, skylit former barge with an outdoor terrace is anchored at the river's edge. The view is among the best in town. The frenzied activity of the valet parking and fluttering triangular flags give the entrance the feel of a fancy yacht club. The cocktail lounge area opens into a terraced dining room with a panorama of the East River and the Queens skyline. Naturally enough, the seafood is the best choice, and the many varieties of oysters and clams are dependably spectacular. Although the service can be harried and the noise level a bit too much for intimate conversation, the place, with its vacation atmosphere, is well worth many visits. It's also a great venue for weddings and other big occasions. ◆ American ◆ E. 30th St at East River (access from E. 34th St). Reservations required. 683.3333

93 Kips Bay Plaza These twin 21-story slabs facing an inner, private park were the first exposed concrete apartment houses in New York. The complex, completed in 1965, was designed by **I.M. Pei Associates** and **S.J. Kessler.** ◆ E. 30th to E. 33rd Sts (between First and Second Aves)

94 Marchi's ★$$$$ Not much has changed since this restaurant opened in 1930. The menu is fixed, and the food keeps coming in a relentless procession, defying even the most indomitable diner to stagger through to the final stage of fruit, cookies, and coffee. Prepare to spend the evening progressing through an excellent meal that includes fish, meat, pasta, dessert, and more—much more. ◆ Italian ◆ Dinner. Closed Sunday. 251 E. 31st St (between Second and Third Aves). Jacket required; reservations recommended. 679.2494

95 Sumptuary Restaurant ★$$ The word *sumptuary* actually has to do with regulating expenses, and the check here won't upset your budget. But *sumptuous* is a better word

for this lavish setting and its creative menu, which some call California-style. There is a charming garden on the ground floor. ◆ American ◆ Lunch and dinner; dinner only on Tuesday, Saturday, and Sunday. Closed Monday. 400 Third Ave (between E. 28th and E. 29th Sts). 889.6056

96 H. Kauffman & Sons You can have your boots custom-made here, or choose from the huge selection of riding equipment that includes anything a horse or its owner could possibly need, even gifts for your horse-owning friends who think they have everything. ◆ M-W, F-Sa 10AM-6:30PM; Th 10AM-7PM. 419 Park Ave South (at E. 29th St). 684.6060

96 Les Halles ★$$$ Here, the owners of **Park Bistro** set out to re-create the nameless hangouts that once surrounded the great wholesale food market in Paris, and succeeded quite well. Enter the dining room through the butcher shop and enjoy onion soup, garlicky sausage, steak with *pommes frites,* or cassoulet. Expect to wait for your table—along with advertising and publishing execs who work nearby. ◆ French ◆ Lunch and dinner. 411 Park Ave South (between E. 28th and E. 29th Sts). Reservations recommended. 679.4111

97 Park Bistro ★★★$$$$ Black-and-white photos of 1950s Paris line the walls in this friendly, French-style bistro. Chef **Jean-Michel Diot's** specialties include a warm potato salad topped with goat cheese and served with a small green salad, and fresh codfish with onion sauce and fried leeks. ◆ French ◆ Lunch and dinner; dinner only on Saturday and Sunday. 414 Park Ave South (at E. 29th St). 689.1360

98 Martha Washington $ One of the last remaining women-only hotels in the city, the establishment has an informal, homelike atmosphere and a dining room. Rooms are small, and not all have private baths, but they are cheerfully decorated and some have kitchenettes. ◆ 30 E. 30th St (between Park Ave South and Madison Ave). 689.1900; fax 689.0023

99 Church of the Transfiguration/The Little Church Around the Corner When actor **George Holland** died in 1870, a friend went to a nearby church to arrange for the funeral. "We don't accept actors here," he was told, "but there's a little church around the corner that will." They did, and the Church of the Transfiguration—built in 1849 and later expanded—got both a new name and a new reputation among actors, some of whom, including **Edwin Booth, Gertrude Lawrence,** and **Richard Mansfield,** are memorialized among the wealth of stained glass and other artifacts inside. During World War I and in the years following, it was the scene of more wedding ceremonies than any other church in the world. This Episcopal church is home to the **Heidelburg Chamber Orchestra,** which performs Vivaldi concerts at Christmas and other times throughout the year. ♦ 1 E. 29th St (between Madison and Fifth Aves). 684.6770

100 Marble Collegiate Church This Gothic Revival church has not been changed since the day it was built in 1854 by **Samuel A. Warner.** The clock is still wound by hand every eight days, and the cane racks behind the pews are still waiting to receive your walking stick. A Dutch Reform church (the oldest denomination in the city), established here by **Peter Minuit** in 1628, it has served under the flags of Holland, England, and the U.S. The most famous minister to use its pulpit was **Dr. Norman Vincent Peale,** author of *The Power of Positive Thinking.* ♦ 272 Fifth Ave (at W. 29th St)

101 The Olde Garden $$ Here, you can still get the kind of food we ate before the gourmands took over—shrimp cocktail, fruit cup, veal cutlet Parmesan, and hot turkey sandwiches. Before the restaurant was established in 1912, the building housed a stable, then an antique shop. ♦ American/Continental ♦ Lunch and dinner. Closed Sunday. 15 W. 29th St (between Fifth and Sixth Aves). 532.8323

102 Greeley Square **Alexander Doyle's** statue of **Horace Greeley,** founder of the *New York Tribune,* was donated by members of the newspaper unions—which says something about Greeley's management style. The area around the square offers the best buys in cameras and related merchandise. The site across Sixth Avenue, now the home of the **Abraham & Straus** department store, is where Gimbels kept its secrets safe from Macy's, which is only a block away on **Herald Square.** ♦ Bounded by W. 32nd and W. 33rd Sts (between Sixth Ave and Broadway)

103 Stanford $ This small, newly renovated hotel is convenient to **Madison Square Garden** and shopping, and has color TVs in all rooms. ♦ 43 W. 32nd St (between Fifth and Sixth Aves). 563.1480

103 M. Steuer Hosiery Co. Here's a great source for discounted fitness attire (leotards and leggings by **Marika, Baryshnikov,** and **Capezio**), hosiery, and lingerie. ♦ M-F 7:45AM-5:20PM. 31 W. 32nd St (between Fifth Ave and Broadway). 563.0052

104 Kyoto Book Center This is one of several bookstores in the neighborhood serving the Korean community. Cosmetics, too, are sold here. ♦ M-Sa 10AM-8PM. 22 W. 32nd St (between Fifth Ave and Broadway). 465.0923

105 Grolier Once an exclusive hideaway for the bibliophiles of the **Grolier Club,** then a private home, and most recently a private club, this turn-of-the-century landmark building now hosts and caters private parties. ♦ Open to sightseers by appointment. 29 E. 32nd St (between Fifth and Madison Aves). 679.2932

106 The Empire State Building Yes, Virginia, this is the once-upon-a-time World's Tallest Building (if you count the twin towers of the World Trade Center as two, it now ranks fourth), famous in fact and fiction, icon of New York City, and the first place from which to study the city. It has an impressive collection of statistics: 1,250 feet to the top of the (unsuccessful) dirigible mooring mast; 102 floors; 1,860 steps; 73 elevators; 60 miles of water pipes; five acres of windows; 365,000 tons of material—and it was under construction for only 19 months. Built by **Shreve, Lamb & Harmon Associates** in 1931, during the Depression, it was known for many years as the "Empty State Building," and the owners relied on income from the Observation Deck to pay their taxes. Oh yes—on a good day you can see for at least 50 miles.

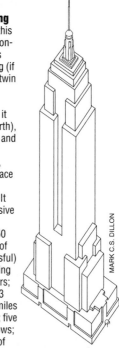

MARK C.S. DILLON

The architects must be lauded for the way in which they handled the immense and potentially oppressive bulk of this building. The tower is balanced, set back from the street on a five-story (street-scale) base. The subtly modulated shaft rises at a distance, terminating in a conservatively geometric crown. The limestone and granite cladding, with its steel mullions and flush windows, is restrained, with just a touch of an Art Deco air (compared to the exuberant ornamentalism of the Chrysler Building, for example). This is *dignity.* Belying the fears of the general public, the tower has not yet cracked or toppled, although it does sway quite a bit in high winds, and only once has a plane crashed into it (in 1945 a bomber broadsided the 79th floor). There have been a few suicides, and a lot of birds have been knocked out of the sky during their migrating season, one of the reasons it always stays illuminated.

The site, too, has a lively history. Between 1857 and 1893 it was the address of a pair of mansions belonging to members of the **Astor** family and the center of New York social life. In the early 1890s a feud erupted, and **William Waldorf Astor,** who had the house on W. 33rd Street, moved to Europe and replaced the house with a hotel—the Waldorf. His aunt across the garden, **Mrs. William Astor,** moved within the year, and had a connecting hotel completed by 1897. The **Waldorf** and **Astoria Hotels** immediately became a social center and operated as one hotel for many years, under the agreement that Mrs. Astor could have all connections between them closed off at any time. When the original structures were demolished in 1929, the **Waldorf-Astoria** moved uptown to Park Avenue. ♦ 350 Fifth Ave (at W. 34th St)

Within The Empire State Building:

Empire State Observatories There is an open platform on all four sides of the 86th floor, well protected with heavy mesh and metal bars. A few steps above it is a glass-enclosed area with food service and a souvenir shop. An elevator takes you higher, to the all-enclosed 102nd-floor lookout, where the view, surprisingly, is slightly different. Tickets are available on the concourse, one level below the street. ♦ Admission. Daily 9:30AM-midnight. Enter on W. 34th St. 736.3100 ext 73

Guinness World Records Exhibit Hall Exhibitions, dioramas, videotapes, replicas, and photographs document the achievements of humankind that possibly wouldn't have happened if there were no *Guinness Book of World Records.* ♦ Admission. Daily 9AM-9PM. Concourse level. 947.2335

107 D. Sokolin This shop boasts a highly touted selection of wines and spirits. ♦ M-F 9:30AM-6PM; Sa 10AM-5PM. 178 Madison Ave (at E. 33rd St). 532.5893

108 Astro Gallery With a collection of minerals and gems from 47 countries, ranging from amethyst crystals to zircons, this is a paradise for collectors and a good source of fine jewelry at low prices. ♦ M-W, F 10AM-6PM; Th 10AM-8PM; Su 11AM-6PM. 185 Madison Ave (at E. 34th St). 889.9000

109 Complete Traveller Bookstore This small store has an amazingly large selection of books—enough to satisfy even the most jaded traveler. ♦ M-F 9AM-7PM; Sa 10AM-6PM; Su 11AM-5PM. 199 Madison Ave (at E. 35th St). 685.9007

110 Church of The Incarnation Episcopal Built in 1864 by **Emlen T. Littel,** this modest church seems to be trying to hide the fact that it contains windows by **Louis Comfort Tiffany** and **John LaFarge,** sculpture by **Daniel Chester French** and **Augustus Saint-Gaudens,** and a Gothic-style monument designed by **Henry Hobson Richardson.** Fortunately, the church provides a folder for a self-guided tour. ♦ 209 Madison Ave (at E. 35th St). 689.6350

111 Dolci On Park Caffe ★★$$ You can get a full meal here, but the best part is the desserts. Enjoy them, along with a cup of espresso, at one of the sidewalk tables. ♦ Italian ♦ Breakfast, lunch, and dinner. Closed Sunday. 12 Park Ave (between E. 34th and E. 35th Sts). 686.4331

112 2 Park Avenue This better-than-average office building is particularly stunning at the top, where the basic structural pattern gives way to some jazzy, colorful Art Deco tile. **Ely Jacques Kahn** designed the building in 1927, with **Leon Solon** as color consultant. ♦ Between E. 32nd and E. 33rd Sts

112 An American Place ★★$$$$ Larry Forgione, the wunderkind of New American cooking, gives this cheery brasserie-style place culinary oomph with a menu of homey, New Wave dishes. The three-fish terrine, roasted duck in cornmeal pancakes, and bread pudding with bourbon sauce are highly recommended. ♦ American ♦ Lunch and dinner; dinner only on Saturday. Closed Sunday. 2 Park Ave (between E. 32nd and E. 33rd Sts). Reservations recommended. 684.2122

113 1 Park Avenue When Fourth Avenue below E. 34th Street had its designation upgraded to "Park Avenue South," this and 2 Park Avenue across the street kept their original addresses. Until 1925, when **York & Sawyer** built on this site, the area wasn't considered upscale. In the 19th century, it was the location of Peter Cooper's glue factory and later of barns for the livestock and horsecars of the New York and Harlem Railroad. ♦ Between E. 32nd and E. 33rd Sts

114 3 Park Avenue No. 3 Park Avenue is a brick tower turned diagonally against its companions and the city. Compare this straight-up tower, built in 1976, and its stylized mansard roof with the careful, soaring composition of the Empire State Building two blocks away—they were designed by the same firm, **Shreve, Lamb & Harmon Associates.** A plaque on the terrace wall at E. 33rd Street marks this as the site of the **71st Regiment Armory.** ♦ Between E. 33rd and E. 34th Sts

115 Dumont Plaza Hotel $$$ All the studios and one- and two-bedroom suites here have their own kitchens. ♦ 150 E. 34th St (between Third and Lexington Aves). 481.7600, 800/637.8483; fax 889.8856

116 Nicola Paone ★$$$ The serious and traditional Northern Italian menu is enlivened by some imaginative offerings. Service is courtly and helpful. The restaurant also has an enviable wine cellar—but only if you ask will you receive. ♦ Italian ♦ Lunch and dinner; dinner only on Saturday. Closed Sunday. 207 E. 34th St (between Second and Third Aves). Reservations recommended. 889.3239

Restaurants/Clubs: Red   **Hotels:** Blue
Shops/ 🌳 Outdoors: Green   **Sights/Culture:** Black

117 St. Vartan Cathedral This is the seat of the Armenian Orthodox Church in America, with a Romanesque design inspired by churches in Asia Minor. It was built in 1967 by **Steinman & Cain,** and its dome was re-covered in 18-karat gold leaf in 1993. ♦ Second Ave (between E. 34th and E. 35th Sts)

118 El Parador ★★$$$ Opened long before the current craze for Mexican food, this spot has remained popular among those who really know Mexican food as well as those who come just to have a good time. Expect to wait at the bar with a margarita so potent it will take the edge off any fidgeting or hunger pangs. Once you are seated, the wait will have been worthwhile. The host has a knack for making you feel like the most important person in his life. After a second margarita, you'll believe him. ♦ Mexican ♦ Lunch and dinner. 325 E. 34th St (between First and Second Aves). Reservations recommended. 679.6812

119 Island Helicopter Sightseeing Choose from four aerial tours of the city. ♦ Daily 9AM-8PM Jan-Mar; daily 9AM-9PM Apr-Dec. E. 34th St at East River. 683.4575

120 Quark International Discover gadgets galore, from Swiss army knives, folding bicycles, and talking translators to video camera tie clips and proton TVs. ♦ M-F 10AM-6:30PM; Sa 11AM-4PM. 537 Third Ave (at E. 35th St). 889.1808

121 Sniffen Court This charming and unusually well-preserved mews of 10 carriage houses was built around the time of the Civil War (1850-60) and was designated a **Historic District** in 1966. ♦ 150-158 E. 36th St (between Third and Lexington Aves)

122 Shelburne Murray Hill $$$ This all-suite hotel has a kitchen in every room. ♦ 303 Lexington Ave (at E. 37th St). 689.5200, 800/637.8483; fax 779.7068

123 Doral Court Hotel $$$$ The rooms here are sunny and quiet, and the staff is enthusiastic. Kitchenettes are available on request. Visit the nearby fitness center or even have a bike brought to your room. **The Courtyard Cafe and Bar** is always a pleasure. ♦ 130 E. 39th St (between Lexington and Park Aves). 685.1100, 800/223.6725; fax 889.0287

123 Doral Tuscany Hotel $$$ The refrigerators in the rooms here are stocked with refreshments, and if you run out, room service will replenish them. Leave your shoes outside your door at night and they'll be shined by morning. And when you rise and shine, you can visit the hotel's squash club and sports training institute. ♦ 120 E. 39th St (between Lexington and Park Aves). 686.1600, 800/223.6725; fax 779.7822

Within the Doral Tuscany Hotel:

Time and Again ★$$$ The turn-of-the-century decor provides an extremely comfortable setting for a weekend breakfast or quiet dinner. If you're in the mood for game, order the pheasant tureen. ♦ American/French ♦ Breakfast, lunch, and dinner; breakfast and dinner only on Saturday and Sunday. 116 E. 39th St (between Lexington and Park Aves). Reservations recommended. 685.8887

124 Rossini's $$$ Hot antipasto is a specialty of this casual, friendly restaurant. A strolling guitarist serenades diners Monday through Thursday; a pianist performs on Friday; an opera trio entertains on Saturday. ♦ Italian ♦ Lunch and dinner. 108 E. 38th St (between Lexington and Park Aves). Reservations required. 683.0135

124 Church of Our Savior This perfect example of Romanesque Gothic architecture was built by **Paul C. Reilly** in 1959, a time when architects were tossing off glass boxes with the excuse that there were no craftsmen left to do this kind of work. The interior of this Roman Catholic church proves that there must have been at least a few in New York in the '50s. ♦ 59 Park Ave (at E. 38th St). 679.8166

125 Sheraton Park Avenue $$$$ This hotel was originally the Russell, after **Judge Horace Russell,** who once had a home on this site. An oak-paneled lobby with book-lined shelves, spacious rooms—some with fireplaces—decorated with antiques, and the always attentive service make it seem like a private club or country home. An intimate bar, where a dramatic confrontation scene between **Paul Newman** and **Charlotte Rampling** was filmed for *The Verdict,* looks like all the movie's mellow Boston locales. ♦ 45 Park Ave (at E. 37th St). 685.7676, 800/325.3535; fax 889.3193

Within the Sheraton Park Avenue:

Judge's Chamber Jazz tunes are piped into the hotel's wood-paneled cocktail lounge. Light snacks are served in the evening. ♦ Daily noon-12:30AM. 685.7676

Tin Pan Alley, once located on W. 28th Street between Broadway and Fifth Avenue, was the heart of the world-famous music publishing industry.

Doral ♟ Park Avenue

126 Doral Park Avenue Hotel $$$ Here's an old-world-style hotel with modern touches, including access to a fitness center up the street on Park Avenue. The rooms are well furnished, the atmosphere gracious and traditional. ♦ 70 Park Ave (at E. 38th St). 687.7050, 800/223.6725; fax 949.5924

Within the Doral Park Avenue Hotel:

Saturnia Restaurant ★$$$ The atmosphere is warm and candlelit. In season, service extends out to a sidewalk cafe. ♦ American ♦ Breakfast, lunch, and dinner. Reservations recommended. 687.7050

127 Madison Towers Hotel $$ Completely modernized, this comfortable hotel offers meeting facilities and more than 200 rooms. A small fee gives guests access to a sauna, health club, and gym. Ask for a room with a view of the Empire State Building. ♦ 22 E. 38th St (at Madison Ave). 685.3700, 800/225.4340; fax 447.0747

Within the Madison Towers Hotel:

The Whaler Bar High-beamed ceilings and a huge working fireplace make this a favorite midtown meeting place. ♦ American ♦ Lunch and dinner. 685.3700

128 Morgans $$$ Former discotheque owner **Ian Schrager** runs this trendy hotel (he also refurbished the **Royalton** and the **Paramount**), with rooms and furnishings created by French designer **André Putman.** The hotel prides itself on getting you whatever you want—if the urge for sushi strikes at midnight, no problem. All rooms have VCRs, stereos, blackout shades on the windows, and phones in the bedrooms and bathrooms. ♦ 237 Madison Ave (between E. 37th and E. 38th Sts). 686.0300, 800/334.3408; fax 779.8352

129 Consulate General of the Polish People This opulent mansion was built by **C.P.H. Gilbert** for a Dutch sea captain in 1905. The equally decorative interiors are largely intact. ♦ 233 Madison Ave (at E. 37th St)

129 231 Madison Avenue This 45-room freestanding brownstone mansion, built in 1852 for banker **Anson Phelps Stokes,** was bought by **J.P. Morgan** for his son in 1904. In 1944, it became the property of the Evangelical Lutheran Church, which is responsible for the sacrilegious brick addition on the E. 37th Street side. It is being restored for incorporation into the **Morgan Library.** ♦ At E. 37th St

Seventy-five percent of New York City's restaurants change hands or close before they are five years old.

130 The Pierpont Morgan Library Financier **J.P. Morgan** began collecting books, manuscripts, and drawings in earnest in 1890, and eventually had to construct this magnificent small palazzo to house his treasures. It was designed in 1906 by **C.F. McKim** of **McKim, Mead & White.** The building itself is a treasure, and the 1928 annex on the Madison Avenue side complements it perfectly. Inside, Morgan's library and office have been preserved exactly as they were when he died in 1913. The collection includes more than 1,000 illuminated medieval and Renaissance manuscripts, the finest in America. It also contains the country's best examples of printed books, from **Gutenberg** to modern times, as well as an extensive collection of fine bookbinding. And its collection of autographed manuscripts, both literary and musical, is considered one of the best in the world. Art historian **Kenneth Clark** summed it all up perfectly when he said, "every object is a treasure, every item is perfect." On your way out, visit the bookshop, where you'll find wonderful books, toys, and cards. The **Morgan Court Cafe,** which serves a light lunch and afternoon tea, is a nice place to relax. ♦ Donation requested. Tu-Sa 10:30AM-5PM; Su 1-5PM. 29 E. 36th St (between Park and Madison Aves). 685.0610

131 Yarn Connection Here you'll find everything from Phildar and Classic Elite to Filatura di Crosa. There's always a cardboard box of odds and ends and great deals to dig through. Reasonably priced beginner to advanced classes are available. ♦ M-F 10AM-6PM; Sa 10AM-5PM. 218 Madison Ave (between E. 36th and E. 37th Sts). 684.5099

132 Lord & Taylor This store has made a specialty of stocking clothing by American designers, but it goes beyond fashion in its furniture and antiques departments, featuring sofas from **Henredon,** Chinese porcelain lamps, and reproductions of Louis XV tables. There is an occasional flash of innovation, particularly in avant-garde designs of the '30s and '40s by **Eileen Gray.** Its shoe department is legendary, as is the caring quality of its sales help, which is quite a rarity these days. Lord & Taylor is also justly famous for its Christmas window displays, without which the holidays in New York wouldn't be the same. The store was the first in the history of retailing to devote its window displays to anything but merchandise during the holiday season. The custom began during the unusually warm December of 1905, when customers didn't seem to feel Christmasy. Lord & Taylor got them into the proper mood by filling its windows with a snowstorm the likes of which New Yorkers hadn't seen since the famous Blizzard of '88. If you arrive 15 minutes before the store opens in the morning, Lord & Taylor provides seating, free coffee (there are also three restaurants within the store), and music just inside the front door. ◆ M-Tu, Sa 10AM-7PM; W-F 10AM-8:30PM; Su noon-6PM. 424 Fifth Ave (between W. 38th and W. 39th Sts). 391.3344

133 Goldberg's Marine Distributors Most of the stores on this block sell trimmings and ribbons, but if you need a stout coil of rope, Goldberg's has it. New York is America's biggest seaport, but it still comes as a surprise to find a place selling anchors, depth finders, fishing equipment (including the tournament reels that are so much more expensive in Europe), and other gear for yacht enthusiasts and sailors. It is a perfect store for the shoes and foul-weather clothes and other outfits you need if you want to look like you belong to the yacht club set. ◆ M-Sa 9:30AM-5:30PM; Su 9:30AM-4PM. 12 W. 37th St (between Fifth and Sixth Aves). 594.6065

134 M&J Trimming Though this well-known chockablock trimmings store looks like the kind traditionally open to the trade only, M&J has always been a retail-shopper's dream. Countless buttons, tassles, piping, frogs, and decorative borders will transform the most nondescript garment into an award-winner. Aspiring and professional designers come here for inspiration, resourcefully using buttons and beads for everything from jewelry to shoe decoration, kitsch to elegant. A new **M&J Decorator Collection** next door at 1014 Sixth Avenue makes the same treasure trove of braiding and trimming available for home design. ◆ M-F 9AM-6PM; Sa 10AM-5PM. 1008 Sixth Ave (between W. 37th and W. 38th Sts). 391.9072

Getting to the top is the literal object of the annual Empire State Building Run Up, a marathon race of unusual proportions. Entrants must negotiate the building's 1,575 steps. People from around the globe enter the event, held each February. Average winning time is 12 to 14 minutes, with winners and losers alike earning a splendid view from the 86th floor and an elevator ride down.

Merce Cunningham
Artistic Director, Merce Cunningham Dance Company

The sight—in early summer on a Sunday morning, the traffic sounds becoming muted—of 10,000 bicycles coming up Sixth Avenue, most of the riders wearing orange jackets, and some of them in tandem. Occasionally an oddity such as a unicycle or a two-wheeled vehicle, the front one small, the back one enormous.

The **Union Square Greenmarket** on any market day, but particularly in the late spring through fall when the fresh produce and flowers and people are at their best. Beware the pickpockets, the signs say.

This one doesn't repeat. The vision of **King Kong** strapped to the **Empire State Building** a few years ago, the huge balloon-animal wrapped around the tower, flattened by the wind.

The vision of a large cruise ship through the windows of **Westbeth,** making a stately, steady progress down the Hudson to the open sea, when I am teaching a class of dancers. The ship's rhythm and movement is a delicious addition, however brief, to the bustle of the class, particularly in late afternoon, with the rays of the polluted sunset over New Jersey.

Being in the theater, backstage or out front, just before the curtain goes up.

Horace Havemeyer III
Publisher, *Metropolis, The Architecture and Design Magazine of New York*

Having lunch on weekends in the winter in SoHo or Midtown before or after visiting galleries or museums. The **MoMA** dining rooms are great for their views.

Browsing in any good bookstore. **Rizzoli's** on 57th Street is open at night so we can drop in, often after a concert. **Doubleday** and **Brentano's** on Fifth Avenue are also favorites.

Walking almost anywhere looking at buildings and their details. Especially:

Park Avenue in the 60s, 70s, and 80s. Look at the detail in the pre-World War II buildings.

TriBeCa. Walk along Greenwich Street and look in at **Duane Square.** Note the continuity between the area's industrial past and residential present.

Along the waterfront looking at the rivers, river traffic, and opposite shores, such as the **Finley Walk** along the East River between 72nd and 90th streets. Going downtown from the East 80s, I always try to take the **East River Drive.**

Queen Anne-style row houses. My favorites are the row of 10 houses at 146-156 E. 89th Street, the **Henderson houses** on East End between 86th and 87th streets, and those between Amsterdam and Columbus on 81st Street.

Gramercy Park, its surrounding buildings, and Park Avenue in the low 20s.

Chelsea

Named for the estate acquired by **Captain Thomas Clarke** in 1750, Chelsea was originally bounded by **W. 14th** and **W. 25th streets**, and **Eighth Avenue** and the **Hudson River**. Today, the Chelsea area, which extends farther north to **W. 34th Street** and east to **Sixth Avenue**, is quite a mixed bag. **Clement Clarke Moore**, who had inherited his grandfather's land—and is best known as the author of the poem *A Visit from St. Nicholas*—divided his family estate and laid out the neighborhood's original building lots in 1830, some of which he donated to the **General Theological Seminary**. The surrounding area was a flourishing middle-class suburb that never quite made it as a desirable address. Once the Hudson River Railroad opened on 11th Avenue in 1851, it attracted breweries and slaughterhouses and their workers' shanties and tenements, which

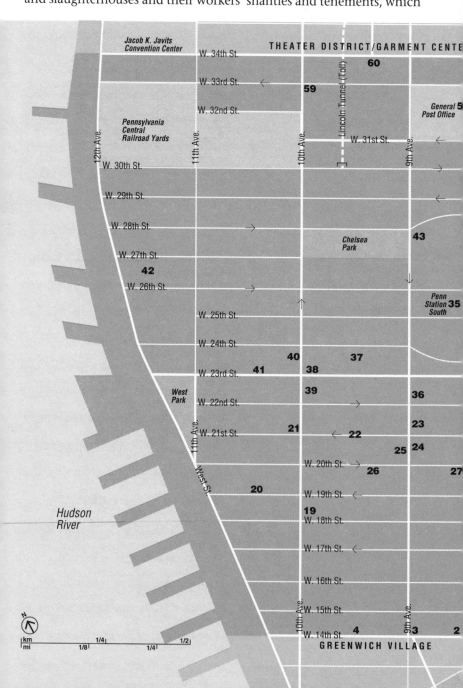

marked the beginning of the area's aesthetic decline. In the 1870s, the remaining town house blocks were invaded by the city's first elevated railroad, on Ninth Avenue.

Despite its industrial image, Chelsea became a creative, as well as a retail, center. A flurry of theatrical activity took over W. 23rd Street in the 1880s, but by 1892 the theater world had moved uptown, leaving behind the artists and writers who eventually departed for the newer bohemia of **Greenwich Village.** The funky **Hotel Chelsea,** on W. 23rd Street, is a remnant of Chelsea's theatrical heyday, when actors and playwrights lodged there. In the 1960s, Andy Warhol's superstars **Viva** and **Edie Sedgewick** lived there, and his film *Chelsea Girls* documented a chapter in the renaissance of the old survivor.

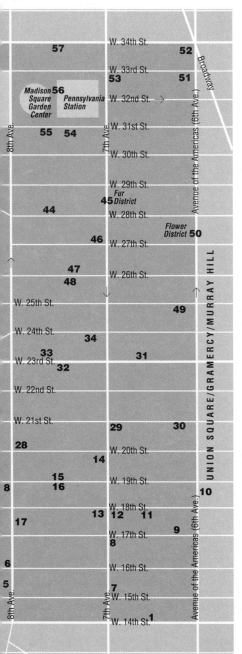

The country's motion picture industry started in Chelsea in 1905, and for a decade flourished in old lofts and theaters used as studios. **Adolph Zukor's Famous Players Studio,** which employed **Mary Pickford** and **John Barrymore,** produced films here. But the **Astoria Studios** in Queens built a better facility, and eventually balmy Hollywood beckoned. The film business also moved on.

In the 1930s, new industry found quarters in the area near the piers. The 11th Avenue railroad was replaced by a less objectionable elevated train, and the Ninth Avenue line shut down. The clean sweep of 1950s and 1960s urban renewal replaced slum housing with housing projects, and renovation started on desirable Federal and Greek Revival town houses. Today, Chelsea is a pastiche of town houses, housing projects, industrial buildings, tenements, secondhand office-furniture stores, and a large number of churches.

Chelsea's retail career was also short-lived. As the gentry pursued their determined course uptown, so did fashionable stores. By the 1870s, W. 23rd Street blossomed, and the blocks on Sixth Avenue south of it became known as the "Ladies' Mile." During the latter part of the century, giant dry goods stores of limestone and cast iron lined Sixth Avenue (now Avenue of the Americas) and Broadway. Many of the buildings that still stand, reminders of past retail glories, are used as lofts and offices. By the early part of the 1900s, the fashion action had moved to W. 34th Street, and by the 1930s, W. 23rd Street was a has-been.

Today, the most interesting shops in Chelsea are those selling antiques on Ninth Avenue between W. 20th and W. 22nd streets, and the **Flower District** on the blocks between W. 27th and W. 30th streets on Avenue of the Americas. Daisies and orchids, rare palms, and exotic bonsai overflow the wholesale and retail stores that supply the city with cut flowers and plants.

1 New York State Armory The 42nd Infantry Division of the **New York National Guard** is headquartered in this building, designed by **Charles S. Kawecki** in 1971 obviously to make its members feel warlike. ♦ 125 W. 14th St (between Sixth and Seventh Aves). 486.6586

2 319 West 14th Street A 20-year-old **Orson Welles** and his first wife, **Virginia Nicholson,** lived in a basement apartment here between 1935 and 1937, during which time he directed the famous all-black *Macbeth* for Harlem's Negro Theater. Their next move was to a country house on the Hudson. ♦ Between Eighth and Ninth Aves

3 Old Homestead ★★$$$$ Established in 1868, this is the oldest steak house in Manhattan, but the interior has been so gussied up that it seems to belong in the suburbs. They must be doing something right to have lasted all these years. The portions are large and the quality is good. At the shop next door, you can buy fresh cuts of beef—1½-inch-thick steaks—sauces, and a variety of gourmet items, including the crème de la crème of chocolates: Valrhona from France and D'Orsay from Belgium. ♦ American ♦ Lunch and dinner. 56 Ninth Ave (at W. 14th St). Reservations recommended. 242.9040

Frank's

4 Frank's ★★$$$ Frank's is a real find. The daytime clientele includes the guys who work in the wholesale meat district, and they're hard to fool with anything less than the best steaks and chops in a plain wrapper. ♦ American ♦ Lunch and dinner; dinner only on Saturday. Closed Sunday. 431 W. 14th St (between Ninth and 10th Aves). Reservations recommended. 243.1349

5 Port of New York Authority Commerce Building/Union Inland Terminal No. 1 The organization now known as the Port Authority of New York and New Jersey had its headquarters in this blockbuster, designed in 1932 by **Abbott, Merckt & Co.,** before moving down to the World Trade Center. The top floors were designed for manufacturing, but the elevators can carry a 20-ton truck to any floor. ♦ 111 Eighth Ave (between W. 15th and W. 16th Sts)

6 Cajun ★$$ The honky-tonk atmosphere and live Dixieland music (every night at 8PM) are fun on occasion; the hearty helpings of Creole-Cajun food generally provide good eating. ♦ Creole/Cajun ♦ Lunch and dinner; dinner only on Saturday. 129 Eighth Ave (at W. 16th St). Reservations recommended for five or more. 691.6174

7 Jensen-Lewis Two floors of creative, colorful merchandise, from sofas and beds to lamps and luggage (even bean-bag chairs), can be found here. This store is especially known for its selection of director's chairs. ♦ M-W, F-Sa 10AM-7PM; Th 10AM-8PM; Su noon-5PM. 89 Seventh Ave (at W. 15th St). 929.4880

BARNEYS NEW YORK

8 Barneys New York This is a New York original. Name a famous designer for either men or women, and the helpful person at the front desk will direct you to their best work, from shoes to hats with every stop between. You can buy antiques, leather goods, jewelry, lingerie, or children's clothes. Downstairs, you can get your hair cut (at **Roger Thompson**) and enjoy a fancy lunch, or cappuccino, surrounded by opulence. Barneys first opened in 1923 as a discount store for men and boys. But a 1986 expansion, particularly the controversial annexation and modernization of town houses behind the original structure, has changed its character completely. A smaller, men's-only branch is at 225 Liberty St (at 2 World Financial Center), 945.1600. ♦ M-Th 10AM-9PM; F 10AM-8PM; Sa 10AM-7PM; Su noon-6PM. Seventh Ave (at W. 17th St). 929.9000. Also at: 660 Madison Ave. 826.8900

9 Da Umberto ★★$$$$ This casual and restful trattoria concentrates on Tuscan dishes, especially wild game (hare, pheasant, venison). Ask to be seated in the skylit back room. ♦ Italian ♦ Lunch and dinner; dinner only on Saturday. Closed Sunday. 107 W.

17th St (between Sixth and Seventh Aves). Reservations required. 989.0303

10 Bed Bath & Beyond You'll find 80 patterns of bed linens, 132 colors and patterns of bath towels, 218 styles of place mats, as well as gadgets ranging from shelf dividers to "banana savers," on the shelves running up to the 28-foot-high ceilings of this overwhelming store, the flagship of the national chain. There are significant discounts on name-brand items, but even if you're not in the market for a new comforter or beach umbrella, it's worth coming into this Victorian-pillared landmark, built in 1896 as the **Siegel-Cooper Dry Goods Store,** just for the experience. ◆ M-F 9:30AM-9PM; Sa 9:30AM-8PM; Su 10AM-6PM. 620 Sixth Ave (between W. 18th and W. 19th Sts). 255.3550

11 Two Worlds Gallery This store is the direct importer of the antiques and unique decorative objects sold here. Paintings and custom artwork from well-known artists are also available. ◆ M-Sa 10AM-6PM. 122 W. 18th St (between Sixth and Seventh Aves). 633.1668

11 Movie Star News Millions of head shots, stills, and lobby cards fill the filing cabinets in this garage space, a popular source for collectors, newspapers, magazines, and TV. **Paula Klaw** and her family also stock movie posters and books on theater and film. ◆ M-F 10AM-6PM; Sa 11AM-6PM. 134 W. 18th St (between Sixth and Seventh Aves). 620.8160

11 Poster America Gallery The selection of vintage posters from 1910 to 1965, mostly original lithographs from Europe and the U.S., is among the best you'll find on either side of the Atlantic. If you like vintage photos, they have those, too. In the 1880s, this space was used as a stable and a carriage house by the department stores along Ladies' Mile. ◆ Tu-Sa 11AM-6PM; Su 1-5PM. 138 W. 18th St (between Sixth and Seventh Aves). 206.0499

12 Le Madri ★★★$$$$ Illustrious crowds flock to **Pino Luongo's** stylish restaurant, which turns out specialties that will remind you of Tuscany. Order roasted vegetables for the whole table. You'll want to return again and again. ◆ Italian ◆ Lunch and dinner; dinner only on Sunday. 168 W. 18th St (at Seventh Ave). Reservations required. 727.8022

Perhaps the most distinguishing feature of the city's streets in the 1880s was the mass of telephone and telegraph wires overhead. After the blizzard of 1888 they were placed underground.

Restaurants/Clubs: Red   **Hotels:** Blue
Shops/ 🌳 Outdoors: Green   **Sights/Culture:** Black

13 Books of Wonder If there are no children in your life, this store will make you wish there were—or at least make you fondly remember when you were a child yourself. Authors and illustrators make frequent appearances to read from their books and to sign copies. These and other special events are described in the store's monthly newsletter. The Hudson Street branch has a story hour every Sunday at 11:30AM (except between Thanksgiving and New Year's). ◆ M-Sa 11AM-7PM; Su noon-6PM. 132 Seventh Ave (at W. 18th St). 989.3270. Also at: 464 Hudson St. 989.3270

14 Claire ★$$$ Although the atmosphere is often flawed by the intensity of the noise, this is a consistently reliable, reasonably priced seafood restaurant that will make you think you have just come in from a sunny Florida beach—the inventive decor is by set designer **Robin Wagner** (*Dream Girls, A Chorus Line*). The sometimes fierce and often intricate flavors are devised by its Thai chef. The choice of accompaniments is limited to one: white rice. There is usually only one vegetable as well, allowing diners to concentrate on the fish and shellfish. ◆ Seafood ◆ Lunch and dinner; late-night meals also on Friday and Saturday. 156 Seventh Ave (between W. 19th and W. 20th Sts). Reservations recommended. 255.1955

15 Bessie Shonberg Theater Operated by the **Dance Theater Workshop (DTW),** this 160-seat theater (named after the dancer, choreographer, and teacher) is one of the most active dance, mime, and poetry houses in the city and offers young performing artists a variety of support services. Famous clown/dancer/mime **Bill Irwin** has often played here. DTW also runs the picture gallery in the lobby of the theater. ◆ 219 W. 19th St (between Seventh and Eighth Aves), second floor. 924.0077

16 The Billiard Club The lush Victorian decor of this vast, 33-table billiard emporium suggests formality, but fun is your cue here (*good clean* fun—no alcohol is served). The light menu of snacks such as sandwiches, hotdogs, and pizza may be ordered at any time and can be enjoyed at small tables interspersed among the playing tables. The weekday lunch special includes nourishment for two and the use of a pool table for an hour. Call for reservations, fee schedule, and party information. ◆ M-F 10AM-2AM; Sa-Su noon-2AM. 220 W. 19th St (between Seventh and Eighth Aves). 206.7665

17 Cola's $ Here you'll find a casual mix of Northern and Southern Italian cuisine, and wine to accompany your meal. Hand-painted, antiqued walls lend a gentle ambience to the room, where a lively downtown crowd comes to take on the pasta. ♦ Italian ♦ Dinner. 148 Eighth Ave (between W. 17th and W. 18th Sts). 633.8020

17 Gascogne ★★$$$ The chef is **Pascal Coudoy,** formerly of the Ambassador Grill. The decor is reminiscent of a French country restaurant with a backyard cafe. The menu, from the southwest of France, offers superb fish soup, foie gras, and an excellent cassoulet. ♦ French ♦ Dinner. Closed Sunday. 158 Eighth Ave (between W. 17th and W. 18th Sts). Reservations required. 675.6564

18 Man Ray ★$$ Guided by skilled chef **Peter Cole,** this bistro serves a clientele who appreciate well-cooked, authentic international cuisine. The decor is sleek and minimal, harking back to the Art Deco age. ♦ International ♦ Lunch and dinner. 169 Eighth Ave (between W. 18th and W. 19th Sts). 627.4220

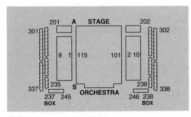

18 The Joyce Theater Renovated in 1981 by **Hardy Holzman Pfeiffer Associates,** this is a theater *for* dancers and the people who love dance; it's elegant, intimate, and deep in the heart of Chelsea. The building was once the decrepit and infamous **Elgin** movie house, but a 1981 remodeling created the current 474-seat venue (see diagram above) by completely replacing the building's interior and re-Deco-izing the exterior. The Joyce Theater is named for the daughter of the principal donor. ♦ 175 Eighth Ave (between W. 18th and W. 19th Sts). 242.0800

19 La Luncheonette ★$$$ The homey bar and open kitchen in this bistro-style restaurant seem familiar enough, but the free-range chicken with mustard, the lamb sausage, and the *gratinée trois poisson* (lobster, crab, and sea scallops) are interesting turns on an honored cuisine. ♦ French ♦ Lunch and dinner; dinner only on Saturday and Sunday. 130 10th Ave (at W. 18th St). Reservations recommended. 675.0342

THE KITCHEN

20 The Kitchen This veteran institution for experimental performing and visual arts presents the works of young artists in dance, film, video, music, and performance art. Programs are scheduled most evenings and some require that tickets be purchased in advance. Call for the current performance schedule. ♦ Box office: M-F 10AM-5PM. 512 W. 19th St (between 10th and 11th Aves). 255.5793

21 Guardian Angel Church This little complex of Italian Romanesque buildings, designed in 1930 by **John Van Pelt,** surrounds what is known as the **Shrine Church of the Sea**. The name reflects the one-time presence of the busiest piers in the Port of New York, a short walk to the west. The church's Renaissance interior is even more impressive than the redbrick-and-limestone facade. The priest in charge of this Roman Catholic church is designated **Chaplain of the Port,** with duties that include assigning chaplains to ships based here. ♦ 193 10th Ave (at W. 21st St). 929.5966

22 West 21st Street Almost all the 19th-century houses on this block follow **Clement Clarke Moore's** requirement of front gardens and street trees. In its earliest years as a residential community, all of Chelsea looked much like this. The building with the unusual peaked roof on the Ninth Avenue corner was built in the 1820s by **James N. Wells** and is the oldest house in the neighborhood. ♦ Between Ninth and 10th Aves

23 Somethin' Else! There are dozens of antique shops scattered around this neighborhood, some authentic, some dubious, all of them browsers' delights. But this one is, indeed, something else. It's a collection of old toys, quilts, jewelry, and an entire wall of crystal glasses. ♦ M-F 11AM-7:30PM; Sa 11AM-6PM; Su 1-6PM. 182 Ninth Ave (between W. 21st and W. 22nd Sts). 924.0006

24 Manhattan Doll House This shop has the largest collection of new and antique dolls, doll houses, and doll accessories in the city—all for sale. ♦ M-F 11AM-5:30PM; Sa 11AM-5PM. 176 Ninth Ave (between W. 20th and W. 21st Sts). 989.5220

25 General Theological Seminary You're welcome to enter this oasis through the library building on Ninth Avenue during public hours or, in summer, to take the free "Grand Design" tour. Land for the Episcopal Seminary was donated by **Clement Clarke Moore** in 1830, on the condition that the seminary should always occupy the site. The **West Building,** built in 1835, is the oldest building on campus, as well as New York's oldest example of Gothic Revival architecture. It predates **Charles C. Haight's** renovation (1883-1900), which includes all the other Gothic buildings. In the center is the **Chapel of the Good Shepherd,** with its outstanding bronze doors and 161-foot-high square bell tower. **Hoffman Hall,** at the 10th Avenue end, contains a medieval-style dining hall complete with a barrel-vaulted ceiling, walk-in fireplaces, and a gallery for musicians. The other end is dominated by the new and very much out-of-place **St. Mark's Library,** built in 1960 by **O'Connor & Kilhan,** containing, along with one of the world's largest collections of Latin Bibles, some 170,000 volumes. ◆ M-F noon-2:30PM; Sa 11AM-3:30PM; Su 2-4PM; closed when school is not in session and on religious holidays. 175 Ninth Ave (between W. 20th and W. 21st Sts). 243.5150

26 406-24 West 20th Street This row of extremely well-preserved Greek Revival houses was built by **Don Alonzo Cushman,** a dry goods merchant who, in 1837, developed much of Chelsea and built these as rental units. The attic windows are circled with wreaths, the doorways framed in brownstone. Even the newel posts, topped with cast-iron pineapples, are still intact. ◆ Between Ninth and 10th Aves

27 St. Peter's Episcopal Church The church and its rectory and parish hall are outgrowths of **Clement Clarke Moore** and **James W. Smith's** 1838 plan to build them in the style of Greek temples. According to legend, the plan was changed when one of the vestrymen came back from England with tales of the Gothic buildings at Oxford. The congregation decided to switch styles, even though the foundations were already in place. The fence that surrounds this charming complex was brought here from **Trinity Church** on lower Broadway, where it had stood since 1790. Renovations are under way to replace the roof, repoint and preserve the masonry, and repair or replace all of the woodwork in the tower and window and door openings. ◆ 346 W. 20th St (between Eighth and Ninth Aves). 929.2390

28 Chelsea Foods This is a gorgeously designed modern store and cafe with many interesting, but expensive, prepared and packaged foods to go. The brownies are terrific. ◆ Cafe/Takeout ◆ Daily 9AM-10PM. 198 Eighth Ave (at W. 20th St). 691.3948

29 Meriken ★$$ New Wave Japanese is served to a trendy crowd in an interesting Art Deco decor in celadon. ◆ Japanese ◆ Lunch and dinner; dinner only on Saturday and Sunday. 189 Seventh Ave (at W. 21st St). Reservations recommended. 620.9684

30 Third Cemetery of the Spanish & Portuguese Synagogue Enclosed on three sides by painted brick loft buildings, this private hideaway is the third cemetery established by the first Jewish congregation in New York; tombstones date from 1829 to 1851. The second cemetery is in Greenwich Village, the first on the Lower East Side. ◆ 98-110 W. 21st St (between Sixth and Seventh Aves)

31 165 West 23rd Street In 1896, *Red Badge of Courage* author **Stephen Crane** moved into a room on the fifth floor of this building. The struggling 24-year-old journalist made his living writing magazine and newspaper articles about poverty and vice in the city. ◆ Between Sixth and Seventh Aves

32 Hotel Chelsea $$ Irish dramatist **Brendan Behan,** who lived here during his New York years, said that there was more space in the Hotel Chelsea than in the whole of Staten Island. It has housed more writers, poets, and musicians than any other hotel in the five boroughs of New York. When the hotel was first built in 1884 by **Hubert, Pirrson & Co.,** Chelsea was the heart of the Theater District, attracting creative people as Greenwich Village would a decade later. In its early days the hotel was home to such writers as **William Dean Howells** and **O. Henry,** and later to **Thomas Wolfe, Arthur Miller, Mary McCarthy, Vladimir Nabokov,** and **Yevgeny Yevtushenko. Sarah Bernhardt** once lived here, and this is where **Dylan Thomas** spent his last days. In the 1960s and 1970s, it was a favorite stopping place for visiting rock stars (including the **Sex Pistols**), who shared the atmosphere with modern classical composers **George Kleinsinger** and **Virgil Thomson.** The Chelsea was originally an apartment building, the first in New York with a penthouse. It was converted into a hotel in 1905. The lobby has been altered, but the stairway, best seen from the second floor, is intact. Rooms with kitchenettes are available upon request. At press time, sorely needed renovations were under way. ◆ 222 W. 23rd St (between Seventh and Eighth Aves). 243.3700; fax 243.3700 ext 2171

32 Manhattan Comics & Cards Here is an extensive collection of new and old comic books and baseball cards. ◆ M-Tu 10AM-6:30PM; W-Th 10AM-7PM; F 10AM-9:30PM; Sa 10AM-7:30PM; Su noon-5:30PM. 228 W. 23rd St (between Seventh and Eighth Aves). 243.9349

33 Unity Book Center "For books that matter" is their tagline; topics include Marxism-Leninism, socialism, African-American literature, and women's equality. ◆ M-F 10:30AM-6PM; Sa 11AM-4PM. 237 W. 23rd St (between Seventh and Eighth Aves). 242.2934

34 McBurney YMCA $ One of the first social workers to deal with the problems of foreign-born New Yorkers, **Robert Ross McBurney** ran a Y at E. 23rd Street and Fourth Avenue in the 1870s. This branch, built in 1904 by **Parish & Schroeder,** is its successor. The building includes a track, a gymnasium, and a rooftop sundeck. Maximum stay is 25 days. ◆ 206 W. 24th St (between Seventh and Eighth Aves). 741.9226; fax 741.0012

35 Penn Station South This 12-square-block complex of 2,820 apartments was built in 1962 by **Herman Jessor** as middle-income housing by the **International Ladies' Garment Workers Union.** As you stroll by, look at the sidewalk on the uptown side of W. 24th Street at Eighth Avenue, where autumn leaves have left a permanent impression. ◆ Bounded by W. 23rd and W. 29th Sts (between Eighth and Ninth Aves)

36 Luma ★★$$$ A new breed of restaurant, Luma caters to health-conscious, and well-heeled, diners. Try the barley risotto and the grilled vegetables with garlic-herb oil. There's not an additive in sight. ◆ American ◆ Dinner. 200 Ninth Ave (between W. 22nd and W. 23rd Sts). Reservations recommended. 633.8033

37 London Terrace Apartments This double row of buildings with a garden in the center contains 1,670 apartments. It was built in 1930 by **Farrar & Watmaugh** at the height of the Depression and stood virtually empty for several years. Its apartments went unrented despite lures such as an Olympic-size swimming pool and doormen dressed as London bobbies. It is the second complex by that name on the site. The original, built in 1845, was a row of Greek Revival buildings with wide front lawns on W. 23rd Street. Behind it, on W. 24th Street, was a row of two-story houses called Chelsea Cottages. The 1845 complex replaced **Clement Clarke Moore's** house, which, though small, had been the only building on the block. ◆ Bounded by W. 23rd and W. 24th Sts (between Ninth and 10th Aves)

38 Chateau Ruggero $$$ The Franco-Italian name comes from the decor, which is French, and the current menu, which is Italian. The charming setting dates back to the London Terrace Apartments of the 1930s. ◆ Italian ◆ Lunch and dinner; dinner only on Saturday. Closed Sunday. 461 W. 23rd St (between Ninth and 10th Aves). Reservations recommended. 242.8641

39 Empire Diner ★$ This 1930s-style diner was refurbished in 1976 by **Carl Laanes** but still has all the trappings of the original, except the grease and the prices. Empire also has a bar. It may be the only diner in America whose late-night customers arrive in stretch limousines. Open 24 hours, it is a favorite of disco and nightclub patrons and of those who want to stay up all night and enjoy the best diner breakfast in town. In summer, sit at one of the tables on the sidewalk for front-row viewing of the street action. ◆ American ◆ Daily 24 hours. 210 10th Ave (between W. 22nd and W. 23rd Sts). 243.2736

40 Chelsea Central ★★$$$ Owner **Larry McIntyre** bills his intimate and cozy old saloon—original tin ceilings, dark wood, old phone booths with folding doors—as an American bistro. The food is terrific. Try the eggplant with mozzarella and roasted peppers, and a slice of chocolate marquis cake. ◆ Continental ◆ Lunch and dinner; dinner only on Saturday. 227 10th Ave (between W. 23rd and W. 24th Sts). Reservations recommended. 620.0230

41 WPA Theater Under the impressive artistic direction of **Kyle Renick,** productions such as *Steel Magnolias, Little Shop of Horrors,* and *The Whales of August* have blossomed into memorable Off-Broadway hits and feature films. The theater seats 122. ◆ 519 W. 23rd St (between 10th and 11th Aves). 206.0523

Restaurants/Clubs: Red   Hotels: Blue

Shops/ 🌳 Outdoors: Green   Sights/Culture: Black

42 Starrett-Lehigh Building A pacesetter in its day, this Art Deco collection of glass, concrete, and brown brick with rounded corners was built over the yards of the Lehigh Valley Railroad, and had elevators powerful enough to lift fully loaded freight cars onto its upper warehouse floors. It was designed in 1931 by **Russell G.** and **Walter M. Cory** and **Yasuo Matsui.** ♦ Bounded by W. 26th and W. 27th Sts (between 11th and 12th Aves)

43 Church of the Holy Apostles The slate-roofed spire of this Episcopal church makes it a standout among the huge brick apartment houses all around it. Built in 1848 by **Minard LaFever** with 1858 transepts by **Richard Upjohn,** it's an unusual feature of the view to the west from the Observation Deck of the Empire State Building. ♦ 300 Ninth Ave (between W. 27th and W. 28th Sts)

44 The Ballroom ★★$$$$ The best place to sit at this authentic Spanish restaurant is at the long food bar, with its rows of hanging sausages, hams, dried cod, and wondrous array of *tapas*—small morsels of traditional appetizers. Adjacent to the restaurant is a charming cabaret theater that showcases musicians and singers Tuesday through Saturday evenings and Sunday afternoons. Call ahead to check the cover policy. ♦ Spanish ♦ Lunch and dinner; dinner only on Saturday. Closed Monday and Sunday. 253 W. 28th St (between Seventh and Eighth Aves). Reservations recommended. 244.3005

45 Fur District Yes, that man you just passed did have a silver fox cape over his arm. No, he didn't steal it, and chances are that no one will steal it from him. It's commonplace in the Fur District for thousands of dollars' worth of merchandise to be delivered in such a casual way. It's all in a day's work for the people who make and sell fur garments in this neighborhood. ♦ Bounded by W. 27th and W. 30th Sts, and Sixth and Eighth Aves

46 Fashion Institute of Technology If there were a competition for the ugliest block in Manhattan, the center of this complex on W. 27th Street would win easily. All the buildings, built between 1958 and 1977, are by the same firm, **De Young & Moscowitz,** but obviously not by the same hand. The prestigious school, part of the **State University of New York,** was created by New York's garment industry to train young people in all aspects of the fashion business. ♦ Seventh Ave at W. 27th St

47 221 West 26th Street This building was originally an armory. It was also once the **Famous Players Studio,** where, in 1915, **Adolph Zukor** paid **Mary Pickford** an unprecedented $2,000 per week as one of his most famous players. Other film studios in the neighborhood were the Reliance, the Majestic, and the Kalem Company. ♦ Between Seventh and Eighth Aves

48 Swedish Institute Clinic If you're seeking relief from arthritis, lower back pain, sciatica, or simple chronic stress, a therapeutic massage may be what the doctor orders. If so, bring your prescription here, where seven half-hour healing treatments can be had for a reasonable rate. ♦ By appointment with a doctor's recommendation only. 226 W. 26th St (between Seventh and Eighth Aves). 924.0991

49 Chelsea Antiques Building If the hundreds of dealers at the weekend Annex Antiques Fair and Flea Market a block away don't satisfy you, this antiques cove is wonderfully convenient and considerably calmer. Twelve floors are filled with quality dealers of art, antiques, and estate treasures, from charming collectibles to serious museum pieces. ♦ Daily 10AM-6PM. 110 W. 25th St (between Sixth and Seventh Aves). 929.0909

50 Flower District The best time to smell the flowers here is the early morning, when florists from all over the city arrive to refresh their stock. If you're in the market for a large plant or a small tree, you'll find it here on the sidewalk soaking up the sun. ♦ Sixth Ave (between W. 26th and W. 29th Sts)

51 A&S Plaza Eight floors of shops plus a food court will make you feel like you're in a mall in the 'burbs. **The Body Shop** (skin-care products), **Accento** (handknit sweaters), and **Moose N' Around** (clothes and accessories adorned with favorite cartoon characters) are of particular interest, but two other reasons to visit this vertical mall, designed by **RTKL Associates,** of Baltimore, in 1989, are the clean bathrooms and the **Visitors Center** on the seventh floor; stop in if you need tourist brochures, transportation information, or assistance in getting theater tickets or making restaurant reservations. ♦ W. 33rd St at Sixth Ave. 465.0500

52 Herald Center Built in 1985 by **Coeland, Novak, Israel & Simmon,** this shopping center, dubbed the "Tall Mall," seems to have suffered in the shadow of A&S Plaza. Once home to 70 stores, at present most are closed except for the food court on the eighth floor, **Toys 'R Us** and **Kids 'R Us** (first and second floors); **10 Dollar Store** on the third floor; and **Half-price** store on the fourth floor. The fate of the remaining space is undetermined. ◆ W. 34th St at Broadway. 244.2555

53 Hotel Pennsylvania $$ Originally designed in 1918 by **McKim, Mead & White,** this hotel was named for the nearby Pennsylvania Station. It is now the hotel closest to the **Jacob K. Javits Convention Center.** In the 1930s, it was a hot stop for the Big Bands: **Glenn Miller** immortalized its phone number with his "PEnnsylvania 6-5000." At press time, all 1,700 rooms were under renovation; completion is scheduled for mid-1994. ◆ W. 33rd St at Seventh Ave. 736.5000, 800/223.8585; fax 502.8798

54 Schoepfer Studios Carrying on an 84-year-old family business started by his grandfather, taxidermist **Jim Schoepfer** stocks a zoo-full of animals, including zebras, armadillos, anteaters, birds, and fish. Perhaps you'll recognize the crocodile from the film *Crocodile Dundee.* A sign on the door welcomes customers, not browsers; fortunately, there's a lot to see in the window display. ◆ M-F 9:30AM-5PM. 138 W. 31st St (between Seventh and Eighth Aves). 736.6939

55 St. John the Baptist Church Designed in 1872 by **Napoleon LeBrun,** this Roman Catholic church is noted for its white marble interior. ◆ 210 W. 31st St (between Seventh and Eighth Aves). 564.9070

56 Madison Square Garden Center America's premier entertainment facility, designed by **Charles Luckman Associates** in 1968, hosts more than 600 events and nearly 6 million spectators each year. Within the center are the 20,000-seat **Arena,** the 5,600-seat **Paramount,** and the **Exposition Rotunda** with a 20-story office building. It is home to the **New York Knicks** and the **New York Rangers.** Throughout the year, the Garden hosts exhibitions and trade shows; boxing;

rodeos; dog, cat, and horse shows; circuses; graduations; rock concerts; tennis, track and field, and gymnastics events; and an occasional presidential convention. ◆ Seventh Ave (between W. 31st and W. 33rd Sts). 465.6741

Within Madison Square Garden Center:

Pennsylvania Station Make connections here for Long Island via the **Long Island Railroad** and for points north, south, and west via Amtrak. ◆ Bounded by W. 31st and W. 33rd Sts (between Seventh and Eighth Aves). Amtrak 582.6875; Long Island Railroad 718/217.5477

57 1 Penn Plaza In 1972, **Charles Luckman Associates** designed this, the tallest of the complex of buildings that replaced the late, great Pennsylvania Station. ◆ W. 34th St (between Seventh and Eighth Aves). 239.7400

58 General Post Office The monumental stairway and columned entrance (shown below) were designed by **McKim, Mead & White** in 1913. Look up for that famous inscription about rain, snow, and the gloom of night that made it the first attraction of visitors arriving by train. Postal services are available here 24 hours daily. ◆ Eighth Ave (between W. 31st and W. 33rd Sts). 967.8585

59 Sky Rink Located on the 16th floor of a huge warehouse building, this Olympic-size ice-skating rink, designed in 1970 by **Davis, Brody & Associates,** features figure skating sessions every day, as well as regular sessions for folks who prefer just going 'round and 'round. The public skating schedule varies; call for current hours. ◆ Fee; skate rental. 450 W. 33rd St (at 10th Ave). 695.6555

60 The Original Improvisation Although it was relocated here in 1992, this is the original, the place that marked the start on the road to stardom for talents like **Richard Pryor, Robin Williams, Stiller & Meara,** and **Rodney Dangerfield.** Light meals are served in casual surroundings. ◆ Cover and drink minimum. Shows: M-Th, Su continuous 9PM-closing; F-Sa 9PM and 11PM. 358 W. 34th St (between Ninth and 10th Aves). Reservations recommended. 582.7442

General Post Office

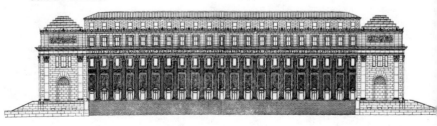

Bests

George Lang
Consultant/Author/Owner of Café des Artistes

Remi—I have rarely eaten Italian food as good as that served in this place, even in the Mother Country. Chef **Francesco Antonucci's** dishes—like the roasted quail wrapped in bacon and served with warm lentil salad—remind me that a good chef is like a good fairy who dispenses happiness. Even the most knowledgeable Italian wine connoisseur will find surprises on the reasonably priced wine list.

Park Bistro—When I stepped through the lace-lined door into the packed, noisy 65-seat restaurant with its plain wood floors, banquettes, posters, and photos of France, it was almost like being in Paris. One of my favorite dishes is lamb shank braised for seven hours with bits of dried apricots, currants, vegetables, and wild mushrooms.

Chef's, Cuisiniere's Club—C.C.C. is truly directed toward the needs of fellow chefs—the three partners are friends from their days together at the **Culinary Institute of America,** and worked together at Côte Basque. You will eat some of the best food anywhere in the unpretentious little dining room. At my last dinner, every dish was a winner.

Carmine's—I think Carmine's reflects the post-Reagan era yearning for an America where the tables had four legs, the light source was not halogen, and the pasta of choice was spaghetti. My recommendations, based on serious soul- and stomach-searching: fried calamari, rigatoni with broccoli, or chicken Contadina.

Helen Gurley Brown
Editor, *Cosmopolitan* magazine

All visitors to New York would enjoy a lunch or dinner at the **Russian Tea Room.** Obviously there are hundreds (maybe more) of fabulous restaurants in New York City, but this one to me captures the warmth, glamour, and charm of our metropolis. Once in a while you will see a movie star seated close to you at a table. If you don't, the food is still worth a visit. It was the first restaurant someone took *me* to when I arrived in New York 30 years ago, and it's better than ever.

Other things to do in New York City: walk the entire length of **East** and **West 57th Street**—that street, to me, as much as Madison Avenue and Fifth and Park, epitomizes our city. A visit to the top of **Rockefeller Center** is always a thriller—**Rainbow and Stars** is the best nightclub in the world, with wonderful entertainers (Rosemary Clooney, Tony Bennett, etc.) in an intimate atmosphere.

Another best restaurant is **Elaine's.** Again, civilians can rub shoulders—well almost—with the famous and the food is great.

Florence Fabricant
Food Columnist/Cookbook Author

Manhattan from 96th Street to Wall Street—Walking, not driving as in most other cities.

Union Square—The bustle of the Greenmarket on Monday, Wednesday, Friday, and Saturday.

Grand Central Oyster Bar—Sitting at the counter for oysters or pan roast.

Rainbow Room—The glamour! The view! The setting! An incomparable experience that's thoroughly New York.

Felissimo—Tea or a mid-afternoon snack in the lovely fifth-floor cafe—quiet, serene.

Madison Square Garden Center—New York Knicks, especially when they're winning.

Flushing Meadow—Tennis at the U.S. Open in September.

Pastrami King/Rego Park—In Queens, but the best pastrami sandwich anywhere.

Arthur Avenue, Bronx—Old-world Little Italy.

Paley Park—For the waterfall.

Le Cirque—The buzz of a celebrity playpen with great food.

Remi—Francesco's bread sticks, risottos, and the gorgeous Venetian mural.

Marilyn J. Appleberg
Writer/Editor/Author, *I Love* guidebooks

The **Metropolitan Museum of Art** Friday or Saturday at 5PM for drinks on the balcony with a classical accompaniment—it's the smartest cocktail lounge in town.

Roetelle A.G.—A German/Swiss restaurant with the best secret garden replete with grape arbor.

Kiev's cheese blintzes, which are without a doubt the world's best.

Bay 1 at Brighton Beach for soft white sand, unpolluted water, and the sound of Russian being spoken. Nearby at **Mrs. Stahl's,** they have the best potato knish.

Zito's whole-wheat bread; I defy you to get it home in one piece.

Stuyvesant Street on the vernal or autumnal equinox, when the sun sets straight down the middle of this, the only *true* east-west street on Manhattan.

Second Avenue Deli with its multicultural countermen and the best pastrami and chopped liver.

The Alice Austin House spring and fall antiques fair on the lawn overlooking the bay.

Le Gamin, best for those moments when you want to be in Paris without leaving New York.

Only in New York: events such as the Empire State Building Run Up, and the wand-breaking ceremony at Houdini's grave the afternoon of Halloween.

Theater District/Garment Center

The Theater District and the Garment Center are among the most important contributors to the New York economy; New Yorkers take their tourism and fashion industries very seriously. For those who love "street theater," no part of town is more entertaining than the Garment Center, which has more than a slight influence over what Atlanta, Kansas City, and Pittsburgh are wearing. Then there's Broadway, which has no equivalent in any other American City. This crucible of fashion design and theater fits in a relatively small area—**W. 34th** to **W. 59th streets**, from **Sixth Avenue** (officially, Avenue of the Americas) to the **Hudson River.**

Before 1900, the garment trade was centered below E. 14th Street on the Lower East Side. By 1915, it had moved north along Broadway and Sixth Avenue as far as W. 30th Street, replacing part of the rough-and-tumble **Tenderloin** district. The merchant princes who were establishing their fine

department stores along Fifth Avenue were distressed to find garment workers mingling with their affluent customers and formed a committee to put a stop to it. The committee's solution was to order the construction of two garment workshop buildings, Nos. 498 and 500 Seventh Avenue, at W. 37th Street, a comfortable distance away. Not long after the 1921 completion of the loft buildings, **Seventh Avenue** came to be synonymous with American fashion.

When the **Metropolitan Opera House** opened at W. 39th Street and Broadway in 1883, the **Floradora Girls** were already packing them in at the Casino Theater across the street. In 1902, the first portion of **Macy's** was built at W. 34th Street and Broadway where it replaced, among other buildings, **Koster & Bial's Music Hall**, where **Thomas Edison** first demonstrated moving pictures.

As the city's center moved uptown, the theaters followed suit. The theatrical quarter moved north across W. 42nd Street in the early 1900s. Theater owners banded together in a syndicate to gain more control over the artists they booked. This gave them control over the competition that remained downtown as well, and those theatrical enterprises were effectively put out of business. The syndicate's power increased greatly in 1916, when the three **Shubert** brothers began to build new theaters in the **Times Square** area, which the subway had put within easy reach of the entire city. Other entrepreneurs joined the rush, and their legacy is still with us.

In 1876, an elevated railroad was built along Ninth Avenue, and thousands of immigrants, chiefly from Ireland, moved to the neighborhood. Work was plentiful in the sawmills, warehouses, stone yards, and stables along the Hudson River. Around this time, the area bordered approximately by W. 30th to W. 59th streets and Eighth to 12th avenues evolved into one of America's roughest neighborhoods: **Hell's Kitchen,** named for the gang that ruled here, thriving on hoodlumism, extortion, and highway robbery. Well into the 20th century—long after gang wars in New York were officially declared over—merchants and property owners west of Eighth Avenue continued to pay "tribute" to the Hell's Kitchen Gang; they didn't have an alternative, until the gang finally disappeared. Today, although porn palaces stand next to Broadway theaters and the streets are filled with hustlers and petty criminals, the area is a far cry from its raucous past and is chiefly inhabited by starving artists yearning to be near the stage.

Reformers tried to clean up the infamous Tenderloin (they called it **Satan's Circus**), which covered Fifth to Seventh avenues from W. 23rd Street to W. 42nd. But the district remained the city's center of vice, as it had for nearly 50 years, until Prohibition closed its watering holes in 1920. Today, the seedy area surrounding Times Square still has its share of adult movie houses, peep shows, and other dens of iniquity, but it is undergoing radical change once again, as developers rush to take advantage of the city's construction incentives that are part of a long-heralded plan to clean up the area.

1 Herald Square During the 1880s and 1890s, this was the heart of the **Tenderloin,** an area of dance halls, bordellos, and cafes adjacent to **Hell's Kitchen.** New York City's theater and newspaper industries were once headquartered here. The square—which, like most of the squares in New York, is anything but—was named for the *New York Herald,* which occupied a Venetian palazzo, completed in 1921 by **McKim, Mead & White,** on the north end. **Greeley Square,** to the south, was named for the founder of the *New-York Tribune.* Note the **Crossland**

Savings Bank by **York & Sawyer**—it has lots of columns inside and out. ♦ Bounded by W. 34th and W. 35th Sts, and Sixth Ave and Broadway

Only a handful of all the semiactuated signals (those chest-high buttons that pedestrians push to make the light change to green) installed on lightpoles around Manhattan actually work; most are located along 12th Avenue.

2 Macy's The Broadway building of this New York institution was built in 1901 by **DeLemos & Cordes;** the Seventh Avenue building was built in 1931 by **Robert D. Kohn.** Although it has always seemed to have more of everything than any other store, Macy's didn't have a compelling fashion image until 1974, when **Ed Finkelstein,** who had been president of Macy's in San Francisco, took charge of the New York branch. Today, the store is both trendy and fashionable. There is a haven for children on the fifth floor, with a vast selection of imported and domestic clothing and even a place to relax over an ice-cream soda. The ninth-floor **Corner Shop** includes a dazzling array of fine antiques. Macy's **Cellar** turns shopping for the kitchen into a heady experience, and even includes fine food to go with the fine kitchenware (**Gene Hovis** creates down-home Southern specialties like buttermilk biscuits and buttermilk-fried chicken as well as a hearty lemon pound cake, macaroni and cheese, and apple pie). You can eat breakfast, lunch, and dinner at Macy's, get a facial and a haircut, mail a letter, have your jewelry appraised, buy theater tickets, and convert foreign currency into dollars. ◆ M, Th-F 10AM-8:30PM; Tu-W, Sa 10AM-7PM; Su 11AM-6PM. Hours may vary with special events and promotions. Bounded by W. 34th and W. 35th Sts, and Broadway and Seventh Ave. 695.4400

3 New York Astrology Center The country's largest source of astrology books, healing books, and Tarot cards can be found here. The center also offers computerized and one-to-one horoscope interpretations. ◆ M-F 10:30AM-6:50PM; Sa 10:30AM-5PM. 545 Eighth Ave (at W. 37th St), 10th floor. 947.3609

4 Hero Boy ★$ According to the **Manganaro** family, who established this enterprise as a satellite of their grocery store next door, the name "hero" sandwich, known as a grinder, a po' boy, and a submarine in other cities, was coined here in 1940 by *Herald-Tribune* food writer **Clementine Paddleford,** who said you have to be a hero to finish one. The Manganaros claim to be the first to sell sandwiches by the foot. They also serve basic hot meals of lasagna, baked ziti, etc. ◆ Italian ◆ Breakfast, lunch, and early dinner; lunch, dinner, and late-night snacks on Sunday. 492 Ninth Ave (between W. 37th and W. 38th Sts). 947.7325

5 Supreme Macaroni Co. ★$$ Stepping into this grocery store leads you back to a time before the words "gourmet" or "nouvelle cuisine" were ever uttered. In the back of the store is a restaurant that serves the best macaroni this side of Naples. The prices are moderate and the service straightforward. ◆ Italian ◆ Lunch and dinner. Closed Sunday. 511 Ninth Ave (between W. 38th and W. 39th Sts). Reservations recommended. No credit cards. 564.8074

6 Jacob K. Javits Convention Center This huge facility—made almost entirely of glass—covering 22 acres between W. 34th and W. Ninth streets, is the largest exposition hall under one roof in North America and one of the biggest buildings in the world. It has 900,000 square feet of exhibition space. The lobby, called the **Crystal Palace,** is 150 feet high. Events are already scheduled into the 21st century. Designed by **I.M. Pei & Partners,** it was called "the center at the center of the world" when it opened in 1986. Crosstown buses on 34th and 42nd streets go right to its front door. Oddly enough, the building appears opaque during the day, while at night the interior lighting makes the structure glow. ◆ 655 W. 34th St (between 11th and 12th Aves). 216.2000

7 Lincoln Tunnel The tunnel, which is 97 feet below the Hudson River, connects Manhattan with Weehawken, New Jersey, and more than 36 million vehicles use it every year. The 8,216-foot center tube was the first to be built. **Aymar Embury** was the architect; **Ole Singstad** completed the engineering in 1937. It was joined by the 7,482-foot north tube in 1945, and the 8,006-foot south tube in 1957, making it the only three-tube vehicular tunnel in the world. Tolls are collected from eastbound cars only—the New Jersey-bound lanes are free. ◆ W. 38th through W. 41st Sts

8 Port Authority Bus Terminal Erected in 1950, the terminal (shown above) was expanded in 1963 and again in 1982 by the **Port Authority Design Staff.** This is the largest and busiest bus terminal in the world, with three levels of platforms serving all of New York's long-distance bus lines and most of the commuter buses between New York and the New Jersey suburbs. A special section on the W. 42nd Street side also serves all three metropolitan airports. For people who prefer driving into Manhattan but not through it, a rooftop parking garage connects directly by ramp to the Lincoln Tunnel. As in any major transportation hub, exercise caution inside the terminal, which sometimes affords temporary shelter to the homeless. Although the situation has greatly improved in recent years, be aware of your belongings at all times, and avoid isolated areas, particularly the restrooms. ◆ Daily 24 hours. Bounded by W. 40th and W. 42nd Sts, and Eighth and Ninth Aves

9 B&J Fabrics, Inc. This store has been at the heart of New York's Garment Center for more than 50 years. Its three floors contain 8,000 square feet of space dedicated to the finest European and American fashion fabrics offered at discount rates. ♦ M-F 8AM-5:45PM; Sa 9AM-4:45PM. 263 W. 40th St (between Seventh and Eighth Aves). 354.8150; fax 764.3355

10 Hotalings News Agency This is *the* stand in New York City for out-of-town and international newspapers and magazines. ♦ 142 W. 42nd St (between Sixth Ave and Broadway). 840.1868

11 Group Health Insurance Building Better known as the original **McGraw-Hill Building,** this 35-story tower was commissioned when growth was expected in this area. Green and glorious, it still stands alone. Built in 1931 by **Hood, Godley & Fouilhoux,** it has the distinction of being the only New York building mentioned in *The International Style,* the 1932 book by **Hitchcock** and **Johnson** that codified modern architecture. In fact, this tower is not strictly glass and steel aesthetics but an individual composition with Art Deco detailing. Eminent architectural historian **Vincent Scully** called it "Proto-jukebox Modern." ♦ 330 W. 42nd St (between Eighth and Ninth Aves)

12 Church of the Holy Cross Although this was built in 1870 by **Henry Englebert** as the parish church of a poor neighborhood, it has several windows and mosaics designed by **Louis Comfort Tiffany. Father Francis P. Duffy,** chaplain of the famous Fighting 69th Division in World War I, fought from the pulpit of this church to break up the gangs of **Hell's Kitchen.** He served here until his death in 1932. ♦ 329 W. 42nd St (between Eighth and Ninth Aves). 246.4732

13 West Bank Cafe ★$$ The upstairs dining room features pasta dishes, seafood specials, salads, and burgers on tables covered with butcher paper; downstairs, enjoy musical comedy and original one-act plays and short full-length plays in a cabaret setting. ♦ American ♦ Lunch and dinner. Theater closed Monday and Tuesday. 407 W. 42nd St (at Ninth Ave). Reservations recommended. 695.6909

14 Chez Josephine ★★$$$ The ebullient **Jean Claude Baker** launched this unique tribute to his late adoptive mother, cabaret legend **Josephine Baker,** in 1986, and has been gratifying critics and public alike ever since. The special decor, an homage to the intimate Parisian nightclubs of the roaring '20s, only adds to the enjoyment of what is considered some of the best *boudin noir* in town, served with red cabbage. Also featured is lobster bisque, goat-cheese ravioli, and rack of lamb. Bluesy lady pianists and a French tap dancer usually lend a musical note to the heady atmosphere. ♦ French ♦ Dinner. Closed Sunday. 414 W. 42nd St (at Ninth Ave). Reservations recommended. 594.1925

15 Theater Row Beginning with the former **West Side Airlines Terminal,** which now houses video recording studios and the National Spanish Television Network, this ambitious project, begun in 1976 by **Playwrights Horizons** (416 W. 42nd Street) includes a dozen Off-Broadway theaters and a revitalized street scene that gives new life to the Lincoln Tunnel exit that cuts the block in half. Tickets for all theaters are available at Ticket Central located at Playwrights Horizons. ♦ Daily 1-8PM. 416 W. 42nd St (between Ninth and 10th Aves). 279.4200

16 Manhattan Plaza These towers, built in 1977 by **David Todd & Associates,** provide subsidized housing for performing artists, whose rent in the 1,688 apartments is based on their income. Their presence pays dividends in the vitality they bring to the neighborhood. ♦ Bounded by W. 42nd and W. 43rd Sts, and Ninth and 10th Aves

Within the Manhattan Plaza:

Good & Plenty to Go At this gourmet catering service and takeout designed by **Milton Glaser, Inc.,** you'll find fresh breads, including whole wheat and sourdough onion rolls; soups and salads; hot and cold pastas; sandwiches and pizza; and homestyle favorites like bourbon-baked ham, jambalaya, crab cakes, and vegetarian chili. A few small tables are placed outside during fair weather. ♦ M-F 7AM-8PM; Sa 7AM-7PM; Su 7AM-6PM. 268.4385

Little Pie Company The aromas here are glorious and the pies are just like Mom's (maybe even better). This small, bright shop offers a selection of 10 all-natural pies—try the fresh fruit ones in summer, the sour cream apple or pumpkin in fall. Take home a five-inch pie if you're alone and can't resist the temptation. ♦ M-F 8AM-8PM; Sa 10AM-6PM; Su noon-6PM. 424 W. 43rd St (between Ninth and 10th Aves). 736.4780

17 World Yacht Cruises ★★$$$$ This fleet of five yachts cruises the harbor year-round. Lunch cruises include light music. The food would make these restaurants impressive even if they were landlocked. Dinner includes music, dancing, and the romance of the harbor. A wonderful place to get married— wedding vows may be exchanged as the boat passes the **Statue of Liberty.** ♦ Continental ♦ Lunch and dinner. Pier 81 (at W. 41st St and 12th Ave). Jacket required for dinner. Reservations required. 929.7090

Restaurants/Clubs: Red   **Hotels:** Blue
Shops/ 🌳 Outdoors: Green   **Sights/Culture:** Black

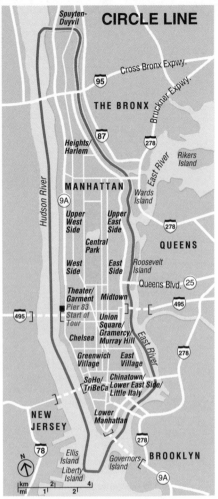

antiques, and film clips of flying machines from the turn of the century through the 1930s. Insights into the future as well as contemporary exploration of the ocean and space are shown in **Technologies Hall**, along with the artifacts of 20th- and 21st-century warfare: jumbo jets, mammoth rockets, and complex weaponry. More aircraft can be inspected on the *Intrepid's* 900-foot flight deck. The newest acquisitions are the guided missile submarine *Growler* and the Vietnam-era destroyer *Edson*. Visitors can climb through the control bridges and command centers of the carrier, but spaces are cramped and there is often a wait. Dress warmly in winter months. ♦ Admission; under 6 and uniformed military free. W-Su 10AM-5PM Labor Day to Memorial Day; daily 10AM-5PM Memorial Day to Labor Day. Last tickets sold at 4PM. Pier 86 (at W. 46th St and 12th Ave). 245.0072

20 Landmark Tavern ★★$$ This is an old waterfront tavern cleaned up and refined for the comfort of modern-day theatergoers and those who seek out its authentic mid-19th-century rooms, where food is served from genuine antique sideboards. Some of the dishes could be better, and the better ones more consistent, but the Irish soda bread is lovable; the fish-and-chips, shepherd's pie, prime rib, and hamburgers are good. ♦ American ♦ Lunch and dinner. 626 11th Ave (between W. 46th and W. 45th Sts). Reservations recommended 757.8595

21 Munson Diner $ The cook at this silver-and-blue relic from 1908 slings a mean corned-beef hash. ♦ American ♦ Daily 24 hours. 600 W. 49th St (at 11th Ave). 246.0964

22 Peruvian Restaurant ★$$ Ignore the fluorescent lighting and Formica tables and concentrate instead on the best and most authentic Peruvian dishes in New York: terrific baked fish with tomatoes and coriander, hearty stews, and good potatoes. The service is pleasant. ♦ Peruvian ♦ Breakfast, lunch, and dinner. 688 10th Ave (between W. 48th and W. 49th Sts). No credit cards. 581.5814

23 Mud, Sweat & Tears This is a cheerful, neat pottery studio for beginning and expert potters. The facilities include 10 Brent & Amaco electric wheels, spacious table areas, basic handbuilding supplies, glazes, a kiln where firings are done frequently, and a small retail area where the potters sell their wares. ♦ 654 10th Ave (at W. 46th St). Call for information on classes. 974.9121

24 Mike's American Bar and Grill ★$$ If you brave the unquestionably sleazy parade down this stretch of 10th Avenue, you'll find a cheerful, intentionally down-at-the-heels joint. Go for the grilled specials, though some faithfuls claim that Mike has the best enchiladas in Manhattan. ♦ American/Mexican ♦ Dinner. 650 10th Ave (between W. 45th and W. 46th Sts). Reservations recommended. 246.4115

18 Circle Line There is simply no better way to orient yourself to Manhattan's wonders. This well-narrated tour heads down the Hudson River, past the **Statue of Liberty,** up the East River to the Harlem River, through Spuyten-Duyvil, and back down the Hudson. The eight vessels are converted World War II landing craft or Coast Guard cutters. When you get on board, try to sit on the port side (left as you face forward). That way, all your views are of Manhattan. The schedule changes often; during summer, there are 12 three-hour cruises a day starting at 9:30AM. ♦ Fee. Closed January and February. Pier 83 (at W. 42nd St and Hudson River). 563.3200

19 Intrepid Sea Air Space Museum The veteran World War II and Vietnam War aircraft carrier *Intrepid* is now a technological and historical museum. Other than the **Air and Space Museum** in Washington, D.C., no other institution gives such a thorough picture of the past, present, and future of warfare and technology in air, space, and sea. The tamer **Pioneers Hall** features mock-ups,

25 Tenth Avenue Jukebox Café ★$$ The menu is called "nouvelle American," and when you see the setting, you'll know why. ◆ American ◆ Lunch and dinner. 637 10th Ave (at W. 45th St). 315.4690

26 The Actors Studio It was in this former Greek Orthodox church that **Lee Strasberg** trained such stars as **Marlon Brando, Dustin Hoffman, Al Pacino,** and **Shelley Winters.** Seats 125. ◆ 432 W. 44th St (between Ninth and 10th Aves). 757.0870

26 The New Dramatists This company, which offers free readings, was founded in 1949 by a group of Broadway's most important writers and producers in an effort to encourage new playwrights; alumni include **William Inge, John Guare,** and **Emily Mann.** The New Dramatists took occupancy of the building, formerly a Lutheran church, in 1968. ◆ 424 W. 44th St (between Ninth and 10th Aves). 757.6960

27 Le Madeleine ★$$$ This casual bistro features salads, pastas, fish, and light meats. Weather permitting, the enclosed garden is open year-round. ◆ French ◆ Lunch and dinner; brunch also on Saturday and Sunday. 403 W. 43rd St (between Ninth and 10th Aves). Reservations recommended. 246.2993

27 Westside Theater For more than 20 years the two theaters in this converted Episcopal church have presented award-winning productions such as *A Shayna Maidel* and *Extremities.* Seats 210 and 190. ◆ 407 W. 43rd St (between Ninth and 10th Aves). Call for performance schedule. 315.2244

28 Rudy's Bar This is one of the area's few remaining neighborhood bars. Locals come for light snacks, conversation, and good drinks. ◆ Daily till 4AM. 627 Ninth Ave (between W. 44th and W. 45th Sts). 974.9169

28 Poseidon Greek Bakery Fans of Greek pastries have kept this tiny shop bustling for more than 50 years. You can have the phyllo specialties mailed anywhere in the U.S. ◆ Tu-Sa 9AM-7PM; Su 10AM-4PM. 629 Ninth Ave (between W. 44th and W. 45th Sts). 757.6173

29 Bali Burma ★$$ Rare are the restaurants that specialize in Balinese and Burmese cuisine. This is the only one in this neighborhood; it's good, and the prices are welcomingly reasonable. ◆ Balinese/Burmese ◆ Lunch and dinner. Closed Sunday. 651 Ninth Ave (between W. 45th and W. 46th Sts). 265.9868

29 Bruno The King of Ravioli Established in 1888, the factory is closed to the public, but the neighboring retail shop sells a vast selection of fresh pastas and sauces, including ravioli, manicotti, canelloni, lasagna, stuffed shells, gnocchi, and cavatelli. ◆ M-Sa 7AM-6PM. 653 Ninth Ave (between W. 45th and W. 46th Sts). 246.8456

29 Zen Palate ★★$$ An oasis in Hell's Kitchen, Zen Palate serves undersize portions of macrobiotic cuisine in an upscale, minimalist setting. It's a bit pricey but worth the culinary and cultural adventure. ◆ Health food ◆ Lunch and dinner. 663 Ninth Ave (at W. 46th St). Reservations required. 582.1669. Also at: 34 Union Sq East (at E. 16th St). 614.9345

30 Film Center Building The pink and black marble in the lobby and the pattern of the orange and blue tiles on the walls helped attract some 75 motion picture distributors, who made this 1929 building by **Buchman & Kahn** their headquarters. The stores on this block rent out moviemaking equipment. ◆ 630 Ninth Ave (between W. 44th and W. 45th Sts). 757.6995

30 Jezebel ★★$$$$ The nondescript entrance does not prepare you for the high-energy New Orleans bordello interior with, among other delights, two-story-high tropical trees, lawn swings, mirrored columns, Egyptian rugs on the walls, and crystal chandeliers. Go for the corn bread and deep-fried whole fish dishes. ◆ Soul food ◆ Dinner. Closed Sunday. 630 Ninth Ave (between W. 44th and W. 45th Sts). Reservations required. 582.1045

31 Thrift and New Shoppe A hodgepodge of stuff—bric-a-brac, American pottery, and silver and gold jewelry—makes this antique shop fun. Treasures await, and the prices are reasonable. ◆ M-Sa 8:30AM-7PM. 602 Ninth Ave (at W. 43rd St). 265.3087

32 The New York Times In 1913, less than 10 years after moving to Times Square, the *Times* had grown so much that this annex was built by **Ludlow & Peabody** around the corner on W. 43rd Street. Its size was doubled in 1924. The building was expanded again in 1945, and the original tower was eventually abandoned. Most copies of the newspaper are printed in a New Jersey plant, although a substantial number come off the presses in the basement here, and the activity on Saturday evening and on both the W. 43rd and W. 44th street sides, as delivery trucks head out with the Sunday edition, is intense. ◆ 229 W. 43rd St (between Seventh and Eighth Aves). 556.1234

CARLOS DINIZ/LEE HARRIS POMEROY

33 Times Square Almost a year before the *New York Times* moved into what had been called **Longacre Square,** the mayor and the board of aldermen passed a resolution in April 1904, changing the name of the area, bounded by W. 42nd and W. 47th streets from Broadway to Seventh Avenue, to Times Square. It quickly became known as "The Crossroads of the World," partly in deference to the *Times,* which certainly could claim that title. It is the heart of the Theater District and the site of some of the most spectacular electric advertising signs ever created. The British novelist **G.K. Chesterton** said of them: "What a glorious garden of wonder this would be to anyone who was lucky enough to be unable to read." It is one of a series of open spaces created as Broadway crosses the straight north-south avenues, in this case Seventh Avenue. Standing at the base of the old Times tower and looking uptown, Broadway comes into Times Square on your left, and leaves it behind you on your right, having cut across Seventh Avenue at the intersection of W. 43rd Street.

33 1 Times Square When this building was under construction as headquarters for the *New York Times,* even the *Times'* archrival, the *Herald,* grudgingly ran a story under the headline "Deepest Hole in New York a Broadway Spectacle," which said that the new *Times* tower was the most interesting engineering feat to be seen anywhere on Manhattan Island. Designed by **Eidlitz & MacKenzie,** it was completed in 1904. The newspaper's pressroom was in the tower's basement, but because the building was being built over the city's biggest subway station, the basement had to be blasted out of solid rock 55 feet down. The presses began printing the *Times* down there on 2 January 1905, after the new year had been welcomed with the dropping of a lighted ball down the flagpole on the roof. The celebration has been repeated every year since (more than 300,000 revelers rang in 1994 here), although in 1966 the *Times* sold the building to **Allied Chemical Co.,** which stripped it bare and refaced it with marble. The building has since been sold again and now houses offices. ♦ W. 42nd St (between Seventh Ave and Broadway)

34 The Town Hall This 1921 landmark, a work of **McKim, Mead & White,** is an elegant building with excellent acoustics. **Joan Sutherland** made her debut here. Today, the hall is constantly in use for one cultural event or another. ♦ 123 W. 43rd St (between Sixth Ave and Broadway). 840.2824

35 National Debt Clock In a frighteningly rapid-fire frenzy, this billboard records our national debt by the mega-second as we sink deeper into the red. In addition to displaying the ever-changing national share (whose increase, as of September 1993, was $13,000 per second), it also shows the average family's share. The 1992 interest cost clocked in at $292 billion. Best not to look. ♦ Sixth Ave (between W. 42nd and W. 43rd Sts)

36 Belasco The eccentric **David Belasco,** whose preferred style of dress was a priest's frock, wrote and produced *Madame Butterfly* and *The Girl of the Golden West* here. Both were later adapted into operas by **Giacomo Puccini.** Belasco's ghost is said to continue to visit backstage. This theater, dating to 1907, was a creation of **George Keister.** ♦ 111 W. 44th St (between Sixth and Seventh Aves). Telecharge 239.6200

36 Cafe Un Deux Trois ★★$$$ The cafe covers the tables with paper cloths and supplies crayons for doodling. The gimmick seems unnecessary, however, as the place provides satisfaction with its simple food: small steaks, heartrending french fries, and fresh seasonal specials. ♦ French ♦ Lunch and dinner. 123 W. 44th St (between Sixth and Seventh Aves). Reservations recommended. 354.4148

37 Hotel Macklowe $$$ This handsome executive-style hotel offers such businesslike amenities as two dual-line speaker phones in each room, phone mail in four languages, and television access to Macktel, an interactive communication system that allows guests to preview restaurant menus, order sporting event and theater tickets, and even check out. In addition, there are a restaurant and bar, a sewing center for last-minute seam repair and button replacement, and a fitness center staffed with private trainers. The **Macklowe Conference Center** encompasses 38 meeting rooms and three boardrooms. At the 650-seat **Hudson Theatre,** a 1902 landmark next door, the hotel maintains a full-service auditorium and 35mm and 70mm screening facilities. ♦ 145 W. 44th St (between Sixth Ave and Broadway). 768.4400, 800/622.5569; fax 768.0847

Restaurants/Clubs: Red	**Hotels:** Blue
Shops/ 🌳 Outdoors: Green	**Sights/Culture:** Black

38 Paramount Building The bank on the corner of W. 43rd Street replaced the entrance to the famous **Paramount Theater,** built in 1926 by **Rapp & Rapp.** The great glass globe on its pinnacle and the four-sided clock make the building an attraction, as does its lavish lobby. Before the theater closed in 1964, its stage had been graced by such stars as **Mae West, Pola Negri, Tommy Dorsey, Bing Crosby,** and, of course, **Frank Sinatra.** ♦ 1501 Broadway (between W. 43rd and W. 44th Sts)

39 Shubert It will be hard to imagine anything but *A Chorus Line* here (after 6,137 performances, the longest-running musical on Broadway closed on 28 April 1990), but that's what they said about **Katharine Hepburn** in *The Philadelphia Story,* and **Barbra Streisand** in *I Can Get It for You Wholesale.* Hoping to reach that legendary status is the current *Crazy for You.* The theater itself was built in 1913 by **Henry B. Herts.** ♦ 225 W. 44th St (between Broadway and Eighth Ave). Telecharge 239.6200

39 Shubert Alley The stage doors of the Shubert Theater on W. 44th Street and of the Booth on W. 45th open onto this space. So does the entrance to the offices of the **Shubert Organization,** making this a favorite spot for Broadway hopefuls to casually stroll up and down hoping to be noticed by the right people. A gift shop, **One Shubert Alley** (M-Sa 9AM-11:30PM; Su noon-7PM), specializes in merchandise related to Broadway shows. ♦ Bounded by W. 44th and W. 45th Sts, and Seventh and Eighth Aves

40 Sardi's ★$$$ On rare occasions a celebrity or two can be seen here, but these days there is more seeking than finding. Many of the big Broadway stars have moved on to other galaxies and other eateries, but their presence is still felt in the caricatures that decorate the walls of both floors. At the second-floor bar, the drinks flow with reckless generosity—a compelling reason for it to have remained a favorite hangout for *New York Times* reporters, who search for inspiration among the clinking ice cubes. To encourage the creative process, the *Times* building has a back-door entrance that leads directly into Sardi's. Perhaps management subscribes to the hallowed theory that serious drinking leads to serious thinking. ♦ Continental ♦ Lunch, dinner, and late-night meals. Closed Sunday. 234 W. 44th St (between Broadway and Eighth Ave). Jacket required; reservations recommended. 221.8440

40 Helen Hayes This theater was constructed in 1912 by **Ingalls & Hoffman.** In 1965, when it was known as the **Little Theatre,** it became home to the "Merv Griffin" and "David Frost" shows. It reopened as a Broadway theater in 1974. In 1983, it was dedicated to Helen Hayes. ♦ 240 W. 44th St (between Broadway and Eighth Ave). 944.9450; Ticketmaster 307.4100

40 St. James At this 1927 work of **Warren & Wetmore, Rodgers and Hammerstein's** *Oklahoma!* was followed by **Ray Bolger** in *Where's Charley?,* which in turn was followed by, among others, *The King and I, The Pajama Game,* and the current offering, *The Who's Tommy.* ♦ 246 W. 44th St (between Broadway and Eighth Ave). Telecharge 239.6200

41 Broadhurst It was here, in this 1918 work of **Herbert J. Krapp,** that **Humphrey Bogart** picked up his credentials as a tough guy when he appeared with **Leslie Howard** in *The Petrified Forest.* The theater is now showing *Kiss of the Spider Woman.* ♦ 235 W. 44th St (between Broadway and Eighth Ave). Telecharge 239.6200

41 Majestic *The Music Man, Carousel, A Little Night Music,* and *The Wiz* helped this theater, built in 1927 by **Herbert J. Krapp,** live up to its name. *The Phantom of the Opera,* which has been playing since 26 January 1988, is carrying on the tradition. ♦ 247 W. 44th St (between Broadway and Eighth Ave). Telecharge 239.6200

42 Milford Plaza $$ Built in 1928 by **Schwartz & Gross,** this hotel was originally known as the **Lincoln.** It was built and first operated by the United Cigar Stores Co., which said it catered to the better element of the masses. Today, it is a **Best Western** property advertising itself as the "Lulla-buy of Broadway." Its 1,300 rooms have all been modernized. ♦ 700 Eighth Ave (between W. 44th and W. 45th Sts). 869.3600, 800/221.2690; fax 914.1433

43 Martin Beck The famed **Theatre Guild Studio** used this 1924 house, a work of **G. Albert Lansburgh,** in the '30s. Great performances echo from the stage, including those of the **Lunts** in **Robert Sherwood's** *Reunion in Vienna,* **Katharine Cornell** in *The Barretts of Wimpole Street,* and **Ruth Gordon** in *Hotel Universe.* In the '50s, **Arthur Miller's** *The Crucible* and **Tennessee Williams'** *Sweet Bird of Youth* played here. In 1965, **Peter Brook's** incendiary production of *Marat/Sade* gave audiences a new look at documentary theater. **Liz Taylor** came out of Hollywood to make her Broadway debut in **Lillian Hellman's** *The Little Foxes.* Today's popular hit is *Guys and Dolls.* ♦ 302 W. 45th St (between Eighth and Ninth Aves). Telecharge 239.6200

44 Triton Gallery You'll find theater posters and show cards for current and past performaces on Broadway and elsewhere in this shop that provides custom framing and mail-order, too. Ask for a catalog. ♦ M-Sa 10AM-6PM. 323 W. 45th St (between Eighth and Ninth Aves). 765.2472

45 Frankie and Johnnie's ★$$$ This popular, hectic, and noisy old Broadway chophouse has few discernible charms. ♦ Steakhouse ♦ Dinner. Closed Sunday. 269 W. 45th St (between Broadway and Eighth Ave). Reservations required. 997.9494

45 Sam's ★$ With its exposed brick and very reasonable prix fixe dinners, this place is a popular hangout with theater people. Although stars sup here occasionally, its most devoted fans are "gypsies" of the chorus lines. Maître d' **Craig Dawson** plays a Broadway overture every night at 7:30 to ensure that cast members leave on time, and he and the staff sing Broadway hits at midnight several times a week. ♦ Lunch, dinner, and late-night meals; lunch and dinner only on Sunday. 263 W. 45th St (between Broadway and Eighth Ave). Reservations recommended. 719.5416

46 Golden One of the longest-running shows in history, *Tobacco Road* (1933), played this 1927 house, another work of **Herbert J. Krapp**. *A Party with Comden and Green, At the Drop of a Hat, Beyond the Fringe,* and **Victor Borge** kept audiences laughing here. ♦ 252 W. 45th St (between Broadway and Eighth Ave). Telecharge 239.6200

46 Royale Actress **Mae West** kept house here for three years as *Diamond Lil'*. The theater was used as a radio studio by CBS from 1936 to 1940. **Laurence Olivier** dazzled audiences with his appearances in *The Entertainer* and *Becket. Grease,* Broadway's longest-running musical at the time, settled here during its last years. ♦ 242 W. 45th St (between Broadway and Eighth Ave). Telecharge 239.6200

46 Plymouth *Abe Lincoln in Illinois,* with **Raymond Massey,** opened not long after **John** and **Lionel Barrymore** appeared here together in *The Jest.* The theater was built in 1917 by **Herbert J. Krapp.** ♦ 236 W. 45th St (between Broadway and Eighth Ave). Telecharge 239.6200

46 Booth Although this 1913 theater, created by **Henry B. Herts,** was named for **Edwin Booth, Shirley Booth** also made a name for herself here with **Sidney Blackmer** in *Come Back, Little Sheba.* ♦ 222 W. 45th St (between Broadway and Eighth Ave). Telecharge 239.6200

47 Imperial *Rosemarie* and *Oh, Kay!* set the tone for this theater, which was built by **Herbert J. Krapp** in 1923. Hit musicals have always found a home here: *Babes in Toyland, Jubilee, Leave It to Me, Annie Get Your Gun,* and the incomparable **Zero Mostel** performing "If I Were a Rich Man" in *Fiddler on the Roof.* In October 1990, *Les Misérables* moved here from the Broadway Theater. ♦ 249 W. 45th St (between Broadway and Eighth Ave). Telecharge 239.6200

47 Music Box Composer **Irving Berlin** built this charming theater to accommodate his *Music Box Revue of 1921.* Also presented here were the first musical to win a Pulitzer Prize, **George Gershwin's** *Of Thee I Sing;* **John Steinbeck's** *Of Mice and Men;* **Kurt Weill's** last musical, *Lost in the Stars;* and **Kim Stanley** in *Bus Stop.* ♦ 239 W. 45th St (between Broadway and Eighth Ave). Telecharge 239.6200

48 Marriott Marquis $$$ This hotel boasts the world's tallest atrium, through which its glass-enclosed elevators zip up and down, serving 47 floors. It has a Broadway theater on the third floor, New York's largest ballroom, and its highest lobby (reached by a chain of escalators passing through floor after quiet floor of meeting rooms). The two on-site gyms have Nautilus, sauna, Jacuzzi, and a trainer, if you need a push. Valet parking, concierge, and several restaurants and lounges are also available in this 1985 creation of **John Portman.** ♦ 1535 Broadway (at W. 45th St). 398.1900, 800/228.9290; fax 704.8930

Within the Marriott Marquis:

Marquis New York's youngest Broadway theater is operated by the famed **Nederlanders.** Many expected it to suffer from its somewhat untheatrical surroundings—and the bad press caused by the demolition of several old theaters to make way for it. The ill will seems to have been forgotten during the almost four-year run of the Marquis' first production, *Me and My Girl.* ♦ 382.0100; Ticketmaster 307.4100

The View ★$$$$ Except for one at the old World's Fair site in Queens, this is New York's only revolving restaurant. It has a limited view, as do the revolving lounges above it, but when the turntable takes you past Rockefeller Center and the skyline to the east and uptown, you'll be glad you took a ride in that glass elevator. ♦ Continental ♦ Dinner; lunch also on Sunday. Closed Monday. Reservations required. No sneakers or jeans. 704.8900

49 Minskoff In 1973, **Debbie Reynolds** opened this house with a revival of *Irene.* **Kahn & Jacobs** designed the theater to provide access for handicapped patrons. ♦ 200 W. 45th St (at Broadway). 869.0550; Telecharge 239.6200

Restaurants/Clubs: Red   **Hotels:** Blue
Shops/ 🌳 Outdoors: Green   **Sights/Culture:** Black

50 Roundabout Theatre This theater was built in 1928 by **Thompson, Holmes & Converse.** Under the leadership of producing director **Todd Haimes,** the Roundabout has won recognition as one of the city's finest theatrical organizations. It remains committed to producing classics by the world's greatest playwrights at affordable prices—**Ibsen's** *Ghosts,* **Pirandello's** *Enrico 4,* **Carson McCullers'** *Member of the Wedding.* ◆ 1530 Broadway (at W. 45th St). 719.9393

50 Xanadu Look no further for New York-inspired kitsch. Xanadu's young Afghani owner is a passionate fan of New York, and it shows in his 2,000-item inventory, which includes everything from King Kong pens to the Statue of Liberty in six sizes and three colors. Yankees jackets, subway-token keychains? It's all here and more. ◆ M-Th 9AM-11PM; F-Sa 9AM-midnight; Su 10AM-11PM. 1528 Broadway (at W. 45th St). 768.2202

51 Lyceum Producer **Daniel Frohman** built the Lyceum in 1903. Now a city landmark, it is the oldest New York theater still used for legitimate productions. It opened with *The Proud Prince.* In 1947, **Judy Holliday** and **Paul Douglas** wise-cracked through *Born Yesterday.* The **A.P.A.-Phoenix Repertory** made this home base for several seasons, and in 1980, *Morning's at Seven* by **Paul Osborn** was revived here. A lyric, neo-baroque structure with banded columns and undulating marquee, it was the first theater designed by **Herts & Tallant,** undisputed kings of theater architecture. Frohman was such a theater fan that he had his apartment above fitted with a trapdoor through which he could see the stage. ◆ 149 W. 45th St (between Sixth and Seventh Aves). Telecharge 239.6200

51 Hamburger Harry's ★$ In addition to the 16 varieties of major league burgers served at this casual grill, the mesquite-grilled seafood and steaks lure New Yorkers in search of the rare and well-done. A Mexican accent adds color to the menu—the Ha-Ha Burger is freighted with chiles, guacamole, *salsa verde,* and cheddar cheese. ◆ American ◆ Lunch and dinner. 145 W. 45th St (between Sixth and Seventh Aves). 840.2756. Also at: 157 Chambers St. 267.4446

52 Cabana Carioca ★★$$ This is a macho place for seriously large servings of Brazilian food. Don't miss the suckling pig, steak dishes, and black beans. ◆ Brazilian ◆ Lunch and dinner. Closed Monday. 123 W. 45th St (between Sixth and Seventh Aves). 581.8088

52 47th Street Photo Old New York reigns supreme at this outpost of the famous W. 47th Street branch. You'll find the same frenzied atmosphere and an equally frenzied, knowledgeable staff. ◆ M-Tu 9:30AM-6PM; W-Th 9:30AM-7PM; F 9:30AM-2PM. 115 W. 45th St (between Sixth Ave and Broadway). 921.1287. Also at: 67 W. 47th St. 398.1410

53 La Topiaire ★$$$ An anomaly for the Times Square area, this new French restaurant offers innovative bistro cuisine in a pretty, contemporary setting. Seared scallops and shrimp or fresh fish simply grilled are very good, and the smiling staff is justified when encouraging you to try any of the desserts. ◆ French ◆ Lunch and dinner; lunch only on Monday; dinner only on Saturday. Closed Sunday. 120 W. 45th St (between Sixth and Seventh Aves). 819.1405

54 American Place This theater was founded with the intention of providing a forum for living American playwrights. It opened originally at St. Clement's Church in 1964 with two memorable plays: **Robert Lowell's** *Old Glory* and **William Alfred's** *Hogan's Goat.* In 1971, a brand new theater with a modified thrust stage was built, adding another dimension to the quality productions. ◆ 111 W. 46th St (between Sixth and Seventh Aves). 840.3074

55 Actor's Equity Building This is the union for all stage actors in America—from the virtually unknown to the most famous. It was founded in 1913 by 112 actors to protect the rights and establish good working conditions for professional stage performers and stage managers. If you're into stargazing, keep your eyes peeled. ◆ 165 W. 46th St (between Sixth and Seventh Aves)

56 I. Miller Building Almost hidden behind advertising signs, on the facade of the building, are sculptures of great women of the theater: **Marilyn Miller, Rosa Ponselli, Ethel Barrymore,** and **Mary Pickford,** none of whom would have thought of appearing on stage in anything but I. Miller shoes. The figures are by **A. Stirling Calder,** whose son, **Alexander Calder,** invented the mobile. The shoe store is gone, but the ladies are still here, at least for now. ◆ W. 46th St (at Seventh Ave)

57 Duffy Square World War I chaplain of the Fighting 69th, **Father Francis P. Duffy** served as pastor of nearby **Holy Cross Church** and is honored in this triangle with a 1937 sculpture by **Charles Keck** at W. 46th Street. He shares the honor with a 1959 statue, by **George Lober,** of **George M. Cohan,** the actor/producer/writer who wrote "Give My Regards to Broadway," among hundreds of other songs. ◆ Bounded by W. 46th and W. 47th Sts, and Seventh Ave and Broadway

57 TKTS The **Theater Development Fund,** housed in this 1973 work of **Mayers & Schiff,** sells tickets to Broadway and Off-Broadway shows and Lincoln Center productions, beginning at 10AM for matinees and 3PM for evening performances, at half-price (plus a nominal fee) for performances on the day of sale. Tickets are not available for every show, but a board tells you what is on sale. A better selection is sometimes available close to curtain time, when producers release unused house seats, and during bad weather, when fewer people venture out. Also try Monday and Tuesday evenings, when most theaters alternate closing. ♦ W. 47th St (between Seventh Ave and Broadway). Cash or traveler's checks only, no credit cards or personal checks. 768.1818

57 Palace Theater "Playing the Palace" was the dream of every vaudeville performer from the theater's 1913 opening well into the '30s. The stage has hosted **Sarah Bernhardt, Will Rogers, Fanny Brice, Harry Houdini, W.C. Fields, Bill "Bojangles" Robinson, Milton Berle, Jack Benny,** and **George Burns** and **Gracie Allen.** The advent of movies brought hard times; but the theater was renovated and reopened as a showcase for big musicals in 1966. *Sweet Charity, Applause, La Cage aux Folles,* and *The Will Rogers Follies* were among its long-running hits. ♦ 1564 Broadway (between W. 46th and W. 47th Sts). 730.8200; Ticketmaster 307.4100

57 Embassy Suites $$$ This modern all-suites hotel is within easy walking distance of Rockefeller Center, Fifth Avenue shopping, Lincoln Center, and Broadway theaters. ♦ 1568 Broadway (between W. 46th and W. 47th Sts). 719.1600, 800/362.2779; fax 921.5212

58 Portland Square Hotel $ This was once home to **James Cagney, Lila Lee,** and **John Boles.** Today, with a renovation completed in June 1993, it offers budget-priced, clean accommodations. ♦ 132 W. 47th St (between Sixth and Seventh Aves). 382.0600; fax 382.0684

59 Dish of Salt $$$$ This Chinese restaurant has a sophisticated two-level, bamboo-decorated setting. The cocktail lounge offers equally sophisticated piano music. ♦ Cantonese ♦ Lunch and dinner; dinner only on Saturday. Closed Sunday. 133 W. 47th St (between Sixth and Seventh Aves). Reservations recommended. 921.4242

60 Gun Fighters Death Clock On 1 January 1994, a digital clock started ticking off the nation's gun killings. The figures on the three-story-high billboard are based on federal statistics and will be adjusted weekly. The first day alone registered 85 deaths, and it is anticipated that one person will be added every 14.8 minutes. The billboard shows an estimation of more than 220 million guns

owned in the U.S. Situated at the northern end of Times Square, it was paid for by **Robert E. Brennan,** a former securities broker from New Jersey whose brother was fatally shot years ago. ♦ W. 47th St (at Seventh Ave)

61 New York Renaissance $$$ Opened in 1992, 10 of this hotel's 305 rooms feature butler service for wake-up, packing, etc. Check out the gym and the on-premises restaurant, **Windows on Broadway.** ♦ 714 Seventh Ave (between W. 47th and W. 48th Sts). 765.7676, 800/628.5222; fax 765.1962

62 The Edison Hotel $ Except for certain aspects of the lobby, a recent renovation has left few vestiges of this 1931 hotel's Art Deco heritage intact. The 1,000 rooms are nice but sometimes nondescript in their contemporary decor. The hotel is popular with large groups, but rooms are often available, and it's well located for those who want to stay in the very heart of the Theater District. Don't miss breakfast in the well-known coffee shop, a longtime hangout for theater people. ♦ 228 W. 47th St (between Broadway and Eighth Aves). 840.5000; fax 596.6850

63 Lunt-Fontanne Both **Mary Martin** and **Theodore Bikel** appeared here in *The Sound of Music,* and **Marlene Dietrich** performed here alone not long afterward. The theater, a work of **Carrère & Hastings,** dates to 1910. ♦ 205 W. 46th St (between Broadway and Eighth Ave). 575.9200; Ticketmaster 307.4100

64 Richard Rodgers This is where **Gwen Verdon** appeared in *Damn Yankees, Redhead,* and *New Girl in Town.* It is also where **Olsen & Johnson** began the long-running *Hellzapoppin'.* Formerly the **46th Street Theater,** built in 1925 by **Herbert J. Krapp,** it was dedicated to Richard Rodgers in March 1990. ♦ 226 W. 46th St (between Broadway and Eighth Ave). 221.1211; Ticketmaster 307.4100

65 Paramount Hotel $$$ This latest venture from hotelier **Ian Schraeger** and French designer **Phillipe Starck** was creating a stir months before its opening in August 1990. Slated as a more affordably priced **Royalton,** the 610-room hotel, in a building erected in 1928 by **Thomas V. Lamb,** leaves some of the less young and trendy guests a bit mystified, although reports from guests are overwhelmingly positive—the staff gets an A+ for service. The focal point in the lobby, which is reminiscent of the set for a movie, is a large gray staircase that looks as though it could lead up to a spaceship but goes only as far as the mezzanine, where food is served. Elevators are illuminated in different colors: purple and orange, for example; and the bathrooms in the very small rooms contain some futuristic Starck designs like silver cone-shaped sinks and lamps that resemble stethoscopes. Amenities include fitness and business centers; VCRs and fresh flowers in every room; a **Dean & DeLuca** gourmet shop; and a newsstand that sells international newspapers and magazines, postcards, and gifts—all in black-and-white. Even if you prefer to put down your suitcases in a more conservative setting, stop in for a peek. ♦ 235 W. 46th St (between Broadway and Eighth Ave). 764.5500, 800/224.7474; fax 354.5237

Within the Paramount Hotel:

Brasseries de Theatres ★★$$ The Paramount Hotel finally has a dining room worthy of its cutting-edge reputation. Bistro meisters **Jean-Michel Diot** and **Max Bernard** (**Les Halles** and **Park Bistro**) now offer French fare "on Broadway." ♦ French ♦ Lunch, dinner, and late-night meals. 243 W. 46th St (between Broadway and Eighth Ave). Reservations recommended. 719.5588

66 **Barbetta** ★★$$$ This romantic Theater District old-timer boasts a beautiful garden and wonderful pasta with truffles, sniffed out by the restaurant's own truffle dogs in Tuscany. ♦ Northern Italian ♦ Lunch and dinner. Closed Sunday. 321 W. 46th St (between Eighth and Ninth Aves). Reservations recommended. 246.9171

67 **Orso** ★$$$ It's easy to relax at this Northern Italian bistro serving pastas, seafood, veal, and wonderful pizzas. The handsome marble bar invites you to make yourself comfortable before or after the theater. ♦ Italian ♦ Lunch and dinner. 322 W. 46th St (between Eighth and Ninth Aves). Reservations recommended. 489.7212

67 **Joe Allen** $$ Gaze upon posters of failed Broadway shows, brick walls, a blackboard menu of simple food, handsome waiters, a stagestruck clientele, and frequently the Broadway stars they idolize and emulate. For nourishment, try a salad, a hamburger, a bowl of chili, or grilled fish. ♦ American ♦ Lunch and dinner. 326 W. 46th St (between Eighth and Ninth Aves). 581.6464

68 **La Vielle Auberge** ★★$$$$ At this casual old-world bistro, the roast veal is always good. ♦ French ♦ Lunch and dinner. Closed Sunday. 347 W. 46th St (between Eighth and Ninth Aves). Reservations required. 247.4284

68 **Becco** ★$$ From the **Bastianich** family, who brought you the terrific **Felidia** restaurant, comes this informal spot on Restaurant Row in the Theater District. A wide variety of flavorful Italian items, such as risotto with wild mushrooms and roast suckling pig, are featured. Best price-value bets are the prix fixe lunch and the daily menus, both under $20. ♦ Italian ♦ Lunch and dinner; dinner only on Sunday. 355 W. 46th St (between Eighth and Ninth Aves). 397.7597

68 **Lattanzi** ★$$$ Enjoy a taste of the Roman Jewish Quarter in a casual atmosphere. Baby artichokes sautéed in olive oil, grilled fish, and homemade pastas are all made to order. ♦ Jewish/Italian ♦ Lunch and dinner; dinner only on Saturday. Closed Sunday. 361 W. 46th St (between Eighth and Ninth Aves). Reservations recommended. 315.0980

68 **Hour Glass Tavern** $$ Like it or not, the hourglass above the table will give you just 60 minutes to savor the reasonably priced, three-course prix fixe dinner. You can expect to see a lot of young Broadway hopefuls in a place like this. ♦ American ♦ Lunch and dinner; dinner only on Saturday and Sunday. 373 W. 46th St (between Eighth and Ninth Aves). No credit cards. 265.2060

69 **Westside Cottage** $ Low prices, good Chinese food, quick service, and a location within walking distance of the Theater District make this spot both convenient and enjoyable for inexpensive dining before or after a show. Despite the plethora of restaurants in this area, there aren't many reliably good Chinese choices—and even fewer in this price category. ♦ Chinese/Hunan/Szechuan ♦ Lunch and dinner. 689 Ninth Ave (between W. 47th and W. 48th Sts). Reservations recommended. 245.0800

70 **Koyote Kate's** $$ Visitors seem to find nothing ironic about traveling long distances to reach New York City and then heading straight to Koyote Kate's for some country-and-western wahoo. If you think a honky-tonk saloon set-up is fun, you'll love the down-home country atmosphere and Tex-Mex/Southern menu, including a good 10-ounce burger or jalapeño shrimp (peppers stuffed with whole shrimp, breaded, and deep fried). Sour cream for dipping takes much of the bite out of the fiery peppers, as do the popular frozen piña coladas and margaritas. Live country-and-western music is performed every night except Wednesday, when the blues reigns. ♦ Tex-Mex ♦ Lunch, dinner, and late-night meals; dinner only and open until 4AM Saturday and Sunday. 307 W. 47th St (between Eighth and Ninth Aves). 956.1091

71 **B. Smith's** ★$$$ The sleek, contemporary decor reflects the style of the people who have made this one of the more popular restaurants in the Theater District. Eclectic cuisine is creatively presented (scampi and sweet potato pecan pie are favorites). Live jazz is offered upstairs; call for changing schedule. ♦ International ♦ Lunch and dinner. 771 Eighth Ave (between W. 47th and W. 48th Sts). Reservations recommended. 247.2222

72 Acropolis $ Enjoy authentic specialties from Greece in a no-nonsense setting, at prices you'll agree are quite sensible. ◆ Greek ◆ Lunch and dinner. Closed Monday. 767 Eighth Ave (at W. 47th St). 581.2733

73 Brooks Atkinson The former **Mansfield,** designed by **Herbert J. Krapp** in 1926, was renamed in 1960 in honor of the *Times* critic. *Come Blow Your Horn,* the first in a series of **Neil Simon** comedy hits, opened here. **Charles Grodin** and **Ellen Burstyn** performed here for three years in *Same Time Next Year.* ◆ 256 W. 47th St (between Broadway and Eighth Ave). 719.4099; Ticketmaster 307.4100

73 Pierre au Tunnel ★★$$$$ Not only does this Theater District standby serve excellent bistro fare (ethnic specials such as *tripes à la mode de Caen* and *tete de veau vinaigrette*), the solicitous staff make sure you're out in time for an eight o'clock curtain. ◆ French ◆ Lunch and dinner. Closed Sunday. 250 W. 47th St (between Broadway and Eighth Ave). Reservations required. 575.1220

74 Barrymore One of the great artists of her era, **Ethel Barrymore** opened this theater (designed by **Herbert J. Krapp**) in 1928 in *Kingdom of God.* The stage has seen the start of many illustrious careers: **Fred Astaire** danced his way to stardom in **Cole Porter's** *The Gay Divorce* (filmed as *The Gay Divorcee*); **Walter Huston** introduced the haunting standard "September Song" in *Knickerbocker Holiday;* **Marlon Brando** first achieved prominence when he costarred with **Jessica Tandy** in *A Streetcar Named Desire.* Today, you can see *The Sisters Rosensweig.* ◆ 243 W. 47th St (between Broadway and Eighth Ave). Telecharge 239.6200

75 Pong Sri ★$$ Manhattan is saturated with Thai restaurants, but this one has long received high marks for being one of the most authentic, though some complain they've toned down their fiery spices to accommodate the American palate. Unless you like extreme heat, you'll enjoy the delicacy of Thai flavors used in the predominantly vegetable and fish dishes. A second more spartan location has recently opened in Chinatown. ◆ Thai ◆ Lunch and dinner. 244 W. 48th St (between Broadway and Eighth Ave). 582.3392. Also at: 106 Bayard St (between Baxter and Canal Sts). 349.3132

75 Longacre In the 1930s, **The Group Theater** premiered three **Clifford Odets** plays: *Waiting for Lefty, Paradise Lost,* and *Till the Day I Die.* **Julie Harris** appeared in *The Lark* and *Little Moon of Alban.* In 1960, theater of the absurd invaded Broadway with the brilliant **Zero Mostel** in *Rhinoceros* by **Eugene Ionesco.** In 1980, *Children of a Lesser God* won a Tony. The 1913 building is the work of **Henry B. Herts.** ◆ 220 W. 48th St (between Broadway and Eighth Ave). Telecharge 239.6200

76 Walter Kerr It took precisely 66 days for the **Shubert Organization** and eminent theater designer **Herbert J. Krapp** to build the former **Ritz Theatre** in 1921. It opened with **Clare Eames** in **John Drinkwater's** *Mary Stuart* and spellbound audiences in 1924 with **Sutton Vane's** eerie *Outward Bound* starring **Alfred Lunt** and **Leslie Howard.** Other standout performances include **Claudette Colbert** in the 1925 production of *The Kiss in a Taxi,* **Helen Hayes** in *Young Blood,* and a young **Bette Davis** making her Broadway debut in the late 1920s in *Broken Dishes.* After years of being used for live radio and TV broadcasts, the theater underwent restoration and returned to legitimacy in 1971 with the rock opera *Soon.* Heavily restored again in 1983, the Walter Kerr easily ranks as one of Broadway's most beautiful theaters and authentically executed restorations, a showcase of Italian Renaissance detail. It is currently the home of **Tony Kushner's** unqualified hit *Angels in America,* a two-part AIDS epic (*Millennium Approaches* and *Perestroika*) that has brought integrity back to Broadway drama. ◆ 219 W. 48th St (between Broadway and Eighth Ave). Telecharge 239.6200

77 Holiday Inn Crowne Plaza $$$ The arrival of the ultracontemporary Holiday Inn's crown jewel in 1989 gave a major boost to the ongoing effort to revamp the Times Square area. The 770 rooms are ideally situated for sightseeing and theatergoing. For a view of Broadway, book a room on the east side; to see the Hudson River, book the west side. Indulge in one of the popular on-premise restaurants—**Broadway Grille, Samplings,** or **The Balcony**—and work off those calories at the pool or fitness center. ◆ 1605 Broadway (between W. 48th and W. 49th Sts). 977.4000; fax 333.7393

78 Cort Many fine plays have opened on this stage, including *The Swan, Merton of the Movies, Charley's Aunt,* and *Lady Windermere's Fan.* But one of the most poignant was *The Diary of Anne Frank,* by famed Hollywood writers **Frances** and **Albert Hackett,** which won a Pulitzer in 1955. The theme of children living under political oppression returned here in the 1980s with *Sarafina!* In 1990, *The Grapes of Wrath* took the Tony for best play. ◆ 138 W. 48th St (between Sixth and Seventh Aves). Telecharge 239.6200

78 Sam Ash Drums Orchestral and rock 'n' roll musicians—from those struggling at the bottom of the heap to those celebrating at the top of the charts—come here for state-of-the-art supplies and equipment. Wander in just to see who's buying. ◆ M-Sa 10AM-6PM. 160 W. 48th St (between Sixth and Seventh Aves). 719.2661

79 Drama Bookshop Established in 1923, this is one of the city's most comprehensive sources of books on the dramatic arts (the Library of Performing Arts at Lincoln Center is another). Subject areas include domestic and foreign theater, performers, music, dance, makeup, lighting, props, staging, even puppetry and magic. ◆ M-Tu, Th-F 9:30AM-7PM; W 9:30AM-8PM; Sa 10:30AM-5:30PM; Su noon-5PM. 723 Seventh Ave (between W. 48th and W. 49th Sts). 944.0595

80 Caroline's Comedy Club Recently transplanted from its original home at South Street Seaport, upscale Caroline's is a major stop on the comedy club circuit for up-and-coming talent. **Jerry Seinfeld, Jay Leno,** and **Billy Crystal** all cut their teeth here. Dinner is served, but you can just order drinks. ◆ Cover; two drink minimum. Shows nightly at 8PM; Saturday and Sunday 8PM and 10:30PM. 1626 Broadway (between W. 49th and W. 50th Sts). Reservations required. 757.4100

81 The Brill Building At the turn of the century, publishers of popular songs were all located on 28th Street west of Broadway. The noise of pianos and raspy-voiced song pluggers gave the name **Tin Pan Alley** to the street. When the action moved uptown, the publishers moved to this building and brought the name with them. The bust of the young man over the door is a memorial to the son of the building's original owner, who died just before construction began. ◆ 1619 Broadway (between W. 49th and W. 50th Sts)

Within The Brill Building:

Colony Records An institution for recordings and sheet music for soundtracks, shows, and jazz, this is a fun stop for post-theater browsing. ◆ Daily 9:30AM-1AM. 265.2050

82 Ambassador Built in 1921, this is another work of **Herbert J. Krapp.** In 1939, **Imogene Coca, Alfred Drake,** and **Danny Kaye** began their careers here in the *Strawhat Review.* ◆ 215 W. 49th St (between Broadway and Eighth Ave). 735.0500; Telecharge 239.6200

83 Eugene O'Neill This 1925 work of **Herbert J. Krapp** was the site of **Arthur Miller's** first major success, *All My Sons,* which opened here in 1947 with **Ed Begley** and **Arthur Kennedy.** ◆ 230 W. 49th St (between Broadway and Eighth Ave). 382.2790; Telecharge 239.6200

84 Worldwide Plaza Changes in zoning laws encouraged the construction of this mixed-use complex of residences and offices on the site of the second Madison Square Garden (1925-66). The apartment towers were designed by **Frank Williams;** the office tower by **Skidmore, Owings & Merrill.** Both were built in 1989. Commercial occupants include **Ogilvy & Mather** and **Polygram Records.** ◆ Bounded by W. 49th and W. 50th Sts, and Eighth and Ninth Aves

85 Chez Napoléon ★★$$$ This casual bistro is hidden away at the edge of the Theater District. It pays homage to **Napoléon** in its decor, and to Paris in its classic menu. ◆ French ◆ Lunch and dinner. Closed Sunday. 365 W. 50th St (between Eighth and Ninth Aves). Reservations required. 265.6980

86 Café Des Sports ★$$$ This is one of New York's better-kept secrets because regular customers like it the way it is. But you don't have to come often to find a warm welcome. ◆ French ◆ Lunch and dinner; dinner only on Saturday and Sunday. 329 W. 51st St (between Eighth and Ninth Aves). 974.9052

86 Rene Pujol ★★$$$$ Enjoy this truly old-fashioned bistro complete with French country atmosphere and decor. The crème brûlée is highly recommended, as is the good, reasonably priced wine list. ◆ French ◆ Lunch and dinner; dinner only on Saturday. Closed Sunday. 321 W. 51st St (between Eighth and Ninth Aves). Reservations recommended. 246.3023

87 Les Pyrénées ★★$$$ Check out this casual country restaurant with a setting made cozier by its working fireplace. ◆ French ◆ Lunch and dinner; dinner only on Sunday. 251 W. 51st St (between Broadway and Eighth Ave). Reservations recommended. 246.0044

88 Gershwin In its short history, such stars as **Tommy Tune, Alfred Drake, Bing Crosby, Frank Sinatra,** and **Rudolf Nureyev** have appeared on this stage, formerly the **Uris Theater,** which was also the home of *Sweeney Todd.* The theater was built in 1972 by **Ralph Alswang.** ◆ 222 W. 51st St (between Broadway and Eighth Ave). 586.6510; Ticketmaster 307.4100

89 Circle in the Square In the past three decades, the Circle has produced more than 100 plays—many in the company's original house in Greenwich Village—and has earned a national reputation for excellence. In 1972, directors **Theodore Mann** and **Paul Libin** built the present arena stage in response to what they saw as a need for classic theater on Broadway. In recent years, *Present Laughter* with **George C. Scott,** *The Caine Mutiny Court Martial* with **John Rubinstein,** and *A Streetcar Named Desire* with **Blythe Danner** achieved critical acclaim. ◆ 1633 Broadway (between W. 50th and W. 51st Sts). Telecharge 239.6200

Restaurants/Clubs: Red **Hotels:** Blue
Shops/ 🌳 Outdoors: Green **Sights/Culture:** Black

90 Winter Garden This beautiful theater, designed by **W.A. Swasey,** opened with **Al Jolson** in 1911. The **Shuberts** produced 12 annual editions of their revue *The Passing Show.* **Fanny Brice, Bob Hope,** and **Josephine Baker** were featured in the *Ziegfeld Follies.* Other hit musicals were *Plain and Fancy, West Side Story, Funny Girl,* and, currently, those fabulous felines in *Cats.* ♦ 1634 Broadway (between W. 50th and W. 51st Sts). Telecharge 239.6200

91 Sheraton Manhattan $$$ A heated indoor swimming pool, a sun deck, and a gym furnished with modern exercise equipment are features of this conveniently located hotel, the handsome result of a major overhaul completed in 1992. Children stay here free if no extra bed is required. ♦ 790 Seventh Ave (at W. 51st St). 581.3300, 800/325.3535; fax 541.9219

92 Equitable Center A huge mural created by **Roy Lichtenstein** for this 1985 building by **Edward Larrabee** brings you in off the street. When you get inside there are other works of art to be seen, the most striking of which are the murals in the corridor to the left, which were painted in 1930 by **Thomas Hart Benton** and moved here from the New School for Social Research. Also off the Equitable's lobby are the **Equitable Gallery** and the **Brooklyn Museum Shop.** ♦ Gallery and shop: M-F 11AM-6PM; Sa noon-5PM. 787 Seventh Ave (between W. 51st and W. 52nd Sts). 554.4818

Within the Equitable Center:

Le Bernardin ★★★★$$$$ When this brilliant seafood restaurant first exploded onto the scene in 1986, it was acclaimed by everyone who dined here. Years later, it is still receiving rave reviews, and it is as difficult as ever to get a reservation. The dining room is distinguished and the prices breathtaking, but the experience justifies the tab, especially if someone else is paying. ♦ French ♦ Lunch and dinner; dinner only on Saturday. Closed Sunday. 155 W. 51st St. Reservations required. 489.1515

Palio ★★$$$$ Named for a horse-racing festival in the town of Siena, Italy, Palio is well worth a visit, if only to see the stunning graphics by **Vignelli Associates** and **Skidmore, Owings & Merrill** and the wrap-around **Sandro Chia** mural that dominates the ground-floor bar. The restaurant itself is on the second floor. From the crystal to the perfection of each rose petal, everything strives for the utmost opulence and luxury. It is a pity the food does not always soar to the same heights. The bar, however, is an experience. ♦ Italian ♦ Lunch and dinner; dinner only on Saturday. Closed Sunday. 151 W. 51st St. Jacket and tie recommended, even in the bar. Reservations required. 245.4850

93 Bellini ★$$$$ A first cousin of the famous **Harry's Bar** in Venice, this ultrachic cafe/restaurant attracts a crowd of the rich and famous. The food is mediocre (although the calf's liver is perfection), but mostly it's the superb service that keep them coming. Stick to champagne. ♦ Italian ♦ Lunch and dinner; dinner only on Saturday. Closed Sunday. 777 Seventh Ave (between W. 50th and W. 51st Sts). Reservations required. 265.7770

93 Michelangelo $$$ Some of the space of the old **Taft Hotel** has gotten a new lease on life in the form of this 178-room marble and crystal palace with 24-hour room service, a concierge, a complimentary 24-hour fitness center, and access (for a fee) to a health club across the street. The larger-than-average rooms have TVs enclosed within hand-inlaid armoires (there are smaller TVs in the bathrooms). Large terry robes, hand cream, Crabtree & Evelyn soaps, Dukar razors, bidets, powder rooms, and valet parking are among the amenities. Another plus: management *likes* children. ♦ 152 W. 51st St (at Seventh Ave). 765.1900, 800/237.0990; fax 541.6604

94 Cité ★$$$$ Restrained waiters serve good food in the main restaurant, but excellent (and less expensive) bistro-cum-cafe fare is available in the adjoining lunch brasserie. ♦ French ♦ Lunch and dinner. 120 W. 51st St (between Sixth and Seventh Aves). Reservations recommended. 956.7100

95 Looking Toward the Avenue Installed in 1989, artist **Jim Dine's** three enormous bronze *Venuses* (ranging in height from 14 to 23 feet) are a humanizing presence amid the impersonal towers that surround them. ♦ 1301 Sixth Ave (between W. 52nd and W. 53rd Sts)

96 Ben Benson's Steakhouse ★★$$$$ This is a classic New York restaurant in a relatively new building. American antiques and prints help do the trick. The steaks are properly aged, too, and the service is old-fashioned friendly. ♦ American ♦ Lunch and dinner; dinner only on Saturday and Sunday. 123 W. 52nd St (between Sixth and Seventh Aves). Reservations recommended. 581.8888

D.W. Griffith's controversial landmark film *The Birth of a Nation* opened on 3 March 1915 at the Liberty Theater, 234 W. 42nd Street.

97 Sheraton New York $$$ This efficient, modern hotel has excellent convention facilities for the mainly corporate clientele. The 1,700 rooms and public areas were completely restored in 1992; the original building, by **Morris Lapidus & Associates**, dates to 1962. Guests have use of the indoor swimming pool across the street at the **Sheraton Manhattan.** There are several restaurants and lounges, and room service is available until 1AM. ♦ 811 Seventh Ave (between W. 52nd and W. 53rd Sts). 581.1000, 800/325.3535; fax 262.4410

98 Rosie O'Grady's ★$$$ The lively nouvelle Irish pub attracts a convivial crowd from the nearby hotels. ♦ Irish ♦ Lunch and dinner. 800 Seventh Ave (between W. 52nd and W. 53rd Sts). Reservations recommended. 582.2975

99 Novotel $$$ Part of a respected French chain, the hotel begins on the seventh floor of this 1984 building by **Gruzen & Partners,** and many of its 474 rooms and suites look down into the heart of Times Square. Room service runs until midnight. ♦ 226 W. 52nd St (between Broadway and Eighth Ave). 315.0100, 800/221.4542; fax 765.5369

Within Novotel:

Cafe Nicole ★$$$ This restaurant and wine bar has a seventh-floor view of the Theater District. You'll find jazzy piano entertainment on the terrace at dinner. Steamed salmon and roast duck are sure bets. ♦ French/American ♦ Breakfast, lunch, and dinner. Reservations recommended. 315.0100

Gallagher's

99 Gallagher's Steak House ★★$$$$ The entrance to this vintage New York restaurant—a huge refrigerated locker (visible from the street) filled with steaks and baskets of strawberries—sets the stage for a restaurant that has hardly changed since it opened here in 1927. If you want to know what New York restaurants were like in the good old days, this is the place to do it. The front room with its huge bar can be noisy. It's quieter in back, where most of the sound comes from sizzling steaks. ♦ American ♦ Lunch and dinner. 228 W. 52nd St (between Broadway and Eighth Ave). 245.5336

100 Roseland The legendary ballroom, which opened in 1919, still plays host to big bands and aspiring Fred Astaires and Ginger Rogerses, although only two days a week now—Thursday, when there is a DJ, and Sunday, when there is live music. ♦ Admission. Th, Su 2:30-11PM. 239 W. 52nd St (between Broadway and Eighth Ave). 247.0200

100 Virginia Formerly called the **ANTA,** it was built in 1925 by **Howard Crane** for the **Theatre Guild. Pat Hingle** and **Christopher Plummer** starred here in **Archibald MacLeish's** *J.B.,* which won the Pulitzer Prize in 1959. Sir Thomas More was brilliantly played by **Paul Scofield** in **Robert Bolt's** *A Man for All Seasons* in 1961. *No Place To Be Somebody* moved here from the **Public Theater** after its author, **Charles Gordone,** won the Pulitzer in 1969. ♦ 245 W. 52nd St (between Broadway and Eighth Ave). Telecharge 239.6200

101 Neil Simon When this theater was erected in 1927 by **Herbert J. Krapp, Fred** and **Adele Astaire** were in the first production, **George** and **Ira Gershwin's** *Funny Face.* A more recent hit was *Annie,* which arrived here exactly 50 years later. ♦ 250 W. 52nd St (between Broadway and Eighth Ave). 757.8646; Ticketmaster 307.4100

101 Russian Samovar ★$$$ Staples and specialties of Slavic cooking—*blini* with caviar, grilled fish, and lamb—lead the menu here. A four-course prix fixe dinner helps attract regulars, who enjoy the Russian decor and music nightly. ♦ Russian ♦ Lunch and dinner; dinner only on Monday and Sunday. 256 W. 52nd St (between Broadway and Eighth Ave). Reservations recommended. 757.0168

102 King Crab ★$$ Spacious it's not, but this pretty seafood restaurant's charm is augmented by gaslight lamps and a helpful staff. The daily specials follow the Fulton Fish Market's whims. Don't pass up the soft-shell crabs when in season. King Crab is one of the nicest fresh fish restaurants in the Theater District, so reserve in advance for a preshow dinner. ♦ Seafood ♦ Lunch and dinner; dinner only on Saturday and Sunday. 871 Eighth Ave (at W. 52nd St). 765.4393

103 Bangkok Cuisine ★★$$$ The best dishes at this excellent Thai restaurant are the seafood soups spiced with pepper and lemon-grass and the baked fish smothered with hot spices. It's crowded in the early evening but more peaceful later on. ♦ Thai ♦ Lunch and dinner; dinner only on Sunday. 885 Eighth Ave (between W. 52nd and W. 53rd Sts). Reservations recommended. 581.6370

104 Broadway Ethel Merman filled this theater with sound and ticket-holders as the star of *Gypsy.* This theater, built in 1924 by **Eugene DeRosa,** is also where **Barbra Streisand** performed in *Funny Girl,* and where **Yul Brynner** gave his final performance in *The King and I. Miss Saigon* opened here on 11 April 1991. ♦ 1681 Broadway (between W. 52nd and W. 53rd Sts). Telecharge 239.6200

The United Nations has a peace garden that boasts more than 1,000 rose bushes.

All the Town's a Stage: The New York Theater Scene

Center Stage: Broadway

The name Broadway has become synonymous with theater in America, but *Broadway* has many other meanings. Geographically, it is the street that runs the entire length of Manhattan. Theatrically, it is the area around **Times Square,** where most of the commercial theaters are located. Legally, it is the place where only members of theatrical trade unions can work. But most important, Broadway symbolizes the whole complex of qualities associated with the glittering world of the theater: stars, polished performances, sophisticated plays, and the all-American musical.

Known as "The Great White Way," Broadway has been the heart of American theater for over 100 years. The reasons are obvious: The audience is here. The production money is here. The best actors, directors, playwrights, designers, choreographers, and critics work here. To be accepted by Broadway is the ultimate recognition of one's talent.

Drama: New Yorkers experienced their first real season in 1753, when the **Hallam Company** of London visited. A favorite theme of dramas of that period was the triumph of native honesty and worth over foreign affectation, as seen in plays such as **Royall Tyler's** *The Contrast* (1787). By the 1830s, **Washington Irving** and **Walt Whitman,** in their roles as theater critics, advised that the stage offer more than just escape.

From 1850 to 1900, commercial houses featured melodramas, spectacle plays, comic operas, vaudeville, and burlesques. The most popular play of the period was *Uncle Tom's Cabin.* It was during these years that the star system was born, with **Joseph Jefferson** in the title role in *Rip Van Winkle,* **Edwin Booth** in *Hamlet,* and **James O'Neill** (father of Eugene) in *The Count of Monte Cristo.* **John Drew, Maude Adams, Richard Mansfield,** and the **Barrymores** made their names in various roles.

Around the time of World War I, producer **Arthur Hopkins** transformed Broadway by revitalizing the classics and by presenting the first modern war play, *What Price Glory?* Hopkins introduced **Katharine Hepburn, Barbara Stanwyck,** and **Clark Gable** to the stage.

Homegrown drama received a welcome stimulus with the emergence of a group of New York City playwrights who were interested in social satire, dramatic realism, and psychological expressionism. **Eugene O'Neill,** preoccupied with man's struggles with his own psyche and with the universe, expressed himself in such plays as *Beyond the Horizon, Anna Christie,* and *Strange Interlude.* Later writers, influenced by O'Neill, went on to create a powerful stage legacy of their own: **Elmer Rice, Clifford Odets, Arthur Miller,** and **Tennessee Williams.**

In the early '20s, an extraordinarily successful organization, **The Theatre Guild,** brought to Broadway the works of new European dramatists including **Tolstoy, Ibsen, Strindberg,** and **Shaw.** Many of America's best-known actors appeared in their productions: **Lynn Fontanne** and **Alfred Lunt, Edward G. Robinson, Helen Hayes,** and **Ruth Gordon.** Around this time, **Brooks Atkinson** became drama critic for the *New York Times,* and artist **Al Hirschfeld** began to capture the essence of the theater world with his caricatures, which still appear today.

In the '30s and '40s, **The Group Theater,** founded by **Harold Clurman,** explored and translated the theater of **Stanislavski,** while **Lee Strasberg** redefined his acting method and created **The Actors Studio** (see page 137 for graduates). The **Mercury Theater,** founded by **Orson Welles** and **John Houseman,** presented provocative works such as **Marc Blitzstein's** *The Cradle Will Rock.* Dramas on Broadway at the time were *Abe Lincoln in Illinois* by **Robert E. Sherwood,** *The Little Foxes* by **Lillian Hellman,** and *Our Town* by **Thornton Wilder.** **Katharine Cornell** became one of the most popular actresses in the American theater. In 1947, **Elia Kazan** directed two plays that exemplified American realism: *A Streetcar Named Desire* by **Tennessee Williams** and *Death of a Salesman* by **Arthur Miller.**

In the '60s, **Edward Albee's** *Who's Afraid of Virginia Woolf?* deeply impressed audiences, and **Eugene Ionesco's** *Rhinoceros* illustrated the theater of the absurd, which dramatized an illogical and incongruous world. Political assassinations, the Vietnam War, and social problems of the '60s and '70s were reflected in plays such as *Hair, The Great White Hope, Streamers,* and *That Championship Season.* Many of these started Off Broadway (a trend that continues today). Many Broadway hits, such as *Fences* by **August Wilson,** also come from regional theaters. English productions are still popular today; the works of writers **Peter Shaffer, Tom Stoppard, David Hare, Michael Frayn,** and director **Peter Hall** are among the favorite British imports.

Comedy: Stage comedy as we know it began in the mid-1800s with the debut of the satirical play *A Glance at New York.* In 1926, *Abie's Irish Rose,* a romantic comedy, closed after a record-setting four-year run. Fine examples of literary comedy in the '30s and '40s included **Marc Connelly's** *The Green Pastures* and **Philip Barry's** *The Philadelphia Story.* **George S. Kaufman,** a master of the wisecrack, wrote (alone and with **Moss Hart**) a series of zany comedies such as *You Can't Take It with You* and *The Man Who Came to Dinner.* England's **Noel Coward** produced a string of frothy hits for the Broadway stage. The present-day king of comedy is **Neil Simon,** whose gift is creating hilarious situations with urbane one-liners. **Harvey Fierstein, David Mamet,** and **John Guare** have also brought often-blistering comedies to Broadway in recent years.

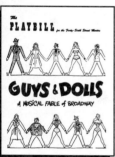

Musical Comedy: The American musical has traveled a long way since *The Black Crook* was presented at **Niblo's Garden** in 1866. The opening performance lasted five and a half hours, and the 100 undraped females and sexy songs proved irresistible to audiences.

Another genre of musical theater was the minstrel show, a revue with performers in blackface (later replaced by vaudeville). The first play to be called a "musical comedy" was *Evangeline* in 1874. During that time, European operettas by **Offenbach, Strauss,** and **Gilbert and Sullivan** dominated the scene. *H.M.S. Pinafore* was such wholesome entertainment that it finally brought women and children into the audience. The first great composer of operettas for the American stage was **Victor Herbert;** the last was **Sigmund Romberg. Harrigan and Hart** wrote hilarious farces about immigrant

groups. **Charles Hoyt's** *A Trip to Chinatown* featured two hit songs, "After the Ball" and "The Bowery." **George Lederer** introduced the "revue" in 1894 with his *Passing Show,* which created opportunities for comedians like **Weber and Fields** and stars like **Lillian Russell** and **Anna Held. Florenz Ziegfeld's** *Follies* and **Irving Berlin's** *Music Box Revues* were the rage.

Meanwhile, **George M. Cohan** romanticized the American identity in shows like *Little Johnny Jones.* In the '20s, **Rodgers** and **Hart, George** and **Ira Gershwin, Cole Porter,** and **Oscar Hammerstein II** wrote some of the most beautiful songs for musical comedy stage. It was in **Jerome Kern's** *Showboat,* however, that music and lyrics were first combined with the sophisticated adult libretto. All these musicians and lyricists worked in **Tin Pan Alley,** where sheet music was turned out by the pound. Political satire was introduced by the Gershwins in *Of Thee I Sing* and *Strike Up the Band.* In 1935, the folk opera *Porgy and Bess,* also by the Gershwins, brought musical theater to a new plateau.

The collaboration of **Rodgers** and **Hammerstein** started with the artistic triumph of *Oklahoma!* in the 1940s. This musical was brilliantly choreographed by **Agnes de Mille.** *Carousel, South Pacific, The King and I,* and *The Sound of Music* also gave new meaning to the musical play. This tradition continued in the '50s and '60s with classics such as *Guys and Dolls* by **Loesser,** *My Fair Lady* by **Lerner** and **Lowe,** *West Side Story* by **Bernstein** and **Sondheim,** and *Fiddler on the Roof* by **Boch** and **Harnick.**

Musicals have dominated the Broadway stage over the last three decades. *Camelot, Funny Girl,* and *Hello, Dolly!* opened a period of romanticism. In 1967, *Hair* represented the radical psychedelic movement of the Vietnam War years. In the mid-1970s, *A Chorus Line,* directed by **Michael Bennett,** dazzled audiences with the energy of its dance. Almost every major director of musicals in the last 15 years has been a choreographer. An exception is producer/director **Harold Prince.** In recent years, his productions of *Cabaret, Sweeney Todd,* and *Evita* brought a fresh political and social viewpoint to musical theater. On the nostalgic side, *Ain't Misbehavin', 42nd Street,* and *Anything Goes* provided grand entertainment. The English musical was the trend of the '80s: **Cameron Macintosh's** *Les Misérables* and fellow Brit **Andrew Lloyd Webber's** *Cats* and *The Phantom of the Opera* took the city by

storm; Webber's 1990 *Aspects of Love* was not as great a success. Macintosh's controversial *Miss Saigon* was the talk of the town that year.

Stage Left: Off Broadway and Off Off Broadway

As the whetstone for theatrical talent, the reservoir for Broadway, and the mechanism for probing the desires of an ever-changing audience, Off Broadway and Off Off Broadway have thrived in New York since the 1950s. There are currently more than 200 small theaters scattered throughout the city.

The **Provincetown Playhouse** and the **Washington Square Players** set the tone of the little-theater movement in the '20s. Decades later, the **Circle in the Square** was the leader of the alternative dramatic scene in Greenwich Village. **Geraldine Page** appeared there in **Tennessee Williams'** *Summer and Smoke,* and **Jason Robards** starred in **Eugene O'Neill's** *The Iceman Cometh.* The Circle also helped **George C. Scott, Colleen Dewhurst, Dustin Hoffman, Cicely Tyson,** and **James Earl Jones** establish their reputations.

The late **Joseph Papp,** head of the **New York Shakespeare Festival** at the **Public Theater,** was the most dynamic theater impresario in America in recent years. With his multistage Public Theater on Astor Place, the outdoor Shakespeare Festival at the **Delacorte Theater** in Central Park, and productions at **Lincoln Center's Beaumont Theater,** he nurtured artists such as writers **Sam Shepard, David Rabe,** and **Israel Horovitz,** and actors **Meryl Streep** and **Raul Julia.** Papp's productions that went on to Broadway include *A Chorus Line, Plenty,* and *The Mystery of Edwin Drood.*

As part of the revitalization of W. 42nd Street, **Theater Row** was established several years ago between Ninth and 10th avenues. Thanks to the vision of **Fred Papert,** this once run-down part of the Times Square area has been transformed into an attractive addition to Off Broadway. Tenants include the **Harold Clurman Theater,** the **South Street Theater,** and **Playwrights Horizons.**

As Off-Broadway productions moved uptown, some artists felt the need to explore subjects forbidden by the traditions of Broadway and Off Broadway, such as politics, profanity, nudity, and sexuality—creating a marvelous spirit of experimentation. **The Living Theater,** founded by **Judith Malina** and **Julian Beck,** was the most controversial of the politically oriented groups. Troupes such as **Mabou Mines, The Wooster Group,** and the **Ridiculous Theatrical Company** are alive and well today.

105 Ed Sullivan This landmark theater, which was built by **Herbert J. Krapp** in 1927 and is full of Gothic details inside and out, has showcased vaudeville, music hall, stage shows, radio, and TV. It was a casino-style nightclub in the '30s, then was the broadcast home of the Fred Allen radio show, and, from 1948 to 1971, "The Ed Sullivan Show." Under its vaulted cathedral ceiling, American audiences got their first look at the **Beatles, Elvis Presley,** and **Rudolf Nureyev.** CBS bought and completely restored the theater in 1993; it is now home to **David Letterman's** *Late Show.* ♦ 1697 Broadway (between W. 53rd and W. 54th Sts)

106 Au Cafe ★$$ This is an idea whose time has certainly come: a coffee bar with a variety of sandwiches, salads, soups, pastas, burgers, and pastries. Au Cafe is the ideal place to relax with your thoughts and a newspaper. Soft jazz, high black stools, and small marble pedestal tables create an airy, laid-back environment with a spacious outdoor palm-lined seating area. ♦ American ♦ Breakfast, lunch, and dinner. 1700 Broadway (at W. 53rd St). 757.2233

107 Stage Delicatessen $$ Looking every bit the sellout that it is, this once-great spot for **Damon Runyon** Broadway characters is now in high disrepute among New Yorkers. The pastrami is still good, but the sandwiches are high-priced. ♦ Deli ♦ Breakfast, lunch, dinner, and late-night meals. 834 Seventh Ave (between W. 53rd and W. 54th Sts). 245.7850

108 Remi ★★★$$$$ Fresh antipasti, Venetian-style pastas, and grilled meats and fish please both the dealmakers from nearby Time-Warner and Orion who lunch here and the city's esteemed chefs, who reserve tables for their nights off. The desserts are worth the splurge; be sure to sample one of the 45 varieties of grappa. ♦ Italian ♦ Lunch and dinner; dinner only on Saturday and Sunday. 145 W. 53rd St (between Sixth and Seventh Aves). Reservations recommended. 581.4242

109 New York Hilton $$$ The quintessential luxury convention hotel in town is this tower of more than 2,000 well-appointed rooms, each with a private bar, with services for businesspeople such as quick checkout, a copy center, rental pocket beeper phones, and a multilingual staff. **Executive Tower** rooms offer a refrigerator, radio alarm, electric shoe polisher, and a free copy of *USA Today* with breakfast. A battery of restaurants and cocktail lounges includes **Club 53,** a comedy club, and **Grill 53,** a fine restaurant. ♦ 1335 Sixth Ave (between W. 53rd and W. 54th Sts). 586.7000, 800/445.8667; fax 315.1374

110 Rhiga Royal Hotel $$$$ Every room is a suite in this new 54-story luxury hotel with great views and meeting facilities to accommodate up to 110. Amenities in each suite include VCRs and two independent phone lines. Most rooms have computer and facsimile ports. Chef **John Halligan,** from the **St. James's Club** in San Francisco, prepares Continental nouvelle cuisine in **The Halcyon,** and there is 24-hour room service. ♦ 151 W. 54th St (between Sixth and Seventh Aves). 307.5000, 800/937.5454; fax 765.6530

111 Carnegie Delicatessen ★★$$ Indulge yourself at *the* classic kosher-style deli, a legend in New York, serving sandwiches named after most of the other New York legends. The menu may seem a bit pricey at first—but then the sandwiches arrive, massive affairs that inevitably provide tasty leftovers to be shared or carted home. Owner **Leo** died recently, but not before seeing the Carnegie immortalized in **Woody Allen's** *Broadway Danny Rose.* It's still a leader in the ongoing New York deli wars. Leave room for the cheesecake. ♦ Deli ♦ Breakfast, lunch, dinner, and late-night meals. 854 Seventh Ave (between W. 54th and W. 55th Sts). No credit cards. 757.2245

112 Pet Department Store Don't have a thing for your dog to wear to your wedding? Or just want to stop in for a cup of tea, check out the exotic multicolor fish, and commiserate about your cat's recurring cough? Bet your Siamese is dying for a Chanel choker, or that your greyhound doesn't have a Burberry to match yours. This fun shop is definitely more for pet owners than for the pets and serves as an unofficial center for the local animal-owners community. ♦ M-Sa 10AM-7PM; Su 1-5PM. 233 W. 54th St (between Broadway and Eighth Ave). 489.9195

113 Siam Inn ★$$ Spicy, authentic fare is offered in the humdrum dining room of this noisy and fashionable Thai restaurant. Fish and seafood dishes are best. The service isn't good. ♦ Thai ♦ Lunch and dinner; dinner only on Saturday and Sunday. 916 Eighth Ave (between W. 54th and W. 55th Sts). 974.9583

114 Broadway Diner ★$ This upscale, 1950s-style diner with lots of tables and a counter features a wide variety of daily specials, such as good salads, steaks, and fresh fish. ♦ American ♦ Breakfast, lunch, dinner, and late-night meals. 1726 Broadway (at W. 55th St). No credit cards. 765.0909. Also at: 590 Lexington Ave. 486.8838

115 MONY Tower When built in 1950 by **Shreve, Lamb & Harmon,** this was the headquarters of the insurance company known as Mutual of New York. It has since become **MONY Financial Services.** The mast on top of the tower is all about change of another kind. If the light on top is green, look for fair weather. Orange means clouds are coming, and flashing orange signals rain. When it flashes white, expect snow. If the lights on the mast itself are rising, so will the temperature, and when they descend, it is going to get cold. ♦ 1740 Broadway (between W. 55th and W. 56th Sts)

116 Omni Park Central $$$ When the '20s roared, a lot of the sound and fury echoed through the halls of the Park Central, which was a meeting place for bootleggers and small-time gangsters. The ghosts have all been exorcised, and the 1927 hotel by **Groneburg & Leuchtag** has a new lease on life. You'll find a lovely on-site bistro, **Nicole,** plus a lounge, a drugstore, a newsstand, and a barbershop. ♦ 870 Seventh Ave (between W. 55th and W. 56th Sts). 247.8000, 800/843.6664; fax 484.3374

117 Hotel Wellington $ This 1930s gem is often overlooked, even though it has 650 rooms, a coffee shop, a restaurant, and a cocktail lounge. A renovation of all rooms was completed in early 1993. ♦ 871 Seventh Ave (between W. 55th and W. 56th Sts). 247.3900, 800/652.1212; fax 581.1719

118 Christer's ★★$$$ After garnering rave reviews during his tenure as chef at the nearby **Aquavit,** Swedish-born **Christer Larsson** opened his new venture in late 1993. The rustic decor of split logs and plaid-covered banquettes is centered around a stone fireplace, and the American menu with a Scandinavian touch spotlights salmon and other fresh fish and seafood. ♦ American/Scandinavian ♦ Lunch, dinner, and late-night meals. Closed Sunday. 145 W. 55th St (between Sixth and Seventh Aves). Reservations recommended. 974.7224

118 City Center of Music and Drama This somewhat unlikely Moorish emporium was built as a Shriners' temple in 1924 by **H.P. Knowles** and converted to City Center in 1943. It was the home of the **New York City Opera** and the **New York City Ballet** before they moved to Lincoln Center. The 2,731-seat City Center has been splendidly renovated. With new raking and improved sightlines, audiences no longer have to strain their necks to see. Regular performers include the **Alvin Ailey, Martha Graham,** and **Merce Cunningham** dance companies. ♦ Box office noon-8PM. 131 W. 55th St (between Sixth and Seventh Aves). 581.7907

119 Castellano ★$$$$ This is a re-creation of **Harry's Bar** in Venice, serving authentic Venetian cuisine. Ravioli with vegetables is a relatively simple dish made extraordinary by a just-right combination of flavors and textures. ♦ Italian ♦ Lunch and dinner; dinner only on Saturday and Sunday. 138 W. 55th St (between Sixth and Seventh Aves). Reservations required. 664.1975

119 Gorham Hotel $$ First opened in 1929, this 120-room hotel was renovated to the tune of $16 million in 1993. It's a lovely and convenient Midtown choice for visitors and particularly families, since contemporary-style rooms are large and come with a fully equipped kitchenette—and there's no charge for children under 16. If you've opted for one of the 45 suites, you can look forward to a whirlpool bath at the end of a long day. ♦ 136 W. 55th St (between Sixth and Seventh Aves). 245.1800, 800/735.0710; fax 582.8332

120 Corrado ★★$$$ The tortellini in *brodo* are as good as they are in Bologna; the pasta is homemade; the sauces light and skillfully spiced; the desserts excellent, especially the flavorful ice creams. Next door is the **Corrado Kitchen,** a popular take-out place. ♦ Italian ♦ Lunch and dinner; dinner only on Saturday and Sunday. Corrado Kitchen: M-F 6:30AM-9PM; Sa-Su 8AM-8PM. 1373 Sixth Ave (between W. 55th and W. 56th Sts). Reservations recommended. 333.3133

120 Ellen's Stardust Diner $ Ellen's burgers won't win any culinary awards, but they're delivered by friendly waiters to the shake, rattle, and roll of vintage '50s music. The menu gets as fancy as grilled swordfish, but your best bet is a Velveeta cheeseburger and strawberry malt topped off by an ice-cream sundae. ♦ American ♦ Breakfast, lunch, dinner, and late-night meals. 1377 Sixth Ave (at W. 56th St). 307.7575

121 The Mysterious Bookshop If you want to know *whodunit,* the amazingly well-informed staff here won't spoil the fun by telling you, but they will guide you to the exact book that you're looking for. There are thousands of mystery books, both new and out-of-print, in this two-level shop. ♦ M-Sa 11AM-7PM. 129 W. 56th St (between Sixth and Seventh Aves). 765.0900

Restaurants/Clubs: Red   Hotels: Blue

Shops/ ♣ Outdoors: Green   Sights/Culture: Black

New York City hosts the consulates or missions of 125 nations.

122 Joseph Patelson Music House
Musicians, from beginners to world-renowned maestros, have been coming to this former carriage house for their music needs (sheet music and books, orchestral and opera scores) ever since it opened in 1920. With the widest selection of music (mostly classical, with some jazz, pop, and Broadway) in New York, it's no surprise that Patelson's receives orders from as far away as Japan, Australia, and Saudi Arabia. The knowledgeable staff is always available to help; feel free to browse. This is a highly recommended attraction for music lovers. ◆ M-Sa 9AM-6PM. 160 W. 56th St (between Sixth and Seventh Aves). 582.5840

123 Lee's Studio Sleek, contemporary lighting fixtures and table and floor lamps like those you'd expect to find at the Museum of Modern Art, as well as a selective choice of chairs, sofas, and accessories, fill this shop. ◆ M-Sa 10AM-7PM; Su noon-5:30PM. 1755 Broadway (at W. 56th St). 581.4400. Also at: 1069 Third Ave. 371.1122

124 Indian Pavilion ★$ With its low-profile decor, this small restaurant gives curry-lovers a lift before or after the theater. Underestimated for its flavorful Indian and Pakistani food, Indian Pavilion is the best choice for inexpensive Indian food in the Theater District, and will save you the time and expense of a trip downtown to Little India's E. Sixth Street. ◆ Indian ◆ Lunch and dinner. 240 W. 56th St (between Broadway and Eighth Ave). 243.8175

125 Symphony Cafe ★★$$ The *New York Times* calls this a "splendid grand cafe," and the spacious setting, professional service, and menu of fresh seafood and great steaks are indeed impressive. Striking a high note in an otherwise nondescript area, it's located equidistant from Lincoln Center, Carnegie Hall, and the Theater District. The antithesis of the nearby Hard Rock Cafe, the candlelit restaurant with fresh table linens and flowers features memorabilia from the Songwriters' Hall of Fame Museum. ◆ American ◆ Lunch and dinner; late-night meals Saturday and Sunday. 950 Eighth Ave (at W. 56th St). Pre-theater reservations required. 397.9595

126 Hearst Magazine Building Architect **Joseph Urban's** bizarre 1928 concoction is reminiscent of the Viennese Secession with strange obelisks standing on a heavy base and rising over the roof of the six-story pile.

Apparently, this was intended to be the plinth for another seven stories; it would have remained a folly nonetheless. ◆ 959 Eighth Ave (between W. 56th and W. 57th Sts). 644.2000

127 Parc Vendome Apartments This was one of the sites considered for a second Metropolitan Opera House. The scheme died when opera patrons were told that a skyscraper would be built to help support it. "We don't need that kind of help," they sniffed and took their money elsewhere. The 570-unit apartment house, a 1931 creation of **Henry Mandel,** contains a private dining room, a gymnasium and pool, a music room, and terraced gardens. ◆ 340 W. 57th St (between Eighth and Ninth Aves). 247.6990

128 Coliseum Books Here you'll find a huge mix of both general interest and scholarly books: academic, trade, and mass-market paperbacks; sports; how-to books; scholarly journals; and oversize paper and hardcover remainders. Computer reference, a helpful staff, and late hours are also pluses. ◆ M 8AM-10PM; Tu-Th 8AM-11PM; F 8AM-11:30PM; Sa 10AM-11:30PM; Su noon-8PM. 1771 Broadway (at W. 57th St). 757.8381

129 Hard Rock Cafe ★★$$ Look for the tail end of a 1958 Cadillac that doubles as its marquee, or follow the young crowd that considers a visit to this branch of the Hard Rock that opened in London in 1971 a transcendental experience. If you're one of the few without a Hard Rock sweatshirt, you can buy one in the gift shop next door. But if you skip the restaurant you won't see the guitar-shaped bar or the rock memorabilia that includes dozens of gold records, **Prince's** purple jacket, and **Jimi Hendrix's** guitar. ◆ American ◆ Lunch, dinner, and late-night. 221 W. 57th St (between Seventh Ave and Broadway). 459.9320

129 Art Students League The three central panels on this French Renaissance palace represent the **Fine Arts Society,** the **Architectural League,** and the **Art Students League,** all of which originally shared this facility and made it the scene of nearly every important exhibition at the turn of the century. Dating to 1892, this is a work of **Henry J. Hardenburgh.** ◆ 215 W. 57th St (between Seventh Ave and Broadway). 247.4510

130 Lee's Art Shop, Inc. "The Department Store for Artists" is appropriately located directly across the street from the Art Students' League. The extensive materials department attracts artists and architects, and the pens, stationery, and picture frames make great gifts. ◆ M-F 9AM-7PM; Sa 9:30AM-6:30PM; Su noon-5:30PM. 220 W. 57th St (between Seventh Ave and Broadway). 247.0110

131 The Osborne Except for the removal of its front porch and the addition of retail stores, this wonderful apartment building has hardly changed since it was built by **James E. Ware** in 1885. The lobby was designed by **Louis Comfort Tiffany.** ♦ 205 W. 57th St (at Seventh Ave)

131 Cafe Europa ★$ Bright and pretty, with dreamy trompe l'oeil ceilings, this cafe is convenient for a sandwich made with the freshest of ingredients or such hot dishes as pizza and pasta. The muffins, tarts, and cakes accompanied by full-flavored coffees are great for a quick lift. ♦ Cafe/Takeout ♦ Breakfast, lunch, dinner, and late-night meals. 205 W. 57th St (at Seventh Ave). 977.4030

132 Trattoria Dell'Arte ★★$$$ Here, opposite **Carnegie Hall,** in a colorful restaurant designed by **Milton Glaser,** presides the largest antipasto bar in the world, according to its proud management. The casual Italian menu features delicate thin-crust pizza. In addition to other sources, Glaser drew inspiration from the noses of some 32 famous Italians and Italian-Americans—**Joe DiMaggio** and **Geraldine Ferraro** among them. ♦ Italian ♦ Lunch and dinner. 900 Seventh Ave (between W. 56th and W. 57th Sts). Reservations required before and after Carnegie Hall performances. 245.9800

CARNEGIE HALL ARCHIVES

133 Carnegie Hall This landmark (interior shown above) was built in 1891 by **William B. Tuthill; William Morris Hunt** and **Dankmar Adler** served as consultants. **Peter Ilyich Tchaikovsky** conducted at the opening concert, and during the next 70 years, the **New York Philharmonic** played here under such greats as **Gustav Mahler, Bruno Walter, Arturo Toscanini, Leopold Stokowski,** and **Leonard Bernstein.** Considered to have acoustics matched by few others in the world, the hall has attracted all of the 20th century's great musicians, and not just the classical variety. **W.C. Handy** brought his blues here in 1928, and was followed by **Count Basie, Duke Ellington, Benny Goodman,** and others. When it was announced in the 1950s that the New York Philharmonic would be moving to

Lincoln Center, Carnegie Hall was put up for sale. Violinist **Isaac Stern** and a group of concerned music lovers waged a successful campaign to save it. Their effort eventually resulted in a restoration, completed in 1986 by **James Stewart Polshek and Partners,** which rendered it as glorious visually as it is acoustically. The corridors are lined with scores and other memorabilia of the artists and composers who have added to Carnegie Hall's greatness. The space above the auditorium contains studios and apartments favored by musicians and artists. Another part of the space is occupied by the **Weill Recital Hall,** used by soloists and small chamber groups. In the spring of 1991, **The Rose Museum at Carnegie Hall** took over yet another part of the building. ♦ Tours M-Tu, Th-F 11:30AM, 2PM, and 3PM. Museum: M-Tu, Th-Su 11AM-4:30PM. 154 W. 57th St (at Seventh Ave). 247.7800

133 The Russian Tea Room ★★$$$$ This may be the happiest place in town, with year-round Christmas decorations, paintings, samovars, and bright colors trimmed with gleaming brass. The Tea Room also offers the exhilaration of celebrity-watching and mingling with beautifully dressed people. The dining experience often begins with caviar and ends with baklava, and includes other traditional Russian fare. In the old country they call it peasant food, but here it is served in a setting that would warm the heart of a czar. In the '30s and '40s, the Tea Room had a cabaret, the **Casino Russe;** in the fall of 1990, a new cabaret opened above the restaurant, featuring performers such as **Julie Wilson, David Staller, Peter Duchin,** and **Anne Hampton Callaway.** ♦ Russian ♦ Lunch and dinner. 150 W. 57th St (between Sixth and Seventh Aves). Jacket and tie recommended; reservations required. 265.0947

134 Uncle Sam's Umbrella Shop This shop has been protecting New Yorkers from the elements for more than 120 years with umbrellas in all different sizes, shapes, and prices, and repairs while you wait. All of the umbrellas for the musical *My Fair Lady* were made here. ♦ M-F 9:30AM-6:15PM; Sa 10AM-5PM. 161 W. 57th St (between Sixth and Seventh Aves). 582.1977

Most shipping these days is done by air, but the Port of New York, which handles more than 150 million tons a year, is far and away the most important seaport in America. New York Harbor is at the apex of a triangle that extends more than 100 miles to the east and south like a giant funnel. The Hudson River, once connected to the Great Lakes by the Erie Canal, gives access to inland America and the East River and, with 771 miles of shoreline, offers more space for anchorage than any other port in the U.S.

135 Planet Hollywood ★$$ This mecca of movie memorabilia with an interior created by the set designer of the original *Batman* film is owned (though not managed) by the omnipotent trio of **Sylvester Stallone, Bruce Willis,** and **Arnold Schwarzenegger.** A hot new eatery that is forever loud, packed, and fun, Planet Hollywood often demands a wait (no reservations are taken), and even though on weekends it may seem that everyone is Romper Room age, the crowd is slightly older than at the equally trendy **Hard Rock Cafe** down the block. The pizza and burger selections are good, but everyone leaves room for the apple strudel, especially Arnold: it's made from his mother's secret recipe. A gift shop next door will supply you with souvenirs for the friend who has everything. ♦ American ♦ Lunch, dinner, and late-night meals. 140 W. 57th St (between Sixth and Seventh Aves). 333.7827

135 Poli Fabrics Fine fabrics at fair prices are well labeled with the price, fiber content, and, often, the name of a designer who has used it: **Carolyn Roehm** or **Ellen Tracy,** for example. ♦ M-Sa 9AM-6PM. 132 W. 57th St (between Sixth and Seventh Aves). 245.7750

136 Parker Meridien $$$$ Its main entrance is on W. 56th Street, but they've included an attractive corridor leading to the other side, which gives it a more uptown address. When making a reservation, ask for an odd-numbered room above the 26th floor, and you'll be rewarded with a wonderful view of Central Park. The 42-story hotel has two restaurants (**Le Patio** turns out a sumptuous buffet breakfast; **Shin's** is the more elegant of the two), a rooftop swimming pool with a jogging track, and racquetball and squash courts. The 24-hour room service has a European flair, as does everything else about the Meridien. ♦ 118 W. 57th St (between Sixth and Seventh Aves). 245.5000, 800/543.4300; fax 307.1776

136 New York Delicatessen $$ The building housing this 420-seat, 24-hour restaurant featuring corned beef, blintzes, and the like is one of the few remaining of dozens like it that housed **Horn & Hardart** automats a half-century ago. It was built by **Ralph Bencker** in 1938. ♦ Deli ♦ Daily 24 hours. 104 W. 57th St (between Sixth and Seventh Aves). 541.8320

137 Salisbury Hotel $$ Most of the 320 large rooms here have serving pantries and individual safes. Guests are served a complimentary Continental breakfast, and an ice cream shop is open during the summer. A renovation is now under way; about half of the rooms have been completed. ♦ 123 W. 57th St (between Sixth and Seventh Aves). 246.1300, 800/223.0680; fax 977.7752

137 Steinway Hall Look through the concave window into the showroom of this prestigious piano company, housed, appropriately, in a domed hall with a huge crystal chandelier. The 12-story building, built in 1925, with a three-story Greek temple on the roof, also includes a recital salon. The relief of **Apollo** over the central arch is by **Leo Lentelli;** the building is by **Warren & Wetmore.** ♦ M-W, F-Sa 9AM-5PM; Th 9AM-6PM; Su noon-5PM. 109 W. 57th St (between Sixth and Seventh Aves). 246.1100

138 Alwyn Court The terracotta dragons and other decorations that cover every inch of this 1909 apartment house by **Harde and Short** are in the style of the great art patron of the Renaissance, **Francis I.** His symbol, a crowned salamander, is prominently displayed above the entrance at the 58th Street corner. Almost no one ever passes by without stopping for a lingering look. ♦ 180 W. 58th St (at Seventh Ave)

138 Petrossian ★★★$$$$ In Paris, Petrossian is the leading source for caviar. It may also be true in New York, thanks to this Art Deco-influenced marble and mink-trimmed room, where you can sample caviar in all its varieties as well as smoked salmon and foie gras, along with champagne or frosty vodka. Take-home delicacies are available in the adjoining retail shop. ♦ Continental ♦ Lunch and dinner. 182 W. 58th St (at Seventh Ave). Jacket and reservations required. 245.2214

139 Freed of London Best known to beginning and professional ballet dancers for their handmade shoes from England and Spain, Freeds also sells tap, ballroom, and theatrical shoes, plus dancewear. ♦ M-F 10AM-5:45PM; Sa 10AM-5PM. 922 Seventh Ave (at W. 58th St). 489.1055

140 The New York Athletic Club This 22-story building, designed by **York & Sawyer** in 1930, houses handball and squash courts and other exercise facilities, including a swimming pool. The club itself was founded in 1868 and has sent winning teams to many Olympic Games. There are guest rooms in the club, but visitors who want to begin their day running in Central Park are not permitted to go through the lobby in jogging outfits. ♦ 180 Central Park South (at Seventh Ave). 247.5100

The *New York World* printed the first crossword puzzle in 1913. The first comic strip serial, *The Yellow Kid,* ran in an 1896 *New York Journal.*

140 Essex House $$$$ The two-year renovation completed in fall 1991 was so extensive that trucks were driving through the lobby. The only remaining parts of the original 1930 grand hotel by **Frank Grad** are the exterior walls and bronze Art Deco elevator doors. Still, the Art Deco details of the facade and the artful use of setbacks make it one of Manhattan's more pleasing towers. The Essex House now boasts a small spa facility with exercise room, massage, facials, and body wraps. There are two restaurants, both overseen by famed chef **Christian Delouvrier**—the gourmet dining room **Les Célébrités,** and the more casual **Cafe Botanica.** A Japanese restaurant is due to open soon. A third of the rooms have Central Park views. ♦ 160 Central Park South (between Sixth and Seventh Aves). 247.0300, 800/645.5687; fax 315.1839

Within the Essex House:

Les Célébrités ★★★★$$$$ Certainly among New York's best new restaunts. Chef **Christian Delouvrier's** beautiful creations include an appetizer of fresh duck foie gras with Granny Smith apples and two superlative main courses—tender beef stew with a tarte of carrot confit, and lobster with asparagus and snow peas with sweet pea butter and grated truffles. ♦ Classical French ♦ Dinner. Closed Monday and Sunday. Reservations and jackets required. 247.0300

141 Hampshire House A hotel converted to cooperative apartments, this building has a peaked roof of copper turned a marvelous shade of green that is one of the highlights of the skyline bordering Central Park. Its lobby is one of the joys of the neighborhood. When the cornerstone was put in place, it was filled with the best books and music of 1931. The time capsule will never have to be opened because the building, a work of **Caughey & Evans,** does the job of explaining what 1931 was all about. ♦ 150 Central Park South (between Sixth and Seventh Aves)

141 Ritz-Carlton $$$$ Until its 1982 refurbishing by **Parrish-Hadley,** which included the charming bow to another era of putting awnings over the windows, this was known as the **Navarro.** The new owner also owns the **Boston Ritz,** among other properties that follow the tradition of the great **Cezar Ritz,** who changed British tradition when he opened a hotel in London in 1898. The design of the hotel is in the style of English manor houses. Amenities include 24-hour room service, robes, twice-daily housekeeping,

turndown service, refrigerators upon request, and no fewer than three phones in every room. ♦ 112 Central Park South (between Sixth and Seventh Aves). 757.1900, 800/241.3333; fax 757.9620

142 Gainsborough Studios In 1908, **Charles W. Buckham** designed this apartment building—now one of the oldest in the city—as an artists' cooperative. It is worth passing by for a look at the frieze by **Isadore Konti** across the second floor—a festival procession with a bust of Gainsborough at the center. In addition, the building has one of the best facades—this one just restored in 1992. ♦ 222 Central Park South (between Seventh Ave and Broadway)

142 San Domenico ★★★$$$$ **Gianluigi Morino** brought his baby to New York from a suburb of Bologna, where they have been dazzling international food critics since 1970. A marble bar, a terracotta floor imported from Florence, and smooth, ocher-tinted stucco walls applied by artisans from Rome put the diner firmly in a better world, where opulent splendors of Italian cuisine can temporarily create the illusion of perfection. The owner is **Anthony May,** who once owned **Palio.** ♦ Italian ♦ Lunch and dinner; dinner only on Saturday and Sunday. 240 Central Park South (between Seventh Ave and Broadway). Reservations and jacket required. 265.5959

143 Urban Grill ★$$ At this Italian and American mix, the pasta, hamburgers, and grilled chicken make a fine quick lunch or pretheater bite. ♦ Italian/American ♦ Lunch and dinner; dinner only on Saturday and Sunday. 330 W. 58th St (between Eighth and Ninth Aves). 586.3300

144 CBS Broadcast Center A TV production center and headquarters of **CBS News,** this was originally the headquarters of a dairy, and CBS old-timers still call it the "Cowbarn." ♦ 524 W. 57th St (between 10th and 11th Aves). 975.4321

145 Copacabana In the 1940s and 1950s, you could be thrilled by the **Copa Girls** and entertained by such personalities as **Sammy Davis, Jr.,** and **Jerry Vale.** Nightclub shows like those are a thing of the past, but the Copa is still a bright spot on Tuesday night, when Latin music is the lure, and Friday and Saturday nights, when the Latin beat is augmented by an upstairs disco. Shows usually begin around 10:30PM. The rest of the time it is used for private parties. In 1993, the Copacabana moved here from the East Side. ♦ Cover. Tu 6PM-8AM; F 9:30PM-4AM; Sa 10:30PM-4AM. 617 W. 57th St (between 11th and 12th Aves). 582.2672

146 IRT Powerhouse The original subway line, **Interboro Rapid Transit,** began running under Broadway in October 1904. It got its electric power from this building, built in 1904 by **McKim, Mead & White,** which now

generates electricity for Con Edison.
♦ Bounded by W. 58th and W. 59th Sts, and 11th and 12th Aves

147 Passenger Ship Terminal The last of the great ocean liners, known as the "Cunard Queens," the SS *France* and the USS *United States* used piers in this neighborhood. But before this terminal complex was finished in 1976, except for the *QE2*, only cruise ships called here regularly. Most arrive Saturday morning and leave the same afternoon. The facility is used at other times as exhibition space. ♦ 711 12th Ave (between W. 48th and W. 55th Sts). 246.5451

Bests

Alexandra Penney
Editor-in-Chief, *Self* magazine

The **Four Seasons.** Best place to take a European.

Little Italy. Nonduplicable delights for your kitchen.

Hayden Planetarium. When the gridlock gets to you.

San Domenico restaurant. When you want to feel you're in the most sophisticated city in the world.

Flea Market at Sixth Avenue and 26th Street. At 8AM on Sunday—best way to buy Christmas presents.

Florent. For 7AM breakfast to get energized.

Strand Bookstore. A place to hang out and find great book deals.

Il Cantinori restaurant. You can't ever tire of it!

Grand Central Terminal. The most delicious soft ice in the world (by the baggage stand).

Drinks under the blue whale in the **American Museum of Natural History.**

Renting a rowboat in **Central Park.**

Charles Gwathmey
Architect

A helicopter ride crossing Manhattan from river to river, from the **George Washington Bridge** to the **Verrazano-Narrows Bridge.** A boat ride around Manhattan. A run around **Central Park,** the only major outdoor space in the city.

A walk through **SoHo** and **TriBeCa, Wall Street** and **Lower Manhattan,** and Madison and Fifth avenues from 90th Street down to 42nd Street.

The Frick Collection and the **Cloisters** are still the most civilized museums.

Stay at **Morgans Hotel.** Eat inexpensively at **Vico** and **Due** (Italian), **Odeon** and **Cafe Luxembourg** (Continental), and **Phoenix Garden** (Chinese). Breakfast at **E.A.T.,** and dine at **Le Bernardin** for an elegant, expensive, and great meal.

A visit to the **International Design Center (IDC/NY)** to see the furniture showrooms and the architecture,

and when in Queens, the **American Museum of the Moving Image.** Finally, see Frank Lloyd Wright's **Solomon R. Guggenheim Museum.**

André Emmerich
Owner, André Emmerich Gallery

Lunch uptown at **Les Plèiades,** watching the passing parade of half of the art world.

Lunch midtown in the **Grill Room** of the **Four Seasons** with its unequaled spa cuisine and sparkling fellow guests.

Early, pretheater dinner at **Le Bernardin**—the best food in the world that stays safely within Pritikin limits.

Sunday night dinner at **Elaine's,** the most relaxing setting for the tensest people in the world—New York's intelligentsia.

Shopping the gentleman's quarter-mile along Madison Avenue from **Chipp, Brooks Brothers, Paul Stuart, Orvis, Tripler,** and on, ending at **Saks Fifth Avenue** on 49th Street.

The antique furniture shops around Broadway below 13th Street.

The revived **Brooklyn Museum**—as the French guidebooks say, well worth the "detour" to see its spectacular exhibitions.

A harbor cruise on a party boat, especially when the ship sails close to the floodlit **Statue of Liberty,** still the grandest public sculpture in the world.

The newly installed galleries of ancient Greek and Roman art at the **Metropolitan Museum.**

The drive into Manhattan from the north along the **Henry Hudson Parkway.**

Finally, New York at sunset seen from my apartment, 380 feet above the avenue right behind the Guggenheim.

George Page
Host, PBS "Nature" series

The **Hudson River.** One of the world's greatest and most beautiful estuaries—a natural wonder and a highway of American history. Take the **Dayliner** cruise to **Bear Mountain State Park** or, better still, rent a yacht for the trip. The **Circle Line** cruise around Manhattan is also recommended and only takes three hours.

The **Metropolitan Museum.** Simply the world's most glorious museum.

The **Palm Court,** the **Oak Room,** and the **Oak Bar,** at **The Plaza Hotel.** All retain an ageless elegance and gentility that is quintessential old New York.

Lutèce. Splurge. It's still the best restaurant in New York, if not the world.

Under no circumstances should you visit New York in July or August unless you enjoy walking around in the world's largest steambath.

Midtown

A sense of power pervades Midtown, the heart of Manhattan. Giant high-rises stand shoulder to shoulder, creating solid walls of concrete and glass that seem to stretch to the sky. Each weekday morning on the crowded sidewalks below, briefcase-toting people in business suits and well-shined shoes race to their offices with definite purpose, emerging at midday—to head for power lunches at some of the finest restaurants in the city or to grab a sandwich from a corner deli—and again in the evening, to jump in a cab for a night on the town or to hurry home, only to begin the cycle again bright and early the next morning.

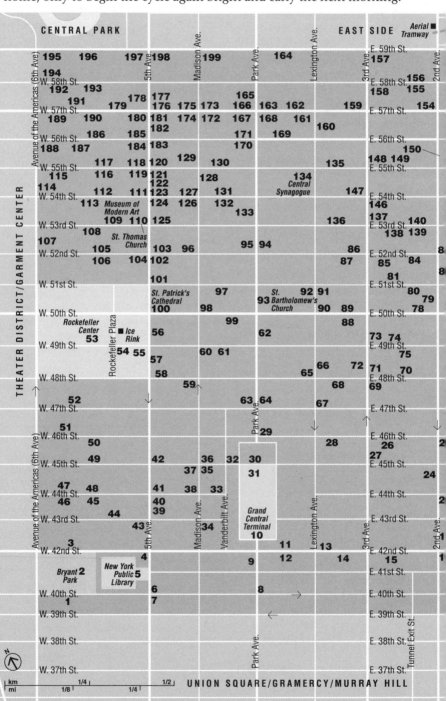

Midtown's weighty importance begins with a concentration of office buildings around **Grand Central Terminal**, touches on **Rockefeller Center** to the west, encompasses the headquarters of the **United Nations** to the east, and extends to the border of **Central Park** to the north. Over on **Fifth Avenue**, the tote of choice is more often a classy shopping bag than a briefcase. The street is home to some of the world's most exclusive stores, including **Saks**, **Henri Bendel**, **Cartier**, **Tiffany**, and **Bergdorf Goodman**. Also within Midtown's boundaries (roughly 40th and 59th streets, Sixth Avenue, and the East River) are world-class hotels (the **Plaza**, the **Waldorf-Astoria**, the **Palace**, the **St. Regis**), the many galleries of 57th Street, and the incomparable **Museum of Modern Art**.

It's a good bet that 90 percent of the people who jam Midtown's streets live elsewhere. But the area is actually a great place to live. The possibilities include the huge **Tudor City** complex overlooking the UN; **Turtle Bay**, with its blocks of brownstone houses in the 50s east of Third Avenue; and dozens of pre-war apartment buildings standing proud throughout. **Beekman Place**, two blocks of town houses on E. 49th to E. 51st streets between First Avenue and the East River, is a hidden treasure. **Sutton Place**, a longer residential street above E. 50th Street along the river, was part of a plan for English-style houses for the well-to-do developed in 1875 by **Effingham B. Sutton**. Morgans, **Vanderbilts**, and **Phippses**, among other notables, lived here.

But it wasn't always that way. When Sutton Place was built, it was in wild territory overlooking what was then called **Blackwell's Island** (now **Roosevelt Island**) in the East River, where the city maintained an almshouse, workhouse, prison, and insane asylum. Although there was a horsecar line running along Second Avenue between Fulton and 129th streets, Sutton's riverfront property was a long way from the mainstream. The neighborhood didn't become "acceptable" until **J.P. Morgan's** daughter moved here in 1921.

Before then, society generally stayed west of Park Avenue. In fact, in the 19th century anyone who suggested that Fourth Avenue would one day be called Park would have been laughed out of the city. In 1832, a railroad line was built in the center of the dirt road, and steam trains huffed and puffed their way in and out of New York past squatters' shacks with goats in the front yards and pigs out back.

Little by little roofs were constructed over the tracks, but it wasn't until the present Grand Central Terminal was designed in 1903 that anything was done about covering the railroad yards that had grown up between Madison and Lexington Avenues from 42nd to 45th streets. When the UN moved into the area in 1947, the cattle pens disappeared and Midtown East became a neighborhood in its own right.

From the day Fifth Avenue was first established in 1837, the rich and famous began to arrive. Railroad tycoon **Jay Gould** was one of the first. He built a mansion at 47th Street and Fifth Avenue and began taking important friends like **Russell Sage, Morton F. Plant**, and **William H. Vanderbilt** to business dinners at the nearby **Windsor Hotel.**

By the late 1800s, Vanderbilt had built three mansions on the west side of Fifth Avenue at 51st Street. His son, **William K. Vanderbilt,** built a fourth palace a few doors uptown. Another son, **Cornelius II,** tried to upstage them with an even grander house at 58th Street. In their quest to outdo one another, they ended once and for all the idea of the traditional New York row house with a brownstone front. And who would have thought of living anywhere but on Fifth Avenue in the blocks between 40th and 59th streets?

Mrs. Astor, that's who. When her husband's nephew, **William Waldorf Astor,** built a hotel next to her house on Fifth Avenue at 33rd Street, she retaliated by tearing down the house and building another hotel next to his. Then she built a Renaissance palace for herself at Fifth Avenue and 65th Street. After her inaugural ball there in 1896, "Millionaire's Row," as Fifth was called, began moving uptown.

Only a few reminders of the 19th-century mansions remain on Fifth Avenue, including the one that houses Cartier at 52nd Street, which, according to one story, Morton F. Plant traded to **Pierre Cartier** for a string of pearls. But many of the fine public buildings survive. Houses of worship include such landmarks as **St. Thomas Church, St. Patrick's Cathedral,** the Romanesque **St. Bartholomew's Church,** and the vaguely Moorish **Central Synagogue**—the oldest building in the city in continuous use as a synagogue. Secular monuments also remain, such as the vast **New York Public Library** and, of course, Grand Central Terminal, which was saved after a long battle.

Except for St. Bartholomew's Church, the Waldorf-Astoria Hotel, and a few more holdouts, today Park Avenue north of Grand Central Terminal is wall-to-wall office buildings, including important examples of the "glass box" genre built in the 1950s: the **Seagram Building** by **Ludwig Mies van der Rohe** and **Philip Johnson,** and **Skidmore, Owings & Merrill's Lever House.**

Impressive office buildings and complexes on the other avenues range from the classic Rockefeller Center to the contemporary **Olympic Tower, Citicorp,** and **IBM** buildings. Madison Avenue above 50th Street has seen an office-building boom, but it's Third Avenue in the 20-block strip from 39th to 59th streets that has had the real mega-office building explosion.

Unexpected pockets of distinctive apartment buildings and town houses continue to cling to the side streets of Midtown (54th Street near the Museum of Modern Art, for example). In combination with small parks such as **Greenacre** and **Paley,** they bring greenery and human scale to what might seem at first glance to be a solid concentration of masonry.

1 American-Standard Building Originally known as the **American Radiator Building,** this 1923 tower was **Raymond Hood's** first major project in New York City (he had just won the **Chicago Tribune** commission). He later had his hand in the **McGraw-Hill, Daily News,** and **Rockefeller Center** buildings. This 21-story midblock high-rise is a stylized variation of the Tribune design, with Gothic details tempered by Art Deco lines. Hood used black brick so that the window holes would fade into the sculpted mass and the gold ornamented top would be that much more spectacular. When lit, it has been compared to a glowing coal. The plumbing showroom in the lobby is not part of the original design. ♦ 40 W. 40th St (between Fifth and Sixth Aves)

2 Bryant Park The only park in the city designed like a formal garden was named for the poet **William Cullen Bryant,** a prime mover in the campaign to establish Central Park and a champion of the Hudson River School of painters, which established the fashion for wild, naturalistic parks. Before becoming a park, the land was a potter's field, and in 1853 it was the site of America's first World's Fair, held in a magnificent domed pavilion of iron and glass known as the Crystal Palace. Among the wonders unveiled to the world there were **Elisha Graves Otis'** elevator, **Peter Cooper's** steel wire, and **Isaac Merritt Singer's** sewing machine. The building stood here until 1858, when it burned to the ground. After the ruins were cleared, the space was used as a parade ground for troops getting ready to defend the Union in the Civil War. When the war was over, it was dedicated as a public park. But the site was little more than a two-block vacant lot until the public library was built and a terrace was added.

In 1934, as the result of a competition to aid unemployed architects, the park was redesigned by **Lusby Simpson,** whose plan was executed under the direction of **Robert Moses.** In the Depression years, the area was a gathering spot for the unemployed, and in the 1960s it became a retail space for marijuana peddlers. In 1980, the Bryant Park Restoration Corporation (Hanna/Olin Ltd.) began a massive restoration program, and today Bryant Park is a safer and friendlier spot, with new landscaping and lighting, restored monuments, footpaths and benches, food service, and public events. A $4.2 million glass and steel pavilion designed by **Hardy Holzman Pfeiffer Associates** is being built behind the library and should be completed in 1995. ♦ Sixth Ave (between W. 40th and W. 42nd Sts)

Within Bryant Park:

Music & Dance Tickets Booth Stop here for same-day half-price tickets for music and dance performances in all five boroughs. Also available are full-price advance tickets for TicketMaster sports and entertainment events. Cash and traveler's checks are accepted. ♦ Tu-Su noon-2PM, 3-7PM. W. 42nd St (at Sixth Ave). 382.2323

3 W.R. Grace Building Some people actually like this sloping, ski-jump, wind-loading building, but it is generally considered a poor interruption of the street wall. Designed in 1974 by **Skidmore, Owings & Merrill,** it has a barren little plaza on the corner of W. 43rd Street and Sixth Avenue—an alleged public amenity in exchange for which the developers were allowed extra floors. The architects built an identical structure for a different client on 57th Street at the same time. ♦ 43 W. 42nd St (between Fifth and Sixth Aves)

4 Nat Sherman's Tobacconist to the stars, Nat Sherman's customers include **Frank Sinatra, Milton Berle,** and **Sylvester Stallone.** His specialty is the pure tobacco cigarette wrapped in brown or in such trendy colors as shocking pink, turquoise, or scarlet. He also stocks cigars and Dunhill lighters. There is a humidor on the premises. ♦ M-Sa 8:30AM-6:30PM. 500 Fifth Ave (at W. 42nd St). 246.5500

5 New York Public Library Treat your soul to one of New York's greatest experiences, the sight of the front of the **New York Public Library's Central Research Building,** designed in 1911 by **Carrère & Hastings.** The familiar lions, Patience and Fortitude, are the work of **Edward Clark Potter.** But there is much more to see: the bases of the 95-foot-high, tapered steel flagposts (by **Thomas Hastings**) on the terrace; the lampposts; the balustrades; the urns; the sculpture by **Paul Bartlett, George G. Barnard,** and **John Donnelly** high above; and the fountains in front, both by **Frederick MacMonnies** (the one on the right represents Truth, the other Beauty). The library was built with the resources of two privately funded libraries, combined in 1895 with the infusion of a $2 million bequest by **Samuel J. Tilden. John Jacob Astor's** library, the first general reference library in the New World, was enhanced by **James Lenox's** collection of literature, history, and theology. (In 1891,

Andrew Carnegie donated $52 million for the establishment of 80 more branches in the New York Public Library system.) This grand building is completely dedicated to research, and none of its more than six million books or 17 million documents can be checked out, so vast is the collection that the original four floors of stacks beneath the building and behind the reading rooms have been supplemented by a new space underneath Bryant Park, which can hold up to 92 miles of stacks.

The main lobby, **Astor Hall,** contains the information desk, the bookshop, and an exhibition area. Marble from floor to ceiling, the hall is lavishly decorated with carved garlands, ribbons, and rosettes. The room directly behind Astor Hall is the **Gottesman Exhibition Hall,** which has the most beautiful ceiling in the city. The hall's changing exhibitions are built around special themes, such as children's books, bird prints, and architectural history, and are usually based on the library's own impressive collection of rare books and prints.

The **Third Floor Hall** and the rooms it serves are rich with carved wood panels and vaulted ceilings. The murals, by **Edward Lanning,** were executed as part of a WPA project. The library's art collection, including paintings by **Gilbert Stuart, Sir Joshua Reynolds,** and **Rembrandt Peale,** is displayed in the **Edna B. Salomon Room.** Directly across the hall is **Room 315,** the **Catalogue Room,** where you can request books. Room 315 leads into the **Main Reading Room,** 51-feet high and one-and-a-half-blocks long. The room is divided in half by the facilities for delivering books, but the ceiling soars above it all with paintings of blue skies and white clouds and carved scrolls, masks, flowers, dolphins, cherubs, and satyrs.

The library has been undergoing extensive restoration since 1963 by such design firms as **Davis, Brody & Associates.** One recently completed room is the **Celeste Bartos Forum,** which opens directly onto the library's 42nd Street entrance. It is used for lectures, concerts, films, and special events. Take one of the free tours—Tuesday to Saturday at 11AM and 2PM—which meet at the front desk. ♦ Main Reading Room: M, Th-Sa 10AM-6PM; Tu-W 10AM-7:30PM. Fifth Ave (between W. 40th and W. 42nd Sts). 661.7220, 930.0800

6 Journey's End Hotel $$$ Ten of this hotel's 189 rooms are specially designed for disabled guests. Amenities include complimentary morning coffee and newspaper, in-room movies, and laundry and dry-cleaning services. ♦ 3 E. 40th St (at Fifth Ave). 447.1500, 800/668.4200; fax 213.0972

7 New York Public Library, Mid-Manhattan Branch Once housing **Arnold Constable,** the department store that provided trousseaux for fashionable brides in the 1890s, the building was redesigned in 1981 by **Giorgio Cavaglieri.** (You can see pictures of the brides in the library's collection of microfilm editions of old newspapers.) Mid-Manhattan has the largest circulating collection of any of the branch libraries. The ground floor includes a branch of the gift shop of the **Metropolitan Museum of Art.** Free tours—Monday, Wednesday, and Friday at 2:30PM—meet at the ground-floor information desk. ♦ M, W 9AM-9PM; Tu, Th 11AM-7PM; F-Sa 10AM-6PM. 455 Fifth Ave (at W. 40th St). 340.0833

8 101 Park Avenue Designed in 1983 by **Eli Attia & Associates,** this speculative tower of black glass rises, angled and tucked, above a granite plaza on an awkward corner. Its slick outline and sheer height, which may be fun from the inside, are somewhat disturbing from the outside. ♦ E. 40th St

9 Philip Morris Headquarters **Ulrich Frazen & Associates'** light gray granite-clad building, designed in 1983, is a glass box hiding behind a postmodernist/historicist appliqué of Palladian patterns. The main facade, rather oddly, faces the Park Avenue viaduct. The enclosed garden and lobby of the building contains an espresso bar, a gift shop featuring contemporary Native American art, a chocolate shop, a magazine stand, and the **Whitney Midtown,** a satellite exhibition space of the **Whitney Museum of Modern Art.** The museum showcases a permanent sculpture exhibition in a vast, high-ceilinged area, while a smaller, more intimate space houses changing exhibitions of 19th- and 20th-century American art, sometimes relating to Midtown life (paintings by the **Ashcan School** depicting New York street life, for instance). Gallery talks take place Monday, Wednesday, and Friday at 1PM. The site was originally the home of the Art Moderne **Airlines Building** (built in 1940 by **John B. Peterkin**). ♦ Museum free. M-W, F 10AM-6PM; Th 10AM-7:30PM. 120 Park Ave (between E. 41st and E. 42nd Sts). 878.2550

The task of cleaning Rockefeller Center's rentable area of 15,000,000 square feet is equivalent to cleaning almost 11,000 six-room apartments. Some 65,000 people work in Rockefeller-owned or -operated buildings daily, and approximately 175,000 visit each day for business or pleasure, giving it a daily population of 240,000. Only 60 cities in the U.S. exceed this total.

Restaurants/Clubs: Red   **Hotels:** Blue
Shops/ ♥ Outdoors: Green   **Sights/Culture:** Black

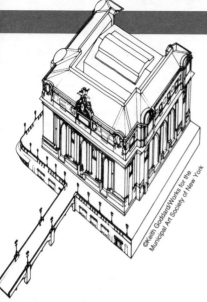

©Keith Godard/Works for the Municipal Art Society of New York

10 **Grand Central Terminal** This extra-ordinary complex (pictured above) may appear slightly tarnished today, but it is a true jewel nonetheless (long-awaited renovations are under way). In 1913, **Reed & Stem's** designs for the new terminal to replace the New York Central and Hudson River Railroads' Grand Central Station were chosen in a competition that included submissions by **Daniel Burnham** and **McKim, Mead & White.** The firm of **Warren & Wetmore** was hired as the associate architect and it was largely responsible for the design of the elaborate public structure. Reed & Stem and railroad engineer **William Wilgus** devised the still-efficient multilayered organization of the immense amount of traffic that flows through the terminal: trains (on two levels), subways, cars, and people.

The main, southern facade of the terminal is dominated by **Jules Coutan's** sculptures of Mercury, Hercules, and Minerva (Glory of Commerce, Moral Energy, and Mental Energy). At the center of the facade is a bronze figure of **Commodore Cornelius Vanderbilt,** founder of the railroad. The building's other major facade fronts Vanderbilt Avenue and what was a genteel residential neighborhood to the west; the tenements to the east were disregarded. In building the terminal, 32 miles of new tracks were laid, 18,000 tons of steel were used, and 2.8 million cubic yards of earth were excavated.

The inner workings of the terminal are organized around the impressive **Main Concourse.** When entered by way of the arcades from Lexington Avenue, the soaring vault is particularly striking. But the space may be better appreciated as a whole from the marble stairs at the Vanderbilt Avenue end. The hall is 160 feet wide, 470 feet long, and 150 feet high at its apogee—larger than the nave of **Notre-Dame** in Paris. The ceiling, a

plaster vault suspended from steel trusses, is decorated with a zodiac representing the winter sky. Designed by **Paul Helleu,** the 2,500 stars used to be lit. They are painted backward—"as God would see it," painter **Whitney Warren** is reported to have remarked. The floors of the Main Concourse are Tennessee marble and the trim is Italian Bottocino marble. The great arched windows are 60 feet tall and 33 feet wide; recently cleaned, they now let in massive amounts of light.

Grand Central Terminal was the centerpiece of a gigantic real-estate development that included eight hotels and 17 office buildings by 1934. When the railroad was forced to electrify, engineer Wilgus realized that if the trains were run underground and the tracks covered over, the air rights could be leased to developers. Thus Park Avenue was born. Tours are conducted by the **Municipal Art Society** for a small fee; they meet at the Chemical Bank in the Main Concourse on Wednesday at 12:30PM. ♦ E. 42nd St (at Park Ave)

Within Grand Central Terminal:

OYSTER

Oyster Bar and Restaurant ★★$$$ It looks exactly like what it is—the basement of a railroad station with tables—and at the height of the lunch hour, the tiled, vaulted ceilings make it impossibly noisy. Nicely prepared, absolutely fresh seafood, including a large variety of oysters, is served in the main dining room, at a counter bar next to it (where you can grab a quick bowl of the delicious and inexpensive clam chowder), and in a somewhat less hectic bar through swinging doors. The extensive wine list is exclusively American. ♦ Seafood ♦ Lunch and dinner. Closed Saturday and Sunday. Reservations recommended. 490.6650

Transit Museum Gift Shop The perfect way to while away a minute or an hour between trains, this modern gift shop celebrates something most Americans and certainly most Manhattanites take for granted: transportation. A host of subway and train-related souvenirs are handsomely displayed beneath a contemporary mural by **Brian Cronin,** including adorable plastic trains, jewelry made from old tokens, and tokens made from milk chocolate. ♦ M-F 8AM-8PM; Sa 8AM-1PM. 682.7572

11 **Grand Hyatt Hotel** $$$ The 1934 **Warren & Wetmore**-designed **Commodore Hotel** was remodeled in 1980 by **Gruzen & Partners,** and is now a bustling commercial hotel with glamorous dining and watering holes visible from the lobby, including the **Crystal Fountain** and **Sun Garden Restaurant,** which is cantilevered over 42nd Street. **Trumpets**

serves its signature nouvelle American cuisine. The rooms are attractive, although some are small, and the hotel is affiliated with a nearby health club, which can be used for a moderate fee. The hotel is the first cornerstone of what was developer **Donald Trump's** "I'll Take Manhattan" empire. ♦ Between E. 42nd and E. 43rd Sts (between Lexington and Park Aves). 883.1234, 800/223.1234; fax 697.3772

12 Home Savings of America Resembling a Roman basilica, the main banking room is 160 feet long, 65 feet high, and definitely worth a visit. The walls are limestone and sandstone, and the mosaic floors are French and Italian marble. The building was designed in 1923 by **York & Sawyer.** ♦ 110 E. 42nd St (between Lexington and Park Aves)

12 Chanin Building The headquarters of the Chanin real-estate empire is an Art Deco triumph built in 1929 by **Sloan & Robertson.** At the third-floor level is an exuberant terracotta frieze. The detailing of the lobby is extraordinary, particularly the convector grilles and elevator doors. ♦ 122 E. 42nd St (between Lexington and Park Aves)

13 The Chrysler Building Built by **William Van Alen** in 1929 for the **Chrysler Automobile Company,** this tower (shown at right), which many consider the ne plus ultra of skyscrapers, is an Art Deco monument. The building has many car-oriented decorative elements: abstract friezes depicting automobiles, flared gargoyles at the fourth setback resembling 1929 radiator hood ornaments, and the spire modeled after a radiator grille. The lobby, decorated with African marble and once used as a car showroom, is another Deco treasure. Use the Lexington Avenue entrance and look up at the representation of the building on the ceiling of the lobby, and be sure to peek into an elevator cab. The lighting of the spire at night—with specially fitted lamps inside the triangular windows—was an idea of Van Alen's that was rediscovered and first implemented in 1981. The Chrysler Building was briefly the tallest building in the world until surpassed by the Empire State. ♦ 405 Lexington Ave (at E. 42nd St)

BILL LACY

14 Mobil Building The self-cleaning stainless-steel skin on this monolith is 37 thousandths of an inch thick—self-cleaning because the creased panels create wind patterns that scour them. The building was designed by **Harrison & Abramovitz** in 1955. ♦ 150 E. 42nd St (between Third and Lexington Aves)

15 New York Helmsley Hotel $$$$ If you are looking for the **Harley Hotel,** this is it. **Harry Helmsley** is the present owner. He and his wife, **Leona,** have maintained the old-fashioned service—breakfast is delivered quickly, checkout is speedy, and room service is available around the clock. Other niceties include **Harry's New York Bar** for drinks and **Mindy's Restaurant** for elegant dining. ♦ 212 E. 42nd St (between Second and Third Aves). 490.8900, 800/221.4982; fax 986.4792

15 Daily News Building This clean, purely vertical, undecorated plastic mass was designed in 1930 by **Howells & Hood,** the pair responsible for the **Chicago Tribune Tower** (in all its Gothic wonder). The stringent composition even has a flat top—a bold step in 1930. The building tells its own story in the frieze over the entrance and in the lobby, where a globe is a center of an interplanetary geography lesson. (When the globe was first unveiled, it was spinning the wrong way.) The 1958 addition on Second Avenue, by **Harrison & Abramovitz,** is not up to the original. ♦ 220 E. 42nd St (between Second and Third Aves)

16 The Tudor $$$ Reopened in the spring of 1991, the renovated Hotel Tudor (once notorious for the smallest rooms in the city) boasts 303 expanded rooms, each with a new marble bathroom, a trouser press, two-line telephones, and fax and PC ports. Within the hotel are a restaurant, a bar and lounge, meeting rooms, conference and banquet facilities, a business center, and a small health club facility. ♦ 304 E. 42nd St (between First and Second Aves). 986.8800, 800/879.8836; fax 297.3440

17 Tudor City Soaring over E. 42nd Street, this Gothic development on its own street was built in 1925 by the **Fred F. French Company** and **H. Douglas Ives.** It comprises 11 apartment buildings, a hotel, shops, a restaurant, a church, and a park. The complex's orientation toward the city seems ill-considered today, but when this enclave was planned, the East River shore below was a wasteland of breweries, slaughterhouses, glue factories, and gasworks. At the turn of the century, the bluff, known as **Corcoran's Roost,** was the hideout of the infamous **Paddy Corcoran** and the **Rag Gang.** Now it provides a good vista of the UN. ♦ Bounded by E. 40th and E. 43rd Sts, and First and Second Aves

18 Ford Foundation Building This 1967 design by **Kevin Roche** and John Dinkeloo &

Associates is probably the oldest and certainly the richest and least hermetic re-creation of a jungle in New York City. Though the building is small with a rather typical entrance on 43rd Street, the 42nd Street side is much more extroverted. It appears as if a container had been opened, leaving the black piers barely restraining an overflowing glass and Cor-Ten steel box of offices that contains a luxuriant park inside a 12-story atrium. Although economically foolhardy and somewhat noisy, this building is handsome and very definitely not to be missed. ♦ 320 E. 43rd St (between First and Second Aves). 573.5000

19 The Lighthouse This is the headquarters of the **New York Association for The Blind.** The on-site gift shop, staffed by volunteers, sells items made by blind persons, and all proceeds benefit the blind. ♦ Hours vary; call ahead. 800 Second Ave (between E. 42nd and E. 43rd Sts). 808.0077

20 Sichuan Pavilion ★★$$$ The Chinese menu is one of the most interesting in the city, though the quality of the ingredients and service can disappoint. UN delegates crowd the handsome dining rooms and get preferential treatment at lunch, making dinner a better choice for others. ♦ Chinese ♦ Lunch and dinner. 310 E. 44th St (between First and Second Aves). Reservations required for lunch, recommended for dinner. 972.7377

21 UNICEF House At the **Danny Kaye Visitors Center** on the ground floor, visitors can watch *Within Our Reach,* a film about the challenges that face children all over the world, narrated by a larger-than-life parrot and a newscaster. The center's retail shop has an extensive collection of UNICEF cards and gifts. ♦ Tours M-F 10AM-4PM. Gift shop M-F 10AM-6PM; Sa 10AM-3PM. 3 UN Plaza (between First and Second Aves). 326.7706

21 1 United Nations Plaza This combination office building, apartment house, and hotel with a striking glass-curtain wall was designed by **Kevin Roche** and **John Dinkeloo & Associates** in 1976. It was so successful that it was duplicated in **2 UN Plaza,** adjoining it to the west, in 1980. ♦ E. 44th St (between First and Second Aves)

Within 1 United Nations Plaza:

United Nations Plaza Hotel $$$ Beginning on the 28th floor of 1 UN Plaza, this comfortable hotel includes a lounge and restaurant, and a swimming pool and health club with a dazzling view. Complimentary limousine service to Wall Street, the Garment District, and theaters is also available. ♦ 355.3400, 800/228.9000; fax 702.5051

Within the United Nations Plaza Hotel:

Ambassador Grill Restaurant ★★$$$ The dramatic mirrored dining room with luxuriously comfortable upholstered

banquettes is run by a top-notch team of chefs from Gascony. In an open kitchen, they prepare excellent American food, including such specialties as salmon in mushroom crust, grilled rack of lamb with goat cheese in tequila sauce, and warm apple tart with cinnamon ice cream. The weekend brunch is an event in itself. ♦ American ♦ Dinner; lunch also on Saturday and Sunday. Reservations recommended. 355.3400

22 The United Nations The UN complex (illustrated below) was designed in 1952 by an international committee of 12 architects that included **Le Corbusier** of France, **Oscar Niemeyer** of Brazil, and **Sven Markelius** of Sweden; the committee was headed by American **Wallace K. Harrison.** The site—once the actual Turtle Bay where the Saw Kill ran into the East River—was a run-down area with slaughterhouses, light industry, and a railroad barge landing when **John D. Rockefeller, Jr.,** donated the money to purchase the land for the UN project. The complex, an enclave apart from the city and in formal contrast to it, has had tremendous influence on its surroundings as well as on the direction of architecture.

Housing the staff bureaucracy, the 39-story **Secretariat** was New York's first building with all-glass walls (these are suspended between side slabs of Vermont marble), and is the only example that approaches the tower-in-the-park urban ideal of the 1940s. (To make way for the UN building, the city diverted the traffic on First Avenue into a tunnel under UN Plaza and created a small landscaped park, **Dag Hammarskjold Plaza.**) Measuring 544 feet high and 72 feet wide, this anonymously faced building is a remarkable sight seen broadside from 43rd Street, where it was set in deliberate opposition to the city grid. The **General Assembly** meets in the limestone-clad, flared white building to the north under the dome.

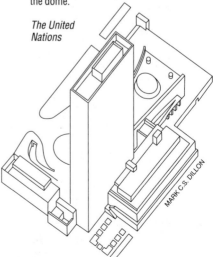

The United Nations

MARK C.S. DILLON

Visitors enter through the north side of the **General Assembly Building** at 45th Street. Outside, flags of all member nations fly in alphabetical order, the same order in which delegates are seated in the General Assembly. More than a million visitors come here every year to see the physical presence of this forum of nations, but also in search of the elusive spirit of peace it symbolizes. Taking a tour (call ahead for hours) is a good idea if you want to explore more than the grounds (don't miss the gardens) and the **Chagall** stained-glass windows in the lobby of the General Assembly Building. But don't expect to witness more than real estate if the General Assembly isn't in session (regular sessions are from the third Thursday in September through mid-December).

Tours, conducted by young people from around the world, steer large groups through the elegant **Assembly Hall** (note the **Léger** paintings on the walls); the Secretariat Building; and the **Conference Building,** which houses media, support systems, and meeting rooms, including the **Security Council Chamber** (donated by Norway), the **Trusteeship Council Chamber** (donated by Denmark), and the **Economic and Social Council Chamber** (donated by Sweden). But you can find out more about how the UN actually functions by witnessing the public part of the UN's business as it takes place in the General Assembly and at meetings of the various councils. It is possible to obtain free tickets to these sessions at the **Information Desk** in the General Assembly lobby on a first-come, first-served basis. They are usually held at 10AM and 3PM. Call for information. ♦ E. 45th St at First Ave. 963.7713

Within The United Nations:

Delegates' Dining Room ★$$ The UN dining room is open to the public during the week offering a very good luncheon buffet and an à la carte menu. The view of the East River is the best of any restaurant in Manhattan. ♦ Continental ♦ Lunch. Closed Saturday and Sunday. UN Conference Building. Jacket required. Reservations recommended. 963.7625

23 **International Education Information Center** The information center is for foreign nationals interested in studying in the United States, and U.S. nationals who wish to study abroad. Staffed primarily by volunteers, the center provides guidebooks, brochures, and university catalogs, as well as materials describing scholarships, internships, and teaching opportunities. ♦ 809 UN Plaza (between E. 45th and E. 46th Sts). 984.5413

Restaurants/Clubs: Red   Hotels: Blue
Shops/ 🌳 Outdoors: Green   Sights/Culture: Black

24 **Palm** ★★$$$$
Along with **Palm Too** across the street (697.5198), this place is ranked as one of the city's best steakhouses. Serious carnivores don't seem to mind the close and chaotic premises, the long wait for a table, or the surly, often rushed service. Caricatures of famous New York journalists are painted right on the walls, but you're more likely to recognize faces at the next table. The steaks and lobsters are huge, and the cottage-fried potatoes are addictive. ♦ Steakhouse ♦ Lunch and dinner; dinner only on Saturday. Closed Sunday. 837 Second Ave (between E 44th and E. 45th Sts). Reservations required. 687.2953

25 **Captain's Table** ★$$$ Superb fresh fish is offered in mostly Mediterranean preparations, both elegant and rustic. The dining room is not very prepossessing, but the service is pleasant. ♦ Seafood ♦ Lunch and dinner; dinner only on Saturday. Closed Sunday. 860 Second Ave (at E. 46th St). Reservations recommended. 697.9538

26 **Sparks** ★★$$$$ Beef, the main business at hand, is as consistently cooked to order as at the other great steak houses, and the wine list is among the best in the country. Not only is the selection extraordinary, but the prices are fair, making it a must stop for oenophiles. Sparks is best known for the murder of mobster **Paul Castellano** out front years ago. ♦ Steakhouse ♦ Lunch and dinner; dinner only on Saturday. Closed Sunday. 210 E. 46th St (between Second and Third Aves). Reservations required. 687.4855

27 **Pen & Pencil** ★$$$$ A steakhouse with a Continental accent, this gracious old-timer still has a capable kitchen. It's getting genteelly shabby around the edges—and unfashionable—so it's a good place for a quiet little table in the corner. ♦ Steakhouse ♦ Lunch and dinner. 205 E. 45th St (between Second and Third Aves). 682.8660

28 **Christ Cella** ★★$$$$ One of the oldest steakhouses in New York, Christ Cella has for years enjoyed a reputation among visiting salesmen as the best in town. The food makes up for the uninspiring decor. When you call for a reservation, ask to sit downstairs; it isn't any more elegant, but it's cozier. There are no printed menus, so feel free to ask the waiter about prices, which are high. The lobsters, steaks, and chops make clear why it's popular with the power lunch crowd. ♦ Steakhouse ♦ Lunch and dinner; dinner only on Saturday. Closed Sunday. 16 E. 46th St (between Third and Lexington Aves). Reservations required. 697.2479

29 Colors ★★$$$$ Immediately discovered by the elite business crowd in search of the perfect executive lunch, this attractive newcomer is the turf of talented chef **Erik Blauberg,** who worked with New York's culinary maestro **David Bouley.** The menu leans toward perfectly prepared interpretations of fish and seafood, such as a delicately marinated salmon, lobster salad with a hint of mussels and lovage, and pasta stuffed with lobster, crabmeat, and artichoke. Also excellent is the lamb with a potato and fig tart, and the sublime chocolate soufflé with caramel and vanilla ice cream is an absolute must. ◆ American/French ◆ Lunch and dinner; dinner only on Saturday. Closed Sunday. 237 Park Ave (entrance on E. 46th St). Reservations required. 661.2000

30 The Helmsley Building Designed in 1929 by **Warren & Wetmore,** this fanciful tower was originally the **New York Central Building,** then **New York General.** An example of creative, sensitive urban design, it was a lively addition to the architects' own **Grand Central Terminal** and the hotels that surrounded it. Built above two levels of railroad tracks, it essentially "floats" on its foundations—those inside feel nary a vibration. The gold-leafed building is worth a special viewing at night. Pause to appreciate the distinct separation of automobile and pedestrian traffic in the street-level arcades, and stop for a look at the wonderful rococo lobby. ◆ 230 Park Ave (between E. 45th and E. 46th Sts)

Within The Helmsley Building:

Snaps ★★$$ Scandinavian favorites—pickled and creamed herring, poached salmon, and the like—are available in this big, comfortable room, perfect for a relaxing lunch. This is **Aquavit's** casual cousin. ◆ Scandinavian ◆ Lunch and dinner; dinner only on Saturday. Closed Sunday. Reservations recommended. 949.7878

31 Metropolitan Life Building Formerly the **Pan Am Building,** this 59-story monolith set indelicately between the **Helmsley Building** and **Grand Central Terminal** started in 1963 as a purely speculative venture and became the largest commercial office building ever built, with 2.4 million square feet. It was not well-received. The siting is problematic, to say the least. But there is

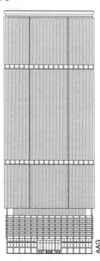

a positive, efficient connection with the terminal that forms an unintentionally ironic mating of the then-expanding airline and the failing railroad. Art in the lobby includes a mural by **Josef Albers** and a space sculpture by **Richard Lippold.** The shape of the tower is supposedly derived from an airplane wing section. There used to be a heliport on the roof, but one too many helicopters had trouble. The architects were **Emery Roth & Associates, Pietro Belluschi,** and **Walter Gropius.** Bauhaus founder and High Modernist Gropius could have done better. ◆ 200 Park Ave (between E. 44th and E. 45th Sts)

Within the Metropolitan Life Building:

Tropica ★★$$$ Chef **Eddie Brown's** standout Caribbean/Key West-style seafood lights up the former Pan Am Building. ◆ Regional American/Tropical ◆ Lunch and dinner. Closed Saturday and Sunday. 867.6767

32 Takesushi ★$$$$ The long line at lunch attests to the fact that this is one of the best sushi bars in the city. Come after 5:30PM to avoid the crowd. The solicitous staff is more than willing to introduce you to the world of raw fish. ◆ Japanese ◆ Lunch and dinner; dinner only on Saturday. Closed Sunday. 71 Vanderbilt Ave (at E. 45th St). Reservations required. 867.5120

33 The Yale Club In a neighborhood crowded with clubs waving the old school tie, this one boasts easy access to trains headed to New Haven for the over-nostalgic. The building was designed in 1913 by **James Gamble Rogers.** Only Yalies are allowed in. ◆ 50 Vanderbilt Ave (between E. 44th and E. 45th Sts)

34 Worth & Worth Hat lovers know top quality when they see it, and it doesn't get any better in the city. The staff is knowledgeable, patient, and friendly, and the merchandise ranges from classic to cutting-edge. ◆ M-F 9AM-6PM; Sa 10AM-5PM. 331 Madison Ave (between E. 42nd and E. 43rd Sts). 867.6058

35 Orvis Fishing equipment and gear, a wide selection of books on such topics as fly-fishing, trout streams, and duck decoys, and outdoor clothing and accessories that complement the country way of life are sold. ◆ M-F 9AM-6PM; Sa 10AM-5PM. 355 Madison Ave (entrance on E. 45th St). 697.3133

36 The Roosevelt Hotel $ Built in 1924 by **George M. Post,** this old hotel was prestigious when railroads were the main form of transportation and the location near Grand Central was highly valued. Popular with those doing business nearby, it has soundproof rooms and a multilingual staff. A bar and a lobby lounge are located within the hotel. ♦ E. 45th St (at Madison Ave). 661.9600, 800/223.1870; fax 687.5064

37 Paul Stuart Classic, well-made clothing for the conservative gentleman is the specialty. Look for jackets and suits in herringbone, Shetland, and tweed; handknit sweaters in alpaca, cashmere, and Shetland wool; and shirts of Sea Island cotton. Women have a tiny niche to themselves on the mezzanine level, where there are tailored skirted suits, Shetland sweaters, and cotton shirts. If you're not the one shopping, a 17th-century Flemish tapestry and comfortable leather chairs make waiting quite pleasant. ♦ M-W, F 8AM-6PM; Th 8AM-7PM; Sa 9AM-6PM. E. 45th St (at Madison Ave). 682.0320

38 Brooks Brothers The home of the Ivy League look—the natural-shoulder sack suit, worn with an oxford cloth shirt and silk rep tie—Brooks Brothers is an American institution. Founded in 1818, it is the country's oldest menswear shop, and continues to offer traditional, conservative clothing. Some wares have become classics, such as the trench coats, Shetland sweaters, oxford cloth shirts, and bathrobes of soft wool and cotton. Boys can choose from shirts, slacks, and sweaters; and women will find a feminine version of all the above. ♦ M, Th 8:30AM-7PM; Tu-W, F 8:30AM-6PM; Sa 9AM-6PM. 346 Madison Ave (at E. 44th St). 682.8800

39 Zen Oriental Bookstore Most of the books and magazines are in Japanese. Those in English cover Buddhism and Zen, Japanese language, history, society, and literature, Japanese and Zen cooking, origami, and bonsai. There's even a guide to job hunting in Japan. ♦ M-F 10AM-7PM; Sa 11AM-7PM. 521 Fifth Ave (between E. 43rd and E. 44th Sts). 697.0840

40 Chikubu ★★★$$$$ If you love Japanese food and can afford the high prices, sit at the counter and get the *omakase*—the chef will make the fabulous choices for you. ♦ Japanese ♦ Lunch and dinner; dinner only on Saturday. Closed Sunday. 12 E. 44th St (between Madison and Fifth Aves). Reservations recommended. 818.0715

41 J. Press This clothier has been dressing Ivy League men in well-made classics and calico patchwork shorts and slacks since 1902. ♦ M-Sa 9AM-6PM. 7 E. 44th St (between Madison and Fifth Aves). 687.7642

42 Fred F. French Building The colorful glazed tiles in the tower call out from across the street. Answer the call; the lobby is a stunner. The building was designed in 1927 by **Fred F. French Company** and **H. Douglas Ives.** ♦ 551 Fifth Ave (at E. 45th St)

Within the Fred F. French Building:

Morton's of Chicago ★★★$$$ It breaks a New Yorker's heart to admit that the city's best steak can be found at this recently arrived out-of-towner. The extra-thick, extra-aged, extra-tender porterhouse led *New York Magazine* to hail Morton's as the city's best in 1994, a title shared with Brooklyn's historic **Peter Luger** restaurant. Noncarnivores will swoon at an equally whalish lobster cooked in butter and sage. ♦ Steakhouse ♦ Lunch and dinner; dinner only on Saturday and Sunday. 551 Fifth Ave (entrance on E. 45th St). Reservations recommended. 972.3315

43 Chemical Bank This 1954 edifice was the first bank to depart from the tradition of rock-solid architecture, and just to make sure potential customers would recognize it as a bank, architects **Skidmore, Owings & Merrill** put the safe in the window. ♦ 510 Fifth Ave (at W. 43rd St). 997.0770

44 Century Association McKim, Mead & White designed this 1891 Palladian clubhouse for men of achievement in arts and letters (McKim and Mead were members). The large window above the entrance was originally a loggia. ♦ 7 W. 43rd St (between Fifth and Sixth Aves). 944.0090

45 General Society Library of Mechanics and Tradesmen More than 140,000 books of fiction, nonfiction, and history are stocked in this private library. The comfortable, elegant surroundings are worth the low membership fee. Within the library are the **Small Press Center,** a nonprofit facility exhibiting books by independent publishers, and the **John M. Mossman Collection of Locks,** where 375 different locks—antique padlocks, powder-proof key locks, and friction locks—are on display. ♦ 20 W. 44th St (between Fifth and Sixth Aves). 840.1840

45 Grove Decoys Both antique and new duck decoys are part of this extensive collection, which also includes bird carvings and rare fish decoys. ♦ M-F 10AM-5:30PM. 36 W. 44th St (between Fifth and Sixth Aves). 391.0688

46 Hotel Royalton $$$ The Royalton's block-long lobby is the setting for a dramatic space (cognac mahogany and green-gray slate) by French designer **Phillipe Starck.** The front desk is discreetly tucked away, as is the bar, patterned after **Hemingway's** favorite at the Paris Ritz. The **Round Bar** is forever full of networking hipsters, and the rooms, many with working fireplaces, are on the cutting edge of modern design and comfort. Amenities include daily newspaper delivery, con at bedside and in the bath, **Kiehl** shampoos and bathcubes, and valet parking. The original structure, built in 1898 by **Ehrick Rossiter,** was renovated in 1988 by **Gruzen, Samton, Steinglass.** ♦ 44 W. 44th St (between Fifth and Sixth Aves). 869.4400; fax 869.8965

Within Hotel Royalton:

Restaurant 44 ★★$$$ Phillipe Starck's decor and the Beautiful People (with a regular contingent of top editors from nearby *Condè Nast*) who inhabit it create a dramatic backdrop for the American nouvelle cuisine. Recommended are crisp filet of grilled salmon flavored with cucumber and dates, or roasted scallops served with a variety of mushrooms. For dessert, try the warm chocolate bread pudding. ♦ American ♦ Lunch and dinner. Reservations required. 944.8844

47 The Algonquin Hotel $$$ Built in 1902 by **Goldwyn Starrett**, this hotel was a gathering place for literary types even before the famous Round Table of such writers as **Alexander Woollcott, Robert Benchley**, and **Dorothy Parker** began meeting regularly in the **Rose Room.** What the Round Table members had in common, besides their razor-sharp wit, was that they were contributors to *The New Yorker,* whose offices at 25 W. 43rd Street conveniently open into the hotel at 44th Street. Few nearby places are as comfortable as the hotel's lobby, where you can summon a cocktail with the ringing of a bell. Guests find all the comforts and friendliness of a country inn here. (Visiting writers favor Room 306; the suite's walls are adorned with *Playbill* magazine covers.) A two-year effort to restore this landmark to its original splendor was completed in 1991. ♦ 59 W. 44th St (between Fifth and Sixth Aves). 840.6800; fax 944.1419

Within The Algonquin Hotel:

Oak and Rose Rooms ★$$$ The dark paneling in the Oak Room contrasts with the brighter Rose Room. But the menu is the same in both, and the quality doesn't vary. The plate-size apple pancake topped with tart lingonberries is a perfect after-theater snack. The Oak Room provides supper club entertainment after 8PM from Tuesday through Saturday. ♦ American ♦ Breakfast, lunch, and dinner. Reservations recommended. 840.6800

47 The New York Yacht Club This unusually fanciful, sculptured work was the creation of **Warren & Wetmore** in 1899. The highlight of the eccentric facade is the sailing-ship sterns in the three window bays, complete with ocean waves and dolphins. The setback above the cornice used to be a pergola. This was the home of The America's Cup from 1857 to 1983, when it was lost to Australia (San Diego reclaimed it in 1987). ♦ 37 W. 44th St (between Fifth and Sixth Aves). 382.1000

48 Harvard Club The interior of this 1894 Georgian-style building by **McKim, Mead &**

White is much more impressive than its facade indicates. If you're not a Harvard alum, go around the block and see it through the magnificent window in back. ♦ 27 W. 44th St (between Fifth and Sixth Aves). 840.6600

49 Train Shop Electronics stores dominate this block, but this basement shop, along with **The Red Caboose** on the fourth floor at 16 W. 45th Street, makes it a major stop on the railroad lines that run in a child's imagination. ♦ M-F 10AM-6PM; Sa 10AM-5PM. 23 W. 45th St (between Fifth and Sixth Aves). 730.0409

50 Via Brasil ★★$$ West 46th Street is known as "Brazil Row" for its unusually high concentration of restaurants and businesses rich in the flavors of that country. Of all the reasonably good Brazilian restaurants squeezed into the same block, Via Brasil is your best bet for sampling the national dish, *feijoada,* a hearty, delicious stew of black beans, sausage, beef, bacon, and pork served on rice—perfect for a blustery winter day. You might want to try the lighter grilled meats or poultry in warmer weather, when a *caipirihna,* the potent national drink made of rum and fresh lime juice, will have you daydreaming of points farther south. There's live music Wednesday to Saturday evenings. ♦ Brazilian ♦ Lunch and dinner. 34 W. 46th St (between Fifth and Sixth Aves). 997.1158

51 Wentworth $ This modest, recently renovated Art Deco hotel has comfortable rooms with color TVs, air-conditioning, and all the modern amenities. Gem-loving guests will like the location next door to the **Jewelry Exchange,** where 60 dealers offer treasures like those sold in the nearby **Diamond Center** on 47th Street. ♦ 59 W. 46th St (between Fifth and Sixth Aves). 719.2300; fax 768.3477

52 47th Street Photo The city's greatest bargains on cameras (including **Canon, Hasselblad, Nikon,** and **Minox**) can be found at this discount store. It also offers New York's best prices on computers, TVs, VCRs, and other electronic appliances, as well as wristwatches and gold chains. The salesmen—from various Hasidic families—look harried, and so do the customers. ♦ M-Th 8:30AM-6PM; F 8:30AM-2PM; Su 10AM-5PM. 67 W. 47th St (between Fifth and Sixth Aves). Also at: 115 W. 45th St. 921.1287

52 Gotham Book Mart & Gallery Founded by **Frances Steloff** in 1920, the Gotham has long been a mecca for New York City's literati: **Theodore Dreiser, Eugene O'Neill, George Gershwin,** and **Charlie Chaplin** all shopped here; **Tennessee Williams** worked as a clerk, but was not that good at his job and lasted only one day. **Edmund Wilson** cashed his checks here; and when **Henry Miller** wrote to Miss Steloff of his financial hardship, she taped his letter to the wall and her customers provided what he needed (a small cart to carry his groceries, a shirt, and socks) and what he wanted (lox). Today, this New York equivalent to Paris' Shakespeare & Company is a bibliophile's heaven: a messy hodgepodge of books, mostly literature (especially 20th century), poetry, drama, art, and literary journals as well as small press and used and rare books. In the upstairs gallery, you'll find changing art exhibitions, including a summer show of vintage postcards from the extensive collection of the store's owner, **Andy Brown.** ♦ M-F 9:30AM-6:30PM; Su 9:30AM-6PM. 41 W. 47th St (between Fifth and Sixth Aves). 719.4448

53 Rockefeller Center This is the largest privately owned business and entertainment complex in the world, with 18 buildings covering 21 acres (see facing page). It all began when **John D. Rockefeller, Jr.,** secured leases on land in the area to provide a setting for the Metropolitan Opera House, which was going to move from the Garment Center in 1928. The Great Depression changed the Opera's plans and left the philanthropist with a long-term lease on 11.7 acres of Midtown Manhattan. He decided to develop it himself, and demolition of 228 buildings to make way for the project began in May 1931. The last of Rockefeller's original 14 buildings, the **Paramount Publishing Building** at 1230 Sixth Avenue, was opened in April 1940. Construction started again in 1957, when **Marilyn Monroe** detonated the first charge of dynamite to begin excavation for the **Time & Life Building,** designed by **Harrison & Abramovitz,** at 1271 Sixth Avenue. Since then, the building at 1211 Sixth Avenue and the **McGraw-Hill Building** at 1251 Sixth Avenue, also by Harrison & Abramovitz, have been added along Sixth Avenue.

The original complex was designed by **Associated Architects,** a committee made up of **Reinhard & Hoffmeister; Corbett, Harrison and MacMurray;** and **Hood and Fouilhoux.** At its head, representing the Rockefeller interests, was **John R. Todd** of Todd, **Robertson & Todd Engineering Corp.** Their ideas included a north-south, midblock private street (**Rockefeller Plaza**) between 48th and 51st streets, underground pedestrian and shopping passageways connecting all the buildings, and off-street freight delivery 30 feet underground, capable of handling a thousand trucks a day. The art that enhances the lobbies and exteriors is the work of 30 of the finest artists of the century. The crown jewel of the original Rockefeller Center complex is the 70-story **GE Building** (formerly the RCA Building), at 1256 Avenue of the Americas. Todd told the architects that no desk anywhere in the building should be more than 30 feet from a window. They obliged him by placing all the rentable space no farther than 28 feet from natural light. About one quarter of the available space has been left open—unusual for an urban development—and much of it has been landscaped. Rockefeller Center's gardeners are kept busy with more than 20,000 flowering plants that are moved periodically as well as two acres of formal gardens on the rooftop. A complete description of the buildings can be found in a walking tour guide available free at the information desk in the lobby at 30 Rockefeller Plaza. A free exhibition chronicling the history of the center through photographs, models, an 11-minute video presentation, and period memorabilia is located on the concourse level of 30 Rockefeller Plaza. ♦ Bounded by W. 48th and W. 51st Sts, and Fifth and Sixth Aves. 632.3975

At Rockefeller Center:

Radio City Music Hall Since 1932, this Art Deco palace has maintained a tradition of spectacular entertainment. When it opened as a variety house operated by entrepreneur **Roxy Rothafel,** it was the largest theater in the world and included such features as a 50-foot turntable on the 110-foot stage, sections of which changed level, 75 rows of fly lines for scenery, a network of microphones, six motor-operated light bridges, a cyclorama 117 feet by 75 feet, and a host of other controls and effects. The scale was overwhelming. "What are those mice doing on stage?" someone asked on opening night. "Those aren't mice, those are horses," his neighbor replied.

The opening of the Music Hall in December 1932 drew such celebrities as **Charlie Chaplin, Clark Gable, Amelia Earhart,** and **Arturo Toscanini.** The premiere performance had 75 stellar acts, including **Ray Bolger, The Wallendas,** and the **Roxyettes** (later known as the **Rockettes**).

The hall was soon turned into a movie house with stage shows, featuring the Rockettes, the **Corps de Ballet,** the **Symphony Orchestra,** and a variety of guest artists. The premiere feature film was **Frank Capra's** *The Bitter Tea of General Yen* with **Barbara Stanwyck.** From 1933 until 1979, when it was *the* place to open a film, more than 650 features debuted at the Music Hall, including *King Kong, It Happened One Night, Jezebel, Top Hat, Snow White and the Seven Dwarfs, An American in Paris,* and *Mister Roberts.* In 1979, a new format was introduced. Musical spectaculars, special film showings, and pop

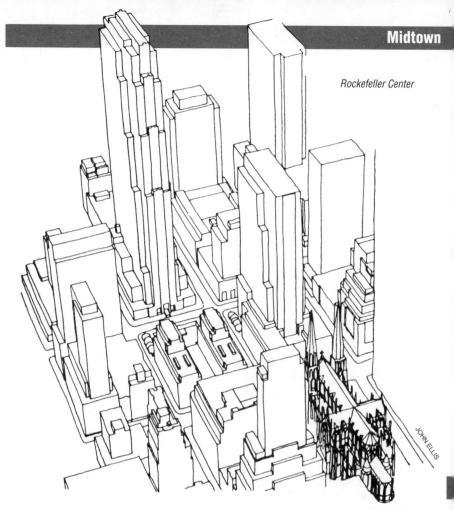

Rockefeller Center

JOHN ELLIS

personalities in concert are the current bill of fare, with an occasional one-shot such as the **George Gershwin** classic *Porgy and Bess*.

The 5,882-seat Radio City Music Hall was awarded landmark status and completely restored in 1979. The public areas, designed largely by **Donald Deskey,** are grand: a plush foyer rises 50 feet, overlooked by a sweeping stair and three mezzanine levels lined with gold mirrors and topped by a gold-leaf ceiling. The restrooms retain much of their fine Deco detailing—tilework, trim, and fixtures— although most of the original art is gone. (A painting by **Stuart Davis** that once hung in a men's room is now at the **Museum of Modern Art.**) The auditorium is everything a theater should be: a plaster vault of overlapping semicircles lit from the inside edge in a rainbow of colors provides sunsets and sunrises as the lights go down and up.
♦ Tours: fee; schedule varies according to show presented: M-Sa 10:15AM-4:45PM; Su 11:15AM-4:45PM. W. 50th St at Sixth Ave. 247.4777

NBC Studio Tours Tours of the radio and television facilities of the **National**

Broadcasting Co. are offered. Children under six are not admitted. ♦ Admission. Daily 9:30AM-4:30PM. 30 Rockefeller Plaza. 664.4000

The Rink at Rockefeller Center The summertime outdoor restaurant becomes an ice-skating rink every October, staying slick and smooth right through April. Ice skates can be rented at the rink. ♦ Admission; fee for skate rental. Daily 8:30-10AM, 10:30AM-noon, 12:30-2PM, 2:30-4PM, 4:30-6PM; 6:30-8PM; 8:30-10PM; 10:30-midnight. Lower Plaza. 757.5730

Librairie de France and Librería Hispanica French and European Publications provides one of the best—albeit expensive—selections of books in French and in English about France, with a smaller offering of Spanish books. ♦ M-Sa 10AM-6:15PM. 610 Fifth Ave. 581.8810

Teuscher Chocolates of Switzerland Teuscher sells some of the city's best (and most expensive) chocolate bonbons. The window displays are stupendous and change with the season. ♦ M-W, F-Sa 10AM-6PM; Th 10AM-7:30PM. 620 Fifth Ave. 246.4416

171

Nikon House Nikon's showroom also contains a photography gallery and repair center for Nikon cameras. Film is not sold. ♦ Tu-Sa 9:30AM-5:30PM. 620 Fifth Ave. 586.3907

Metropolitan Museum of Art Gift Shop
At three floors and 6,000 square feet, this is the largest of the museum's nine gift shop outposts. The merchandise, for the most part inspired by the museum's permanent collections and special exhibitions, includes prints and posters, stationery, jewelry, tabletop accessories, sculpture reproductions, and educational gifts for children. Especially popular are the Met's signature items, which include William, a reproduction of the 12th-dynasty Egyptian hippo (the Met's unofficial mascot), and Venus earrings, one black and one white teardrop, worn by the goddess of love in **Rubens**' *Venus Before the Mirror.* ♦ M-F 10AM-7PM; Sa-Su 10AM-6PM. 610 Fifth Ave. 332.1380

The Sea Grill ★★★$$$$
Fresh seafood is served in a lush setting of cherrywood and rich fabrics. A favorite is the fresh cavatelli with shrimp and pancetta. Among the many gorgeous desserts is golden-dusted Prometheus chocolate cake. In winter, request a window seat so you can watch the skaters. ♦ Seafood ♦ Lunch and dinner; dinner only on Saturday. Closed Sunday. 19 W. 49th St (Rockefeller Plaza). Reservations required. 246.9201

American Festival Cafe ★★$$$ The menu is constantly changing in this festival of regional American cuisine. As part of its annual celebration of the wine harvest, **Barbara Ensrud,** the author of many books on food (including the outstanding *American Vineyards*), has designed a regional wine list and selected dishes for an accompanying menu. ♦ American ♦ Breakfast, lunch, and dinner. 20 W. 50th St (Rockefeller Plaza). 246.6699

The Rainbow Room ★★★★$$$$ When it reopened in 1987 after two years of restoration, the *New York Times* said the Rainbow Room was "exactly what you've always dreamed was on top of Rockefeller Center . . . a room that wants to be filled with people in formal dress and the sounds of Gershwin and Cole Porter." The redesign (architecture by **Hardy Holzman Pfeiffer Associates;** graphic design by **Milton Glaser**) was supervised by restaurateur **Joseph Baum,** whose other New York accomplishments have included **The Four Seasons, Windows on the World,** and **Aurora.** Start with a Kir Royale (made at the table) and a cold seafood platter. Then move on to grilled swordfish in red wine and marrow sauce, roast guinea hen with potato galette and sweet garlic sauce, or, when in season, soft-shell crabs. Even without a view the Rainbow Room would be a romantic place for dining and dancing, but as the song says, the great big city's a wondrous toy, and it's here glittering at your feet. A wonderful place for native New Yorkers as well as visitors, the later it gets the more "New York" it becomes. The view is at its best from the bar on the south side. ♦ Continental ♦ Lunch and dinner; dinner only on Saturday. Closed Sunday. 30 Rockefeller Plaza (at Fifth Ave), 65th floor. Jacket and tie required. Reservations required well in advance. 632.5100

New York Bound Bookshop More than 3,000 books (new and out-of-print) on both the city and the state—from guidebooks to literature, architecture, city planning, performing arts, and politics—fill the shelves of this shop. Maps, photographs, and prints are sold as well. Linger awhile—chairs are provided for your comfort. ♦ M-F 10AM-6PM; Sa noon-4PM. 50 Rockefeller Plaza (between W. 50th and W. 51st Sts). 245.8503

54 **Dean & DeLuca Cafe** ★$ Here's the place for a culinary break from the high-priced, mediocre coffee shops around Rockefeller Center. The latest in Dean & DeLuca's line of eight Italian gourmet takeouts/restaurants, this airy cafe is a welcome, convenient place to stop for either a full lunch or afternoon tea in Midtown Manhattan. The selection of soups, salads, and fresh panini sandwiches is reliably innovative. ♦ Italian/Takeout ♦ Breakfast, lunch, and early dinner. 9 Rockefeller Plaza (at W. 49th St between Fifth and Sixth Aves). 664.1363

55 **La Reserve** ★★★$$$$ Handsome and spacious La Reserve is the right place for a romantic dinner. Since **Dominique Peyraudeau,** the former chef of **La Terrace,** took over the reins, the classic French food has taken on new dimensions. Sample the delicate marinated onions and the scrumptious saddle of lamb. Among the desserts, the chocolate basket filled with a chocolate mousse and raspberries is a must. ♦ French ♦ Lunch and dinner; dinner only on Saturday. Closed Sunday. 4 W. 49th St (at Fifth Ave). Reservations required. 247.2993

55 **Goelet Building** Ignore the ground-floor shops in this crisp, early-modern structure, built in 1932 by **E.H. Faile & Co.** But do stop in the elevator lobby: the highly ornamented space is a hidden Art Deco gem all the way to the paneling of the elevator cabs. Note the lighting in the pilasters and cornices. ♦ 608 Fifth Ave (at W. 49th St)

56 **Saks Fifth Avenue** Fashionable and always in good taste, Saks has another asset few other stores can offer: service. Great designer

collections throughout the store will please any woman's sense of style, and the men's department is legendary. The selection for children is heaven-on-earth for parents and grandparents who enjoy seeing the little ones turned out in style. The small luxury selection of candies, liqueur cakes, and chocolates includes beautiful truffles from Joseph Schmidt and decadent chocolate- and caramel-covered apples from Mrs. Prindables. ♦ M-W, F-Sa 10AM-6:30PM; Th 10AM-8PM; Su noon-6PM. 611 Fifth Ave (between E. 49th and E. 50th Sts). 753.4000

57 Brentano's Bookstore Formerly **Scribner's Bookstore,** the entire 10-story French Renaissance-inspired composition is worth studying, but the two-story wrought-iron and glass storefront takes the prize, along with the vaulted space inside. On the facade, medallions honor printers **Franklin, Caxton, Gutenberg,** and **Manutius;** also note the cherubs holding the former establishment's name. The two-story, plaster-vaulted interior is equally impressive. The building was designed by **Ernest Flagg** in 1913. ♦ M-F 8AM-7PM; Sa 9AM-6PM; Su 11AM-6PM. 597 Fifth Ave (between E. 48th and E. 49th Sts). 826.2450

58 Hatsuhana ★★★$$$ Sushi lovers rate this bar at the top of the list. Sit at a table or at the counter where you can watch the sushi chef in action. Either way, sushi by the item adds up quickly; the prix fixe lunch menu is a good buy. Tempura and some skewered grilled items are also available. ♦ Japanese ♦ Lunch and dinner; dinner only on Saturday. Closed Sunday. 17 E. 48th St (between Madison and Fifth Aves). Reservations recommended. 355.3345

59 Crouch & Fitzgerald This store is an old New York institution for luggage, handbags, and business cases. ♦ M-Sa 9AM-6PM. 400 Madison Ave (at E. 48th St). 755.5888

60 Richard Metz Golf Studio Learn the basics or just improve your swing with the help of a PGA pro and an instant replay TV. Equipment and clothing are for sale. ♦ M-Th 10AM-8PM; F 10AM-7PM; Sa 10AM-5PM. 425 Madison Ave (at E. 49th St). 759.6940

62 Dolce ★$$ Pasta, pasta, pasta is served in one of the cushiest rooms in town. Well-spaced oversize tables are ideal for private conversations. The moderately priced food is popular with midday Midtowners. ♦ Italian ♦ Lunch and dinner; dinner only on Saturday. Closed Sunday. 60 E. 49th St (between Madison and Park Aves). Reservations recommended. 692.9292

62 Waldorf-Astoria Hotel $$$$ The incomparable Waldorf (shown above) has been home to permanent guests such as the **Duchess of Windsor** and the American representative to the UN, as well as temporary guests like **King Faisal** of Saudi Arabia and every U.S. president since 1931, when it was built. Taking up nearly the entire block between Park and Lexington avenues and 49th and 50th streets, it has almost 2,000 spacious rooms, and is now administered by the **Hilton** hotel chain. Designed by **Schultze & Weaver,** the building is considered by many to be the best on this stretch of Park Avenue. The base is in proper relation to the surrounding buildings, while the unique twin towers are still noteworthy additions to the skyline.

The hotel epitomized the good life of New York in the 1930s, carrying on in the tradition of its fashionable predecessor at 34th Street. (The hotel's tony guests often arrived underground in their private railway cars on a specially constructed spur off the tracks under Park Avenue.) The luxurious Art Deco interiors have suffered some mistreatment and neglect over the years—the burled walnut elevator cabs, for example, were lined with brocade—but have been meticulously restored. Of particular interest are the **Louis Rigel** murals in the lobby and the *Wheel of Life* mosaic in the floor. The ornate gilded and marble lobby teems with businesspeople and travelers from all over the world. A transportation desk handles logistical strategies, an international desk assists foreign guests, and the Waldorf's **Boutique Row** caters to the silk-stocking trade with shops such as **Doris Boutique** and **Sulka Men's Shop.** Decent fare can be had at the **Bull and Bear** and the pretty **Peacock Alley.** ♦ 301 Park Ave (between E. 49th and E. 50th Sts). 355.3000, 800/445.8667; fax 872.7272

Within the Waldorf-Astoria Hotel:

Inagiku Japanese Restaurant ★$$$$ When **Emperor Hirohito** stayed at the Waldorf, he was right at home at Inagiku, which features sushi, sashimi, tempura, and teriyaki in a setting that would be considered among the nicest in Tokyo. ♦ Japanese ♦ Lunch and dinner; dinner only on Saturday and Sunday. Jacket and reservations required. 355.0440

Restaurants/Clubs: Red   Hotels: Blue
Shops/ ♥ Outdoors: Green   **Sights/Culture:** Black

63 Chemical Bank World Corporate Headquarters This 53-story monster was built in 1960 by **Skidmore, Owings & Merrill** for **Union Carbide,** which has since moved to the suburbs. Railroad yards under the building made it necessary to begin the elevator shafts on the second floor, which is why the ground-floor lobby looks forgotten. ♦ 270 Park Ave (between E. 47th and E. 48th Sts). 270.6000

64 ChemCort at Chemical Bank World Headquarters The plants and mini-waterfalls in this greenhouse lobby have a soothing effect. **Emery Roth & Sons** designed the main building in 1962; **Haines Lundberg Wachler** executed the ChemCort addition in 1982. At the E. 48th Street entrance is *Taxi,* a sculpture of a businessman hailing a taxi by **J. Seward Johnson, Jr.** ♦ 277 Park Ave (between E. 47th and E. 48th Sts)

65 Hotel Inter-Continental New York $$$ Once known as the **Barclay,** this hotel designed by **Cross & Cross** in 1927 was the most luxurious of the hotels built by the New York Central Railroad. Now part of the Inter-Continental chain, it's as prestigious as ever, with special amenities to make life easier for visiting businesspeople (24-hour room service, concierge, valet service, and health spa). The Barclay name lives on in the **Barclay Restaurant** and in the gracious **Barclay Terrace** overlooking the lobby; the name of the clubby bar off the lobby was changed to **Bar One Eleven.** American and Continental cuisine is featured in the restaurant; the Terrace specializes in afternoon tea. Both recommend reservations. ♦ 111 E. 48th St (between Lexington and Park Aves). 755.5900, 800/332.4246; fax 644.0079

65 Caswell-Massey Established in 1752 and considered to be America's oldest chemist and perfumer, Caswell-Massey has been called everything from "the Disneyland of drugstores" to "a beauty browser's paradise." The historic flagship store, here since 1926, no longer boasts the soda fountain where Bogart and Bacall were once regulars. But it's still worth the trip to pick up any of the nostalgically packaged bath items and toiletries. ♦ Daily 9AM-7PM. 518 Lexington Ave (at E. 48th St). 755.2254. Also at: South Street Seaport. 608.5401; World Financial Center. 945.2630

66 New York Marriott East Side $$$ Originally the **Shelton,** a club/hotel for men, this 34-story tower designed by **Arthur Loomis Harmon** in 1924 was the first major building to reflect the 1916 zoning regulations. Its set-back massing is admirable, and the design became particularly famous as the winner of architectural awards and as the subject of many paintings by **Georgia O'Keeffe.** The hotel's recently renovated rooms have character but are sometimes cramped. Each has a bathroom telephone, AM/FM alarm radio, scale, remote-control color TV, and wall safe. Another helpful touch is a babysitting service. Within the hotel are a coffee shop, the **Shelton Grill** for more serious dining, and the **Champion Sports Bar.** ♦ 525 Lexington Ave (between E. 48th and E. 49th Sts). 755.4000, 800/228.9290; fax 751.3440

67 Roger Smith Winthrop Hotel $$$ The Winthrop's long-term renovation program is finally complete. All of the 183 rooms and suites have been redecorated and the lobby has been redone with mahogany and free-form bronze sculptures by hotel president/artist **James Knowles.** Rooms come with their own coffeemakers, and most rooms on the **Concierge Floor** have granite bathrooms with Jacuzzis and hair dryers. ♦ 501 Lexington Ave (at E. 47th St). 755.1400, 800/455.0277; fax 319.9130

68 Helmsley Middletowne $$$ Part of the Helmsley chain, this is an apartment hotel with rooms and junior and large suites, some with kitchenettes, terraces, and fireplaces. ♦ 148 E. 48th St (between Third and Lexington Aves). 755.3000; fax 832.0261

69 767 Third Avenue This squeaky-clean curved tower designed in 1981 by **Fox & Fowle** is high-tech clothed in brick instead of aluminum, and wood instead of steel. The chessboard on the side wall of the building next door was provided by the developer, **Melvyn Kauffman,** so that people would have something to look at. A new move is made each week; ask the concierge at No. 767 for the bulletin and a short description of how to play the game. ♦ At E.48th St

70 Turtle Bay Gardens When planning began for the UN complex just east of here, these blocks were slated for demolition. Cooler heads prevailed, and this little development, dating from 1870 and remodeled in 1920 by architect **Clarence Dean,** was saved. The Gardens, not open to the public, were created for **Mrs. Walton Martin,** who bought a back-to-back row of 10 houses on each street, then ripped out all the walls and fences behind them to create a common garden. She left a 12-foot strip down the middle for a path, at the center of which she installed a fountain copied from the **Villa Medici** in Rome. She redesigned the 20 houses so that their living rooms faced the private garden rather than the street and began attracting such tenants as **Tyrone Power** and **Leopold Stokowski. Katharine Hepburn** still lives here. ♦ 227-247 E. 48th St and 226-246 E. 49th St (between Second and Third Aves)

71 Lescaze Residence Glass blocks, stucco, and industrial-pipe railings replaced the original brownstone front of this town house when modernist architect **Paul Lescaze** converted it to his combination office/residence in 1934. Lescaze is well known as the co-designer of Philadelphia's extraordinary **PSFS Building** with **George Howe.** He also participated in the design of **1 New York Plaza** overlooking the harbor, and the **Municipal Courthouse** at 111 Centre Street. ♦ 211 E. 48th St (between Second and Third Aves)

72 780 Third Avenue This 50-story tower is clad in brick, but the cross patterns are the structure showing through—a sort of dressed version of Chicago's **John Hancock Tower.** A plaza on three sides is a relief in a crowded area. **Raul de Armas** was the partner in charge of the 1983 **Skidmore, Owings & Merrill** design. ♦ Between E. 48th and E. 49th Sts

73 Smith & Wollensky ★★$$$$ Young corporate types prefer this meat palace above all others. The steak doesn't disappoint, and the restaurant's extraordinary American wine list won the 1988 *Wine Spectator* award. The more casual, less expensive **Smith & Wollensky Grill** next door (753.0444) offers a limited steak selection and the best burgers in the city. ♦ American ♦ Lunch and dinner; dinner only on Saturday and Sunday. 797 Third Ave (at E. 49th St). Reservations required. 753.1530

74 David K's Noodle Road ★$$ Bowing to the economy, **David Keh** closed his two pricey Chinese restaurants (**Auntie Yuan** and **David K's**) in lieu of this noodle joint. It's short on atmosphere and long on noodles. ♦ Chinese ♦ Lunch and dinner; dinner only on Saturday and Sunday. 209 E. 49th St (between Second and Third Aves). 486.1800

75 Chin Chin ★★$$$ Chinese cuisine takes an innovative turn in this handsome restaurant with a decidedly un-Oriental ambience. Chin Chin is one of the nicest Midtown spots for fresh and exotic Cantonese food. ♦ Cantonese ♦ Lunch and dinner. 216 E. 49th St (between Second and Third Aves). 888.4555

76 Beekman Tower Hotel $$$ Originally called the **Panhellenic Hotel,** catering to women belonging to Greek-letter sororities, this is now an all-suite hotel catering to visitors looking for reasonably priced accommodations with fully equipped kitchens. **John Mead Howells** designed the

building in 1928. For a wonderful view of the East River, have a drink in the **Top of the Tower.** ♦ 3 Mitchell Pl, E. 49th St (at First Ave). 355.7300, 800/637.8483; fax 753.9366

79 Wylie's ★$$ Rib fans can be finicky, so it's not surprising that devotees and detractors call this both the best and worst rib joint in town. Wylie's has been around for 15 years and is always crowded with a rather satiated-looking crowd of happy habitués. Specialties are the juicy beef or pork ribs, or the moist barbecued chicken with a side of onion rings, all calling out for a pitcher of Wylie's tasty hallmark dipping sauce. ♦ Barbecue/Ribs ♦ Lunch, dinner, and late-night meals. 891 First Ave (between E. 50th and E. 51st Sts). 751.0700

Lutèce

78 Lutèce ★★★★$$$$ Consistently rated as the best French restaurant in the United States since its opening in 1961, Lutèce has especially wonderful Alsatian dishes, including a fragrant onion tart, fresh trout in a heady cream sauce, and *anything* with noodles. The man responsible is **André Soltner,** the owner and original chef, who can be seen at work in his kitchen and often chatting with diners. In spite of its awesome reputation, this is one of the friendliest restaurants in New York, and first-time diners are made to feel as welcome as celebrity regulars. ♦ French ♦ Lunch and dinner; dinner only on Monday and Saturday. Closed Sunday. 249 E. 50th St (between Second and Third Aves). Reservations required, often weeks in advance. 752.2225

79 Zarela ★★$$$ Queen of the city's Mexican chefs, **Zarela Martinez** runs the top spot for regional Mexican cuisine in New York (although **Rosa Mexicano** has its rabid fans as well). Don't leave without trying a fresh margarita and Zarela's famous red snapper hash. ♦ Mexican ♦ Lunch and dinner; dinner only on Saturday and Sunday. 953 Second Ave (between E. 50th and E. 51st Sts). Reservations required. 644.6740

80 Hotel Pickwick Arms $ The 370 redecorated rooms in this hotel are popular for their Midtown location; other pluses are a roof garden, a cocktail lounge, and a gourmet deli. ♦ 230 E. 51st St (between Second and Third Aves). 355.0300

81 Greenacre Park Another "vest pocket park," Greenacre is slightly larger and more elaborate than its cousin, **Paley Park.** Designed in 1971 by **Sasaki, Dawson, DeMay Associations,** it was a gift to the city by **Mrs. Jean Mauze,** daughter of **John D. Rockefeller, Jr.** ♦ 217-221 E. 51st St (between Second and Third Aves)

82 Artichoke Consistently fresh and delicious salads, as well as a small selection of meats, cheeses, packaged goods, breads, cakes, and pastries are stocked in this immaculate store. Prices are fair, and the knowledgeable service is a high point. ◆ M-F 8AM-7PM; Sa 8AM-6PM. 968 Second Ave (between E. 51st and E. 52nd Sts). 753.2030

82 Fu's ★★$$$ Hostess **Gloria Chu** presides over this upscale Chinese restaurant. You can't go wrong ordering the Grand Marnier shrimp, the lemon chicken, or the crabs in black-bean sauce. ◆ Chinese ◆ Lunch and dinner. 972 Second Ave (between E. 51st and E. 52nd Sts). Reservations recommended. 517.9670

83 Eamonn Doran $$ An Irish pub gone Continental, this place has too much carpeting, comfort, and Muzak for **James Joyce** fans. But rugby players and other assorted real and would-be Irish folk carouse here and take advantage of the extensive list of imported beers. The food is pleasant, but the occasional brogue at the bar is even more so. ◆ Irish ◆ Lunch, dinner, and late-night meals. 998 Second Ave (at E. 52nd St). 752.8088

84 242 East 52nd Street Like the **Lescaze Residence**, this 1950 **Philip Johnson** design is a quintessentially modern composition in a row house lot. Commissioned by **John D. Rockefeller, Jr.,** as a guesthouse for the **Museum of Modern Art,** it was also used at one time by Johnson as a New York City pied-à-terre. The base is Wrightian brick, the top Miesian steel and glass, and the whole composition is almost Oriental in its simplicity and mystery. ◆ Between Second and Third Aves

85 Bridge Kitchenware Corp. Pros like **Craig Claiborne** and **Julia Child** pick up their copper pots, knife sets, and pastry tubes at this exceptional store. The staff is very knowledgeable, in case you don't happen to be a pro yourself. ◆ M-F 9AM-5:30PM; Sa 10AM-4:30PM. 214 E. 52nd St (between Second and Third Aves). 688.4220

86 Nippon ★★★$$$$ Reserve a formal tatami room and experience the best in Japanese elegance. ◆ Japanese ◆ Lunch and dinner; dinner only on Saturday. Closed Sunday. 155 E. 52nd St (between Third and Lexington Aves). Reservations recommended. 758.0226

87 Beijing Duck House ★$$ It's usually necessary to order Peking duck in advance, but not here. The duck is carved at your table, then rolled in a rice pancake with *hoisin* sauce, scallions, and cucumbers. Since it's a whole duck, take a hungry friend along. ◆ Chinese ◆ Lunch and dinner. 144 E. 52nd St (between Third and Lexington Aves). Reservations required. 759.8260

87 Rand McNally Map and Travel Center The well-stocked book department also has travel videos, road maps, wall maps, globes, travel games, map puzzles, beachballs, pillows, and geography games. Call 800/234.0679 for 24-hour mail-order service. ◆ M-W, F 9AM-6PM; Th 9AM-7PM; Sa 11AM-5PM. 150 E. 52nd St (between Third and Lexington Aves). 758.7488

88 San Carlos Hotel $$ Most of the comfortably furnished rooms at the San Carlos have kitchenettes. ◆ 150 E. 50th St (between Third and Lexington Aves). 755.1800, 800/722.2012; fax 688.9778

89 Tatou ★$$$ Once an opera house and then the famous **Versailles** where **Edith Piaf** and **Judy Garland** performed, this building now houses a large supper club (although lunch is served Monday through Friday) featuring French and Cajun-spiced food. A blues pianist provides the entertainment at dinner. For further merry-making, head upstairs to the disco and private club. ◆ American Provençale ◆ Lunch, dinner, and late-night meals; dinner and late-night meals only on Saturday. Closed Sunday. 151 E. 50th St (between Third and Lexington Aves). Jacket and reservations required. 753.1144

90 The Beverly $$ Most accommodations are suites or junior suites with kitchenettes in this homey and comfy hotel. **Kaufman Pharmacy** within the hotel is one of the few left in New York open 24 hours a day (but its prices are exorbitant). Decent steak can be had at **Kenny's Steak and Seafood House.** ◆ 125 E. 50th St (at Lexington Ave). 753.2700, 800/223.0945; fax 753.2700

91 Loews Summit Hotel $$$ **Morris Lapidus** and **Harle & Liebman's** 1961 plastic modern design for this hotel is nonetheless cheery and comfortable inside. The Summit offers an in-hotel garage; barbershop; beauty salon for manicures, pedicures, and waxing; and jewelry shop. There is also a coffee shop and the **Lexington Avenue Grill** for breakfast and dinner. ◆ 569 Lexington Ave (at E. 51st St). 752.7000, 800/223.0888; fax 758.6311

92 General Electric Building This 51-story tower was designed in 1931 by **Cross & Cross** to harmonize with the Byzantine lines of **St. Bartholomew's Church,** and is still best seen with the church at its feet. But it's a beauty from any angle, lavishly decorated with what may have been intended to be stylized lightning bolts in honor of its first tenant, the **Radio Company of America,** which moved soon after to the new Rockefeller Center. ♦ 570 Lexington Ave (at E. 51st St)

M. SHREWSBURY

93 St. Bartholomew's Church This richly detailed Byzantine landmark (shown above) with a charming little garden is a breath of fresh air on a high-rise-lined block. But it has been the object of a long-running battle between preservationists and church fathers, who want to sell off the **Community House** for commercial development. The portico was a **Vanderbilt**-financed, **Stanford White**-designed addition (1903) to a church by **James Renwick.** In 1919, **Bertram Goodhue** inherited the portico and designed the church—a confabulation handled with style. The site was a **Schaefer** brewery in the 1860s. ♦ Park Ave (between E. 50th and E. 51st Sts)

94 Seagram Building The ultimate representation of pure modernist reason, this classically proportioned and exquisitely detailed 1958 bronze, glass, and steel box by **Ludwig Mies van der Rohe** and **Philip Johnson** is the one everybody copied (see Sixth Avenue and other parts of Park Avenue)—but it's still the best. The immutable object (ignore the back bit) is a vestigial column set back on a plaza that was an innovative relief when it was conceived. ♦ 375 Park Ave (between E. 52nd and E. 53rd Sts)

Within the Seagram Building:

The Four Seasons ★★★★$$$$ Power lunches got their name at The Four Seasons, a city institution with sublime service and innovative cuisine. The **Bar Room Grill** becomes *the* power center midday, when the top echelon of New York's publishing world gathers to exchange notes and gossip. The new and improved **Grill Room** now features the "Grill at Night," offering a true fine dining bargain—an under-$40 three-course meal, including coffee. The classic **Pool Room** next door has been going strong since 1958. Sublime service and innovative continental eclectic cuisine are the hallmarks of both. ♦ Eclectic ♦ Lunch and dinner; dinner only on Saturday. Closed Sunday. 99 E. 52nd St (between Park and Lexington Aves). Jacket, tie, and reservations required. 754.9494

The Brasserie ★$$$ The pretty, upbeat Brasserie has a menu to match—omelets, quiche, filet mignon, a fabulous onion soup, and copies of *The Wall Street Journal* to peruse while you're waiting for your food. They take outgoing orders over the phone and by fax—and guarantee no mistakes. ♦ French/American ♦ Daily 24 hours. 100 E. 53rd St (between Lexington and Park Aves). Reservations recommended. 751.4840; fax 308.3973

95 Racquet and Tennis Club A somewhat uninspired Florentine palazzo, this 1918 **McKim, Mead & White** design is an appropriate foil for the **Seagram Building** across the street. "Men only" partake in tennis, squash, racquets (an English game similar to squash but faster), and swimming. ♦ 370 Park Ave (between E. 52nd and E. 53rd Sts). 753.9700

96 Omni Berkshire Place $$$ The old Berkshire has become one of the city's best European-style hotels, known for its personal service. Many of its generously proportioned rooms have sitting areas. The lobby's gracious sunlit **Atrium** serves drinks and tea; the **Rendez-Vous,** a pricey, popular bistro for new American and French nouvelle cuisine, can be hectic for lunch, but quiets down at dinnertime. ♦ 21 E. 52nd St (at Madison Ave). 753.5800, 800/843.6664; fax 355.7646

97 Sushisay ★$$$ *Sushisay* means fresh sushi and that's what you'll get at this branch of the Tokyo original, complete with white walls and shoji screens. It's filled with Japanese businessmen at lunch. Good luck getting a seat at the sushi bar. ♦ Japanese ♦ Lunch and dinner; dinner only on Saturday. Closed Sunday. 38 E. 51st St (between Park and Madison Aves). Reservations required. 755.1780

97 Tse Yang ★★$$$$ Like the original Tse Yang in Paris, this stateside outpost offers outstanding Peking cuisine and European-style service. The wine list is appropriate to its Gallic connection. Try the Peking hot-and-sour soup, orange beef (served cold), and pickled cabbage, and for dessert, caramelized apples for two. ♦ French/Chinese ♦ Lunch and dinner. 34 E. 51st St (between Park and Madison Aves). Jacket and reservations required. 688.5447

Restaurants/Clubs: Red	**Hotels:** Blue
Shops/ 🌳 Outdoors: Green	**Sights/Culture:** Black

The New York Palace

98 The New York Palace Hotel $$$$
"Queen" **Leona Helmsley** once stood guard
over New York's tallest hotel, a 55-story glass
tower designed in 1980 by **Emery Roth &
Sons.** The Palace looms over the restored
110-year-old **Villard Houses,** parts of which
are incorporated into the hotel's public rooms,
resulting in an uneasy but interesting
marriage. The bars and dining rooms in the
old section are opulent—even excessively
so—with the ornate woodwork, marble,
frescoes, and fireplaces from the Gilded Age
all intact. The main dining room, **Le Trianon,**
is tricked out as New York's answer to
Versailles, but the **Gold Room,** with a vaulted
ceiling and a harpist playing from a musician's
balcony is, with all its ostentatiousness, a
splendid spot for high tea (held every day of
the year, including Christmas, from 2PM to
5PM). **Harry's New York Bar** is slickly
contemporary, unlike the more atmospheric,
paneled upstairs bar. Rooms are spacious,
comfortably—if overly—decorated, and
thoughtfully appointed. Among other nice
touches is 24-hour room service. In 1993, the
royal family of **Brunei** agreed to buy the hotel
(which had become a major liability after
Helmsley was sentenced to prison for tax
evasion in 1989) for $202 million. ◆ 455
Madison Ave (at E. 50th St). 888.7000,
800/221.4982; fax 303.6000

98 The Villard Houses This collection of six
houses (illustrated below) was designed in
1884 by **McKim, Mead & White** to resemble a
single Italian palazzo at the request of the
original owner, publisher **Henry Villard.** They
were later owned by the **Archdiocese of New
York,** which sold them to **Harry Helmsley.** In
a precedent-setting arrangement, Helmsley
incorporated two of the landmark houses into
his **Palace Hotel** and restored the interiors to
their turn-of-the-century rococo splendor—
although you might wonder if they ever looked
as new as they do now. ◆ 451-455 Madison
Ave (between E. 50th and E. 51st Sts)

Within The Villard Houses:

Urban Center The Municipal Art Society,
Parks Council, Architectural League of New
York, and the **New York Chapter of the
American Institute of Architects** share the
north wing of the Villard Houses, where they
frequently host exhibitions that are open to
the public. The **Information Exchange,** a
service project of the Municipal Art Society
that helps find answers to questions about
New York City, "the built city," is also here.
The service will, for example, field queries
about the history of Central Park or how to
clean brownstones and repair old plasterwork.
◆ M-F 10AM-1PM. 935.3960

Urban Center Books As you would expect,
the emphasis is on books, periodicals, and
journals about architecture, historic
preservation, and urban design. ◆ M-Th
11AM-7PM; F-Sa 10AM-6PM. 935.3595

99 Sky Books International Originally a mail-
order business run by a former RAF flight
instructor, this shop has the world's largest
collection of books and magazines on military
history and aviation. ◆ M-Sa 10AM-7PM. 48
E. 50th St (between Park and Madison Aves).
688.5086

100 St. Patrick's Cathedral Now dwarfed by
its surroundings—particularly by **Rockefeller
Center**—this church was considered too far
out of town when **James Renwick, Jr.,** built it
in the 1880s. (**Charles T. Matthews** added
Lady Chapel in 1906.) The 11th-largest
church in the world, St. Patrick's is a finely
detailed and well-proportioned but not very
strict adaptation of its French-Gothic

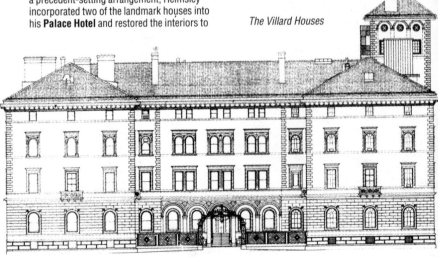

The Villard Houses

predecessors. There are no flying buttresses, for example, but there are pinnacles. The spires rise to 330 feet, and the rose window above the center portal is 26 feet in diameter. More than half of the 70 stained-glass windows were made in Chartres and Nantes. Renwick also designed the high altar. ♦ Fifth Ave (between E. 50th and E. 51st Sts)

101 Olympic Tower This black glass box full of exclusive apartments was designed in 1976 by **Skidmore, Owings & Merrill.** The hospitable interior arcade is complete with a waterfall and a Japanese restaurant, **Shin-wa,** plus a foreign currency exchange office. Reflections of **St. Patrick's** are a nice bonus. ♦ 645 Fifth Ave (at E. 51st St)

Since 1931, the Rockefeller Center Christmas tree has been one of New York City's most beloved traditions. The tree for 1993 was spotted by helicopter in the front yard of a private home in Nantucket, Massachusetts. At 10 tons and 85 feet tall, the Norway spruce measures in as one of the city's largest, decorated with more than 27,000 multicolored lights on five miles of wire.

Thaddeus Hyatt dramatically changed the sidewalks of New York in 1845, when he invented iron vault covers with glass inserts that allowed daylight to filter into building basements. Before electric lights, basement space was all but useless. Cast-iron buildings incorporated Hyatt's invention into light platforms that were raised a step or two off the sidewalk so window-shoppers could indulge themselves without stopping pedestrian traffic on narrow sidewalks. The platforms usually had round, pink-tinted translucent windows on the risers of the steps to allow light into the below-ground floor. Most of them have either been removed, paved over, or turned into truck loading docks.

You've seen them in every movie about New York, from *Breakfast at Tiffany's* to *Taxi Driver.* The yellow Checker cab will forever be nostalgically associated with bygone New York City. With more than 11,000 yellow cabs, only 10 Checkers are still on the road, each having clocked an average of 500,000 miles on New York's pockmarked streets. To be lucky enough to find and flag down an available one is enough to make your day. With an ocean of leg room, two jump seats, and a taxi driver who is bound to feel like something of a national treasure, passengers sit high above the potholes and surrounding traffic. In the 1970s, as many as 5,000 Checkers cruised the streets of New York. The remaining 10 will grace New York for at least a few more years, their disappearance a result of their drivers' retirements, not their own deterioration.

Cartier

102 Cartier Lovely baubles for the body and the home, mostly at astronomical prices, are Cartier's stock in trade. The originator of the tank watch is always coming up with original designs, and there are all those rings of diamonds, emeralds, and pearls. Don't miss **Les Musts,** the more affordable boutique collection of gifts, such as cigarette lighters. Once the residence of businessman **Morton F. Plant,** the Renaissance palazzo-style Cartier building is a rare survivor of the days when Fifth Avenue was lined with the houses of such people as **William Vanderbilt,** who lived diagonally across the street. **Robert W. Gibson** designed the building in 1905; **William Welles Bosworth** supervised the conversion to a store in 1917. Note the detailing of the entrance and centralized composition on 52nd Street. ♦ M-Sa 10AM-5:30PM. 2 E. 52nd St (at Fifth Ave). 753.0111

103 La Grenouille ★★★$$$$ The budget for flowers is close to $100,000 a year, mirrors sparkle everywhere, and the lighting is nearly perfect, making the Beautiful People who frequent La Grenouille look even more beautiful. But the food is an even better reason to reserve a table—grilled turbot with *beurre blanc* is particularly delicate and fragrant. The best time to go is at lunch, fashionably, at 1 o'clock. ♦ French ♦ Lunch and dinner. Closed Monday and Sunday. 3 E. 52nd St (at Fifth Ave). Jacket and tie required. Reservations required days in advance. 752.1495

104 B. Dalton Bookseller The flagship store of the Dalton chain is organized by subject and arranged by author with hardcover, paperback, and backlist included in each section. Computer software is downstairs. ♦ M-F 8:30AM-7PM; Sa 9:30AM-6:30PM; Su noon-6PM. 666 Fifth Ave (between W. 52nd and W. 53rd Sts). 247.1740. Also at: 396 Sixth Ave. 674.8780

104 Top of the Sixes Don't come here for dinner—only out-of-towners with no great expectations do—but do come for a frozen strawberry daiquiri and the best sunset or night-time view of Midtown in its illuminated glory, 39 floors above it all. ♦ M-Th 11:30AM-10PM; F 11:30AM-11PM; Sa 11:30AM-midnight. 666 Fifth Ave (between 52nd and 53rd Sts). 757.6662

105 21 Club ★★$$$$ During the 1920s, every house on 52nd Street between Fifth and Sixth avenues had a speakeasy, and this is the only survivor. In 1967, it was purchased by **Marshall Cogan** (for $21 million) and in 1987 was renovated by **Charles Pfister** to cater to a younger clientele. The downstairs bar is as active as ever, and nothing was done to change the iron fence and jockeys that have been outside since this was a private mansion. It is still a gathering place for entertainers, politicians, and society types who don't seem to mind the wildly uneven menu and sky-high prices. The famous 21 Burger is a truly amazing twist on an old standby. ♦ Continental ♦ Lunch and dinner. Closed Sunday. 21 W. 52nd St (between Fifth and Sixth Aves). Jacket, tie, and reservations required. 582.7200

105 Museum of Television and Radio Originally called the Museum of Brodcasting, this gallery was founded in 1965 by the late **William S. Paley,** the founder of CBS. Only the winners air here, such as a **Hitchcock** retrospective or a tribute to **Henry Fonda.** You can select TV and radio programs of your choice from the museum's vast archives— everything from **Edward R. Murrow** to "Mr. Ed"—and screen or listen for hours if you wish. In 1990, the museum (shown here) moved from its longtime home next to Paley Park on 53rd Street into this building designed by **John Burgee Architects** that more than doubled the museum's size and added two theaters, a screening room, a gallery space, an expanded library with computer access to catalogs, and a museum shop. Docent-led tours are held at 1:30PM on Tuesday. ♦ Admission. Tu-W, Sa-Su noon-6PM; Th noon-8PM; F noon-9PM. 25 W. 52nd St (between Fifth and Sixth Aves). 621.6600

105 Hines Building In 1986, while designing this building, architect **Kevin Roche** was also working on plans for the new zoo in Central Park. The zoo has covered walkways supported by columns with sliced edges, an effect called chamfering. Roche and co-architect **John Dinkeloo & Associates** used the same idea here and put the building on similar columns. In 1989, with the support of neighboring cultural institutions, including the American Craft Museum and the Museum of Television and Radio, the occupants established the ground-floor **Lobby Gallery,** a nonprofit exhibition space that mounts about 10 shows a year. ♦ 31 W. 52nd St (between Fifth and Sixth Aves). 754.5880

106 Traveller's Bookstore Owners **Candace Olmsted** and **Jane Grossman** don't stock every book in print on a certain destination. Instead, they read (and use, if possible) all of the available books and sell only the very best. Stop in for guidebooks and related fiction and nonfiction, phrase books, practical maps from all over the world, and sound advice from the congenial and knowledgeable staff. An extensive mail-order catalog is available. ♦ M-F 9AM-6PM; Sa-Su 10AM-3PM. 22 W. 52nd St (between Fifth and Sixth Aves). 664.0995

106 Bombay Palace ★$$$ The crisp and light Indian breads are delightful, the curries are mild, and the tandoori chicken is properly moist and tender at this pleasant Indian restaurant with friendly service. For dessert, try the mango ice cream or the Indian rice pudding, if you don't mind the subtle taste of rosewater. ♦ Indian ♦ Lunch and dinner. 30 W. 52nd St (between Fifth and Sixth Aves). 541.7777

106 Cesarina ★$$$ Owned and run by the proprietors of Italy's legendary Villa d'Este Hotel, this airy, elegant restaurant has an efficient and friendly staff eager to make suggestions about the carefully prepared risottos or pastas. The veal cutlet Milanese and osso buco are as delicious as the simple fish specialties that change depending on the market's catch of the day. This is a popular lunch spot for Midtown execs, but is more comfortable and quiet for a pretheater dinner. ♦ Northern Italian ♦ Lunch and dinner. Closed Saturday and Sunday. 36 W. 52nd St (between Fifth and Sixth Aves). Reservations recommended for lunch. 582.6900

107 CBS Building This is **Eero Saarinen's** only high-rise building, although he didn't live to see its completion in 1965. Known as Black Rock, the dark gray granite mass is removed from the street, and its surface is given depth by triangular columns. With the top the same as the bottom, the tower is the image of mystery (even the entrances are hard to identify)—the monolith from *2001* landed on Sixth Avenue. ♦ 51 W. 52nd St (between Fifth and Sixth Aves)

Within the CBS Building:

China Grill ★★$$$$ Although not related to Wolfgang Puck's Santa Monica landmark, Chinois on Main, the cuisine—an amalgam of Oriental, French, and California influences—is similarly inspired. It comes as no surprise that China Grill was opened by Chinois expatriates. The modern, airy space, with the story of

---

Restaurants/Clubs: Red   **Hotels: Blue**
Shops/ ♥ Outdoors: Green   **Sights/Culture: Black**

Marco Polo's journey to China recounted on the floor and on the menu, is beautiful, as are the food and the people. ♦ Pan Asian ♦ Lunch and dinner; dinner only on Saturday and Sunday. Reservations required. 333.7788

108 The MoMA Design Store Merchandise is inspired by the Museum of Modern Art collections, including educational toys (Colorforms, kaleidoscopes, architectural blocks), furniture (designs by **Frank Lloyd Wright** and **Charles Eames,** plus a reproduction of the famous butterfly chair by **Antonio Bonet, Jorge Farrari,** and **Juan Kurchen**), housewares, and desk accessories. ♦ M-W, Sa 10AM-6PM; Th-F 10AM-9PM; Su 11AM-6PM. 44 W. 53rd St (between Fifth and Sixth Aves). 767.1050

108 American Craft Museum The appreciation of American crafts has grown in recent years, partly due to an interest in things that are *not* machine-made and partly due to the pioneering of the **American Crafts Council** and its New York City museum, built in 1986 by **Fox & Fowle Architects.** Works in glass, fiber, wood, clay, metal, and paper by America's most talented craftspeople, either from the museum's collection (from 1900 to the present) or from changing loan exhibitions, are displayed. Sometimes the shows are amusing, sometimes serious, but the taste level is always high. ♦ Admission. Tu 10AM-8PM; W-Su 10AM-5PM. 40 W. 53rd St (between Fifth and Sixth Aves). 956.6047

108 New York Public Library, Donnell Library Center When he died in 1896, textile merchant **Ezekiel Donnell** left his estate to the New York Public Library to establish a place where young people could spend their evenings away from demoralizing influences. Thanks to Donnell's legacy, this library has the best collection of children's literature in the United States. Each department has its own hours; call for specific times. ♦ Main floor: M, W noon-6PM; Tu, Th 9:30AM-8PM; Sa 10AM-5:30PM; Su 1-5PM. 20 W. 53rd St (between Fifth and Sixth Aves). 621.0618

Before construction on Central Park began in 1856, Fifth Avenue from 59th to 120th streets was called "Squatters' Sovereignty." This stretch contained poor people living in shacks made of wooden planks and flattened tin cans. When construction on the park started, the poor were evicted and soon the area housed the city's richest and most powerful people.

When Radio City Music Hall opened during the Depression, the populace was so poor and the charge for entry so extravagant that it closed on opening night.

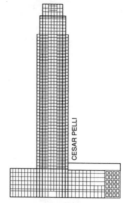

CESAR PELLI

109 Museum Tower This prestigious apartment building (shown above), designed in 1983 by **Cesar Pelli & Associates,** was built to raise funds for the **Museum of Modern Art** next door. ♦ 15 W. 53rd St (between Fifth and Sixth Aves)

109 Museum of Modern Art (MoMA) When the Museum of Modern Art was founded in 1929, a few days after the big stock market crash, the idea of a museum dedicated to the understanding and enjoyment of contemporary visual arts was novel. Founders **Abby Aldrich Rockefeller** (wife of **John D., Jr.**), **Lillie P. Bliss,** and **Mrs. Cornelius J. Sullivan** were joined by other collectors and philanthropists in the venture, and the collections have grown through the largesse of the early benefactors and others.

The original sleek white horizontal building with its marble veneer and tile-and-glass facade was designed in 1939 by **Philip L. Goodwin** and **Edward Durell Stone** in the International Style—a striking statement by an innovative institution, practicing what it preached in a row of brownstones. There was (briefly) a plan to cut a street through the two blocks from Rockefeller Center leading directly to the museum (the Rockefellers controlled the land in the vicinity). **Philip Johnson's** 1951 and 1964 additions, black glass wings to the east and west, not only expanded the gallery space and improved the **Sculpture Garden** (designed in 1953 by Johnson and **Zion & Breen**), but were an effective frame for the original front. The tower and addition by **Cesar Pelli** in 1984 replaced Johnson's west wing; Pelli also replaced the garden facade with a glassed-in **Garden Court** full of escalators. The somewhat banal condominium tower rising above the base of the museum wing is a source of income for MoMA and of contention for those who appreciated the sunny garden and low-rise side streets. The tower's cladding consists of 11 shades of glass. The expansion doubled the space available for loan shows and for the permanent collection.

One of MoMA's most important contributions to the art world is its embracing of disciplines previously considered unworthy of museum status, resulting in a collection that is not only strong in 20th-century painting and sculpture, but also photography, film, theater, music, industrial design, and architecture. When the museum's first director, **Alfred H. Barr, Jr.,** espoused this multidepartmental concept in 1929, the idea of including practical as well as fine art was considered radical. At first MoMA displayed only 19th-century paintings, but soon began a slow and steady implementation of Barr's idea. Today, MoMA also includes a publishing house, movie theater, and film department.

MoMA is strongest in art of the first half of the century—Impressionists, Cubists, and Realists such as **Picasso, Matisse, Miró,** and **Hopper**—but it also has good examples of post-World War II Abstract Expressionists through Conceptualists, including **de Kooning, Rothko, Lichtenstein, diSuvero,** and **LeWitt.** The photography galleries are worth seeing, as are the galleries of architecture and design, where you will find such 20th-century classics as **Thonet** bentwood chairs, **Tiffany** glass, **Bauhaus** textiles, and **Marcel Breuer** furniture. Among the most important paintings in the collection are **van Gogh's** *Starry Night,* **Mondrian's** *Broadway Boogie Woogie,* **Matisse's** *Dance,* **Picasso's** *Les Demoiselles d'Avignon,* **Andrew Wyeth's** *Christina's World,* and **Jackson Pollock's** *One (Number 31, 1950).*

With MoMA's newfound spaciousness, the unrivaled multidepartmental museum has truly fulfilled Barr's dream. The lower level holds the **Roy and Niuta Titus Theaters,** showing off the **Department of Film,** the largest international collection of its kind. The ground floor leads to temporary exhibitions and the **Abby Aldrich Rockefeller Sculpture Garden.** Stretching across MoMA's second floor is the **Painting and Sculpture Collection,** with separate rooms allotted to Picasso and Matisse, among others. The **Drawing Collection** on the third floor has its own exhibition space. Acquisitions include **Max Pechstein's** *Reclining Nude with Cat* and Picasso's 1913 *Head.* The **Prints and Illustrated Books** collection owns a 1968 etching by Picasso, the first of a series of 347 intaglio prints, and the only self-portrait of him as an old man. The **Architecture and Design Collection** on the fourth floor features two designs for houses by **Frank Lloyd Wright** and a **Mindset Computer.** ◆ Admission; members and children under 16 accompanied by an adult free; voluntary contribution Th-F 5:30-8:30PM. M-Tu, Sa-Su 11AM-6PM; Th-F noon-8:30PM. 11 W. 53rd St (between Fifth and Sixth Aves). 708.9480; film schedule 708.9490

Within the Museum of Modern Art:

 The Sculpture Garden One of the most pleasant outdoor spaces in the city, the garden has sculpture by **Rodin, Renoir, Miró, Matisse,** and **Picasso,** among others. Weather permitting, it's open the same hours as the museum and holds a variety of concerts in the summer. The **Garden Cafe** overlooks the garden and offers a variety of snacks and light meals. ◆ M-Tu, F-Su 11AM-6PM; Th-F noon-8:30PM. 708.9480

The MoMA Bookstore Be sure to peruse the bookstore's extensive assortment of books, posters, and cards relating to the museum's collection. ◆ M-W, Sa 11AM-5:45PM; Th-F 11AM-8:45PM. 708.9480

Sette MoMA ★★$$$ MoMA mia! The inevitable combination of great art and great food finally came together here with the 1993 opening of this restaurant by the owners of the successful Upper East Side's **Sette Mezzo** and **Vico.** Though the dining room is cool and contemporary, with art from the museum's permanent collection, ask for a table on the outdoor terrace for a lovely view of the sculpture garden. Best bets include the simply grilled vegetables or pasta filled with goat cheese and eggplant. During museum hours, enter through the museum; after 5PM use the entrance on W. 54th Street. ◆ Italian ◆ Lunch and dinner. Closed Wednesday. Reservations recommended. 708.9710

110 St. Thomas Church Cram Goodhue & Ferguson designed this picturesque French Gothic edifice (illustrated above) on a tight corner in 1914. You have to wonder why a second tower wasn't included; the single one is rather awkward in an otherwise symmetrical composition. A dollar sign next to the "true lover's knot" over the **Bride's Door** is presumably a sculptor's comment on the social standing of the congregation. The Episcopal Church has a world-renowned boys choir that makes the services here a memorable experience from October through May; call in advance for a schedule. ♦ 1 W. 53rd St (at Fifth Ave). 757.7013

111 University Club Considered by many to be the finest work of **Charles Follen McKim** (of **McKim, Mead & White**), this 1899 building is an original composition with a bow to a half-dozen Italian palaces. When it was built, in the days before air-conditioning, it had striped awnings in the windows, which made the pink marble exterior even more interesting. The interior is just as lavish. This club set the style for all the others that followed for decades. ♦ 1 W. 54th St (at Fifth Ave). 247.2100

112 Aquavit ★★★$$$$ **Nelson Rockefeller** once lived in this town house, but he wouldn't recognize the eight-story atrium, complete with birch trees and a waterfall, that is now the main dining room of this lovely, modern restaurant. The namesake potent liquor is one of the stars at the street-level bar, which offers light meals, including a wonderful smorgasbord platter that is so varied and each morsel so sublime that it always seems new. The Swedish decor—contemporary and antique Scandinavian art and exquisite table settings—adds greatly to the pleasure of the fine food. ♦ Scandinavian ♦ Lunch and dinner; lunch only on Saturday. Closed Sunday. 13 W. 54th St (between Fifth and Sixth Aves). Reservations and jacket recommended. 307.7311

112 Rockefeller Apartments When **John D. Rockefeller, Jr.** was assembling the site for **Rockefeller Center,** he lived on this block. By the end of 1929 he owned 15 of the block's houses, having joined his neighbors, most of whom were members of his family, in protecting the street from commercial use. But he wasn't above a little commercialism himself, and hired **Harrison & Fouilhoux** to design this building in 1936, a few months before he moved over to Park Avenue. Its bay-windowed towers overlook the garden of the **Museum of Modern Art,** a site donated by Rockefeller through his wife, **Abby Aldrich Rockefeller,** one of the museum's founders. ♦ 17 W. 54th St (between Fifth and Sixth Aves)

113 Suarez High-end designer bags—most of them European and all top-of-the-line—at 20 percent below standard retail are the specialty of this well-stocked boutique. ♦ M-F 10AM-6PM; Sa 10AM-5PM. 26 W. 54th St (between Fifth and Sixth Aves). 315.5614

113 Hotel Dorset $$$ This attractive, unassuming hotel has a very loyal following and a prime location—next door to the **Museum of Modern Art.** The bar and restaurant are jovial and popular. ♦ 30 W. 54th St (between Fifth and Sixth Aves). 247.7300; fax 581.0153

Within the Hotel Dorset:

Park Cafe ★★$$$ Bay scallops in cream sauce with white wine and wonderful cold appetizers are some of the always delicious choices. The room is large, bright, and comfortable. ♦ Continental ♦ Lunch and dinner. Reservations required. 247.7300

114 Warwick Hotel $$ The **Beatles** holed up in this European-style hotel when they were looking for peace and quiet in New York. Amenities include babysitting and interpreting services. A bar and restaurant are also on the premises. ♦ 65 W. 54th St (at Sixth Ave). 247.2700, 800/522.5634; fax 957.8915

115 Allegria ★$$ If warm weather allows you to sit outside and you stick to the simpler dishes or variety of good pizzas and pastas, you'll experience something of the "happiness" implied in this popular Italian restaurant's name. Brightly tiled and painted indoors with idyllic scenes of the Italian countryside and celebrations, this newcomer offers a basic Mediterranean menu: rigatoni with eggplant, pasta with seafood, and a number of chicken dishes such as a grilled version topped with artichokes and fresh tomatoes. ♦ Italian ♦ Lunch and dinner. 66 W. 55th St (between Fifth and Sixth Aves). 956.7755

116 La Bonne Soupe ★$$ Soups, omelets, a variety of chopped beef dishes and daily specials of provincial French food are good buys. ♦ French ♦ Lunch and dinner. 48 W. 55th St (between Fifth and Sixth Aves). 586.7650

116 Michael's ★$$ Sleek and airy Michael's is a popular place for healthy breakfasts and is always full at lunch with Midtown business types. The sunny, spare setting is an understated backdrop for an impressive collection of modern art, one that sets an appropriate tone for a light menu of imaginative California-style cuisine. Michael's signature dish is warm grilled chicken on a bed of Montrachet goat cheese, grilled peppers and red onions, vine-ripened tomatoes, and baby greens—covered in olive oil seasoned with jalapeño and cilantro. ♦ American/California ♦ Breakfast and lunch; dinner only on Saturday. Closed Sunday. 24 W. 55th St (between Fifth and Sixth Aves). 767.0555

117 J.P. French Bakery Stop in for perhaps the best croissant in town, plus excellent French breads in several sizes—from *ficelle* (a thin baguette) to large, round loaves—all baked on the premises. ♦ M-F 7AM-7PM; Sa 8AM-6PM; Su 9AM-5PM. 45 W. 55th St (between Fifth and Sixth Aves). 765.7575

Restaurants/Clubs: Red   **Hotels:** Blue
Shops/ ♥ Outdoors: Green   **Sights/Culture:** Black

117 La Fondue $$ Swiss chocolate, cheese, and filet mignon fondues, plus steaks, seafood, and incredible desserts are served in the warm, casual atmosphere of a European cellar. ♦ Swiss ♦ Lunch, dinner, and late-night meals. 43 W. 55th St (between Fifth and Sixth Aves). 581.0820

117 Menchanko-tei ★$ Japanese businessmen frequent this cozy noodle emporium. After Tokyo prices, the tab here must seem rock bottom. The hearty soups fortified with a host of ingredients and noodles are as authentic as it gets in Midtown Manhattan. Stop by for one of the steamy broths after a winter's afternoon at the nearby Museum of Modern Art. ♦ Japanese ♦ Lunch, dinner, and late-night meals. 39 W. 55th St (between Fifth and Sixth Aves). 247.1585

117 La Caravelle ★★$$$$ Although this eatery was consistently rated as one of New York's best French restaurants after its 1960 opening, in recent years standards began to slip and it started to lose the accolades it once wore with such distinction. Fortunately, La Caravelle is experiencing a renaissance and is once again a superb spot with excellent service. ♦ French ♦ Lunch and dinner; dinner only on Saturday. Closed Sunday. 33 W. 55th St (between Fifth and Sixth Aves). Jacket, tie, and reservations required. 586.4252

117 Shoreham Hotel $$ This small hotel has only 75 rooms, each with its own serving pantry. ♦ 33 W. 55th St (between Fifth and Sixth Aves). 247.6700, 800/553.3347; fax 765.9741

118 Fifth Avenue Presbyterian Church When society moved uptown, this church, which had been at 19th Street since 1855, moved with it to this 1875 building designed by **Carl Pfeiffer.** Future president **Theodore Roosevelt** was one of the original parishioners, along with the **Auchinclosses, Livingstons,** and **Walcotts.** It was called the most influential congregation in New York. ♦ 7 W. 55th St (at Fifth Ave). 247.0490

THE PENINSULA
NEW YORK

119 The Peninsula New York $$$$ This hotel was built in 1905 by **Hiss & Weeks** and for many years, as the **Gotham Hotel,** was a favorite stopping place for movie stars. Then it briefly became **Maxim's** and was completely restored in the Belle Epoque tradition of the original Maxim's in Paris. The latest incarnation reflects the "Peninsula" style. The 250 oversize rooms are outfitted with marble baths and Art Nouveau decor. Services range from newspaper delivery to 24-hour room service, and the hotel includes three restaurants and a tri-level fitness center and spa with a glass-enclosed rooftop swimming pool. ♦ 700 Fifth Ave (at W. 55th St). 247.2200, 800/262.9467; fax 903.3943

Within The Peninsula New York:

Adrienne

Adrienne ★★★$$$ Fine Continental cuisine is offered in this comfortable yet elegant dining room overlooking Fifth Avenue. A typical choice is grilled Long Island duckling with soy glaze. Good service justifies the prices. ♦ Continental ♦ Lunch and dinner; lunch only on Monday and Sunday; dinner only on Saturday. Jacket, tie, and reservations required. 247.2200

Penn-Top Bar and Terrace The beautiful view of the Manhattan skyline from this glass-enclosed bar can't be beat. Lunch is served buffet-style on the terrace during the warmer months. ♦ M-Sa 5PM-1AM. 23rd floor. 247.2200

120 Christian Dior Boutique Reminiscent of Dior's Paris headquarters at 30 Avenue Montaigne, the luxurious 4,500-square-foot space is large enough to display **Gianfranco Ferre's** complete haute couture and ready-to-wear collections. ♦ M-Sa 10AM-6PM. 703 Fifth Ave (at E. 55th St). 223.4646

120 La Côte Basque ★★★$$$$ This is considered by many to be one of the top restaurants in New York. Chef/owner **Jean Jacques Rachou** provides food that is technically perfect and exquisitely served in a setting reminiscent of a French seaside village. The presentation of the lobster terrine, a combination of shellfish, green beans, tomato, shredded carrots, and *celerie rémoulade*, is stunning and sure to please. The cream of New York society occupies their regular tables, but newcomers are also treated graciously. It's an inspired choice for celebrating a special occasion, *if* you can secure a reservation. ♦ French ♦ Lunch and dinner; dinner only on Saturday. Closed Sunday. 5 E. 55th St (between Madison and Fifth Aves). Jacket and tie required. Reservations required days in advance. 688.6525

The section of Fifth Avenue currently named Museum Mile used to be called Millionaire's Row. The introduction of income tax, however, had such a tragic effect on the wealthy that this high-priced name soon fell away.

121 The St. Regis Sheraton $$$$ When **Trowbridge & Livingston** built the St. Regis for **John Jacob Astor** in 1904, Astor said he wanted the finest hotel in the world, a place where guests would feel as comfortable as they did in a gracious private home. Today, this is the only hotel in New York that offers 24-hour butler service. A three-year, $100 million renovation, completed by **Brennan, Beer Gorman** in 1991, has produced one of New York's most elegant hotels. The capacity has actually been lowered, from more than 500 rooms to 322, 86 of them suites. The spectacular landmark exterior remains, with its stone garlands and flowers and its slate mansard roof. But now it's complemented inside by state-of-the-art technology, computerized phones, and other comforts. Besides the elegant **Lespinasse**, the hotel contains the **Astor Court**, which serves light meals and tea, and the **King Cole Bar and Lounge.** ♦ 2 E. 55th St (at Fifth Ave). 753.4500; fax 787.3447

Within The St. Regis Sheraton:

Lespinasse ★★★$$$$ The newly renovated hotel's gourmet restaurant is about as elegant as it gets in New York. In fact, the room may be a little too grand for comfort. The food, while a touch fussy, is nonetheless sublime. Chef **Grey Kunz** is a master of unusual spices from the Far East, and his plates often include little pots of wondrous exotics. ♦ International ♦ Breakfast, lunch, and dinner; breakfast only on Sunday. 2 E. 55th St (between Madison and Fifth Aves). Jacket and reservations required. 339.6719

122 Takashimaya Japan's largest retail conglomerate launched a unique venture in April 1993 when it opened this elegant 20-story building designed by New York architect **John Burgee.** A distinctive array of products are sold on the third through fifth floors, ranging from home furnishings and fashion accessories to table and bed linens, specialty gifts, and objets d'art. The ground floor consists of a 4,500-square-foot gallery as well as a multilevel atrium, used as an exhibition space for contemporary Asian and American art and artisanal crafts. A Zen-like tearoom has just opened in the basement, guaranteed to relax shoppers' jangled nerves. ♦ M-W, F-Sa 10AM-6PM; Th 10AM-8PM. 693 Fifth Ave (between E. 54th and E. 55th Sts). 350.0115

123 Elizabeth Arden Salon The famous red door leads to a world apart, filled with designer fashions, lingerie, and sportswear and a salon that has made pampering a fine art. The salon offers exercise facilities, massages, facials, hair styling, and more, all calculated to make you look as terrific as you feel. ♦ M-W, F-Sa 8AM-6PM; Th 8AM-8PM. 691 Fifth Ave (between E. 54th and E. 55th Sts). 546.0200

123 Façonnable With more than 40 stores throughout Europe and Japan, this French men's apparel company has just opened its first store in the U.S. in the coveted Fifth Avenue location formerly occupied by Gucci. Replicating the Façonnable store on Rue Royale in Paris, this shop has already become a destination for well-heeled and well-dressed professional men who like the grouping of items by color and pattern. If you want to pick up "a little something" on Fifth, come here to choose from more than 7,000 ties and shirts in some 200 patterns. ♦ M-W, F-Sa 10AM-7PM; Th 10AM-8PM; Su noon-6PM. 689 Fifth Ave (at W. 54th St). 319.0111

124 Indonesian Pavilion This is one of the few remaining buildings from the time when 54th Street east and west of Fifth Avenue was called "The Art Gallery of New York Streets." It was designed in 1900 by **McKim, Mead & White** and built by **W.E.D. Stokes,** who sold it to **William H. Moore,** a founder of the **United States Steel** and **American Can** companies. Note the massive balcony and strong cornices—evidence of **Charles McKim's** interest in Renaissance architecture. Currently uninhabited, its future is in limbo. ♦ 4 E. 54th St (at Fifth Ave)

124 Gucci A staff that ranges from very pleasant to downright snooty sells shoes and leather goods for men and women, as well as suits, topcoats, dresses, ties, and scarves. The famed red and green stripe is omnipresent on handbags, boots, and luggage. ♦ M-W, F-Sa 9:30AM-6PM; Th 9:30AM-7PM. 685 Fifth Ave (at E. 54th St). 826.2600

124 Fortunoff You would never expect to find a reasonably priced jewelry and silver store on Fifth Avenue, but here is one (complete with a glitzy facade) that offers good prices on strings of pearls, gold chains, hammered silver pitchers, urns, chalices, sterling silver, and silver plate flatware by Oneida and Towle, Reed & Barton, and stainless-steel flatware by Fraser and Dansk. The sales help is remarkably courteous. ♦ M-Th 10AM-7PM; F-Sa 10AM-6PM. 681 Fifth Ave (between E. 53rd and E. 54th Sts). 758.6660

125 Samuel Paley Plaza Named for the father of its benefactor, the late **William S. Paley** of CBS, this park is a spare, very welcome anomaly in the densest part of town. Good furniture and a wonderful waterfall provide the perfect spot to steal a moment's peace. A counter sells light food and beverages. The park was designed in 1967 by landscape architects **Zion & Breen** and consulting architect **Albert Preston Moore.** ♦ 3 E. 53rd St (at Fifth Ave)

125 Seryna ★★$$$ Avoid the crowds at lunch and visit Seryna for dinner to enjoy any of the excellent steak dishes. The sushi and sashimi are good, too. ♦ Japanese ♦ Lunch and dinner; dinner only on Saturday. Closed Sunday. 11 E. 53rd St (between Madison and Fifth Aves). Reservations recommended. 980.9393

126 San Pietro ★★$$$ Italy's Amalfi Coast is the inspiration for the seafood specialties at **Sistina's** sister. The elegant setting caters to a crowd of Italian cuisine cognoscenti. ♦ Neopolitan ♦ Lunch and dinner. 18 E. 54th St (between Fifth and Madison Aves). Jacket, tie, and reservations required. 753.9015

127 Bice ★★$$$$ **Bill Blass, Calvin Klein, Oleg Cassini,** and **Gianfranco Ferre** frequent this trendy Milanese trattoria. The long, curved white marble bar, multilevel seating, bright lighting, and exquisite flower arrangements create a luxurious setting. Among the more rewarding main courses are roast rack of veal with new potatoes, and grilled fish (salmon, swordfish, or sole). Bice is every bit as elegant as its Milan counterpart. ♦ Italian ♦ Lunch and dinner. 7 E. 54th St (between Madison and Fifth Aves). Reservations recommended. 688.1999

128 Morrell & Company, The Wine Emporium A playground for oenophiles, this large, well-organized store carries practically every worthwhile label, including many direct imports. Service is knowledgeable but occasionally impatient. ♦ M-F 9AM-6:45PM; Sa 10AM-6:30PM. 535 Madison Ave (between E. 54th and E. 55th Sts). 688.9370

129 The Sony Building Known as the AT&T Headquarters until 1992, this pinkish granite building designed by **Philip Johnson** and **John Burgee** in 1984 continues to be recognized by its top, often referred to as "Chippendale" in style. At press time, the base was being enclosed by the new Japanese owners; it will eventually feature a branch of the popular **City Bakery.** The building is one of the more recognizable elements in Manhattan's urban fabric. ♦ 550 Madison Ave (between E. 55th and E. 56th Sts)

130 Friars Club This is the private club for actors who invented the famous roasts, in which members poke fun at celebrity guests. ♦ 57 E. 55th St (between Park and Madison Aves). 751.7272

131 Oceana ★★$$$$
Lovers of interesting seafood preparations revel in the varied selection of fish and crustaceans served in Oceana's comfortable pastel surroundings. Creative dishes range

from grilled yellowfin tuna steak with foie gras in a juniper vinaigrette to a flan of lobster and cod with mashed potatoes, savoy cabbage, and chanterelles. ♦ Seafood ♦ Lunch and dinner; dinner only on Saturday. Closed Sunday. 55 E. 54th St (between Park and Madison Aves). Jacket and reservations required. 759.5941

131 Bill's Gay Nineties ★$$$ The sirloin steak special in this holdover from the 1890s is named for **Diamond Jim Brady,** who would be right at home here. A pianist plays in the dining room, where American cuisine is served. ♦ American ♦ Lunch and dinner; dinner only on Saturday. Closed Sunday. 57 E. 54th St (between Park and Madison Aves). 355.0243

132 Hotel Elysée $$$ **Tallulah Bankhead** used to be a regular here, as was **Tennessee Williams.** Recently renovated, the hotel still retains its old-world atmosphere in spite of the modern buildings rising around it. Each of the 110 rooms has its own personality, and most go by names as well as numbers. Renovation of the once-renowned **Monkey Bar** is currently underway. ♦ 60 E. 54th St (between Park and Madison Aves). 753.1066; fax 980.9278

133 Lever House **Gordon Bunschaft** was the partner in charge of this 1952 **Skidmore, Owings & Merrill** design. The first glass wall on Park Avenue, built when **Charles Luckman** was president of Lever Brothers, has, after a long battle, been awarded landmark status and saved from possible destruction or disfigurement. The articulate building (at right) displays the tenets of orthodox Corbusian Modernism: it is raised from the ground on columns, it has a roof garden, and there is a free facade on the outside and free plan on the inside. With the **Seagram Building** across the street, this is a landmark corner that changed the face of the city. ♦ 390 Park Ave (between E. 53rd and E. 54th Sts)

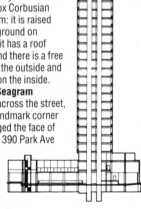

Restaurants/Clubs: Red   Hotels: Blue
Shops/ 🌿 Outdoors: Green   Sights/Culture: Black

134 Central Synagogue This 1872 Moorish Revival building designed by **Henry Fernbach** is the oldest continuously used synagogue in the city. The onion domes on the 222-foot towers and the brightly stenciled interior add a bit of fancy to the mottled brownstone facade. ◆ 652 Lexington Ave (at E. 55th St)

135 Enoteca Iperbole ★★$$$ The management calls this America's first wine library/restaurant. The setting is charming, the food is well-prepared, and there are more than 500 wines available. ◆ Italian ◆ Lunch and dinner; dinner only on Saturday. Closed Sunday. 137 E. 55th St (between Third and Lexington Aves). Reservations recommended. 759.9720

135 Shun Lee Palace ★★★$$$ The late **T.T. Wang,** founder of this fine restaurant, was the man who introduced America to Chinese cuisine that went beyond egg rolls and chow mein. The menu represents several regions of China, and the kitchen does justice to all of them. ◆ Chinese ◆ Lunch and dinner. 155 E. 55th St (between Third and Lexington Aves). Reservations required. 371.8844

136 Citicorp Center Designed in 1978 by **Hugh Stubbins & Associates,** the rakish angle of the building's top was planned as a solar collector but is now nothing more than a vent for the cooling system, which provides a steamy effect for the night lighting. Also under the roof is a 400-ton computer-operated **Tuned Mass Damper** ("earthquake machine" to most of us). They don't expect an earthquake any time soon, but the building (shown here) is cantilevered on 145-foot columns that allow it to sway in the wind. Those 10-story-high stilts also make it possible for Citicorp Center to be the world's only skyscraper with skylights in the basement, where free concerts and other programs take place in the center of a gaggle of shops and restaurants. ◆ 153 E. 53rd St (between Third and Lexington Aves). 559.1000

Within Citicorp Center:

St. Peter's Lutheran Church St. Peter's is a major reason for the engineering and formal antics of Citicorp Center's design. The church refused to sell its air rights to Citicorp unless the bank agreed to build a new church clearly distinct from the tower. In contrast to the high-tech tower, the church is granite, with wooden furnishings and interior detailing by **Massimo** and **Lella Vignelli.** Within the church, the **Erol Beaker Chapel** was created by sculptor **Louise Nevelson.** Watch for jazz vespers at St. Peter's, known as the city's jazz ministry. But the interior is well worth a look under any circumstances. ◆ E. 54th St at Lexington Ave. 935.2200

Theatre at St. Peter's Church Two productions began in this excellent 165-seat space in the basement of Citicorp Center and went on to Broadway: *Tintypes* and *The Elephant Man.* ◆ 534.5366

The Market at Citicorp Center Accessible from the sunken plaza at the corner of 53rd Street and Lexington Avenue, this international bazaar offers three levels of dining as well as culinary and housewares shopping. Slate floors and an all-glass front add a homogeneity to the potpourri of shops. Midtown office workers fill up the tables, where you can bring food from the shops and restaurants at lunch or just sit and read a newspaper. Semi-regular free entertainment enlivens the atrium: weeknight cabaret and pop concerts at 6PM, Saturday night jazz at 8PM, Sunday classical concerts at noon, and often Saturday programs for kids at 11AM.

Nyborg-Nelson ★★$ The Scandinavian specialties here include packaged goods and prepared salads and fish. They'll assemble a lunch or supper for eating in the Citicorp atrium. ◆ Scandinavian ◆ Lunch and early dinner. Closed Sunday. 223.0700

137 Fisher & Levy Caterers **Chip Fisher** and **Doug Levy** opened this decidedly upscale food store, where breakfasts as well as California-style pizzas are served—or delivered. Their lunches are available for delivery throughout Manhattan. This is also one of the few Midtown shops that makes and serves fresh doughnuts. ◆ Continental/Pizza ◆ Breakfast and lunch. Closed Saturday and Sunday. 875 Third Ave (at E. 53rd St), concourse level. 832.3880

138 Solera ★★$$ Tapas and other Spanish delicacies top the list in this stylishly redesigned town house. The soft lighting and colorful tiling is the ideal stage for chef/owner **Dominick Cerrone's** food and wine. ◆ Spanish ◆ Lunch and dinner; dinner only on Saturday. Closed Sunday. 216 E. 53rd St (between Second and Third Aves). Reservations recommended. 644.1166

139 Quest Book Shop of the New York Theosophical Society The stated purpose of the society is: "To form a nucleus of the Universal Brotherhood of Humanity, without distinction of race, creed, sex, caste, or color. To encourage the study of Comparative Religion, Philosophy, and science. To investigate unexplained laws of Nature and the powers latent in man." ♦ M-F 10AM-6PM; Sa noon-5PM. 240 E. 53rd St (between Second and Third Aves). 758.5521

140 Il Nido ★★$$$$ Excellent Italian food is served in a stylish yet comfortable atmosphere. Special care is taken with service: dishes are adorned with last-minute garnishes by an expert waiter at your table. ♦ Italian ♦ Lunch and dinner; dinner only on Saturday. Closed Sunday. 251 E. 53rd St (between Second and Third Aves). Jacket, tie, and reservations required. 753.8450

141 Brazilian Pavillion ★★$$ People argue about whether this restaurant has the best Brazilian kitchen in town, but not about whether it's the most pleasant setting for this bold cuisine. It's light, modern, and bright, and there's a fully garnished *fejoada* (a black-bean stew with pork) every night and at lunch on Wednesday and Sunday. ♦ Brazilian ♦ Lunch and dinner. 316 E. 53rd St (between First and Second Aves). Reservations recommended. 758.8129

142 Le Perigord ★★$$$ UN ambassadors often frequent this cozy French restaurant. The decor is rather dull, but the extravagant flower arrangements add a sense of luxury. The Dover sole is excellent, and the crepes-soufflés are a good bet for dessert. ♦ French ♦ Lunch and dinner; dinner only on Saturday. Closed Sunday. 405 E. 52nd St (at First Ave). Jacket, tie, and reservations required. 755.6244

143 River House This 26-story, twin-towered, limestone and gray brick cooperative, built in 1931 by **Bottomley, Wagner & Whitee,** has always been one of the most exclusive apartment buildings in the city (when there was a dock on the river, only the best yachts used it). The lower floors house the **River Club,** which includes squash and tennis courts, a pool, and a ballroom. ♦ 435 E. 53rd St (between the East River and First Ave)

144 Sutton Place and Sutton Place South Until colonized by **Vanderbilts** and **Morgans** moving from Fifth Avenue in the early 1920s, this elegant end of York Avenue was a run-down area. The town houses and apartment buildings are by such architects as **Mott Schmidt, Rosario Candela, Delano & Aldrich,** and **Cross & Cross.** Visit the park at the end of 55th Street and the terrace on 57th Street for views of the river and the **Queensboro Bridge.** Also peek in from 58th Street, where **Riverview Terrace,** one of New

York's last private streets, runs along the river lined with five ivy-covered brownstones. The secretary-general of the United Nations lives at Nos. 1 to 3. ♦ E. 54th to E. 59th Sts

145 54th Street Recreation Center These turn-of-the-century enclosed public bathhouses built by **Werner & Windolph** in 1906 now offer an indoor running track, gymnasium facilities, and an indoor swimming pool open all year. ♦ Sunday for children only (parents welcome). 348 E. 54th St (between First and Second Aves). 397.3154

146 Vong ★★★$$$ Superchef **Jean-Georges Vongerichten** (of **JoJo** and **Lipstick Cafe**) weighs in with his own wonderful interpretation of Thai/French cuisine in the onetime home of **Toscana,** transformed into an elegant Asian space by **David Rockwell.** Appetizers sometimes outshine entrées, especially the fried crab roll and sublime coconut milk soup. ♦ Thai/French ♦ Lunch and dinner; dinner only on Saturday. Closed Sunday. 200 E. 54th St (at Third Ave). 486.9592

146 Lipstick Cafe ★★$ In his "free time," **Jean-Georges Vongerichten** (of **JoJo** and **Vong**) throws a tasty bone to hungry Midtown workers on a dining-out budget. Delicious homemade soups, salads, sandwiches, breads, and pastries are made to go or stay. ♦ American ♦ Breakfast and lunch. Closed Saturday and Sunday. 885 Third Ave (at E. 54th St). 486.8664

147 900 Third Avenue The aluminum section at the base of this brick-clad tower and the silhouette of the greenhouse at the top are a reference to the neighboring **Citicorp Center** across 54th Street. It was built in 1983, five years after Citicorp, by **Cesar Pelli & Associates** with **Rafael Vinoly.** ♦ E. 54th St

148 P.J. Clarke's ★$$ Few better places exist to witness the slow pickling of Midtown's younger and more rambunctious crowd during the cocktail hour. Mysteriously, the hamburgers are famous, although that's not the meat the young singles come here to get. ♦ American ♦ Lunch, dinner, and late-night meals. 915 Third Ave (at E. 55th St). 759.1650

149 Michael's Pub ★$$$ Well-known jazz singers and instrumentalists, including **Mel Torme,** perform nightly at **Gil Wiest's** restaurant, and on Monday nights when he's in town, **Woody Allen** puts in an appearance with his clarinet to play a few sets with the **Dixieland New Orleans Funeral and Ragtime Band.** ♦ American ♦ Lunch and dinner; dinner only on Saturday. Closed Sunday. 211 E. 55th St (between Second and Third Aves). Reservations recommended. 758.2272

150 The Manhattan Art & Antiques Center More than a hundred dealers spread their quality wares over three large floors at Manhattan's specialized antiques "mall." One-stop shopping offers every imaginable item from affordable to exorbitant, from tiny pillboxes to magnificent chandeliers. Bargains are hard to come by and much of the merchandise is museum quality and pricey, but the variety is extensive and prices are competitive. ♦ M-Sa 10:30AM-6PM; Su noon-6PM. 1050 Second Ave (between W. 55th and W. 56th Sts). 355.4400

151 March ★★★$$$ A hideaway in a fin-de-siècle town house, this romantic restaurant is decorated with elegant banquettes and a tapestry on the wall. The eclectic menu features such exciting appetizers as confit of rabbit with foie gras and white beans. Among the best entrées are Atlantic salmon with Middle Eastern spices and barley risotto, and rack of lamb with sweet mustard and herbed crust. Save room for desserts like crispy pancakes with vanilla ice cream, mango, and berries. Wines are affordable. ♦ American ♦ Dinner. Closed Sunday. 405 E. 58th St (between First Ave and Sutton Pl). Reservations recommended. 838.9393

151 Ararat Dardanelles ★$$ The specialty of this restaurant is kebabs, at least one of which is made with yogurt, another staple in the Armenian kitchen. The menu also includes moussaka and stuffed dolmas. Live music is performed six days a week. ♦ Russian/Armenian ♦ Dinner and late-night meals. 1076 First Ave (between E. 58th and E. 59th Sts). Reservations required. 752.2828

152 Rosa Mexicano ★★$$$ The menu is light on tortilla dishes, but the grilled meats and avocado-based appetizers at this popular spot are standouts, and the frozen margaritas are wonderfully toxic. ♦ Mexican ♦ Dinner. 1063 First Ave (at E. 58th St). Reservations recommended. 753.7407

153 Café Nicholson ★$$$ Dining at this intimate, romantic hideaway is a theatrical experience. The fanciful decor includes huge marble slabs, ornate hand-painted 19th-century tiles, and antique furniture, paintings, and pottery. The eccentric owner only opens the restaurant when he feels like it, so be sure to confirm your reservation. On arrival, don't be surprised if you're immediately asked whether you want the vanilla or chocolate soufflé. If you say no to both, expect a decided chill in the atmosphere. Either way, the tip will be included in the bill. ♦ French ♦ Dinner. Closed Monday and Sunday. 323 E. 58th St (between First and Second Aves). Reservations required. 355.6769

154 Iris Brown's Victorian Doll and Miniature Shop Brown specializes in miniature furniture and toys, dollhouses, and Christmas ornaments of the Victorian era. ♦ M-F 11AM-5:30PM; Sa 12:30-5:30PM. 253 E. 57th St (between Second and Third Aves). 593.2882

154 Les Sans-Culottes ★$$$ Each meal opens with a basket overflowing with charcuterie. The main courses will make you wish you'd had a bit more restraint—the filet of sole is exceptionally light and the chicken cordon bleu well prepared. ♦ French ♦ Lunch and dinner; dinner only on Sunday. 1085 Second Ave (between E. 57th and E. 58th Sts). Reservations recommended. 838.6660

155 Bruno ★$$$ As with many of the better Midtown Italian restaurants, most of the antipasti, pastas, vegetables, and seafood are done to perfection, while prime quality meats can suffer from overthickened, undercooked wine-based sauces. A smart-looking modern room and gracious service make up for the lapses. ♦ Italian ♦ Lunch and dinner; dinner only on Saturday. Closed Sunday. 240 E. 58th St (between Second and Third Aves). Reservations recommended. 688.4191

156 Felidia ★★$$$$ *Connoisseur* magazine says this Italian restaurant serves the best martini in the world, which is just as well since the food is erratic—sometimes great and at other times less so. Despite its ranking among the top establishments serving the food of Trieste, critics note that a native of that city would not recognize many of the offerings on the menu. Nevertheless, the place is almost always full of people having a good time. ♦ Italian ♦ Lunch and dinner; dinner only on Saturday. Closed Sunday. 243 E. 58th St (between Second and Third Aves). Jacket and reservations required. 758.1479

156 Silk Surplus Those in the know shop here and at the annex at 223 E. 58th Street for generous discounts on Scalamandre and other luxurious fabrics used for upholstery, tablecloths, draperies, wallpapers, and trimmings. ♦ M-Sa 10AM-5:30PM. 235 E. 58th St (between Second and Third Aves). 753.6511

157 Morton Books Books and periodicals on architecture, gardening, and interior design are the specialty of this small shop. ♦ M-Sa 11AM-7PM. 989 Third Ave (at E. 59th St). 421.9025

158 Dawat ★★$$$ One of New York's best upscale Indian restaurants, Dawat offers entrées from every region of India, from mild to flamingly hot. Vegetarians will be delighted with the choices. ♦ Indian ♦ Lunch and dinner; dinner only on Saturday and Sunday. 210 E. 58th St (between Second and Third Aves). Reservations recommended. 355.7555

158 Girafe ★$$$$ The oily deliciousness of much of the cooking is at odds with the recherché tone of the place and high civility of the staff, but the contrast is what makes it all interesting. Try the veal in lemon with white wine sauce. ♦ Italian ♦ Lunch and dinner; dinner only on Saturday. Closed Sunday. 208 E. 58th St (between Second and Third Aves). Reservations recommended. 752.3054

159 Royal Athena Galleries Ancient, European, Oriental, pre-Columbian, and tribal works of art are sold here. Each object is labeled and has a price tag, but the staff enjoys answering questions from browsers as well as from serious collectors. ♦ M-Sa 10AM-6PM. 153 E. 57th St (between Third and Lexington Aves). 355.2034

159 Nesle, Inc. The wealth that was India's during the heyday of the maharajas is here in the form of extraordinary lavish chandeliers, mirrors, and thrones. **Albert Nesle** combed the great houses of India, London, and Paris to put together the greatest collection of chandeliers in the city, and has sold them to the White House and the State Department. ♦ M-F 9AM-5PM. 151 E. 57th St (between Third and Lexington Aves). 755.0515

159 Hammacher Schlemmer Unintentionally one of the funniest stores in the city, it carries gadgetry to the limits of credibility with such items as a solar-powered ventilated golf cap, an electronic home casino, and an interactive talking chess game. On the practical side, it was the first store to introduce the steam iron, electric razor, and pressure cooker. The mail-order catalog is a kick, too. ♦ M-Sa 10AM-6PM. 147 E. 57th St (between Third and Lexington Aves). 421.9000

160 The Fitzpatrick Manhattan Hotel $$$ One of the few hotels in this part of Midtown—and just two blocks from Bloomingdale's—this hotel is the only U.S. representation of a small Irish chain. A welcome attention to detail, tastefully furnished rooms and public areas, marbled whirlpool baths, a smiling top-hatted bellman, and Irish-inspired hospitality make this a veritable oasis in the chaos of Midtown Manhattan. ♦ 687 Lexington Ave (between W. 56th and W. 57th Sts). 355.0100, 800/367.7701; fax 308.5166

161 Allerton Hotel for Women $ The Allerton has a homelike atmosphere in a good location. Not all the rooms have baths or air-conditioning, but there is a sunroof and a restaurant. ♦ 130 E. 57th St (at Lexington Ave). 753.8841

162 The Gazebo Hundreds of old and new quilts fill this airy shop, which also features baskets, charming white wicker indoor and outdoor furniture, appliquéd and patchwork pillows, and unusually wide (11 feet) rag rugs. New quilts are produced to the Gazebo's specifications with American fabrics in Haiti. Both quilts and rugs can be custom-made. ♦ M-Sa 10AM-7PM; Su noon-6PM. 127 E. 57th St (between Lexington and Park Aves). 832.7077

162 The Galleria This midblock tower, designed in 1975 chiefly by **David Kenneth Specter** and **Philip Birnbaum,** comprises luxury apartments above a health club, retail facilities, and a public through-block arcade. At least at the Galleria—unlike at Olympic Tower—the passerby knows there is something inside. Also worthwhile is the individualistic silhouette created by a multi-greenhouse quadriplex (considered Manhattan's most expensive apartment) custom-built for philanthropist **Stewart Mott.** He never lived here, however. Apparently Mott had such passion for fresh milk that he wanted to keep cows on the roof, and the building's board turned him down. ♦ 117 E. 57th St (between Lexington and Park Aves)

163 Mitsukoshi ★★★$$$$ Follow the lead of Japanese businessmen and come here for perfect sushi in a comfortable setting. ♦ Japanese ♦ Lunch and dinner. Closed Saturday and Sunday. 461 Park Ave (at E. 57th St). Reservations recommended. 935.6444

163 Ritz Tower **Emery Roth** and **Carrère & Hastings** built this 42-story tower in 1925 as part of the **Hearst** apartment-hotel chain. Its stepped spire is still a distinctive mark in the skyline. ♦ 465 Park Ave (at E. 57th St)

164 Argosy Gallery Few places in the United States have a better selection of historical pictures: photographs, posters, playbills, maps, engravings, lithographs, etchings, and woodcuts. ♦ M-F 9AM-5:30PM; Sa 10AM-4:30PM. 116 E. 59th St (between Lexington and Park Aves). 753.4455

165 Helene Arpels The pampered feet of **Jacqueline de Ribes** and **Marie-Helene de Rothschild** are among those sporting Helene Arpels designs. Shoes for both men and women can be custom-decorated with hand embroidery, bead appliqué, stone studding, or exotic leathers. ♦ M-Sa 10AM-6:30PM. 470 Park Ave (between E. 57th and E. 58th Sts). 755.1623

166 Four Seasons Hotel $$$$ Opened in 1993 and the tallest hotel in town, the 52-story world-class Four Seasons was designed by the revered **I.M. Pei.** The sparse limestone lobby with its 33-foot onyx ceiling and serene public areas has been compared to a soaring marble mausoleum, cool and Zen-like in its simplicity. But the 367 elegant and spacious (600-square-foot) rooms are considerably cozier and warmer, with Art Deco-influenced decor and wonderful views of the city and Central Park. Services befitting of such a deluxe operation include 24-hour concierge, well-equipped fitness facilities, an executive business center, and **"5757,"** a contemporary American grill/restaurant serving breakfast, lunch, and dinner. If you're not content with your room's 120-square-foot bathroom, look into the heart-stopping $4,000-a-night **Presidential Suite.** ♦ 57 E. 57th St (between Park and Madison Aves). 758.5700, 800/332.3442; fax 758.5711

166 Louis Vuitton Luggage and leather accessories with the familiar LV signature fill the store. ♦ M-F 10AM-5:30PM; Sa 10AM-5PM. 51 E. 57th St (between Park and Madison Aves). 371.6111

167 Buccellati Silver New York's most opulent handcrafted silver, including flatware, is sold in this store. ♦ M-F 9:30AM-5:30PM; Sa 10AM-6PM. 46 E. 57th St (between Park and Madison Aves). 308.2507

167 David Saity If you don't think of New York as being the right source for authentic Native American jewelry, you haven't seen the window display of this well-known jeweler. Possibly the country's largest collection of rare, antique, and contemporary jewelry and accessories, each piece is of exceptional quality, handcrafted by past and present master artisans of the Zuni, Hopi, and Navajo tribes. ♦ M-Sa 10AM-6PM. 48 E. 57th St (between Madison and Park Aves). 223.8125. Also at: Trump Tower, 725 Fifth Ave, fifth floor. 308.6570

167 Sherle Wagner International Film stars, industrialists, and kings and queens are among the clientele of this purveyor of the most luxurious bathtubs, toilets, and sinks, including tubs of rose quartz, counters of tigereye, bidets of marble, and gold-plated basins. ♦ M-F 9:15AM-5PM. 60 E. 57th St (between Park and Madison Aves). 758.3300

168 Le Chantilly ★★$$$$ The vast room, bustling with service people who somehow never seem to be near your table when you need them, makes you feel as if you're dining on a deluxe ocean liner. But that doesn't keep Le Chantilly's affluent clientele away. Technically, the classic cuisine is excellent. ♦ French ♦ Lunch and dinner; dinner only on Sunday. 106 E. 57th St (between Lexington and Park Aves). Jacket required. Reservations recommended. 751.2931

168 Universal Pictures Building This 1947 building by **Kahn & Jacobs** is noteworthy as the first office building on this previously residential section of Park Avenue and as the first to be built to the "wedding cake" outline of the then-current zoning regulations. It is perhaps the best example of pre-glass-curtain wall design. Compare it to its 1972 counterpart across the street at 450 Park Avenue. ♦ 445 Park Ave (between E. 56th and E. 57th Sts)

169 The Lombardy $$ Built in 1927 by **Henry Mandell,** this residential hotel has transient suites and studios, each with a different decor and all with serving pantries and refrigerators. ♦ 111 E. 56th St (between Lexington and Park Aves). 753.8600; fax 754.5683

170 Mercedes-Benz Showroom One of New York City's rare works by **Frank Lloyd Wright,** this 1955 design is a curious exercise in glass, ramp, plants, and fancy cars in a too-tight space. ♦ 430 Park Ave (at E. 56th St)

171 The Drake Swissôtel $$$ Built by **Emery Roth** in 1927, this hotel was purchased by real-estate entrepreneur **William Zeckendorf** in the 1960s and became the home of the city's first discotheque, **Shepheards.** In 1980, it was restored by the Swissôtel chain to its original elegance, and is more a setting for chamber music than rock. Amenities include refrigerators in every room, 24-hour room service, concierge, and parking facilities. ♦ 440 Park Ave (at E. 56th St). 421.0900, 800/372.5369; fax 688.8053

172 The Pace Gallery Among the heaviest of the city's heavy hitters, Pace represents a formidable roster of artists and artists' estates, including **Jim Dine, Chuck Close, Louise Nevelson, Mark Rothko,** and **Lucas Samaras.** Housed in the same building are the gallery's many offspring—**Pace Prints, Pace Master Prints, Pace Primitive Art,** and **Pace/MacGill** for 20th-century photography. ♦ Tu-Sa 10AM-6PM. 32 E. 57th St (between Madison and Park Aves). 421.3292. Also at: 142 Greene St. 431.9224

172 Guy Laroche The city's only outpost for the ready-to-wear collection of this French label carries everything from silk camisoles to full-length ball gowns. ♦ M-Sa 10AM-6PM. 36 E. 57th St (between Madison and Park Aves). 759.2301

173 Fuller Building The identification over the entrance of this black-and-white Art Deco tower, designed in 1929 by **Walker & Gillette,** is graced with a pair of figures by sculptor **Elie Nadelman.** The building is home to many art galleries, including **Marisa del Re, André Emmerich,** and **Susan Sheehan.** ♦ 41 E. 57th St (at Madison Ave)

173 Ronin Gallery This is the place to see Japanese art, including woodblock prints, ivory netsuke, and metalwork from the 17th through 20th centuries. The gallery offers free appraisals of Japanese art. ♦ M-Sa 10:30AM-5:30PM. 605 Madison Ave (between E. 57th and E. 58th Sts). 688.0188

174 IBM Building This 43-story green granite building, designed in 1982 by **Edward Larrabee Barnes,** rises dramatically over a high atrium containing tables and chairs for relaxing and lots of bamboo to take your mind off Midtown's hectic pace. That water rushing by outside the 56th Street entrance is a horizontal fountain designed by **Michael Helzer.** In a small space downstairs, high-quality exhibits of art, science, and technology are mounted. ♦ 590 Madison Ave (between E. 56th and E. 57th Sts)

175 James II Galleries Edwardian and Victorian jewelry, Spode pottery, ironstone, majolica, brass, silver plate, and Art Nouveau and Art Deco silver are featured. ♦ M-F 10AM-5PM; Sa 10:30AM-4:30PM. 15 E. 57th St (between Madison and Fifth Aves). 355.7040

175 Hermès Saddlery, scarves, and silk shirts are sold at this Parisian original. ♦ M-Sa 10AM-6PM. 11 E. 57th St (between Madison and Fifth Aves), ground floor. 751.3181

176 Burberrys The Burberrys raincoat has incomparable style, but the rest of the clothes for men and women, including hats, coats, jackets, trousers, and skirts, do not—unless you like to look the way the British royal family does on a rainy day in Scotland. ♦ M-W, F-Sa 9:30AM-6PM; Th 9:30AM-7PM; Su noon-5PM. 9 E. 57th St (at Fifth Ave). 371.5010

176 Chanel A main-floor boutique and second-floor showroom display the increasingly popular Chanel fashions. ♦ M-W, F 10AM-6:30PM; Th 10AM-7PM; Sa 10AM-6PM; Su noon-5PM. 5 E. 57th St (at Fifth Ave). 355.5050

176 Warner Brothers Studio Store Smack in the middle of a tony enclave of luxury stores and sky-high real estate is this three-story Hollywood-inspired shopping center that resembles a high-tech back lot, with TV screens playing old Warner Brothers movies. The gift-shop area is filled with watches, address books, posters, ties, mugs, and more. But if you're not in the mood to buy any of the 3,000 items (much of it apparel), just come for the experience. ♦ M-F 10AM-8PM; Sa 10AM-6PM; Su noon-6PM. 1 E. 57th St (at Fifth Ave). 754.0300

177 David McKee Gallery This small but very smart gallery boasts an impressive list of youngish artists like sculptor **Martin Puryear** and painters **Sean Scully** and **Jake Berthot,** as well as the estate of the influential **Philip Guston.** ♦ Tu-Sa 10AM-6PM. 745 Fifth Ave (between E. 57th and E. 58th Sts). 688.5951

177 Forum Twentieth-century figurative American paintings and sculpture are featured in this gallery. ♦ Tu-Sa 10AM-5:30PM. 745 Fifth Ave (between E. 57th and E. 58th Sts). 355.4545

177 Bergdorf Goodman Men According to Bergdorf's chairman, **Ira Neimark,** this store is "for the sort of men who dine at the best restaurants, stay at the best hotels, and join the best clubs." What do these men wear? Shirts from **Turnbull & Asser** and **Charvet;** suits from **Brioni, Luciana Barbera,** and **St. Andrews;** sportswear from **Willis & Geiger.** Additional boutiques within the store include the **London Tack Shop, W & H Gidden, Hermès, Lacoste,** and **Kentshire Antiques.** ♦ M-W, F-Sa 10AM-6PM; Th 10AM-8PM. 745 Fifth Ave (between E. 57th and E. 58th Sts). 753.7300

178 Bergdorf Goodman Bergdorf's is the most luxurious of the city's legendary department stores. Although there is some moderately priced merchandise, the idea that living well is the best revenge permeates the store, partly because of the architecture (high ceilings, delicate moldings, arched windows) and partly because of the wares. Bergdorf's was the first store to promote the designers of Milan with a vengeance. All the merchandise bears the stamp of luxury, whether it's the impeccable clothes of **Donna Karan** and **Sonia Rykiel,** the iridescent jewelry of **Ted Muehling,** the aromatic scents from London's **Penhaligon,** delicate candies from **Manon Chocolates,** or glove-leather bags by **Paloma Picasso. Van Cleef & Arpels** has its inexpensive boutique in this store, meaning that you can find a bauble for a little less than a small fortune. The salespeople are helpful, low-key, and candid. There is also a beauty salon (**Frederic Fekkai**) and a cafe. ♦ M-W, F-Sa 10AM-6PM; Th 10AM-8PM. 754 Fifth Ave (between W. 57th and W. 58th Sts). 753.7300

178 Van Cleef & Arpels When the late **Shah of Iran** needed a tiara made for his **Empress Farah,** he came here. The boutique department, where jewelry ranges from moderate to expensive, is actually in **Bergdorf's** main store next door, while gemstones that cost more are sold here. Jewelry can be custom-designed. Estate jewelry is also bought and sold. The guard is formidable, but the salespeople at least deign to acknowledge customers who make it past him. ♦ M-W, F-Sa 10AM-5:45PM; Th 10AM-7:30PM. 744 Fifth Ave (at W. 57th St). 644.9500

179 9 West 57th Street Designed in 1974 by **Skidmore, Owings & Merrill,** the best feature of this black glass swoop—built at the same time and by the same designers as the **W.R. Grace Building** on 42nd Street—is its address: the big red "9" is by graphic designer **Ivan Chermayeff.** ♦ Between Fifth and Sixth Aves

180 The Crown Building At 26 stories, this was once the tallest building on Fifth Avenue above 42nd Street. Originally called the **Heckscher Building,** it was designed by **Warren & Wetmore** and built in 1922 as a wholesale center for women's fashions. In 1929, the **Museum of Modern Art** opened its first gallery here. The gold leaf on the facade and tower is recent, as is the lighting of this entire intersection. ◆ 730 Fifth Ave (between W. 56th and W. 57th Sts)

181 Galeries Lafayette This 85,000-square-foot space is home to a branch of France's largest department store. ◆ M-Sa 10AM-6:30PM; Su noon-6PM. 4 E. 57th St (at Fifth Ave). 355.0022

181 Tiffany & Co. Built in 1940 by **Cross & Cross,** this store has become so famous for quality and style that many of its well-designed wares are now classic gifts: the all-purpose wineglass, the Wedgwood drabware, a sterling silver baby rattle in the shape of a dumbbell—all enhanced by the cachet of a gift in a Tiffany box. There is also elegant jewelry by **Elsa Peretti** and **Paloma Picasso,** plus three floors of gems, stationery, crystal, porcelain, clocks, and watches at all prices. Tiffany windows are worth going out of your way to see—especially at Christmas. ◆ M-W, F 10AM-5:30PM; Th 10AM-7PM. 727 Fifth Ave (between E. 56th and E. 57th Sts). 755.8000

182 Trump Tower Donald Trump, the developer whose name this building bears, currently lives here in a triplex. Offices fill the lower floors, along with a glitzy six-story atrium with pricey boutiques and restaurants. Built in 1983, the tower was designed by **Der Scutt** of **Swanke, Hayden, Connell & Partners.** ◆ 725 Fifth Ave (at E. 56th St). 832.2000

183 Steuben More like a museum than a store, Steuben showcases engraved sculptures featuring Chinese calligraphy, animals, or even a forest of spreading pine. All are displayed in backlit glass cases in a gray-walled sanctuary. The hoi polloi find crystal in the shape of dolphins, elephants, and hippopotamuses. ◆ M-W, F-Sa 10AM-6PM; Th 10AM-8PM. 717 Fifth Ave (at E. 56th St). 752.1441, 800/424.4240

184 Henri Bendel The windows are among the most imaginative in New York, but don't stop there. This exclusive store is filled with unique merchandise, including tabletop wares by **Frank McIntosh,** and it's still fun to kick up your heels and announce you just got those stunning shoes at Bendel's (be sure to say "BEN-dls," as the natives do). ◆ M-W, F-Sa 10AM-6:30PM; Th 10AM-8PM; Su noon-6PM. 712 Fifth Ave (between W. 55th and W. 56th Sts). 247.1100

184 Harry Winston, Inc. The father of this world-famous seller of diamonds owned a little jewelry store on Columbus Avenue, but Harry went into business for himself while he was still a teenager and eventually established what may be the most intimidating diamond salon in the city. It is the only store on Fifth Avenue that processes diamonds from rough stones to finished jewelry. ◆ M-Sa 9AM-5PM. 718 Fifth Ave (at W. 56th St). 245.2000

FELIϟϟiMO

184 Felissimo Located within a turn-of-the-century town house built by **Warren & Wetmore** in 1901, this store is the first U.S. outlet of one of the most successful retailers in Japan. It carries men's and women's clothing, accessories, and gifts. ◆ M-W, F-Sa 10AM-6PM; Th 10AM-8PM. 10 W. 56th St (between Fifth and Sixth Aves). 956.4438

185 Grace Borgenicht Masters of 20th-century art and promising newcomers are shown here. ◆ Tu-F 10AM-5:30PM; Sa 11AM-5:30PM. 724 Fifth Ave (at W. 56th St), eighth floor. 247.2111

185 Virginia Zabriskie American and European painting, sculpture, and photography of the 20th century are shown in this quality gallery. ◆ Tu-Sa 10AM-5:30PM. 724 Fifth Ave (at W. 56th St), 12th floor. 307.7430

185 Doubleday The larger of the 2 Manhattan Doubledays keeps a high profile of new releases, backlist, audio and magazines on 4 well-arranged floors. Especially good for fiction, cookbooks, and art. ◆ 724 Fifth Ave (at W. 56th St). 397.0550. Also at Citicorp Center, 153 E. 53rd St. 223.3301

185 OMO Norma Kamali Kamali is the designer who put many American women into high-fashion sweatshirt dresses, blouses, slit skirts, and cocoon wraps. The bottom floor of the store carries less expensive cottons and knits, while the upstairs floor has one-of-a-kind evening gowns, loose or skin-tight dresses, outerwear, and her famous, provocatively cut swimsuits. ◆ M-F 10AM-6:30PM; Sa 11AM-6PM. 11 W. 56th St (between Fifth and Sixth Aves). 957.9797

186 Kiiroi Hana ★★★$$ Good sake meets excellent service in this great Japanese restaurant with a simple but carefully selected menu. Sit at the sushi bar for fresh and beautifully arranged fish prepared by pleasant chefs. ◆ Japanese ◆ Lunch and dinner; dinner only on Sunday. 23 W. 56th St (between Fifth and Sixth Aves). Reservations recommended for dinner. 582.7499

Articles for sale in the United Nations gift shop are duty-free because the UN is not officially in any country. The gift shop offers items from every member nation.

187 Darbar Indian Restaurant ★★★$$$ Darbar is easily one of the best Indian restaurants in town, from every point of view. The decor is authentic and beautiful, and if you want a quiet little table in the corner, there are several downstairs, separated by screens that give complete privacy. The staff is friendly and helpful, and the kitchen thoroughly professional. To start, try the delightful *pakoras* (fried spinach fritters) and move on to the *josh vindaloo*, a lamb stew cooked with potatoes in a hot curry sauce. ♦ Indian ♦ Lunch and dinner; dinner only on Saturday and Sunday. 44 W. 56th St (between Fifth and Sixth Aves). Reservations recommended. 432.7227

188 Harley Davidson Cafe ★$$ Welcome to Harleywood. First there was the Hard Rock and Planet Hollywood, then this highly hyped restaurant with a $3 million-plus price tag roared into town. Located in the formerly staid American Savings Bank building, the cafe seats up to 300 (with room for as many as 100 in Midtown's largest outdoor seating area). And yes, Harleys dangle from the ceiling in an atmosphere somewhere between Mardi Gras and mayhem. The menu features "great American road food." ♦ American ♦ Lunch, dinner, and late-night meals. 1370 Sixth Ave (at W. 56th St). 245.6000

189 Frumkin/Adams Gallery The blue-ribbon stable of contemporary artists includes **Jack Beal, Robert Arneson,** and **Luis Cruz Azaceta.** ♦ Tu-F 10AM-6PM; Sa 10AM-5:30PM. 50 W. 57th St (between Fifth and Sixth Aves), second floor. 757.6655

189 Marlborough Gallery One of New York's old-line establishments represents some of the most important names in European and American art, including **Larry Rivers, Fernando Botero, Red Grooms,** and **Magdalena Abakanowicz.** ♦ M-Sa 10AM-5:30PM. 40 W. 57th St (between Fifth and Sixth Aves), second floor. 541.4900

189 Kennedy Galleries Works by American artists from the 18th century on, including **John Singleton Copley, Edward Hopper, Georgia O'Keeffe,** and **John Marin,** are shown at this gallery, founded in 1874. Its catalogs are wonderful, too. ♦ Tu-Sa 9:30AM-5:30PM. 40 W. 57th St (between Fifth and Sixth Aves), fifth floor. 541.9600

190 J.N. Bartfield Galleries & Books Nineteenth-century American and European art, including works by **Remington, Russell,** and other masters of the American West, are displayed here, along with elegantly bound antiquarian books by famous authors such as **Shakespeare** and **Dickens.** ♦ M-F 10AM-5PM; Sa 10AM-3PM. 30 W. 57th St (between Fifth and Sixth Aves), third floor. 245.8890

190 Galerie St. Etienne This import from Vienna features Austrian and German Expressionists as well as European and American folk art. ♦ Tu-Sa 11AM-5PM. 24 W. 57th St (between Fifth and Sixth Aves), eighth floor. 245.6734

190 William H. Schab Gallery Master prints and drawings by such artists as **Delacroix, Dürer, Piranesi,** and **Rembrandt** are showcased. ♦ Tu-Sa 9:30AM-5:30PM. 24 W. 57th St (between Fifth and Sixth Aves). 974.0337

Small-Fry in the Big Apple: Ten Terrific Things for Kids

1 Young audiences are encouraged to participate when the **Little People's Theater Company** stages such favorites as *Humpty Dumpty Falls in Love* at the **Courtyard Playhouse.**

2 Feel like a shrimp under the 10-ton blue whale or get lost in the stars at the planetarium, both at the **American Museum of Natural History.**

3 Little sweet teeth will love the fabulously tasty **Bocce Ball** (Italian ice cream covered with chocolate), but even the simple two-scoop cone is grand when eaten at **Rumpelmayer's.**

4 The **New York City Ballet's** *Nutcracker Suite* brings dancing toy soldiers, evil mice, and sugarplum fairies to **Lincoln Center.**

5 The **New York Philharmonic's Young People's Concerts** at **Avery Fisher Hall** include talks to introduce kids to classical music.

6 Getting into the **Brooklyn Children's Museum** through a 180-foot tunnel and waterway is half the fun.

7 You can climb up on a mushroom and join Alice, the Cheshire Cat, and the Mock Turtle at **José de Creeft's** statue overlooking **Central Park's Conservatory Water.**

8 One of the best ways to enjoy **Lower Manhattan** is with a view from the river of a replica of an 18th-century steamboat at the **South Street Seaport.**

9 Hear readings from your favorite book by the author at **Books of Wonder.**

10 Produce your own newscasts and public affairs programs at the **Time Warner Center for Media** at the **Children's Museum of Manhattan.**

New York traffic engineers have not taken on the project of installing Walk/Don't Walk lights (a.k.a. "ped" lights) on Park Avenue between 46th and 56th streets because of what lies barely eight inches below: the tunnels in and out of Grand Central Station.

190 Marian Goodman Gallery Goodman's stark but generous space is devoted to a host of weighty imported talents, including the German painter **Anselm Kiefer** and British sculptor **Tony Cragg.** Don't miss the gallery's new space, where **Multiples,** Goodman's print-publishing arm, displays its wares. ◆ M-Sa 10AM-6PM. 24 W. 57th St (between Fifth and Sixth Aves), fourth floor. 977.7160

190 Grand Central Art Galleries Begun by artists **John Singer Sargent, Walter Clark,** and **Edmond Greacen** in 1922, the exhibitions include Realist portraits, still lifes, sculpture, and the work of more than a hundred artists. ◆ W-F 10AM-5:30PM; Sa 10AM-4PM. 24 W. 57th St (between Fifth and Sixth Aves), second floor. 867.3344

190 Susan Bennis/Warren Edwards The designers of this collection of shoes for men and women use such exotic skins as baby crocodile, ostrich, and emu. Styles include sexy hot-weather sandals, tasseled loafers, evening pumps of lace and *peau de soie* for women, patent leather for men, and boots in unusual materials and colors. ◆ M-W, F 10AM-6:30PM; Th 10AM-8PM; Sa 10AM-6PM; Su noon-6PM. 22 W. 57th St (between Fifth and Sixth Aves). 755.4197

190 Blum Helman Gallery This unusually large space features contemporary American painting and sculpture. ◆ Tu-Sa 10AM-6PM. 20 W. 57th St (between Fifth and Sixth Aves), second and eighth floors. 245.2888

191 Rizzoli Bookstore The ultimate bookstore, Rizzoli is reminiscent of an oak-paneled library in an opulent Italian villa, with classical music playing (records are for sale) and a hushed, unhurried atmosphere. Rizzoli is known for foreign-language, travel, art, architecture, and design books. It also has an outstanding foreign and domestic general interest and design periodical department and a small gallery upstairs. All is well looked after by president and publisher **Gianfranco Monacelli.** The building dates from the turn of the century, and was restored in 1985 by **Hardy Holzman Pfeiffer Associates.** ◆ M-Sa 9AM-8PM; Su 10AM-7:30PM. 31 W. 57th St (between Fifth and Sixth Aves). 759.2424

191 Brewster Gallery The graphics at this gallery are by such important European artists as **Picasso, Miró,** and **Chagall.** ◆ Tu-Sa 10:30AM-5:30PM. 41 W. 57th St (between Fifth and Sixth Aves), second floor. 980.1975

191 Hacker Art Books This store features in- and out-of-print books and reprints, plus some excellent bargains on the literature of the visual arts. ◆ M-Sa 9:30AM-6PM. 45 W. 57th St (between Fifth and Sixth Aves). 688.7600

Restaurants/Clubs: Red
Shops/ 🌳 Outdoors: Green

Hotels: Blue
Sights/Culture: Black

192 Jean Lafitte ★$$ This cozy Parisian-style neighborhood bistro in the heart of Manhattan is no flash in the pan—it's been around for years, thanks to a reliably good menu and loads of charm. Soups on a wintery day and an authentic *choucroute* come highly recommended. A visit to Jean Lafitte is a lovely way to start or finish an evening at nearby Carnegie Hall. ◆ French ◆ Lunch, dinner, and late-night meals; dinner only on Saturday and Sunday. 68 W. 58th St (between Fifth and Sixth Aves). 751.2323

193 Wyndham Hotel $$ This remarkably comfortable hotel is a favorite with stars appearing on Broadway, many of whom, such as **Peter Falk, Hume Cronyn,** and the late **Ingrid Bergman,** could easily have afforded to stay at the Plaza. Some stars, planning for a long Broadway run, have been known to arrive with their own furniture. ◆ 42 W. 58th St (between Fifth and Sixth Aves). 753.3500; fax 754.5638

194 The Manhattan Ocean Club ★★★$$$$ The excellent seafood here reflects an often overlooked fact—that New York is still a port, with access to the treasures of the sea. Try the appetizer of seared tuna with lattice potatoes and salsa verde or the main course of grilled swordfish with cream of lentil curry and crisp onions. The owner's personal collection of more than a dozen **Picasso** ceramics is on display. ◆ Seafood ◆ Lunch and dinner; dinner only on Saturday and Sunday. 57 W. 58th St (between Fifth and Sixth Aves). Jacket, tie, and reservations recommended. 371.7777

195 St. Moritz on the Park $$ Designed in 1931 by **Emery Roth & Sons,** this strictly business hotel has small but comfortable rooms. A fax machine is available. Other niceties are room service, a newsstand, and a gift shop. ◆ 50 Central Park South (at Sixth Ave). 755.5800, 800/221.4774; fax 751.2952

Within St. Moritz on the Park:

Cafe de la Paix ★$$$ Take a breather at possibly the best sidewalk cafe in the neighborhood, which is to be expected, considering the location. Have an anisette or orange cappuccino and soak up the atmosphere and the parade of people. ◆ Continental ◆ Lunch and dinner. 755.5800

Rumpelmayer's $$ Viennese pastries and ice-cream concoctions are served in the company of a collection of stuffed animals at this perennial kiddie-pleaser. Anyone under 50 who grew up in Manhattan will tell you that

195

Rumplemayer's is the place to go for hot chocolate. ♦ Continental ♦ Breakfast, lunch, dinner, and late-night meals. 755.5800

196 Mickey Mantle's ★★$$ This is a great place to bring the kids. They can watch the day's big game or memorable moments in the world of sports on huge video screens, study the restaurant's collection of uniforms and memorabilia and, if they're lucky, catch sight of the man himself, who is often around to say "hi" and sign postcards. The food—gigantic burgers, ribs, hot-fudge sundaes—will please a not-too-finicky sports fan. ♦ American ♦ Lunch and dinner. 42 Central Park South (between Fifth and Sixth Aves). 688.7777

196 Park Lane Hotel $$$ A relative newcomer to the neighborhood, the arches at the top of this 46-story building designed by **Emery Roth & Sons** in 1971 add interest to the block. The always controversial **Harry** and **Leona Helmsley,** who own several hotels and a lot of real estate in Manhattan, once picked this as their own home address. Marble and chandeliers abound, and the multilingual staff is alert and eager to please. ♦ 36 Central Park South (between Fifth and Sixth Aves). 371.4000, 800/221.4982; fax 319.9065

197 Grand Army Plaza One of the city's few formal pedestrian spaces, the plaza acts as both a forecourt to the **Plaza Hotel** and as an entrance terrace to **Central Park.** Although the wall of the square has been weakened by the **GM Building,** the center has held strong, solidly anchored by the circular **Pulitzer Memorial Fountain,** built with funds provided in **Joseph Pulitzer's** will and designed by **Carrère & Hastings.** The sculpture on top is by **Karl Bitter,** and the equestrian statue of **General William Tecumseh Sherman** (by **Augustus Saint-Gaudens**) was displayed at the World Exhibition in Paris in 1900 and was erected here in 1903. Tradition still survives in the horse-drawn carriages. They were the limousines of another era, and in the 1930s, Hollywood loved to send romancing couples off in them for jaunts in Central Park. You can still take a romantic ride through the park in a carriage, many with top-hatted drivers. ♦ Fifth Ave (between W. 58th and W. 60th Sts)

In the movie *The House on Carroll Street,* there is a scene in which Nazi spies run on beams above the ceiling of Grand Central Station; one of them falls through, 125 feet to the floor.

197 The Plaza Hotel $$$ The Plaza (shown above) is a legend in its own time, a landmark that has hosted **Teddy Roosevelt,** the **Beatles,** and **F. Scott Fitzgerald** and his wife, **Zelda** (who, it's rumored, danced nude in the fountain out front). **Solomon R. Guggenheim** lived for years in the **State Suite** surrounded by fabulous paintings, and **Frank Lloyd Wright** made the Plaza his New York headquarters. A book called *Eloise*—about a precious little girl who lived at the Plaza—was even written about it. Its latest extravaganza was the Christmas 1993 wedding of mega-developer **Donald Trump** and **Marla Maples,** attended by 1,000 VIP guests.

This stylish Edwardian/French pile dating from 1907 is considered one of architect **Henry J. Hardenbergh's** masterpieces (he also did the **Dakota** apartments). **Warren & Wetmore** oversaw the 1921 addition. Located on a unique site with two sides of the building equally exposed, the dignified hotel has survived many years as the center of high social activity. Rooms vary wildly. Many of the lovely high-ceilinged ones are still in top condition, but some face air shafts. Request an outside room—or better still, a park view. The 24-hour room service remains, and so do the flags outside representing countries of important foreign guests. **Donald Trump** bought the Plaza in 1988; his now ex-wife, **Ivana,** oversaw a major renovation and hired several of New York's top hotel personnel, but she has since left. The **Oak Bar and Restaurant** is still in its original (woody, elegant, and comfortable) condition; the **Oyster Bar** still opens sparkling fresh clams and oysters to order; and the venerable, paneled **Edwardian Room** is still a fashionable spot for dining and dancing. The fabled **Palm Court** in the lobby is fine and festive, particularly as a choice for high tea. Also in the lobby are an art gallery and a **Neuchatel** chocolate shop. ♦ W. 59th St at Fifth Ave. 759.3000, 800/759.3000; fax 759.3167

198 FAO Schwarz Because this is the best-stocked toy store in the United States, some parents never bring their kids here; the sight of so many toys can turn children into monsters of greed. The inexhaustible stock includes Madame Alexander dolls, Steiff stuffed animals, LGB electric trains, outdoor swings, magic tricks, video games, and hundreds of other amusements. At Christmastime you may have to wait in line just to go inside. ♦ M-Sa 9AM-9PM; Su 10AM-8PM. 767 Fifth Ave (between E. 58th and E. 59th Sts). 644.9400

199 Baccarat The world-famous crystal, plus **Limoges** china and fine glassware and silver, are sold. ♦ M-Sa 10AM-6PM. 625 Madison Ave (between E. 58th and E. 59th Sts). 826.4100

Bests

Ed Levine
Author, *New York Eats*

The **Second Avenue Deli** is one of the last old-time Jewish delis in New York. Have mushroom barley soup, a pastrami sandwich, and an order of fries. Then wander around the East Village and the Lower East Side. There you'll find what's left of our melting pot. Ukrainian shops coexist peacefully with Muslim meat markets, Polish bakeries, and pasta stores.

Have a meal at the **Union Square Cafe.** They're serious about food without being in the least bit pretentious. It's one of the few great restaurants in New York that treats everyone like a regular.

Go to **Madison Avenue** and window shop at the **Valentino** and the **Armani** boutiques. Don't even think about buying anything, unless you plan on taking out a second mortgage on your home. Then head up to the **Lexington Candy Shop** and have a shrimp salad sandwich and either a lemonade or a coffee malt. There you'll get a feel of what a real New York luncheonette is all about.

Fairway Market has a wonderful selection of produce, cheese, bread, and coffee. Next, wander up Broadway to **Zabar's** and check out the smoked fish and the cookware. Then walk over to the **Museum of Natural History** and see the dinosaurs.

Wander around **SoHo** checking out the shops and galleries. Then go to **Melampo Imported Foods** for the best focaccia sandwich you've ever eaten. Take your sandwich next door to the playground and sit at one of the booths the city has conveniently constructed for Melampo sandwich buyers.

Fred Ferretti
Columnist, *Gourmet* magazine

A bowl of fresh and thick barley soup with mushrooms in **Ratner's Dairy Restaurant** on the Lower East Side. With onion rolls.

The cooking, on any day, in the very best of the city's French restaurants—**Lutèce**, where André Soltner remains a municipal treasure; **La Reserve**, an outpost of elegant restraint under Jean-Louis Missud; and **Montrachet**, where Debra Ponzek creates the most intense of flavors.

Some of the best Italian cooking, in a place overrun by Italian restaurants, in, of all places, **Le Cirque**, where Sirio Maccioni is teaching its bright young French chefs the niceties of *la cucina rustica*.

There is nothing better than a hot dog, boiled on a street cart, served with a lot of mustard and a bit of sauerkraut, and eaten while sitting with **General Sherman** at the entrance to **Central Park.**

The 100-year-old Spanish tiles, the Tiffany lamp, the marble statuary, the lure of the city's most romantic restaurant, **Café Nicholson.**

Breakfast, lunch, or dinner, provided they have slabs of that rough country pâté, at **Café des Artistes**, just outside Central Park's western border.

The upper right-field stands of **Yankee Stadium** on a hot Sunday afternoon with a cold beer, hoping that Don Mattingly will hit one near you.

The best steak in the city at **Sparks Steak House,** with a selection from what may well be New York's best list of American wines.

Jimmy Breslin
Writer, *New York Newsday*

Rao V in the rain, looking up the steps at the sidewalk. Probably Manhattan's oldest restaurant.

Cafe 2000 on 101st Avenue and 103rd Street in Ozone Park, Queens, where you sit at a table over espresso in the morning and watch old women come down stone steps of a great old church while bells toll. Europe in Queens.

Meat market by the **Howard Beach Station** of the A train. Women sit on stools and talk in the morning while the butchers work and the women sit facing the counter and watch like hawks.

Walk in **Rockaway** at dusk from 116th Street to the end of **Riis Park** and back with the sky rose on purple and the waves spitting white into the cold air.

Sit at night on **Shore Road** and watch the *Queen Elizabeth II* slide under the Verrazano Bridge. The ship at first seems to be part of another shore. Then you see it moving so quickly.

Don Peppe Vesuvio Restaurant, Lefferts Boulevard and South Conduit Avenue in Richmond Hill, Queens. Look into the kitchen as the waiters and chefs scream at each other. A fight, at first. Then you hear that the bitterness is over a horse that lost at Aqueduct, right around the corner. Then the waiters bring out tubs of mussels and clams. One of the world's great restaurants. Caters to racetrack people with taste.

Coming from Queens to Manhattan at night over the **Queensboro Bridge.**

Living anywhere on the water in Brooklyn Heights, Williamsburg, Long Island City, or up on the hill in Maspeth and Middle Village in Queens and looking over at Manhattan. The people in Manhattan can only see Queens with its Pepsi-Cola signs. The smart people live in Queens and get a view that is unique in the world, even to photos, for the most sophisticated camera people don't know where these neighborhoods are.

The **May Wave** in the **Ramble** at **Central Park** and in the **Bird Sanctuary** at **Jamaica Bay.** The flocks come north again and on 10 May the same birds are in the same places. For decades the same type of bird is in the same spot, in the Ramble or at the bird sanctuary. So many types that even the best books cannot have them all cataloged. They are en route to Canada and as far as the North Pole.

Third Avenue and **42nd Street** and all the sidewalks in every direction at 5PM. Crowds of such size that it is hard to think that one place can hold them.

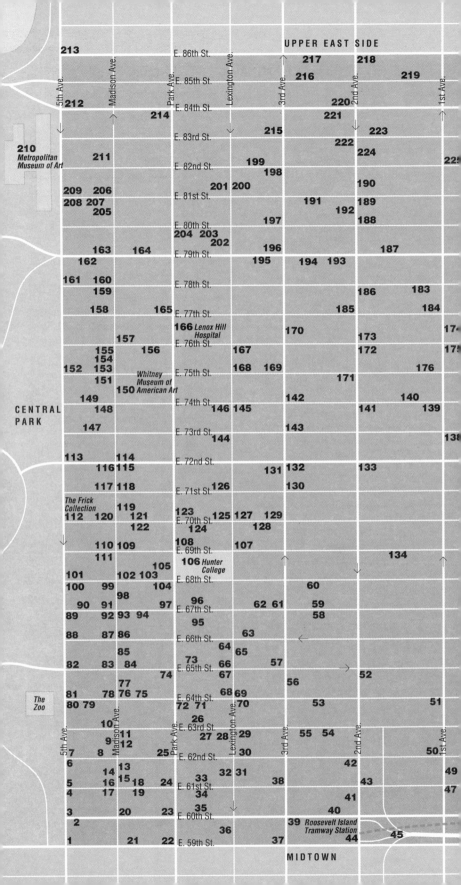

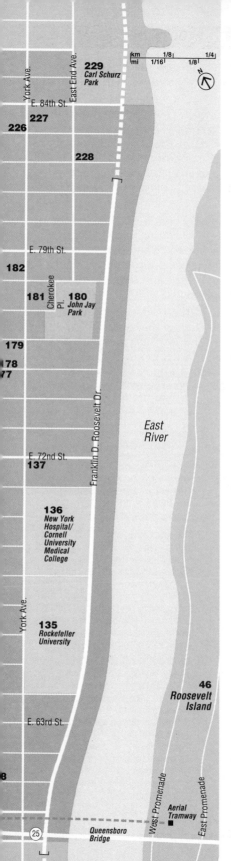

East Side

In the 1920s, the *New York Times* described the East Side as "a string of pearls: each pearl is a double block of millionaires, and Madison Avenue is the string." Like everything else about New York, the East Side has been altered by time. But there are few places in the city where memory is as intact as in the blocks bounded by **E. 59th** and **E. 86th streets**, and **Fifth Avenue** and the **East River.**

Until the close of the Civil War, this was the part of New York where the fashionable gathered to escape city summers—the counterpart of today's Hamptons on Long Island's South Shore. At the end of the 18th century, a necklace of mansions in parklike settings followed the shore of the East River all the way to Harlem. The Boston Post Road, now Third Avenue, made access to the city below Canal Street convenient, and summer residents with lots of leisure time traveled downtown on steamboats. By the late 1860s, the old summer houses were converted to year-round use for pioneering commuters, and, a few years later, the coming of elevated railroads on Second and Third avenues opened the area to working-class people.

The improved transportation brought summer fun-seekers as well. The area bounded by E. 66th and E. 75th streets from Third Avenue to the East River became **Jones's Wood.** It included such attractions as a beer garden, a bathhouse, an athletic club, and a block-long coliseum for indoor entertainment.

High society became firmly ensconced on the East Side when **Caroline Schermerhorn Astor** built a mansion on Fifth Avenue at 65th Street in 1896. (She had been forced uptown from 34th Street when her nephew built the **Waldorf Hotel** next door to her house.) Her presence here was only part of the draw for people such as the **Fiskes,** the **Havemeyers,** the **Armours,** and jeweler **Charles Tiffany.** Just as important were **Central Park** (providing a buffer on the west) and the railroad that ran down what is now **Park Avenue**, which kept the riffraff in their place to the east.

Society had its heyday on the East Side between 1895 and the outbreak of World War I. The state of American architecture was superb at the time, and the super rich had the financial resources to hire the best. Technology was very much in vogue then, and it was a rare four-story house that didn't have at least one elevator. Nearly every house had an elaborate intercom system, and all installed dumbwaiters, usually electrically operated, to make life simpler for the servants.

But the showplace was the bathroom—no New York house had indoor plumbing until the **Croton Aqueduct** began operating in 1842. Until the turn of the century, the style had been to bathe in dark, wood-paneled rooms designed to conceal their use. As the East Side developed after 1895, elaborate ceramic fixtures, imported tiles, gold-plated pipes, and showers that sprayed water in several directions at once were considered absolute necessities.

Up until 1900, any family sharing a house with other families (except servants, of course) was labeled déclassé. But when the barrier fell, the "best of the best" apartment buildings appeared on the East Side, especially along Park Avenue, which after 1915 became what one contemporary called "a mass production of millionaires." The huge apartment houses created a kind of leveling effect among the wealthy, as well as a guarantee that this would remain *their* kind of neighborhood. They didn't even budge during the Great Depression, when armies of the unemployed took up residence across the way in Central Park.

The 1960s brought construction of uninspiring white and yellow brick apartment houses to the area; many of the elegant town houses had already been broken up into multiple-unit dwellings years before. Despite the turmoil, the neighborhood continues to be what it has been for nearly a century: New York City's elite enclave.

1 Sherry-Netherland Hotel $$$$ One of the grandes dames rimming Central Park, the Sherry, designed in 1927 by **Schultze & Weaver** and built by **Louis Sherry** of ice cream fame, was once the centerpiece of an elegant trio, sitting between the **Pierre** and the **Savoy-Plaza** (whose site now hosts the **General Motors** tower). Its high-peaked roof sports gargoyles and chimneys like a Loire Valley confection. On the walls lining the entrance are panels rescued from a **Vanderbilt** mansion by **Richard Morris Hunt**. The 65-room hotel reopened in 1993 after a two-year total renovation that cost $18 million. Service is continental luxury class, and the rooms are large, many with park views. ♦ 781 Fifth Ave (at E. 59th St). 355.2800; fax 319.4306

Within the Sherry-Netherland Hotel:

Harry Cipriani ★★$$$$ If you can't get to Venice to see the original Harry's Bar, this spin-off will do. Pastas and peach Bellinis are specialties of the house, as is glamorous people-watching. ♦ Northern Italian ♦ Breakfast, lunch, and dinner. Reservations recommended; jacket required. 753.5566

2 The Harmonie Club In 1852, wealthy German Jews, excluded from most other men's clubs, formed the *Harmonie Gesellschaft*, which was described at the time as "the most homelike of all clubs" because its members made it a practice to bring along their wives. Today, the home of this private club is located in a 1906 building designed by **McKim, Mead & White.** ♦ 4 E. 60th St (between Madison and Fifth Aves)

3 Metropolitan Club Designed by **McKim, Mead & White** in 1894, this is a good example of **Stanford White** in an enthusiastic mood. Note particularly the extravagant, colonnaded carriage entrance behind the gates of the château. An addition was built in 1912 by **Ogden Codman.** The Metropolitan was organized by **J.P. Morgan** for his friends who were not accepted at other clubs. Ignore all rules of etiquette and see if you can get a glimpse through a main-floor window. ♦ 1 E. 60th St (at Fifth Ave). 838.7400

Restaurants/Clubs: Red	**Hotels:** Blue
Shops/ ♥ Outdoors: Green	**Sights/Culture:** Black

4 The Pierre $$$$ Designed in 1930 by **Schultze & Weaver,** the architects of the **Sherry-Netherland,** this is another of the grand old European-style hotels with many permanent guests and a loyal following of the rich and the powerful. A stretched mansard roof clothed in weathered bronze at the top of the tower gives the Pierre a distinctive silhouette; it and the Sherry-Netherland next door make a romantic couple. It is a wee bit intimidating, perhaps, with all those limos in front and the miles of mural-lined lobby, but the Pierre offers the kind of luxury one could get used to: enormous rooms (good Central Park views from the upper floors) and vast bathrooms; 24-hour room service; an attentive, multilingual staff; twice-daily maid service; complimentary shoe shine; even an unpacking service. And you don't have to go out to find a notary public, beauty salon or barbershop, or the **House of Bulgari** jewelers. Afternoon tea is served daily in the **Rotunda;** the **Cafe Pierre** is open daily and features a pianist nightly. ♦ 2 E. 61st St (at Fifth Ave). 838.8000, 800/268.6282; fax 940.8109

5 800 Fifth Avenue Until her death in 1977, **Mrs. Marcellus Hartley Dodge,** a niece of **John D. Rockefeller, Jr.,** lived here with her famous collection of stray dogs in a five-story brick mansion that was a mate to the nearby **Knickerbocker Club.** In 1978, **Ulrich Frazen & Associates** moved in, promising a tasteful building that would be a credit to the neighborhood. This 33-story building is how the promise was kept. The zoning law forced them to build a three-story wall along Fifth Avenue. Unfortunately, it isn't high enough to hide the building behind it. ♦ At E. 61st St

6 The Knickerbocker Club In the 1860s, some members of the Union Club proposed that its membership be restricted to men descended from the colonial families of New York, known as the Knickerbockers. When their suggestion was rejected, they started their own club. But one of its most influential founders was **August Belmont,** a German immigrant. Today, the club is located in this 1914 building by **Delano & Aldrich.** ♦ 2 E. 62nd St (at Fifth Ave). 838.6700

7 810 Fifth Avenue Former residents of this 13-story limestone building designed in 1926 by **J.E.R. Carpenter** include **William Randolph Hearst** and **Mrs. Hamilton Fish,** one of the last of the grandes dames of New York society. Before he moved to the White House in 1969, **Richard M. Nixon** lived here. His neighbor on the top floor was **Nelson Rockefeller,** who had New York's only fully equipped bomb shelter. ♦ At E. 62nd St. 838.0266

8 Arcadia ★★★★$$$$ Chef/owner **Anne Rosenzweig** is as impressive as ever. Signature dishes on her seasonal menu include corncakes with crème fraîche and caviar, chimney-smoked lobster with tarragon butter, and a chocolate bread pudding swimming in a brandy custard sauce. The dining room's focal point—aside from the food—is the wraparound mural of the countryside as the seasons change. ♦ American ♦ Lunch and dinner. Closed Sunday. 21 E. 62nd St (between Madison and Fifth Aves). Jacket, tie, and reservations required. 223.2900

9 Addison on Madison Subdued yet interesting men's shirts of fine French cotton are offered in appealing, gentle stripes and checks, with a few bolder stripes. Sleeves come short, regular, and extra long. Collars come button-down, regular, and white. Accessories include silk ties and crystal cuff links. ♦ M-Sa 10:30AM-6:30PM. 698 Madison Ave (between E. 62nd and E. 63rd Sts). 308.2660. Also at: 725 Fifth Ave. 752.2300

10 Le Relais ★★$$$ This is one of those East Side places where models, soap-opera players, and other chic and beautiful trendies while away evenings sipping white wine and Perrier, eating French food, and looking at one another. It's fun to observe the outdoor cafe scene in the warmer months. ♦ French ♦ Lunch and dinner. 712 Madison Ave (at E. 63rd St). Reservations required. 751.5108

Metropolitan Club

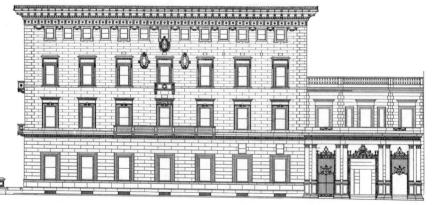

10 Laura Ashley Home Furnishings Ashley is the Welsh designer who put nosegays and sprigs of flowers on pure cotton, and created an empire by whipping up the fabric into sweet Victorian dresses, petticoats, nightgowns, peasant skirts, and little girls' dresses. Here her signature prints are available on furniture, in fabric by the roll, in wallpaper, and in home accessories. ♦ M-W, F-Sa 10AM-6PM; Th 10AM-7PM. 714 Madison Ave (between E. 63rd and E. 64th Sts). 735.5000. Also at: 21 E. 57th St (clothing). 752.7300; 398 Columbus Ave (clothing and furnishings). 496.5110; 4 Fulton St (clothing and furnishings). 809.3556

THE
LOWELL

11 The Lowell $$$$ White-glove treatment is the norm in this small, charming hotel. Many of the 61 rooms and suites in this 1926 building by **Henry S. Churchill** have serving pantries and wood-burning fireplaces, and some can accommodate formal board meetings. Room service meals arrive on a silver tray, or, if you prefer company, the second-floor dining room is both cheerful and serene. One of New York City's very best. ♦ 28 E. 63rd St (between Park and Madison Aves). 838.1400; fax 319.4230

Within The Lowell:

The Post House ★★★$$$$ A classic New York steakhouse in a classic New York setting, possibly the most handsome in the city. And the atmosphere is ultracivilized. ♦ American ♦ Lunch and dinner; dinner only on Friday, Saturday, and Sunday. Reservations required. 935.2888

12 Margo Feiden Galleries The specialty here is the work of caricaturist **Al Hirschfeld** (see page 150), who has been capturing the essence of famous faces for the *New York Times* since the 1920s. The list of subjects ranges from **Marlon Brando** to **Madonna, Thomas E. Dewey** to **Albert Einstein.** The trick is to find all the Ninas in each drawing. Hirschfeld hides his daughter's name within folds of clothing, pompadours, wherever. One clue: the number of times "Nina" appears is indicated next to his sign-off. Original pen and ink drawings, limited editions, etchings, and lithographs are shown. ♦ Daily 10AM-6PM. 699 Madison Ave (between E. 62nd and E. 63rd Sts). 677.5330

13 Julie: Artisans' Gallery Clothes conceived as art to wear: **Julie Hill's** jackets of hand-painted silk, **Linda Mendelson's** scarves and coats knitted in geometric patterns, **Janet Lipkin's** loom-knitted and hand-dyed

garments, and many other flights of fancy. Some of the items are more for display than to be worn. Not for the timid. ♦ M-Sa 11AM-6PM. 687 Madison Ave (between E. 61st and E. 62nd Sts). 688.2345

13 Georg Jensen/Royal Copenhagen Silver, including flatware and exquisite jewelry, is featured here: sleek, gleaming bangles and cuffs, Art Nouveau pins shaped like leaves and trimmed with precious stones. This is also a good source for crystal glassware and the entire collection of Royal Copenhagen china. ♦ M-Sa 9:30AM-5:30PM. 683 Madison Ave (between E. 61st and E. 62nd Sts). 759.6457

14 Fogal of Switzerland You'll find an impressive selection of fine hosiery in this shop. ♦ M-Sa 10AM-6PM. 680 Madison Ave (between E. 61st and E. 62nd Sts). 759.9782. Also at: 510 Madison Ave. 355.3254

15 Sherry Lehman One of the top wine merchants in America—certainly the most famous in New York—offers courteous, expert advice. It's a handsome store for browsing. ♦ M-Sa 9AM-7PM. 679 Madison Ave (at E. 61st St). 838.7500

16 Maxim's ★★$$$ Although the decor is a faithful homage to the Belle Epoque original, the food doesn't quite measure up. But for romance, Maxim's is hard to beat. Downstairs is **L'Omnibus de Maxim's,** more casual but just as elegant. ♦ Continental ♦ Lunch and dinner. Closed Monday and Sunday. 21 E. 61st St (at Madison Ave). Jacket and tie required Friday; black tie required Saturday. Reservations required. 751.5111. L'Omnibus de Maxim's: reservations recommended. 980.6988

17 Barneys This nine-story, 230,000-square-foot fashion temple designed by minimalist architect **Peter Marino** opened to much hoopla in September 1993, three years—and $100 million—after the **Pressman** family decided to bring their downtown clothing mecca for men and women to Midtown. The largest specialty store to be built in Manhattan since the Depression, it's light and airy, with large stretches of loftlike space. The women's side measures more than twice the size of its quarters in the flagship store in Chelsea. ♦ M-F 10AM-8PM; Sa 10AM-7PM; Su noon-6PM. 660 Madison Ave (at E. 61st St). 826.8900. Also at: Seventh Ave (at W. 17th St). 929.9000; 2 World Financial Center. 945.1600

Within Barneys:

mad. 61

Mad. 61 ★★$$$ Following a parallel trend of top-quality restaurants appearing in the city's major museums, acclaimed restaurateu **Pino Luongo** (of **Le Madri** and **Coco Pazzo**) has opened his latest eatery inside Barneys.

Centered around a marble mosaic pool, the restaurant lures shoppers with Luongo's trademark rich and rustic Italian cuisine. Surrounding the dining room are a more informal wine bar (serving 160 kinds) and an Italian espresso bar area where you can order from a less expensive but equally delicious menu. The restaurant is open even when the store is closed. ◆ Italian ◆ Lunch and dinner. Reservations required. 833.2200

18 Mme. Romaine de Lyon ★★$$$ With more than 500 kinds to choose from, it's safe to say that this is New York's ultimate place for an omelet. The setting is charming and comfortable, the staff is friendly, and the kitchen has turned omelets into an art form. ◆ French ◆ Lunch and dinner; brunch only on Sunday. 29 E. 61st St (between Park and Madison Aves). Reservations recommended. 759.5200

19 Aureole ★★★$$$$ A contrast to the quaint twig baskets scattered throughout the restaurant are the plaster reliefs of animals on the walls and ceiling, which, to say the least, are humorous. Treat yourself to Aureole's own chocolates and cookies. ◆ Continental ◆ Lunch and dinner. Closed Sunday. 34 E. 61st St (between Park and Madison Aves). Reservations required. 319.1660

20 Bogner You expect slick, well-made active sportswear from this Austrian manufacturer of ski clothing. The surprise is the line of leisurewear for men and women—jackets, coats, sweaters, pants, skirts, shoes, bags—all in the same sensible, hardy mode. ◆ M-Sa 10AM-6PM. 655 Madison Ave (at E. 60th St). 752.2282

20 Boyd's Madison Avenue Legions of well-known women, including **Jackie Onassis** and **Cher,** have come here to choose from a vast, international collection of makeup brushes, lip glosses, feather powder puffs, rouges, combs, hairbrushes, and toothbrushes. ◆ M-F 8:30AM-8PM; Sa 9:30AM-7PM; Su noon-6PM. 655 Madison Ave (at E. 60th St). 838.6558

21 Kaplan's $$ This large, clean, modern delicatessen isn't big on atmosphere but has fair prices and better-than-average salads, sandwiches, soups, and service. ◆ Deli ◆ Daily 7AM-10PM. 59 E. 59th St (between Park and Madison Aves). 755.5959

22 Caviarteria This caviar and champagne bar has an on-site retail store with a huge variety of caviar, pâtés, chocolates, and other delicacies. The staff is very helpful—if you don't understand the mystique of caviar, don't be shy about asking. Also ask about mail-order service. Caviarteria is a direct importer and wholesaler, which keeps prices down. ◆ M-Sa 9AM-6PM. 502 Park Ave (at E. 59th St). 759.7410

22 Christie's The New York headquarters of the famous London auction house specializes in old masters, Impressionists, 19th- and 20th-century European and American art, and 22 other areas of art including antiques and Chinese art. Tickets, available without charge a week or two before an auction, are required for evening auctions. Previews of items to be auctioned are held five days prior to the auction itself, and catalogs are available. *Auction Talks,* a series of free lectures on fine and decorative arts, is presented during the auction seasons. Call for schedule. ◆ M-F 9:30AM-5:30PM; Sa 10AM-5PM; Su 1-5PM. 502 Park Ave (at E. 59th St). 546.1000

23 The Grolier Club Named for the 16th-century bibliophile **Jean Grolier,** this Georgian structure, designed by **Bertram G. Goodhue** in 1917, houses a collection of fine bookbindings and a specialized library open only to scholars and researchers. Regularly changing exhibitions display books, prints, and rare manuscripts. ◆ Free. M-Sa 10AM-5PM. 47 E. 60th St (between Park and Madison Aves). 838.6690

23 Christ Church Built in 1932 by **Ralph Adams Cram,** this is an interesting limestone-and-brick Methodist church. One of the best ecclesiastical structures of the 1930s, it was designed to look hundreds of years old. ◆ 520 Park Ave (at E. 60th St)

24 The Regency $$$$ This elegant hotel is the scene of some of New York's most important power breakfasts, at which the city's movers and shakers get together to start their business day. Guests can take advantage of 24-hour room service for their breakfast, but it isn't as exciting. Other advantages include a well-equipped fitness center and a large, multilingual staff. The hotel is furnished with French antiques, which gives it a feeling of luxury uncommon in newer buildings. ◆ 540 Park Ave (at E. 61st St). 759.4100, 800/233.2356; fax 826.5674

25 The Colony Club The building, which houses an exclusive club for society women, presents a solid, neo-Georgian, Federal redbrick face, settled on a limestone base. It was designed in 1924 by **Delano & Aldrich.** ◆ 564 Park Ave (at E. 62nd St). 838.4200

26 101 East 63rd Street Remodeled in 1970 by **Paul Rudolph,** the tripartite composition of the dark-glass front of this carriage house is a reflection of its interior. ◆ Between Lexington and Park Aves

27 Park Avenue Cafe ★★★$$$$ **David Burke** whips up high-end, creative American fare such as his famous swordfish chop. The bar and stylish, kitsch-filled dining rooms are usually packed, but service is snappy. ◆ American ◆ Lunch and dinner; dinner only on Saturday; brunch also on Sunday. 100 E. 63rd St (between Park and Lexington Aves). Reservations required. 644.1900

27 Society of Illustrators Built in 1875, this museum of American illustration features changing exhibitions of advertising art, book illustration, editorial art, and other contemporary work. ♦ Free. M, W-F 10AM-5PM; Tu 10AM-8PM; Sa noon-4PM. 128 E. 63rd St (between Park and Lexington Aves). 838.2560

28 Saint-Remy Produits de Provence Pale, muted floral and paisley fabrics are sold here, mainly by the yard (but can be ordered made up into napkins, lamp shades, and place mats), along with fragrant spices, hand-painted pottery, and bath oils. ♦ M-F 10:30AM-7PM; Sa 10:30AM-6:30PM. 818 Lexington Ave (between E. 62nd and E. 63rd Sts). 486.2018

GUY BILLOUT. COURTESY MILTON GLASER

29 The Barbizon Hotel $$$ Its richly detailed brickwork and fine interiors have made this former residence for women—actresses **Candice Bergen, Gene Tierney,** and **Grace Kelly** stayed here at various times—one of the East Side's better-known buildings (shown above); it was designed in 1927 by **Murgatroyd & Ogden.** Until 1981—when it was converted to a hotel open to both sexes, with interiors by **Milton Glaser**—its upper floors were off-limits to men. But the rooftop arcades framed skyline views that were made famous by photographer **Samuel Gottscho.** The view also inspired painter **Georgia O'Keeffe.** Among its amenities are 12 tower suites, a multilingual staff, a cafe (**Cafe Barbizon**), and an oak-paneled meeting room with a pipe organ, stained-glass windows, and a fireplace. The Morgan's Hotel Groups (**Morgan's, The Royalton, The Paramount**) purchased this fine old hotel in the fall of 1988, but it is now operating independently. Some restorations have taken place, mainly in the lobby, and more are on the way. ♦ 140 E. 63rd St (at Lexington Ave). 838.5700, 800/223.1020; fax 753.0360

30 Tender Buttons Featured here are millions and millions of buttons, new and antique, made of brass, stoneware, taqua nut, Lucite, wood, abalone, seashell, agate, plastic, silver—you name it. They come in every shape, from Betty Boop to ponies, butterflies, mice, cats, and dogs, and are as practical as buttons for shirts or as esoteric as gold-colored filigree fasteners for antique Chinese robes. ♦ M-F 11AM-6PM; Sa 11AM-5PM. 143 E. 62nd St (between Lexington and Third Aves). 758.7004

31 New York Doll Hospital Even if your doll isn't sick, don't miss this experience. They buy and sell antique dolls and toys here, but what makes it so much fun is the collection of spare parts. ♦ M-Sa 10AM-6PM. 787 Lexington Ave (between E. 61st and E. 62nd Sts), second floor. 838.7527

32 Brio ★$$$ Conveniently located near Bloomingdale's, this attractive, wood-paneled trattoria is almost always full, thanks to Italian-style home cooking. If the only thing you taste is the first course of hearty polenta with porcini mushrooms or aromatic fusilli with pesto, it'll be enough to bring you back again and again. ♦ Italian ♦ Lunch, dinner, and late-night meals. 786 Lexington Ave (between E. 61st and E. 62nd Sts). Reservations recommended. 980.2300

33 Il Valletto ★$$$$ If **Nanni** (the owner) is around when you visit, let him order for you. If he's not, here are some good choices: bruschetta, tender baked clams, eggplant Siciliana with light ricotta and spinach, or linguine with delicate, tender clams in a light white sauce. For dessert, try the baked pear with zabaglione or the fresh fruit salad. ♦ Italian ♦ Lunch and dinner; dinner only on Saturday. Closed Sunday. 133 E. 61st St (between Park and Lexington Aves). Reservations and jacket required. 838.3939

34 The Pillowry Owner/designer **Marjorie Lawrence** sells kilims and Oriental rugs and makes pillows from antique rugs and textiles collected from all over the world. ♦ M-F 11:30AM-5:30PM. 132 E. 61st St (between Park and Lexington Aves). 308.1630

35 Le Veau d'Or ★$$$$ Longtime East Siders still flock to this great old bistro for well-prepared, basic French fare and unpretentious, efficient service. ♦ French ♦ Lunch and dinner. Closed Sunday. 129 E. 60th St (between Park and Lexington Aves). Reservations recommended. 838.8133

36 The Original Levi's Store An icon in the annals of American fashion, the Levi's jean is here in every model, size, color, and interpretation imaginable. This spacious store is always filled with foreign shoppers having a field day. Jeans, jackets, vests, and sweatshirts for men and women are stocked to the rafters. ♦ M-Sa 10AM-8PM; Su noon-5PM. 750 Lexington Ave (between W. 59th and W. 60th Sts). 826.5957

Restaurants/Clubs: Red	**Hotels:** Blue
Shops/ ♥ Outdoors: Green	**Sights/Culture:** Black

37 Bloomingdale's No store promotes its products better or with more verve, imagination, and sizzle. The store's buyers plumbed the heartland of China and came back with Bloomie's-inspired dishes, rugs, and ashtrays the Chinese artisans would never have conceived of on their own. They went to India, Israel, and the Philippines and brought back mirrored elephants, swimsuits, and salty fish sauces. Bloomingdale's is show business. It caters to those who like to buy their clothes, food, and sofas in an atmosphere that is a cross between a discotheque and a Middle Eastern suk. Ladies threaten to squirt perfume at you and TV screens show endless tapes of designer fashion shows. Every object seems to catch your eye. For children, there are layettes, strollers, **Oshkosh** overalls, and hand-knit sweaters. For women, there are slinky knits by **Missoni,** seductive knits by **Sonia Rykiel,** the American chic of **Ralph Lauren,** and the luxe of **Yves Saint Laurent.** For men, there are clothes by **Cacharel, Ralph Lauren,** and **Calvin Klein.** The **Main Course** is a cornucopia of kitchenware and gadgets. **Descamps** has a boutique in the linen department. There is a shop devoted solely to **Petrossian** caviar. Special shopping services are extensive; the store once delivered an entire household of brand-new furniture to the home of a Russian diplomat's wife. ♦ M-W, F 10AM-7PM; Th 10AM-9PM; Sa 10AM-6:30PM; Su 11AM-6:30PM. 1000 Third Ave (at E. 59th St). 705.2000

Within Bloomingdale's:

Le Train Bleu ★$$ Designed to re-create the dining car on the famous **Orient Express,** this "train" has spectacular views of the **Queensboro Bridge.** The food is of indeterminate origin and dubious merit, but the restaurant itself is comfortable and a welcome resting ground for emotionally and financially drained Bloomingdale's shoppers. ♦ Continental ♦ Lunch and dinner. Closed Sunday. Sixth floor. Reservations recommended. 705.2100

38 Trump Plaza You can easily pass this 1987 building by **Philip Birnbaum & Associates.** It is another attempt to immortalize the name of developer **Donald Trump.** But don't pass up the waterfall or the open space to the left of the entrance that make it so pleasant. ♦ 167 E. 61st St (at Third Ave)

38 Matthew's ★★$$$ Replacing the once-popular **Alo Alo,** this immediately successful descendant showcases the same talented chef, **Matthew Kenney.** Then specializing in Italian cuisine, Kenney is now doing an American stint, creating his own trends while adhering to the whims of the season. The setting is rustic yet elegant—white linen, rattan chairs, ceiling fans, and big baskets of fruit. All this is finished off by terrific desserts. ♦ American ♦ Lunch and dinner. 1030 Third Ave (at E. 61st St). 838.4343

39 Yellowfingers ★★$$$ A perfect place to recover after a splurge at Bloomingdale's. The open kitchen turns out generous salads, sandwiches (all served on thick focaccia) and a hearty entrée called *fa'vecchai,* a pizzalike bread baked with toppings—grilled mushrooms, braised onions, olives, and eggplant. ♦ American/Italian ♦ Lunch and dinner. 200 E. 60th St (at Third Ave). 751.8615

Above Yellowfingers:

Contrapunto ★★$$$ Fresh pasta squares filled with lobster, scallops, fresh fennel, and leeks in a lemon-cream sauce, and delicate angel hair pasta with littleneck clams, are among the best choices. ♦ American/Italian ♦ Lunch and dinner. 751.8615

39 Arizona 206 ★★★$$ Authentically ensconced in lots of adobe, bare wood, and desert flowers, this cavelike place serves up imaginative Southwest fare. To the right is the **Cafe,** a more casual restaurant with an inventive tasting-menu—depending on the size of your party, up to 12 dishes are served family-style. ♦ Southwestern ♦ Lunch and dinner. 206 E. 60th St (between Second and Third Aves). Reservations recommended. 838.0440

40 Serendipity ★$$ It's an ice cream parlor and informal restaurant named after *The Three Princes of Serendip,* **Horace Walpole's** retelling of a Persian myth, and it will, as they say, delight children from eight to 80. The overdone Victorianesque decorations, the decadent desserts—including the famed frozen hot chocolate—and the fine, simple food—from shepherd's pie to barbecued chicken casserole—have made it a prime attraction since its opening in 1954. The novelty boutique keeps you busy while you wait for a table. ♦ American ♦ Lunch, dinner, and late-night meals. 225 E. 60th St (between Second and Third Aves). 838.3531

40 Betsey Johnson Johnson has been ahead of her time for more than two decades. Her fashion statement is fun, sexy, and excessive. ♦ M-W, F-Sa 11AM-7PM; Th 11AM-8PM; Su 1-7PM. 251 E. 60th St (between Second and Third Aves). 319.7699. Also at: 72 Columbus Ave. 362.3364; 130 Thompson St. 420.0169

41 Joia As antique clothes from the 1930s and 1940s become more scarce, this shop is carrying fewer Oriental robes and more **Clarice Cliff** china. Although the stock is mostly clothes for men and women, the treasure here is the jewelry. ♦ M-Sa 11AM-7PM. 1151 Second Ave (between E. 60th and E. 61st Sts). 754.9017

42 Pushbottom for Kids This shop carries outfits for children by the famous purveyor of quality sweaters. The little fashion plate in your family will turn everyone's head in one of Pushbottom's crocheted bow ties. ♦ M-F

11AM-6PM. 252 E. 62nd St (between Second and Third Aves). 888.3336. Also at: 46 E. 59th St. 759.6200

43 Darrow's Fun Antiques This is a place for grownups to become children: toy soldiers; cigar store Indians; antique windup monkeys, dogs, and bears; movie star memorabilia; and even the occasional funhouse mirror. ♦ M-F 11:30AM-7PM; Sa noon-4PM. 309 E. 61st St (between First and Second Aves). 838.0730

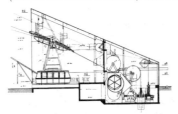

44 Roosevelt Island Tramway Station The Swiss-made tram (see diagram), designed in 1976 by **Prentice & Chan, Ohlhausen,** would be more at home on a snow-covered mountain. It takes you across the East River's West Channel at 16mph and provides wonderful views of the **East Side** and the **Queensboro Bridge.** Until October 1989, when the subway finally opened (after 25 years of planning and construction), the tram was the only way to get to or from Roosevelt Island, except for a short automobile bridge on the Queens side. ♦ Nominal fee. M-Th, Su 6AM-2AM; F-Sa 6AM-3AM. Second Ave (between E. 59th and E. 60th Sts). 832.4543

45 Queensboro Bridge Designed by engineer **Gustav Lindenthal** and built in 1909 by **Palmer & Hornbostel,** the distinctive triple span of this bridge is the image of a machine, an intricate web of steel that speaks of power, if not finesse. Under the Manhattan ramp are great vaulted spaces now used for storage and parking; there are continual plans afoot to restore them to their original use as a farmers' market. ♦ From E. 59th St at Second Ave, Manhattan, to Queens Plaza, Queens

46 Roosevelt Island This island is separated from Manhattan by 300 yards and more than a few decibels, but politically it is very much a part of it. The community, built in the 1970s, is accessible from Manhattan by tramway and subway, and from Queens by a small bridge at 36th Avenue, Queens Plaza. The master plan for a series of U-shaped housing projects facing the river was designed by **Philip Johnson** and **John Burgee.** Only the southern section was built, and it's taller and denser than they recommended. Until the 1970s, when rental agents needed a name change, it was known as **Welfare Island** because of the island's many hospitals and sanitariums. Before 1921, it was **Blackwell's Island,** named for the family that farmed it for two centuries. A prison was built in 1828, and over the next several years, a workhouse, an almshouse,

and an insane asylum were added. A century later those institutions were swept away and hospitals were substituted. The present city has reminders of each of the island's former lives. The ruin at the southern end was the **Smallpox Hospital,** designed in 1856 by **James Renwick, Jr.** Just above it are the remains of the 1859 **City Hospital,** and under the Queensboro Bridge is **Goldwater Memorial Hospital.** Not far from the tramway station is the **Blackwell Farmhouse** (1796-1804). Nearby are the **Eastwood Apartments,** built for low- and middle-income tenants in 1976 by **Sert, Jackson & Associates.** On the Manhattan side are **Rivercross Apartments,** built in 1975 by **Johansen & Bhavnani,** for people who can afford to pay more. There are two more luxury complexes: **Westview,** built in 1976 by Sert, Jackson & Associates, and **Island House,** built in 1975 by Johansen & Bhavnani, which has a glassed-in swimming pool overlooking Manhattan.

Cars are not allowed on the island except in the garage complex known as **Motorgate.** Garbage is removed through vacuum tubes to the **AVAC (Automated Vacuum Collection) Building**—where it is sorted, sanitized, and packed for removal. Near this monument to a "Brave New World" is the **Chapel of the Good Shepherd,** originally built in 1889 by **Frederick Clarke Withers** and restored by **Giorgio Cavaglieri** in 1976, now used as a recreation center. Landmarks at the northern end include the **Octagon Tower,** an 1839 building by **Alexander Jackson Davis,** all that's left of the **New York City Lunatic Asylum,** and a 50-foot stone lighthouse designed in 1872 by James Renwick, Jr. (According to an inscription on the lighthouse, it was built by **John McCarthy,** an asylum inmate who busied himself by building a fort to defend himself against the British but was persuaded to replace it with a more attractive lighthouse instead.) The hospital at the uptown end of the island is the 1952 **Bird S. Coler Hospital for the Chronically Ill.** A complex of 1,104 apartments, **Northtown II** was completed by **Starrett Housing** in 1989. Currently, plans are under way for 15-acre **Octagon Park,** just south of the Coler Hospital, and **Southtown,** a complex of 2,000 mixed-income apartments. Transportation on Roosevelt Island is provided by bus, but probably the best way to enjoy it is by walking on its riverside promenades. ♦ East River

One of the more colorful inmates at Roosevelt Island's New York City Lunatic Asylum was Mae West, who was locked up there for 10 days in 1926 and fined $500. She had been appearing locally in a lewd play called *Sex* that raised one too many eyebrows. Upon her request, she was permitted to wear her silk undergarments beneath her prison uniform.

47 Magique Home of Chippendale's You think clubs with male go-go dancers are only in the suburbs? Not so. At Chippendale's, chiseled hunks titillate Manhattan's ladies. There's also a large, circular disco with high-tech, black glittery walls and floor. ♦ Cover. Shows: W-Th 8PM; F-Sa 8:30PM. You must arrive 45 minutes in advance. 1110 First Ave (at E. 61st St). 935.6060

48 Abigail Adams Smith Museum The daughter of **John Quincy Adams,** for whom this 1799 house/museum is named, never even slept here. But she and her husband, **Colonel William Smith,** did own the land it was built on. They bought 23 choice acres on the bank of the East River in 1786 with the idea of building a country estate called **Mt. Vernon** (Col. Smith served under George Washington). Because of financial reverses, they sold the estate in 1799. The stone stable that is now the museum was remodeled as an inn in the 1820s, then used as a private dwelling until the neighborhood fell on hard times. The **Colonial Dames of America** rescued it in 1924, furnished it in the style of the Federal period, planted an 18th-century garden, and opened the house as a museum. Colonial Dames members, well versed in the contents of the house (but not necessarily about antiques or the history of the period), show visitors the nine rooms filled with delicate **Aubusson** rugs, graceful **Sheraton** chests, a framed letter from George Washington, a mannequin wearing a simple summer dress that Abigail had made for herself (she had indeed fallen on hard times), and unexpected touches such as a cardroom set up with a game of loo. ♦ Admission. M-F noon-4PM; Su 1-5PM. 421 E. 61st St (between York and First Aves). 838.6878

49 Dangerfield's This club, which showcases new and established comic talent, is owned and operated by well-known comedian **Rodney Dangerfield.** It has a typical Las Vegas/Atlantic City atmosphere and caters to suburbanites, known as the "bridge and tunnel" crowd. ♦ Cover, minimum. Shows: M-Th 9PM-1AM; F 9PM, 11:15PM; Sa 8PM, 10:30PM, 12:30AM. 1118 First Ave (between E. 61st and E. 62nd Sts). 593.1650

50 Il Vagabondo ★$$ A noisy, good-humored neighborhood trattoria with robust Italian cooking, mostly in the Southern style, this place has the city's only indoor boccie court—perfect for working off rich homemade gnocchi. (Other specials include tuna steak, a fragrant veal stew, and filet of sole.) Boccie, a type of bowling, has been a favorite Italian sport since the days of the Roman Empire. If you ask to be seated in the room with the court, you can watch the players throw the boule while you dine. ♦ Italian ♦ Lunch and dinner; dinner only on Saturday and Sunday. 351 E. 62nd St (between First and Second Aves). 832.9221

50 Carol Rollo/Riding High You'll find bold, luxurious—and expensive—clothing for men and women, including designs from **Jean Paul Gaultier, Chloe,** and **Sitbon.** ♦ M-W, F 10AM-7PM; Th 10AM-8PM; Sa 10:30AM-7PM. 1147 First Ave (at E. 62nd St). 832.7927

51 Manhattan Cafe ★$$$ This is the place to get late-night traditional steakhouse fare in a comfortable, posh setting. Just for the record, they also have decent veal and pasta dishes. ♦ American ♦ Lunch, dinner, and late-night meals. 1161 First Ave (at E. 64th St). Reservations recommended. 888.6556

52 Silver Star $$ This glorified diner attracts a curious mix, from local moviegoers to celebs in the mood for a hearty bite. The spaghetti with meatballs is a triumph of engineering; the meatballs are the size of tennis balls. ♦ American/Greek ♦ Daily 24 hours. 1236 Second Ave (at E. 65th St). 249.4250

53 Jackson Hole ★$ Delicious, juicy burgers the size of Wyoming are the specialty of this restaurant, one of five in the city. Any (or many) of the 12 toppings can be requested to adorn the standard seven-ounce hamburger, and sides of onion rings or french fries are part of the ritual. Vegetarians won't be disappointed with the equally large selection of good omelets. This is a favorite with kids on weekends (it can get noisy). ♦ Hamburgers ♦ Lunch, dinner, and late-night meals. 232 E. 64th St (between Second and Third Aves). 371.7187

54 Bravo Gianni ★★$$$ Although this is an elegant place—gray suede walls, velvet banquettes, and lots of smoked mirrors—you may be treated a bit cavalierly unless you're one of the regulars. ♦ Italian ♦ Lunch and dinner; dinner only on Saturday. 230 E. 63rd St (between Second and Third Aves). Reservations recommended. 752.7272

55 Lolabelle ★$$ After leaving her namesake restaurant, **"Lola"** transferred her tropical cuisine and gospel music uptown to this bilevel space where **John Clancy's East** previously stood. Unfortunately, something was lost in the move. Lola's trademark calamari and onion rings are now soggy, and the service is just as sloppy. Considerably better are the Caribbean fried chicken with yams and swamp greens, cod with buttermilk whipped potatoes, and grilled jerked quail. Still spectacular is Lola's Sunday gospel brunch with live singers. ♦ Southern American/Tropical ♦ Lunch, dinner, and late-night meals; brunch only on Sunday. 206 E. 63rd St (between Second and Third Aves). 755.5652

56 New York Women's Exchange Established in 1878 to help women support themselves without sacrificing their pride, this is an excellent source of handmade children's articles, lingerie, and gifts. ♦ M-Sa 10AM-6PM. 1095 Third Ave (between E. 64th and E. 65th Sts). 753.2330

57 The Sign of The Dove ★★★$$$$ The garden setting here is a knockout, the furnishings are real antiques, and the dining experience is memorable. In its early years, the restaurant was regarded as a tourist attraction and nothing more. The romantic atmosphere hasn't changed, but the kitchen now turns out quite good food. Try the shellfish stew with saffron. A cafe menu is also available. ♦ American ♦ Lunch and dinner; dinner only on Monday, Saturday, and Sunday. 1110 Third Ave (at E. 65th St). Jacket required. Reservations recommended. 861.8080

57 Ecce Panis True connoisseurs of fresh bread—crispy outside, chewy and deeply flavored inside—come here for their daily fix. A sampling of the day's bounty—sourdough, rye, whole-wheat currant—sits in a basket on the counter. ♦ M-F 9AM-8PM; Sa-Su 9AM-6PM. 1120 Third Ave (between E. 65th and E. 66th Sts). 535.2099

58 Solow Houses Developer **Sheldon Solow,** who built the innovative office building at 9 W. 57th Street in 1983, created these 11 houses (designed by **Attia & Perkins**), the first new town house row in the city since the end of the 19th century. The granite facade, which binds them together between flat and slightly bowed fronts, barely articulates each individual house. The front is fortresslike, hiding luxurious interiors. ♦ 222-242 E. 67th St (between Second and Third Aves)

59 Le Comptoir ★$$$ The menu, as close as can be to true French bistro fare, includes frisee with *lardons,* steak in red wine sauce, *pommes frites,* and pâtés. Desserts are simple: fruit tarts and ice cream. ♦ French ♦ Lunch and dinner; dinner only on Saturday and Sunday. 227 E. 67th St (between Second and Third Aves). 794.4950

60 Neikrug Photographica Contemporary and vintage photos, daguerreotypes, and photographic equipment are featured here. At press time, it's open by appointment only, so call ahead. ♦ 224 E. 68th St (between Second and Third Aves). 288.7741

61 Soleil ★★★$$$ Gone are the dark carpets and Cantonese cuisine of Fortune Garden, and in their place are bright yellow walls and a Mediterranean menu. Try the Thai seafood salad or the orrechiette pasta tossed with tomatoes, spinach, and pine nuts. And don't miss the focaccia with olive oil and rosemary. ♦ Contemporary American ♦ Lunch and dinner. 1160 Third Ave (between E. 67th and E. 68th Sts). Reservations required. 717.1177

61 Janovic Plaza This is just one of several outlets of the most thorough paint store in the city. It offers not only 8,000 colors and finishes but fabrics from design houses such as **Country Gear, Jack Prince,** and **Schumacher,** pure cotton towels, and made-to-order curtains, bedspreads, comforter covers, draperies, Roman shades, canopies, and shower curtains. ♦ M-F 7:30AM-6:30PM; Sa 8AM-5:45PM; Su 11AM-5PM. 1150 Third Ave (at E. 67th St). 772.1400

62 Park East Synagogue Designed in 1890 by **Schneider & Herter,** this Moorish extravaganza has a more sedate Victorian interior. ♦ 163 E. 67th St (between Third and Lexington Aves). 737.6900

63 131-135 East 66th Street The two apartment blocks, designed in 1905 by **Charles Adams Platt,** are most noted for dignified grandeur and Mannerist porticoes. ♦ Between Third and Lexington Aves

64 Cosmopolitan Club Cast-iron balconies give a New Orleans flavor to this 1932 Greek Revival building, designed by **Thomas Harlan Ellett.** It is the headquarters of a prestigious women's club for those interested in the arts and sciences. ♦ 122 E. 66th St (between Lexington and Park Aves). 734.5950

64 126 East 66th Street This Romanesque-style carriage house was built by **W.J. Wallace** and **S.E. Sage** in 1895 for **H.O. Havemeyer,** the sugar magnate, who lived at 1 E. 66th Street. Apparently it was too far from his house, because he sold it before it was finished to **Oliver H. Payne,** brother-in-law of **William C. Whitney.** It is now owned by **John Hay Whitney.** ♦ Between Lexington and Park Aves

64 The Forgotten Woman This unfortunately named store offers handsome designer clothing for the larger woman (sizes 14 to 24). There are tailored suits, pure cashmere sweaters, cocktail dresses, and leather skirts. Large-size teenagers can find preppy-looking pleated skirts, casual jackets, and Shetland sweaters. The service is exceptionally good. ♦ M-W, F-Sa 10AM-6PM; Th 10AM-7:30PM; Su noon-5PM. 888 Lexington Ave (at E. 66th St). 535.8848

65 Church of St. Vincent Ferrer When New York's Roman Catholic elite make wedding plans, **St. Patrick's Cathedral** is their first choice. If the cathedral is booked, this is where they turn. It was designed by **Bertram G. Goodhue** in 1923. ♦ Lexington Ave (between E. 65th and E. 66th Sts). 744.2080

66 Ashanti This shop offers sophisticated dresses of pure cotton, silk, and wool for the larger woman (sizes 14 to 24); also featured are accessories such as scarves and wrap belts. ♦ M-W, F-Sa 10AM-6PM; Th 10AM-8PM. 872 Lexington Ave (at E. 65th St). 535.0740

67 Ségires à Solanée Classic Provençal designs—hand-painted wood furniture, iron furniture, faience from Moustiers-Sainte-Marie, and linen place mats and napkins—abound in **Georgette Buckner's** sunny shop. ♦ M-Th 10AM-5:30PM; F 10AM-5PM; Sa 11AM-5PM. 866 Lexington Ave (at E. 65th St). 439.6109

68 The Elder Craftsmen Shop Men and women age 55 and over make wooden toys, dollhouses, crib quilts, hand-knit sweaters, picture frames, and hand-smocked dresses that are sold by volunteers of all ages in this tiny, cheerful store. ♦ Daily 10AM-5:30PM. 846 Lexington Ave (at E. 64th St). 535.8030

69 Renny **Renny Reynolds,** one of the city's top florists and party designers, stocks a staggering array of plants and flowers—wild country flowers, graceful lilies, numerous species of orchids—and the crystal and bamboo vases to hold them. Reynolds has designed parties for celebrities from **David Letterman** to **Calvin Klein.** ♦ M-Sa 9AM-6PM. 159 E. 64th St (between Third and Lexington Aves). 288.7000

70 Jojo ★★★$$$ Hailed as a creative genius and forerunner in the movement to replace cream- and butter-based sauces with more healthful infused oils and vegetable juices, chef **Jean-Georges Vongerichten** left the formal **Lafayette** restaurant in 1991 to open this casual spot. The limited menu offers unique interpretations of bistro fare. Favorites include shrimp in carrot juice with Thai spices and a spectacular chocolate cake. ♦ French ♦ Lunch and dinner; dinner only on Saturday. Closed Sunday. 160 E. 64th St (between Third and Lexington Aves). Reservations recommended. 223.5656

71 Edward Durell Stone House Designed by **Edward Durell Stone** in 1956, the concrete grillwork covering the facade of the late architect's home is similar to the screen he used in his design for the American Embassy in New Delhi two years earlier. ♦ 130 E. 64th St (between Lexington and Park Aves)

72 Central Presbyterian Church To build this former Baptist church, which was designed by **Henry C. Pelton** and **Allen & Collens** in 1922, **John D. Rockefeller, Jr.,** matched every contribution, dollar for dollar; he also taught Bible classes here. In 1930, the congregation moved to **Riverside Church,** also largely funded by Rockefeller. ♦ 593 Park Ave (at E. 64th St). 838.0808

73 China House Gallery/China Institute in America This gift of publisher **Henry R. Luce,** the son of missionaries to China, reflects his lifelong interest in Sino-American cultural and political exchange. Along with changing exhibitions on Chinese fine arts and folk traditions, the institute, housed in a 1905 building by **Charles A. Platt,** conducts educational programs. ♦ Voluntary contribution. Hours vary, so call ahead. 125 E. 65th St (between Lexington and Park Aves). 744.8181

74 Mayfair Baglioni Hotel $$$$ Originally an apartment house designed by **J.E.R. Carpenter** in 1925, it was converted to a small European-style hotel (shown above) in 1934—one of the few in the city with 24-hour staffed elevator service. The lobby exudes an air of old money with its mellow marble and antique mahogany. Most of the recently renovated, elegantly decorated rooms are large enough to include a sitting area, a working fireplace, and a butler's pantry. Guests are offered an array of soaps, terry robes, and an umbrella on rainy days. Recently purchased by Italy's prestigious **Baglioni** chain, with **Dario Mariotti** as general manager, this is possibly the finest hotel of its size in the city. ♦ 610 Park Ave (at E. 65th St). 288.0800, 800/223.0542; fax 737.0538

Within the Mayfair Baglioni Hotel:

Le Cirque ★★★$$$$ Actors, high-fashion models, and other representatives of the rich and powerful favor this bustling, posh restaurant. **Sirio Maccioni,** owner and

---

Restaurants/Clubs: Red   **Hotels: Blue**

Shops/ 🍴 Outdoors: Green   **Sights/Culture: Black**

ringmaster, is the city's best host, and regulars—whether titled or not—get royal treatment, though unknowns are treated well too. Chef **Sylvain Portay** produces both standard haute cuisine and many original dishes. For the choicest morsels, concentrate on the specials rather than the printed menu. Pasta primavera, first popularized here, is never on the menu or an announced special, but is ordered by patrons in the know. Heavenly desserts include chocolate mousse cake and crème brûlée. Power tables: the front banquettes or the bar tables. ♦ French ♦ Lunch and dinner. Closed Sunday. 58 E. 65th St (between Park and Madison Aves). Jacket and tie required; reservations required days in advance. 794.9292

75 Hotel Plaza Athénée $$$$ Formerly the **Alrae Apartments,** designed by **George F. Pelham** in 1927, this intimate, ultraclassy hotel is modeled after the famous Paris original. Its moderate size (160 spacious rooms and suites) and residential location attract guests, such as the **Princess of Wales,** in search of serenity rather than the hustle of Midtown. The lobby is a combination of French period furnishings, Italian marble floors, and hand-painted mural tapestry walls. Amenities include 24-hour concierge and room service, kitchenettes, **Porthault** robes, **Crabtree & Evelyn** toiletries, in-room safes (the hotel itself is extremely secure, with only one entrance), and fax machines available upon request. Each of the four duplex penthouse suites includes a terrace and solarium. ♦ 37 E. 64th St (between Park and Madison Aves). 734.9100; fax 772.0958

Within the Hotel Plaza Athénée:

Le Regence ★★★★$$$$ Run by the expert **Rostang** family and guided by resident chef **Marcel Agnez,** Le Regence continues to excel in all categories. The service is impeccable and the food top flight. At lunch, choose from the extensive à la carte menu—lamb chops, veal, or anything from the sea. At dinner, go à la carte as well, or order either of two elaborate prix fixe meals. Duck liver salad, Mediterranean seafood soup, and Dover sole are frequent offerings. There is also a private dining room available for parties up to 25. ♦ French ♦ Breakfast, lunch, and dinner. Jacket, tie, and reservations required. 606.4647

76 Boutique Descamps A French company devoted to the luxury of bed and bath, this store carries plush toweling and robes, cotton sheets in delicate prints, and down comforters and pillows. ♦ M-Sa 10AM-6PM. 723 Madison Ave (at E. 64th St). 355.2522

77 Walter Steiger This women's shoe salon features the newest silhouettes from Europe by one of the leading designers. ♦ M-Sa 10AM-6PM. 739 Madison Ave (between E. 64th and E. 65th Sts). 570.1212

78 Chase Manhattan Bank A brick wall to the left of this Georgian bank, designed by **Morrel Smith** in 1932, conceals a colonial garden—a rarity on this busy street. ♦ 726 Madison Ave (at E. 64th St)

78 Wildenstein & Co. In 1932, **Horace Trumbauer** designed the building housing this gallery, which is known for the depth of its collections of old and contemporary paintings and objets d'art. Exhibitions often rival museum shows. ♦ M-F 10AM-5PM. 19 E. 64th St (between Madison and Fifth Aves). 879.0500

79 Emilio Pucci This boutique for the Italian designer is in a house that was once owned by **Consuela Vanderbilt Smith,** daughter of **William K. Vanderbilt.** It was built in 1882 by **Theodore Weston,** with a 1920 facade by **Mott B. Schmidt.** Pucci, whose designs became popular in the '50s, passed away in 1992. ♦ M-Sa 10AM-6PM. 24 E. 64th St (between Madison and Fifth Aves). 752.4777

80 Berwind Mansion This Venetian Renaissance mansion was the home of coal magnate **Edwin J. Berwind,** who was the sole supplier of coal for America's warships. Today, the building, which was designed in 1896 by **N.C. Melton,** contains cooperative apartments. ♦ 2 E. 64th St (at Fifth Ave)

80 820 Fifth Avenue Designed in 1916 by **Starrett & Van Vleck,** this is one of the earliest luxury apartment buildings on Fifth Avenue. Among its first tenants was New York's governor **Al Smith.** ♦ At E. 64th St

81 India House This unusually wide (65 feet) mansion, designed by **Warren & Wetmore** in 1903, would be right at home on the streets of Paris. It was built for banker **Marshall Orme Wilson,** whose wife was **Carrie Astor,** daughter of *the* **Mrs. Astor,** who lived around the corner. It is now owned by the government of India. ♦ 3 E. 64th St (at Fifth Ave)

82 Temple Emanu-El Designed by **Robert D. Kohn, Charles Butler,** and **Clarence Stein** in 1929, this impressive gray limestone edifice on the site of a mansion belonging to **Caroline Schermerhorn Astor** is the temple of the oldest Reform congregation in New York. Resembling only the nave of a cathedral, the structure has masonry-bearing walls. In style, it is Romanesque with Eastern influences; these are repeated on the interior with Byzantine ornaments. The hall is 77 feet wide, 150 feet long, and 403 feet high; it seats 2,500—more than St. Patrick's Cathedral. ♦ 1 E. 65th St (at Fifth Ave). 744.1400

83 Cambridge Chemists Any top-of-the-line European product can be found here, including **Cyclax of London, Innoxa, Roc,** and **Vichy.** ♦ M-F 9AM-7PM; Sa 10AM-5PM. 21 E. 65th St (at Madison Ave). 734.5678

84 Sarah Delano Roosevelt Memorial House In 1908, when her son, **Franklin,** was married, **Sarah Delano Roosevelt** commissioned **Charles A. Platt** to design this pair of houses; one was for herself, the other for the newlyweds. The houses are identical, with a common entrance. Several of their rooms were connected by folding doors to make them larger when necessary, as well as to give interior access between the two houses. It was in the fourth-floor front bedroom of the house on the right that Roosevelt went through his long recovery from polio in 1921-22. The future president's mother wanted him to go to their estate in Hyde Park, New York, but his wife, **Eleanor,** persuaded him to stay in the city. She felt he had a future in politics and needed to be closer to the centers of power, even though bedridden. Her decision doomed her to live under the thumb of her mother-in-law, not one of her favorite people. The buildings are now a community center for **Hunter College** students. ♦ 45-47 E. 65th St (between Park and Madison Aves)

84 American Federation of the Arts (AFA) Located in a 1910 building that was designed by **Trowbridge & Livingston,** the AFA provides traveling exhibitions for small museums around the country. The interior of the building, designed by **Edward Durell Stone** in 1960 and now devoted to office space, is richly detailed. The walls are French limestone, the ceilings sculpted in plaster. Some rooms have oak-paneled walls. It was originally the home of stockbroker **Benson B. Sloan.** ♦ 41 E. 65th St (between Park and Madison Aves)

85 LS Collection Elegant high-design housewares, such as leather desk accessories by **Arte Cuoio,** sterling silver desk accessories and vases from **Zucchi & Pampaloni,** and perfume bottles from Canadian sculptor **Max Leser** are found here. ♦ M-W, F-Sa 10AM-6PM; Th 10AM-7PM. 765 Madison Ave (between E. 65th and E. 66th Sts). 472.3355

86 45 East 66th Street Designed in 1900 by **Harde & Short,** this building displays a lacy pastry exuberance at an even higher level than the **Alwyn Court Apartments,** designed by the same firm. Note the Elizabethan and Flemish Gothic detailing and the sensuous ease of the round tower on the corner. ♦ At Madison Ave

87 North Beach Leather Whether they prefer trendy or classic styles, male and female leather aficionados will find all manner of leather jeans, jackets, shirts, overblouses, coats, bras, bikini pants, and dresses—some punched out, others adorned with feathers, beads, or studs. ♦ M-W, F 10AM-6:30PM; Th 10AM-7PM; Sa 10AM-6PM; Su noon-5PM. 772 Madison Ave (at E. 66th St). 772.0707

Restaurants/Clubs: Red   Hotels: Blue
Shops/ 🌱 Outdoors: Green   **Sights/Culture:** Black

88 The Lotos Club Designed by **Richard H. Hunt** in 1900, this was once the home of **William J. Schieffelin,** head of a wholesale drug firm and a crusader for civil rights at the end of the 19th century. The rusticated limestone base supports a redbrick midsection and a double-story mansard roof. A vigorous Second Empire composite on the verge of being excessive, it is now head-quarters of the Lotos Club, an organization of artists, musicians, actors, and journalists. ♦ 5 E. 66th St (between Madison and Fifth Aves)

89 4 East 67th Street This is an ornate Beaux Arts mansion, built for banker **Henri P. Wertheim** in 1902 and designed by **John H. Duncan.** It is now the residence of the **Consul General of Japan.** ♦ Between Madison and Fifth Aves

90 13 and 15 East 67th Street This is a curious pair, particularly in contrast to the Modernist red-granite face at No. 17. No. 13, designed in 1921 by **Henry Allan Jacobs,** is an Italian Renaissance concoction that was built for theatrical producer **Martin Beck.** No. 15, a 1904 building by **Ernest Flagg,** now the **Regency Whist Club,** was the **Cortland Field Bishop House.** Concocted of stone and restrained ironwork, this rather Parisian house was designed by the man who did **Scribner's Bookstore.** ♦ Between Madison and Fifth Aves

91 Ronaldo Maia Ltd. Maia's party designs—tables wrapped with rose moiré and ceilings turned into topiaries—are much sought-after. He is the author of *Decorating with Flowers.* ♦ M-F 9:30AM-6PM. 27 E. 67th St (at Madison Ave). 288.1049

92 Sonia Rykiel Rykiel's fashions are expensive but timeless. The colors, cut, and workmanship make them seem an investment, and Rykiel's followers say her clothes make them feel special. ♦ M-W, F-Sa 9:30AM-6:30PM; Th 9:30AM-7:30PM. 792 Madison Ave (between E. 66th and E. 67th Sts). 744.0880

93 Montenapoleone Fabulously silky and embroidered Italian and French lingerie is sold here. ♦ M-Sa 10AM-6PM. 789 Madison Ave (between E. 66th and E. 67th Sts). 535.2660

malo

93 Malo If you have to ask how much these sumptuous cashmere items for men and women cost, you best not enter. This is the company's first American boutique, featuring their remarkably lightweight—if heavy-priced—items of ultimate luxury. It takes one year's production from three to four cashmere goats to produce one sweater. ♦ M-Sa 10AM-6PM. 791 Madison Ave (at E. 67th St). 717.1766

94 Gallery of Wearable Art Everything here makes a statement. Whether it is a statement you'd care to make is something you'll have to decide. In addition to daily—though hardly quotidian—clothes, there's a unique collection of wedding gowns and bridal accessories. ♦ Tu-Sa 10AM-6PM. 34 E. 67th St (between Park and Madison Aves). 425.5379

94 Koos Van Den Akker Along with the elaborate feminine skirts, jackets, and blouses of patchwork and collage for which he is known, Koos also offers an exclusive collection of handmade sweaters, along with such one-of-a-kind extravaganzas as a wedding dress with a lace top and a voluminous Scarlett O'Hara skirt of appliquéd silk and net. Sometimes he comes up with an unadorned silk or jersey dress for those not enamored of pattern-on-pattern. ♦ M-F 9AM-5PM; call for Saturday hours. 34 E. 67th St (between Park and Madison Aves). 249.5432

95 Seventh Regiment Armory Designed by **Charles W. Clinton** in 1880, this is a crenelated, almost cartoonish fort in a very proper neighborhood. The interiors were furnished and detailed by **Louis Comfort Tiffany.** The hall is immense: 187 feet by 290 feet. It is the site of the **Winter Antiques Fair** and other huge events. ♦ E. 66th to E. 67th Sts (between Lexington and Park Aves). 439.0300

96 115 East 67th Street Designed in 1932 by **Andrew J. Thomas,** this building is a happy place with owls, squirrels, and other animals in the decorative panels and huge arched entry. ♦ Between Lexington and Park Aves

97 660 Park Avenue Architect **Philip Sawyer,** of **York & Sawyer,** carved a reputation for himself as a designer of banks, but his work on the rustication of this handsome 1927 apartment building is worthy of any of them. ♦ At E. 67th St

98 Frette This sleek Italian shop features extravagant linens for bed and table, including piqué bedspreads, linen sheets, and damask tablecloths. ♦ M-Sa 10AM-6PM. 799 Madison Ave (between E. 67th and E. 68th Sts). 988.5221

98 Thomas K. Woodard At the city's premier shop for high-quality antique and early 20th-century quilts, you'll find sizes ranging from crib to king. Designs include stars, postage stamps, and "drunkard's path." There are also baskets, spongeware, painted furniture, and rag and hooked rugs. ♦ M-Sa 11AM-6PM. 799 Madison Ave (between E. 67th and E. 68th Sts), second floor. 988.2906

98 Emanuel Ungaro Here is the city's largest grouping of the designer's pret-a-porter collection for women, including his opulently printed, jewel-toned fabrics—paisleys, stripes, florals, and checks—in surprising combinations as seemingly weightless dresses, separates, and evening gowns. The shop also sells such accessories as boots, shoes, belts, and shawls. ♦ M-Sa 9:30AM-6:30PM. 803 Madison Ave (between E. 67th and E. 68th Sts). 249.4090

Cerutti

98 Cerutti This may be the most useful children's clothing store in the city, due to its broad and well-chosen range. There are the practical, the perky, and the extravagant (hand-knit sweaters and leggings sets from Italy). Little boys will find navy blue blazers, and little girls handmade, lavishly smocked dresses. ♦ M-Sa 9AM-5:30PM. 807 Madison Ave (between E. 67th and E. 68th Sts). 737.7540

99 Joseph Tricot The latest knits from London are here—some crude, some romantic, all representing the world of street chic. Also, hats and leather bags. ♦ M-W, F-Sa 10AM-6PM; Th 10:30AM-6:30PM. 804 Madison Ave (between E. 67th and E. 68th Sts). 570.0077

99 Billy Martin's Western Wear Yes, it's the late **Billy Martin** who used to pace the dugout at Yankee Stadium. This one-stop source of cowboy boots, fancy belts, and other expensive duds will make you look at home on the range. ♦ M-F 10AM-7PM; Sa 10:30AM-6PM; Su noon-5PM. 812 Madison Ave (at E. 68th St). 861.3100

100 6, 8, and 10 East 68th Street These three houses, designed by **John H. Duncan** in 1900, were bought by financier **Otto Kuhn,** of **Kuhn, Loeb & Co.,** in 1916, and altered in 1919 with a French Renaissance limestone facade designed by **Harry Allen Jacobs.** He refurbished the interiors and sold them to, among others, banker **Edward W. Harriman.** ♦ Between Madison and Fifth Aves

101 9 East 68th Street Designed in 1906 by **Heins & LaFarge,** this was formerly the **George T. Bliss House,** now the **Center for Marital Therapy.** Four giant columns hold up nothing but that little balcony and a brave front to the world. Remarkably out of scale, the house is noteworthy because it is engaging and not overly pretentious. ♦ Between Madison and Fifth Aves

102 MaxMara The upscale Italian women's clothing company purchased this six-story building and is restoring it to the tune of $1 million. Designed and built in 1882 in the neo-Greco style with Federal elements, the first two floors will provide elegant retail space for the well-known manufacturer. Opening is scheduled for fall of 1994. ♦ 813 Madison Ave (at E. 68th St)

102 Giorgio Armani Boutique The Italian designer's complete avant-garde ready-to-wear and couture lines for men and women are now under one roof. ♦ M-W, F-Sa 10AM-6PM; Th 10AM-7PM. 815 Madison Ave (at E. 68th St). 988.9191

102 Valentino In this hushed and lavish setting, you can see the ready-to-wear collection of Valentino, including classic pants, beautifully shaped jackets, and luxurious dresses for day and night. Fabrics are intensely sensuous—linens are weightless, cottons silken. Prices are out of this world. ♦ M-Sa 10AM-6PM. 825 Madison Ave (between E. 68th and E. 69th Sts). 772.6969

103 45 East 68th Street In the 1950s and 1960s, **Richard Kollmar** and his wife, **Dorothy Kilgallen,** used a fourth-floor studio in this house, which was designed by **C.P.H. Gilbert** in 1912, to broadcast their popular radio program, "Breakfast with Dorothy and Dick." After their divorce, Kollmar's second wife, fashion designer **Anne Fogarty,** used the room as her studio. ♦ Between Park and Madison Aves

104 Council on Foreign Relations This building, designed in 1920 by **Delano & Aldrich,** was built by **Harold I. Pratt,** son of **Charles Pratt,** a partner of **John D. Rockefeller, Jr.,** and founder of Brooklyn's **Pratt Institute.** The present owner is an organization that promotes interest in foreign relations and publishes the influential magazine *Foreign Affairs.* ♦ 58 E. 68th St (at Park Ave)

105 Americas Society In the late 1940s and early 1950s, this was the **Soviet Delegation to the United Nations,** which made this corner the scene of almost continuous anti-Communist demonstrations. Before the Russians arrived, it was the home of banker **Percy Rivington Pyne.** The building, designed in 1909 by **McKim, Mead & White,** now houses a gallery specializing in Central, South, and North American art. ♦ Tu-Su noon-6PM. 680 Park Ave (at E. 68th St). 249.8950

105 680-690 Park Avenue A lively but not exceptional collection of brick and limestone neo-Georgian buildings, this ensemble is special because it is the only full block of town houses surviving on Park Avenue. No. 680: **Center for Inter-American Relations,** formerly the **Soviet Delegation to the UN,** originally the **Percy Pyne House,** was designed in 1909 by **McKim, Mead & White;** No. 684: **Spanish Institute,** the house of Pyne's son-in-law, **Oliver D. Filey,** was built in Pyne's garden in 1926, by McKim, Mead & White; No. 686: **Institute Italiano di Cultura,** formerly the **William Sloane House,** was designed in 1918 by **Delano & Aldrich;** No.

690: **Italian Consulate,** originally the **Henry P. Davidson House,** was designed in 1917 by **Walker & Gillette.** ♦ Between E. 68th and E. 69th Sts

106 Hunter College One of the colleges of the **City University of New York,** Hunter was founded in 1870 as a school for training teachers. Today, the school emphasizes such practical disciplines as science, premed and nursing, and education. It also offers bachelor's degrees in the arts, humanities, and social sciences. The **Hunter College Theater** (772.4000), in the main building, is used for lectures, political forums, and music and dance programs. ♦ E. 68th to E. 69th Sts (between Lexington and Park Aves). 772.4000

107 S. Wyler This shop celebrated its 100th birthday in 1990. It is an excellent source of 18th- and 19th-century English sterling silver and Victorian and old Sheffield plate, as well as antique porcelain. ♦ M-Sa 10AM-5:30PM. 941 Lexington Ave (at E. 69th St). 879.9848

108 The Union Club Limestone and granite in a conservative and rather dry palazzo composition (compare with the University or Metropolitan clubs) looks the way you would expect the oldest men's club in New York City to look. This building was designed in 1932 by **Delano & Aldrich.** ♦ 101 E. 69th St (at Park Ave). 734.5440

109 Pratesi One of the more sybaritic bed-and-bath shops in town, Pratesi sells sheets of linen, silk, and Egyptian cotton, as well as comforters filled with goose down or cashmere and covered in silk. Upstairs there are terry cloth robes and towels to match the printed sheets. ♦ M-Sa 10AM-6PM. 829 Madison Ave (at E. 69th St). 288.2315

109 Madison Avenue Bookshop It looks deceptively small, but the two no-nonsense floors are packed with a wide range of literary criticism, art, current fiction, and cookbooks. It stocks the full line of every major publisher, including a lot of first novels. Service is a strong point: mailing, delivery, special orders, out-of-print searches, and fancy gift-wrapping. ♦ M-Sa 10AM-6PM. 833 Madison Ave (at E. 69th St). 535.6130

109 Maraolo Italian-made shoes for men, women, and children can be found here at reasonable prices, considering the location and the quality. ♦ M-W, F-Sa 10AM-6:30PM; Th 10AM-7PM; Su noon-5PM. 835 Madison Ave (between E. 69th and E. 70th Sts). 628.5080. Also at: 782 Lexington Ave. 832.8182; 1321 Third Ave. 535.6225

110 Minna Rosenblatt An enchanting collection of **Tiffany** lamps and other glass antiques are offered here. ♦ M-Sa 10AM-5:30PM. 844 Madison Ave (between E. 69th and E. 70th Sts). 288.0250

The Frick Collection

110 Missoni The whole store is devoted to the Missoni signature Italian knits on what is becoming "European Designers' Row." The recognizable blend of subtle color combinations and patterns is worked up in all kinds of dashing sportswear for men and women. ♦ M-Sa 10AM-6PM. 836 Madison Ave (at E. 69th St). 517.9339

110 The Westbury Hotel $$$$ There is a Westbury in London with an American flavor, but its American counterpart is decidedly British. Amenities include 24-hour room service, in-room safes, PC and fax ports, same-day valet service, and a multilingual staff. The Chippendale furniture and 17th-century Belgian tapestries in the lobby are genuine. All of its large 235 rooms and suites are handsomely decorated. ♦ 15 E. 69th St (at Madison Ave). 535.2000, 800/321.1569; fax 535.5058

Within The Westbury Hotel:

The Polo Lounge ★★$$$ The atmosphere is appropriately clublike—plush leather chairs, banquette seating, dark mahogany walls with equestrian prints, brass sconces. Try the fresh foie gras terrine—a memorable appetizer. The balance of the menu, American with French touches, has greatly improved. Service is polite and attentive. ♦ American/French ♦ Breakfast, lunch, and dinner. Jacket required. Reservations recommended. 439.4835

111 MacKenzie-Childs Madison Avenue's newest purveyor of high-end domestic goods is no place for the minimalist-minded. Designed and decorated with *objets* that are hand-painted with spots, checks, stripes, and flowers, this charming three-level store is supplied by artisan workshops in upstate New York. Hand-painted dinnerware in myriad designs and mix-and-match possibilities is a particular strength. Gift ideas abound, and an unusually friendly staff is eager to help with the decision-making. ♦ M-Sa 10AM-6PM. 824 Madison Ave (at E. 69th St). 570.6050

111 D. Porthault This shop can weave tablecloths that will go the entire length of a ballroom, sheets to fit the beds of private airplanes, and duvet covers of fine linen. **Queen Elizabeth II** has slept on Porthault's sheets. Wealthy children wear its overalls of the silkiest cotton. ♦ M-F 10AM-5:30PM; Sa 10AM-5PM. 18 E. 69th St (at Madison Ave). 688.1660

112 The Frick Collection When the old Lenox Library was torn down, **Henry Clay Frick,** chairman of the Carnegie Steel Corp., bought the site, wanting a place to display his art. He had **Thomas Hastings** design the Beaux Arts house in 1914—one of the last great mansions on Fifth Avenue—with apartments for the family and reception rooms for the art. In his will, Frick decreed that his wife could continue living there until her death, at which time it would be renovated and expanded as a museum (illustrated above). **John Russell Pope,** who later designed the **National Gallery** in Washington, D.C., designed in 1935 what is now the museum. He is responsible for its unique character, especially the glass-covered courtyard, a rewarding retreat from city anxieties if ever there was one. The east wing was added in 1977, designed by **John Barrington Bayley** and **Harry Van Dyke;** the great landscape architect **Russell Page** designed the garden.

Visiting here is like being asked into the sumptuous private home of a collector who bought only the crème de la crème of the old masters, and then hung them, amid fine furniture, porcelains, and bronzes, in the most restful, well-lit rooms. Treasures here include **Rembrandt's** *The Polish Rider,* **Van Eyck's** *Virgin and Child with Saints, and Donor,* **Bellini's** *Saint Francis in the Desert,* **Titian's** *Man in a Red Cap,* **El Greco's** *Saint Jerome,* **Piero della Francesca's** *Saint Simon the Apostle,* and a whole room of **Fragonard.** There are occasional free lectures and chamber music concerts. (Call or write for ticket information.) Absolutely worth a visit. Children under 10 not admitted. ♦ Admission. Tu-Sa 10AM-6PM; Su 1-6PM. 1 E. 70th St (at Fifth Ave). 288.0700

113 Lycee Français The French school now occupies two French Renaissance mansions: No. 7, designed in 1899 by **Flagg & Chambers,** was the **Oliver Gould Jennings House;** No. 9, created in 1896 by **Carrère & Hastings,** was the **Henry T. Sloane House.** ♦ 7 and 9 E. 72nd St (between Madison and Fifth Aves). 861.9400

114 Au Chat Botté Expensive charm pervades this shop, which sells baby furniture, including cribs, changing tables, chairs, chests of drawers, clothes racks, and bumper guards, as well as children's clothes. ♦ M-Sa 10AM-6PM. 903 Madison Ave (at E. 72nd St). 772.7402

115 Polo-Ralph Lauren If you like the Polo look, you'll love the wonderland **Ralph Lauren** created here. Designed in 1898 by **Kimball & Thompson,** the French Renaissance building was commissioned by **Gertrude Rhinelander Waldo,** a descendant of one of New York's most influential families. She lived here for a few months, but preferred to live across the street with her sister. She offered it to her son, but he preferred to live elsewhere too, and the house stood empty until it was sold in a foreclosure in 1920. Before Lauren moved in, it was the **Philips Auction Gallery.** It's well worth a visit even if you don't buy anything. ♦ M-W, F-Sa 10AM-6PM; Th 10AM-8PM. 867 Madison Ave (at E. 72nd St). 606.2100

116 Polo Sport-Ralph Lauren Ralph Lauren has extended his fashion emporium across the street to this 10,000-square-foot activewear shop. In addition to the high-tech, performance-oriented clothing for outdoor sports (skiing, rock-climbing, golf, etc.), there's a boutique featuring Lauren's new "RRL" division of weathered classics: jeans, motorcycle jackets, flannel shirts, and the like. ♦ M-W, F-Sa 10AM-6PM; Th 10AM-8PM. 888 Madison Ave (at E. 72nd St). 434.8000

117 Pierre Deux The French family **Demery** has spent 300 years creating richly colored paisley and floral fabrics that are quintessentially Provençal. They sell their best designs—the **Souleiado** line—to Pierre Deux. Fabric is sold by the yard or made up into tablecloths, napkins, place mats, quilts, pillows, scarves, shawls, neckties, shirts for men, and dresses for women and little girls. ♦ M-Sa 10AM-6PM. 870 Madison Ave (at E. 71st St). 570.9343. Also at: 369 Bleecker St. 243.7740

118 St. James Episcopal Church Originally designed in 1884 by **R.H. Robertson,** this church was established on the East Side before the invasion of the millionaires, but its future was secured when families such as the **Schermerhorns,** the **Rhinelanders,** and the **Astors** became members of its vestry. In 1924, the church was rebuilt by **Ralph Adams Cram;** the steeple was added by **Richard Kimball** in 1950. ♦ Madison Ave at E. 71st St. 288.4100

119 Yves Saint Laurent-Rive Gauche Neighboring stores combine to offer the entire Saint Laurent line for men and women. Together, they have the city's largest variety of his collections, including hats, umbrellas, shirts, slacks, dresses, suits, and ball gowns. ♦ M-Sa 10AM-6PM. 855-859 Madison Ave (between E. 70th and E. 71st Sts). 988.3821

120 Hirschl & Adler Top-quality shows of 18th-, 19th-, and 20th-century American and European art appear here. Also featured are American prints and contemporary paintings and sculpture. ♦ Tu-F 9:30AM-5:15PM; Sa 9:30AM-4:45PM. 21 E. 70th St (between Madison and Fifth Aves). 535.8810

120 Knoedler Gallery The oldest New York-based art gallery, founded in 1846, Knoedler handles contemporary greats such as **Richard Diebenkorn, Nancy Graves, Robert Motherwell, Frank Stella,** and **Robert Rauschenberg.** Located in a 1910 building by **Thornton Chad,** this gallery is always worth checking out. ♦ Tu-Sa 9:30AM-5:30PM. 19 E. 70th St (between Madison and Fifth Aves). 794.0550

121 45 East 70th Street Originally the home of investment banker **Arthur S. Lehman,** this nondescript town house was designed by **Aymar Embury II** in 1929. His wife was the former **Adele Lewisohn,** a philanthropist and champion tennis player. It is now the home of **Joseph** and **Estee Lauder.** ♦ Between Park and Madison Aves

122 46 East 70th Street This ornate neo-Jacobean house, designed in 1912 by **Frederick Sterner,** was built for **Stephen C. Clark,** whose family owned the **Singer Sewing Machine Co.** Parts of his extensive art collection are in the **Metropolitan Museum of Art.** Among his many interests was baseball—he founded the **Baseball Hall of Fame** at Cooperstown, New York. The former residence is now the **Lowell Thomas Building of the Explorers Club.** ♦ Between Park and Madison Aves

123 The Asia Society The permanent collection of Asian art assembled by **John D. Rockefeller III** between 1951 and 1979 was moved in 1981 to this building designed by **Edward Larrabee Barnes.** It is known for its outstanding Southeast Asian and Indian sculpture, Chinese ceramics and bronzes, and Japanese ceramics and wood sculptures. Other galleries in this serene albeit extravagant building feature changing exhibits ranging from Chinese snuff bottles to Islamic books from the collection of **Prince Salruddin Aga Kahn.** The Asia Society also sponsors lectures here on Asian arts and adventures, as well as films and performances. A large bookstore is well stocked with books, periodicals, and prints from or about Asia. ♦ Admission. Tu-W, F-Sa 11AM-6PM; Th 11AM-8PM; Su noon-5PM. Free tours: Tu-Sa 12:30PM; Su 2:30PM. 725 Park Ave (at E. 70th St). 288.6400

Restaurants/Clubs: Red	Hotels: Blue
Shops/ ♛ Outdoors: Green	Sights/Culture: Black

123 Visiting Nurse Service of New York This organization is located in a Tudor Revival mansion, designed in 1921 by **Walker & Gillette,** that was once home to **Thomas W. Lamont,** chairman of **J.P. Morgan & Co.** ♦ 107 E. 70th St (between Lexington and Park Aves). 794.9200

124 124 East 70th Street Built for financier **Edward A. Norman** in 1941 by **William Lescaze,** this International-style house was cited by the **Museum of Modern Art** for its innovative design. ♦ Between Lexington and Park Aves

125 123 East 70th Street Designer **Samuel Trowbridge,** whose works include the B. Altman department store (which closed in 1989), the St. Regis Hotel, and other Beaux Arts gems, built this house for himself in 1903. ♦ Between Lexington and Park Aves

125 Paul Mellon House This French Provincial town house, right at home in New York, was built for the industrialist and art collector in 1965 by **H. Page Cross.** ♦ 125 E. 70th St (between Lexington and Park Aves)

126 131 East 71st Street America's first interior decorator, **Elsie de Wolfe,** lived here and used the house as a showcase for her talents. The house was built in 1867, but she designed the present facade in 1910 with **Ogden Codman, Jr.** ♦ Between Lexington and Park Aves

127 La Petite Ferme ★★$$$ A great place to go for simply cooked, fresh French food—if only the prices were more reasonable. ♦ French ♦ Lunch and dinner. Closed Sunday. 973 Lexington Ave (between E. 70th and E. 71st Sts). Reservations recommended. 249.3272

127 Sette Mezzo ★★$$$ Pasta is numero uno at this Northern Italian boîte, where the beautiful people rub elbows with loyal neighborhood regulars. ♦ Italian ♦ Lunch and dinner. 969 Lexington Ave (between E. 70th and E. 71st Sts). Reservations required. 472.0400

128 The Lenox School This Tudor house, built in 1907 by **Edward P. Casey** for **Stephen H. Brown,** governor of the New York Stock Exchange, was considered one of the area's showplaces before it was converted to a school in 1932. ♦ 154 E. 70th St (between Third and Lexington Aves)

129 Gracious Home The ultimate neighborhood hardware store: TVs, woks, umbrellas, dishwashers, typewriters, radiator covers, mason jars, and all the expected basics. Gracious Home will also custom-order radiator enclosures. At the store across the street (No. 1217), you will find a complete bath shop—everything from sinks and faucets to shower curtains and bath mats—decorative hardware, moldings, wallpaper, bedding, and gift items. ♦ M-F 8AM-7PM; Sa 9AM-7PM; Su 10AM-6PM. 1220 Third Ave (at E. 70th St). 517.6300

130 Grace's Marketplace This is an uptown version of **Balducci's** gourmet food store in Greenwich Village, and an East Side answer to the West Side's **Zabar's.** ♦ M-Sa 7AM-8:30PM; Su 8AM-7PM. 1237 Third Ave (at E. 71st St). 737.0600

131 Fay & Allen's Cafe $$ Light snacks and sandwiches are served here in a relaxed setting. ♦ Cafe ♦ Dinner. 1240 Third Ave (between E. 71st and E. 72nd Sts). 794.1359

132 Evergreen Antiques Scandinavian country furniture and accessories as well as Continental and Biedermeier furniture are available here. ♦ M-F 11AM-7PM; Sa 11AM-6PM. 1249 Third Ave (at E. 72nd St). 744.5664

133 Cafe Greco ★$$$ This lively, flower-filled restaurant orients its cuisine around the Mediterranean. Spanish, Italian, French, and Moroccan dishes all find their way to the table. ♦ Continental ♦ Lunch and dinner. 1390 Second Ave (between E. 71st and E. 72nd Sts). 737.4300

134 First Reformed Hungarian Church Hungarian-born architect **Emery Roth** gave us a taste of the old country in 1915 when he designed this ornamented white stucco church topped by an 80-foot, conical-roofed bell tower. ♦ 344 E. 69th St (between First and Second Aves)

135 Rockefeller University This collection of buildings was originally known as the **Rockefeller Institute for Medical Research.** The site, which was a summer estate of the **Schermerhorn** family, was acquired in 1901; the first building, **Founder's Hall,** opened in 1903 as a laboratory. Most striking are the gray hemisphere of **Caspary Auditorium,** built in 1957, and the **President's House,** built in 1958, both by **Harrison & Abramovitz.** It's worth a visit. Ask the guard for permission to enter, and while you're here, stroll toward the river for a look at the gardens. ♦ E. 64th to E. 68th Sts (between FDR Dr and York Ave). 327.8000

136 New York Hospital/Cornell University Medical College What appears to be a singular, almost solid, well-balanced mass is actually 15 buildings, designed in 1932 by **Coolidge, Shepley, Bullfinch & Abbott.** The strong vertical lines are offset by Gothic arches. The site is reported to have been the location of **Smuggler's Cave**—the hiding place of famous smuggler **David Provoost,** cousin of the first Episcopal bishop of New York City. The first smallpox vaccination was given here in 1799, by **Dr. Valentine Seaman.** ♦ 525 E. 68th St (between FDR Dr and York Ave). 746.5454

137 Sotheby's The London-based Sotheby's is the largest and oldest fine-arts auctioneer in the world. With its original Madison Avenue headquarters closed, it has relocated here in a larger but less personal shop, where there is a full round of important sales, exhibitions, and free seminars. Admission to some auctions is by ticket only, but all viewings are open to the public. ◆ M-Sa 10AM-5PM; Su 1-5PM. 1334 York Ave (at E. 72nd St). 606.7000

138 Petaluma ★★$$$ Fallen from the graces of the chic and trendy, this eclectic cafe still attracts a decent following. Singles flock to the bar, while folks of all shapes and sizes dine in the vast, pastel-colored postmodern space. The food is good, and don't skip the chocolate cake if you're a confirmed chocoholic. ◆ Italian ◆ Lunch and dinner. 1356 First Ave (at E. 73rd St). Reservations required. 772.8800

139 Cafe Crocodile ★$$$ The fresh, home-cooked taste of everything—be it of Greek, French, Italian, or North African origin—is the main appeal. The owner is also the chef, in the best sense of the word—someone who cooks for the love of it, and it shows. The upstairs dining room is available for private parties of 16 to 24. ◆ Mediterranean ◆ Lunch and dinner. Closed Sunday. 354 E. 74th St (between First and Second Aves). Reservations recommended. 249.6619

140 Jan Hus Church This 1914 Presbyterian church was founded by the Czech community, whose presence in the neighborhood led it to be known as Little Bohemia in the 1920s and 1930s. The parsonage is furnished to resemble a Czech peasant's house. ◆ 351 E. 74th St (between First and Second Aves). 879.0929

Within Jan Hus Church:

Chicago City Limits Established in New York in 1980, this is one of the oldest, and probably the only self-sustaining, comedy improvisation groups in the city. It was formed in Chicago in 1977 by **George Todisco** and actors participating in workshops at that city's renowned **Second City. Paul Zuckerman** and **Eddie Ellner** are standards. ◆ Shows: W-Th 8:30PM; F-Sa 8PM, 10:30PM. 772.8707

141 AccScentiques Decorative and fragrant accents for the home—tapestry and moiré pillows, hand-painted boxes and mirrors, a bamboo desk and chair, sachets, dried flowers, and potpourri—are squeezed into this petite boutique. ◆ Tu by appointment only; W-Su 11AM-7PM. 1418 Second Ave (at E. 74th St). 288.3289

142 Mezzaluna ★$$ This tiny restaurant is quite popular among East Siders who like to be seen in all the right places. Pizzas baked in wood-burning ovens are featured at lunch and after 10PM. ◆ Italian ◆ Lunch, dinner, and late-night meals. 1295 Third Ave (between E. 74th and E. 75th Sts). 535.9600

143 BBQ ★$ Cheap barbecued chicken and ribs are served with corn bread and coleslaw in this bargain hunter's paradise. Beat the dinner crowd for early-bird specials. ◆ American ◆ Lunch, dinner, and late-night meals. 1265 Third Ave (at E. 73rd St). 772.9393

144 Kamdin Designs In six to 12 months a custom-designed rug can be yours. Bring in a wallpaper or fabric swatch, a picture, or just an idea. Also sold here are Indian dhurries, Portuguese needlepoint, and Chinese petits points. ◆ Tu-F 11AM-6:30PM. 1020 Lexington Ave (at E. 73rd St). 772.2140

144 May We ★★$$$ Chef/owner **Mark May** and his wife, **Nini,** do the most they can in this cramped duplex space. Fine Mediterranean-inspired cuisine is served in the airy second-floor dining room, while singles dine and drink cocktails in the small cafe/bar downstairs. There's also a new outdoor cafe. ◆ French ◆ Lunch and dinner. Closed Sunday. 1022 Lexington Ave (at E. 73rd St). Reservations required. 249.0200

145 Paraclete Theological (mainly Christian) works are this bookstore's specialty. ◆ Tu-F 10AM-6PM; Sa 10AM-5PM. 146 E. 74th St (at Lexington Ave). 535.4050

146 Vivolo ★$$$ This is one of the city's most popular Italian restaurants, and that's the problem. Crowded and noisy, the cafe's system is overtaxed, and the ambience suffers. With all the rush, there doesn't seem to be time to create dishes that are better than merely ordinary. Fine if you're in the neighborhood. ◆ Italian ◆ Lunch and dinner. Closed Sunday. 140 E. 74th St (at Lexington Ave). Reservations required. 737.3533. Also at: 222 E. 58th St. 308.0112

147 La Maison du Chocolat From the acclaimed Parisian chocolatier **Robert Linxe** comes a shop for the true connoisseur. If the prices make you flinch, remember that these are among the best chocolates in the world. ◆ M-F 10AM-6:30PM; Sa 10AM-6PM. 25 E. 73rd St (between Fifth and Madison Aves). 744.7117

148 Trois Pommes French children's clothing from a variety of designers, including **Petit Bateau, Dan Jean,** and **Tartine et Chocolat,** are sold here. You'll find pure cotton footsies, T-shirts, nightgowns, and pants in mushroom, dolphin, polka dot, and stripe patterns, plus classic sweaters, snowsuits, dresses, pants, and rompers. ◆ M-W, F-Sa 10AM-6PM; Th 10AM-8PM. 930 Madison Ave (at E. 74th St). 288.1444

149 Coco Pazzo ★★★$$$ **Pino Luongo** has done it again! After **Le Madri**, he opened this, the most popular in his line of Italian restaurants. Judging from the highly talented Tuscan chef, **Cesare Casella**, and the illustrious crowds that flock here, Coco Pazzo's future is assured. ◆ Italian ◆ Lunch and dinner; dinner only on Sunday. 23 E. 74th St (between Fifth and Madison Aves). Reservations recommended. 794.0205

150 Books & Co. This is a general bookstore with the focus on literature, literary periodicals, and the complete works of many major writers. The leather sofa in the philosophy section is a welcome retreat for weary shoppers and museumgoers. ◆ M-Sa 10AM-7PM; Su noon-6PM. 939 Madison Ave (at E. 74th St). 737.1450

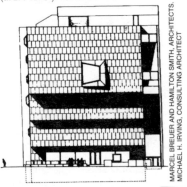

MARCEL BREUER AND HAMILTON SMITH, ARCHITECTS. MICHAEL H. IRVING, CONSULTING ARCHITECT

150 Whitney Museum of American Art Sculptor **Gertrude Vanderbilt Whitney** founded this museum in 1931 to support young artists and increase awareness of American art. The nucleus of its collection was 600 of the works she owned by **Thomas Hart Benton, George Bellows, Maurice Prendergast, Edward Hopper, John Sloan,** and other American artists of the era. The present building (shown above), designed by **Marcel Breuer** with **Hamilton Smith** in 1966, is the museum's third home. Like the **Guggenheim,** the Whitney is more sculpture than building. A dark, rectilinear, Brutalist mass steps out toward the street, almost threatening those who want to enter. Only the drawbridge entrance seems protective. The museum, perched on the corner, is isolated from its surroundings by sidewalls. You can peer down into the sunken sculpture garden and see through to parts of the lobby. But otherwise, the interior's workings are a mystery, guarded by angled trapezoidal windows that refuse to look you in the eye.

The vast gallery spaces are surprisingly flexible, and can be quite appropriate for a variety of types of art—an important quality for a museum dedicated to temporary exhibitions of contemporary art. The permanent collection, which has been increased to 10,000 pieces through gifts and acquisitions, includes works by **Alexander Calder, Louise Nevelson, Georgia O'Keeffe, Robert Rauschenberg, Ad Reinhardt,** and **Jasper Johns,** among others, and a portion of it is always on display. Special exhibitions often concentrate on the output of a single artist. It could be video artist of the '80s **Nam June Paik,** or Realist of the '30s Edward Hopper. The Whitney's regular invitational **Biennial,** which critics often pan, is a mixed bag of what's going on across the country. The museum has an aggressively independent series for American film and video artists and makes adventurous forays into the performing arts. For information on these and gallery lectures, check the information desk. The restaurant overlooking the sculpture garden is a pleasant place for refreshments and light meals. The museum operates two branches, including one at **Champion International Corp.** in Stamford, Connecticut, and one at the **Philip Morris Building,** Park Avenue at 42nd Street. **David Ross** was appointed director in 1991. ◆ Admission; free Th 6-8PM. W, F-Su 11AM-6PM; Th 1-8PM. Madison Ave at E. 75th St. 570.3676

Within the Whitney Museum of American Art:

Sarabeth's at the Whitney ★★$$ This branch of the Sarabeth's restaurant family is the perfect place to relax after touring the museum. Try her now-famous desserts. ◆ American ◆ Lunch; brunch on Saturday and Sunday. Closed Monday. 570.3670

151 The Chocolate Soup Charming children's clothes and accessories are crammed into this minuscule store. The most renowned item is the **Danish Souperbag,** an imported schoolbag that's as popular with adults as with children. Great sales. ◆ M-Sa 10AM-6PM; Su 1-6PM. 946 Madison Ave (between E. 74th and E. 75th Sts). 861.2210

152 Harkness House This 1905 building by Hale & Rogers was built for **Edward S. Harkness,** son of a **Standard Oil Co.** founder. It is now headquarters of the **Commonwealth Fund,** a philanthropic foundation. ◆ 1 E. 75th St (at Fifth Ave). 535.0400

153 Givenchy For women who want their haute couture brought to their doorsteps, this boutique sends fitters from the **House of Givenchy** in Paris to New York each spring and fall to measure their local clients from stem to stern. Their clothes can be picked up on either side of the Atlantic. For others, there are blouses, skirts, sweaters, coats, suits, ball gowns, and hats from both ready-to-wear and couture adaptations, which feature the same styles as in the couture collection but in less expensive fabrics. ◆ M-Sa 10AM-6PM. 21 E. 75th St (at Madison Ave). 772.1040

153 **Delorenzo** Furniture of the Art Deco era, sometimes including pieces by such designers as **Emile Rouhlmann, Jean Dunand,** and **Pierre Chareau,** is available here. ◆ M-Sa 10AM-6PM. 958 Madison Ave (at E. 75th St). 249.7575

154 **Time Will Tell** More than 1,000 antique watches and timepieces by such prestigious manufacturers as Rolex and Tiffany fill this specialty store. Pocket watches from the 1800s join more "modern" pieces from the turn of the century, a variety of Art Deco models, and even some of the early Mickey Mouse numbers. An array of quality watchbands in unusual skins are also for sale, and a full repair service is available. ◆ M-Sa 10AM-6PM. 962 Madison Ave (between E. 75th and E. 76th Sts). 861.2663

155 **The Surrey** $$$ This small apartment-hotel, part of the Manhattan East group, has large tastefully decorated rooms. The room service is from **Restaurant Daniel,** a favorite spot of the staff of the nearby Whitney Museum and other art-world movers and shakers. ◆ 20 E. 76th St (between Fifth and Madison Aves). 288.3700, 800/637.8483; fax 628.1549

Within The Surrey:

Restaurant Daniel ★★★$$$$ The most heralded debut of 1993 belonged to young master-chef **Daniel Boulud,** who opened his own restaurant after an illustrious six-year run at the legendary **Le Cirque.** Boulud has successfully re-created the same inimitable kitchen, much to the delight of the loyal, well-heeled society patrons who followed him. Getting dinner reservations often requires a month's wait, but it's well worth it. ◆ French ◆ Lunch and dinner. Reservations and jackets required. 288.0033

156 **William Secord Gallery** William Secord, former director of the **Dog Museum** (now located in St. Louis), operates this gallery devoted to man's best friend. Exhibitions may also include cats and barnyard animals. ◆ M-Sa 10AM-5PM. 52 E. 76th St (between Park and Madison Aves), third floor. 249.0075

157 **Carlyle Hotel** $$$$ John F. Kennedy used to stay here, and the jet set still does. At 38 stories, the Carlyle, designed in 1929 by **Bien & Prince,** soars above the East Side. Decorous charm and easy elegance pervade the premises; it is always at the top of someone's list of best New York City hotels, and is one of the few hotels tolerated by those who are used to the grand European style. For them, the Tower apartments seem to fill the bill for short stays or as permanent residences. From the custom-blended soap to the Chinese red-lacquered **Gallery,** it's a class act. Pianist **Bobby Short** has made the **Cafe Carlyle** famous, but his frequent substitutes are popular, too. The more relaxed and less expensive **Bemelmans Bar,** named for illustrator **Ludwig Bemelmans,** who painted the murals here, features jazz singer/pianist **Barbara Carroll,** but the music is more for background than is the case in Cafe Carlyle, where the audience maintains complete silence. The Gallery is recommended for people-watching at tea time. The **Carlyle Restaurant** serves an elegant dinner. ◆ 35 E. 76th St (at Madison Ave). 744.1600, 800/227.5737; fax 717.4682

158 **The Mark** $$$$ This elegant and intimate luxury hotel boasts 18th-century Piranesi prints, feather pillows, VCRs, marble bathrooms, terry cloth robes, and heated towel racks. Most of the 180 rooms have their own kitchens. ◆ 25 E. 77th St (between Madison and Fifth Aves). 744.4300, 800/843.6275; fax 744.4586

Within The Mark:

Mark's ★$$$$ Here you'll find a spacious, tranquil, softly lit dining room attended by a gracious staff. Recommended are sirloin steak with three peppers, roasted red snapper, farfalle with chanterelles and mixed vegetables, and a lobster baked potato. ◆ French ◆ Lunch and dinner. Reservations recommended. 879.1864

159 **Sant Ambroeus** ★★$$$ This Milanese institution is known on both sides of the ocean for its elegant Italian fare followed by the best cappuccino and espresso around. Fusilli with onions and vegetables is a particularly well-turned-out first course. Try the wonderful pastries to go—chestnut cake or chocolate mousse. ◆ Italian ◆ 1000 Madison Ave (between E. 77th and E. 78th Sts). Reservations recommended. 570.2211

160 **Stuyvesant Fish House** Designed by **McKim, Mead & White** in 1898, this Renaissance palace was once the scene of the city's most lavish parties. It was owned by **Stuyvesant Fish,** who was president of the Illinois Central Railroad. He and his wife, **Marion,** were prominent social leaders. ◆ 25 E. 78th St (at Madison Ave)

161 **James B. Duke House** A copy of an 18th-century château in Bordeaux, this mansion, designed in 1912 by **Horace Trumbauer,** was built for the founder of the **American Tobacco Co.** It was given to **New York University** in 1959 by Duke's widow and her daughter, **Doris** (who, along with **Barbara Hutton,** was known as a "poor little rich girl" in the 1930s), and is now NYU's **Institute of Fine Arts.** Many of the original furnishings are still here, including a **Gainsborough** portrait in the main hall. ◆ 1 E. 78th St (at Fifth Ave)

161 French Embassy Created in 1906 by **McKim, Mead & White,** this Italian Renaissance mansion, built for financier **Payne Whitney,** is typical of upper Fifth Avenue at the turn of the century, before the arrival of massive apartment houses. ◆ 972 Fifth Ave (between E. 78th and E. 79th Sts)

162 Acquavella One of the uptown heavy hitters, this gallery shows 19th- and 20th-century European masters and postwar American and European artists. ◆ M-F 9:30AM-5:30PM. 18 E. 79th St (between Madison and Fifth Aves). 734.6300

162 Salander-O'Reilly Galleries Twentieth-century Modernist American painters of the **Stieglitz** group (**Alfred Maurer, Arthur Dove, Stuart Davis**) as well as bold, contemporary ones (**Susan Roth, Dan Christensen, John Greifen**) are shown here. ◆ M-Sa 9:30AM-5:30PM. 20 E. 79th St (between Madison and Fifth Aves). 879.6606

163 Hanae Mori A striking balance of stucco front and off-center chrome cylinder, this slightly mysterious 1969 storefront is **Hans Hollein's** first work in Manhattan. Inside is the retail outlet for Mori's sophisticated, Japanese-influenced women's clothing. ◆ M-Sa 10AM-6PM. 27 E. 79th St (between Madison and Fifth Aves). 472.2352

164 New York Society Library Often confused with the New York Historical Library, this is New York City's oldest circulating library, founded in 1754 by a civic-minded group who believed that the availability of books would help the city to prosper. Housed since 1937 in a handsome Italianate town house built in 1917 by **Trowbridge & Livingston,** today it is a local landmark boasting a collection of more than 200,000 volumes, as well as first editions and rare books and manuscripts. The library's particular strengths are in English and American literature, biography, history, art history, travel and exploration, and works relating to the Big Apple. There is also a children's section. ◆ M 1-5PM; Tu, Th 9AM-7PM; W, F-Sa 9AM-5PM; closed Saturday and Sunday in summer. 53 E. 79th St (between Madison and Park Aves). 288.6900

165 870 Park Avenue This 1898 town house has been completely remodeled. The tripartite division of the facade alludes to that era's tradition and the scale of the surrounding buildings. In terms of styling, this is the next step after Modernism (see the **Lescaze Residence** and **112 E. 64th Street**), and it holds its own. This structure was designed in 1976 by **Robert A. M. Stern** and **John S. Hagmann.** ◆ At E. 77th St

Rockefeller University, at York Avenue in the east 60s, has the lowest teacher-pupil ratio of any university in the United States.

166 Lenox Hill Hospital A compound of modern buildings extends from the hospital's nucleus, the **Uris Pavilion,** built in 1975 by **Rogers, Butler, Burgun & Bradbury.** Ranked as one of the city's—and the nation's—best, Lenox Hill is a forerunner in obstetrical and neonatal care (its **Prenatal Testing Center** is one of the most comprehensive in the country), cardiology (the first balloon angioplasty in the country was performed here in 1978), and sports medicine (the **Nicholas Institute of Sports Medicine and Athletic Trauma** was the first such hospital-based center in the U.S.). ◆ E. 76th to E. 77th Sts (between Lexington and Park Aves). 439.2345

167 St. Jean Baptiste Church This Roman Catholic church, designed by **Nicholas Serracino** in 1913, was founded by French Canadians in the area. It is a little overwrought, but charming. Among its best features is the French-style organ, one of the finest in any New York church. ◆ Lexington Ave at E. 76th St. 288.5082

168 Mortimer's ★★$$$ This is the neighborhood watering hole of one of the wealthiest neighborhoods in the world. Nothing pretentious, just a tavern with simple food that is good, but not so good that it distracts from conversation. The bar is kept busy by captains of industry, fashionable ladies—many with well-known wardrobes—and as gossip columnist **Suzy** would say (and often does about the crowd here), "others too rich and famous to mention." Mortimer's is always crowded evenings and for Sunday brunch. ◆ Continental ◆ Lunch and dinner. 1057 Lexington Ave (at E. 75th St). Reservations required for five or more. 517.6400

169 Bonté There is hardly a pastry or cake that you won't find divine, but the specialty is extravagantly decorated cakes with exquisite marzipan and spun-sugar work. One of the two or three best bakers, and definitely the best eclairs, in Manhattan. ◆ M-Sa 9AM-6:30PM. 1316 Third Ave (at E. 75th St). 535.2360

170 Jim McMullen's ★★$$$ A handsome, modern tavern and an enduring singles—and networking—spectacle, this is more a place to experience than to dine in. The simply grilled fish, meat, and poultry are all fresh and adequately prepared, but one doesn't come for gastronomic satisfaction. Sustenance and a good time seem quite enough. **Dustin Hoffman** waited tables here at the beginning of the film *Tootsie.* ◆ American ◆ Lunch and dinner. 1341 Third Ave (between E. 76th and E. 77th Sts). Reservations recommended. 861.4700

Restaurants/Clubs: Red **Hotels:** Blue
Shops/ 🌳 Outdoors: Green **Sights/Culture:** Black

171 Baraonda ★★$$$ First there was **Mezzaluna,** then **Ciao Bella,** and now Baraonda, owner **Enrico Proiotti's** latest contribution to the beautiful people and pasta scene. ♦ Northern Italian ♦ Lunch and dinner. 1439 Second Ave (at E. 75th St). Reservations required. 288.8555

171 Pamir ★$$ The latest in ethnic invasions presents exotic Afghani cuisine. Lots of skewered meats—lamb and chicken—are served with moist rice pilaf and side dishes of yogurt and sautéed eggplant. ♦ Afghani ♦ Dinner. Closed Monday. 1437 Second Ave (between E. 74th and E. 75th Sts). Reservations recommended. 734.3791

172 Galleria Hugo Owner **Hugo Ramirez** is a master of restoration of 19th-century antique lighting. His work (all done by hand) can be found in Gracie Mansion, city museums, and historic homes around the country. ♦ By appointment only. 304 E. 76th St (between First and Second Aves). 288.8444. Also at: 341 E. 76th St. 228.8444

173 Il Monello ★★$$$$ The in-depth Italian wine list is not only laudable, it's applaudable. The food is for those who like showbiz at the table. The decor is of a type sometimes called Bronx Renaissance. Try the saltimbocca (veal sautéed in wine, with prosciutto and sage). ♦ Italian ♦ Lunch and dinner. 1460 Second Ave (between E. 76th and E. 77th Sts). Reservations required. 535.9310

174 Et Cetera $ Although the oversize neon sign in the window and the Miami motif are a bit much, the crowd, food, service, and jukebox are all quite decent. Most, however, come for the bar. ♦ Mexican ♦ Lunch and dinner; bar open until 4AM. 1470 First Ave (between E. 76th and E. 77th Sts). 382.0122

175 Voulez Vous ★$$ This glass-fronted French bistro with tinted mirrors features comfortable seating and a handsome bar where you can sample wine while waiting for your table. Try the excellent brunch on Sunday with cheese soufflés, couscous salad, and steak tartare. Dinners include traditional fare such as steak *pommes frites,* stews, baked fish, and, for dessert, excellent crème brûlée and flaky homemade fruit tarts. ♦ French ♦ Lunch and dinner. 1462 First Ave (at E. 76th St). Reservations required. 249.1776

176 Vasata $$ A bistro straight from the streets of Prague, this place serves thick schnitzels in a comfortable setting with gaily colored pottery and beamed ceilings. ♦ Czech ♦ Dinner; lunch also on Sunday. Closed Monday. 339 E. 75th St (between First and Second Aves). 988.7166

177 Marlo Flowers, Ltd. Here you'll find everything from tiny bouquets to dinner arrangements for 10,000, with a romantic, totally artistic approach to compositional floristry. ♦ M-F 10AM-6PM; Sa-Su by appointment only. 428A E. 75th St (between York and First Aves). 628.2246

178 The Red Tulip ★$$ Pleasant, if you appreciate the nearly relentless live Hungarian—and otherwise—folk music. The bright dining room in back of the dimly lit bar is gaily decorated with old, hand-painted pottery, wooden shelves, and cabinets. Booths around the sides of the room provide romantic privacy with high-backed natural-wood banquettes. All the food is amply portioned, made with fresh ingredients and lots of cooked-in depth of flavor: rich goulash soup, sour cream and double-smoked bacon, Hungarian sausage, braised veal shank with vegetables, stuffed cabbage and delicate spaetzle (noodles). ♦ Hungarian ♦ Dinner. Closed Monday and Tuesday. 439 E. 75th St (between York and First Aves). Reservations recommended. 734.4893

179 Frederic York Avenue Patisserie The inventive chef **Frederic Piepenburg** fills his shop with an interesting array of pastries, including oregano croissants, brioches, and reduced-calorie apple tarts. He also does low fat "diabetic baking" with low or no sugar. ♦ M-F 7AM-9PM; Sa-Su 8AM-7PM. 1431 York Ave (at E. 76th St). 628.5576

180 John Jay Park This neighborhood park has an outdoor public pool open from the end of the school year until Labor Day. Bring a padlock. ♦ E. 77th St at FDR Dr

181 Cherokee Apartments Built as model housing for the working class, these apart-ments are distinguished by the amount of light and air admitted by large casements and balconies—an unusual commodity in the days of "dumbbell" tenements; these were designed in 1909 by **Henry Atterbury Smith.** Walk through the vaulted tunnels into the central courtyards and study the detailing on the sheltered stairs at each corner that allow tenants to walk up in style. ♦ Between E. 77th and E. 78th Sts (between York Ave and Cherokee Pl)

182 City Cafe ★★$$$ Solid American fare with a healthy bent in what began as a neighborhood hangout is now drawing diners from around the city. The grilled vegetable plate, roast chicken, hamburger, and mashed potatoes are standouts. ♦ American ♦ Dinner; brunch only on Sunday. 1481 York Ave (between E. 78th and E. 79th Sts). Reservations recommended. 570.9810

183 Rigo Hungarian Pastry The strudels, cakes, tortes, and other attractions here are legendary. ♦ M 8AM-4PM; Tu-Sa 8AM-6PM; Su 9AM-4PM. 318 E. 78th St (between First and Second Aves). 988.0052

184 Maruzzella ★$$ The simple stucco interior and wood-burning oven add to the cheery charm. Start with the heady *ricotta di bufala* cheese with strips of roasted bell pepper, then move on to the pastas. Chef **Giovanni Pinato** does wonders with ravioli stuffed with spinach and cheese. Of course, there are the pizzas—perfect crusts topped with creamy mozzarella, ham, sausages, and vegetables. ♦ Italian ♦ Lunch and dinner. 1479 First Ave (at E. 77th St). 988.8877

coconut grill

185 Coconut Grill ★$$ The roast chicken is required eating at this tropical grill, whose real focus is on fun and socializing. ♦ American ♦ Lunch and dinner; brunch on Saturday and Sunday. 1481 Second Ave (at E. 77th St). 772.6262

186 Caffe Bianco ★$$ The entrées are fine—pastas, salads, chicken dishes—but the desserts, especially the Valencia orange cake, and cappuccinos are sublime. The pretty decor is as authentic as it gets this side of the Atlantic. ♦ Italian ♦ Lunch and dinner; late-night on Friday and Saturday. 1486 Second Ave (between E. 77th and E. 78th Sts). No credit cards. 988.2655

186 Lusardi ★★$$$ This is one of several informal, clublike, uptown trattorias that attract a sleek, affluent crowd. The food at this one, however, is more reliable than at others, and the service more concerned. ♦ Italian ♦ Lunch and dinner; dinner only on Saturday and Sunday. 1494 Second Ave (at E. 78th St). Reservations recommended. 249.2020

187 Fourteen Bis ★★$$$ **Peter Meltzer** and **Mark DiGuilio** have taken their love of French bistro uptown. The new place, until recently known as Quatorze Bis, is a touch more elegant than the original downtown but serves the same excellent bistro food. Here you should sample the best *choucroute garnie* (sauerkraut with smoky sausages, ham, and pork chops) in town or the excellent sautéed *boudin blanc* (a white veal sausage served with a strong Dijon mustard). Roast chicken also tastes quite interesting, simply roasted with herbs. ♦ French ♦ Lunch and dinner; dinner only on Saturday and Sunday. 323 E. 79th St (between First and Second Aves). Reservations recommended. 535.1414. Also at: 240 W. 14th St. 206.7006

188 Istanbul Cuisine ★$ This is a small Turkish restaurant with no decor to speak of, but excellent kebabs and rich honey-soaked desserts. Also good are the stuffed grape leaves, eggplant dishes, and broiled fish, which are authentic and cheap. ♦ Turkish ♦ Dinner. 303 E. 80th St (between First and Second Aves). 744.6903

189 Pig Heaven ★$$ The theme is *pig*—on the walls, the menus, you name it. But the food is fairly typical Chinese, not restricted to pork dishes as the name seems to indicate. The prices are higher than for standard Chinese fare, presumably for the pleasure of dining in this silly and fun pig-infested place. ♦ Chinese ♦ Lunch and dinner; late-night meals on Friday and Saturday. 1540 Second Ave (between E. 80th and E. 81st Sts). Reservations recommended. 744.4333

189 Divino Ristorante ★$$$ Service and pasta are the high points of this unpretentious favorite of Italian expatriates. The best second course is the breaded veal chop Milanese. Try also the more casual **Cafe Divino** (1544 Second Ave, 517.9269) and the homey **Gastronomia Divino** (1542 Second Ave, 861.1533), a trattoria that also offers a take-out menu. All three serve wonderful cappuccino and are conveniently located on the same block. ♦ Italian ♦ Dinner. 1556 Second Ave (between E. 80th and E. 81st Sts). Reservations required. 861.1096

190 Paprikas Weiss Paprika is among the hundreds of imported spices you'll find here, but the store is named for its founder, a Hungarian immigrant who first sold spices from a pushcart. The store sells prepared foods, imported ingredients for Hungarian cooking, gourmet cooking utensils, and fresh condiments. Everything they sell is available by mail. Ask for the catalog. ♦ M-F 9AM-7PM; Sa 9AM-6PM; Su 11AM-5PM. 1572 Second Ave (between E. 81st and E. 82nd Sts). 288.6117

190 The Comic Strip A showcase club for stand-up comics and singers. **Eddie Murphy**, **Jerry Seinfeld**, and **Paul Reiser** started here, and sometimes a big name will drop by. ♦ Cover, minimum. Shows: M-Th 9PM; F 8:30PM, 10:45PM; Sa 8PM, 10:30PM, 12:30AM; Su 8:30PM. 1568 Second Ave (between E. 81st and E. 82nd Sts). 861.9386

191 Etats-Unis ★★$$$ The name is French for the United States, which provides a good indication of the memorable eclectic cuisine. The **Rapp** family has no professional culinary training, so the success of their ever-changing, highly personal menu is all the more exciting. The only invariable is the delicious outcome, served by an eager and well-informed staff in casual but sophisticated surroundings. ♦ American/Eclectic ♦ Dinner. Closed Saturday and Sunday. 242 E. 81st St (between Second and Third Aves). 517.8826

192 Sistina ★★$$$ The attractive clientele makes up for the minimal but subtly pretty decor, which has become so typical of East Side restaurants. Even if you speak fluent Italian, the menu is annoyingly difficult to decipher. But if you can figure out what to order, the food is quite good. Try the excellent *Sisto IV* (grilled herbed chicken) as your main dish. ◆ Italian ◆ Dinner. 1555 Second Ave (between E. 80th and E. 81st Sts). Reservations required. 861.7660

193 Border Cafe $ Fajitas, nachos, chilis, chicken wings, and, of course, frozen margaritas are the main draw here. ◆ Southwestern ◆ Dinner; brunch also on Saturday and Sunday. 244 E. 79th St (between Second and Third Aves). Reservations recommended. 535.4347

194 New York Public Library, Yorkville Branch This rather academic neoclassical building, designed in 1902 by **Mames Brown Lord,** is the earliest of what are known as the Carnegie Libraries. There are 65 of these small branch libraries throughout the city, established by a donation from **Andrew Carnegie.** Later ones, similar in style, were designed by Lord and other distinguished architects such as **McKim, Mead & White, Carrère & Hastings,** and **Babb, Cook & Willard.** ◆ M noon-8PM; Tu 10AM-6PM; W-Th noon-6PM; Sa 10AM-5PM. 222 E. 79th St (between Second and Third Aves). 744.5824

195 Trois Jean ★$$$ An inviting boîte, Trois Jean is an ideal spot to drop in for a light snack or pastry, or a full bistro meal. The romantic second floor usually requires reservations. ◆ French ◆ Lunch and dinner. 154 E. 79th St (between Lexington and Third Aves). Reservations recommended. 988.4858

196 Parma ★$$$ This plain-looking room was the first of the "in" uptown Italian trattorias. Newer places have surpassed it in popularity, but even so, the kitchen maintains its standards. The pastas are well prepared, the Italian-style vegetables—fully cooked, served at room temperature—are brightly flavored. Have a grappa instead of dessert. ◆ Italian ◆ Dinner. 1404 Third Ave (at E. 79th St). Reservations recommended. 535.3520

197 Tirami Su ★$$ Although the crowd that fills this fashionable Italian cafe is determined to have a good time, they really do care for the food: excellent homemade pastas with strong zesty sauces, pizzas with classic and unusual toppings, some acceptable salads, and authentic Italian desserts served with excellent espresso. ◆ Italian ◆ Dinner; brunch also on Sunday. 1410 Third Ave (at E. 80th St). 988.9780

Café Metairie

198 Cafe Metairie ★$$$ An expensive bistro with an authentic French country decor and a fireplace. The unmistakably French menu includes a correct cassoulet, a tender steak *aux poivres* with thin *frites*, a well-spiced rare rack of lamb, and the traditional coq au vin. For dessert, there are excellent fruit tarts and crème caramel. ◆ French ◆ Lunch and dinner. 1442 Third Ave (at E. 82nd St). 988.1800

198 Le Refuge ★★$$$ Bare wooden tables, kitchen towels for napkins, American stoneware, and etched stemware provide a mood of romantic, rustic elegance. The ever-changing menu is prepared with carefully chosen fresh ingredients and cooked and seasoned with a sure and brilliant hand. Fish dishes are particularly delectable, and some consider the bouillabaisse the best in town. ◆ French ◆ Lunch and dinner. 166 E. 82nd St (between Third and Lexington Aves). Reservations recommended. 861.4505

199 Girasole ★$$$ Conservative East Siders dine at this dependable, noisy Italian restaurant located on the ground floor of a brownstone. Poultry and game dishes, such as chicken sautéed with lemon, and grilled organic Cornish hens with peppercorns, are best. ◆ Italian ◆ Lunch and dinner. 151 E. 82nd St (between Third and Lexington Aves). Dinner reservations required. 772.6690

200 Big City Kite Co., Inc. More than 150 kinds of kites are sold here. They come in a variety of shapes, including tigers, teddy bears, sailboats, sharks, dragons, and bats. The proprietors, whose stock is about as ambitious as you're likely to find, can arrange parties for kite-flying lessons and shows. They will also guide you to nearby kite flights. ◆ M-W, F 11AM-6:30PM; Th 11AM-7:30PM; Sa 10AM-6PM. 1201 Lexington Ave (between E. 81st and E. 82nd Sts). 472.2623

201 Rosenthal Wine Merchant Here you'll find unique wines from California and Europe (particularly Burgundies). ◆ M-F 9:30AM-7PM; Sa 9:30AM-6PM. 1200 Lexington Ave (between E. 81st and E. 82nd Sts). 249.6650

202 Tiny Doll House All the teeny, tiny furniture and accessories it takes to make a doll's home, including mini Degas paintings, handmade English houses, and furniture, are here under one roof. If you think you can make something better yourself, all the supplies you need are available. ◆ M-F 11AM-5:30PM; Sa 11AM-5PM. 1146 Lexington Ave (between E. 79th and E. 80th Sts). 744.3719

203 Junior League of The City of New York One of a trio of perfect neighbors, this sophisticated 1928 Regency-style mansion by **Mott B. Schmidt** was built for **Vincent Astor.** The other two are Schmidt's Georgian house for **Clarence Dillon** (1930) at 124 E. 80th Street, and the Federal-style **George Whitney House** (1930) at 120 E. 80th Street, by **Cross & Cross.** ◆ 130 E. 80th St (between Lexington and Park Aves). 288.6220

204 Lewis Spencer Morris House The original owner, a direct descendant of a signer of the Declaration of Independence, significantly chose the Federal style for this 1923 town house by **Cross & Cross.** ♦ 116 E. 80th St (between Lexington and Park Aves)

205 E.A.T. ★★$$$ All the breads here are made with a sourdough starter, including the famous *ficelle*, a crusty 22-inch-long loaf with a diameter that is barely larger than a silver dollar. The prices are stunning, but so is the quality of most of the cheeses, breads, salads, pastries, cakes, etc., in this informal eatery owned by **Eli Zabar.** ♦ American ♦ Breakfast, lunch, and dinner. 1064 Madison Ave (between E. 80th and E. 81st Sts). 772.0022

206 Frank E. Campbell Funeral Chapel In this building, possibly the most prestigious funeral chapel in the world, we have said farewell to **Elizabeth Arden, James Cagney, Jack Dempsey, Tommy Dorsey, Judy Garland, Howard Johnson, Robert F. Kennedy, John Lennon, J.C. Penney, Damon Runyon, Arturo Toscanini, Mae West,** and **Tennessee Williams,** to name-drop just a few. ♦ 1076 Madison Ave (at E. 81st St). 288.3500

206 Burlington Book Shop This neighborly bookstore, a fixture for the last 50 years, is run by **Jane Trichter.** Upstairs is the out-of-print department. Downstairs is **Burlington Antique Toys,** a dusty basement shop full of antique and vintage racing cars, tin soldiers, wooden boats, and more. ♦ M-F 9:30AM-6PM; Sa 10AM-6PM; Su noon-5PM. The hours downstairs vary but are usually M-Sa 11:30AM-6PM. 1082 Madison Ave (between E. 81st and E. 82nd Sts). 288.7420

207 Parioli Romanissimo ★★★$$$$ Here is one of the most refined Italian kitchens in New York City, located in a charming town house. The delicate egg pasta is seriously divine, and the fish entrées are impeccable. Because it is run like a private club for favored patrons, it is often difficult to get a reservation. ♦ Italian ♦ Dinner. Closed Sunday. 24 E. 81st St (between Madison and Fifth Ave). Jacket, tie, and reservations required. 288.2391

208 The Stanhope Hotel $$$$ Created in 1926 by **Rosario Candela,** the Stanhope is strategically located across the street from the **Metropolitan Museum of Art** and **Central Park.** The Stanhope has been freshened up without great disturbance to its gentility. The 148 rooms (nearly all suites), decorated in the French style, have such amenities as in-room safes and multiple telephones. Room service and valet service are available 24 hours, and limousine service is provided to **Lincoln Center** and the **Theater District.** Rooms facing the museum and the park are particularly choice. **Le Salon** and the **Dining Room** are favorite escapes from museum overload. **Gerard's** is for those in need of stronger medicine. ♦ 995 Fifth Ave (at E. 81st St). 288.5800, 800/828.1123; fax 517.0088

209 998 Fifth Avenue This 1912 apartment building in the guise of an Italian Renaissance palazzo was built by **McKim, Mead & White** when the bulk of society lived in mansions up and down the avenue. The largest apartment here has 25 rooms; it was originally leased by **Murray Guggenheim.** ♦ At E. 81st St

209 1001 Fifth Avenue Designed in 1978 by **Philip Birnbaum,** this average apartment tower has been upgraded with a limestone facade by **Philip Johnson** and **John Burgee.** Half-round ornamental molding relates horizontally to the neighboring 998 Fifth Avenue, while the mullions struggle for a vertical emphasis, pointing at the mansard-shaped cut-out roof. The distinctive silhouette is best admired from across the park. Up close, its one-dimensional character takes precedence; from the back, you can see the struts bracing the facade like stage jacks bracing a scenery flat. ♦ Between E. 81st and E. 82nd Sts

210 Metropolitan Museum of Art The first, original section was built in 1880 by **Calvert Vaux** and **Jacob Wrey Mould.** Additions and renovations were as follows: southwest wing 1888, **Theodore Weston;** north wing 1894, **Arthur Tuckerman;** central facade 1902, **Richard Morris Hunt, Richard Howland Hunt,** and **George B. Post;** Fifth Avenue wings 1906, **McKim, Mead & White;** stairs, pool, Lehman Wing, and Great Hall renovations 1970, **Kevin Roche, John Dinkeloo & Associates;** later additions 1975-87, Kevin Roche, John Dinkeloo & Associates; Andre Meyer Gallery renovation 1993, **David Harvey, Gary Tinterow,** and **Philippe de Montebello** with **Alvin Holm** and Kevin Roche. Ten years after the first section was finished at the edge of Central Park, **Frederick Law Olmsted,** the park's designer, said he regretted having allowed it to be built there. He should see it now. The Met (pictured below) has grown to 1.4 million square feet of floor space (more than 32 acres), with some 3.3 million works of art, making it the largest art museum in the Western Hemisphere. It seems to be expanding and getting better every day (much of this growth must be credited to director **Philipe de Montebello**).

Founded in 1870 by a group of art-collecting financiers and industrialists who were on the art committee of New York's **Union League Club,** the Metropolitan's original collection consisted of 174 paintings, mostly Dutch and Flemish, and a gift of antiquities from **General di Cesnola,** the former U.S. consul to Cyprus.

The more recent additions, including the **Lila Acheson Wallace Wing** (20th-century art) with its beautiful roof garden, provide a dramatic contrast of high-tech glass curtain walls to the solid limestone Beaux Arts front. The interiors are spectacular, too, contrasting but not fighting with Richard Morris Hunt's equally spectacular **Great Hall,** just inside the main entrance.

The list of benefactors who have swelled the museum's holdings over the years reads like a *Who's Who* of the city's First Families— **Morgan, Rockefeller, Altman, Marquand, Hearn, Bache, Lehman.** The push to house the collection in style has produced the **Sackler Wing** (1979) for the **Raymond R. Sackler Far East Art** collection; the entire Egyptian **Temple of Dendur** (1978), given to the people of the United States for their support in saving monuments threatened by the construction of the Aswan High Dam; the **Egyptian Galleries** (1983) for the Met's world-class permanent collection; the impressive **Michael C. Rockefeller Wing** (1982) for the art of Africa, the Americas, and the Pacific Islands; the **Douglas Dillon Galleries of Chinese Painting** (1983) and the **Astor Chinese Garden Court** (1980), with a reception hall from the home of a 16th-century scholar; an expanded and dramatically redesigned **American Wing** (1980); and the **Lehman Wing** (1975), which displays its collection of paintings, drawings, and decorative objects in rooms re-created from the original Lehman town house on W. 54th Street. Don't miss the beautifully renovated **Andre Meyer Galleries** (1993), where you'll see the premier collection of 19th-century European paintings and sculpture in the world, rivaling the Musée d'Orsay in Paris.

The permanent collection (about a third of which can be displayed at any one time) is expanding in every department. The museum already has the most comprehensive collection of American art in the world, and excels in Egyptian, Greek and Roman, and European art, including arms and armor, ranging from medieval times to the 20th century. The list of priceless art and artifacts within these walls is almost impossible to comprehend.

The **Costume Institute** displays its 35,000 articles of clothing in stylish themes, with special temporary blockbuster exhibits you won't want to miss.

The information desk in the center of the Great Hall has floor plans and a helpful staff to direct you. The staff also has information about concerts and lectures in the museum's **Grace Rainey Rogers Auditorium** and will help you

arrange for a guided tour, available in several languages. At the north end of the Great Hall, tape-recorded tours of most of the exhibits are available for rental. Just off the Great Hall is the justly famous book and gift shop.

The museum restaurant is a hectic, cafeteria-style arrangement with tables around a pool. A little-known resource is weekend brunch in the elegant upstairs dining room, which, during the week, is only open to sponsors and patrons.

The Iris and B. Gerald Cantor Roof Garden, a lovely sculpture garden with grand views from the roof of the museum, has a limited beverage service.

The Friday and Saturday evening hours have added a touch of civility and grace to the busy city scene. Many of the museum's employees take advantage of the tranquil twilight hours, when, beginning at 5PM, a string quartet serenades from the Great Hall balcony, where a bar and candlelit tables are set up for relaxation. Evening educational offerings— art lectures and documentaries—coincide with the concerts in the Grace Rainey Rogers Auditorium. ♦ Admission. Tu-Th, Su 9:30AM-5:15PM; F-Sa 9:30AM-8:45PM. Fifth Ave at E. 82nd St. 535.7710

211 William Greenberg, Jr., Inc. Towering chocolate cakes decorated with whipped cream and chocolate wafers must be ordered months ahead. All the other buttery American-style goods go fast. ♦ M-Sa 9AM-6PM. 1100 Madison Ave (between E. 82nd and E. 83rd Sts). 744.0304. Also at: 1377 Third Ave. 861.1340; 518 Third Ave. 686. 3344

212 3 East 84th Street This jewel of a small apartment house, in gray stone with Art Deco details, was designed in 1928 by **Raymond Hood**—before **Rockefeller Center.** ♦ Between Madison and Fifth Aves

213 The YIVO Institute for Jewish Research (Yidisher Visnshaftlekher Institut) The explorations of this organization cover all aspects of Jewish life. It has the world's largest collections of books, letters, and manuscripts in Yiddish, some dating back to 1600, and its extensive library is open for browsing. Since 1955 it's been housed here in one of the last great Fifth Avenue mansions, designed by **Carrère & Hastings.** The **Serge Sabarsky Foundation** is planning to buy the building and open a museum of Austrian and German Expressionist art. YIVO's future location is unknown. ♦ M-Th 9:30AM-5:30PM. 1048 Fifth Ave (at E. 86th St). 535.6700

Metropolitan Museum of Art

McKIM, MEAD & WHITE

214 Church of St. Ignatius Loyola The overscaled Vignoia facade on Park Avenue was designed by **Ditmars & Schickel** in 1898. Its flat limestone late-Renaissance style looks very comfortable here—and it is a welcome change from all that Gothic. ♦ 980 Park Ave (at E. 84th St). 288.3588

215 Polo Grounds ★$$ Like SoHo's Sporting Club, this sports fanatic's dream is the place to watch every imaginable televised event on three giant screens and 16 TVs. Come for the camaraderie and bonhomie, not the food, though if you stick with the buffalo wings and burgers you'll be happy—especially if your team wins. ♦ American ♦ Daily 4PM-1AM. 1472 Third Ave (between E. 83rd and E. 84th Sts). Reservations required for major sporting events. 570.5590

216 Apex Fitness Club Fitness facilities around the city have turned into urban country clubs, and this is one of the hottest. In addition to standard long-term membership, single-visit coupons are available. The range of classes is enormous. Use Apex as a meeting ground, but don't mistake its seriousness. ♦ M-F 6AM-9PM; Sa-Su 8AM-6PM. 205 E. 85th St (between Second and Third Aves). 737.8377

217 Kleine Konditorei ★$$ Sauerbraten, Wiener schnitzel, roast goose, and *natur schnitzel* are the specialties here, along with potato pancakes and pastries. Not for the diet-conscious. ♦ German ♦ Lunch and dinner. 234 E. 86th St (between Second and Third Aves). 737.7130

217 Elk Candy Company Search for the moist, chocolate-covered marzipan behind the sweet disorder of this East Side institution. ♦ M-Sa 9AM-6:45PM; Su 10AM-5:45PM. 240 E. 86th St (between Second and Third Aves). 650.1177

218 Schaller & Weber This incredible store is filled from floor to ceiling with cold cuts. They are piled on counters, packed into display cases, and hung from the walls and ceilings. ♦ M-Sa 9AM-6PM. 1654 Second Ave (between E. 85th and E. 86th Sts). 879.3047

218 Estia ★★$$$ Here you'll find fresh and always satisfying Greek food in a typical, noisy trattoria setting. At about 8:30PM, the live music starts; by about 10PM, when the instrumentalists are joined by singers, conversation becomes impossible. The Greek antipasto for two is the best introduction to a hearty meal. Also recommended is the fried zucchini with a wondrous almond-garlic sauce for dipping. The standard specialties are all first-rate, which is why Greeks throng here. ♦ Greek ♦ Dinner. Closed Monday and Sunday. 308 E. 86th St (between First and Second Aves). Reservations required on weekends. 628.9100

219 Paola ★★$$$ Excellent pasta, especially tortellini, good hearty soups, good veal dishes, and creamy cheesecake are featured in this delightful Northern Italian restaurant. The room is noisy but the atmosphere is pleasant and intimate. ♦ Italian ♦ Lunch and dinner. 347 E. 85th St (between First and Second Aves). Reservations required for lunch, recommended for dinner. 794.1890

220 Elio's ★★$$$ Serious Wall Streeters and bankers mix easily with media types and celebs at this "in" neighborhood eatery, a spin-off of the ever-popular **Elaine's**. It's always crowded, always noisy, and the food is always good. Stick with the specials, which seem to steal the kitchen's attention away from the regular menu. ♦ Italian ♦ Dinner. 1621 Second Ave (between E. 84th and E. 85th Sts). Reservations required. 772.2242

221 Azzurro ★★$$$$ In a neighborhood chock-a-block with formula Italian trattorias, this family-run Sicilian operation puts an emphasis on homemade pastas. ♦ Italian ♦ Dinner. 245 E. 84th St (between Second and Third Aves). Reservations recommended. 517.7068

222 Erminia ★★$$$ The crowning achievements of this restaurant are Tuscan grilled lamb and pasta in lush sauces. The romantic candlelit atmosphere makes Erminia a popular place, so reserve your table a couple of days in advance. ♦ Italian ♦ Dinner. Closed Sunday. 250 E. 83rd St (between Second and Third Aves). Reservations required. 879.4284

223 Trastevere ★★$$$ When you open a place that's small enough to legitimately exclude almost everyone from tasting your hearty Italian cooking, everyone and his cousin will want to come. So call way ahead, then expect an affluent, casual crowd of heavy-duty garlic eaters, lots of noise, confusion, and—despite it all—good humor. ♦ Italian ♦ Dinner. 309 E. 83rd St (between First and Second Aves). Reservations required. 734.6343

224 Mocca Hungarian ★$ Treat yourself to hearty Hungarian home cooking that will please your purse as well as your palate. The portions are more than generous and the prices are impossibly low. As expected, the Wiener schnitzel and strudel are most satisfying. ♦ Hungarian ♦ Dinner. 1588 Second Ave (between E. 82nd and E. 83rd Sts). No credit cards. 734.6470

225 Primavera ★★$$$$ This is one of the great watering holes for the older, distinguished smart set—people whose money is so quiet, you can hear a diamond drop. They find honest food here, but nothing extraordinary. ♦ Italian ♦ Dinner. 1578 First Ave (at E. 82nd St). Jacket, tie, and reservations required. 861.8608

226 Wilkinson's 1573 Seafood Cafe ★★$$$ The interior of this little gem of a restaurant is relaxed and intimate, with pastel-colored murals adorning the bare-brick walls. Chinese chicken in raspberry vinegar is just one of the winning dishes. ♦ Seafood ♦ Dinner. 1573 York Ave (at E. 83rd St). Reservations recommended. 535.5454

227 Szechuan Hunan Cottage ★$$ They don't come for the decor—sometimes they don't come at all and instead order from home for some of the fastest delivery in town—but the regular line outside this small restaurant is a testimony to Chinese food that doesn't get any better in this price range. If the selection overwhelms you, try the house specialty, "Cottage Chicken," made with carrots, snow peas, and scallions. ♦ Chinese ♦ Lunch and dinner. 1590 York Ave (between E. 83rd and E. 84th Sts). 535.5223. Also at: 1433 Second Ave (between 74th and 75th Sts). 535.1471

228 Sirabella ★★$$ This neighborhood Italian restaurant is always packed because of its authentic home cooking, especially the fresh pasta made-in-*casa*. On cold winter nights the rich textured soups are a must, as is the crisp calamari. The osso buco is delectable, and the vegetables—the cooked escarole, for example—are redolent of garlic and olive oil. ♦ Italian ♦ Lunch and dinner. 72 East End Ave (between E. 82nd and E. 83rd Sts). Reservations recommended. 988.6557

229 Carl Schurz Park The park, on land acquired by the city in 1891, was named in 1911 for the German immigrant who served as a general during the Civil War, was a senator from Missouri and secretary of the interior under President Hayes, and went on to become editor of the *New York Evening Post* and *Harper's Weekly*. The park, which was remodeled in 1938 by **Harvey Stevenson** and **Cameron Clark**, is a delightful edge to the neighborhood of Yorkville. It is not very large, but its distinct sections and the varied topography make a walk here rewarding. The promenade along the East River above FDR Drive is named for **John Finley,** a former editor of the *New York Times* and an enthusiastic walker. **Gracie Mansion,** the residence of the mayor of New York City, occupies the center of the north end of the park.

Across the river is Astoria, Queens; spanning the river are the **Triborough Bridge** and **Hell's Gate** railroad trestle; also visible are **Ward's**

Island and **Randall's Island;** the yellow building is **Manhattan State Mental Hospital,** and the little island that looks like an elephant's head is known as **Mill Rock.** This point of the river is a treacherous confluence of currents from the Harlem River, Long Island Sound, and the harbor—hence the name Hell's Gate. ♦ East End Ave (between E. 84th and E. 90th Sts)

Bests

Cindy Adams
Syndicated Columnist for the *New York Post*/ WNBC-TV "Today in New York" Correspondent

For celebrity-watching: Lunch at **Le Cirque.**

For jewelry-watching: The **Diamond Center,** 47th Street between Fifth and Sixth avenues.

For people-watching: Bench in front of the **Plaza Hotel** around noon.

For kid-watching: **FAO Schwarz.**

For view-watching: **Rainbow Room.**

For lox/bagel/pastrami/salami-watching: **Stage Deli.**

For window-shopping: **Madison Avenue** going uptown from 57th Street.

For shopping: **Trump Tower.**

For culture: **Lincoln Center.**

For color: **Greenwich Village.**

For architecture: **Seagram's Building** (supermodern glass and chrome), **Chrysler Building** (Art Deco), **Guggenheim Museum** (Frank Lloyd Wright), **World Trade Center** (tallest).

For VIP high-rises, where people from Phil Donahue to Jackie O to me dwell: Walk **Fifth Avenue.**

For caviar: **Petrossian's.**

For seafood: **Sea-Grill.**

For steaks: **Gallagher's.**

For Chinese: **Fu's.**

For Japanese: **Inagiku** at the Waldorf.

For Spanish: **Pamplona.**

For Mexican: **Rosa's Place.**

For Indian: **Akhbar.**

For Italian: **Tre Scalini.**

For French: **La Reserve.**

For Russian: **Russian Tea Room.**

For atmosphere: **The Water Club.**

For what's no place else in the whole world but in New York: **Statue of Liberty, Radio City Music Hall, United Nations, Rockefeller Center** skating rink, the **Theater District, Empire State Building.**

And read the *New York Post.*

Restaurants/Clubs: Red	Hotels: Blue
Shops/ ♥ Outdoors: Green	Sights/Culture: Black

Upper East Side

The upscale and largely residential Upper East Side, which is bounded by **E. 86th** and **E. 110th streets**, and **Fifth Avenue** and the **East River**, has a heavy concentration of town houses, deluxe apartment buildings, elitist hotels, and elegant mansions, interspersed with churches, clubs, museums, boutiques, restaurants, and gourmet take-out stores.

Most of the great mansions of Park and Fifth avenues and the cross streets between them, the first constructions in this part of New York, were built between 1900 and 1920, when the classical tradition was in flower—they all exhibit neo-Georgian, neo-Federal, neo-French, or neo-Italian Renaissance styling. The original owners, families such as the **Whitneys**, the **Astors**, the **Straights**, the **Dillons**, the **Dukes**, the **Mellons**, the **Pulitzers**, and the **Harknesses**, all moved here from downtown. It was an era of lavish balls and of "the 400" (so named because **Mrs. William Astor** could accommodate only 400 of her closest friends comfortably at one time).

Construction of apartment houses and hotels began in 1881 and ended in 1932. Almost all the churches were erected between 1890 and 1920. Although there are still isolated blocks of row houses that date from the late 1860s to 1880s as well as a few colonial relics and some contemporary buildings, the

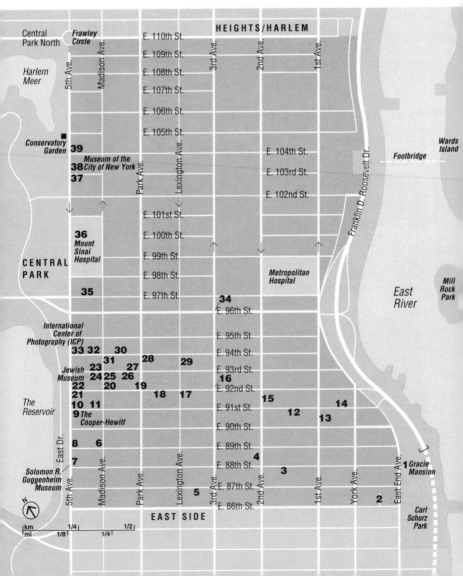

look, especially in the western part of the district, is generally more uniform than elsewhere in the city. The reason for the relatively late start in populating this area is that, except for the German village of **Yorkville**, it was all open country. When work started on **Central Park** in 1857, the neighborhood consisted mainly of farms and squatters' shanties, and pigs grubbed on Fifth Avenue. Even after the park opened in 1863, steam trains chugging along Park Avenue made this an undesirable residential neighborhood. But in 1907, when the **New York Central Railroad** electrified the trains and covered the Park Avenue tracks, the Upper East Side became an attractive place for the well-to-do to live.

Fifth Avenue facing Central Park is New York City's "street of parades," and the most elegant of the avenues. A few new buildings have been slipped into the unbroken frontage that progresses up Fifth Avenue north of Grand Army Plaza at 58th Street. Museum Mile begins at the heroic **Metropolitan Museum of Art** on the park side of Fifth Avenue and ends with the **Museum of the City of New York** at 103rd Street. In between are the **International Center of Photography**, the **Cooper-Hewitt Museum**, the **Solomon R. Guggenheim Museum**, and the **Jewish Museum.** The vertical palace on E. 92nd Street that was the former home of **Marjorie Merriwether Post** is only one of the numerous outstanding apartment buildings and town houses in the neighborhood.

Among the many churches on the Upper East Side are the **Episcopal Church of the Holy Trinity** and **St. Christopher Home and Parsonage** at E. 88th Street, which form a neo-Gothic grouping around a courtyard built on land donated by **Serena Rhinelander** that had been in her family since 1798.

Madison Avenue has become largely a street of important art galleries, jewelry stores, antique shops, clothing boutiques, and restaurants. Although the Saturday afternoon stroll is still a diversion for East Siders, Madison Avenue now seems sedate compared to SoHo with its newer galleries and boutiques and the trendy Columbus Avenue shops.

Park Avenue, with its landscaped center island and legions of dignified apartment houses and old mansions (most of which are now occupied by foreign cultural missions or clubs), is still an address to conjure with.

Lexington Avenue is a Madison Avenue without the cachet—and often without the quality. Shops, restaurants, and singles bars line Third, Second, and First avenues, and, farther north, more high-rise "people boxes" border these thoroughfares. The side streets are a mix of tenements—some gentrified, some not—and modest town houses.

Yorkville, which extends from the East River to Lexington Avenue, from E. 77th to E. 96th streets, continued to receive immigrants from Germany over the first half of the 20th century, but the ethnic heart is shrinking. Once, E. 86th Street was filled with German restaurants, beer gardens, and grocery, pastry, and dry goods stores. Now, there are inexpensive chain stores and fried chicken and pizza parlors, and a new Eastern European presence can be felt. A few of the old restaurants, groceries, and record stores remain. **Gracie Mansion** has been the official mayoral residence since the 1942 term of **Fiorello La Guardia.**

1 Gracie Mansion The site was known to the Dutch as **Hoek Van Hoorm;** when the British captured it during the Revolutionary War, the shelling destroyed the farmhouse that was there. The kernel of the present house was built in 1799 by Scottish-born merchant **Archibald Gracie** as a country retreat.

Acquired by the city in 1887, it served, among its many uses, as the first home of the **Museum of the City of New York,** a refreshment stand, and a storehouse. In 1942, at the urging of Parks Commissioner **Robert Moses, Fiorello La Guardia** accepted it as the mayor's official residence. (The 98 men who

preceded him in the office had lived in their own homes.) In 1966, an addition to the house was designed by **Mott B. Schmidt.** Currently it is the home of **Mayor Rudolph Giuliani.** The **Gracie Mansion Conservancy** has restored the mansion to something better than its former glory, and conducts tours and special programs there.
♦ Voluntary contribution. Tours (by appointment only) W 10AM, 11AM, 1PM, 2PM Mar-Nov. East End Ave (at E. 88th St). 570.4751

2 **Henderson Place** These 24 Queen Anne houses were commissioned by **John C. Henderson,** a fur importer and hat manufacturer, and designed by **Lamb & Rich** in 1882 as a self-contained community with river views. Symmetrical compositions tie the numerous pieces together below an enthusiastic profusion of turrets, parapets, and dormers. There are rumors in the neighborhood that some of these houses are haunted. The ghosts may be looking for the eight houses from the group that were demolished to allow for a yellow apartment block. ♦ Off East End Ave (between E. 86th and E. 87th Sts)

3 **Church of the Holy Trinity** Built in 1897 by **Barney & Chapman,** this picturesque gold, brown, and red Victorian church modestly slipped into this side street encloses a charming garden. The sleek tower with its fanciful Gothic crown is rather nice, too. ♦ 316 E. 88th St (between First and Second Aves). 289.4100

4 **Elaine's** ★★$$$ If you absolutely must see celebrities eating steamed mussels, you will most likely accomplish that mission here. It's a kind of club for media celebrities, gossips, and so-called literati, but not necessarily for food. Try to sit near **Elaine**— all the action revolves around her. ♦ Italian ♦ Lunch, dinner, and late-night meals. 1703 Second Ave (between E. 88th and E. 89th Sts). Reservations required. 534.8103

5 **The Franklin Hotel** $$ Built in 1931 and recently refurbished top-to-toe, this 53-room hotel is quite stylish for the price. The rooms are small but nicely decorated, the service is good, and the buffet breakfast is complimentary. East Side residents often book rooms for their guests here. ♦ 164 E. 87th St (between Lexington and Third Aves). 369.1000, 800/600.8787; fax 369.8000

6 **Personal Pursuit** The young students from the prestigious private schools in the neighborhood are a captive audience for the personalized toys, toy chests, and frames sold here. ♦ M-Sa 10AM-6PM. 1242 Madison Ave (at E. 89th St). 722.3222

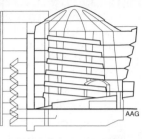

7 **Solomon R. Guggenheim Museum** When **Solomon R. Guggenheim** wanted a museum that would "foster an appreciation of art by acquainting museum visitors with significant painting and sculpture of our time," he founded this repository, which has remained a testament to his personal taste. Guggenheim collected old masters at first, but in the 1920s he began acquiring the avant-garde work of painters such as **Delaunay, Kandinsky,** and **Léger.** Soon his apartment at the Plaza was bursting at the seams (the old masters were relegated to his wife's bedroom), and he began to look for other quarters for his burgeoning collection. During two sojourns in rented space, his new museum began to buy more of everything by both established and new talent. Finally, the need for a permanent home was realized in a building (shown above) designed in 1959 by **Frank Lloyd Wright.**

The museum, Wright's only New York building, is one of the architect's fantasies, first dreamed of in the mid-1940s. It is an extraordinary structure: a massive concrete spiral sits atop one end of a low horizontal base, expanding as it ascends, dominating not only its plinth and a counterweight block of offices at the other end but the site itself and the blocks around it.

The display of art was clearly not Wright's main concern. The essence of architecture for the sake of architecture, the Guggenheim is a building that everyone seems to have an opinion about. Wright personally handled all the details, down to the Fifth Avenue sidewalk. The first addition, built in 1968 by **Taliesin Associates,** was not up to snuff. That firm, Wright's successors and keepers-of-the-flame, never had the touch of the Master.

Construction of the second addition, by **Gwathmey Siegel & Associates,** was completed in 1992 and doubles the museum's gallery space.

Dean & DeLuca is the new museum cafe, where you'll find their trademark uncompromising quality, unique selections, and innovative combinations. ♦ Admission. M-W, F-Su 10AM-8PM. Cafe: breakfast, lunch, and early dinner; lunch and early dinner only on Thursday. Museum shop: M-W, F-Su 10AM-8PM; Th 11AM-6PM. Fifth Ave (at E. 88th St). 360.3500

Restaurants/Clubs: Red   **Hotels:** Blue
Shops/ 🌳 Outdoors: Green   **Sights/Culture:** Black

8 National Academy of Design Since its
founding in 1825 by **Samuel F.B. Morse,**
painter and inventor of the telegraph, the
National Academy has been an artist-run
museum, a fine-arts school, and an honorary
organization of artists. Headquartered in a
town house that was remodeled in 1915 by
Ogden Codman, Jr., and located around the
corner from its **School of Fine Arts,** the
academy is the second-oldest museum school
in the country. In addition to an annual
exhibition (alternately open to member artists
and all artists), the academy presents special
exhibitions of art and architecture. Painters,
sculptors, watercolorists, graphic artists, and
architects number among its members today.
♦ Admission. W-Th, Sa-Su noon-5PM; F
noon-8PM. 1083 Fifth Ave (at E. 89th St).
369.4880

9 The Cooper-Hewitt There could be no
better setting for the **Smithsonian
Institution's National Museum of Design**
than this splendidly decorated mansion
designed in 1903 by **Babb, Cook & Willard.** It
was built on the northern fringe of the well-
heeled stretch of Fifth Avenue mansions for
industrialist **Andrew Carnegie,** who requested
"the most modest, plainest, and most roomy
house in New York City." The rather standard
Renaissance-Georgian mix of red brick and
limestone trim on a rusticated base is most
noteworthy for the fact that it is freestanding
in quite an expansive garden. The richly
ornamented rooms of the sumptuous
mansion, which was renovated in 1977 by
Hardy Holzman Pfeiffer Associates,
sometimes compete with the exhibitions; the
conservatory is particularly pleasant. Also
notice the very low door to what was once the
library at the west end—Carnegie was a short
man, and this was his private room.

The permanent collection of the Cooper-
Hewitt—based on the collections of the
Cooper and Hewitt families and now under the
stewardship of museum director **Diane**

Pilgrim—encompasses textiles dating back
3,000 years, jewelry, furniture, wallpaper, and
metal-, glass-, and earthenware. It also
includes the single largest group of
architectural drawings in this country. The
library is a design student's reference paradise
of picture collections, auction catalogs, and
17th- and 18th-century architecture books.
Lectures, symposia, summer concerts, and
classes for school groups take place on a
regular basis. A gift shop sells design
objects, catalogs, postcards, and museum
publications. ♦ Admission; free Tuesday 5-
9PM. Tu 10AM-9PM; W-Sa 10AM-5PM; Su
noon-5PM. 2 E. 91st St (between Madison and
Fifth Aves). 860.6868

10 The Convent of the Sacred Heart
Originally built in 1918 by **C.P.H. Gilbert** and **J.
Armstrong Stenhouse,** this extravagant Italian
palazzo was one of the largest private houses
built in New York City, and the last on
"Millionaire's Row." It was the home of **Otto
Kahn,** banker, philanthropist, and art patron.
Now it's a private school for girls. ♦ 1 E. 91st
St (at Fifth Ave). 722.4745

11 Mrs. James A. Burden House When
Vanderbilt heiress **Adele Sloane** married
James A. Burden, heir to a steel fortune, they
moved into this freestanding mansion, which
was built in 1902 by **Warren & Wetmore.** The
spiral staircase under a stained-glass skylight
is one of the city's grandest, and was called the
"stairway to heaven." ♦ 7 E. 91st St (between
Madison and Fifth Aves)

11 Mrs. John Henry Hammond House When
Hammond saw the plans for this house,
designed in 1906 by **Carrère & Hastings,** he
said that this gift from his wife's family made
him feel "like a kept man." He moved in
anyway, along with a staff of 16 full-time
servants. The couple's musicales were
legendary. **Benny Goodman** came here
frequently in the 1930s to play **Mozart's**
clarinet works. ♦ 9 E. 91st St (between
Madison and Fifth Aves)

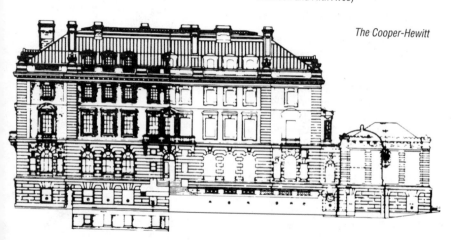

The Cooper-Hewitt

12 Playhouse 91 Plays that relate to the Jewish experience are given standard to excellent treatment here by the **Jewish Repertory Theatre,** which stages revivals (of **Chekhov, Neil Simon**), originals (*Crossing Delancey* premiered here), and musicals. ◆ 316 E. 91st St (between First and Second Aves). 831.2000

13 El Pollo ★★$ This tiny storefront lacks atmosphere, but you can't beat the South American barbecued chicken served with a side order of fried plantains. Wash it down with **Inca Kola** and top it all off with an exotic pudding made of raisins, cinnamon, and quinoa (a 5,000-year-old nutty grain that tastes a bit like brown rice). ◆ Peruvian ◆ Lunch and dinner. 1746 First Ave (between E. 90th and E. 91st Sts). No credit cards. 996.7810

14 Vinegar Factory The timely brainchild of E.A.T.'s owner **Eli Zabar** (his father founded the legendary Zabar's gourmet food store) is located in an old mustard and vinegar factory. This is the ultimate in recycling, as prepared foods find new life when unsold products get cooked: Eli's famous focaccia is wonderful when fresh, twice as delicious when made into Parmesan toast; loaves of brioche are dried to make a scrumptious bread pudding. And the waste not, want not axiom of the '90s goes on. Fresh breads baked daily on the premises are sold here for a fraction above wholesale. Eli plans to open a 70-seat cafe with a rooftop garden and a bagel factory here in 1994. ◆ Daily 9AM-8PM. 431 E. 91st St (between York and First Aves). 987.0885

15 Ruby's River Road Cafe ★★$ Some people might be turned off by the idea, but Ruby's patrons love to down a shot or two of Jell-O. Here, the normally benign wiggly matter is spiked with vodka. After a couple of them, you'll be ready to dive into a bowl of gumbo. ◆ American ◆ Lunch and dinner; bar open until 4AM. 1754 Second Ave (between E. 91st and E. 92nd Sts). 348.2328

16 Yura and Company ★★$$ One of the neighborhood's best cafes, this place features gourmet takeout and catering kitchens. Try the excellent bouillabaisse and decadent desserts. ◆ American/French ◆ Market: M-Sa 7AM-8PM; Su 8AM-6PM. Cafe: M-Sa 7AM-11PM; Su 8AM-11PM. 1650 Third Ave (at E. 92nd St). 860.8060

17 92nd Street Y This branch of the **Young Men's/Women's Hebrew Association** is one of the city's cultural landmarks. Under music director **Gerard Schwartz,** its **Kaufman Concert Hall** has become New York's best place to hear chamber music and recitals. Such groups as the **Guarneri, Cleveland,** and **Tokyo quartets** are regulars here. The renowned **Poetry Center** has offered readings by every major poet in the world since its founding in 1939, and the tradition continues with such writers as **Saul Bellow, Joseph Brodsky,** and **Isaac Bashevis Singer.** The **American Jewish Theater** is sponsored by the Y, as are lectures, seminars, and workshops, even unusual tours of the city. ◆ 1395 Lexington Ave (at E. 92nd St). 427.6000

17 De Hirsch Residence $ Because of its affiliation with the well-known cultural and community center next door, the De Hirsch Residence tends to attract an interesting international crowd as compared to what you'd expect to find at a Y. Men and women are accommodated in dorm-style rooms on separate floors with shared bathrooms and kitchens, or in simple private rooms for shorter stays. Guests receive discounted admission to the cultural center's events. Unlike at many Ys, the De Hirsch Residence has no student or age qualifications or a maximum-stay requirement. ◆ 1395 Lexington Ave (at E. 92nd St). 427.6000

18 120 and 122 East 92nd Street Because fire laws made the construction of wooden houses illegal in the 1860s, there are very few of them in Manhattan. This pair (and the frame houses at 160 E. 92nd Street and 128 E. 93rd Street), built in 1850, are a reminder of what this neighborhood was like in the mid-19th century. ◆ Between Lexington and Park Aves

19 Night Presence IV The intentionally rusty steel sculpture is by the late **Louise Nevelson.** The view down the avenue from here is picture-perfect. ◆ Park Ave at E. 92nd St

20 Busby's $$$ This all-American, California-influenced restaurant has an imaginative menu that features such appetizers as roasted goat cheese wrapped in grilled eggplant. ◆ American ◆ Lunch and dinner; brunch only on Sunday. 45 E. 92nd St (at Madison Ave). Reservations recommended. 360.7373

20 Wales Hotel $$ This small, moderately priced European-style hotel is ideally located if you plan to spend a lot of time on Museum Mile or in Central Park. All the rooms have been renovated, but ask for a large, bright room or you may end up with the opposite. ◆ 1295 Madison Ave (between E. 92nd and E. 93rd Sts). 876.6000; fax 860.7000

20 Sarabeth's Kitchen ★★$$$ Many a New Yorker has stood on line for a weekend brunch of Sarabeth's gourmet comfort foods: homemade waffles and pancakes crowned with fresh fruit, hot porridge, and warm-from-the-oven muffins. On your way out, pick up homemade brownies and cookies. ◆ American ◆ Breakfast, lunch, and dinner. 1295 Madison Ave (between E. 92nd and E. 93rd Sts). Dinner reservations recommended. 410.7335. Also at: 423 Amsterdam Ave. 496.6280

21 1107 Fifth Avenue Built in 1925 by **Rouse & Goldstone,** this was a perfectly ordinary apartment building except for a few anomalies on the facade—evidence of an era past. **Marjorie Merriwether Post** (at the time married to stockbroker **E.F. Hutton**) purchased a 54-room apartment here. The Palladian window near the top center of the facade opened onto the main foyer of this apartment. ♦ At E. 92nd St

22 Jewish Museum Recently reopened in 1993 after a two-year renovation and expansion, this museum (shown above) holds the country's largest collection of Judaica. Besides permanent and rotating exhibits, it has classrooms, a delightful kosher cafe, and an attractive book and gift shop. This French Renaissance mansion, designed by **C.P.H. Gilbert** in 1908, was the home of financier **Felix M. Warburg.** Two annexes have been added: the first, in 1963, is by **Samuel Glazer,** and the second, finished in 1993, is by **Kevin Roche.** ♦ Admission. M, W-Th, Su 11AM-5:45PM; Tu 11AM-8PM. 1109 Fifth Ave (at E. 92nd St). 423.3230

23 Military Bookman This store specializes in used and out-of-print books on just about every aspect of the armed forces of the world. ♦ Tu-Sa 10:30AM-5:30PM. 29 E. 93rd St (between Madison and Fifth Aves). 348.1280

23 The Wicker Garden Wicker furniture, both new and antique, plus quilts and hand-painted furniture is offered here. Across the street, **Wicker Garden's Baby** (348.1166) sells white wicker cribs, bassinets, and high chairs, along with pure cotton clothes for newborns to six-year-old kids. ♦ M-Sa 10AM-5:30PM. 1318 Madison Ave (between E. 93rd and E. 94th Sts). 410.7000

24 Bistro du Nord ★$$$ Hearty meals and warm service are the hallmarks of this cozy little bistro. ♦ French ♦ Lunch and dinner. 1312 Madison Ave (at E. 93rd St). Reservations required. 289.0997

25 Corner Bookstore Featuring a wide selection of books, over a third of them for children, this store has an atmosphere conducive to browsing. Works on literature, art, and architecture are well represented. ♦ M-F 10AM-8PM; Sa 11AM-6PM; Su 11:30AM-6PM. 1313 Madison Ave (at E. 93rd St). 831.3554

25 Island ★$$$ You might expect to find this sort of place on the West Side: plenty of young people wolfing down quite good if slightly overpriced pasta and grilled dishes. ♦ Continental ♦ Lunch and dinner. 1305 Madison Ave (between E. 92nd and E. 93rd Sts). Reservations recommended. 996.1200

25 Paul Bott This is the perfect place if you want your living room to look like an English garden, or have a passion for roses (more than 30 varieties flown in daily from France and Holland), peonies, or wildflowers. A day's advance notice is usually sufficient for parties. ♦ M-F 9AM-5PM; Sa 9AM-2PM. 1305 Madison Ave (between E. 92nd and E. 93rd Sts). 369.4000

26 Smithers Alcoholism Center This former home of showman **Billy Rose** was the last of the large, great mansions to be built in New York. It is in the delicate style of the 18th-century Scottish brothers **Lambert** and **Nicholas Adam,** who created most of the best houses in Edinburgh and London. This one, however, was designed in 1932 by **Walker & Gillette.** ♦ 56 E. 93rd St (between Park and Madison Aves)

By the 1800s, Yorkville had become a haven for middle-class Germans, although the majority of Manhattan Germans still lived on the Lower East Side in an area around Thompkins Square Park called "Kleindeutschland." By the turn of the century, many German families were leaving the southern part of the island to resettle in Yorkville in order to avoid the waves of immigrants from Eastern Europe and Italy. The single greatest event, however, that brought New York Germans to Yorkville was the General Slocum disaster of 1904. This excursion steamer was filled with passengers, mostly women and children from Kleindeutschland. It burned and sank in the East River, killing more than a thousand people. The men of these families, who had not been on board because they could not get away from work that day, found their empty homes unbearable. They moved to Yorkville to help them forget.

26 60 East 93rd Street After **Mrs. William K. Vanderbilt** divorced her husband, she leased an apartment on Park Avenue, only to discover that her ex-husband had one in the same building. She broke the lease and had **John Russell Pope** build this beautiful French Renaissance mansion in 1930. ◆ Between Park and Madison Aves

27 Synod of Bishops of the Russian Orthodox Church Outside Russia Built in 1917 for **Francis F. Palmer** and renovated in 1928 by **Delano & Aldrich** for banker **George F. Baker,** this unusually large Georgian mansion has remained virtually unchanged, except for the introduction of exquisite Russian icons. A small cathedral occupies the former ballroom. ◆ 1180 Park Ave (at E. 93rd St). 534.1601

28 1185 Park Avenue Designed in 1929 by **Schwartz & Gross,** this is the only East Side version of the full-block courtyard apartment house typified by the **Belnord, Astor Court,** and **Apthorp** across town. The Gothicized entrance adds needed levity to the otherwise traditional composition. ◆ Between E. 93rd and E. 94th Sts

29 Kitchen Arts & Letters Approximately 9,000 cookbooks and books on the subject of food and wine are displayed here. You'll also find paintings and photographs of food, reproduction tin biscuit boxes, and other culinary memorabilia. ◆ M 1-6PM; Tu-F 10AM-6:30PM; Sa 11AM-6PM. 1435 Lexington Ave (between E. 93rd and E. 94th Sts). 876.5550

30 Squadron A and Eighth Regiment Armory/Hunter High School When the armory—a distinctly businesslike fortress built in 1895 by **John Rochester Thomas**—was on the verge of being torn down, community protest saved at least the facade on Madison Avenue. The school's architects, **Morris Ketchum, Jr. & Associates,** did a marvelous task in 1971 of using it as both a backdrop to the playground and as a formal inspiration for the new building. ◆ Bounded by E. 94th and E. 95th Sts (between Park and Madison Aves)

Directly after the Revolution, New York City had a short career as the capital of the young United States. George Washington was inaugurated in Lower Manhattan.

31 Dollhouse Antics Here you'll find all the necessary Lilliputian accessories for dollhouse decorating: playpens, paint easels, overstuffed sofas, sterling silver knives and forks, copper pots and pans, and hundreds of other minute items. Houses can be custom-ordered and even wired for electricity. ◆ M-F 11AM-5:30PM; Sa 11AM-5PM. 1343 Madison Ave (at E. 94th St). 876.2288

32 Saranac ★$$ This small American restaurant has the feel of a lodge in the Adirondacks. The reasonable prices belie its *Bonfire of the Vanities* location, and the menu lists well-prepared steaks, hamburgers, and grilled fish. ◆ American ◆ Lunch and dinner; brunch also on Saturday and Sunday. 1350 Madison Ave (between E. 94th and E. 95th Sts). 289.9600

33 International Center of Photography (ICP) Here you'll find the only museum in New York City—and perhaps the world—devoted entirely to photography. The ICP, designed in 1914 by **Delano & Aldrich,** is an ebullient and hospitable home for practitioners of the art, where the best and the brightest are given shows and encouragement. Every inch of the Georgian town house it occupies is used in the service of photography: four galleries for revolving shows; workshops and photo labs; a screening room; and a gallery for the permanent collection, which includes works by 20th-century photographers **W. Eugene Smith** and **Henri Cartier-Bresson,** among others. A gift shop sells books, catalogs, posters, and, of course, picture postcards. The center maintains additional gallery space at 1133 Sixth Avenue. ◆ Admission; free Tuesday 5-8PM. Tu 11AM-8PM; W-Su 11AM-6PM. 1130 Fifth Ave (at E. 94th St). 860.1777

34 Islamic Center of New York A computer was used to ensure that this mosque faces Mecca, as Islamic law requires. Built in 1991 by **Skidmore, Owings & Merrill,** it is New York's first major mosque, and is intended as the spiritual home of the city's 400,000 Moslems and to serve diplomats from Islamic countries. ◆ Third Ave (at E. 96th St). 722.5234

Label Vishinsky, inventor of an early automatic bagelmaker, claimed that the first New York bagel emerged from 15 Clinton Street in 1896.

Restaurants/Clubs: Red **Hotels:** Blue
Shops/ 🌳 Outdoors: Green **Sights/Culture:** Black

35 Russian Orthodox Cathedral of St. Nicholas Built in 1901-02, this church is unusual because, set above the polychromatic Victorian body, there are five onion domes. ♦ 15 E. 97th St (between Madison and Fifth Aves). 289.1915

36 Mount Sinai Hospital The latest construction project, completed in 1992 by **Cobb Freed & Partners,** includes three hospital towers in one grand pavilion. These new facilities replace 10 older buildings—some dating as far back as 1904—all of which have been demolished. Also of architectural interest is the **Annenburg Building,** a 436-foot Cor-Ten steel box that gets its color from a coating of rust that protects the steel from further corrosion. ♦ Bounded by E. 98th and E. 101st Sts (between Madison and Fifth Aves)

37 New York Academy of Medicine Built in 1926 by **York & Sawyer,** this charming combination of Byzantine and Romanesque architecture contains one of the most important medical libraries in the country. The collection includes 4,000 cookbooks, a gift of **Dr. Margaret Barclay Wilson,** who believed that good nutrition was the key to good health. ♦ M-F 9AM-5PM. 2 E. 103rd St (at Fifth Ave). 876.8200

38 Museum of the City of New York The story of New York City is told through historical paintings, **Currier & Ives** prints, period rooms, costumes, **Duncan Phyfe** furniture, **Tiffany** silver, ship models, and wonderful toys and dolls, all handsomely displayed in a roomy neo-Georgian building. The structure, red brick with white trim, designed by **Joseph Freedlander** in 1932, was built for the museum after it moved from **Gracie Mansion.** Puppet shows are staged for children, concerts and lectures for adults. ♦ Free. W-Sa 10AM-5PM; Su 1-5PM. 1220 Fifth Ave (between E. 103rd and E. 104th Sts). 534.1672

39 El Museo del Barrio This culture center and showcase for the historic and contemporary arts of Latin America (especially Puerto Rico) began as a neighborhood museum in an East Harlem classroom. Video, painting, sculpture, photography, theater, and film are featured. Permanent collections include pre-Columbian art and hand-carved wooden saints, one of the culture's most important art forms. ♦ Admission. W-Su 11AM-5PM. 1230 Fifth Ave (between E. 104th and E. 105th Sts). 831.7272

Bests

Marcia Tucker
Director, The New Museum of Contemporary Art

Studio Museum in Harlem. Sunday afternoon openings; among the most exciting shows in town (plus a fabulous gift shop).

A cappuccino at **Caffè Dante.** The closest you can get to Italy in the Village.

A Sunday visit to the **Lower East Side,** particularly the shops on **Orchard Street.** Unbelievable bargains, great knishes at **Yona Schimmel's** on Houston Street on your way there or back.

Radio City Music Hall's Easter and Christmas shows. The best kitsch anywhere in the world, destined to make you weep for the good old days.

Taking any six-year-old girl to the **Plaza** for tea. Makes you see the world somewhat differently—a little better and brighter.

The **Cowgirl Hall of Fame.** Ranks tops among eating and drinking establishments for the name alone, but the rest lives up to it. The decor provides instant respite from city overload.

Beverly Sills
Diva/Former Director of the New York City Opera

The **New York City Opera.**

The best restaurants in the world.

The greatest theater district in the world.

Brooklyn, where I was born.

Quentin Crisp
Actor (In the smiling and nodding racket)

I live on the Lower East Side of Manhattan because that is where they put me. I eat where I am invited (occasionally at the **Sumptuary,** 400 Third Avenue—but not often, as that would not befit my lowly station in life). I go to art galleries though I do not understand art—chiefly to the **Leslie Lohman** gallery on Prince Street because they give me a drink and there is somewhere to sit.

What I love about New York is the people, but I am not a connoisseur of anything. In fact, I have no taste whatsoever!

Jacob Walton, the owner of the Gracie Mansion area in 1770, was loyal to the King of England. When the Revolution began, he built a tunnel leading to the East River so he could escape to a waiting ship if necessary. The tunnel wasn't discovered until 1913.

"There are two million interesting people in New York—and only 78 in Los Angeles."

Neil Simon

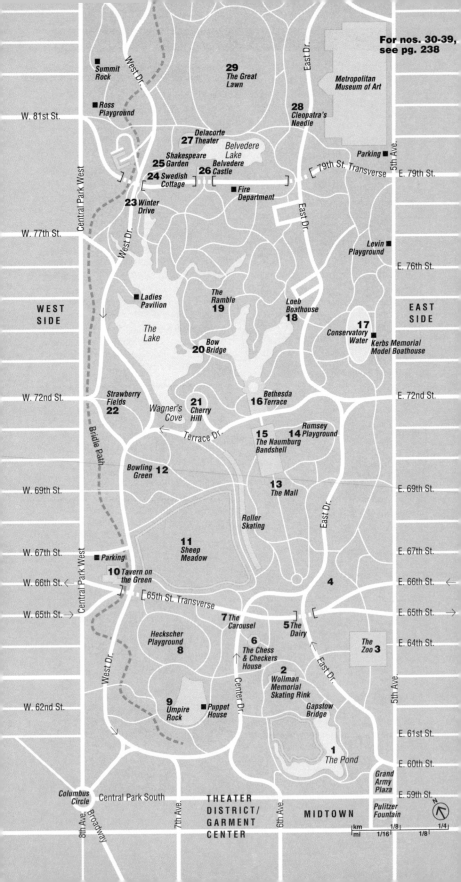
For nos. 30-39, see pg. 238

Metropolitan Museum of Art

29 The Great Lawn

28 Cleopatra's Needle

Parking ■

5th Ave.

E. 79th St.

79th St. Transverse

27 Delacorte Theater

Belvedere Lake

25 Shakespeare Garden

26 Belvedere Castle

24 Swedish Cottage

■ Fire Department

23 Winter Drive

W. 81st St.

■ Summit Rock

■ Ross Playground

West Dr.

Central Park West

W. 77th St.

West Dr.

Levin ■ Playground

E. 76th St.

WEST SIDE

■ Ladies Pavilion

The Lake

19 The Ramble

20 Bow Bridge

Loeb **18** Boathouse

17 Conservatory Water

Kerbs Memorial ■ Model Boathouse

EAST SIDE

W. 72nd St.

Strawberry Fields **22**

Wagner's Cove

21 Cherry Hill

Terrace Dr.

Bethesda **16** Terrace

E. 72nd St.

15 The Naumburg Bandshell

14 Rumsey Playground

Bowling Green **12**

13 The Mall

W. 69th St.

E. 69th St.

Bridle Path

Roller Skating

11 Sheep Meadow

W. 67th St.

East Dr.

E. 67th St.

■ Parking

10 Tavern on the Green

W. 66th St. ←

4

E. 66th St. ←

W. 65th St. →

65th St. Transverse

E. 65th St. →

Central Park West

Heckscher Playground **8**

7 The Carousel

5 The Dairy

6 The Chess & Checkers House

The Zoo **3**

E. 64th St.

2 Wollman Memorial Skating Rink

West Dr.

9 Umpire Rock

■ Puppet House

Center Dr.

Gapstow Bridge

W. 62nd St.

E. 61st St.

5th Ave.

1 The Pond

E. 60th St.

Columbus Circle

Central Park South

Grand Army Plaza

E. 59th St.

8th Ave.

Broadway

7th Ave.

THEATER DISTRICT/ GARMENT CENTER

6th Ave.

MIDTOWN

Pulitzer Fountain

km
mi   1/16   1/8   1/8   1/4

Central Park

"This different and many smiling presence," is how **Henry James** once referred to Central Park, bounded by **59th** and **110th streets, Fifth Avenue**, and **Central Park West**. The completely man-made park, unlike any other urban park in the United States, certainly elicits smiles from the more than 14 million people who wander through it every year. And 250 species of birds are regularly sighted here.

Not long after work began to clear the site on 12 August 1857, a friend suggested to journalist **Frederick Law Olmsted**, whose avocation was landscaping, that he should compete for the job of superintendent of the new Central Park. He quickly found backers in newspaper editors **Horace Greeley** and **William Cullen Bryant**, and when writer **Washington Irving** added his name to the list, Olmsted got the job. Later that same year, the Parks Commission announced a design competition for the new park, and Olmsted's friend, architect **Calvert Vaux**, suggested they join forces. Olmsted—concerned that the commissioners might consider his participation a conflict of interest—wasn't interested at first. But when his superiors convinced him otherwise, he accepted Vaux's proposal, and the two men went to work. Olmsted would later become known as the nation's foremost landscape architect. His legacy includes Yosemite National Park (he lobbied for its designation as the first national park in 1864); Fairmont Park in Philadelphia; the Capitol grounds in Washington, D.C.; George W. Vanderbilt's estate in Asheville, North Carolina; and the grounds of the 1893 World's Columbian Exposition in Chicago.

On 28 April 1858, after Olmsted and Vaux submitted what they called their **Greensward** plan, Olmsted wrote: "Every foot of the Park's surface, every tree and bush, as well as every arch, roadway, and walk, has been placed where it is with a purpose." In the years since, buildings have been added, monuments put in place, and playgrounds, roads, even parking lots have been constructed. But the original purpose is still well served.

The groundswell of support for the park had begun in 1844 when William Cullen Bryant warned that commerce was devouring Manhattan inch by inch. He pointed out that there were still unoccupied parts of the island, but that "while we are discussing the subject, the advancing population of the city is sweeping over them and covering them from our reach." By the mayoral election of 1851, Bryant and others had moved the cause forward to the point where it was the only issue both candidates could agree on. The winner of the race, **Ambrose C. Kingsland**, immediately recommended buying a 153-acre tract known as **Jones's Wood**, between the East River and Third Avenue, from 66th to 75th streets. His proposal was attacked from all sides: park supporters argued it was too small; influential businessmen objected to giving up the waterfront property to any purpose but commerce. In 1853, the state legislature authorized the city to buy the larger and much more central present site. The price tag was $5 million.

The land was no bargain. A swampy pesthole filled with pig farms and squatters' shacks, it was used as a garbage dump and served as a prime location for bone-boiling plants. After surveying it, Olmsted called it a "pestilential spot where miasmatic odors taint every breath of air." But he succeeded in turning it into what New Yorkers today proudly call the "lungs of the city."

Actual work began in 1857, and by the time the park was considered finished 16 years later, nearly five million cubic yards of stone and dirt had been rearranged and almost five million trees planted. Before construction started, 42 species of trees grew on the site, and by the time it was completed, 402

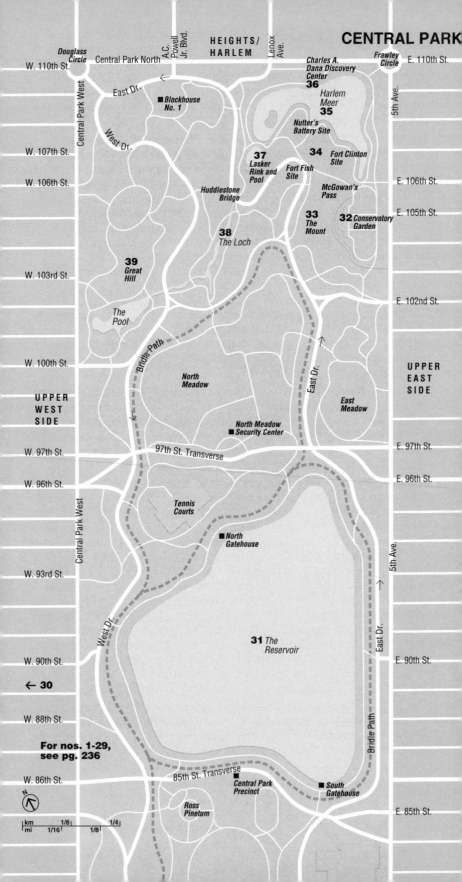

HEIGHTS/
HARLEM

Douglass
Circle

Central Park North

A.C. Powell Jr. Blvd.

Lenox Ave.

Frawley
Circle

W. 110th St.

E. 110th St.

Charles A.
Dana Discovery
Center
36

East Dr.

Blockhouse
No. 1

Harlem
Meer
35

Nutter's
Battery Site

5th Ave.

West Dr.

W. 107th St.

34 Fort Clinton
Site

W. 106th St.

E. 106th St.

37
Lasker
Rink and
Pool

Fort Fish
Site

McGowan's
Pass

Huddlestone
Bridge

E. 105th St.

33
The
Mount

32 Conservatory
Garden

38
The Loch

E. 102nd St.

39
Great
Hill

W. 103rd St.

The
Pool

Bridle Path

W. 100th St.

North
Meadow

**UPPER
EAST
SIDE**

East Dr.

East
Meadow

**UPPER
WEST
SIDE**

North Meadow
Security Center

97th St. Transverse

W. 97th St.

E. 97th St.

W. 96th St.

E. 96th St.

Tennis
Courts

Central Park West

North
Gatehouse

W. 93rd St.

West Dr.

5th Ave.

31 The
Reservoir

W. 90th St.

E. 90th St.

← **30**

East Dr.

W. 88th St.

Bridle Path

**For nos. 1-29,
see pg. 236**

W. 86th St.

85th St. Transverse

Central Park
Precinct

South
Gatehouse

E. 85th St.

N

Ross
Pinetum

km 1/8 1/4
mi 1/16 1/8

kinds of deciduous trees thrived, along with 230 species of evergreens and 815 varieties of shrubs. There were also 58 miles of pedestrian walks, six and a half miles of roads, and a bridle path four and a half miles long. A reservoir covered one hundred and six acres and a sprawling lake occupied another 22 acres. A series of smaller lakes and ponds were also created and some 62 miles of pipe installed to carry off unwanted water. In those days, earthmovers consisted of gangs of men with picks and shovels and teams of horses pulling wagonloads of dirt.

Olmsted was single-minded about what he wanted, and as superintendent of construction, he usually, but not always, got his way. He opposed buildings on park grounds, not related to the park itself: "Reservoirs and museums are not part of the park, but deductions from it," he said. The **Metropolitan Museum of Art** hasn't stopped deducting from the park since Calvert Vaux designed the original building in 1880. Olmsted was also testy about monuments: "The Park is not a place for sepulchral memorials. The beautiful cemeteries in the vicinity of the city offer abundant opportunities to commemorate the virtues of those who are passing away." Today, there are more than 80 monuments in Central Park. Frederick Law Olmsted may well be turning over in his grave, which, by the way, is not in the park.

Fortunately, Central Park is alive and well in spite of countless schemes to "improve" it. In 1918, someone in all seriousness suggested digging trenches in the **North Meadow** to give people an idea of what the doughboys were going through "over there." A year later, plans were submitted for an airport near **Tavern on the Green**, which was then a sheepfold. There have been several proposals to use some of the space for housing projects, and plans for underground parking garages have been coming and going since the 1920s. Not only have the **Parks Department** and the **Central Park Conservancy** resisted encroachment, they've been working for a decade or more to restore the park to what it once was. The result is that one of the best things about New York is getting better every day.

1 The Pond A shot of the reflection of the nearby buildings, especially the Plaza Hotel, in this crescent-shaped haven for ducks and other waterfowl may be among the best pictures you'll take home. The view is from the **Gapstow Bridge,** which crosses the northern end. The Pond was created to reflect the rocks in what is now a bird sanctuary on its western shore and is a favorite lunch spot for nearby office workers. From the time the park opened until 1924, swan boats like the ones still used in the Boston Garden dodged real swans here. The Pond was reduced to about half its original size in 1951 when the Wollman Memorial Skating Rink was built. ♦ Between 59th and 62nd Sts (near Fifth Ave)

2 Wollman Memorial Skating Rink The original rink lasted less than 30 years, and when the city attempted to rebuild it, the project became mired in so much red tape that it began to look as though it might take another 30 years to replace it. In 1986, real estate and casino tycoon **Donald Trump** took it upon himself to do the job—without the regulations the city imposes on itself—and finished it in record time. Trump occasionally appears here on winter weekends to accept the warm thanks of the skaters. Though an encroachment on the park, it is a hugely popular one, and space on the ice is usually at a premium. Ice-skating is generally from October to April, with roller-skating at other times. ♦ Admission; skate rental. M 10AM-5PM; Tu-Th, Su 10AM-9:30PM (closed to public for classes W-Th 6-7:30PM); F-Sa 10AM-11PM. 63rd St (off East Dr). 517.4800

3 The Arsenal The 10 acres of land around this building were a park before Central Park was even a dream. Designed by **Martin E. Thompson** and completed in 1851, the Arsenal's original use as a storehouse for arms and ammunition accounts for the iconography of cannons and rifles around the Fifth Avenue entrance. It became the citywide headquarters of the **Parks and Recreation Department** in 1934, following use as a police precinct, a weather bureau, a menagerie, and the first home of the **American Museum of Natural History**. A third-floor gallery contains, among other exhibits, the original Greensward plan, whose results are all around you. ♦ M-F 9AM-5PM. 64th St (at Fifth Ave). 360.8111

THE ZOO

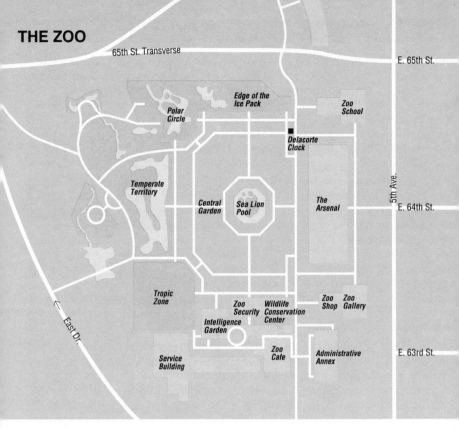

65th St. Transverse

E. 65th St.

Polar Circle

Edge of the Ice Pack

Zoo School

Delacorte Clock

Temperate Territory

Central Garden

Sea Lion Pool

The Arsenal

5th Ave.

E. 64th St.

Tropic Zone

Zoo Security

Wildlife Conservation Center

Zoo Shop

Zoo Gallery

Intelligence Garden

Service Building

Zoo Cafe

Administrative Annex

E. 63rd St.

East Dr.

3 The Zoo After four years of construction and $35 million of expense, this new home for 450 animals representing more than a hundred species reopened in 1988. The zoo it replaced had elephants, antelopes, and other animals too large for such cramped quarters; they were given to other zoos with more hospitable facilities. The bears and sea lions have been given new, more natural homes here, and two flocks of penguins cavort under a simulated ice pack in a pool with glass walls that allow you to watch their underwater antics. Monkeys swing in trees in a reproduction of an African environment, bats fly through their own naturalistic cave, and alligators swim in the most comfortable swamp north of the Okefenokee. The five-and-a-half-acre complex, encompassing three climatic zones, is now officially known as the **Central Park Wildlife Center**. A cafeteria and a gift shop at the southern edge are accessible without entering the grounds. The zoo was designed by **Kevin Roche** and **John Dinkeloo Associates**.
♦ Admission. M-F 10AM-5PM, Sa-Su and holidays 10:30AM-5:30PM Apr-Oct; daily 10AM-4:30PM Nov-Mar. 64th St (at Fifth Ave). 861.6030

4 Balto One of the most popular monuments in the park, this 1925 bronze portrait by **Frederick G.R. Roth** represents the husky who led his team of dogs from Anchorage to Nome (a thousand miles) to deliver serum to stem a diphtheria epidemic. ♦ 66th St (at East Dr)

GLENN WOLFF

5 The Dairy When this Gothic building (shown here) was constructed in 1870, fresh milk was a relative luxury. The park's planners, following European models, added milkmaids and a herd of cows to enhance the sylvan setting and to provide children with a healthy treat. After the turn of the century, the cows were sent off to the country, the milkmaids retired, and the building became a storehouse. In 1981, it was restored and its wooden porch replaced and painted in Victorian colors. It is now the park's central **Visitor Center**, with an information desk, exhibitions, and a sales desk. Weekend walking tours, led by the **Urban Park Rangers**, usually begin here.
♦ Visitor Center Tu-Th, Sa-Su 11AM-5PM; F 1-5PM. 65th St (west of the Zoo). Tour information 427.4040; special events 360.1333

6 The Chess & Checkers House A gift of financier **Bernard Baruch** in 1952, this mecca for checkers-playing retirees sits on top of a rock known as the *Kinderberg* (Children's Mountain), named for a rustic summerhouse that once stood here as a retreat for children. ♦ 64th St (southwest of the Dairy)

7 The Carousel There has been a merry-go-round here since 1871. The original was powered by real horses that walked a treadmill in an underground pit. The present one, built in 1908 at Coney Island, was moved here in 1951. Its 58 horses were hand-carved by **Stein & Goldstein,** considered the best woodcarvers of their day. Don't just stand there—climb up and go for the ride of your life. ♦ Nominal admission. Daily 10:30AM-4:30PM. 65th St Transverse (at Center Dr). 879.0244

8 Heckscher Playground The original park plan didn't include sports facilities, but this was one of three loosely connected areas for children who had secured the proper permits to play games like baseball and croquet. In the 1920s, adults wanted to get into the game and pressured the city into building them five softball diamonds with backstops and bleachers. At about the same time, the former meadow was converted into an asphalt-covered playground to give the kids something to do while the adults were running bases. It was the first formal playground in the park. The softball fields are available by permit only, and are used by teams from corporations, Broadway shows, and other groups. ♦ 63rd St (between Center and West Drs). Call 427.6100 to see who's playing today; for a permit for your own team, call 408.0209

9 Umpire Rock Central Park is laced with rocky outcrops like this one, left behind some 20,000 years ago by the Laurentian Glacier. The boulder on top is called an erratic, and was carried down with the ice from the Far North. The tracks on the face of the rock, called striations, were formed by the scraping of large stones embedded in the glacier as it moved southeast across Manhattan. Most of the rocky outcrops in the park are a type of mica-rich shale called Manhattan schist. About 400 million years ago, they formed the base of a mountain chain about as high as the present-day Rocky Mountains. The rocks were already here when the park was built, of course, but **Olmsted** exposed many that had previously been below the surface. Most experts agree that the erratic on Umpire Rock was moved here by Olmsted's construction crews. But many of the erratics in the park were left where the glacier had deposited them. ♦ 62nd St (overlooking ballfields)

TAVERN ON THE GREEN

10 Tavern on the Green ★★$$$$ Designed by **Jacob Wrey Mould** in 1870, this building, added over **Olmsted's** strenuous objection by parks commissioners controlled by **Boss Tweed** and **Tammany Hall,** was originally the Sheepfold, which housed the herd of Southdown sheep that grazed on the nearby meadow. In 1934, the sheep were exiled to Brooklyn's Prospect Park, and the building was converted into a restaurant. It was reconverted in 1976 by **Paul K.Y. Chen** and **Warner LeRoy** along the lines of LeRoy's late lamented Maxwell's Plum, which closed in 1988. The outdoor garden is a wonderful place to spend a summer evening and is spectacularly lit by twinkling lights in the trees from November to May. But any time of year, the **Crystal Room,** dripping with chandeliers, is an unforgettable experience, especially for Sunday brunch. If you're lucky enough to be here when snow is falling outside, you'll never want to go home. ♦ American ♦ Lunch and dinner; dinner only on Saturday and Sunday; late-night meals also on Saturday. 67th St (at Central Park West). Reservations required. 873.3200

11 Sheep Meadow The original park design called for a meadow here to enhance the view from the gentle hill to the north. The 15-acre hill was resodded in 1980 after concerts and other crowd-pleasing events had reduced it to hardpan. On the first warm day of the year, New Yorkers flock here for picnicking, sunbathing, and quiet recreation. The view from the hill with the city skyline in the background is in some ways more breathtaking than the park's architects ever envisioned. ♦ Tu-F, Su 11AM-5PM; Sa 1-5PM. 67th St and West Dr

12 Bowling Green Lawn bowling and croquet were first played on the Green in the 1920s. The folks who play here today take their games very seriously, which explains why the greens are so well-maintained. You can get a permit to join them by calling. ♦ Games start at 1PM and 1:30PM Tu-Sa May-1 Nov. 70th St (at West Dr). 360.8133

12 Mineral Springs The concession stand overlooking Sheep Meadow also houses a comfort station. It replaced the **Mineral Springs Pavilion,** built in 1868 by a mineral water company that used it to dispense some 30 varieties of water. ♦ 70th St (at West Dr)

Appointed in 1911, Samuel Battle was New York's first black police officer. He was promoted to lieutenant and later became a member of the Parole Commission.

Restaurants/Clubs: Red   **Hotels:** Blue
Shops/ 🌳 Outdoors: Green   **Sights/Culture:** Black

13 The Mall This formal promenade was largely the work of **Ignaz Anton Pilat,** a plant expert who worked with **Olmsted** and **Vaux** on the overall design of the park. He deviated from the romantic naturalism of the plan by planting a double row of elm trees along the length of the Mall, but in the process created a reminder of what country roads and New England villages were like a century ago. The promenade was placed on a northwest angle to provide a sightline directly to a high outcropping above 79th Street known as **Vista Rock.** Vaux designed a miniature castle for the top of the rock to create an impression of greater distance. The bandshell in the northeast corner was designed in 1923 by **William G. Tachau** and donated by **Elkan Naumburg,** who presented concerts here for many years. It replaced an 1862 cast-iron bandstand that included a sky-blue cupola dotted with gold-leaf stars. The current bandshell is still used for dance, music, and opera performances, as well as special events. ♦ Between 66th and 72nd Sts (off East Dr). 860.1355

14 Rumsey Playground A 1938 sculpture of *Mother Goose* by **Frederick G.R. Roth** and **Walter Beretta** provides a welcome to this walk-up playground with a wisteria-covered pergola at its western edge. Its location at the top of a hill and a less-than-inviting design make it unattractive to parents of small children. A recent decline in the number of children living near the park has reduced the use of all the park's playgrounds. This one is used primarily as an athletic field for nearby private schools. It was built on the site of the **Central Park Casino,** a cottage originally designed as a ladies' house of refreshment. In the 1920s, it was turned into a restaurant, designed by **Joseph Urban,** which became the most popular place in town for the likes of **Gentleman Jimmy Walker,** whose basic rule of life was that the only real sin was to go to bed on the same day that you got up. ♦ 71st St (at East Dr)

15 The Naumburg Bandshell The bandshell is a vital summertime center for jazz, folk dance, and theatrical performances. ♦ Call ahead for showtimes. 72nd St (at the Mall). 360.2756

If you get lost in the park, find the nearest lamppost. The first two numbers signify the nearest numbered (east-west) street.

There are 22 playgrounds, 26 ball fields, and 30 tennis courts in Central Park.

Restaurants/Clubs: Red   **Hotels:** Blue
Shops/ 🌳 Outdoors: Green   **Sights/Culture:** Black

16 Bethesda Terrace Located between the Lake and the Mall, this terrace has always been considered the heart of Central Park. It was named for a pool in Jerusalem that the Gospel of St. John says was given healing powers by the annual visitation of an angel. The *Angel of the Waters,* **Emma Stebbins'** statue on top of the magnificent fountain (shown above), re-creates the event. It was unveiled in 1873, but Bethesda Terrace itself had opened in 1861. The basic design is the work of **Calvert Vaux.** But the arcade ceiling, tile floors, and elaborate friezes and other ornamentation are by **Jacob Wrey Mould,** whose early background was in Islamic architecture—which explains why the terrace is so much like a courtyard in a Spanish palace. ♦ 72nd St (at Terrace Dr)

17 Conservatory Water The name for this pond comes from a conservatory that was never built. The space is occupied by the **Kerbs Memorial Model Boathouse,** designed by **Aymar Embury II** in 1954. It houses model yachts that race on the pond every Saturday in the summer. At the north end is **José de Creeft's** fanciful *Alice in Wonderland* group, given to the park in 1960 by publisher **George Delacorte.** At the western edge is **George Lober's** 1956 bronze statue of **Hans Christian Andersen,** a gift of the Danish people. During the summer, a storyteller appears here every Saturday at 11AM. A small snack bar with outdoor tables overlooks the water on the east side. ♦ Between 73rd and 75th Sts (off Fifth Ave)

18 Loeb Boathouse Built in 1954, this is the third boathouse on the lake. It was tucked away here in the northeast corner so it wouldn't spoil lake views. Besides rowboat and bicycle rentals, there is also an authentic Venetian gondola that holds six people. The Venetians gave a gondola to the park in 1862, but for lack of a gondolier, it rotted away. This one, a more recent gift, includes the services of an expert to pole it around the lake. Bicycle rentals are also available; call 861.4137 for information. ♦ Rowboat rentals: M-F 11AM-5PM; Sa-Su 11AM-6PM. Gondola rides: fee. M-F 5-10PM; Sa-Su 3-10PM Mar-Oct. 74th St (at East Dr). Reservations required. 517.2233

Within Loeb Boathouse:

Boathouse Cafe ★★★$$$ Light fare is served in this restaurant, one of New York's best settings. In good weather, sit on the outdoor terrace with a peaceful view of the lake. But the view from inside is just as good, and it's unusually pleasant (and uncrowded) on rainy days, when the landscape outside becomes dramatic. ♦ Northern Italian ♦ Lunch and dinner. Closed Dec-Feb. 517.2233

19 The Ramble This 37-acre wooded section of the park was conceived as a wild garden preserve for native plants and was also intended as a foreground for Vista Rock as seen from the Mall. The Ramble has seen better days, but it is still a wild place, with a brook meandering through and tumbling over several small waterfalls, and a perfect place for bird-watching. One of the winding paths led to a man-made cave at the edge of the lake, but the cave was walled up in the 1920s. There are few better places to get away from it all. Because this little forest can be relatively deserted, it may be best to share its pleasures with a friend. ♦ From 74th to 79th Sts (between East and West Drs)

20 Bow Bridge Calvert Vaux designed most of the park's bridges, and no two are alike. This one, crossing the narrowest part of the lake, is considered one of the most beautiful. When the cast-iron bridge was put in place, it was supposedly set on cannonballs to allow for expansion caused by temperature changes. But when it was restored in 1974, no cannonballs were found. ♦ 74th St (between the Ramble and Cherry Hill)

21 Cherry Hill Designed as a vantage point with a view of the Mall, the lake, Bethesda Terrace, and the Ramble, Cherry Hill also provided a turnaround for carriages and a fountain for watering the horses. It was converted into a parking lot in 1934 but restored with 8,500 new trees and shrubs and 23,000 square feet of new sod in 1981. ♦ Terrace Dr (west of Bethesda Terrace)

22 Strawberry Fields This is a teardrop-shaped memorial grove, rehabilitated and maintained with funds provided by Yoko Ono in memory of her late husband, John Lennon. The former Beatle was assassinated in front of the Dakota apartment house, which overlooks this tranquil spot. ♦ 72nd St (at Central Park West)

23 Winter Drive Evergreens were originally planted in all parts of the park to provide color in the winter months, but the heaviest concentration is here, where 19th-century gay blades entered the park for ice-skating. When the ice on the lake was hard enough, a red ball was hoisted on the flagpole above Belvedere Castle, and horsecars on Broadway carried the message downtown by displaying special flags. The parks commissioners estimated that as many as 80,000 people a day crowded the 20-acre frozen lake during the 1850s. The **Arthur Ross Pinetum,** added in 1971 at the north end of the Great Lawn, enhances the original plantings with unusual species of conifers from all over the world. ♦ West Dr (between 77th and 100th Sts)

24 Swedish Cottage Moved here from Philadelphia after the 1876 Centennial Exposition, this building was used as a comfort station until Swedish-Americans mounted a protest. After many years, it was converted into a marionette theater in 1973. ♦ Admission. General public: shows at Sa noon and 3PM; school groups: shows at Tu-F 10:30AM and noon. Hours vary according to months, so it's best to call ahead. 79th St Transverse (at West Dr). Reservations required. 988.9093

25 Shakespeare Garden In this lovely secluded garden, you'll find a series of pathways, pools, and cascades among trees and plants mentioned in the works of **William Shakespeare.** ♦ 80th St (at West Dr)

GLENN WOLFF

26 Belvedere Castle A scaled-down version of a Scottish castle (pictured above) was placed here to become part of the view. Its interior is just as impressive. The building houses a **National Weather Service** station and the **Central Park Learning Center.** ♦ Tu-F, Su 11AM-5PM; Sa 1-5PM. 79th St Transverse (between West and East Drs). 772.0210

Particularly evident from Central Park are a flurry of twin-towered buildings on Central Park West. Landmark luxury apartment complexes that are a favorite element in New York City's distinctive skyline, they were built from 1929 to 1931 during the peak of the Art Deco period when zoning laws allowed taller buildings if setbacks and towers were used. That period's prolific architect, the imminent Emery Roth, designed the San Remo at 145 Central Park West as well as the Eldorado at 300 Central Park West. The twin-towered 55 Central Park West was featured in the film *Ghostbusters.*

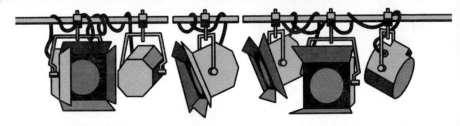

New York City on Screen

New York was a booming film production city even before the sunny skies of Hollywood began to woo producers and filmmakers west in the early 1900s. **D.W. Griffith** loved to shoot here, and **Mack Sennett's Keystone Cops** ran rampant through Coney Island.

The City goes out of its way to court the film industry, providing a special mayor's office to act as an industry liaison, police protection to stars and production crews, and even help arranging scenes ranging from helicopter chases to historical location settings. The number of feature films shot here has quadrupled since 1977, and movie, TV, and commercial production ranks among the city's top five growth industries.

It is no wonder then that many visitors to movieland's Gotham get a feeling of déjà vu. Here are a few of the movies and locations you may remember:

1941 *Citizen Kane* rallies political support at Madison Square Garden in **Orson Welles'** classic.

1942 Alfred Hitchcock's chilling *Saboteur* includes a dangling climax from the Statue of Liberty's crown.

1945 Ray Milland seeks solace at Bellevue Hospital after enduring *The Lost Weekend*. ♦ A troubled family discovers that *A Tree Grows in Brooklyn*.

1947 Macy's Santa Claus proves he's real to a jury and to young **Natalie Wood** in *Miracle on 34th Street*.

1948 Jules Dassin directed **Barry Fitzgerald, Howard Duff,** and **Don Taylor** in the oft-imitated police thriller *The Naked City*, which has a famous last scene on the Williamsburg Bridge.

1949 In the quintessential New York picture, *On the Town*, **Frank Sinatra, Gene Kelly,** and **Ann Miller** dance from Wall Street to Rockefeller Center.

1953 Fred Astaire and **Cyd Charisse** go *Dancing in the Dark* through Central Park in *The Band Wagon*. ♦ **Richard Widmark** stars in the Cold War thriller *Pickup on South Street*, whose location shots include the Bowery.

1954 Judy Holliday and **Jack Lemmon** reside at 115 West 69th Street in *It Should Have Happened to You*.

1957 Tony Curtis and **Burt Lancaster** dine at 21 in *The Sweet Smell of Success*.

1961 Director **Robert Wise** shoots the opening scene of *West Side Story* between Amsterdam and West End avenues at 68th Street. ♦ **Audrey Hepburn** and **George Peppard** find love (and silver toenail clippers) on Fifth Avenue in *Breakfast at Tiffany's*.

1963 *America, America,* **Elia Kazan's** portrayal of immigration to the United States, incorporates Ellis Island locales.

1965 Rod Steiger stars as a Jewish concentration camp survivor running a pawnshop in Harlem in Sidney Lumet's melodrama *The Pawnbroker*.

1966 Astor Place plays host to the wedding party in the film version of **Mary McCarthy's** novel *The Group*.

1967 Newlyweds **Jane Fonda** and **Robert Redford** meet in Washington Square in *Barefoot in the Park*. ♦ Harren High School at 59th Street and 10th Avenue hosts the teenagers of *Up the Down Staircase* (and the kids looking for *Fame* some 13 years later).

1968 *Funny Girl* **Barbra Streisand** shares the spotlight with the Statue of Liberty. ♦ Spanish Harlem hostility creates controversy for production crews and star **Richard Widmark** in the tough-cop story *Madigan*. ♦ **Frank Sinatra** and **Lee Remick** meet at the Columbia Law Library in *The Detective*. ♦ **Roman Polanski** directs **Mia Farrow, John Cassavetes,** and **Ruth Gordon** in *Rosemary's Baby*, most of which takes place in the Dakota Apartments.

1969 Director **Gene Kelly** and crew convert the village of Garrison's Landing to 1890 Yonkers for *Hello, Dolly!* ♦ **Dustin Hoffman** and **Jon Voight** jam up traffic at 58th Street and Sixth Avenue in *Midnight Cowboy*.

1970 A rich kid becomes the owner of a tenement in a black neighborhood in Brooklyn in **Hal Ashby's** *The Landlord*, starring **Beau Bridges, Pearl Bailey, Lou Gossett,** and **Lee Grant**.

1971 The *Panic in Needle Park* strikes heroin addicts at Broadway and Amsterdam Avenue. ♦ Unforgettable cop Popeye Doyle (**Gene Hackman**) chases drug smugglers along Brooklyn's Stillwell Avenue to discover *The French Connection*.

1972 A small restaurant in the Bronx is the setting for a key scene in **Francis Ford Coppola's** *The Godfather*, the first in his Corleone family trilogy. **Marlon Brando, James Caan, Diane Keaton, Robert Duvall,** and **Richard Castellano** star, and **Al Pacino** makes a memorable debut.

1973 Al Pacino fights corruption in the NYPD in *Serpico*, with location shots at New York University.

♦ A slice-of-life look at three losers in Little Italy is provided by *Mean Streets,* with **Robert De Niro.**

1974 Robert De Niro returns to Little Italy as young mob boss Don Corleone in *The Godfather, Part II.* ♦ Extortionists demand $1 million for the lives of subway passengers on the Pelham Bay Line in *The Taking of Pelham 1-2-3.*

1975 Al Pacino and two cohorts turn a simple Manhattan bank robbery into a *Dog Day Afternoon.* ♦ **Jack Lemmon** and **Anne Bancroft** are victims of the vicious city in *Prisoner of Second Avenue.*

1976 *Next Stop, Greenwich Village* captures the lure of artsy bohemia for a Brooklyn boy. ♦ **Robert De Niro** finds his own way of cleaning up New York's crime-ridden streets in **Martin Scorsese's** *Taxi Driver.*

1977 Woody Allen grows up under the Cyclone roller coaster at Coney Island in *Annie Hall.* ♦ **Liza Minnelli's** the singer, **Robert De Niro's** the sax player, and this is the town in *New York, New York.* ♦ **John Travolta** escapes his futureless reality as a disco dance king in *Saturday Night Fever.* His identity crisis reaches a climax atop the Verrazano-Narrows Bridge when a friend falls to his death. ♦ Unexpected and totally unwelcome, **Richard Dreyfuss** moves into **Marsha Mason's** apartment at 78th Street and Amsterdam Avenue in *The Goodbye Girl.*

1978 Christopher Reeve, that *Superman,* disguises himself as a mild-mannered reporter at the *Daily Planet.* The actual New York Daily News Building is used. ♦ Yellow linoleum tile transforms the Brooklyn Bridge into Oz in *The Wiz,* with **Diana Ross.** ♦ **Jill Clayburgh** portrays the trauma of becoming *An Unmarried Woman* on the Upper East Side.

1979 Dustin Hoffman drops his son off at school (P.S. 6 on Madison Avenue at 81st Street), while his soon-to-be-ex-wife **Meryl Streep** watches from across the street at The Copper Lantern, in *Kramer vs. Kramer.* ♦ Hippies dance through Central Park in **Milos Forman's** film version of *Hair.* ♦ **Woody Allen's** tribute to *Manhattan* features a tour of the Hayden Planetarium.

1980 Dustin Hoffman shocks **Sydney Pollack** in the Russian Tea Room, as *Tootsie* drops in for lunch.

1981 Paul Newman is a policeman overwhelmed by out-of-control crime in *Fort Apache, The Bronx.* ♦ **Dudley Moore** questions his date's profession just a bit too loudly in the Oak Bar at the Plaza in *Arthur.*

1982 Meryl Streep and **Kevin Kline** live together in a Victorian house in Flatbush (101 Rugby Road) in *Sophie's Choice.* ♦ **Peter O'Toole** tests the firehose by rappelling down the side of the Waldorf-Astoria in *My Favorite Year.*

1983 Four thousand extras attend a protest staged at Union Square for *Daniel,* **Sidney Lumet's** adaptation of **E.L. Doctorow's** novel. ♦ In *Splash,* mermaid **Daryl Hannah** tries to tell **Tom Hanks** her name while shopping at Bloomingdale's. The resulting fish-squeal shatters every TV set in the store. She later chooses the name "Madison" while walking down that avenue with him.

1984 Suburban housewife **Rosanna Arquette** finds unexpected adventure in Battery Park with **Madonna** in *Desperately Seeking Susan.* ♦ *Ghostbusters* **Bill Murray, Dan Aykroyd,** and **Harold Ramis** move into (and blow the roof off of) the 8 Hook and Ladder Firehouse in TriBeCa.

1985 This time **Rosanna Arquette** is the adventurous one, leading **Griffin Dunne** to SoHo and the most hellish date of his life in *After Hours.* ♦ At the Brooklyn Heights Promenade, **Jack Nicholson** debates whether he should marry **Kathleen Turner,** or ice her, in *Prizzi's Honor.*

1986 Carrie Fisher, Diane Wiest, and **Sam Waterston** take a tour of Manhattan architecture in **Woody Allen's** *Hannah and Her Sisters,* also starring **Mia Farrow, Barbara Hershey,** and **Michael Caine.**

1987 Paul Hogan resides at the Plaza while visiting from Down Under, in *Crocodile Dundee.* ♦ **Cher** is *Moonstruck* on the streets of Brooklyn.

1988 Michael J. Fox finds the New York fast lane to be moving just a little too fast in the film version of **Jay McInerney's** novel, *Bright Lights, Big City.* ♦ In *Big,* **Tom Hanks** and **Robert Loggia** perform a charming impromptu musical number at F.A.O. Schwarz.

1989 Bernadette Peters portrays an aspiring hat designer lost in the artificiality of the SoHo art world in the film version of **Tama Janowitz's** *Slaves of New York.* ♦ In **Rob Reiner's** *When Harry Met Sally,* Sally demonstrates to Harry the art of sexual deception while they share a meal at Katz's Delicatessen on the Lower East Side. ♦ **Woody Allen** studies life, death, and infidelity against the backdrop of the New York City skyline in *Crimes and Misdeamors.* ♦ Bedford-Stuyvesant is the setting for director **Spike Lee's** tale of racial strife *Do the Right Thing,* starring **Danny Aiello, Ossie Davis, Ruby Dee,** and **Giancarlo Esposito.**

1990 Gerard Depardieu and **Andie MacDowell** get to know each other in **Peter Weir's** tale of love after marriage, *Green Card.* ♦ Sherman McCoy's world of Upper East Side privilege is shattered after a hellish ride through the Bronx in *Bonfire of the Vanities.* ♦ Audiences get an unglamorous view of the Mafia in **Martin Scorsese's** *GoodFellas.*

1991 Barbra Streisand and **Nick Nolte** portray a New York psychiatrist and a high school football coach from South Carolina who discover that beyond their differences lie the commonalities of human joy and suffering, in the film version of **Pat Conroy's** best-selling novel, *Prince of Tides.*

1992 Al Pacino wins an Oscar for his portrayal of a blind man in **Martin Brest's** *Scent of a Woman,* costarring **Chris O'Donnell** and **Gabrielle Anwar.** ♦ **Macauley Culkin** is lost in New York in *Home Alone II,* directed by **Chris Columbus.** Joe Pesci, **Daniel Stern,** and **Brenda Fricker** costar.

1993 Winston Chao, Mitchell Lichstenstein, and **May Chin** concoct a plan for a marriage of convenience in *The Wedding Banquet,* shot at various locations, including Chinatown. ♦ **Robert De Niro** makes his directorial debut in *A Bronx Tale.*

27 Delacorte Theatre A 1960 addition to the park provides a modern home for the late **Joseph Papp's New York Shakespeare Festival.** Obtaining one of the 2,000 tickets (which are given out to the general public only on the day of the performance) is a time-consuming process that begins early in the day when would-be audience members queue up for several hours in order to receive line numbers, which are handed out after the first 200 people have arrived. Holders of line numbers are then required to return to stand in line until about 6:15PM, when the numbers are exchanged for actual tickets. Although it is possible to obtain a line number for one other person, no one can obtain an admission ticket for someone else. With good friends and a picnic, it can be a pleasant experience. Two Shakespeare plays are chosen for performance each summer. ◆ Free performances Tu-Su at 8PM late June to early Sept. 80th St (at West Dr). 861.7277

28 Cleopatra's Needle The **Khedive of Egypt** gave this obelisk to New York in 1881 and presented its mate to **Queen Victoria,** who had it placed on the Thames Embankment in London. When the 200-ton granite shaft was delivered to New York, it was placed in a special cradle and rolled here from the Hudson River on cannonballs. Because it had stood for many centuries in front of a temple built by Cleopatra, New Yorkers immediately dubbed it Cleopatra's Needle. It was, however, built by Egypt's **King Thotmes III** in 1600 BC. The hieroglyphics on its sides had survived for 3,500 years, but New York's air pollution has rendered them unreadable in fewer than a hundred. Movie producer **Cecil B. De Mille** thoughtfully provided plaques translating the tales they told of Thotmes III, **Rameses II,** and **Osorkon I.** ◆ 82nd St (at East Dr)

29 The Great Lawn The largest field in the park was formerly a rectangular reservoir that was drained just in time to provide a location for a Depression-inspired collection of squatters' shacks known as a Hooverville. By 1936 it was cleared again, and the oval-shaped lawn, with Belvedere Lake at the south end and two playgrounds to the north, was fenced off to create a cooling patch of green. It didn't stay that way long. It is now surrounded by ball fields with their backstops where the lawn should be, and overuse has almost completely eliminated the grass. In 1980, **Elton John** drew 300,000 people here for a concert; **Simon & Garfunkel** attracted 500,000 a year later; in 1982, an antinuclear rally brought out 750,000; and in 1993, **Pavarotti** sang before an audience of 500,000. The **New York Philharmonic** and the **Metropolitan Opera** give several free performances here every summer, each of which attracts about 100,000 people. ◆ Between 80th and 85th Sts (between East and West Drs)

30 Claremont Stables Though not actually in the park, the stables are very much a part of it. Riders experienced with English saddles rent horses here and enjoy Central Park from its bridle path. ◆ M-F 6:30AM-10PM; Sa-Su 8AM-5PM. 175 W. 89th St (between Columbus and Amsterdam Aves). Reservations required. 724.5100

31 The Reservoir Designed as part of the Croton Water System, this still-active receiving reservoir, covering nearly 107 acres, is better known for the soft-surface track that encircles it, providing a perfect amenity for serious runners. Once around is 1.58 miles. ◆ Between Fifth Ave and Central Park West (between 86th and 96th Sts)

32 Conservatory Garden A park nursery was replaced in 1899 by a glass conservatory, which was removed in 1934 to create this series of gardens. It remains one of Central Park's best-kept secrets, even though its presence is announced by an elaborate iron gate that once stood in front of the **Cornelius Vanderbilt II** mansion. The roofs of the buildings set into the hillside overlook three formal gardens, one of which is planted with seasonal flowers, another with perennials, and a third with grass surrounded by yew hedges and flowering trees and featuring a wisteria-covered pergola. Each is enhanced by a fountain. ◆ Daily 8AM-dusk. 105th St (at Fifth Ave). 581.0896

33 The Mount When **General Washington's** army was retreating through Manhattan in 1776, the British were held at bay here from a small fortress overlooking McGowan's Pass. The Mount was named for a tavern on top of the hill, which in 1846 became, of all things, a convent. The sisters moved out when the park was created, and the building was converted back into a tavern. It was one of the city's better restaurants in the late 19th century, but was demolished on orders of **Mayor John Purroy Mitchel** in 1917. ◆ 105th St (at East Dr)

34 The Forts During the War of 1812, three forts were built on the future park site to fend off an anticipated British attack. None was actually used, but their now-barren sites are marked with plaques and are waiting for a history buff to re-create them. A little farther to the north, an 1814 blockhouse, the oldest structure in the park, is also waiting for renovation. These days, its thick walls, laced with gunports, look into groves of trees. But when they were placed there, men inside could spot an enemy miles away. None ever came, and few people climb the hill to see the site today. ◆ Between 106th and 108th Sts (off East Dr)

35 Harlem Meer The park's original northern boundary was at 106th Street until 1863, when it was extended another four blocks northward, at which time this 11-acre lake was created. It uses the Dutch word for lake, although it hardly qualified for a lake or a meer for a long time. In 1941, the Parks Department altered its shoreline to eliminate the natural coves and inlets the original designers had placed there, and the whole thing was rimmed and lined with concrete. Fortunately, this once beautiful corner of the park, desperately in need of loving care, has now been restored to its natural appearance. Work is also underway to rebuild the boathouse, create a playground and discovery center for children, and build an esplanade for small concerts at 110th Street. ◆ 110th St (at Fifth Ave)

36 Charles A. Dana Discovery Center This is the newest of the park's **Visitor Centers**, opened in 1993, with exhibits and programs on environmental issues for all ages. ◆ Tu-Su 11AM-4PM. E. 110th St (at the Harlem Meer). 860.1370

37 Lasker Rink and Pool Built in 1964, this shallow swimming pool doubles as an ice-skating rink from Thanksgiving through March (M-Th, Su 10AM-9:30PM; F-Sa 10AM-11PM). It gets considerably less traffic than the downtown Wollman Rink, even though it costs less to use. It was built at the mouth of the stream that feeds Harlem Meer. ◆ July-Sept. 107th St (at Lenox Ave). 996.1184

38 The Loch This natural pond, undisturbed by the original designers, has been left alone to the point of being silted almost out of existence. A brook leading from the north end forms a small waterfall near the Huddleston Bridge, which carries the East Drive over it. ◆ Between 103rd and 105th Sts (off East Dr)

39 Great Hill The mansion of the **Bogardus** family that once stood on the crest of this 134-foot hill was home to **Frederick Law Olmsted** during the park's construction. He considered replacing it with a lookout tower because of the view, not only of the park, but of the Hudson River to the west. The view is gone and so is the charm of Great Hill, which, although recently resodded and replanted, remains capped with asphalt. ◆ 103rd St (at Central Park West)

"In its influence as an educator, as a place of agreeable resort, as a source of scientific interest, and in its effect upon the health, happiness, and comfort of our people may be found its chief value."

Frederick Law Olmsted, *Report of the Commissioners of Central Park,* 1870

The first New York City Marathon took place in 1970, when 127 runners circled Central Park four times. The meager $1,000 budget left no room for extravagance: to save money, post-race sodas were purchased in the Village and lugged uptown, where soda was more expensive.

Corky Pollan
Contributing Editor, *New York* magazine

The Frick Collection—this is probably on everyone's list of favorites, but where else in New York can you view some of the greatest works of art without having to jockey for position?

The **Seal Pond** at the renovated **Central Park Zoo.**

Lunch at the **Post House** for old-world elegance and service.

Tea at the **Mayfair Baglioni** for soothing teas, delectable sandwiches, and comforting sofas.

The **Conservatory Garden** any spring day.

The **Museum of the City of New York** for its enchanting collection of antique and vintage dolls, dollhouses, and toys.

Lower Broadway on a Saturday or Sunday to catch the hottest and trendiest fashion looks.

Rizzoli, even when you're not looking for a book.

Little Rickie on First Avenue for nostalgic toys from the '50s and '60s.

Drinks at the **Top of the Tower** at sunset—one of the city's most romantic spots.

Joan Juliet Buck
Novelist/Film Critic/Journalist

Walter Reade Theater when a strange film is playing.

The **27th Street Flea Market** for relics from the '20s.

Eat on Madison Avenue for the deep-fried baby artichokes.

Schweitzer Linen for decently priced bedclothes.

The **Fifth Avenue bus** all the way downtown.

Strand Bookstore, because you don't know what you don't know till you find it here, usually from the top of a ladder and slightly out of reach, definitely out of print.

Weekend lunch at **Petaluma** because it's bright and the *quattro stagione* pizza is perfect.

Sam Hilu's warehouse/showroom on Fifth: the world as textiles.

Fresh & Plus Korean Grocers on Third Avenue because it's both.

Ballet lessons at any reliable ballet school.

The Russian Samovar because it's Roman Kaplan's Moscow—poets, dancing dervishes, jazzmen from Kiev.

St. Ambroeus for cappuccino because the tablecloths are so clean.

Sirio Maccioni
Owner/Manager, Le Cirque

Lutèce.

Bouley.

Mayfair Baglioni Hotel.

West Side

Bisected by **Broadway** and its casual jumble of bookstores, delis, theaters, and restaurants, Manhattan's West Side is more laid-back than its fashionable East Side counterpart across Central Park. The area was first settled by Eastern European Jews and other immigrants from the Lower East Side in the early part of this century. Today, this vibrant neighborhood, bounded by the **Hudson River**, **Central Park**, and **59th** and **86th streets**, is characterized by roller bladers zipping past patrons at sidewalk cafes, young mothers pushing baby carriages, and well-dressed crowds pouring in and out of the concert halls and restaurants. Highlights include **Lincoln Center for the Performing Arts**, the ever-changing mix of clothing stores and sidewalk cafes on **Columbus Avenue** and Broadway, and numerous architecturally noteworthy buildings.

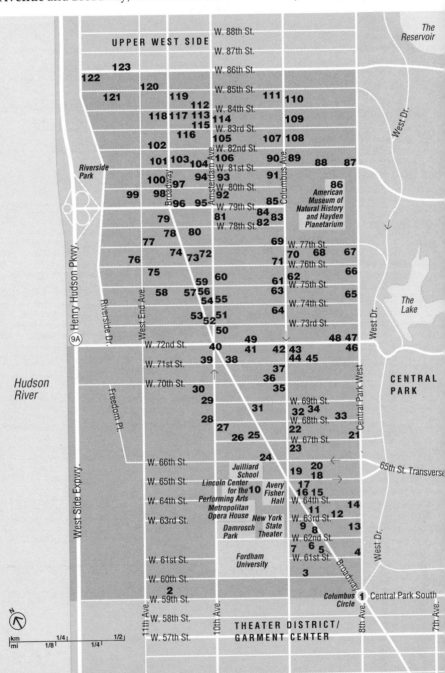

Riverside Drive, along the neighborhood's western edge, was originally a street of upper-middle-class town houses, and although it had spectacular river views, it lacked the cachet of Fifth Avenue, where "the 400" (**Mrs. William Astor's** most intimate circle, so called because her home could only accommodate that number) were erecting their palazzi and châteaux. Riverside Drive only had a few grand mansions like the one **Charles Schwab** built in 1906 at 73rd Street (now an apartment house). Many of the private homes were replaced in the 1920s by the 15-story apartment buildings of today, their faces sometimes curving to follow the shape of the street.

Some argue that **Central Park West**, skirting the neighborhood's eastern edge, is finer than Fifth Avenue, which borders the other side of the park, because the buildings are more distinguished and the street wider and more elegant. Most of the buildings on Central Park West were originally apartments rather than houses, including the wonderfully eclectic **Dakota** (the city's first luxury apartment house, built in 1884) at 72nd Street and the Art Deco **Century** (built in 1931) at 25 Central Park West.

The park blocks—the numbered streets between Central Park West and Columbus Avenue—contain interesting collections of brownstones and apartments. Particularly noteworthy are the six buildings with artists' studios on 67th Street, including the **Hotel des Artistes** (home of the **Café des Artistes**), in whose plush apartments many well-known artists, actors, and writers have lived, among them **Isadora Duncan**, **Noel Coward**, and **Fannie Hurst**.

West End Avenue, once lined with Romanesque and Queen Anne-style row houses and now apartment houses, was supposed to be the West Side's commercial street, while Broadway was slated to be the residential area, hence the avenue's generous width and mall in the center. But the reverse happened, and Broadway became the neighborhood's "Main Street."

1 Columbus Circle This traffic circle (today a real runaround for pedestrians) was built after the commissioners of Central Park were empowered to develop the West Side from 55th to 155th streets in 1887. Around the edges are the Moorish white block of the **New York City Department of Cultural Affairs**, designed in 1962 by **Edward Durell Stone** and originally built by A&P heir **Huntington Hartford** for his abortive **Gallery of Modern Art**; the grayish lump of the **Coliseum**, designed in 1956 by **Leon & Lionel Levy**; and the black-and-white tower of the **Gulf + Western Building** and its sunken plaza, designed in 1970 by **Thomas E. Stanley**—all in all a dismal landscape in a difficult space that planners have been trying to solve for years. The most imaginative suggestion yet was to make an arcade with the columns from the demolished **Penn Station**. In the center stands *Christopher Columbus*, a 700-ton monument by **Gaetano Russo**, installed in 1892. At the corner of Central Park is the **Maine Memorial**, designed by **H. Van Buren Magonigle** in 1913 and sculpted by **Attilio Piccirilli**. ♦ Central Park South at Central Park West

At Columbus Circle:

Visitors Information Center Stop by the offices of the **New York Convention and Visitors Bureau** for brochures about attractions and lists of restaurants, shops, and hotels. Warning: only organizations that are members of the bureau are listed. The center also has information regarding free tickets to TV shows and half-priced tickets to Broadway shows. ♦ M-F 9AM-6PM; Sa-Su and holidays 10AM-6PM. 2 Columbus Cir (between Broadway and Eighth Ave). 397.8222

2 West 59th Street Public Pool The outdoor public pool provides much relief in the summer. Call for hours and bring a padlock. ♦ 533 W. 59th St (between 10th and 11th Aves). 397.3159

3 Gabriel's ★★$$$ Probably the best homemade pastas, risottos, grilled dishes, and desserts on the Lincoln Center restaurant scene are served. Gabriel himself is a great source for wine and food recommendations. ♦ Northern Italian ♦ Lunch and dinner; dinner only on Saturday. Closed Sunday. 11 W. 60th St (between Broadway and Columbus Ave). Reservations recommended. 956.4600

Congregation Shearith Israel at W. 70th Street is the oldest Jewish congregation in the United States. The first house of worship was built in 1730 by descendants of 23 men, women, and children who arrived from Nieuw Amsterdam in 1654. It was moved uptown three times until the current synagogue at W. 70th Street was built in 1897.

4 Mayflower $$$ Well-located for **Lincoln Center,** the Mayflower offers roomy, styleless accommodations, all with color TVs and most with serving pantries. The **Conservatory Restaurant** serves breakfast, lunch, and dinner, plus an after-theater supper, often with classical music. ♦ 15 Central Park West (at W. 61st St). 265.0060, 800/223.4164; fax 265.5098

5 Bible House/American Bible Society
The American Bible Society tries to make the Holy Scripture available in every language on earth. Its headquarters has a gallery for exhibitions from its collection of rare and unusual bibles, which includes pages from the **Gutenberg Bible.** ♦ Free. M-F 9AM-4:30PM. 1865 Broadway (at W. 61st St). 408.1200

6 Harkness Atrium Designed by **Philip Birnbaum** in 1980, the large open space has plenty of tables and chairs for public use. Potted palms decorate the atrium, which holds various art exhibitions, shows, and demonstrations. ♦ W. 61st St (between Broadway and Columbus Ave)

7 45 Columbus Avenue Designed by **Jardine, Hill & Murdock** in 1930, this 27-story building was originally the **Columbus Circle Automatic Garage.** It is a tremendous Art Deco sampler: all the walls are embellished with ornament. ♦ Between W. 61st and W. 62nd Sts

8 The Ballet Shop This favorite shop of balletomanes specializes in dance publications—in- and out-of-print—and records, videos, and souvenirs. ♦ M-Sa 11AM-7PM; Su noon-5PM. 1887 Broadway (between W. 62nd and W. 63rd Sts). 581.7990

At the corner of Washington Place and Greene Street, a plaque commemorates the deaths of 146 people in the infamous fire at the Triangle Shirtwaist Company. The victims were predominantly Jewish and Italian immigrant women. When the fire broke out, the workers were unable to escape because the owners locked them into the building during shifts, a common industry practice. The fire brought attention to the despicable conditions of employment in the sweatshop industry, and the state enacted many reforms in the fire code and workplace safety regulations. The owners of the Triangle Shirtwaist Company were acquitted of any responsibility for the deaths in a court of law, despite the outrage of the community.

9 The Radisson Empire Hotel $$ A $70 million renovation, completed in 1992, has brought the 375 rooms into the electronic age: each is equipped with a cassette and CD player, a VCR, and a two-line telephone. Other highlights are the ballroom, corporate lounge, and **Empire Restaurant.** ♦ 44 W. 63rd St (between Broadway and Columbus Ave). 265.7400, 800/545.7500; fax 315.0349

9 Iridium ★★$$ Modern, amorphic shapes, undulating walls, gilt surfaces, and deep burnished woods create a Memphis-movement-cum-Wonderland atmosphere in this new and immediately popular restaurant where O'Neals' reigned for so many years. In addition to its important location across the street from Lincoln Center, it boasts the innovative talents of chef **John DiLeo,** formerly of SoHo's Zoey. Try his signature grilled hangar steak with warm potato salad, or seared loin of tuna in a distinctive Indonesian plum wine sauce. A changing roster of jazz musicians play the downstairs room nightly from 9:30PM to midnight. ♦ Eclectic American ♦ Lunch and dinner. 44 W. 63rd St (at Columbus Ave). 582.2121

10 Lincoln Center for the Performing Arts
Robert Moses, planner and New York powerbroker, initiated the idea of a center for the city's major performing arts institutions in the 1950s, and this conglomeration of travertine halls came slowly into existence. Massed on a plaza above the street, the buildings have been called an **Acropolis,** but the arrangement around the fountain is actually a static version of **Michelangelo's Capitoline Hill** in Rome. Although the main theaters all take their formal cues from images of classical architecture, critics claim they never really come together as a whole, and remain, at best, individual *tours de trite.* Although **Wallace K. Harrison** coordinated the project and designed the master plan, individual architects designed the buildings in the 1960s. ♦ W. 65th St and Broadway. 875.5000

At Lincoln Center for the Performing Arts:

Avery Fisher Hall Standing opposite the State Theater, this building was designed in 1966 by **Max Abramovitz.** Originally **Philharmonic Hall,** it has been reconstructed several times in the hopes of improving the acoustics, and a final touch-up in 1992 turned it into an acoustic gem. The stabile in the foyer is by **Richard Lippold.** The **New York Philharmonic** is in residence here from September through May. Music director **Kurt Masur** is the latest in an illustrious line that has included the late **Leonard Bernstein, Zubin Mehta, Arturo Toscanini,** and **Leopold Stokowski.** The informal **Mostly Mozart** concerts are held in July and August; **Great Performances** concerts are held September through May. Both are presentations of

Lincoln Center Productions. The Philharmonic's **Young People's Concerts** have been letting kids in on the motives behind the music since 1898; performances take place four times a year. Don't miss the regularly scheduled open rehearsals, which usually occur on Thursday morning. ♦ Broadway at W. 65th St. 875.5030

Panevino ★$$ This is a pleasant place for dinner, pastry and coffee, or just drinks. During the summer, the cafe spills out onto the plaza. ♦ Italian ♦ Dinner. Closed Sunday. Avery Fisher Hall, lobby. 874.7000

Metropolitan Opera House Home to the **Metropolitan Opera Company,** the plaza's magnificent centerpiece (designed by **Wallace K. Harrison**) opened in 1966 with **Samuel Barber's** *Anthony and Cleopatra.* Behind the thin, 10-story colonnade and sheer glass walls, two wonderful murals by **Marc Chagall** beam out onto the plaza. The interior is filled with a red-carpeted lobby, a dramatic staircase lit by exquisite Austrian crystal chandeliers, and an equally plush auditorium. The opera season, from mid-September to April, leaves the stage available for visiting performers and companies, including the **American Ballet Theater,** during the rest of the year. ♦ Broadway at W. 65th St. 362.6000

Metropolitan Opera Shop Imaginative opera- and music-related gifts and clothing are sold, most of them exclusive to this shop. Pick up hard-to-find books, records, posters, and libretti, with proceeds going to the Metropolitan Opera. ♦ M-Sa 10AM-second intermission (usually 9:30PM); Su noon-6PM. Next to the Met box office. 580.4090

New York State Theater Located on the plaza's south side, this theater was designed in 1964 by **Philip Johnson** and **Richard Foster.** At the culmination of a series of increasingly grand entrance spaces is a striking four-story foyer with balconies at every level, a pair of white marble sculptures by **Elie Nadelman,** and a gold-leaf ceiling. The rich red and gold auditorium was designed for both ballet and musical theater. From 1964 to 1968, under the artistic directorship of **Richard Rodgers** of the Music Theater of Lincoln Center, revivals of musical classics were staged here. Now it's home to the **New York City Ballet** and the **New York City Opera.** In March 1989, conductor **Christopher Keene** took over the opera company's direction from former opera star **Beverly Sills,** who assumed the position in 1979. The Ballet's season is usually late November through February and April through June. *Nutcracker* season runs from 1 to 31 December. The City Opera performs from July through November. Note the diamond-shaped floodlights surrounding the building. ♦ W. 63rd St (at Columbus Ave). 870.5570

Guggenheim Bandshell South of the Met, within **Damrosch Park,** the bandshell is a beautiful space for free concerts. It was designed by **The Eggars Partnership** in 1969 and seats 2,500. ♦ SW corner of Lincoln Center. 875.5000

Vivian Beaumont Theater North of the Met, behind a tree-studded plaza and reflecting pool (with a sculpture by **Henry Moore**), this theater was designed by **Eero Saarinen & Associates** and first opened in 1965. Recently reconstructed from a thrust to a proscenium stage, it had been plagued by trouble since the **Repertory Company of Lincoln Center** opened here under the direction of **Robert Whitehead** and **Elia Kazan** with **Arthur Miller's** apologia *After the Fall.* After several mediocre productions, there was a change of leadership. The new team, **Jules Irving** and **Herbert Blau** of the **Actor's Workshop** in San Francisco, had trouble adjusting to the thrust stage for the first few seasons but produced some fine plays, including **Bertolt Brecht's** *Galileo,* **Heinar Kipphardt's** *In the Matter of J. Robert Oppenheimer,* and a revival of **Tennessee Williams'** *A Streetcar Named Desire.* The theater, however, was losing money, and after eight years, impresario **Joseph Papp** took over. His **New York Shakespeare Festival at Lincoln Center** presented many innovative productions here and at the **Mitzi E. Newhouse,** including **David Rabe's** *Streamers,* Brecht's *Threepenny Opera,* **Miguel Pinero's** *Short Eyes,* and **Anton Chekov's** *The Cherry Orchard* (directed by **André Serban**). After continued deficits and power struggles, however, Papp left in 1977. The Beaumont was dark for three years, until director **Richmond Crinkley** formed a sextet of famous entertainment-world personalities to chart a new course for the theater, including writer/actor/director **Woody Allen,** opera director **Sarah Caldwell,** playwright **Edward Albee,** and directors **Robin Phillips, Ellis Rabb,** and **Liviu Ciulei. André Bishop** is the Beaumont's current, extremely successful, director. ♦ 150 W. 65th St (at Broadway). 239.6277

Mitzi E. Newhouse Theater Directly below the Beaumont, this smaller theater is for experimental and workshop productions, such as **Mike Nichols'** controversial *Waiting for Godot* starring **Steve Martin, Robin Williams,** and **Bill Irwin.** The 334-seat theater itself was designed by **Eero Saarinen & Associates** and opened in 1965. ♦ 150 W. 65th St (at Broadway). 239.6277

Juilliard School Located across a large terrace/bridge over 66th Street, Juilliard was founded in 1905 by **Augustus D. Juilliard** and is one of the nation's most acclaimed performing arts schools. Enrollment is limited to less than a thousand, making acceptance in itself a career achievement for gifted students of music, dance, and drama. The building, a Brutalist contrast to Lincoln Center's classicism, was designed by **Pietro Belluschi** with **Eduardo Catalano** and **Westerman & Miller,** and opened in 1968. ♦ Theaters: Juilliard Theater (seats 933); Drama Theater (seats 206); C. Michael Paul Recital Hall (seats 278). 60 Lincoln Center Plaza, W. 65th St (at Broadway). 799.5000

Alice Tully Recital Hall South of Juilliard, entered from Broadway, Alice Tully is the most intimate and best of the auditoriums at Lincoln Center. Designed for chamber music and recitals by **Pietro Belluschi** in 1969, it is the home of the **Chamber Music Society of Lincoln Center** from October through May. Students of the Juilliard School perform here, too. Films from around the world are shown every late September and October at the **New York Film Festival.** ♦ 1941 Broadway (at W. 66th St). 875.5050. Film Society: 875.5610

New York Public Library/Library and Museum of the Performing Arts The two galleries at this popular branch of the New York Public Library were part of the 1965 creation of **Skidmore, Owings & Merrill.** They exhibit costume and set designs, music scores, and other tools and tricks of the trade, as well as art. The 212-seat **Bruno Walter Auditorium** presents showcase productions and music recitals. In addition to the most extensive collection of books on the performing arts in the city, the library is equipped with state-of-the-art audio equipment and a vast collection of recordings. ♦ M, Th noon-8PM; W, F-Sa noon-6PM. Lincoln Center Plaza, 111 Amsterdam Ave (at W. 65th St). 870.1630

Lincoln Center Guided Tours Take a tour to see the physical plant, hear the legends and history, and peek at whatever else is going on, perhaps a rehearsal of the Philharmonic. Another plus: the expertise and enthusiasm of the tour guides, who are often performers themselves. Tours, which last about one hour, are offered daily; the schedule varies, so call ahead. ♦ Fee. Main Concourse (accessible through the lobby of the Met). 875.5350

Performing Arts Gift Shop Records, music boxes, jewelry, clothing, and toys, all tuned into the performing arts, are sold here. Many items, such as the composer signature mugs and a belt with a music staff brass buckle, are designed for and sold exclusively at Lincoln Center. ♦ M-Sa 10AM-8PM; Su 10AM-6PM. Main Concourse. 580.4356

Lincoln Center Poster Gallery This is the sales outlet for specially commissioned Lincoln Center prints and posters by such artists as **Josef Albers, Marc Chagall, Robert Indiana,** and **Andy Warhol.** ♦ M-Sa 11AM-8PM. Main Concourse. 580.4673

Samuel B. & David Rose Building
Tenants on the first 10 floors of this tower designed by **Davis, Brody & Associates** and completed in 1990 include the Riverside branch of the **New York Public Library,** the **Walter Reade Theater,** the **Film Society of Lincoln Center,** and Lincoln Center, Inc. offices. Floors 12 to 29 are dormitories for students at Juilliard and the School of American Ballet. In order to finance construction of this building, Lincoln Center sold $50 million worth of air rights to the developers of the neighboring condominiums at 3 Lincoln Plaza. ♦ Between W. 65th St and Amsterdam Ave

11 Fiorello's ★$$$ The location across from Lincoln Center is one of the main reasons Fiorello's tables continue to fill. The lighter offerings—pasta, salads—are quite good as a pre- or post-performance meal. ♦ Italian ♦ Lunch and dinner; brunch also on Saturday and Sunday. 1900 Broadway (at W. 63rd St). Reservations required. 595.5330

12 West Side YMCA $ In 1966, the city planned to raze this building, designed by **Dwight James Baum** and built in 1930, to clear the entire block up to Central Park West for a Lincoln Center Mall. Plans fell through when the YMCA refused to sell out. The Y offers single and double rooms to both men and women. In addition to a popular sports/fitness center, it has a family and youth services department. ♦ 5 W. 63rd St (between Central Park West and Broadway). 787.4400

13 Century Apartments Brother of the Majestic (No. 115, designed in 1930), this is the southernmost pair of the sets of twin towers designed by the office of **Irwin S. Chanin** that make the skyline of Central Park West so distinctive. The Century was built in 1931, when **Jacques Delamarre** was the director of Chanin's office. The apartment house occupies the site of the resoundingly unsuccessful (but magnificent) **Century Theater,** a 1909 building by **Carrère & Hastings,** which first failed as a national theater, then as an opera house, and finally as a Ziegfeld vaudeville theater. ♦ 25 Central Park West (between W. 62nd and W. 63rd Sts). 265.1608

Restaurants/Clubs: Red   Hotels: Blue
Shops/🌳 Outdoors: Green   Sights/Culture: Black

14 New York Society for Ethical Culture
It's refreshing to find this example of Art Nouveau in New York. Although the structure lacks the brilliance of the best European examples, you can't help but be grateful that it's not neoclassical. **Robert D. Kohn,** who was also the architect of **Temple Emanu-El,** was the president of the society at the time he designed this building in 1910. ♦ 2 W. 64th St (at Central Park West). 874.5210

O'NEALS'

15 O'Neals' ★★$$$ Fans of the recently closed O'Neals' will be glad to see it has relocated just a block away. The menu is straight-forward and predictably good, from hamburgers to tarragon chicken and Chicago-style ribs. Waiters are visibly calmer around 8PM, when the crowds empty out to catch curtain time across the street at Lincoln Center. ♦ American ♦ Lunch, dinner, and late-night meals. 49 W. 64th St (between Broadway and Central Park West). 787.4663

16 The Saloon $$ Service in the cavernous dining room and street cafe is as erratic as the food on the enormous snack and dinner menu. The waiters may not always be efficient, but the outdoor tables are a great vantage point for people-watching. **The Saloon Grill** next door serves the same food in a slightly calmer atmosphere. ♦ Continental ♦ Lunch and dinner. 1920 Broadway (at W. 64th St). Reservations recommended. 874.1500

16 World Gym If you've taken advantage of one too many New York restaurants, this popular bodybuilding gym offers mini memberships by the day, week, or month. This is serious stuff, obvious from the pumped-up late-night workaholics who take advantage of the 24-hour schedule. ♦ Daily 24 hours. 1926 Broadway (between W. 64th and W. 65th Sts), second floor. 874.0942. Also at: 404 Lafayette St. 260.2534

17 Sfuzzi ★★$$$ Dramatic decor and fun food are served in this lively addition to the Lincoln Center area. The bar is packed before and after the theater with smart, young trendy types sipping frozen *Sfuzzis*—a combination of fresh peach nectar, champagne, and peach schnapps, which comes in small, medium, and ridiculous sizes. You can also sit in the elevated dining area and try one of the inventive pastas, salads, or pizzas. ♦ Italian ♦ Lunch and dinner. 58 W. 65th St (between Central Park West and Broadway). Reservations recommended. 873.3700. Also at: 2 World Financial Center. 385.8080

18 Shun Lee ★$$$ Long a favorite of the Lincoln Center crowd, the kitchen does many regional Chinese cuisines justice. The vast dining room is comfortable and gracious, though not as fancy as the prices. ♦ Chinese ♦ Lunch and dinner. 43 W. 65th St (between Central Park West and Broadway). Reservations required. 595.8895

19 Museum of American Folk Art/Eva and Morris Feld Gallery at Lincoln Square
The best of American folk art from the 18th century to the present, including paintings, sculpture, textiles, furniture, and decorative arts, is displayed here. The museum holds regular lectures and workshops and has an adjacent gift shop that's worth a visit. ♦ Voluntary contribution. Tu-Su 11AM-7:30PM. 2 Lincoln Sq (Columbus Ave between W. 65th and W. 66th Sts). 496.2966

20 First Battery Armory, New York National Guard Today, **ABC TV** studios hide behind this fortress facade, designed in 1901 by **Horgan & Slattery** and altered in 1978 by **Kohn Pederson Fox.** ♦ 56 W. 66th St (between Central Park West and Broadway)

21 Hotel des Artistes An early studio building designed by **George Mort Pollard** in 1913 specifically for artists—duplexes with double-height main spaces—this overscaled Elizabethan building is now one of the more lavish co-ops around. It has always attracted noteworthy tenants, among them **Isadora Duncan, Alexander Woollcott, Norman Rockwell, Noel Coward,** and **Howard Chandler Christy.** ♦ 1 W. 67th St (between Central Park West and Columbus Ave). 362.6700

Within the Hotel des Artistes:

Café des Artistes ★★★★$$$$ The West Side's most charming and romantic restaurant is entered through the hotel's lobby. Light streams through the leaded-glass windows by day, and the original 1934 murals of ethereal female nudes by **Howard Chandler Christy** are an inspiration. Owner **George Lang** updates the menu and wine list daily as well as seasonally (his renowned asparagus festival occurs every May and June). Don't leave without sampling sweets beyond your wildest dreams on the **Great Dessert Plate.** The famous weekend brunch is a must. ♦ French ♦ Lunch and dinner; brunch also on Saturday and Sunday. Jacket and tie required after 5PM. Reservations required. 877.3500

America's first patent was issued in New York City on 31 July 1790. It was granted to a Samuel Hopkins for a process that involved the making and purifying of potash, an ingredient used in soap. The patent was signed by President George Washington, Secretary of State Thomas Jefferson, and Attorney General Edmund Randolf.

22 Vince & Eddie's ★★$$$ Locals pack this comfy spot that specializes in homestyle fare such as lamb shank with cherries, and bass in a flavorful veal stock. Don't pass up side dishes like Swiss chard, mashed potatoes, and turnips. ◆ American ◆ Lunch and dinner; brunch on Sunday. 70 W. 68th St (between Columbus Ave and Central Park West). Reservations recommended. 721.0068

22 67 Wine & Spirits Service could sometimes be more personal, but it's hard to find a wider selection of fine wines and spirits at decent prices. ◆ M-Th 9AM-9PM; F-Sa 9AM-10PM. 179 Columbus Ave (at W. 68th St). 724.6767

23 American Broadcasting Company Facilities (ABC) Fortunately, these two buildings don't intrude on this quiet, low-scale street: 30 W. 67th Street, the technical center, is set back respectfully, and the limestone, tan brick, and glass are in harmony with the surroundings. In 1979, architects **Kohn Pederson Fox** used a lot of glass to create an inviting lobby for the local television studios at 7 Lincoln Square. Try to see the atrium at night with its flying staircase on the top three floors. ◆ 30 W. 67th St and 7 Lincoln Sq (between Central Park West and Broadway)

24 Tower Records Along with nearby **Tower Video,** these sister stores to the larger downtown branch are the West Side's most complete resource for audio and video home entertainment. ◆ Daily 9AM-midnight. 1961 Broadway (at W. 66th St). 799.2500. Tower Video: daily 9AM-midnight. 1977 Broadway (at W. 67th St). 496.2500

25 Café Bel Canto ★$ This restaurant in a plant-filled three-story atrium is serviced by a personable staff. The pasta specials and sandwiches are good, but if you just want to hang out, you don't have to order a thing. ◆ Italian ◆ Breakfast, lunch, and dinner. 1991 Broadway (between W. 67th and W. 68th Sts). 362.4642

Above Café Bel Canto:

Andiamo! ★★$$$ This dramatic room with a soaring skylight is adorned with the owner's collection of modern art. But don't let the flash put you off—the kitchen is refreshingly on target, with inventive risotto specials and a knack for perfectly grilled meats. No smoking. ◆ Italian ◆ Dinner. Closed Sunday. Reservations recommended. 362.3315

26 Merkin Concert Hall Concert series are held here, including ensemble programs and contemporary and chamber music. The 457-seat hall is located in the **Abraham Goodman House.** ◆ 129 W. 67th St (between Broadway and Amsterdam Ave). 362.8719

27 The Good Earth You can get everything from all-natural allergy pills to free-range chicken in this health-food supermarket. ◆ M-F 9:30AM-9:30PM; Sa 9:30AM-6:30PM; Su noon-6PM. 167 Amsterdam Ave (at W. 68th St). 496.1616

28 Sweetwater's One of the few remaining cabaret rooms in town, Sweetwater's occasionally forays into R&B and jazz. It's known for consistently solid bookings, some big-name singers and groups, and an audience that knows talent. ◆ Cover. Call for performance schedule. Closed Monday and Tuesday. 170 Amsterdam Ave (at W. 68th St). Reservations recommended. 873.4100

29 Lincoln Square Synagogue Designed in 1970 by **Hausman & Rosenberg,** this is a mannered, curved building with fins and rectangular block attached, all clad in travertine, à la neighboring Lincoln Center. It's one of Manhattan's most popular Orthodox synagogues. ◆ 200 Amsterdam Ave (at W. 69th St). 874.6100

30 Cafe Luxembourg ★★$$$ A people-watcher's Art Deco brasserie, Cafe Luxembourg is affiliated with TriBeCa's trendy **Odeon.** The zinc-topped bar draws a stylish, international crowd, and the menu is a mélange of French, Italian, and regional American offerings. Order the duck cassoulet or any salad. ◆ French ◆ Lunch, dinner, and late-night meals; brunch on Sunday. 200 W. 70th St (between Amsterdam and West End Aves). Reservations recommended. 873.7411

31 Christ and St. Stephen's Church This charming country church, built in 1880 to the designs of **William H. Day** and altered in 1897 by **J.D. Fouguet,** is holding up well in the big city. ◆ 120 W. 69th St (between Columbus Ave and Broadway). 787.2755

La Boîte en Bois

32 La Boîte en Bois ★★$$$ Located a few steps downstairs and far from the madding crowd on Columbus Avenue, this charming French bistro has a country atmosphere and a Provençale-accented menu. ◆ French ◆ Dinner. 75 W. 68th St (between Central Park West and Columbus Ave). Reservations recommended. No credit cards. 874.2705

33 19 West 68th Street In 1953, at the age of 22, **James Dean** moved into his first New York apartment on the top floor of this building. A year later he moved to California to begin his first movie, *East of Eden.* ◆ Between Central Park West and Columbus Ave

34 Santa Fe ★$$$ The refurbished old town house dining room is painted in flattering soft desert tones and fitted with fine detailing and Southwestern arts and crafts, making it a pleasure to sit in. The mostly Mexican food—with some original American dishes—is good. ♦ Mexican ♦ Lunch and dinner; dinner only on Saturday and Sunday. 72 W. 69th St (between Central Park West and Columbus Ave). Reservations recommended. 724.0822

35 Rikyu ★$$ Predating the trendy invasion of Columbus Avenue, this restaurant is still popular with the locals and the Lincoln Center crowd for good sushi and traditional dishes. Competition from the neighboring sushi bars keeps the prices reasonable. ♦ Japanese ♦ Lunch and dinner. 210 Columbus Ave (between W. 69th and W. 70th Sts). Reservations recommended. 799.7847

35 Soutine A tiny bake shop with the feel of a French *boulangerie,* this is one of the neighborhood's favorites. ♦ M-F 8AM-7PM; Sa 9AM-7PM; Su 9AM-3PM. 106 W. 70th St (at Columbus Ave). 496.1450

36 Ying ★$$ Though this restaurant has pretty flowers and food, unusual salads, and tasty chicken dishes, it's not quite up to Chinatown standards. ♦ Chinese ♦ Lunch and dinner. 117 W. 70th St (between Columbus Ave and Broadway). 724.2031

37 Dapy Objets de pop art or designer bric-a-brac? Your call. ♦ Daily 11AM-9PM. 232 Columbus Ave (between W. 70th and W. 71st Sts). 877.4710. Also at: 431 W. Broadway. 925.5082

37 Havana ★$$$ The former Victor's continues to offer Cuban cuisine at its best if you're fond of simple fare like black beans and rice. Sit in the enclosed terrace for a front-row seat on Columbus Avenue while sampling plantain and chicken stews. After the theater, try the *Cubano* (Cuban sandwiches): saffron bread filled with ham, roast pork, pickles, and a touch of mayonnaise. The coffee is almost as rich as the espresso served in Little Havana in Miami. ♦ Cuban ♦ Dinner; lunch and late-night meals also on Saturday and Sunday. 240 Columbus Ave (at W. 71st St). 595.8599

38 The Dorilton When this Beaux Arts masterpiece, designed by **Janes & Leo,** was completed in 1902, critic **Montgomery Schuyler** was so displeased with its design that he wrote the following in *Architectural Record:* "The incendiary qualities of the edifice may be referred, first to violence of color, then to violence of scale, then to violence of 'thingness,' to the multiplicity and importunity of the details." When the Landmarks Preservation Commission granted it landmark status in 1974, they described it as "exceptionally handsome." ♦ 171 W. 71st St (at Broadway)

39 Applause Theater Books For thespians, this is a good place to find an obscure play or movie scenario. Books on other performing arts are also sold. ♦ M-Sa 10AM-8PM; Su noon-6PM. 211 W. 71st St (between Broadway and West End Ave). 496.7511

40 Sherman Square Another one of those places where Broadway crosses the city grid to form a bow tie, not a square, Sherman Square is occupied by an **IRT Subway Control House,** which was designed by **Heins & LaFarge** in 1904. This is one of two surviving ornate entrances to the original IRT subway line (the other is at the **Battery Park Control House** in Lower Manhattan). Note the stylish detailing of the neo-Dutch, somewhat baroque shed. Directly to the north, the other half of the tie is **Verdi Square,** where a patch of trees surrounds a statue of composer **Giuseppe Verdi** with characters from four of his operas; this 1906 work by **Pasquale Civiletti** was a gift from the local Italian community. ♦ W. 72nd St (at Broadway and Amsterdam Ave)

40 Gray's Papaya $ An international cast of characters frequents this round-the-clock takeout that boasts hot dogs that are "tastier than filet mignon" and a papaya drink that is "a definite aid to digestion." ♦ Hot dogs ♦ Daily 24 hours. 2090 Broadway (at W. 72nd St). 799.0243

41 Acker-Merrall-Condit Experts on Burgundy, these established liquor merchants boast a reputation for good service. The store design is nice, too. ♦ M-Sa 9AM-10PM. 160 W. 72nd St (between Columbus Ave and Broadway). 787.1700

41 Fine & Schapiro ★$$ This long-established classic kosher delicatessen makes one nostalgic for the days before cholesterol counts. (As a concession, there's a salt-free corner on the menu.) Their hot dogs may cost more than the street-corner version, but they're theologically correct. ♦ Jewish deli ♦ Lunch and dinner; deli hours 9AM-10PM. 138 W. 72nd St (between Columbus Ave and Broadway). 877.2874

42 Blades West Rent a pair of rollerblades and protective gear, then set off for a day of blading in the park. The blades, as well as ice skates, skateboards, snowboards, helmets, and accessories, are also for sale. ♦ M-Sa 10AM-8PM; Su 10AM-6PM. 120 W. 72nd St (at Columbus Ave). 787.3911

42 Betsey Johnson The West Side branch of this trendy boutique is full of the designer's whimsical and colorful outfits and accoutrements. ♦ M-W, F-Su 11AM-7PM; Th 11AM-8PM. 248 Columbus Ave (at W. 72nd St). 362.3364. Also at: 130 Thompson St. 420.0169; 251 E. 60th St. 319.7699

42 To Boot New York This West Side landmark specializes in cowboy boots but also stocks the best in men's and women's footwear—casual, business, and formal. Handwoven ties and scarves are also available. ◆ M-Sa noon-8PM; Su 1-6PM. 256 Columbus Ave (at W. 72nd St). 724.8249

43 Charivari 72 An intriguing mix of expensive fashion-forward and evening clothes for men and women, ranging from leather coats and hand-knit sweaters to evening dresses, is sold. ◆ M-W, F 11AM-8PM; Th 11AM-9PM. 257 Columbus Ave (at W. 72nd St). 787.7272

44 Harry's Burrito Junction ★$ If you've splurged on Lincoln Center tickets or you're just in the market for some great budget-friendly nachos, Harry's is the West Side answer. A young crowd fills the three-level space for the '60s *chotchkas* and the foot-long bay burrito oozing with black beans and shredded beef. ◆ Mexican ◆ Lunch, dinner, and late-night meals; brunch also on Saturday and Sunday. 241 Columbus Ave (at W. 71st St). 580.9494

45 Fishin Eddie ★★$$$ Courtesy of the folks behind **Vince & Eddie's**, this restaurant specializing in seafood is ideal for a pre- or post-Lincoln Center meal, especially if you don't want to breathe cigarette smoke (smoking is not allowed). ◆ Seafood ◆ Dinner. 73 W. 71st St (between Central Park West and Columbus Ave). Reservations recommended. 874.3474

45 Café La Fortuna ★$ A mainstay of the neighborhood for years—and one of the late **John Lennon's** hangouts—this pleasant, unassuming cafe serves excellent Italian coffees and a mouth-watering array of traditional Italian pastries and other sweets. The garden in the rear is an ideal respite from summer's heat, especially when sipping the favorite seasonal drink: unparalleled iced cappuccino laced with homemade chocolate or coffee ice. ◆ Cafe ◆ Lunch, dinner, and late-night meals. 69 W. 71st St (between Central Park West and Columbus Ave). No credit cards. 724.5846

46 Sidewalkers ★$$$ You don't have to go all the way to the Chesapeake Bay to find a crab shack, just to the rear of this old residential hotel lobby. ◆ Seafood ◆ Dinner. 12 W. 72nd St (between Central Park West and Columbus Ave). 799.6070

47 Dakota Apartments Built in 1884, the Dakota was one of the first luxury apartment houses in the city (along with the **Osborne** on W. 57th Street and **34 Gramercy Park East**). The building (pictured above) was christened when someone remarked to its owner, **Edward Clark,** president of the Singer Sewing Company, that it was so far out of town, "it might as well be in Dakota Territory." Clark, not without a sense of humor, went on to instruct the architect, **Henry J. Hardenbergh,** to embellish the building with symbols of the Wild West; arrowheads, sheaves of wheat, and ears of corn appear in bas-relief on the building's interior and exterior facades. Hardenbergh later designed the **Plaza Hotel,** and the same skill is evident here, though the style is very different. The Dakota is a highly original masonry mass with echoes of the Romanesque and German Renaissance. Recent cleaning has revealed the rich creamy brown stone of the facade. Victorian details and miscellaneous pieces sprout at every turn—turrets, gables, oriels, dormers, pinnacles—but all are under control. The top three floors, once servants' quarters and a playroom and gymnasium for children, are now some of the most prized apartments in Manhattan. The building has gained notoriety not only as the setting for the film *Rosemary's Baby* but as the home of **Boris Karloff, Judy Garland, Lauren Bacall, Leonard Bernstein, Rex Reed, Roberta Flack, Yoko Ono** and **John Lennon, Kim Basinger,** and **Chris Whittle.** ◆ 1 W. 72nd St (at Central Park West)

48 Dallas Barbecue ★★$ The barbecued ribs and chicken are well-seasoned, tender, juicy, and handily inexpensive. But for many the most wonderful thing at this large, informal, and noisy restaurant—well-populated with locals—is the *huge* loaf of greasy onion rings ◆ Barbecue ◆ Lunch and dinner; late-night meals also on Friday and Saturday. 27 W. 72nd St (between Central Park West and Columbus Ave). 873.2004

49 Eclair $$ Open since 1939, this venerable cafe is the last remnant of the time when W. 72nd Street was home to a wave of Middle European immigrants and was known as **Little Vienna.** The restaurant is not what it used to be, but a traditional mid-afternoon *kaffee und kuchen* is wonderful (try the *Schwarzwalder* kirsch torte or Linzer torte). ♦ Cafe ♦ Breakfast, lunch, and dinner. 141 W. 72nd St (between Columbus Ave and Broadway). 873.7700

50 Star Magic If you're in the market for crystals, New Age-inspired accessories, and trinkets for the astral traveler, stop by this shop. ♦ M-Sa 10AM-10PM; Su 11AM-9PM. 275 Amsterdam Ave (at W. 73rd St). 769.2020. Also at: 745 Broadway. 228.7770

51 Vinnie's Pizza ★$ This favorite pizzeria deserves its first-rate reputation—the thin-crust pizza is loaded with cheese and super-fresh toppings. The parlor itself wouldn't win any prizes, so be sure to get your pie to go. ♦ Pizza ♦ Lunch and dinner. 285 Amsterdam Ave (between W. 73rd and W. 74th Sts). 874.4382

52 Apple Bank A Florentine palace seems like an appropriate model for a bank. This one, designed in 1928 by the masters **York & Sawyer** (who also designed the **Federal Reserve Bank of New York**), skillfully contains a proper rectangular banking hall within the trapezoidal building necessary on the site. The additional triangular wedge inside is filled by alcoves and mezzanines behind the arches. ♦ 2100 Broadway (between W. 73rd and W. 74th Sts). 573.6551

53 Ansonia Hotel Designed by **Graves & Duboy** and built in 1904, this lyric masterpiece, bristling with ornament, balconies, towers, and dormers, is the grande dame of the Belle Epoque apartment buildings in New York. (As with the **Hotel des Artistes,** this was never a hotel at all; the appellation is from the French *hôtel de ville.*) The thick walls and floors required for fireproofing have made the 16-story cooperative apartment building a favorite of musicians. Among those who have lived here are **Enrico Caruso, Arturo Toscanini, Lily Pons, Igor Stravinsky,** and **Ezio Pinza.** Other famous tenants have included **Florenz Ziegfeld, Sol Hurok, Theodore Dreiser,** and **George Herman (Babe) Ruth.** ♦ 2109 Broadway (between W. 73rd and W. 74th Sts). 724.2600

54 Coastal ★★$$$ Fresh ingredients and a certain degree of inventiveness in the kitchen keep Coastal a cut above its similarly noisy and crowded neighbors. Try the appetizers (especially the grilled vegetables), fish with interesting sauces, and homemade ice creams. ♦ American ♦ Dinner. 300 Amsterdam Ave (at W. 74th St). Reservations recommended. 769.3988

55 Freddy and Pepe's Gourmet Pizza ★$ A good tomato base under myriad toppings makes for a filling meal at this popular no-frills pizza place. Try the unusual seafood smorgasbord pie. ♦ Pizza ♦ Lunch and dinner. 303 Amsterdam Ave (between W. 74th and W. 75th Sts). No credit cards. 799.2378

56 China Club A fun dance bar with a young, energetic crowd, China Club features sounds from Motown to Prince. There's live music every night except Monday. ♦ Cover. Daily 10PM-3AM or 4AM. 2130 Broadway (at W. 75th St). 877.1166

56 Beacon Theatre Special films, dance groups, and foreign performing arts groups, as well as mainstream soul and rock artists, are featured in this 2,700-seat theater. Some say the magnificent interior by **Walter Ahlschlager** is second only to **Radio City's.** ♦ 2124 Broadway (at W. 75th St). 496.7070

57 Fairway Residents swear by this all-purpose market, which has the best produce, freshest cheese, and zaniest service. Best times to shop: early morning or after 8PM. ♦ Daily 7AM-midnight. 2127 Broadway (between W. 74th and W. 75th Sts). 595.1888

57 Citarella Fish This retail fish store and raw seafood bar is ideal for a quick stand-up snack before a show at the **Beacon Theatre.** The elaborate fish-sculpture displays add a new dimension to window dressing. A new location specializing in meats has recently opened next door. ♦ M-Sa 8AM-9PM; Su 9AM-7PM. 2135 Broadway (at W. 75th St). 874.0383

58 254 West 75th Street Distinguished by three arches and excellent brick, stone, and ironwork, this 1885 house stands out among the many fine homes in the area. ♦ Between Broadway and West End Ave

59 Ernie's $$$ Table-hopping is the key word here, although you'll have to shout to get any networking done. The angel-hair pasta and grilled baby chicken are good enough to eat; the rest of the menu is just an excuse to congregate beneath the high ceilings of this spacious, postmodern watering hole. ♦ Italian ♦ Lunch and dinner; brunch also on Saturday and Sunday; late-night meals also on Friday and Saturday. 2150 Broadway (at W. 75th St). Reservations recommended. 496.1588

60 Bennie's $ Pick up an inexpensive lunch to bring to nearby Central Park. There's also a small sit-down area. ◆ Lebanese/Takeout ◆ Lunch and dinner. 321½ Amsterdam Ave (between W. 75th and W. 76th Sts). No credit cards. 874.3032

61 Mughali $$ For Indian food that's not too spicy or far out, this is the place. The *tandoori* is best, and there's always a good mango chutney served with the curry, which is on the mild side. Desserts are plain, except for the highly recommended rice pudding with rosewater. ◆ Indian ◆ Dinner. 320 Columbus Ave (at W. 75th St). Reservations recommended. 724.6363

62 Memphis ★★$$$ Very good Southern and Cajun-style cuisine is the draw. The nondescript, slate-gray entrance is easy to overlook; not so the eats. ◆ American ◆ Dinner. 329 Columbus Ave (between W. 75th and W. 76th Sts). Reservations recommended. 496.1840

63 Pappardella $$ This is a popular destination for pasta and *secondi* with a Tuscan accent. Try a thin-crusted pizza with a glass of Chianti, and relish the escape from the bustle of Columbus Avenue. ◆ Italian ◆ Lunch and dinner. 316 Columbus Ave (at W. 75th St). Reservations recommended. 595.7996

64 Red River Grill ★$$$ Yet another entry in the ever-popular Southwestern trend sweeping the city. Best bets are eggplant cobbler with goat cheese drop biscuit and fennel-crusted rib eye steak. ◆ Southwestern ◆ Lunch and dinner. 302 Columbus Ave (at W. 74th St). Reservations required. 721.6000

65 San Remo In contrast to the streamlined **Century** and **Majestic** apartments by **Irwin Chanin**, **Emory Roth's** twin towers, constructed in 1930, are capped with Roman temples surmounted by finials. ◆ 145-146 Central Park West (between W. 74th and W. 75th Sts)

66 Central Park West/76th Street Historic District This district, designated a historic area in 1973, comprises the blocks on Central Park West between W. 75th and W. 77th streets and about half of W. 76th Street. It includes a variety of row houses built at the turn of the century; the neo-Grecian Nos. 21-31 by **George M. Walgrove** are the earliest, and the baroque Nos. 8-10 by **John H. Duncan** are the most recent. Of interest as well are the **Kenilworth** apartment building (151 Central Park West), designed in 1908 by **Townsend, Steinle & Haskell,** noteworthy for its convex mansard roof and highly ornamented limestone, and the Oxfordish **Universalist Church of New York** (W. 76th Street at Central Park West), designed in 1898 by **William A. Potter.** Also included in the designated area is 44 W. 77th Street, designed in 1909 by **Harde & Short,** a Gothic-style building used as artists' studios; much of the ornament was removed in 1944. ◆ Central Park West (between W. 75th and W. 77th Sts)

67 New-York Historical Society The society is housed in a fine neoclassical French building, the central portion of which was designed by **York & Sawyer** in 1908, with unimaginative 1938 additions by **Walker & Gillette.** Inside, the collection is rich with such Americana as wall-to-wall silver, rare maps, antique toys, splendid carriages, portraits by **Gilbert Stuart** and **Benjamin West,** watercolors by **John James Audubon,** and landscapes by again-popular **Frederic Church** and the rest of the **Hudson River** boys. The society also has stunning 17th-, 18th-, and 19th-century furniture arranged in chronological order. Changing shows touch on cast-iron stoves, American bands, or early women's magazines. The society's library is one of the major reference libraries of American history in this country. If you're wondering about the hyphen in New-York Historical Society, it's a point of pride for the museum: when it was founded in 1804, everybody spelled New York that way. In 1993, the **Jewish Museum,** temporarily housed here, returned to its newly renovated building on Fifth Avenue at 92nd Street. The New-York Historical Society is now closed for renovation and is scheduled to reopen in Fall 1994. ◆ Admission. New hours are expected to be M-F 10AM-5PM; for weekend hours, call ahead. 170 Central Park West (between W. 76th and W. 77th Sts). 873.3400

68 Scaletta ★★$$$ A large dinner menu, fast and efficient service, and excellent pasta and antipasto (especially the prosciutto) are highlights of this lovely Northern Italian restaurant. Try the specials of the day, often Italian dishes usually found only in Italian homes. Desserts are of the rich Italian variey, and the espresso is good. ◆ Italian ◆ Dinner. 50 W. 77th St (between Central Park West and Columbus Ave). 769.9191

69 Museum Cafe ★$$ Just across the street from the **American Museum of Natural History,** this is a perfect stop for a quick lunch or dinner. The interior is a dull, restful pink with wood trimmings; try to eat in the enclosed sidewalk cafe. The restaurant stays open all night on Thanksgiving Eve, when the **Macy's Day Parade** floats are inflated out front. Stick to the Grecian chicken salad or the gargantuan bowls of pasta. ◆ American

♦ Lunch and dinner; brunch also on Saturday and Sunday. 366 Columbus Ave (at W. 77th St). 799.0150

70 Isabella $$ This typical West Side Italian restaurant is well-liked for its simple, pleasant decor and inviting sidewalk cafe. The menu sports good pasta and grilled dishes, such as veal chops and chicken. Salads are ordinary and desserts erratic, but the espresso is good. It's always jammed with a young crowd in the spring and summer. ♦ Italian ♦ Lunch and dinner; brunch also on Saturday and Sunday. 359 Columbus Ave (at W. 77th St). 724.2100

70 Kenneth Cole Shoes by the self-promoting designer are sold in this shop. Copies of his print ads, which address the political and social issues of the moment—one suggests that customers buy one less pair of shoes and, instead, donate the money to AIDS research—are displayed along the right-hand wall as you enter. ♦ M-Sa 11AM-8PM; Su noon-7PM. 353 Columbus Ave (between W. 76th and W. 77th Sts). 873.2061. Also at: 95 Fifth Ave. 675.2550

70 Putumayo Fashions from developing countries around the world—Thailand, Peru, Guatemala—are here in vivid, eye-appealing colors. Create complete outfits of chiffonlike skirts and crisp linen blouses and shirts, or use one piece, such as the classic llama sweaters, to match any wardrobe. ♦ M-Sa 11AM-7PM; Su noon-6PM. 341 Columbus Ave (between W. 76th and W. 77th Sts). 595.3441. Also at: 857 Lexington Ave. 734.3111; 147 Spring St. 966.4458

GreenFlea

71 GreenFlea/IS 44 Market If you can't make the trek down to the larger weekend flea market at W. 26th Street and Sixth Avenue, you'll fare well here, though the pickings aren't as extensive. Weather dictates the turnout of vendors and crowd at this outdoor market, but on rainy days an indoor section offers refuge. The emphasis is on new, used, and vintage clothing and accessories, with a nice mix of antiques, collectibles, and furniture. It's not unusual to see New York's upscale personalities rummaging alongside more common folk in search of that one-of-a-kind find. ♦ Free. Su 10AM-6PM. Columbus Ave and W. 76th St. 316.1088

72 Equinox Fitness Club Ideal for visitors, this cutting-edge mega-gym opens its doors for one-time-use admission. A huge success since its 1991 debut, the Equinox is as famous for its social scene as for its unsurpassed fitness programs. A killer 10-week program is available for those who plan to stay on in New York. ♦ M-Th 6AM-11PM; F 6AM-10PM; Sa-Su 8AM-9PM. 344 Amsterdam Ave (between W. 76th and W. 77th Sts). 721.4200

73 Promenade Theatre New plays and revivals of lesser-known plays by established playwrights are featured at this intimate 399-seat theater, often with big-name stars returning to the boards to hone their craft. ♦ 2162 Broadway (between W. 76th and W. 77th Sts). 580.1313

74 Pizza Joint ★$ Terrific pies are served with all the fixins. ♦ Pizza ♦ Daily 24 hours. 2165 Broadway (at W. 77th St). No credit cards. 724.2010

75 Milburn Hotel $ Handsome prewar apartment buildings are common in this residential area, and the Milburn was one of them until a recent multimillion-dollar refurbishing converted it to a gracious 70-suite hotel. All the traditionally furnished rooms have fully equipped kitchens with microwaves, making this a good choice for families and long-term visitors. ♦ 242 W. 76th St (between Broadway and West End Ave). 363.1006, 800/833.9622; fax 721.5476

76 343-357 West End Avenue Built in 1891 and designed by **Lamb & Rich,** this complete block-front on West End and around both corners is a lively, well-ordered collection typical of Victorian town houses, and the only West Side block without high-rises between West End Avenue and Riverside Drive. (Rumor has it that **Mayor Jimmy Walker's** mistress lived at W. 76th Street and Broadway and the block was supposedly zoned to protect his river view.) The variety of shapes and materials—gables, bays, dormers, and limestone, red, and tan brick—is clearly under control, resulting in a stylish, humorous energy with no dissonance. ♦ Between W. 76th and W. 77th Sts

77 West End Collegiate Church and School The school, established by the Dutch in 1637, is housed in a copy of the market building in Haarlem, Holland. Designed in 1893 by **Robert W. Gibson,** this is a particularly good example of Dutch detailing; note the stepped gables and the use of long bricks. ♦ 245 W. 77th St (at West End Ave). 787.1566

78 La Caridad $ Expect a wait at this popular and inexpensive Cuban/Chinese beanery. ♦ Cuban/Chinese ♦ Lunch and dinner. 2199 Broadway (at W. 78th St). No credit cards. 874.2780

Restaurants/Clubs: Red   **Hotels:** Blue

Shops/ 🌳 Outdoors: Green   **Sights/Culture:** Black

79 Apthorp Apartments Designed by **Clinton & Russell** and built in 1908, this is the best of the three big West Side courtyard buildings (the **Belnord** on 86th Street and **Astor Court** on Broadway between W. 89th and W. 90th streets are the others). The ornate ironwork here is especially wonderful. It was built by **William Waldorf Astor,** who owned much of the land in the area, and was named for the man who had owned the site in 1763. ♦ 2101-2119 Broadway (between W. 78th and W. 79th Sts)

80 Stand-Up NY Up-and-coming and established merchants of the one-liner play this comedy club. ♦ Cover, minimum. Shows: M-Th, Su 9PM; F 9PM, 11:30PM; Sa 8PM, 10PM, midnight. 236 W. 78th St (between Amsterdam Ave and Broadway). Reservations required. 595.0850

81 Aris Mixon & Co. A wonderful mix of antique and vintage stemware, jewelry, turn-of-the-century prints, collectible salt and pepper shakers, ceramics, and handmade toys fills this store. At Christmas, it becomes a wonderland of ornaments and small gifts. ♦ M-F noon-7PM; Sa 11AM-6PM; Su 1-5:30PM. 381 Amsterdam Ave (between W. 78th and W. 79th Sts). 724.6904

82 21-131 West 78th Street Built in 1886 by **Raphael Gustavino,** an Italian mason famous for his vaults (see the **Oyster Bar** at **Grand Central Terminal**), these six red and white houses are unified by their symmetrical arrangement and cheery details. ♦ Between Columbus and Amsterdam Aves

83 Alice Underground Climb down into this large basement store for an eclectic mix of inexpensive, wearable separates and outerwear for men and women, much of it unisex fashion, from the 1950s to the 1970s. In addition to the typical Hawaiian and tuxedo shirts, you'll find tablecloths, flowered curtains, chenille bedspreads, and costume jewelry. ♦ M-F, Su 11AM-7:30PM; Sa 11AM-8PM. 380 Columbus Ave (between W. 78th and W. 79th Sts). 724.6682. Also at: 481 Broadway (at Broome St). 431.9067

83 Only Hearts Silky lingerie, sweet-smelling sachets, jewelry, books about hearts and kissing, and heart-shaped waffle irons and fly swatters are sold in this pretty shop for the shameless romantic. ♦ M-Sa 11AM-8PM; Su noon-7PM. 386 Columbus Ave (between W. 78th and W. 79th Sts). 724.5608

84 Bag One Arts Named after the interviews that **John Lennon** and **Yoko Ono** gave from the inside of a black bag, this gallery sells limited-edition graphics by the ex-Beatle. ♦ By appointment only. 110 W. 79th St (between Columbus and Amsterdam Aves). 595.5537

85 Laura Ashley Floral patterns, frilly trim, and classic understatement are the Laura Ashley trademark. Home furnishings and fashions are also available. It's as if **Louisa May Alcott** had gone into retailing a century later. ♦ M-W, F-Sa 11AM-7PM; Th 11AM-8PM; Su noon-6PM. 398 Columbus Ave (at W. 79th St). 496.5110

86 American Museum of Natural History This preeminent scientific research institution is one of the top cultural draws in New York City. Its collections—more than 34 million artifacts and specimens—constitute a priceless record of life, illuminating millions of years of evolution from the birth of the planet through the present day. In 1994-95, the museum (shown above) will observe its 125th anniversary with special events and exhibitions reflecting the concerns of its scientific staff: biodiversity, global climate change, and loss of species.

Built in 1872 in the middle of a landscape of goats and squatters, the original building (designed by **Jacob Wrey Mould** and **Calvert Vaux**) can now be glimpsed only from Columbus Avenue. The body of the museum (built in 1899 by **J.C. Cady & Co.** and **Cady, Berg & See** with later additions by **Charles Vos** and **Trowbridge & Livingston**), an example of Romanesque Revival at its grandest, can best be admired from 77th Street. The building itself is nothing if not a piecemeal reflection of changing tastes in style. In between the turreted extensions, a massive carriage entrance passes under a sweeping flight of stairs: the heavy red-brown brick and granite add to the medieval aura and positive strength typified by the seven-arch colonnade. That welcoming entrance is now ignored, and the main facade of the museum has been shifted to the newly renovated **Theodore Roosevelt Memorial** facing Central Park West—a rather pompous Beaux Arts triumphal arch and terrace designed by **John Russell Pope** in 1936. On top of the four giant Ionic columns are statues of explorers **Boone, Audubon,** and **Lewis and Clark** (these and the attic frieze are by **James Earle Fraser;** the animal relief is by **James L. Clark**). Behind this facade is an equally intimidating **Memorial Hall.**

The museum is widely recognized as having the greatest collection of fossil vertebrates in the world. However, the dinosaur and fossil halls are currently closed while the museum undergoes a $45 million remodeling that will restructure the entire fourth floor, adding six exhibition halls to tell the story of the evolution of vertebrates (throughout the renovation period, dinosaurs will be on view somewhere in the museum; *Barosaurus,* the world's tallest freestanding dinosaur exhibit, stands majestically in the Theodore Roosevelt Hall). The museum is returning the halls to their original splendor—expanding exhibition spaces, revealing architectural details that include grand arches and columns, and providing panoramic views of Central Park.

The **Wallace Wing,** housing two new fossil halls, displays an extraordinary assemblage of fossil mammals, including saber-toothed cats, woolly mammoths, and giant sloths, as well as some of our earliest relatives, bizarre reptilelike creatures with three-foot sails on their backs. An interactive computer system allows visitors to explore different locations and time periods and the animals that inhabited them. The four exhibitions under construction include two dinosaur halls (slated for opening in spring of 1995) that will showcase Tyrannosaurus rex and Apatosaurus, dramatically remounted to reflect new scientific thinking, along with Triceratops, a duck-billed dinosaur mummy, and dozens more. The final two halls, plus an orientation center and a hall of primitive vertebrates will open in spring of 1996. The **Hall of Human Biology and Evolution,** the newest permanent exhibit, examines the heritage we share with other living things and traces the patterns of human evolution using the latest multimedia technology and exhibit techniques. The *New York Times* predicted the hall will be "the most popular museum exhibition New York City has seen."

The museum has an ongoing program of lectures, films, plays, workshops, and concerts. Free **Museum Highlights Tours** assemble at the second-floor information desk every hour. Two gift shops, one just for children, offer Mexican and Indian crafts, microscopes, puppets, books, petrified wood, and other surprises. There are three restaurants: the **Whale's Lair** (cocktails and snacks), the **Garden Cafe** (lunch and dinner in a greenhouse setting), and **Dinersaurus** (cafeteria). Limited paid parking is available in the museum lot, on W. 81st Street.
♦ Suggested admission. M-Th, Su 10AM-5:45PM; F-Sa 10AM-8:45PM. Central Park West at 79th St. 769.5000

At the American Museum of Natural History:

Nature Max Theater Super-spectacular films are shown daily on a four-story-high screen that puts you right into the action. Call for schedule. ♦ Admission. 769.5000

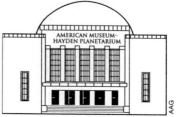

Hayden Planetarium The copper dome on the brick box outside is an obvious reflection of the spaces inside, which house astronomy exhibitions such as the **Hall of the Sun,** the **Laserium** and **Astronomia.** The **Sky Theater** auditorium is 75 feet in diameter and 48 feet to the top of the dome, and hosts the famous **Sky Shows** that keep you in touch with what the heavens are up to. Imbedded into the concrete in front of the planetarium is **Michele Oka Doner's** *Celestial Plaza,* a sculpture comprised of 300 cast bronze pieces that represent astronomical bodies. Shows last one hour. Admission charge covers museum admission. Call for schedule.
♦ Admission. Central Park West (at W. 81st St). 769.5920

87 The Beresford On a street of twin-towered landmarks, this deluxe 1939 apartment building designed by **Emery Roth** distinguishes itself by having three rather squat baroque turrets that give it a double silhouette from two directions. Famous residents have included poet **Sara Teasdale,** underworld crime leader **Meyer Lansky, Margaret Mead,** and **Rock Hudson.** Tennis great **John McEnroe** and newscaster **Peter Jennings** are among the current residents.
♦ 211 Central Park West (at W. 81st St). 787.2100

88 Excelsior $ In a classy block across the street from the grounds of the **American Museum of Natural History,** this budget hotel is attractive and well-maintained. ♦ 45 W. 81st St (between Central Park West and Columbus Ave). 362.9200, 800/368.4575; fax 721.2994

89 Charivari Workshop The latest inspirations from such designers as **Matsuda, Paul Smith,** and **Katharine Hamnett** are sold here. Taken together, the five Charivari stores offer the West Side's best clothes shopping. ♦ M-W, F 11AM-8PM; Th 11AM-9PM; Sa 11AM-7PM; Su 12:30-6PM. 441 Columbus Ave (between W. 81st and W. 82nd Sts). 496.8700. Also at: 18 W. 57th St. 333.4040; 1001 Madison Ave. 650.0078; 58 W. 72nd St. 787.7272; 201 W. 79th St. 799.8650

89 Maxilla & Mandible When they say you can find anything in this city, they mean it. This shop specializes in selling all types of bones. Definitely worth a visit. ♦ M-Sa 11AM-7PM; Su 1-5PM. 453 Columbus Ave (between W. 81st and W. 82nd Sts). 724.6173

90 Endicott Booksellers You can browse leisurely among shelves lined with university and small press books, literary greats, recent fiction and nonfiction, and a backlist of authors in paperback. Seating is provided for casual perusing. Readings by nationally known authors are often held here, too. ♦ M, Su noon-8PM; Tu-Sa 10AM-9PM. 450 Columbus Ave (between W. 81st and W. 82nd Sts). 787.6300

90 Penny Whistle Toys The Pustefix teddy bear out front is forever blowing bubbles to get your attention. If he could talk, he'd tell you all about the quality classics inside: board games, stuffed animals, dolls, cars, indoor gyms, table soccer games, rattles for infants, and—surprise—no electronic video games! The shop is owned by **Meredith Brokaw**— yes, she's related to Tom. ♦ M 10AM-6PM; Tu, Th-Sa 10AM-7PM; W 10AM-8PM; Su 11AM-6PM. 448 Columbus Ave (between W. 81st and W. 82nd Sts). 873.9090. Also at: 1283 Madison Ave. 369.3868; 132 Spring St. 925.2088

90 Greenstones & Cie European clothing for children, including brightly colored French sportswear from **Petit Boy** and **Maugin** and dressy duds from Italy's **Mona Lisa**, are sold. Happily, nothing is so extravagant that it's unwearable. ♦ M-Sa 10AM-7PM; Su noon-6PM. 442 Columbus Ave (between W. 81st and W. 82nd Sts). 580.4322. Also at: 1184 Madison Ave. 427.1665

91 Pizzeria Uno $ The deep-dish, Chicago-style pizza is decent and quite reasonable. Pizzeria Uno is one of the very few places near the **American Museum of Natural History** where people with small children can manage. The express lunch is ready in five minutes flat. ♦ Pizza ♦ Lunch, dinner, and late-night meals. 432 Columbus Ave (at W. 81st St). 595.4700. Also at: South Street Seaport. 791.7999; 391 Sixth Ave. 242.5230

91 Street Life This shop caters to the hip and not-over-twentysomething female who aspires to **Yohji** and **Matsuda**—someday. In the meantime Street Life offers a more affordable statement. ♦ M-Sa 11AM-7PM; Su noon-6PM. 422 Columbus Ave (between W. 80th and W. 81st Sts). 769.8858. Also at: 470 Broadway. 219.3764; 310 Columbus Ave. 875.1844

92 Roman Ruins Two friendly "empresses," **Ivette** and **Madeline,** rule over this gallery/store devoted to art and decoration related to ancient Rome and Greece. Architectural and sculptural reproductions, wrought-iron chairs, hand-painted jewelry, and other unique items are sold. ♦ M-W, F-Sa noon-7:30PM; Th noon-9PM; Su noon-6PM. 417 Amsterdam Ave (at W. 80th St). 496.7390

93 Sarabeth's Kitchen ★★$$ Sarabeth's is one of the better—and busier—brunch spots (breakfast during the week is less hectic). Pancakes and waffles served with fresh fruit are delicious, and in winter, Sarabeth's hot porridge is a cure. Dinner is also served. ♦ American ♦ Breakfast, lunch, and dinner; brunch also on Saturday and Sunday. 423 Amsterdam Ave (between W. 80th and W. 81st Sts). Reservations recommended, but accepted for dinner only. 496.6280. Also at: 1295 Madison Ave. 410.7355

94 Amsterdam's Bar and Rotisserie ★$$ The bar crowd is noisy and young, and the roast chicken with french fries and generous salads better than average. Take a table in the back, keep it simple, and skip dessert. ♦ American ♦ Lunch and dinner. 428 Amsterdam Ave (between W. 80th and W. 81st Sts). 874.1377. Also at: 454 Broadway. 925.6166

95 Baci ★★$$ Zippy Sicilian fare is served in an upbeat, handsome room. Best pasta bets are the fettuccine with sardines and fennel and the linguine *Trapanese,* rich with black olives and olive paste. Chicken and veal dishes are prepared with a light, well-seasoned touch. Save room for the wickedly rich homemade *tiramisù.* ♦ Italian ♦ Lunch and dinner. 412 Amsterdam Ave (between W. 79th and W. 80th Sts). No credit cards. 496.1550

95 Dublin House Tap Room At night, the area's younger, newer residents take over this former workingman's retreat, and the place gets very lively indeed. The brilliant neon harp over the door beckons you to have a lager, and the separate back room makes you wish you'd invited the whole team. ♦ 225 W. 79th St (between Amsterdam Ave and Broadway). 874.9528

96 Filene's Basement This longtime Boston tradition came first to New York via Queens, and at press time was opening another store on Broadway. Filene's is known for selling perfect and slightly damaged clothing and shoes for men and women from the country's best department stores at bargain prices, which gave rise to the expression "bargain basement." ♦ M-Sa 9AM-9PM; Su 11AM-6PM. 2220 Broadway (at W. 79th St). 875.0161

In 1826, Elisha Otis demonstrated his "safety holster" (or elevator-braking device) at America's first World's Fair, held at the Crystal Palace in New York City. His invention cleared the way for the construction of tall buildings.

97 VideoTown Laundrette Come here to make copies, rent videos or a mailbox, send or receive a fax, soak up some rays in the tanning salon and, oh yes, do your laundry. While you're waiting for the clothes to dry, you can munch on the popcorn and candy for sale at the counter, sit out back on the patio and read a book, or watch music videos. ♦ Daily 7AM-midnight. 217 W. 80th St (at Broadway). 721.1706

97 Gryphon Book Shop Used and rare books are sold at decent prices. Look for general humanities plus theater, performing arts, and children's books, especially the *Oz* series by **L. Frank Baum.** An annex is located around the corner at 246 W. 80th Street. ♦ Daily 10AM-midnight. 2246 Broadway (between W. 80th and W. 81st Sts). 362.0706

98 H&H Bagels West They never stop baking here—60,000 bagels a day, shipped nationwide and to London! Stop in for one fresh from the oven 24 hours a day. While you're at it, check out the section of kosher and nonkosher products. H&H is one of the last Manhattan bastions of the "baker's dozen" (buy 12, get 13). ♦ Daily 24 hours. 2239 Broadway (at W. 80th St). 595.8000, 800/692.2435. Also at: 1551 Second Ave. 734.7441

99 411 West End Avenue Built in 1936 to the designs of **George F. Pelham II,** this building has basic yellow brick, but with streamlined details and Art Deco massing at the top. Of special note are the steel drapes on the facade. ♦ At W. 80th St

100 Zabar's This three-star food bazaar is like no other in the world. Though it grew from a small Jewish appetizing store to become this giant grocery and housewares store—with cookware, appliances, and packaged, prepared, and fresh foods from all over the world—it retains a distinctly New York character. On weekends, a line forms for the Western Nova Salmon (if you're lucky, the counter help will pass you a slice to nosh on). Prices are usually better than the competition, and the quality is unrivaled. ♦ M-F 8AM-7:30PM; Sa 8AM-10PM; Su 9AM-6PM. 2245 Broadway (at W. 80th St). 787.2000

Next door to Zabar's:

Zabar's Cafe ★$ The West Side's finest cappuccino is served in the neighborhood's most undistinguished interior. Try a warm knish or a pastry with your coffee for a superlative afternoon delight. Stop in for a restorative espresso after a whirlwind trip through Zabar's. ♦ Cafe/Takeout ♦ Breakfast, lunch, and early dinner. 787.2000

100 Shakespeare & Co. A huge selection of quality and hard-to-find paperbacks line the shelves in this large bookstore. Children's and cookbook sections are in the rear, and gift books and a wing for the performing arts are upstairs. ♦ M-Th, Su 10AM-11:30PM; F-Sa 10AM-12:30AM. 2259 Broadway (at W. 81st St). 580.7800. Also at: 716 Broadway. 529.1330

101 Teachers Too $$ Originally an annex of the now defunct **Teachers,** this restaurant features the same pub menu, the same good spinach salad, and more or less the same crowd. ♦ American ♦ Lunch and dinner; late-night meals also on Friday and Saturday. 2271 Broadway (between W. 81st and W. 82nd Sts). 362.4900

BARNES & NOBLE

102 Barnes & Noble Though this mega-bookstore chain has more than 900 stores around the country, including the B. Dalton, Doubleday, and Scribner's chains, no branch has opened to such hype and acclaim. One of 110 "superstores" throughout the U.S.—this vast two-story space has late hours that encourage the neighborhood's singles to cruise in an intelligent environment, and an interior designed to look like a library, with varnished wood, brass lighting fixtures, and Shaker-style chairs and tables where you can sit for hours. A cafe on the mezzanine serves coffee and cakes, and the children's section is straight out of "Romper Room." ♦ M-Th, Su 9AM-11PM; F-Sa 9AM-midnight. 2289 Broadway (at W. 82nd St). 362.8835

103 The Yarn Co. In addition to being one of the best sources for yarn and expert knitting instruction in the city, this is one of the most pleasant yarn shops, with a big wooden farm table and chairs in the center of the room and an abundant stock of high-quality yarns—from **Rowan, Tahki Imports, Missoni,** and others—lining the walls. Also available are needlepoint supplies, a finishing and lining service, and custom-designed sweaters for those who don't knit. ♦ Tu-Sa 11AM-6PM. 2274 Broadway (between W. 81st and W. 82nd Sts), second floor. 787.7878

Restaurants/Clubs: Red
Shops/ 🍴 Outdoors: Green
Hotels: Blue
Sights/Culture: Black

104 **Yellow Rose Cafe** ★$$ The hearty Texas fare appeals to the "more is more" crowd. Try the distinguished barbecue, framed by fresh cornbread and mounds of chunky mashed potatoes drenched in gravy. ♦ American ♦ Lunch and dinner; brunch also on Saturday and Sunday. 450 Amsterdam Ave (between W. 81st and W. 82nd Sts). 595.8760

105 **Bath Island** An oasis for stressed out New Yorkers in search of biodegradable beauty and bath products, this shop is stocked with bubble bath, shampoo, essential perfume oils (the most potent form of fragrance and the base of all perfumes), skin-care products, cotton kimonos, loofah sponges, and, perhaps best of all, great service from two of the friendliest merchants around, **Janet Loeffler** and **Sebastian Rafala.** You can't miss the store; every morning they scent the sidewalk with hot sudsy water and one of the 75 available perfume oils. ♦ Daily noon-8PM. 469 Amsterdam Ave (between W. 82nd and W. 83rd Sts). 787.9415

105 **Shoofly** You may want to only admire, not buy, the adorable children's shoes and accessories here, as many cost more than parents spend on themselves. The European shoes are displayed on low shelves that children can reach (gulp!), and the hats, either from Europe or made by local artisans, are each hung on a different-shaped hook, ranging from a dinosaur to a crab to a corn cob. An old pipe is made to look like a tree, the floor is painted to resemble moss, and a low table and chairs made out of a tree stump and branches are set up for kids who are tired of shopping (you should be so lucky). Styles range from classic to zany. Larger sizes for older kids and moms are sold in the adjoining space. ♦ M-Sa 11AM-7PM; Su noon-6PM. 465 Amsterdam Ave (between W. 82nd and W. 83rd Sts). 580.4390

Underground New York is home to millions of Norway rats. These creatures, who average 18 inches from nose to tail and weigh in at about a pound, can and will eat practically anything, as well as chew their way through such seemingly impenetrable substances as lead insulation and cinder blocks.

105 **Avventura** Exquisite vases, china, and crystal in singular, sculptural shapes and patterns are carried in this small shop. Beautifully and simply displayed and lit, the pieces are cool to the eye and tempting to touch. Don't bring the kids. ♦ M-Th 10:30AM-7PM; F 10:30AM-sunset; Su 11AM-6PM. 463 Amsterdam Ave (between W. 82nd and W. 83rd Sts). 769.2510

106 **The Silk Road Palace** ★$ The name of this small and most unpalatial restaurant is a tad too ambitious, but you've got to admire their aspirations to high cuisine. The crowd forever loitering outside while waiting for a table is proof of the management's success in combining great Chinese food at low prices with friendly service. ♦ Chinese/Hunan/Szechuan ♦ Lunch and dinner; late-night meals also on Friday and Saturday. 447B Amsterdam Ave (between W. 81st and W. 82nd Sts). 580.6294

107 **Poiret** ★★$$$ Designer **Nancy Mah** has re-created the style of turn-of-the-century French designer **Paul Poiret.** The bistro's white walls are stenciled with green branches and red roses, Poiret's trademark. The long list of daily specials gives you much to choose from, but don't leave without sampling the chocolate-mousse cake. ♦ French ♦ Dinner; brunch also on Sunday. 474 Columbus Ave (between W. 82nd and W. 83rd Sts). Reservations recommended. 724.6880

108 **Fujiyama Mama** ★$$$ It's best to sit at the sashimi counter and get friendly with the chef at this high-tech Japanese restaurant where rock music is played much too loud and waitresses wear traditional kimonos. The menu has some interesting offerings, especially the yakitori or broiled dishes. ♦ Japanese ♦ Dinner. 467 Columbus Ave (between W. 82nd and W. 83rd Sts). Reservations recommended. 769.1144

109 **Handblock** For those who like the exotic look of handblocked fabrics, this is an oasis. The owners have asked their suppliers in India to make traditional patterns as well as totally untraditional ones, such as checks and Provençal-inspired florals, and to whip them up into pillowcases, duvet covers, table cloths, placemats, and pillow shams. Fabrics themselves are not stocked. ♦ M-F 9:30AM-8PM; Sa-Su 9:30AM-7PM. 487 Columbus Ave (between W. 83rd and W. 84th Sts). 799.4342

109 **The Hero's Journey** Although this shop carries all the latest crystals, New Age books, trinkets, and paraphernalia, some might feel that spiritualism and commercialism just aren't meant to mix the way they do here. ♦ M-Sa 11AM-7PM; Su noon-6PM. 489 Columbus Ave (between W. 83rd and W. 84th Sts). 874.4630

110 Lucy's $ Up front, the long and narrow bar area is a crowded, noisy, kitschy place. Patrons fill it regularly, holding their blue and pink drinks aloft like riders on a jerky subway. Squeeze into the back, where a Tex-Mex dining room features the same kind of whimsy, but delivers professional, reliable food. The staff is personable and attractive, but if you find yourself waiting in line, there are other choices nearby. ♦ Tex-Mex ♦ Dinner; lunch also on Saturday and Sunday; late-night meals on Friday and Saturday. 503 Columbus Ave (between W. 84th and W. 85th Sts). 787.3009

111 Down & Quilt Shop Reasonably priced quilts and down comforters are this store's specialty. ♦ M-Sa 10AM-7PM; Su noon-6PM. 518 Columbus Ave (at W. 85th St). 496.8980

112 Harriet's Kitchen $ Excellent chicken soup and straightforward family fare—roast chicken, green beans and carrots, fudge layer cake—are available from this unpretentious takeout that opens its doors at 4:30PM, the hour tired parents decide they're not in the mood to cook. ♦ Takeout ♦ Dinner. 502 Amsterdam Ave (between W. 84th and W. 85th Sts). 721.0045

113 206 West 84th Street **Edgar Allan Poe** finished writing *The Raven* in December of 1844 while he and his wife were boarders at **Patrick** and **Mary Brennan's** farmhouse at this site. ♦ At Amsterdam Ave

113 Chez David $ This kosher pizza place has freshly prepared falafel and Middle Eastern specialties. ♦ Kosher ♦ Breakfast, lunch, and dinner; dinner only on Saturday. 494 Amsterdam Ave (at W. 84th St). No credit cards. 874.4974

114 Good Enough to Eat ★★$$ Breakfast and weekend brunch are the best bets at this tiny Vermont-style outpost. Prepare to wait in line for pecan-flecked waffles, cinnamon-swirl French toast, or the lumberjack breakfast—as big as it sounds. Lunch and dinner are prepared with a homemade, if less inventive, touch. ♦ American ♦ Breakfast, lunch, and dinner; no lunch on Saturday or Sunday. 483 Amsterdam Ave (between W. 83rd and W. 84th Sts). Reservations recommended for dinner. 496.0163

Guided Tours of Gotham City

Adventure on a Shoestring According to company founder Howard Goldberg, these are "walking tours that celebrate everything that is wonderful and positive about the city." Chats with members of the community toured are often scheduled. Twelve months a year, rain or shine. ♦ Modest fee. Call for schedule. 265.2663

Doorway to Design Customized behind-the-scenes tours of the interior design, fashion, and art worlds as well as walking tours with an architectural historian. Groups are welcome. ♦ Fee. Call for schedule. 221.1111 (daytime), 718/338.1542 (evenings)

Gray Line of New York Two- to eight-and-a-half-hour Manhattan tours are offered. ♦ Fee. Call for schedule. Departure: 900 Eighth Ave (at 54th St). 397.2600

Harlem Gospel & Jazz Tours Tours include visits to historic sites, gospel church services, soul-food restaurants, and jazz clubs. ♦ Fee. 302.2594

History Walks Manhattan historian **Joyce Gold** conducts walking tours of Lower Manhattan, Greenwich Village, Chelsea, the Ladies' Mile, and Harlem. ♦ Fee. Call for schedule, departures. 242.5762

Municipal Art Society Walking tours (one hour to all day) with an architectural orientation. Meet in the neighborhood of walk. ♦ Fee. Call for schedule. Reservations required. 935.3960

Museum of the City of New York Once or twice a month walks of varying lengths are geared to the museum's current exhibitions. Departure from neighborhood of walk. ♦ Fee. Sunday at 1PM. Reservations recommended. 534.1672 ext 206

92nd Street YM/YWHA Neighborhood walking tours, holiday theme tours, and visits to artists' studios are among the inventive destinations. Also bus tours to Manhattan environs. Most tours (three hours to full weekend) begin at the Y. ♦ Fee. Call for schedule. Reservations required. 415.5628 or 415.5599

River to River Downtown Walking Tours **Ruth Alscher-Green** will tailor a tour of Lower Manhattan (from the Hudson River to the East River) to individuals or groups, and is flexible about scheduling. ♦ Fee. 321.2823

Shortline Bus Tours From two-and-a-half-hour to all-day tours of Manhattan, plus an evening tour of Christmas lights, in season. ♦ Fee. Call for schedule. Departure: 166 W. 46th St (between Sixth and Seventh Aves). 354.5122

Urban Park Rangers The emphasis is on botany, geology, and wildlife on these walking tours of parks in all five boroughs. ♦ Free. Call for schedule. Reservations required for workshops and bicycle or bus tours. 427.4040

115 The Raccoon Lodge West Siders come to this bar for the pool table, friendly atmosphere, great jukebox, and cheap drinks. ♦ M-F 11AM-4AM; Sa-Su 3PM-4AM. 480 Amsterdam Ave (at W. 83rd St). 874.9984. Also at: 59 Warren St. 766.9656

115 Cafe Lalo ★$ This dessert-only cafe with brick walls and a wooden floor has long French-style windows that open onto the street. Although it's quite pleasant to linger over a cappuccino during the day, it can get crowded and loud at night. ♦ Cafe ♦ M-Th noon-2AM; F noon-4AM; Sa 11AM-4AM; Su 11AM-2AM. 201 W. 83rd St (at Amsterdam Ave). 496.6031

116 Children's Museum of Manhattan This educational playground of interactive exhibitions and activity centers is all built around the museum's theme of self-discovery. On the second floor is the **Time Warner Center for Media,** where children can produce their own videotapes, newscasts, and public affairs programs. Exhibition interpreters are always on hand to provide assistance, and entertainers are stationed at key points to provide further understanding through song, dance, or puppetry. There is an art studio where classes in book- and paper-making and other studio arts are held, and a theater where performances are given by theater groups, dancers, musicians, puppeteers, and storytellers, as well as children participating in the museum's education and video programs and workshops. ♦ Admission. M, W-Th 1:30-5:30PM; F-Su 10AM-5PM. 212 W. 83rd St (between Amsterdam Ave and Broadway). 721.1223

117 Loew's 84th Street Showplace Once a grand movie palace, the Loew's 84th Street is now a suburban-style, multiscreened venture tucked rather discreetly onto a row of newly opened retail shops on the ground floor of the **Bromley.** If you remember the old place, you'll be disappointed; if you want to see a movie, you'll go anyway—they're showing them all. The site of former **Mayor Koch's** failed attempt at a boycott of the $7 movie ticket, the price has since climbed even higher. ♦ 2310 Broadway (at W. 84th St). 877.3600

Jack Dempsey's 14-room apartment at 145 Central Park West included a huge kitchen where the fighter practiced his favorite hobby—cooking.

118 Ollie's Noodle Shop ★$ New York would be a better place if every neighborhood had a place like Ollie's. There are three of these lively, unpretentious Chinese noodle joints on the West Side. Cold sesame noodles and scallion pancakes are winners; vegetable, pork, or shrimp dumplings and great spare ribs are the standby favorites. There was a time when you'd have to round up a bunch of friends and head down to Chinatown for food this good at prices this low, but Ollie's has moved that downtown formula uptown. ♦ Chinese ♦ Lunch, dinner, and late-night meals. 2315 Broadway (at W. 84th St). 362.3712. Also at: 2957 Broadway. 932.3300; 200 W. 44th St. 921.5988

119 Patzo $$ The pizza is better than usual at this two-level Italian restaurant. The crust is thin and well-baked and the list of toppings will make you dizzy. Good pasta is also available. It's crowded on the weekends but peaceful at lunchtime during the week. ♦ Italian ♦ Lunch and dinner. 2330 Broadway (at W. 85th St). 496.9240

120 520 West End Avenue Neighborhood residents vehemently defended their many-gabled "castle" when, in 1987, a misled developer proposed building an apartment house on this site. This survivor was built in 1892 to the designs of **Clarence F. True.** ♦ At W. 85th St

121 The Red House Designed by **Harde & Short** and built in 1904, this six-story apartment building is a cross between an Elizabethan manor and a redbrick row house. Note the dragon and crown near the top. ♦ 350 W. 85th St (between West End Ave and Riverside Dr)

122 The Clarendon In 1908, **William Randolph Hearst** moved his family into a 30-room apartment on the top three floors of this 1903 building designed by **Charles Birge.** In 1913, when the landlord refused to ask the residents on the other nine floors to leave so that Hearst, his family, and his art collection could spread out, Hearst simply purchased the building and forced them out himself. Faced with financial woes, he sold the property in 1938. ♦ 137 Riverside Dr (at W. 86th St)

123 La Mirabelle ★$$$ A fresh, inviting decor, efficient service, and food that is a notch above the ordinary keep this French bistro busy. Good choices are escargots, soft-shell crabs cooked with lots of garlic and tomatoes, pink and spicy rack of lamb, and the best steak *pommes frites* on the West Side. Desserts are nothing to write home about. ♦ French ♦ Dinner. 333 W. 86th St (between West End Ave and Riverside Dr). Reservations recommended. 496.0458

Bests

Barbara Cohen and Judith Stonehill
Co-owners, New York Bound Bookshop

Places for book-lovers:

Afternoon tea at **Anglers & Writers Cafe,** on Hudson Street at St. Luke's Place. (Marianne Moore lived nearby and worked in the public library around the corner.)

The **New York Public Library,** with its extraordinary collection of over 6 million books spanning 88 miles of shelves.

Gansevoort Street, where Herman Melville once worked as a customs officer and where you will find authentic French bistro food 24 hours a day at **Florent's.**

The **General Society Library** to see the latest books at the **Small Press Center,** or to borrow a book. The turn-of-the-century Harvard and New York Yacht clubs, en route to the fabled **Algonquin** for tea or a cocktail and a bit of reading.

A drink at the **White Horse Tavern** on Hudson Street after work, to think of Dylan Thomas, Delmore Schwartz, Brendan Behan, and other writers who drank hour after hour there.

The **Morgan Library,** with its priceless medieval and Renaissance manuscripts, rare editions, and unique exhibitions on the book arts. Edith Wharton would have been at home in its old New York splendor.

Edgar Allan Poe's home, a clapboard cottage he rented in 1846, and where he wrote *Annabel Lee.*

A proper afternoon tea and a library of thousands of books on the British Commonwealth can be found at the **English Speaking Union** in its cozy town house.

With breezes from the river and broad vistas, a walk along the grand **Battery** promenade evokes Melville and Whitman, especially after a summer evening reading held there by **Symphony Space.** (In the winter, we go uptown to Symphony Space on 95th Street to hear actors read from literary works.)

Quiet places to read a book: the sculpture garden at the **Noguchi Museum;** the **Temple of Dundur Hall** at the Metropolitan Museum; the **Staten Island Ferry** during the quiet hours of the day.

George Lois
Lois USA

My idea of blowing a Saturday afternoon is doing *The Dirty Dozen,* a hit-and-run look at 12 of the greatest galleries in the world:

Start with **Michael Ward** at 9 E. 93rd, who continually surprises with brilliant shows of scholarship and artifacts, including Celtic art, medieval art, and African weaponry.

Quickly to **Barry Friedman** at 84th Street and Madison, a great young dealer specializing in late 19th-century and early 20th-century decorative arts. If you're looking for original Bauhaus for your house, he's your man.

Then the beginning of a trek down Madison to **Mert Simpson,** probably the world's greatest dealer in tribal art, to study his selection of masterpieces of African, Oceanic, and Northwest Coast Indian art.

A few blocks down to a second tribal arts dealer, **Leloup,** and then to **DeLorenzo,** where you lose your heart to the most sensational Art Deco furniture ever collected in one gallery. The **Ruhlmanns, Dunands,** and **Chareaus** can make (and have made) a grown man cry.

Next door and up the stairs to **Jordan Volpe,** the best dealers in the world for the American Arts and Crafts movement.

A block south is **Galerie Metropol,** which single-handedly reintroduced the arts of the Wiener Werkstätte to America.

At 70th Street, **Hirschl & Adler Folk** (early American folk art), **Hirschl & Adler Modern,** and across the street **Hirschl & Adler,** the leading specialists in American art.

Two blocks south on E. 68th Street is **Primavera,** a miniature version of DeLorenzo but also a treasure house for Art Deco jewelry.

Continuing south to 61st Street is the **Macklowe Gallery,** loaded with Art Nouveau and Art Deco.

Elizabeth Tilberis
Editor-in-Chief, *Harper's Bazaar*

The view of Manhattan from the **Triborough Bridge** at dusk.

Driving through **Central Park.**

Driving down the **FDR Highway.**

Skating at **Wollman Rink.**

Eating outdoors on summer evenings as the sun sets at any restaurant with sidewalk cafes.

The shop windows at Christmastime.

The Egyptian rooms at the **Metropolitan Museum of Art.**

High tea at **Rumpelmayer's.**

Circling Manhattan at sunset before the plane lands at **La Guardia Airport.**

Chinatown for Chinese food—the children love it here.

Little League baseball on Saturday in **Central Park.**

Knicks games on Sunday at **Madison Square Garden**—and the heavenly hot dogs.

To create Lincoln Center—six buildings devoted to theater, music, and dance in an area of 14 acres—it was necessary to demolish 188 buildings and relocate 1,600 people. These were the very slums in which Leonard Bernstein set his famous American musical *West Side Story.* He would later be instrumental in the development and creative organization of Lincoln Center.

Upper West Side

A neighborhood in transition, the Upper West Side (the area bordered by **Central Park**, the **Hudson River**, **W. 86th Street**, and **Cathedral Parkway/110th Street**) is undergoing the same kind of gentrifying process that has taken place farther south. The commercial zone is extending up **Broadway** and **Amsterdam** and **Columbus avenues**, and the residential zone that surrounds **Columbia University** is moving down those same streets. While the Central Park blocks (the numbered streets between Columbus Avenue and Central Park West) contain brownstones and apartments that are in excellent condition as far north as 95th Street, even the blocks of tenements and middle-income apartments between Amsterdam Avenue and Broadway, in disrepair for years, have become desirable residences—if only for their proximity to the burgeoning shopping and dining strips. The residential **West End Avenue** and **Riverside Drive** remain staunchly unchanged, except perhaps for the parade of new windows in the grand old high-rises, most of which have been converted to co-ops as far north as **Duke Ellington Boulevard (106th Street)**.

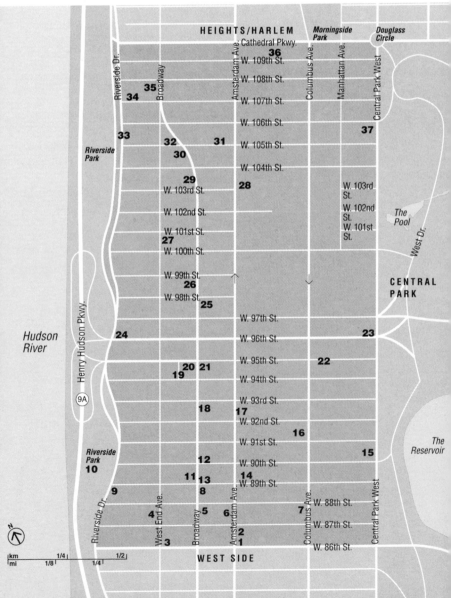

Whereas only a few years ago it seemed to be a fading reminder of the Old World, the West Side north of 86th Street is now a thriving cosmopolitan mix that feels like the best of both worlds. New high-rise buildings fronted by sidewalk cafes and attractive retail stores are graceful and stabilizing elements to a rapidly changing upper Broadway. Columbus Avenue buzzes with life spilling in and out of its restaurants, bars, antique shops, and clothing stores. Even the area from 96th to 110th streets is sprucing up, particularly east of Broadway, where what was once considered part of Harlem has been given a name of its own—**Manhattan Valley**—and has been annexed to the Upper West Side. And while there's easy access to Central Park on the eastern side of this area, to the west is **Riverside Park**, a 50-block oasis designed by **Frederick Law Olmsted**, creator of Central Park.

1 West Park Presbyterian Church Originally the **Park Presbyterian Church,** this church was built in 1890 to the designs of **Henry F. Kilburn.** The rough-hewn red sandstone of the Richardsonian Romanesque mass is enlivened by the lightness of the almost Byzantine details of the capitals and doorways and the fineness of the colonettes in the tower. The church's boldness is emphasized by the asymmetrical massing, with the single tower holding the corner between two strong facades. ◆ Amsterdam Ave (at W. 86th St). 362.4890

2 Barney Greengrass (The Sturgeon King) ★$$ Folksier than **Zabar's,** though not as complete, this Jewish appetizing store has good roots: it opened in 1908, has been in its present location since 1929, and is run by son **Moe** and grandson **Gary Greengrass.** There's a small dining room attached to the take-out store. Though the staff is generally quite rude, it's worth a visit for the vintage New York ambience. ◆ Deli ◆ Breakfast and lunch. 541 Amsterdam Ave (between W. 86th and W. 87th Sts). 724.4707

2 Popover Café ★$$ This is one of the most easygoing of the neighborhood sandwich/salad spots. Best bets are the popovers with strawberry jam, perhaps with a steaming bowl of homemade soup. Keep it simple. ◆ American ◆ Breakfast, lunch, and dinner. 551 Amsterdam Ave (at W. 87th St). 595.8555

3 Church of St. Paul and St. Andrew Built in 1897 and designed by **R.H. Robertson,** this church has overtones of the manners of **Boulee,** particularly in the octagonal tower. Note the angels in the spandrels. ◆ West End Ave (at W. 86th St). 362.3179

4 565 West End Avenue Designed by **H.I. Feldman** in 1937, this is a neo-Renaissance building in Art Deco fabric—brick instead of stone, corner windows instead of quoins. At the bottom, banded brick represents the shadow of a traditional plinth, and the cornice is stainless steel. ◆ Between W. 87th and W. 88th Sts

5 Boulevard ★$$ Excellent hamburgers, good pasta, and a not-so-good grilled chicken are served in this pleasant restaurant with an American menu and the feel of a French outdoor cafe. Service is slow, but when the weather is good does it really matter? ◆ American ◆ Lunch and dinner; late-night meals also from Friday through Sunday. 2398 Broadway (at W. 88th St). 874.7400

6 Ozu ★$ Expect simple Japanese decor and solid macrobiotic fare. ◆ Macrobiotic ◆ Lunch and dinner. 566 Amsterdam Ave (between W. 87th and W. 88th Sts). 787.8316

6 Pandit ★$$ Save yourself the trek down to the East Village's Little India and have a memorable meal here for prices only slightly higher. Pandit is one of the few—and best—Indian restaurants in this neighborhood. Service is friendly, and the waiters steer you along the way to an authentic culinary experience. ◆ Indian ◆ Lunch and dinner. 566 Amsterdam Ave (between W. 87th and W. 88th Sts). 724.1217

7 Grossinger's Uptown Bake Shop This old-fashioned bakery sells traditional Jewish food: *babka, ruggalah,* coffeecake, cheesecake. ◆ M-Th, Su 8:30AM-7PM; F 8:30AM-sundown. 570 Columbus Ave (at W. 88th St). 874.6996

7 East West Books A New Age bookstore is home to the **Himalayan Institute of New York,** which offers instruction in many areas, including yoga, meditation, relaxation and breathing, homeopathy, and stress management. ◆ M-Sa 10AM-6:45PM; Su 11AM-6PM. 568 Columbus Ave (between W. 87th and W. 88th Sts). 787.7552

8 Westside Judaica Religious articles and a large stock of fiction and nonfiction covering all aspects of the Jewish experience are sold, along with cassette tapes, videos, and holiday decorations for children's parties. ◆ M-Th 10:30AM-7:30PM; F 10:30AM-2PM; Su 10:30AM-6PM. 2412 Broadway (between W. 88th and W. 89th Sts). 362.7846

9 Yeshiva Chofetz Chaim Isaac L. Rice had this house built in 1901 and named it Villa Julia for his wife, the founder of the now defunct **Society for the Suppression of Unnecessary Noise.** This and the former **Schinasi Residence** (351 Riverside Drive) are the only two mansions left from the days when Riverside Drive was lined with them.

Note the slightly askew porte-cochère (a porch large enough for wheeled vehicles to pass through). The architects, **Herts & Tallant,** also designed the **Lyceum Theater.** ♦ 346 W. 89th St (at Riverside Dr). 362.1435

10 Riverside Park Originally designed by **Frederick Law Olmsted** from 1873 to 1910, this welcome strip of greenery between the city and the Hudson River stretches for three miles (blessedly covering a rail line below), with space for jogging, tennis, and baseball. When there's snow, people actually sleigh ride. Additions were made to the park in 1888 by **Calvert Vaux** and **Samuel Parsons, Jr.,** and in 1937 by **Clinton F. Lloyd.** Not a monument in itself, as is Central Park, this piece of land is spattered with a few little memorials—most notably the **Soldiers' and Sailors' Monument** designed in 1902 by **Stoughton & Stoughton** and **Paul E.M. Duboy** at 89th Street, modeled after the **Choragic Monument of Lysicrates** in Athens; the **Firemen's Memorial** at 100th Street, designed in 1913 by sculptor **Attilio Piccirilli** and architect **H. Van Buren Magonigle,** and graced by statues of *Courage and Duty;* and the easy-to-overlook but not-to-be-forgotten **Carrère Memorial** (1916), a small terrace and plaque at 99th Street honoring the great architect **John Merven Carrère,** designed by his partner **Thomas Hastings.** Carrère died in an automobile accident in 1911. ♦ Bounded by Riverside Dr and Hudson River, and W. 72nd and W. 145th Sts

11 Docks Oyster Bar and Seafood Grill ★★$$$ Fresh seafood served in a perky black-and-white tiled dining room is featured in this lively neighborhood haunt. The catch of the day varies, but fried oysters coated in cornmeal are a sure bet anytime, and the French-fried yams are an inspiration. One wishes the kitchen were a bit more consistent and the service less slow. ♦ Seafood ♦ Lunch and dinner; brunch also on Saturday and Sunday. 2427 Broadway (between W. 89th and W. 90th Sts). Reservations recommended. 724.5588

11 Murray's Sturgeon The ultimate Jewish appetizing store has maintained its reputation for high-quality herring, lox, whitefish, and all things dairy through more than half a century and the neighborhood's many vicissitudes. ♦ M-F, Su 8AM-7PM; Sa 8AM-8PM. 2429 Broadway (between W. 89th and W. 90th Sts). 724.2650

12 Pumpkin Eater $$ This small restaurant proves that food can be healthful and taste good, too. ♦ Vegetarian/Seafood ♦ Lunch and dinner. 2452 Broadway (between W. 90th and W. 91st Sts). 877.0132

12 Carmine's $$ Come hungry and bring a friend to share the huge portions; all meals are meant for two or more. ♦ Italian ♦ Dinner. 2450 Broadway (between W. 90th and W. 91st Sts). 362.2200

13 The Armadillo $ It's worth a visit just to see the neon cactus that winds its way up the main pillar. The menu is a curious mix of Southern, Southwestern, and Mexican cooking. A typical meal might be Texas-fried chicken. Try the chili. ♦ Tex/Mex ♦ Dinner and late-night meals; brunch also on Saturday and Sunday. 2420 Broadway (at W. 89th St). 496.1066

14 Claremont Riding Academy Designed in 1982 by **Frank A. Rooke,** this multistory stable is the only one left in Manhattan for riding horses. The bridle paths are a few blocks away in Central Park. Lessons are available. ♦ M-F 6:30AM-10PM; Sa-Su 8AM-5PM. 175 W. 89th St (between Columbus and Amsterdam Aves). Reservations required. 724.5100

15 The Eldorado The northernmost of the twin-towered silhouettes on Central Park West, this apartment building, designed by **Margon & Holder** and built in 1931, is characterized by its Art Deco detailing. ♦ 300 Central Park West (between W. 90th and W. 91st Sts)

16 Trinity School and Trinity House The main building was built in 1894 to the designs of **Charles C. Haight;** the east building was designed by **William A. Potter** in 1892; and the apartment tower and school addition were designed by **Brown, Guenther, Battaglia, Seckler** in 1969. Straight, wonderful Romanesque Revival, now locked to an intricate 1960s tower, it is much better than average. ♦ 100 W. 92nd St and 101 W. 91st St (between Columbus and Amsterdam Aves). School: 873.1650. House: 724.1313

17 Les Friandises ★★$$ Trained at world-famous **Le Nôtre,** owner/pâtissiere **Jean Kahn** turns out an impressive variety of elegant cakes and pastries. Her sumptuous breakfast treats with a cup of strong French coffee are worth a detour. ♦ Cafe ♦ Breakfast, lunch, and early dinner. 665 Amsterdam Ave (between W. 92nd and W. 93rd Sts). 316.1515

18 Murder Ink. The grandmother of all mystery bookstores, this is just the way you picture it: cozy and English, with fat fuzzy cats and a clutter of new and out-of-print mysteries, references, and periodicals. Most major mystery authors do signings here. ♦ M-W, F-Sa 10AM-7:30PM; Th 10AM-9PM; Su 11AM-7PM. 2486 Broadway (between W. 92nd and W. 93rd Sts). 362.8905

19 Pomander Walk A surprising little enclave, this double row of mock-Tudor town houses was named after a play that was produced in London and played on Broadway in 1911. The houses, designed in 1922 by **King & Campbell,** were meant to look like the stage set for the New York production. Tenants have included **Rosalind Russell, Humphrey Bogart,** and **Lillian** and **Dorothy Gish.** ♦ W. 94th to W. 95th Sts (between Broadway and West End Ave)

20 Symphony Space Constructed during the first decade of this century, this building began as the **Crystal Carnival Skating Rink** and was converted into a movie house in the 1920s. Under the guidance of artistic directors **Isaiah Sheffer** and **Allan Miller,** it has become a performing arts center that has contributed to a cultural renaissance on the Upper West Side. Marathon musical events such as *Wall to Wall Bach,* a free birthday salute to composer **John Cage,** and a glorious **Aaron Copland** celebration are some items from the bill of fare. Notable supporters include violinists **Itzak Perlman** and **Pinchas Zuckerman,** jazz pianist **Billy Taylor, John Cage,** actor **Fritz Weaver,** and actresses **Estelle Parsons** and **Claire Bloom.** ♦ 2537 Broadway (between W. 94th and W. 95th Sts). 864.5400

21 Key West Diner $$ Finally, upper Broadway has its own *Miami Vice* look-alike. But don't let the salmon-and-turquoise interior fool you—this is an honest-to-goodness diner in the best sense of the term. Omelets with home fries and giant bagels are generous and fresh, as is the light challah French toast. ♦ Diner ♦ Breakfast, lunch, dinner, and late-night meals. 2532 Broadway (between W. 94th and W. 95th Sts). 932.0068

22 West 95th Street These blocks of diverse row houses represent one aspect of the **Upper West Side Urban Renewal** effort. Between the housing projects on the avenues, side streets such as this one, which provide unique and charming character, are being restored. ♦ Between Central Park West and Amsterdam Ave

23 First Church of Christ, Scientist This is, surprisingly, not particularly Beaux Arts, but more in the style of the English Renaissance, with a touch of Hawksmoor in the energetic facade and steeple. The marble interiors are quite impressive. **Carrère & Hastings,** who designed this structure in 1903, were also responsible for the **New York Public Library** and the **Frick Residence.** ♦ 1 W. 96th St (at Central Park West). 749.3088

24 The Cliff Dwellers' Apartments The facade is decorated with a frieze of mountain lions, snakes, and buffalo skulls—symbols of the Arizona cliff dwellers. Designed in 1914 by **Herman Lee Leader,** this is an unusual example of Art Deco interest in prehistoric art and culture. ♦ 243 Riverside Dr (at W. 96th St)

25 The Hunan Balcony ★$ It's hard to ask for more from a neighborhood spot: dependably fresh ingredients, low prices, and clean, bright surroundings—and when they say *spicy,* they mean it. ♦ Chinese ♦ Lunch, dinner, and late-night meals. 2596 Broadway (at W. 98th St). Reservations recommended. 865.0400

26 Health Nuts Natural vitamins, grains, nuts, herbs, honey, and breads are sold here. ♦ M-Sa 9AM-9PM; Su 11AM-7PM. 2611 Broadway (at W. 99th St). 678.0054

27 838 West End Avenue Covered with terracotta decoration, both geometric patterns and stylized natural forms, this structure was designed by **George** and **Edward Blum** in 1914. ♦ At W. 101st St

28 New York International American Youth Hostel (AYH) $ Unlike many other hostels, no work is required in exchange for the clean, safe, and inexpensive accommodations; there is no curfew; and the hostel stays open all day long. Like other hostels, all guests must be members of American Youth Hostels (nonmembers can join on the spot) and must bring a sleeping bag or rent sheets. The building itself, once a home operated by the **Association for the Relief of Respectable Aged Indigent Females,** is a Designated Landmark of the City of New York. **Richard Morris Hunt,** who designed this building in 1883, also created the facade of the **Great Hall** of the **Metropolitan Museum of Art** and the base of the Statue of Liberty. The maximum stay is seven days, but you can apply for an extension. Bathrooms are shared. ♦ 891 Amsterdam Ave (between W. 103rd and W. 104th Sts). 932.2300

29 Broadway Barber Shop The gilt lettering on the windows is fading, but all the other fixtures seem to be intact in this quaint barbershop, which opened in 1907. "It's the oldest barbershop in New York," a heavily accented barber calls out as he circles a supine head in his chair. In addition to a good shave, it's a great photo opportunity. ♦ M-Sa 8AM-7PM. 2713 Broadway (between W. 103rd and W. 104th Sts). 666.3042

30 Positively 104th Street Cafe ★★$$ Specialty foods like grilled Norwegian salmon are served in a cozy cafe-style setting. ♦ American ♦ Breakfast, lunch, and dinner. 2725 Broadway (between W. 104th and W. 105th Sts). Reservations recommended. 316.0372

30 Au Petit Beurre ★$ You'll see signs of student-inspired whole earth consciousness in this pleasant, airy resting spot that calls itself a French cafe. Good cappuccino and excellent muffins are served to a neighborhood clientele—the old and the new. ♦ Cafe ♦ Breakfast, lunch, and dinner. 2737 Broadway (at W. 105th St). 663.7010

31 Santerello ★★$$$ One of the pioneer Italian establishments on the Upper West Side, this intimate, side-street venue continues to serve excellent Northern Italian fare. Try the daily fish specials or the especially flavorful chicken in a pungent Gorgonzola sauce. ♦ Italian ♦ Lunch and dinner; brunch also on Sunday. 239 W. 105th St (between Broadway and Amsterdam Ave). Reservations recommended. 749.7044

32 Birdland ★$$ This jazz/supper club features the likes of pianist **Henry Butler, Mark Morganelli and the Jazz Forum All-Stars**, and **Arthur Taylor's Wailers**. ♦ American/Cajun ♦ Dinner and late-night meals. Call for changing schedule of shows. 2745 Broadway (at W. 105th St). Reservations recommended. 749.2228

33 Riverside Drive/West 105th Street Historic District Riverside Drive between W. 105th and 106th streets (plus some of W. 105th Street) has an excellent collection of turn-of-the-century French Beaux Arts town houses. Of special interest is No. 331, designed in 1902 by **Janes & Leo,** formerly **Marion Davies'** residence and now part of the **New York Buddhist Church** and **American Buddhist Academy.** ♦ Between W. 105th and W. 106 Sts

34 Nicholas Roerich Museum Roerich was well-known in his native Russia and throughout the world as an artist, philosopher, archaeologist, and founder of an educational institution to promote world peace through the arts. This beautiful old town house, one unit of his **Master Institute,** overflows with his landscapes, books, and pamphlets on art, culture, and philosophy. Lectures and concerts take place here. ♦ Free. Tu-Su 2-5PM. 319 W. 107th St (between Broadway and Riverside Dr). 864.7752

35 107 West ★★$$ A mostly young upscale crowd keeps this three-room establishment bustling. Spicy Cajun specialties are best (blackened everything), especially fresh salmon in season, and there's a good wine list. ♦ American ♦ Dinner; brunch also on Sunday. 2787 Broadway (between W. 107th and W. 108th Sts). 864.1555

36 Cathedral Parkway Houses These two massive apartment towers were carefully articulated in an attempt to accommodate them to the much smaller scale of the neighborhood. They were built in 1975 and designed by **Davis, Brody & Associates** and **Roger Glasgow.** ♦ 125 W. 109th St (between Columbus and Amsterdam Aves). 749.1100

37 Towers Nursing Home Typically Victorian with its squat towers and conical roofs, this was originally the **New York Cancer Hospital,** the first in the nation devoted to the care of cancer patients. It was designed in 1887 by **Charles C. Haight,** who was also the architect of the main buildings of the **General Theological Seminary** and **Trinity School.** ♦ 2 W. 106th St (between Central Park West and Columbus Ave)

Restaurants/Clubs: Red   Hotels: Blue
Shops/ 🌳 Outdoors: Green   Sights/Culture: Black

In the Market for a van Gogh? Try New York's Museum Gift Shops

No trip to a New York City museum is complete without a stop at its gift shop. Gone are the days when posters and art books related to the museum's collection were the sole merchandise. Museum shops now emblazon their logos and most famous works of art on everything from T-shirts to toothbrushes. Gift shops generally operate during museum hours, although some may be open on days when the museum is closed. Several have additional outlets throughout the city.

The Asia Society The accent in this well-stocked museum store is on books pertaining to the arts of the major and minor Asian cultures, including travel guides, cookbooks, and volumes on history, the performing arts, languages, philosophy, and religion. A smaller inside room displays a carefully edited selection of crafts and some antiques from such countries as Indonesia, Nepal, Thailand, and India. ◆ Asia Society Shop: M-Sa 11AM-6:30PM. 725 Park Ave (at E. 70th St). 517.6397

Brooklyn Museum Contemporary and antique crafts, jewelry, and objects from around the world make this museum shop seem more like a visit to the United Nations Gift Shop. Representative of the international scope and diversity of the museum's collections, the global merchandising unfortunately overshadows the art books and reproductions from the museum's collections. But it's a great place to browse and, unlike other museum shops, often offers discounts. ◆ Brooklyn Museum Shop: W-Su 10:30AM-5:30PM. 200 Eastern Pkwy (at Washington Ave), Prospect Heights, Brooklyn. 718/638.5000. Also at: Equitable Building, 787 Seventh Ave. 554.4888

The Cooper-Hewitt The small gift shop at the Smithsonian Institution's National Museum of Design, housed in the lovely music room of the former Andrew Carnegie mansion, is filled with a generous, design-oriented collection of objects for the desk, dining room, coffee table, and even the bath (handsomely packaged soaps and designer toothbrushes). A book and postcard selection vies with salt and pepper shakers and flower vases for shelf space, most reflective of the design sensibility of the museum. ◆ Cooper-Hewitt National Museum of Design Shop: Tu 10AM-9PM; W-Sa 10AM-5PM; Su noon-5PM. 2 E. 91st St (between Madison and Fifth Aves). 860.6878

Metropolitan Museum of Art The city's star museum store has recently grown to nearly 19,000 square feet on two floors and is a proud homage to the Metropolitan's unrivaled collections and visiting exhibitions. Downstairs is a huge book selection and jewelry store (jewelry accounts for nearly one-third of the 1,600 items the museum reproduces), and a cornucopia of silver, glass, porcelain, and statues from different centuries and cultures. Upstairs are rugs, the bridal registry, and prints on consignment from contemporary artists. A mail-order catalog is available. Additional branches are located in Rockefeller Plaza, the Public Library at 445 Fifth Avenue, Macy's Herald Square, and the Cloisters. ◆ Metropolitan Museum Gift Store: Tu-Th, Su 9:30AM-5:15PM; F-Sa 9:30AM-8:45PM. Fifth Ave at E. 82nd St. 879.5500

Museum of American Folk Art The museum's focus on American crafts and early Americana is reflected in the gift shop, with how-to books on everything from quilt-making and stenciling to basket-weaving. This store is particularly charming at Christmastime, when scores of handmade tree ornaments and tabletop decorations made by American craftspeople are sold. The Museum of American Folk Art is three blocks away on W. 53rd Street. ◆ Museum of American Folk Art Gift Shop: M-Sa 10:30AM-5:30PM. 62 W. 50th St (between Fifth and Sixth Aves). 247.5611. Also at: 66 Columbus Ave. 496.2966

Museum of Modern Art (MoMA) The Museum of Modern Art now boasts two gift shops: the recently opened MoMA Design Store, an off-site gift shop just across the street from the museum; and the original gift shop off the museum's lobby, now dedicated exclusively to books, magazines, posters, and cards. The extensive selection at the Design Store includes everything to furnish your office, home, and garden, from table-top conversation pieces to such design-collection classics as Charles Eames chairs and Alvar Aalto tables. ◆ MoMA Design Store: M-W, Sa 10AM-6PM; Th-F 10AM-9PM; Su 11AM-6PM. 44 W. 53rd St (between Fifth and Sixth Aves). 767.1050. MoMA Bookstore: M-W, Sa-Su 11AM-5:45PM; Th-F 11AM-8:45PM. 11 W. 53rd St (between Fifth and Sixth Aves). 708.9700

Solomon R. Guggenheim Museum In addition to books, postcards, and posters, the shop has a small selection of hand-crafted jewelry and scarves not related to the museum's collections. The only way into the Guggenheim's new branch museum in SoHo is through its museum store, where merchandise is much the same as in the parent institution. ◆ Solomon R. Guggenheim Museum Gift Shop: M-W, F-Su 10AM-8PM; Th 11AM-6PM. 1071 Fifth Ave (at E. 89th St). 423.3615. Guggenheim Museum SoHo: M-W, Su 11AM-6PM; Th-Sa 11AM-8PM. 575 Broadway (at Prince St). 423.3876

Whitney Museum of American Art As in the Museum of Modern Art, the Whitney's on-site bookstore outgrew its limited space, hence the opening of the adjacent Store Next Door. The museum's lobby shop offers a small but well-focused selection of catalogs and books, while the Store Next Door carries design-conscious lifestyle collections that feature everything from Shaker-influenced objects to handmade ceramics and birdhouses. ◆ Whitney Museum Shop: Tu-W, F-Su 11AM-6PM; Th 11AM-8PM. 945 Madison Ave (at E. 75th St). 606.0202. The Store Next Door: Tu-W, F-Su 10AM-6PM; Th 10AM-8PM. 943 Madison Ave (between E. 75th and E. 74th Sts). 606.0200

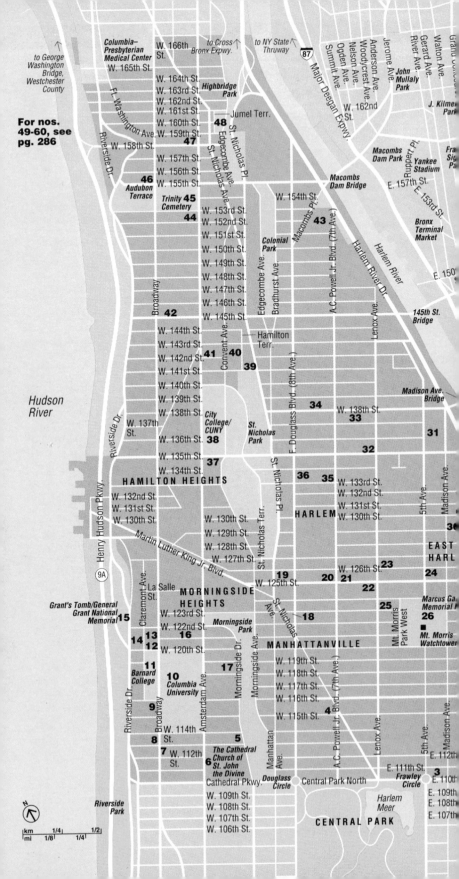

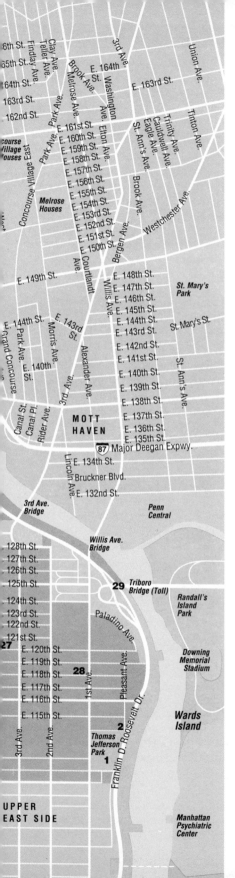

Heights/ Harlem

Located north of **Cathedral Parkway (110th Street)**, the geographical peaks and valleys of the Heights and Harlem more or less define neighborhood boundaries all the way up to **Spuyten-Duyvil**, where the Hudson and East rivers join at 225th Street.

Morningside Heights, the hilly terrain between Cathedral Parkway and 125th Street, was largely undeveloped until the opening of **Morningside Park** in 1887 and of **Riverside Drive** in 1891. World-renowned scholars began to settle in shortly thereafter, and today the area is dominated by educational giants. **Union Theological Seminary**, **Jewish Theological Seminary**, **Columbia University**, and **Barnard College** form the cornerstone of this outstanding academic community. Two other structures stand out in the landscape: the massive work-in-progress of the **Cathedral Church of St. John the Divine**, and the **Riverside Church**, an important religious and cultural center in its own right. While you're in the neighborhood, don't forget **Grant's Tomb**, set high on a hill above the river. **Broadway** is the main drag, just as it is on the Upper West Side, but here it's less prettied up, although Columbia University, a major property owner in the area, has been bringing in more chic—and consequently more expensive—stores and restaurants.

Hamilton Heights, from 125th Street north to **Trinity Cemetery** (155th Street at Riverside Drive), is a former factory and ferry-landing town named for **Alexander Hamilton**, who built a country estate here in 1802. Other 19th-century buildings survive, but most of the development occurred after 1904, when the Broadway IRT subway opened. The area has remained primarily residential, and today, some of the most desirable residences are the turn-of-the-century row houses in the **Hamilton Heights Historic District. City College of New York (CCNY),** the northernmost Manhattan outpost of the **City University of New York (CUNY)** system, moved into the former campus of **Manhattanville College** (now located in Riverdale) in 1950.

Harlem, which becomes **East Harlem** east of Fifth Avenue, is Manhattan's black ghetto, where immigrants from the Caribbean and Africa and economic refugees from the American states live, often in inadequate conditions. Many people of Hispanic origin, mostly from Puerto Rico, have settled in East Harlem, renaming it *El Barrio* ("the neighborhood" in Spanish), while the later wave of Dominicans and Cubans have settled along upper Broadway (Broadway in the 140s is known as "Little Dominica"), and on the east side of Broadway as far north as **Inwood** (207th Street). The two Harlems are older than most black urban communities in this country, as well as larger, taking up six square miles from 110th Street north to the Harlem River and bounded on the east by the East River. Unlike in many other ghettos in the United States, housing stock was once excellent, and although much of it has deteriorated, it's still worth renovating—which is what increasing numbers of middle-class families are doing.

This section of the island was covered with wooded hills and valleys inhabited by Indians when the Dutch started the settlement of *Nieuw Haarlem* in 1658. Black slaves owned by the West India Company helped build a road, later called Broadway, and the *Haarlem* outpost grew. In the early 19th century, affluent Manhattanites, including **James Roosevelt**, built estates and plantations here. It was also a haven for the poor, with Irish immigrants among those who built shantytowns on the East River, where they raised free-roaming hogs, geese, sheep, and goats.

Harlem began to develop as a suburb for the well-to-do when the **New York and Harlem Railroad** started service from Lower Manhattan in 1837. More railway lines followed, and as handsome brownstones, schools, and stores went up, immigrant families who had achieved some degree of success, many of them German Jews, moved up from the Lower East Side.

The announcement that work was starting on the IRT Lenox subway line touched off another round of development, but this time the boom went bust. When the subway was completed in 1905, most of the buildings were still empty. Blacks began renting, often at inflated rates, after having been squeezed out of other parts of the city by commercial development. Eventually the only whites who remained were poor and lived on the fringes, and Harlem became *the* black community in the United States. The subsequent waves of blacks that poured in were often in need of jobs while lacking in skills and education.

Although many blacks in Harlem were existing at poverty level in the 1920s and 1930s, black culture blossomed in dance, drama, literature, and music here. Speakeasies flourished in the area during Prohibition, and the smart set came uptown to the **Sugar Cane Club** and the **Cotton Club** (now a private club) to hear **Count Basie, Duke Ellington**, and other jazz legends. **Lena Horne** got her start here, and literary giants **Langston Hughes** and **James Baldwin** were native sons.

In the 1950s, urban renewal made a dent in the declining housing stock by clearing blocks of slums and replacing them with housing developments. Gentrification began in Harlem in earnest in the 1970s and continues today, as middle-class families move into **Striver's Row** in the **St. Nicholas District** and to the **Mount Morris Park Historic District,** where the brownstones are among the city's finest. Still, Harlem is not a safe place to visit at night and, in some neighborhoods, during the day. (Try not to go alone, and always take taxis to and from your destination.)

Washington Heights, starting at Trinity Cemetery and going north to Dyckman Street, was once an Irish neighborhood. In addition to the descendants of the Irish, the area now has an ethnic mix of blacks, Puerto Ricans and other Latins, Greeks, and Armenians.

Audubon Terrace, a turn-of-the-century Beaux Arts museum complex, seems out of place at 155th and Broadway, where it's surrounded by housing projects and tenements. But the complex is easy to reach by subway and worth a visit. North and east of Audubon Terrace is the **Jumel Terrace Historic District.**

Another important Heights landmark is **Fort Tryon Park** (pronounced TRY-on), the site of **Fort Tryon,** the northernmost defense of **Fort Washington.** Its crowning jewel is the **Cloisters,** which houses the medieval collection of the **Metropolitan Museum of Art.** Just south of the Cloisters is a little-known shrine, the **St. Frances Cabrini Chapel.** Here, under the altar in a crystal casket, lies the body of **Mother Cabrini,** the patron saint of all immigrants. Above her neck is a wax mask, because her head is in Rome. (As the story goes, shortly after her death in 1917, a lock of her hair restored an infant's eyesight. That infant is now a priest in Texas.)

Inwood Hill Park, where Indian cave dwellers once lived, caps the northern end of the island with a rural flourish. Playing fields and open parkland with views over the Hudson and the **George Washington Bridge** and as far as the **Tappan Zee Bridge** are highlights, along with a wilderness of hackberry bushes, maples, Chinese white ash, and Oriental pine trees that stretch to the end of the island, where you can wander the trails and imagine what it was like when the Algonquin Indians had a forest paradise to themselves.

1 Thomas Jefferson Public Pool This outdoor public pool is open from the last Saturday in June until Labor Day. Call for the schedule and bring a padlock. ♦ E. 111th St and First Ave. 397.3112

2 Rao V ★★★$$$$ Judging from the limousines parked outside, you'd think this was the most exclusive Italian restaurant in Manhattan, and in some ways it is. Even with hard-to-come-by reservations, you might get squeezed out by **Sinatra** and his entourage. But take your chances, because this unassuming little bistro, run by the **Rao** family, is first-rate all the way. ♦ Italian ♦ Dinner. Closed Sunday. 455 E. 114th St (at Pleasant Ave). Reservations required well in advance. No credit cards. 534.9625

3 Arthur A. Schomburg Plaza These 35-story octagonal apartment towers, completed in 1975 by **Gruzen & Partners** and **Castro-Blanco, Piscioneri & Feder,** are distinguished markers at the corner of Central Park. The pairing of the balconies creates an original rhythm in moderating the scale. ♦ E. 110th and E. 111th Sts (between Madison and Fifth Aves). 491.2200

4 New York Public Library, 115th Street Branch This 1908 Renaissance composition in limestone, a style favored by architects **McKim, Mead & White,** is one of the finest of the branch libraries. ♦ M, Th-F 1-6PM; Tu 11AM-7PM; W 10AM-6PM. 203 W. 115th St (between Adam Clayton Powell Jr. and Frederick Douglass Blvds). 666.9393

5 St. Luke's Hospital At least the central entrance pavilion and east wing remain of **Ernest Flagg's** classical/baroque composition that includes a little something extra. The 1896 building is charming, dignified, slightly busy, and certainly original. ♦ Morningside Dr (between W. 113th and W. 114th Sts)

All that remains of Revolutionary War-era Fort Washington is the outline of the foundation, marked by paving stones, in Bennett Park. Here at Fort Washington Avenue, between 183rd and 185th streets, is the highest point in Manhattan, 267.75 feet above sea level.

6 The Cathedral Church of St. John the Divine Begun in 1892 under the sponsorship of **Bishop Henry Codman Potter** to designs by **Heins & LaFarge**, this giant, slightly rough Byzantine church (shown above) with Romanesque influences is still a work in progress. By 1911, the apse, choir, and crossing were done, the architects and the bishop were dead, and fashions had changed. Gothic enthusiast **Ralph Adams Cram** of **Cram & Ferguson** drew up new plans to complete the church. The nave and western facade are, therefore, fine French Gothic. Work was discontinued in 1941, but resumed in the 1980s in an effort to complete the cathedral, particularly the towers. In the stone yard in operation next to the church, two dozen artisans, many of them neighborhood youths, are working under a master mason from England to carve blocks in a centuries-old tradition.

When St. John's is finished (a project that will carry over into the next century), it will be the largest cathedral in the world. The nave is 601 feet long and 146 feet wide; when completed, the transepts will be just as wide and span 320 feet. The floor area is greater than **Chartres** and **Notre Dame** together, and the towers will be 300 feet high. Although not entirely complete, four of the five portals have been fitted with Burmese teak doors; the bronze door of the central portal was cast in Paris by **M. Barbedienne,** who cast the Statue of Liberty.

The interior is spectacular, with seven apsidal chapels in a variety of styles by a collection of prominent architects. The finest is that of **St. Ambrose,** a Renaissance-inspired composition by **Carrère & Hastings.** The eight granite columns that ring the sanctuary are 55 feet high and weigh 130 tons each. The dome

over the crossing, intended to be temporary, was erected in 1909. Master woodworker **George Nakashima's** massive heart-shaped **Altar for Peace,** cut from a 125-foot English walnut tree from Long Island and finished with his trademark rosewood inlays, is the site of monthly meditations for peace. The church hosts an impressive schedule of concerts, art exhibitions, lectures, and theater and dance events. ♦ Amsterdam Ave (at W. 112th St). 316.7540; box office 662.2133

7 Symposium $ Greek specialties like moussaka, spinach pie, and *exohiko* (lamb, feta cheese, artichoke hearts, and peas all wrapped up in a phyllo dough) are featured in this popular and comfortable spot. The atmosphere and food are strictly authentic. During spring and summer, the garden is available for dining. ♦ Greek ♦ Lunch and dinner. 544 W. 113th St (between Broadway and Amsterdam Ave). 865.1011

8 West End Gate Cafe Columbia University and the rest of the community are drawn here for the diverse entertainment programs, including jazz on Tuesday and Wednesday and music brunches followed by children's theater every Saturday. The basic American food is secondary. ♦ Cafe ♦ Daily 11AM-4AM. 2911 Broadway (between W. 113th and W. 114th Sts). 662.8830

8 Papyrus Booksellers The paperbacks here are geared to Columbia students, and the fine periodical section leans toward politics and the arts. ♦ M-Sa 9:30AM-11PM; Su 10AM-10PM. 2915 Broadway (at W. 114th St). 222.3350

9 Bookforum A bookstore located near Columbia naturally stocks a lot of scholarly paperbacks and books used in courses. This one also focuses on newly released hardcovers. You'll find older ones marked down on the tables outside. ♦ M-F 10AM-11PM; Sa 10AM-8PM; Su 10AM-7PM. 2955 Broadway (at W. 116th St). 749.5535

"In Manhattan, there are gardens on roofs, gardens outside basement apartments, and minigardens on miniterraces. How do the gardens grow? Expensively. And what do they grow? Almost anything. Apparently, even cash crops. Wildflowers have been tamed on tiny balconies, and families fed on vegetables nurtured in the alien soil bordered by sidewalks."

Ralph Caplan, writer and design consultant

On 21 January 1908, the first ordinance banning smoking was passed—not surprisingly, this ordinance applied to women only.

Restaurants/Clubs: Red   **Hotels:** Blue
Shops/ 🌳 Outdoors: Green   **Sights/Culture:** Black

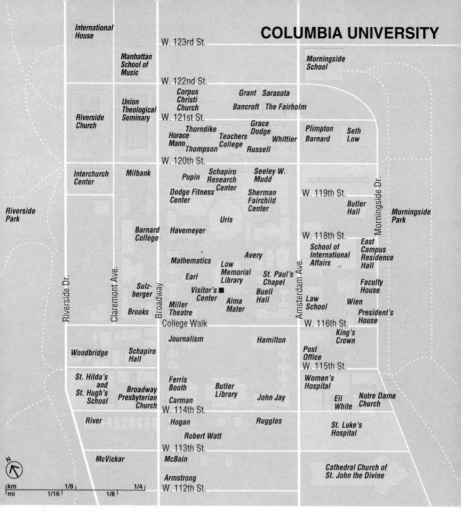

International House

W. 123rd St.

Manhattan School of Music

Morningside School

W. 122nd St.

Corpus Christi Church

Grant   Sarasota

Bancroft   The Fairholm

Riverside Church

Union Theological Seminary

W. 121st St.

Thorndike

Grace Dodge

Horace Mann   Teachers College   Whittier

Thompson

Russell

Plimpton Barnard

Seth Low

W. 120th St.

Interchurch Center

Milbank

Pupin

Schapiro Research Center

Seeley W. Mudd

Dodge Fitness Center

Sherman Fairchild Center

W. 119th St.

Butler Hall

Morningside Dr.

Morningside Park

Barnard College

Havemeyer

Uris

W. 118th St.

Mathematics

Avery

School of International Affairs

East Campus Residence Hall

Riverside Park

Riverside Dr.

Claremont Ave.

Earl

Low Memorial Library

St. Paul's Chapel

Faculty House

Sulzberger

Broadway

Visitor's Center

Buell Hall

Law School

Wien

Brooks

Miller Theatre

Alma Mater

Amsterdam Ave.

President's House

College Walk

W. 116th St.

Journalism

Hamilton

King's Crown

Woodbridge

Schapiro Hall

Post Office

W. 115th St.

St. Hilda's and St. Hugh's School

Broadway Presbyterian Church

Ferris Booth

Butler Library

Women's Hospital

Carman

John Jay

Eli White

Notre Dame Church

W. 114th St.

River

Hogan

Ruggles

St. Luke's Hospital

Robert Watt

W. 113th St.

McVickar

McBain

Cathedral Church of St. John the Divine

Armstrong

W. 112th St.

N

km   1/8   1/4
mi   1/16   1/8

10 Columbia University Founded in 1754, this historic Ivy League school has an enrollment of nearly 20,000. Now less politically outspoken than they were in the 1960s, the students have settled down to their studies in Columbia's three undergraduate schools: **Columbia College, School of General Studies,** and **School of Engineering and Applied Science.** On the site of the **Bloomingdale Insane Asylum** (of which Buell Hall is a remnant), the original design and early buildings of the campus (the third one Columbia has occupied) were planned by **Charles Follen McKim** of McKim, Mead & White in a grand Beaux Arts tradition. Although only a segment of his plan was completed in 1897, most of its elements can be discerned. The Italian Renaissance-inspired institutional buildings—in red brick with limestone trim and copper roofs—are arranged around a central quad on a terrace two stories above the street. There were to be six smaller side courts like the one between **Avery** and **Fayerweather Halls** (somewhat changed now due to the extension of **Avery Library**).

McKim's dominant central element is the magnificent **Low Memorial Library** (1897), a monumental pantheon named after the father of Columbia president **Seth Low** (who was also mayor of New York City from 1902 to 1903). No longer used as a library, Low remains the administrative and ceremonial center of the university. The statue of the *Alma Mater* on the front steps—made famous during the riots of 1968—was unveiled by **Daniel Chester French** in 1903.

Other noteworthy buildings on the Columbia campus include **Butler Library,** a colonnaded box facing Low, completed in 1934 by **James Gamble Rogers.** The **Sherman Fairchild Center for the Life Sciences,** a 1977 **Mitchell/Giurgola** creation, is an interesting contextual essay in which a glass-and-metal building has been hidden behind a screen of quarry tile that resembles the ground pavers. The **Law School** and **School of International Affairs** extension, built in 1963 and 1971 by **Harrison & Abramovitz,** form a great white mass beyond a block-long bridge that spans Amsterdam Avenue. Charming and modest, the Byzantine/Renaissance **St. Paul's Chapel,** a 1907 work by **Howell & Stokes,** has an interior that is lovely, vaulted, and light. Tours of the campus, which originate at Low Library (854.2845), are given according to public interest and the availability of guides. Call in advance. The main entrance is at W. 116th Street. ♦ Bounded by W. 114th and W. 120th Sts, Amsterdam Ave, and Broadway. 854.1754

11 Barnard College The 2,200-student women's school, an undergraduate college of **Columbia University,** offers bachelor's degrees in 27 majors, with an emphasis on liberal arts. Across Broadway from the elegant expanse of Columbia, the Barnard campus appears crowded but somehow more lively. The older buildings at the north end—**Millbank, Brinkerhoff,** and **Fiske Halls**—were designed by **Lamb & Rich** in the 1890s in a sort of New England academic style. More interesting is the heart of the campus today: the limestone counterpoints of **MacIntosh Center** and **Altschul Hall,** both built by Philadelphia architect **Vincent G. Kling** in 1969. In 1989, 400 students moved into **Centennial Hall,** a 17-story tower at the southern end of campus, designed by **James Stewart Polshek & Partners.** ♦ Bounded by W. 116th and W. 120th Sts, Broadway, and Claremont Ave. 854.5262

12 Union Theological Seminary Bookstore Here you'll find any and all in-print books and periodicals that concern theology. ♦ M-F 9AM-5PM. 3041 Broadway (at W. 120th St). 662.7100

13 Union Theological Seminary In a landscape studded with institutions, this is one of the few that truly manages to keep the city at bay. Designed by **Allen & Collens** in 1910 with alterations by **Collens, Willis & Beckonert** in 1952, the building is an example of collegiate Gothic borrowed from Oxbridge and, in that tradition, it has a secluded interior courtyard. ♦ Bounded by W. 120th and W. 122nd Sts, Broadway, and Claremont Ave

Billie Holiday called her home at 108 W. 193rd Street "a combination YMCA, boardinghouse for broke musicians, soup kitchen for anyone with a hard luck story, community center, and after-hours joint where a couple of bucks would get you a shot of whiskey and the most fabulous fried chicken."

Manhattan measures 13.4 miles long and is only 2.3 miles across. Within the total area of the five boroughs, the longest distance between its boundaries is 35 miles, from the northeast to the southwest.

Restaurants/Clubs: Red   Hotels: Blue
Shops/ 🌳 Outdoors: Green   Sights/Culture: Black

14 Riverside Church This church (shown above) was built in 1930 by **Allen & Collens Henry C. Pelton,** and **Burnham Hoyt,** with a south wing added in 1960 by **Collens, Willis & Beckonert.** Funded by **John D. Rockefeller, Jr.,** it is a steel frame in a thin, institutional Gothic skin. The fine nave is almost overpowered by the tower, which rises 21 stories, and the 74-bell carillon is the largest in the world. Visit the **Observation Deck** in the tower, not only to look at the bells on the way up but for a splendid view of the Hudson, Riverside Park, and the surrounding institutions. Forty-five-minute guided tours are offered Sunday at 12:30PM, after services. ♦ Daily 9AM-5PM. Observation deck: Sunday 12:30-4PM. Carillon bell concerts: Sunday 10:30AM, noon, 3PM. Riverside Dr (between W. 120th and W. 122nd Sts). 222.5900

Within Riverside Church:

Theater at Riverside Church For more than a decade, dancers and choreographers tested their mettle on this tiny stage as part of the **Riverside Dance Festival.** These days, the church no longer sponsors performances, but still opens its doors to theater, music, video, and dance productions. ♦ 864.2929

15 Grant's Tomb/General Grant National Memorial Now's the time to pose the infamous college exam question: who is buried in Grant's Tomb? The massive granite mausoleum, designed in 1897 by **John H. Duncan,** is set on a hill overlooking the river, thereby dominating its surroundings. The walk to the tomb is impressive: you pass along the terrace, up the stairs, through the colonnade and bronze doors, and find yourself under a high dome looking down on the identical black marble sarcophagi of the general and his wife in the center of a rotunda—an open crypt similar to **Napoléon's** tomb at the **Hôtel des Invalides** in Paris. It's surrounded by bronze busts of the general's comrades-in-arms and by allegorical figures between the arches representing scenes from his life. Photographs in two flanking rooms fill in with more realistic details. More fun, however, are the benches on the outside, created in 1973 by **Pedro Silva** of the **Cityarts Workshop.** The bright mosaic decorations were done by community residents. Make this trip in daytime only, as Grant's Tomb at night attracts some unsavory characters. Oh, yes, the answer: **Ulysses S. Grant** and his wife, **Julia.** ♦ Free. W-Su 9AM-5PM. Riverside Dr (at W. 122nd St). 666.1640

16 Teachers College, Bancroft Hall A stew of abstracted details—basically Beaux Arts Renaissance but with a touch of Spanish and a pinch of Art Nouveau—enliven the facade of this apartment house, designed in 1911 by **Emery Roth.** ♦ 509 W. 121st St (between Amsterdam Ave and Broadway)

17 The Terrace ★★★$$$$ The views alone—skyscrapers to the south and the glittering **George Washington Bridge** to the northwest—would make a trip to this unusual location worthwhile. But everything, from soup to dessert, is also wonderful. Sometimes the chef's original ideas are high-reaching, but his technical mastery pulls him through. The warm lobster salad, homemade pasta, and chocolate mousse are especially good. ♦ French ♦ Lunch and dinner. Closed Monday and Sunday. 400 W. 119th St (at Morningside Dr). Reservations recommended. 666.9490

18 28th Precinct Station House Architects **Lehrecke & Tonetti** did a particularly good job on a difficult triangular site when designing this station in 1974, which shows a subtle sensibility in terms of material and massing that is similar to the work of the late, great **Louis I. Kahn.** ♦ 2271 Frederick Douglass Blvd (between W. 122nd and W. 123rd Sts)

19 Frank Silvera Writers' Workshop Founded in 1973 by **Garland Lee Thompson,** this workshop/theater is a memorial to the late **Frank Silvera,** who was active in nurturing black writers. Productions include *No Left Turn* by **Buriel Clay II** and *Inacent Black and Five Brothers* by **Marcus Hemphill.** Monday evenings feature readings and critiques of new plays. Check the schedule for seminars on play- and screenwriting. ♦ 317 W. 125th St (at St. Nicholas Ave), third floor. 662.8463

20 The Apollo This former vaudeville house, designed by **George Keister** and built in 1914, became the entertainment center of the black community in the 1930s, and by the 1950s it was *the* venue for black popular music. A decade later, however, the Apollo fell on hard times as big-name acts began playing larger downtown houses. It wasn't until the early 1980s, when it was rescued by **Inner City Broadcasting,** that the faded theater was given a much-needed face-lift and turned into a showplace for black television productions as well as live entertainment. Wednesday

amateur nights are always fun and packed with budding talents. ♦ 253 W. 125th St (between Adam Clayton Powell Jr. and Frederick Douglass Blvds). No credit cards. 749.5838

21 New York State Office Building Ifill-Johnson-Hanchard designed this overbearing monument of glass and concrete on a vast, unpopulated site in 1973. It was more a political gesture than a necessary building. ♦ 163 W. 125th St (at Adam Clayton Powell Jr. Blvd)

22 Studio Museum in Harlem Changing exhibitions of black art and culture from Africa, the Caribbean, and America are featured in this small museum of black fine arts. Year-round education programs, including the well-known *Vital Expression in American Art,* offer lectures, concerts, and poetry readings. ♦ Admission. W-F 10AM-5PM; Sa-Su 1-6PM. 144 W. 125th St (between Lenox Ave and Adam Clayton Powell Jr. Blvd). 864.4500

23 Sylvia's ★★$$ The most renowned soul-food restaurant in Harlem and perhaps in New York City has expanded into a second dining room and, during the warmer months, into an open patio next door. Southern-fried and smothered chicken are standouts, as are the dumplings, "candied sweets" (yams), and dessert puddings. The atmosphere is reminiscent of a luncheonette. ♦ Southern ♦ Breakfast, lunch, and dinner; Sunday 1-7PM. 328 Lenox Ave (between W. 126th and W. 127th Sts). 996.0660

24 National Black Theater Courses, readings, performance workshops, and productions all take place at this 99-seat theater. ♦ 2033 Fifth Ave (at E. 125th St). 722.3800

25 Mount Morris Park Historical District The charming Victorian character of this district, designated historic in 1971, was established during the speculative boom at the end of the 19th century, when it was urbanized by descendants of Dutch, Irish, and English immigrants. After 1900, it became a primarily German-Jewish neighborhood. The houses on Lenox Avenue between 120th and 121st streets, designed by **Demeuron & Smith** in 1888, are particularly captivating. The **Morris Apartments** at 81-85 E. 125th Street, built just a year later by **Lamb & Rich,** now house the **Mount Morris Bank and Safety Deposit Vaults.** The building is distinguished by Richardsonian Romanesque arches and stained glass.

The district also has a fine collection of religious buildings. Dating from 1907, the neoclassical **Mount Olivet Baptist Church,** at 201 Lenox Avenue, was originally designed by **Arnold Brunner** as **Temple Israel,** one of the most prestigious synagogues in the city. **St. Martin's Episcopal Church,** on Lenox Avenue at 122nd Street, is a bulky, asymmetrical Romanesque 1888 composition by **William A. Potter** with a carillon of 40 bells, second in size only to that of Riverside Church. Built in 1889 by Lamb & Rich, the **Bethel Gospel Pentecostal Assembly,** at 36 W. 123rd Street, used to be the **Harlem Club.** The **Greater Bethel AME Church,** built in 1892 by Lamb & Rich, was originally the **Harlem Free Library.** Originally the **Dwight Residence, Frank H. Smith's** 1890 building at 1 W. 123rd Street is now the home of the **Ethiopian Hebrew Congregation.** It is a Renaissance mansion with an unusual round- and flat-bayed front that is a strong addition to the block of fine brownstones on W. 123rd Street. ♦ Bounded by W. 119th and W. 124th Sts, Mt. Morris Park West, and Lenox Ave

26 **Marcus Garvey Memorial Park** When the city purchased this craggy square of land in 1839, it was named **Mount Morris Park.** It was renamed in 1973 for Garvey, who was a brilliant orator and the founder of the **Universal Negro Improvement Association** and of the now-defunct newspaper *Negro World.* The highland in the center supports an 1856 fire watchtower, the only one surviving in the city. Its steel frame and sweeping spiral stairs, once practical innovations, are now nostalgic. ♦ Bounded by W. 120th and W. 124th Sts, Madison Ave, and Mt. Morris Park West

27 **Harlem Courthouse** Constructed with a mix of brick and stone, the Romanesque edifice was built in 1891 to the designs of **Thom & Wilson.** With its gables, archways, and corner tower, the dignified and delicate mass represents the American tradition of great "country" courthouses. ♦ 170 E. 121st St (between Third and Lexington Aves)

28 **Patsy's Pizzeria** ★$ It's still worth a side trip to East Harlem for one of the best slices— and pies—in the city. Countertop connoisseurs will love the thin crust and perfect balance of ingredients. ♦ Pizza ♦ Lunch, dinner, and late-night meals. 2287 First Ave (at E. 118th St). No credit cards. 534.9783

29 **Triborough Bridge** A lift span connects Manhattan and Randalls Island, a fixed roadway springs from Randalls Island to the Bronx, and a suspension span crosses the Hell Gate. The impressive connector-collection was designed by **Othmar Ammann** and **Aymar Embury II** in 1936. ♦ From Harlem River Dr at E. 125th St, Manhattan to Grand Central Expwy, Queens to Bruckner Expwy, the Bronx

30 **All Saints Church** This fine group of buildings shows the Gothic influence of architect **James Renwick, Jr.** The firm he founded, **Renwick, Aspinwall & Russell,** built the church in 1894 and the rectory in 1889, and the school was built by **W.W. Renwick** in 1904. Some say this work is more pleasing than **St. Patrick's Cathedral,** also a Renwick creation. Especially worthwhile is the harmony of the terracotta tracery and buff, honey, and brown brick. ♦ E. 129th St (at Madison Ave)

31 **Riverbend Houses** The complex of 625 apartments for moderate-income families is respectful of context and use of material, while assembled with great style and imagination. Built in 1967 by **Davis, Brody & Associates,** the complex is a landmark in the recent tradition of publicly subsidized housing. ♦ Fifth Ave (between E. 135th and E. 138th Sts)

32 **Schomburg Center for Research in Black Culture** The largest library of black and African culture in the United States, collected by Puerto Rican black **Arthur Schomburg** (1874-1938), is housed in this research center. Occasionally there are shows by African and black American artists. ♦ Free. M-W noon-8PM; Th-Sa 10AM-6PM. 515 Lenox Ave (at W. 135th St). 491.2200

33 **Abyssinian Baptist Church** Built in 1923 by **Charles W. Bolton,** this bluestone Gothic Tudor building is renowned for its late pastor, U.S. Congressman **Adam Clayton Powell, Jr.** Founded in 1808, it is New York's oldest black church. ♦ 132 W. 138th St (between Lenox Ave and Adam Clayton Powell Jr. Blvd)

34 **St. Nicholas Historic District/King Model Houses** In an unusual and highly successful 1891 venture, speculative builder **David King** chose three architects to design the row housing on these three blocks. Nos. 202 to 250 W. 138th Street and 2350 to 2354 Adam Clayton Powell Jr. Boulevard are by **James Brown Lord,** all in simple Georgian red brick on a brownstone base. Nos. 203 to 271 W. 138th Street, 2360 to 2390 Adam Clayton Powell Jr. Boulevard, and 202 to 272 W. 139th Street are by **Bruce Price** and **Clarence S. Luce.** Nos. 203 to 267 W. 139th Street and 1380 to 1390 Adam Clayton Powell Jr. Boulevard are the finest—elegantly detailed, Renaissance-inspired designs by **McKim, Mead & White.** The harmony of the ensemble, achieved through similarity of scale and sensitive design, despite the variety of styles and materials, is extraordinary. The area came to be known as "Striver's Row," the home of the area's young and professionally ambitious. It was designated a historic district in 1967. ♦ Bounded by W. 138th and W. 139th Sts, and Adam Clayton Powell Jr. and Frederick Douglass Blvds

35 Jamaican Hot Pot ★★$ Yvonne Richards and **Gary Walters** turn out fabulous Jamaican specialties—fried chicken and oxtail stew are just two winning dishes. Locals love this place. ♦ Jamaican ♦ Lunch, dinner, and late-night meals. 2260 Adam Clayton Powell Jr. Blvd (at W. 133rd St). 491.5270

36 P.S. 92 This 1965 work of **Percival Goodman** is elegantly articulated and warmly detailed. ♦ 222 W. 134th St (between Adam Clayton Powell Jr. and Frederick Douglass Blvds)

37 135th Street Gatehouse, Croton Aqueduct Built in 1890, this brownstone and granite watchtower, a Roman echo, was the end of the aqueduct over High Bridge. From here, water was taken in pipes to W. 119th Street, by an aqueduct under Amsterdam Avenue, to W. 113th Street, and then by pipe again to the city. Finely crafted gatehouses still stand at W. 119th and W. 113th streets. ♦ At Convent Ave

38 City College/City University of New York Nearly 12,000 students—75-percent of them minorities—attend classes at this 34-acre campus. Bachelor's and master's degrees are offered in liberal arts, education, engineering, architecture, and nursing. The science programs are also noteworthy. The campus is an ornately costumed, energetic collection of white-trimmed, neo-Gothic buildings constructed of Manhattan schist excavated during the construction of the IRT subway. The old campus, completed in 1905 by **George B. Post,** is especially wonderful in contrast to the more recent buildings that have grown up around it. The Romanesque south campus used to be **Manhattanville College of the Sacred Heart,** originally an academy and convent. ♦ Bounded by W. 130th and W. 140th Sts, St. Nicholas Terr, and Amsterdam Ave. 650.7000

Within City College:

Aaron Davis Hall at City College Located in the **Leonard Davis Performing Arts Center,** this multiarts theater hosts, among others, the **Dance Theater of Harlem** and the **Negro Ensemble Company.** ♦ W. 135th St (at Convent Ave)

39 Harlem School of the Arts (HSA) In 1965, soprano **Dorothy Maynor** began teaching piano in the basement of the **St. James Presbyterian Church Community Center.** From that modest beginning, the Harlem School of the Arts has grown to 1,300 students (from four-year-olds to senior citizens, with the majority falling between the ages of four and 18), and has gained national prominence as a performing arts school. Several former students and teachers now have active Broadway careers. With world-famous mezzo-soprano **Betty Allen** as

president, the school now teaches musical instrument study (piano, orchestral string, percussion), ballet and modern dance, and visual and dramatic arts. (The orchestral string department is especially noteworthy; the 23-member **Suzuki Ensemble,** made up of eight- to 17-year-olds, is known throughout the city.) Through the Opportunities for Learning in the Arts program, students from other schools are brought in to take classes during the day. The Community and Culture in Harlem program hosts concerts, art exhibitions, and readings. The school's award-winning building, a 1977 work of **Ulrich Franzen & Associates,** is a complex marriage of classrooms, practice studios, three large dance studios, auditoriums, offices, and an enclosed garden. An adjacent building holds the 200-seat **Harlem School of the Arts Theater.** ♦ 645 St. Nicholas Ave (at W. 141st St). 926.4100

40 Hamilton Heights Historic District The Hamilton Heights area, designated historic in 1974, was once the country estate of **Alexander Hamilton.** His house, the **Grange,** stands at Convent Avenue and W. 141st Street next to **St. Luke's.** The district has a generally high-quality collection of row houses dating from the turn of the century that exhibit a mixture of styles and a wealth of ornament. W. 144th Street is exemplary. The row at Nos. 413 to 423, designed in 1898 by **T.H. Dunn,** has Venetian Gothic, Italian, and French Renaissance elements. Because there is very little through traffic, the neighborhood has always been slightly secluded and desirable. It is occupied primarily by faculty from nearby **City College.** ♦ Bounded by W. 141st and W. 145th Sts, Hamilton Terr, and Convent Ave

The small area known as Marble Hill is actually part of Manhattan. It was originally a peninsula at the northern tip of the island. The Spuyten-Duyvil Creek (Dutch for Spout-Devil), which separated Marble Hill from the mainland (the Bronx), was too narrow for ships. In 1895, the creek was filled (with dirt from the excavation of Grand Central Station), and the channel at the apex of the Harlem River was straightened and deepened. The latter action pushed Marble Hill up into the Bronx. This created a bit of an uproar, as the residents were not thrilled about losing their status as Manhattanites. They quickly drafted a successful petition to remain part of the island politically, if not physically.

40 Aunt Len's Doll and Toy Museum
Although closed indefinitely at press time, do call to see if Aunt Len's has reopened. It's a treat. More than 5,000 dolls and toys, collected by a former school teacher, **Mrs. Lennon Holder Hoyte,** fill up this typical Hamilton Terrace row house. ♦ 6 Hamilton Terr (at W. 141st St). 281.4143

41 Our Lady of Lourdes Church Truly a scavenger's monument, this 1904 church by the **O'Reilly Brothers** is composed of pieces from three other buildings: the Ruskinian Gothic gray and white marble and bluestone facade on 142nd Street is from the old **National Academy of Design,** built in 1865 by **P.B. Wight,** that stood at 23rd Street and Park Avenue South; and the apse and part of the east wall were once the Madison Avenue end of **St. Patrick's Cathedral**—removed for the construction of the Lady Chapel. The pedestals flanking the steps are from **A.T. Stewart's** palatial department store, which stood on 34th Street at Fifth Avenue when it was built by **John Kellum** in 1867. ♦ 467 W. 142nd St (between Convent and Amsterdam Aves)

42 Copeland's ★$$ Southern style goes Continental with Louisiana gumbo, barbecued jumbo shrimp, and live dinner music on Friday, Saturday, and Sunday. ♦ Southern/Continental ♦ Dinner; lunch also on Sunday. Closed Monday. 547 W. 145th St (between Amsterdam Ave and Broadway). Reservations recommended. 234.2357

43 Harlem River Houses This exemplary complex consisting of nine acres of public housing developed by the **Federal Administration of Public Works** was built in 1937 by **Archibald Manning Brown** with **Charles F. Fuller, Horace Ginsberg, Frank J. Forster, Will Rice Amon, Richard W. Buckley,** and **John L. Wilson. Michael Rapuano** was the landscape architect. An energetic variety of building shapes are arranged in three groups around a central plaza and landscaped courts, becoming less formal nearer the river. The sculpture inside the 151st Street entrance is by **Paul Manship,** who also did the *Prometheus* at **Rockefeller Center.** ♦ Bounded by W. 151st and W. 153rd Sts, Harlem River Dr, and Macombs Pl

44 32nd Precinct Station House (Former) Dating from 1872, this Victorian work by **N.D. Bush** features a cast-iron crest and mansard roof. ♦ 1854 Amsterdam Ave (at W. 152nd St)

45 Trinity Cemetery This hilly cemetery used to be a part of the estate of American naturalist **J.J. Audubon,** who is among those buried here. Others include many members of families that made New York, such as the **Schermerhorns, Astors, Bleeckers,** and **Van Burens.** At Christmastime, the grave of **Clement Clarke Moore** draws special attention—he wrote *A Visit from St. Nicholas* ("Twas the night before Christmas"). The boundary walls and gates date from 1876; the gatehouse and keeper's lodge were designed in 1883 by **Vaux & Redford;** and the grounds were laid out in 1881 by **Vaux & Co.** ♦ Daily 8AM-dusk. Bounded by W. 153rd and W. 155th Sts, and Amsterdam Ave and Riverside Dr. 602.0787

At Trinity Cemetery:

Chapel of the Intercession Built in 1914 by **Cram, Goodhue & Ferguson,** this chapel is essentially a large country church set in the middle of rural Trinity Cemetery. The cloister at the W. 155th Street entrance is particularly nice, and the richly detailed interior is marvelous, highlighted by an altar inlaid with stones from the Holy Land and sites of early Christian worship. The ashes of architect **Bertram Goodhue** are entombed in a memorial in the north transept. ♦ Broadway (at W. 155th St)

46 Audubon Terrace This collection of classical buildings was first planned in 1908, and bankrolled by poet and scholar **Archer M. Huntington.** The master plan was created by **Charles Pratt Huntington,** his nephew, who also designed five of the buildings: the **Museum of the American Indian, Heye Foundation,** built in 1916; the **American Geographic Society,** built in 1916; the **Hispanic Society of America** (north building, constructed in 1916; south building, constructed between 1910 and 1926); the **American Numismatic Society,** built in 1908; and the **Church of Our Lady of Esperanza,** built in 1912. The green-and-gold interior of the church is rather nice; the stained glass, skylight, and lamps were gifts of the king of Spain, who also knighted the architect. The two buildings of the **American Academy and Institute of Arts and Letters** are by **William M. Kendall** (administration building, constructed in 1923) and **Cass Gilbert** (auditorium and gallery, built in 1930). ♦ Broadway (between W. 155th and W. 156th Sts)

At Audubon Terrace:

National Museum of the American Indian (Smithsonian Institution) It's worth traveling all the way uptown to see one of the largest collections of American Indian artifacts in the world, though not enough people do. Started from the private collection of **George G. Heye,** the material displayed runs the gamut from prehistoric to contemporary illustrations of the aesthetic contributions and daily lives of the Indians in North, Central, and South America. The dazzling array of items includes Iroquois masks, Apache playing cards, Mexican play figurines, **William Penn's** Wampum belts, personal possessions of **Geronimo** and

Sitting Bull, and shrunken human figures from the Jivaro Indians of Ecuador. The presentations run from excellent to jumbled, so if the often sketchy labels whet your appetite for more information, try the **Museum Shop,** where you'll find an exhaustive stock of books on Indian cultures as well as high-quality jewelry, rugs, paintings, *molas,* and other Indian crafts at fair prices. ♦ Admission. Tu-Sa 10AM-5PM; Su 1-5PM. 3753 Broadway (at W. 155th St). 283.2420

Hispanic Society of America
The museum of the Hispanic Society is in a lavishly appointed building lined with the paintings of old masters—**El Greco, Goya, Velázquez**—archaeological finds, ceramics, and other decorative arts of the Iberian Peninsula. The library in the building across the terrace is an important research center.
♦ Free. Tu-Sa 10AM-4:30PM; Su 1-4PM. 613 W. 155th St (at Broadway). 926.2234

American Numismatic Society
Downstairs are rotating examples of the world's coinage—past and present—and a display of medals and decorations. On the second floor is the most comprehensive numismatic library in America. For collectors, a **Public Inquiry Counter** is staffed by a curator to answer questions. Write or call in advance to get help with investigating a specific type of coinage in the collection.
♦ Free. Tu-Sa 9AM-4:30PM; Su 1-4PM. Broadway (at W. 155th St). 234.3130

American Academy and Institute of Arts and Letters
View regular exhibitions of the work of members and nonmembers of this honor society for American writers, artists, and composers. ♦ Free. M-F 9:30AM-5PM. 633 W. 155th St (between Broadway and Riverside Dr). 368.5900

47 Wilson's Bakery & Restaurant ★★$$
Having a bakery next door ensures the freshest baked goods at the restaurant—the perfect complement to the outstanding baked ribs. Wilson's is a Harlem institution.
♦ Bakery/Southern ♦ Breakfast, lunch, and dinner. 1980 Amsterdam Ave (at W. 158th St). 923.9821

New York City post offices once used underground pneumatic tubes to rush mail between branches at speeds four times faster than could be reached via the streets.

According to New York common law, it is acceptable and even encouraged to sit on a stoop and drink beer from the bottle, as long as it is in a brown paper bag. It is both illegal and a sign of low breeding to drink beer from an uncovered bottle.

48 Morris-Jumel Mansion Built in 1765 by **Roger Morris** as a summer residence on an estate that stretched from river to river, the mansion's two-story portico (shown above) became the model for many houses built in Canada and the United States at the turn of the century. During the Revolution, **George Washington** *did* sleep here, and even briefly used it as a headquarters, until New York City was taken over by the British. After housing a tavern, the mansion was bought and remodeled by French merchant **Stephen Jumel.** The exterior of the house is Georgian Palladian, with some details added in the Federal period; note the conceit of the quoins—a stone form mimicked in wood.

Inside, the elegant home is decorated with excellent Georgian, Federal, and French Empire-style furnishings, silver, and china. Some draperies were woven by master fabric-maker **Franco Scalamandre** using period patterns, and some of **Napoléon's** furniture is here. In 1833, **Aaron Burr** and the newly widowed **Madame Jumel** were married in the front parlor room. Museum educators and volunteers now conduct guided tours of the house, and lectures and concerts are held here as well. Picnickers are welcome to use the colonial herb and rose gardens. Around the mansion is the **Jumel Terrace Historic District,** designated in 1970, a charming neighborhood of well-kept 19th-century row houses. ♦ Admission. Tu-Su 10AM-4PM. 1765 Jumel Terr (Edgecombe Ave at W. 160th St). 923.8008

49 Columbia-Presbyterian Medical Center Affiliated with **Columbia University,** this enormous hospital complex continues to grow. The hospital enjoys the reputation of being a top-notch teaching facility and working hospital, and it has stabilized the neighborhood it serves. ♦ 622 W. 168th St (between Broadway and Riverside Dr). 305.2500

50 High Bridge Originally an aqueduct as well, this footbridge is the oldest bridge extant connecting Manhattan to the mainland. Construction lasted from 1839 to 1849. The architect, **John B. Jervis,** also designed the **Highbridge Tower** in 1872, which was used to equalize pressure in the Croton Aqueduct.
♦ From Highbridge Park at W. 174th St, Manhattan, to W. 170th St at University Ave, the Bronx

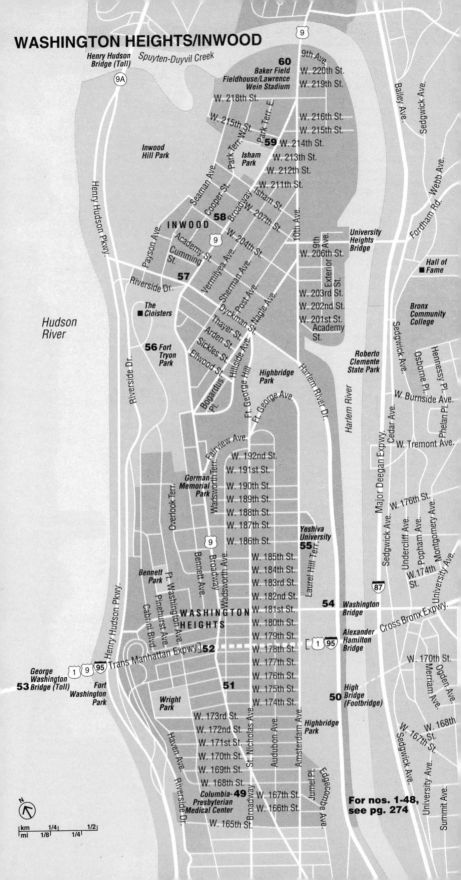

WASHINGTON HEIGHTS/INWOOD

Henry Hudson Bridge (Toll)

Spuyten-Duyvil Creek

60 Baker Field Fieldhouse/Lawrence Wein Stadium

9th Ave
W. 220th St.
W. 219th St.

Bailey Ave.

Sedgwick Ave.

W. 218th St.

Park Terr. E.

W. 216th St.
W. 215th St.

Inwood Hill Park

Park Terr. W.

W. 215th St.

59 W. 214th St.
W. 213th St.
W. 212th St.
W. 211th St.

Isham Park

Isham St.

Fordham Rd.

Webb Ave.

Seaman Ave.

Cooper St.

Broadway

7th Ave

10th Ave

INWOOD

58 W. 207th St.

University Heights Bridge

Payson Ave.

Academy St.

Cumming St.

W. 204th St.

9

W. 206th St.

9th Ave

Exterior St.

Hall of Fame

Parson Ave.

Riverside Dr.

57

Vermilyea Ave.

Sherman Ave.

Post Ave.

Nagle Ave.

W. 203rd St.
W. 202nd St.
W. 201st St.

Academy St.

Bronx Community College

The Cloisters

Dyckman St.

Thayer St.

Arden St.

Sickles St.

Eltwood St.

Hillside Ave.

Highbridge Park

Harlem River Dr.

Roberto Clemente State Park

Sedgwick Ave.

Hennessy Pl.

Osborne Pl.

Phelan Pl.

56 Fort Tryon Park

Bogardus Pl.

Ft. George Hill

Ft. George Ave.

Harlem River

W. Burnside Ave.

Cedar Ave.

Riverside Dr.

W. Tremont Ave.

Hudson River

Fairview Ave.

W. 192nd St.
W. 191st St.
W. 190th St.
W. 189th St.
W. 188th St.
W. 187th St.
W. 186th St.

Wadsworth Terr.

Gorman Memorial Park

Overlook Terr.

Major Deegan Expwy.

Sedgwick Ave.

W. 176th St.

Undercliff Ave.

Popham Ave.

Montgomery Ave.

W. 174th St.

Yeshiva University

55

W. 185th St.
W. 184th St.
W. 183rd St.
W. 182nd St.
W. 181st St.
W. 180th St.
W. 179th St.
W. 178th St.
W. 177th St.
W. 176th St.
W. 175th St.
W. 174th St.

Bennett Park

Ft. Washington Ave.

Pinehurst Ave.

Cabrini Blvd.

Bennett Ave.

Wadsworth Ave.

Broadway

Laurel Hill Terr.

87

54 Washington Bridge

Cross Bronx Expwy.

WASHINGTON HEIGHTS

Alexander Hamilton Bridge

1 95

W. 170th St.

Ogden Ave.

Merriam Ave.

53 George Washington Bridge (Toll)

1 9 95

Trans Manhattan Expwy. **52**

Fort Washington Park

Wright Park

51

St. Nicholas Ave.

Audubon Ave.

Amsterdam Ave.

50 High Bridge (Footbridge)

Highbridge Park

W. 168th St.

Sedgwick Ave.

W. 167th St.

Haven Ave.

Riverside Dr.

W. 173rd St.
W. 172nd St.
W. 171st St.
W. 170th St.
W. 169th St.
W. 168th St.

Jumel Pl.

Edgecombe Ave.

University Ave.

Summit Ave.

Columbia-Presbyterian Medical Center **49**

Broadway

W. 167th St.
W. 166th St.
W. 165th St.

For nos. 1-48, see pg. 274

N

km   1/4   1/2
mi 1/8   1/4

51 The United Church When it was erected in 1930 by **Thomas W. Lamb,** this building was **Loew's 175th Street Theater.** The Miami-Egyptian concoction is movie palace architecture at the height of its glory. It's one of the few remaining movie palaces in Manhattan *not* to suffer from the sixplex syndrome, but the stage has been given over to **Reverend Ike,** the "positive-thinking" preacher. ♦ 4140 Broadway (at W. 175th St). 568.6700

52 George Washington Bridge Bus Station This concrete butterfly is a noteworthy attempt at celebrating the bus station in the shadow of a grand bridge. It was constructed in 1963 by the **Port Authority of New York** in collaboration with architect/engineer **Pier Luigi Nervi.** ♦ W. 178th St (between Broadway and Fort Washington Ave). Bus information 564.1114

53 George Washington Bridge In 1947, French architect and master of Modernism **Le Corbusier** said this spectacularly sited and magnificently elegant suspension bridge with its 3,500-foot span was "the most beautiful bridge in the world . . . it gleams like a reversed arch. It is blessed." If the original plans had been completed, architectural consultant **Cass Gilbert** would have encased the towers in stone. The work of **Othmar Amman,** the bridge took four years to build and was completed in 1931. In 1962, it was expanded to become the world's first 14-lane suspension bridge. The roadway peaks at 212 feet above the water and the towers rise 604 feet. Today, the CMI Engineering landmark is the world's busiest bridge, with a hundred million vehicles traveling across it yearly. For pedestrians, there is a good view of the bridge from W. 181st Street, west of Fort Washington. But the real heart-thumper is a walk across the bridge itself. ♦ From W. 178th St at Hudson River, Manhattan to Fort Lee, New Jersey

54 Little Red Lighthouse Now overshadowed by the eastern tower of the **George Washington Bridge,** this was built in 1921 to steer barges away from **Jeffrey's Hook.** Because navigation lights were put on the bridge, the lighthouse went up for auction in 1951, but the community's support saved it. The pair is the subject of a well-known children's book by **Hildegarde Hoyt Swift** entitled *The Little Red Lighthouse and the Great Gray Bridge.* ♦ Fort Washington Park (at Washington Bridge)

55 Yeshiva University Yeshiva, the oldest Jewish studies center in the country, celebrated its centennial in 1986. The independent university offers both undergraduate and graduate degrees in programs ranging from Hebraic studies to biomedicine, law, and rabbinics. Also part of the university are the **Albert Einstein College of Medicine,** Bronx; **Brookdale Center-Cardozo School of Law,** Greenwich Village; and **Stern College for Women,** Midtown. The main building of its Washington Heights campus was built in 1928 by **Charles B. Meyers Associates.** It's characterized by a fanciful, romantic composition of institutional underpinnings overlaid with a Middle Eastern collection of turrets, towers and tracery, minarets, arches, and balconies—all in an unusual orange, with marble and granite striping. The light in the auditorium is especially extraordinary, with mirrored chandeliers and orange and yellow windows. ♦ W. 186th St (at Amsterdam Ave). 960.5400

56 Fort Tryon Park This 62-acre park, with its sweeping views of the Hudson River, is beyond exquisite. Originally the **C.K.G. Billings** estate (whose entrance was the triple-arched driveway from Riverside Drive), the land was bought by **John D. Rockefeller, Jr.,** in 1909 and given to the city in 1930. (As part of the gift, the city had to agree to close off the ends of several streets above 60th Street to create the site for **Rockefeller University.**) There are still signs of **Fort Tryon,** a Revolutionary War bulwark. Don't miss the magnificent flower gardens. The landscaping is by **Frederick Law Olmsted, Jr.** ♦ Bounded by W. 192nd and Dyckman Sts, Broadway, and Riverside Dr

"Gotham," a term for New York, was coined by Washington Irving in his early 19th-century satire *A History of New York.* In it he also introduced the word "Knickerbockers" for New Yorkers. Also the author of *Rip Van Winkle* and *The Legend of Sleepy Hollow,* Irving's works garnered some of the first serious international recognition for American literature.

"New York had all the iridescence of the beginning of the world."

F. Scott Fitzgerald, *The Crack-up*

Restaurants/Clubs: Red   **Hotels:** Blue
Shops/ 🌳 Outdoors: Green   **Sights/Culture:** Black

Within Fort Tryon Park:

THE CLOISTERS

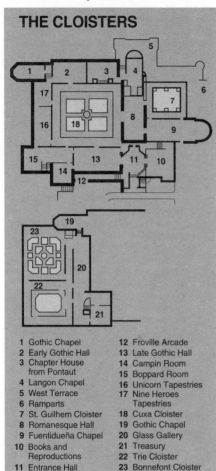

1 Gothic Chapel
2 Early Gothic Hall
3 Chapter House
   from Pontaut
4 Langon Chapel
5 West Terrace
6 Ramparts
7 St. Guilhem Cloister
8 Romanesque Hall
9 Fuentidueña Chapel
10 Books and
   Reproductions
11 Entrance Hall
12 Froville Arcade
13 Late Gothic Hall
14 Campin Room
15 Boppard Room
16 Unicorn Tapestries
17 Nine Heroes
   Tapestries
18 Cuxa Cloister
19 Gothic Chapel
20 Glass Gallery
21 Treasury
22 Trie Cloister
23 Bonnefont Cloister

The Cloisters Both the building and the contents of this branch of the **Metropolitan Museum of Art** were a gift of the munificent **John D. Rockefeller, Jr.** Arranged among cloisters and other architectural elements from monasteries in southern France and Spain, this is very much a medieval ensemble, incorporating both Gothic and Romanesque elements dating from the 12th to 15th centuries. The complex was designed in the mid-1930s by **Charles Collens** to house the Met's medieval collection, and the **Fuentidueña** chapel was added in 1962 by **Brown, Lawford & Forbes.** The best way to see the pastiche of architectural and art fragments is in chronological sequence— discover romantic gardens, ancient stained-glass windows, altar pieces, sculpture, and tapestries along the way. Highlights include the **Treasury,** where precious enamels, 13th- to 15th-century manuscripts, and ivories are on display, and the pièce de résistance, the celebrated **Unicorn Tapestries** from the late

15th and early 16th centuries. Recorded medieval music sets the mood. Special programs, including gallery talks, musical performances, and demonstrations, are scheduled on Saturday at noon and 2PM. A special place to relax is the herb garden (in the Bonnefort Cloister), with a view of the Palisades as **Henry Hudson** might have seen it. (Rockefeller protected the view by also buying the land on the Palisades opposite and restricting development.) The Cloisters are an absolute must. ◆ Voluntary contribution. Tu-Su 9:30AM-5:15PM. Free tours Tu-F 3PM; Su noon. W. 193rd St (at Fort Washington Ave). 923.3700

57 International Gourmet and Gift Center China, cutlery, crystal, appliances, food, and cosmetics imported mainly from Germany can be found in this well-stocked store, one of the last outposts of the German-Jewish community of Washington Heights that was once referred to as the "Fourth Reich." ◆ M-Th 9AM-6PM; F 9AM-2PM; Su 9AM-5PM. 4797 Broadway (between Dyckman and Academy Sts). 569.2611

58 Dyckman House The only 18th-century Dutch farmhouse in Manhattan survives despite the inroads of 20th-century apartment houses and supermarkets. Built in 1783 and given to the city as a museum in 1915, the house has been restored and filled with original Dutch and English family furnishings, and gets high marks for authenticity and charm. An herb garden, smokehouse, and reproduction of a Revolutionary hut are further reminders of life on a farm in the colonies. It's worth a visit. ◆ Free. Tu-Sa 11AM-4PM. 4881 Broadway (at W. 204th St). 304.9422

59 Carrot Top Pastries Owner **Renee Allen Mancino** bakes the single best carrot cake in New York, as well as delicious pecan, sweet-potato, and pumpkin pies. Devoted customers of her two cafes include **Stevie Wonder** and **Richard Pryor.** The outlet near **Columbia-Presbyterian Medical Center** has a small seating area. Special orders are accepted. ◆ M-Sa 6AM-7PM; Su 9AM-4PM. 5025 Broadway (at W. 214th St). 569.1532. Also at: 3931 Broadway. 927.4800

60 Baker Field Fieldhouse/Lawrence Wein Stadium Columbia University's uptown athletic facility features Manhattan's only college football stadium. The views from **Wein Stadium** (**Inwood Hill Park** is just to the west, **Spuyten-Duyvil** just beyond the northern end zone) are a treat. There's also a soccer field closer to Broadway. Call for a schedule. ◆ W. 218th St (between Broadway and Seaman Ave). 567.0404

Restaurants/Clubs: Red   **Hotels:** Blue
Shops/ ♙ Outdoors: Green   **Sights/Culture:** Black

Sam Hall Kaplan
Los Angeles-based Design Critic and Author

Things a person born and bred in New York but living in Los Angeles likes to do when he returns to New York:

On separate weekdays, visit the **Met,** the **Whitney,** the **Guggenheim,** the **Cooper-Hewitt,** and **MoMA.**

At dusk, check out the old neighborhood, walking down **Broadway** from about 96th Street to **Lincoln Center,** catch a concert, then stroll up **Columbus Avenue** and have a late-afternoon snack at a sidewalk cafe.

Any day, anytime, sit on the edge of the **Pulitzer Fountain** at 59th Street and Fifth Avenue and watch the crowds go by, then join them in any direction.

Early on Saturday, wander from **Greenwich Village,** through **Washington Square Park, SoHo, Little Italy,** and **Chinatown** to the **South Street Seaport** and back again, but on different streets, noshing all the way.

On Sunday, have brunch at the **Russian Tea Room** or **Tavern on the Green,** then rent or borrow a bicycle to work off the calories exploring **Central Park.**

Later, especially if it is warm, pedal or walk to the East Side and **Carl Schurz Park,** catch a breeze and watch the boats chug by, or go to the West Side and **Riverside Park** at the 79th Street Boat Basin.

Or spend Sunday at the **Cloisters,** bicycling or busing there.

Anne Rosenzweig
Chef/Owner, Arcadia
Vice Chairperson, 21 Club

An unusual perspective of Manhattan begins with an early-morning breakfast at **Sylvia's** (salmon cakes, grits, deep-fried slab bacon, and biscuits). This is the perfect start to a walking day. Then a stroll through the marvelous but crumbling architecture of Harlem, especially around **Mt. Morris Park.** Then to **La Marqueta,** the Spanish market under the train tracks at Park Avenue and 116th Street. Wonderful and unearthly smells and sights—fresh baby goats, huge aloe vera plants (which soothe kitchen burns and cuts), all sorts of tropical fruits and botanicals, pigs' snouts, love elixirs mixed to order, etc. . . . Then down to the **Conservatory Gardens** at Fifth Avenue and 105th Street. The gardens are completely transformed every season. In spring, huge lilac bushes create an intoxicating aroma under which one can read the Sunday papers. During the summer, they are the setting of some of the most beautiful weddings in New York.

Sitting in the upper decks of **Shea Stadium** on a hot, hot summer night just to catch a good breeze.

The perfect four-and-a-half-minute New York lunch: papaya drink and extra-crispy hot dog at **Papaya King.**

All the museums on upper Fifth Avenue on a Tuesday evening, when they're free.

On the rare occasions when the city is under a deep, fresh blanket of snow—cross-country skiing in **Central Park** and getting hot roasted chestnuts afterward.

The Indian restaurants on Sixth Street in summer—eating outside in back with a gang of friends on picnic tables for the cheapest sums possible.

Buying bags of flattened fortune cookies at one of the many bakeries in **Chinatown**—they're the ones that didn't make it.

Jazz cruises at night up the **Hudson River** and being able to see the skyline at twilight.

Brendan Gill
Writer, *The New Yorker*

Downstairs at the **21 Club.**

A midsummer night's sail from the **South Street Seaport Museum.**

Openings at the **Clocktower Gallery,** high above Broadway.

Sunday brunch at **Mortimer's.**

The latest theater piece at **LaMama E.T.C.,** with **Ellen Stewart** presiding.

A ramble in the **Ramble,** in Central Park.

The **Big Apple Circus.**

The sound of brasses on Sunday morning at the **Cathedral of St. John the Divine.**

Crossing the windswept boardwalk of the **Brooklyn Bridge.**

The successful flagging down of a taxi at twilight on **Park Avenue.**

Books & Company, a shop eager to serve customers even on Sunday.

Architectural exhibitions at the **Urban Center** in the historic **Villard Houses** on Madison Avenue.

Ninth Street, west of **Fifth Avenue.**

Lunch in the **Rose Room** of the **Algonquin.**

The **New York Society Library.**

The annual festival of the **Film Society of Lincoln Center.**

The **Café des Artistes.**

A big winter opening at the **Whitney Museum of American Art.**

Brandy at **Jim McMullen's.**

The delectable smell of **Bendel's.**

The pillared Palladian folly on W. 57th Street that leads one into the **Parker Meridien Hotel.**

Bradley's Bar, on University Place.

Upstairs at the **21 Club.**

Boroughs

Manhattanites refer to **Brooklyn**, **Queens**, the **Bronx**, and **Staten Island** as the "outer" boroughs, while borough residents refer to Manhattan as "the city"; a great deal of attitude is implied therein. The truth is that although they are outside the skyline's media limelight, the boroughs do more than play supporting roles to Manhattan. They lend the city a fair portion of its vitality and character—much of Manhattan's work force commutes from one borough or another—and they hold their own on many fronts, with their own high-caliber restaurants, theaters, parks, and architecture.

Brooklyn

With over 300 years of history and more than 75 square miles of land, Brooklyn has always been a city in its own right. It has been a step up the ladder for immigrant groups, an oceanfront resort, a shipping capital, a cultural mecca, a teeming slum, and the front-runner of an urban renaissance.

Its national reputation is built on vaudeville jokes, an imitable accent, urban conflict, and a host of famous and often comedic natives—**George Gershwin, Woody Allen, Mel Brooks,** and **Beverly Sills** among them. Impressive as it may be, this esteem doesn't begin to do justice to the diverse immensity of what would be, were it still autonomous, America's fourth largest city. Independent until its annexation into New York City in 1898 (Brooklyn-born author **Pete Hamill** calls this the "great mistake"), it has all the earmarks of a major metropolis.

1 River Café ★★★$$$$ The backdrop is unequaled—the towering, glittering Manhattan skyline seen from the foot of the Brooklyn Bridge. Huge bouquets of flowers and a well-dressed crowd offer other visual distractions on this handsome, anchored barge, but only until the food arrives. Chef **John Loughren** has gained a national reputation for creating dishes using the most interesting and freshest American ingredients: buffalo meat, quail, wild greens, intensely flavored berries and fruits, caviar, and wild mushrooms are just some of the bounty with which his kitchen creates.
♦ American ♦ Lunch and dinner; brunch also on Saturday and Sunday. 1 Water St (on the East River under Brooklyn Bridge), Brooklyn Heights. Jacket and reservations required. 718/522.5200

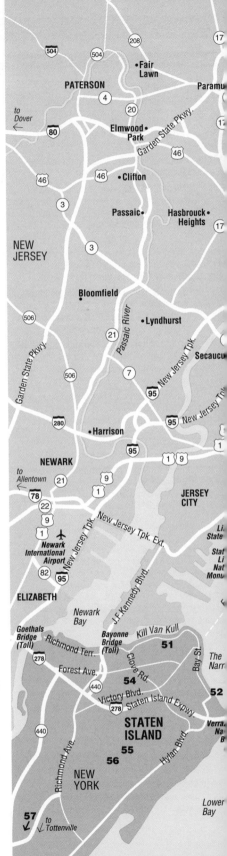

2 Henry's End ★$$$ This small bistro prepares wild game dishes such as elk chops and venison, as well as alligator stew with competence and an inventive style. They also do nice things with fish and fowl. ◆ Continental ◆ Dinner. 44 Henry St (at Cranberry St), Brooklyn Heights. Reservations required for three or more. 718/834.1776

3 Montague Street Saloon ★$$ A friendly, casual atmosphere fills this local hangout. The basic pub fare is good, as is the live entertainment Monday through Thursday evenings. The quaint outdoor cafe is open during the warmer months. ◆ American ◆ Lunch, dinner, and late-night meals. 122 Montague St (between Henry and Hicks Sts), Brooklyn Heights. 718/522.6770

3 Leaf & Bean ★$ Intimate yet lively and filled with neighborhood regulars, this restaurant is Montague Street at its best. The wide selection of coffees and teas are for sale, along with a large assortment of kitchen accessories. Food is served until late afternoon. ◆ American ◆ Breakfast and lunch. 136 Montague St (between Henry and Clinton Sts), Brooklyn Heights. 718/855.7978

4 Brooklyn Borough Hall A palatial sweep of stairs rises to the entrance of this Greek Revival hall of government, designed by **Gamaliel King** and built in 1851. The building, originally fashioned after **Dr. William Thornton's** competition-winning design, was supposed to mimic Manhattan's City Hall, but subsequent design changes dulled the effect. ◆ 209 Joralemon St (at Court St), Downtown. 718/802.3700

4 Gage & Tollner ★★★$$$ The menu, famous for its length, promises "to serve the nostalgic atmosphere that serves to bring back fond recollections," and the place does. The oldest restaurant in the city is still turning out superb seafood. Now at the helm in the kitchen is celebrated chef **Edna Lewis,** whom Gage & Tollner lured back from South Carolina. Among her specialties are Charleston she-crab soup, panfried quail, shrimp and crab gumbo, and the famed chocolate soufflé she originated at Café Nicholson. The gaslights, arched mirrors, dark wood paneling, and well-worn mahogany tables are all 19th century. The waiters, proudly wearing the gold eagles, stars, and bars awarded for 25-, five-, and one-year service, are all professionally humble. Local political powers hold sway at lunch, while a more genteel group gathers at night. Among the extensive list of oyster and clam specialties are clam bellies (the main section of steamer clams) coated in cornmeal and broiled. ◆ Seafood ◆ Lunch and dinner. 372 Fulton St (between Jay St and Boerum Pl), Downtown. Reservations recommended. 718/875.5181

4 New York Transit Museum Popular with young and old transportation buffs, this small museum takes you back in time with one of the world's finest collections of mass transit artifacts, including vintage cars, signal equipment, turnstiles, mosaics, photographs, and an extensive collection of engineering drawings dating to the beginning of the century. ◆ Admission. Tu-F 10AM-4PM; Sa-Su 11AM-4PM. Corner of Boerum Pl and Schermerhorn St, Brooklyn Heights. 718/330.3060

5 Tripoli ★$$ Atlantic Avenue is the center for Middle Eastern cuisine, and among the numerous small restaurants, this one is probably the best and most authentic. Order any of the excellent lamb kebab, falafel, *hummus,* and heavily honeyed desserts. There's live music and entertainment Saturday nights. ◆ Middle Eastern ◆ Lunch and dinner. 156 Atlantic Ave (at Clinton St), Brooklyn Heights. Reservations required Friday and Saturday nights. 718/596.5800

6 Casa Rosa ★$$ Good—and inexpensive—home-style cooking is Casa Rosa's trademark. Have pork chops or lobster *fridilo* (half lobster with mussels, clams, and shrimp on a bed of linguine). ◆ Italian ◆ Lunch and dinner; dinner only on Saturday. Closed Monday. 384 Court St (at Carroll St), Carroll Gardens. Reservations recommended. 718/625.8874

7 Two Toms ★$ There's no sign, and at night from the outside the place looks like a workingman's tavern in a deserted warehouse district. Inside, it's just as plain, and there are no menus. The waiters sometimes forget to wear more than an undershirt, and they may come up to the unsuspecting diner and ask, "Well, what'll youse have?" Why bother, you ask? Because it's one of the better Italian restaurants in the borough. ◆ Italian ◆ Dinner. Closed Monday and Sunday. 255 Third Ave (between Union and President Sts), Carroll Gardens. No credit cards. 718/875.8689

8 Brooklyn Academy of Music This organization, affectionately known as BAM, was founded in 1859 on Montague Street and is housed in a 1908 **Herts & Tallant**-designed building. Among the superlative performers who have appeared at BAM's current home are **Edwin Booth** as *Hamlet* and **Sarah Bernhardt** as *Camille.* **Pavlova** danced and **Caruso** sang in the **Opera House.** BAM is the home of the **Brooklyn Philharmonic.** Over the last decade, impresario **Harvey Lichtenstein** has introduced many innovative programs in music and dance. His annual **Next Wave Festival** has been the launching pad for artists like **Philip Glass, Laurie Anderson,** and choreographer **Mark Morris.** In 1987, BAM reopened the **Majestic,** an 83-year-old theater-turned-movie house that had been lying dormant for nearly 20 years. Interestingly, the shell of the theater was left intact—the wear and tear of the years showing—while two semicircular tiers of seats around a large stage were built, creating an intimate amphitheaterlike space with an exciting medieval feel. The interior was designed by **Hardy Holzman Pfeiffer Associates.** Successful engagements at the Majestic (located on Fulton Street, a block away from BAM's main structure) have included choreographer/director **Martha Clarke's** *Endangered Species* and the musical *Township Fever,* from **Mbongeni Ngema,** the director of *Sarafina!* A shuttle bus leaves from Lexington Avenue at 51st Street in Manhattan; call BAM for a schedule. ♦ Theaters: Opera House (seats 2,100); Helen Carey Playhouse (seats 1,078); Lepercq Space (seats 550); Majestic (seats 900). 30 Lafayette Ave (between St. Felix St and Ashland Pl), Downtown. 718/636.4100

9 Junior's ★$ Some say Junior's cheesecake is the best in New York, and it just may be. The trick is to leave room for it, because copious portions are the house rule. ♦ Deli ♦ Breakfast, lunch, dinner, and late-night meals. 386 Flatbush Ave Ext (at DeKalb Ave), Downtown. 718/852.5257

10 Peter Luger ★★★$$$ One of the oldest and still one of the better, more colorful steakhouses in the city, Peter Luger is great for one thing only: well-charred porterhouse steak made from prime, aged Iowa corn-fed beef. The hefty porterhouses, ordered for two or more, are always cooked perfectly to order and come presliced unless you request otherwise. Potato side dishes are all serviceable, but skip the other vegetables. For dessert, try cheesecake or ice cream. ♦ Steakhouse ♦ Lunch and dinner. 178 Broadway (at Driggs Ave), Williamsburg. Reservations required well in advance. No credit cards. 718/387.7400

11 Architectural Salvage Warehouse If you want to recycle some of the charm and detail of old New York into your new home, this warehouse is stocked with authentic architectural artifacts and elements rescued from the city's condemned buildings. Established in 1980 by the New York City Landmarks Preservation Commission, its purpose is to supply New Yorkers who are restoring their homes with bits and pieces of the past. Architects and interior designers come here looking for old woodwork, shutters, doors, mantels, pedestal sinks, and exterior ironwork; you'll need to arrange the transportation of your acquisitions. ♦ Friday by appointment. 337 Berry St (near Broadway), Williamsburg. 553.1100

12 Pratt Institute Architecture, business, science, and fine arts are the strong suits of this 3,200-student school established in 1887. The 25-acre campus has a satellite in Manhattan. ♦ Bounded by DeKalb and Willoughby Aves (between Classon Ave and Hall St), Downtown. 718/636.3600

13 Brooklyn Children's Museum In this museum, which was built in 1976 to the designs of **Hardy Holzman Pfeiffer Associates,** children visit a greenhouse, work with butterflies and fossils, and learn about how animals get energy from food. They can also participate in a dream sequence inside a 25-foot model of a sleeping head and use their five senses to unlock the mystery of objects, using as tools 20,000 cultural artifacts and natural history specimens from the museum's collection. Special events include films, workshops, field trips, concerts, and storytelling sessions. ♦ Free. W-F 2-5PM; Sa-Su, holidays noon-5PM. 145 Brooklyn Ave (at St. Mark's Ave), Crown Heights. 718/735.4432

14 The New Prospect At Home If you'd rather take out than eat in at the nearby **New Prospect Café,** stop here and pick up a salad or muffin in one of the first of such places to pop up in this increasingly upscale neighborhood. ♦ Takeout ♦ M-F 7:30AM-9PM; Sa-Su 8:30AM-9PM. 52 Seventh Ave (between Lincoln and John's Pls), Park Slope. 718/230.8900

14 Santa Fe Grill ★★$$ A popular spot for the young after-work crowd, the bar offers a variety of fancy concoctions, and the Cajun food is quite respectable for this far north. ♦ Tex-Mex ♦ Dinner. 62 Seventh Ave (at Lincoln Pl), Park Slope. 718/636.0279

15 Aunt Sonia's ★★$$ Perfect after a late-afternoon stroll through Prospect Park or a long visit to the Brooklyn Museum, this small, crowded restaurant has an eclectic menu that depends on the chef's mood. The food is dependably excellent and sometimes quite extraordinary. The service is uneven, but good-humored. ♦ Eclectic ♦ Dinner; brunch also on Saturday and Sunday. 1123 Eighth Ave (at 12th St), Prospect Heights. 718/965.9526

15 Bed & Breakfast on the Park $$ Former antique-store owner **Liana Paolella** has meticulously restored this landmark 19th-century home-turned-inn. A fanatic for details, her guests enjoy eight spacious, beautifully furnished rooms replete with wood-burning fireplaces, canopied beds, stained-glass windows, Oriental rugs, and an extensive collection of museum-quality paintings. A scrumptious breakfast further complements the inn's grand style. ♦ 113 Prospect Park West (between Sixth and Seventh Sts), Park Slope. 718/499.6115; fax 718/499.1385

16 The New Prospect Café ★$$ The spicy corn-and-shrimp chowder is not to be missed in this place, which is always crowded with folks being served tasty meals at very good prices. ◆ American ◆ Lunch and dinner; dinner only on Monday; brunch also on Saturday and Sunday. 393 Flatbush Ave (between Plaza St and Sterling Pl), Park Slope. 718/638.2148

16 Grand Army Plaza Monuments have been added since the plaza was first laid out in 1870 by **Frederick Law Olmsted** and **Calvert Vaux.** The Roman-style **Soldiers' and Sailors' Arch** was raised as a tribute to the Union Army in 1892 and was later encrusted with **Frederick MacMonnies'** massive sculptures and some less exuberant bas-relief forms. The **Bailey Fountain** was added in 1932 by architect **Edgerton Swarthwout** and sculptor **Eugene Savage. Morris Ketchum & Associates** designed the 1965 **John F. Kennedy Memorial.** ◆ Plaza St at Flatbush Ave (between Eastern Pkwy and Prospect Park West), Park Slope-Prospect Heights

16 Prospect Park The **Grand Army Plaza** is the official entrance to this 526-acre park, as loved by Brooklynites as the larger Central Park is by Manhattanites. In fact, these two parks share designers (landscape architects **Olmsted** and **Vaux**), and—not surprisingly—landscaping characteristics (meadowlands, footpaths, skating rink, boating lake, carousel, and the recently opened wildlife center, the country's largest children's zoo). The recipient of a recent multimillion-dollar renovation, the park is close to being returned to its original bucolic state of loveliness. Among other sites, an 18th-century Dutch farmhouse was relocated here to be used as a museum, and an old Quaker cemetery contains **Montgomery Clift's** tomb. ◆ Brooklyn. 718/965.8900

17 Brooklyn Museum This museum always seems to be undergoing construction, which began in 1893 and continued until 1924 by **McKim, Mead & White. Prentice & Chan, Ohlhausen** designed the next addition in 1978, and **Joseph Tonetti** designed the next in 1987. The last addition of this massive five-story museum, part of a major $31 million renovation completed in December 1993, was designed by **Arata Isozaki** and **James Stewart Polshek & Partners.** It includes three floors of new galleries in the West Wing, the new 460-seat **Iris and B. Gerald Cantor Auditorium** (which will serve as the museum's first formal gathering place since the original auditorium was converted into the Grand Lobby in the early 1930s), and two floors of additional art storage space. Excellent collections include the arts of Egypt, the classical Middle East, and Asia. Exhibitions of primitive arts come from Africa, the South Pacific, and the Americas; other displays feature Greek and Roman antiquities. Costumes, textiles,

decorative arts, and period furniture dating from the late 17th century are all beautifully laid out for viewing. The permanent collection includes works by **Rodin, Modigliani, Cassatt, Degas, Monet, Chagall, Gauguin, Toulouse-Lautrec, Homer, Sargent,** and **Bierstadt.** The continuing series of exhibitions by contemporary artists has included **Joseph Kosuth, Alfredo Jarr,** and **Reeva Potoff.** ◆ Voluntary contribution. M, W-Su 10AM-5PM. 200 Eastern Pkwy (at Washington Ave), Prospect Heights. 718/638.5000

17 Brooklyn Botanic Garden Although not as large or as famous as the **New York Botanical Garden** in the Bronx, the Brooklyn Botanic Garden has such celebrated plantings as a Japanese hill-and-pond garden, an herb garden with over 300 specimens, and one of the largest public rose collections in America. A conservatory houses the largest bonsai collection in the country. The 50 acres of flora include a fragrance garden for the blind. The master plan for the garden was designed by **The Olmsted Brothers** and laid down in 1910; the landscaping was completed in 1912 by **Harold Caparn;** and the Steinhardt Conservatory, which was designed by **Davis, Brody & Associates,** was completed in 1988. ◆ Grounds: free; parking fee; Tu-F 8AM-6PM, Sa-Su, holidays 10AM-6PM Apr-Sept; Tu-F 8AM-4:30PM, Sa-Su, holidays 10AM-4:30PM Oct-Mar. Steinhardt Conservatory: admission Apr-Nov; parking fee; Tu-Su 10AM-5PM Apr-Sept; Tu-Su 10AM-4PM Oct-Mar. 1000 Washington Ave (between Empire Blvd and Eastern Pkwy), Prospect Heights. 718/622.4433

18 Kleinfeld's The largest bridal shop in the world stocks 800 to 1,000 models from all the major manufacturers, including **Priscilla of Boston, Carolina Herrera,** and **Scassi.** The mother-of-the-bride shops in the Salon, and bridesmaids go down the street to 8209 Third Avenue. ◆ Appointments are preferred. 8202 Fifth Avenue (between 82nd and 83rd Sts), Bay Ridge. 718/833.1100

18 Areo ★$$ Solid Italian fare is served in this restaurant. The impressively titled Ram's Feast—veal and filet mignon with mushrooms and fried zucchini—will satisfy nearly every gourmand. There's also good cheesecake and *tiramisù.* ◆ Italian ◆ Lunch and dinner. Closed Monday. 8424 Third Ave (at 85th St), Bay Ridge. Reservations recommended. 718/238.0079

The Bronx is the only borough that is part of mainland New York. Manhattan and Staten Island are islands, and Brooklyn and Queens are on the western end of Long Island. New York City is, in fact, an archipelago.

19 Coney Island Rattling over the tracks since 1927, the wooden Cyclone roller coaster still provides thrills, and a Nathan's hotdog with everything on it is still a genuine treat, but the golden days of Coney Island are no longer. The beach has survived somewhat intact, and it sure does beat the tar beaches many Manhattanites settle for on the roofs of their apartment buildings on hot summer weekends. In the 1920s, this was the Riviera, the "World's Largest Playground" for generations of hard-working immigrants and native New Yorkers. For just a few nickels, it provided an escape from the heat of the city during the height of the Depression, and the three huge fairgrounds thrived. It has since faded into neglect, but provides a certain nostalgia with a glimpse of other times, ocean views, and a visit to nearby Brighton Beach for a peek into Little Russia. ♦ Surf Ave (between W. 37th St and Ocean Pkwy)

On Coney Island:

Nathan's Famous ★$ Indeed, this is probably the most famous and elaborate hot dog stand in the world, having served spicy franks and fabulously greasy, crinkle-cut fried potatoes for nearly a century. There are locations all over Manhattan as well, but this was the first. ♦ American ♦ Surf Ave (at Stillwell Ave), Coney Island. 718/946.2202

New York Zoological Society, New York Aquarium Native creatures of the **Hudson River Display** and dramatic denizens of the shark tank are on exhibit in the **Native Sea Life** building. Penguins and sea lions provide comic relief, and **Aquatheater** shows provide great entertainment: dolphins in the summer and whales, walruses, and sea lions in the winter. There's also a **Discovery Cove**, where kids can touch sea stars and horseshoe crabs. ♦ Admission; parking fee. Daily 10AM-4:45PM. Surf Ave (at W. Eighth St), Coney Island. 718/265.3400

20 National Restaurant ★★$$$ Yet another colorful Russian restaurant in this area dubbed "Little Odessa by the Sea." Film buffs will recall it as the location where Soviet defector Robin Williams sang and danced with his compatriots in *Moscow on the Hudson.* Known for its boisterous good times and late-night bonhomie, the restaurant is the place to come with friends for the rivers of vodka that help you forget that the food is not the high point. You'll be singing tunes from the motherland with the live band before you know it. ♦ Russian ♦ Dinner and late-night meals. 273 Brighton Beach Ave (between Second and Third Aves), Brighton Beach. 718/646.1225

20 Odessa ★★$$$ You can come for lunch, but it's better to make a night of it. The Eastern European regulars put on their best duds and indulge in vodka on ice, and more vodka on ice, and endless "appetizers" (the word has a decidedly different meaning in Russian). There's dancing and live music nightly. All in all, this is an extraordinary experience. ♦ Russian ♦ Lunch and dinner. 1113 Brighton Beach Ave (between 13th and 14th Sts), Brighton Beach. Reservations required. 718/332.3223

Queens

Sprawling Queens has always been a conglomeration of towns, villages, model communities, and real-estate developments. Suburban in spirit and design, it has grown far too dense to be anything but urban in essence. And it has, of late, become the type of immigrant staging ground that Manhattan, Brooklyn, and the Bronx used to be (next to Athens, Queens has the world's largest Greek community). But unlike these older boroughs, it is oriented toward the highways that lace it together, toward the airports (Kennedy and La Guardia) that sit on either shore, and toward the suburban reaches of Nassau County.

21 Water's Edge ★★★$$$$ Surrounded by glass walls on three sides, the tables in this swank river restaurant all have spectacular views of Midtown and Lower Manhattan. The menu is heavy on beautifully grilled and sautéed fish with rich and light sauces, as well as a few unexpected touches like tempura vegetables and, at lunch, potpies. ♦ Seafood ♦ Lunch and dinner; dinner only on Saturday. Closed Sunday. 44th Dr (at East River), Long Island City. Jacket, tie, and reservations required. 718/482.0033

22 Manducatis ★$$ Family atmosphere, bravado, and warmth give Manducatis a real Italian trattoria feeling. Chef **Ida's** fine, straightforward hand with fresh ingredients brings people from Manhattan to this out-of-the-way spot. ♦ Italian ♦ Lunch and dinner; dinner only on Saturday and Sunday. 13-27 Jackson Ave (at 47th Ave), Long Island City. Reservations recommended. 718/729.4602

22 P.S. 1 An alternative space of the **Institute for Contemporary Art,** this 19th-century school, under the directorship of **Alanna Heiss,** is used for film, video, and exhibitions of new as well as established artists. Call for a

Restaurants/Clubs: Red   Hotels: Blue
Shops/ Outdoors: Green   Sights/Culture: Black

schedule. ♦ Voluntary contribution. 46-01 21st St (between Jackson Ave and 45th Rd), Long Island City. 718/784.2084

22 Silvercup Studios In 1983, the **Silvercup Bakery** was converted into a movie studio. Eighteen soundstages are contained within a mammoth three-block-long building. In addition to providing space for work on movies (*Garbo Talks, Street Smart, The Purple Rose of Cairo*), commercials (which account for most of the studio's activity), and music videos, Silvercup rents screening rooms, production offices, and a party room on the fourth floor, where windows overlook the New York skyline. ♦ 42-22 22nd St (between Bridge Plaza South and 43rd Ave), Long Island City. 718/784.3390

23 Isamu Noguchi Garden Museum Completed in 1985, this is one of the few museums dedicated to the work of a single artist, created by that artist. **Isamu Noguchi** (1904-88) had a controversial career filled with projects that ranged from immense sculpture gardens to *akari* lamps to set designs for choreographers **Martha Graham** and **George Balanchine.** Some of the greatest examples of Noguchi's work are on display in the museum's 12 galleries and outdoor sculpture garden. ♦ Voluntary contribution. W, Sa-Su 11AM-6PM Apr-Nov. 32-37 Vernon Blvd (at 33rd Rd), Long Island City. 718/204.7088

24 Roumeli Taverna ★$$ Authentic Greek food has made this one of the favorites in Queens' enclave of Greek eateries. Named after a Greek mountain range, Roumeli is a shade fancier than neighboring tavernas, but low prices and high quality attract locals and visitors alike. Before or after eating here, stroll around the streets between Broadway and Ditmars Boulevard and take in the sights, sounds, and smells of Greek grocery stores, bakeries, cafes, and almost a dozen Greek Orthodox churches. ♦ Greek ♦ Lunch and dinner. 33-14 Broadway (between 33rd and 34th Sts), Astoria. 718/278.7533

25 American Museum of the Moving Image Designed by **Gwathmey Siegel & Associates,** and built in 1988, this museum is all that its name advertises and more, with extensive archives, special showings, and exhibitions. There are no snobbish distinctions between film and TV or technology and art, but it's not about junk culture, either. The artifacts displayed leave an indelible impression of Pop history. ♦ Admission. Tu-F noon-4PM; Sa-Su noon-6PM. 36-01 35th Ave (at 36th St), Astoria. 718/784.0077; tours 718/784.4520

25 Kaufman Astoria Studio/U.S. Army Pictorial Center **Rudolph Valentino** and **Gloria Swanson** starred in silent films made here in the heyday of New York City's motion picture boom. **Edward G. Robinson** made the

early talkie *Hole in the Wall* here, and the **Marx Brothers** used the studio for the filming of *The Cocoanuts.* After the studio's 1932 bankruptcy, the property passed through several hands. During World War II, it was used by the army for training and propaganda films done by **Frank Capra.** Now a historic landmark, the studio is back in business. It was a favorite location of director **Sidney Lumet.** ♦ 34-12 36th St (between 34th and 35th Aves), Astoria. 718/392.5600

26 Piccola Venezia ★★$$$ Fish dishes are especially good at this off-the-beaten-track Italian restaurant. ♦ Italian ♦ Lunch and dinner; dinner only on Saturday and Sunday. 42-01 28th Ave (at 42nd St), Astoria. 718/721.8470

27 Taverna Vraka $$ Don't be surprised if your waiter suddenly appears in authentic Greek costume to perform folk dances in the middle of the dining room. This is the *real* thing—patrons are known to shower the dancers with dollar bills. There's live music nightly from Wednesday to Sunday. ♦ Greek ♦ Dinner. Closed Tuesday. 23-15 31st St (between 23rd and 24th Aves), Astoria. Reservations recommended. 718/721.3007

28 Steinway Mansion **William Steinway** was a great friend of **President Grover Cleveland** and presented him with a grand piano as a wedding gift. The Steinway home, built in 1856, was once a lively setting for fairy tale social events. ♦ 18-33 41st St (at Berrian Blvd), Astoria

29 Little India Known as **Jackson Heights,** this area is a solid, family-oriented neighborhood of Argentinians, Thais, Spaniards, Koreans, Italians, and Pakistanis. But the bold colors and pungent smells of India make it the most foreign and exotic to the curious visitor. Some 60,000 Indian immigrants in the New York City area live on this one block of 74th Street north of Roosevelt Avenue, or flock here regularly to shop, eat, and visit. Sari shops, aromatic grocery stores, jewelry stores whose windows are laden with 22K gold wedding jewelry, and about a dozen authentic restaurants are part of the lively scene. ♦ 74th St and Roosevelt Ave

29 Delhi Palace ★★$$ Recently remodeled, this is Little India's most elegant dining choice, with crisp white tablecloths, fresh flowers, attentive service, and quiet background music. An extensive and tantalizing buffet appears at both lunch and dinner, and selections from the menu are equally delicious. Don't miss the chicken with creamy cashew sauce or tandoori shrimp with *masala* sauce. ♦ Indian ♦ Lunch and dinner. 37-33 74th St (between Roosevelt and 37th Aves). 718/507.0666

Restaurants/Clubs: Red   Hotels: Blue

Shops/ 🌳 Outdoors: Green   Sights/Culture: Black

29 Jackson Diner ★$ You'll find no frills and no liquor license in this Indian restaurant, just authentic cuisine made from owner **Gian Saini's** family recipes. Local Indian families pack the place for the excellent tandoori chicken and unusual specialties. ♦ Indian ♦ 37-03 74th St (between Roosevelt and 37th Aves). No credit cards. 718/672.1232

30 Jai Ya Thai ★★$$ An extensive, original Thai menu includes more than 300 choices. Try the pork with chili peppers (very hot) and onions. ♦ Thai ♦ Lunch and dinner. 81-11 Broadway (between 81st and 82nd Sts), Elmhurst. Dinner reservations recommended Friday through Sunday. 718/651.1330

31 London Lennie's $$ Comforting chowder, panfried oysters, and big pots of steamers attract hordes of locals to this wood-paneled, nautically decorated fish house with a long wine list. ♦ Seafood ♦ Lunch and dinner; dinner only on Saturday and Sunday. 63-88 Woodhaven Blvd (between 63rd Dr and Fleet St), Forest Hills. 718/894.8084

32 Shea Stadium Home of the **New York Mets,** this 55,300-seat stadium, built in 1963 and designed by **Praeger-Waterbury,** also hosted **Pope John Paul II** in 1979 and the history-making 1965 **Beatles** concert. The stadium opened for the Mets' 1964 season, which coincided with the World's Fair next door at Flushing Meadow-Corona Park. For its 25th anniversary in 1988, the stadium underwent a modest renovation and now features large neon figures on the outside, new plastic seating to replace old wooden benches, and a **DiamondVision** video screen. Traffic around the stadium is quite congested before and after games; call for directions by public transportation. ♦ 126th St (at Roosevelt Ave), Flushing. 718/507.8499

33 Flushing Meadow-Corona Park Once a garbage dump, this triumph of reclamation, smack dab in the geographic center of New York City, was later chosen for the 1939-40 and 1964-65 New York World's Fairs. ♦ Bounded by Union Turnpike and 44th Ave (between Van Wyck Expwy and Grand Central Pkwy), Flushing

Within Flushing Meadow-Corona Park:

Hall of Science Designed by **Wallace K. Harrison** and built as a science pavilion for the 1964-65 World's Fair, this is New York's only hands-on science and technology museum. The sophisticated collection includes 150 interactive exhibits focusing on color, light, microbiology, structures, feedback, and quantum physics. ♦ Admission. W-Su 10AM-5PM. 47-01 111th St (at 48th Ave). 718/699.0675

Queens Museum of Art Highlights include excellent art and photography shows and the world's largest scale model—a 9,335-square-foot **Panorama of New York City** that includes just about every street, building, bridge, and park at a scale of one inch to 100 feet. ♦ Donation requested. Tu-F 10AM-5PM; Sa-Su noon-5PM. Off Grand Central Pkwy. 718/592.5555

34 Pastrami King ★$$ Manhattanites reminisce about neighborhood delis as good as this one. ♦ Deli ♦ M-F, Su 8AM-9PM; Sa 8AM-10PM. 124-24 Queens Blvd (at 82nd Ave), Kew Gardens. 718/263.1717

35 Aqueduct Thoroughbred racing takes place from October to May. ♦ Rockaway Blvd (at 110th St), Ozone Pk. 718/641.4700

36 Jamaica Bay Wildlife Refuge Within the **Center Gateway National Recreation Area,** these vast man-made tidal wetlands and uplands have become a haven for hundreds of species of birds and plants. The fall migratory season, starting in mid-August, is a particularly good time to come. Dress appropriately. ♦ Free. Daily 8:30AM-5PM. Cross Bay Blvd at Broad Channel. 718/318.4340

37 Patrick's Pub ★$$ The cozy, rustic atmosphere is perfect for enjoying Irish coffee and shepherd's pie. ♦ Irish ♦ Lunch, dinner, and late-night meals. 252-12 Northern Blvd (at Little Neck Pkwy), Little Neck. 718/423.7600

The Bronx

The Bronx stands not only as a study in contrasts, but also typifies the rapid succession of growth and decline experienced throughout New York City—a microcosm of American urban change squeezed into just over half a century. Today it is a mélange of devastated tenements, suburban riverfront mansions, seaside cottages, massive housing superblocks, and fading boulevards of grand Art Deco apartment towers. Although in recent years the Bronx has become a synonym for urban decay, some of the borough remains stable, and heavy philanthropic and governmental investment as well as active community-based groups are helping to restore some of the more run-down areas.

38 Yankee Stadium In 1973, the **Yankees** celebrated their 50th anniversary in this 57,545-seat horseshoe arena designed in 1923 by **Osborn Engineering Co.** Remodeling has kept this home of the frequent World Series champs one of the most modern baseball facilities in the country. It was almost completely rebuilt in 1976 by **Praeger-Kavanagh-Waterbury.** The park is 11.6 acres, 3.5 of which are taken up by the field itself. Within the park are monuments to such Yankee greats as **Lou Gehrig, Joe DiMaggio, Casey Stengel,** and, of course, **Babe Ruth.** ♦ E. 161st St (at River Ave), Highbridge. 718/293.6000

39 Hall of Fame for Great Americans
Bronze busts of nearly a hundred of America's greatest scientists, statesmen, and artists are on display in this handsome building designed in 1901 and 1914 by **McKim, Mead & White.** Sculptures are by **Daniel Chester French, Frederick MacMonnies,** and **James Earle Fraser.** Note the classic arcade by **Stanford White.** ◆ Free. Daily 10AM-5PM. W. 181st St (at University Ave), Bronx Community College, University Heights. 718/220.6003

40 Edgar Allan Poe Cottage From 1846 to 1848 the writer and his dying wife lived in this house, which dates back to 1812. *Annabel Lee* was among the works written here. The museum displays many of Poe's manuscripts and other memorabilia. ◆ Nominal admission. Sa 10AM-4PM; Su 1-5PM. Grand Concourse (at E. Kingsbridge Rd), Fordham. 718/881.8900

41 Fordham University Considered by many to be the nation's foremost Jesuit school, this 85-acre campus has over 13,000 students studying a traditional arts and sciences curriculum. **Rose Hill Manor** (1838), which now forms part of the **Administration Building,** was the home of the original school, **St. John's College,** begun in 1841 by **John Hughes.** Hughes later became New York State's first Catholic archbishop. This beautiful campus has a classic collection of Collegiate Gothic structures, most notably **Keating Hall,** designed in 1936 by **Robert S. Reiley.** ◆ 441 E. Fordham Rd (at Third Ave), Fordham. 718/817.1000

42 Arthur Avenue Retail Market This section of the Bronx is still a vibrant Italian community, much more than Manhattan's Little Italy. An indoor farmers' market and lovely bakeries and import shops provide a great diversion before or after a visit to the zoo. ◆ M-Sa 8AM-6PM. 2344 Arthur Ave (between E. 187th and E. 189th Sts), Fordham. 718/367.5686

42 Calabrea Pork Store Just try and choose among the 500 kinds of sausage dangling from the ceiling. ◆ M-Sa 7AM-6PM. 2338 Arthur Ave (at E. 187th St), Fordham. 718/367.5145

42 Belmont Italian-American Playhouse In a cramped loft above a supermarket in a neighborhood where the newspapers are still read in Italian and social clubs are crowded with old men discussing soccer scores, this 70-seat theater draws crowds from Manhattan for classic and contemporary Italian works, Shakespearean productions, and works by local playwrights of all ethnic backgrounds. The three young Italian-American owners knew their theater would make it when **Robert DeNiro** used their space to audition for his 1993 film *A Bronx Tale.* Call for a schedule. ◆ Shows Thursday through Saturday at 8:30PM; Sunday matinee. 2385 Arthur Ave (between E. 186th and E. 187th Sts), Fordham. 718/364.4700

42 Dominick's ★★$$ Don't bolt when you see the lines outside. Once inside, you'll be greeted with terrific home-style Southern Italian fare and a solicitous staff. Children are welcome. ◆ Italian ◆ Lunch and dinner; dinner only on Sunday. Closed Tuesday. 2335 Arthur Ave (between E. 187th St and Crescent Ave), Fordham. No credit cards. 718/733.2807

42 Calandra Salted braids and unsalted balls of very fresh mozzarella, made on the premises, are sold here. Don't forget to keep them in water. ◆ M-Sa 8AM-6PM. 2314 Arthur Ave (at E. 183rd St). 718/365.7572

43 Bronx Zoo/Wildlife Conservation Park Managed by NYZS/The Wildlife Conservation Society, the zoo is home to almost 4,000 animals—650 species—on 265 acres, making it the largest metropolitan zoo in the United States. At its northernmost end is **Astor Court** (built from 1901 to 1922 to the design of **Heins & LaFarge**), a collection of formal zoo buildings that contains the **Zoo Center** (old elephant house), the renovated **Monkey House,** and **Sea Lion Pool.** These structures, influenced by the 1893 Chicago World's Fair, were built as part of the original plan, which envisioned a formal central court area surrounded by natural park settings. The balance of the zoo's acreage is designed to re-create naturalistic habitats where African and Asian wildlife roam. ◆ Admission. M-F 10AM-5PM; Sa-Su, holidays 10AM-5:30PM Mar-Oct; daily 10AM-4:30PM Nov-Feb. Bronx River Pkwy (Fordham Rd), Northeast. 718/367.1010

Within the Bronx Zoo:

Paul Rainey Memorial Gate Images of bears and deer decorate these imaginative Art Deco gates, which open onto a 200-year-old Italian fountain donated by **William Rockefeller.** The gate was designed by **Charles A. Platt** in 1934, and the sculpture is by **Paul Manship.** ◆ Fordham Rd at Pelham Pkwy

World of Birds Visitors can observe more than 500 birds in the 25 environments of this well-designed aviary, with no bars or fences to obscure the view. It was designed in 1972 by **Morris Ketchem, Jr. & Associates.**

Children's Zoo Children can explore prairie dog tunnels or hop like a wallaby in this hands-on zoo. Kids must be accompanied by an adult. ◆ Nominal admission. Last visitors admitted one hour before zoo closes.

Jungle World This award-winning indoor rain forest has four habitats, five waterfalls, giant trees, and Asian animals separated from humans by bridges and small rivers. Look out for proboscis monkeys, silver-leaf langurs (monkey family), white-cheeked gibbons (ape family), and Indian gharials (a crocodilian relative that is believed to have lived 180 million years ago).

World of Darkness Day and night are reversed for the nocturnal animals who live here, so they are awake and active for daytime visitors. This fascinating exhibit was designed by **Morris Ketchem, Jr. & Associates** in 1972.

44 New York Botanical Garden One of the world's outstanding botanical gardens, its 250 acres include a 40-acre virgin hemlock forest, formal gardens, and the **Enid A. Haupt Conservatory** (built in 1902 and restored in 1978 by **Edward Larrabee Barnes**), which was modeled after the **Great Palm House** at **Kew Gardens** in England. A museum houses an herbarium, accessible only to members, of 5 ½ million dried plants, and a shop that sells plants and gardening books and supplies. The **Lorillard Snuff Mill** (built in 1840) was converted into a cafe in the 1950s. A massive renovation project with an estimated $165 million price tag is underway in an attempt to draw more visitors, and is expected to be completed in the year 2000. The following projects are in the planning stages: a new library and herbarium, a renovated lecture hall, a restoration of the museum exterior, a new restaurant and catering area, extensive renovation to the Enid A. Haupt Conservatory, and a new visitor center. If all goes as planned, the Botanical Garden will be much more visitor-friendly and less like "a museum of plants." Last admission is one hour before closing. ♦ Grounds: voluntary fee; Tu-Su 10AM-6PM Mar-Oct; Tu-Su 10AM-4PM Nov-Feb. Conservatory: admission; Tu-F 10AM-5PM, Sa-Su 10AM-6PM Apr-Oct; Tu-Su 10AM-4PM Nov-Mar. 200th St (at Southern Blvd), Bronx Park. 718/220.8700

45 City University of New York, Herbert H. Lehman College More than 10,000 students attend this school, founded in 1931 as **Hunter College.** The campus' Gothic buildings were designed by **Thompson Holmes & Converse** and **Frank Meyers** in 1928. The **Lehman Center for the Performing Arts,** designed in 1980 by **David Todd & Associates** and **Jan Hird Pokorny,** includes a 2,300-seat concert hall, experimental theater, recital hall, library, dance studio, and art galleries. The Center has become for the Bronx a kind of scaled-down Lincoln Center, attracting many of the same events that normally would play Manhattan only. ♦ Bedford Park Blvd West (between Jerome and Goulden Aves), Bedford Park. 718/960.8000

46 Wave Hill The 28-acre Hudson River estate of financier **George W. Perkins** was given to the city in 1965. **Arturo Toscanini, Theodore Roosevelt,** and **Mark Twain** each lived here for a short time. The 19th-century mansion hosts a chamber music series and family-arts projects and presents vintage recordings of Toscanini concerts. The dazzling gardens and greenhouses put on a display each season. ♦ Admission on weekends. Tu-Su 10AM-4:30PM. 675 W. 252nd St (Independence Ave at W. 249th St), Riverdale. 718/549.2055

47 Van Cortlandt Museum This Georgian-colonial mansion is one of those where **George Washington** actually slept—it was his military headquarters on several occasions. Built in 1748, the mansion has been restored with Dutch, English, and colonial furnishings. ♦ Nominal admission. Tu-F 10AM-3PM; Sa-Su 1-4PM. Broadway at W. 246th St, Riverdale. 718/543.3344

48 Bartow-Pell Mansion Museum This Federal home on beautifully manicured grounds, with views of Long Island Sound and outstanding formal gardens, was built from 1836 to 1842. Run by the **International Garden Club,** it's a rare treat. ♦ Nominal admission. W, Sa-Su noon-4PM or by appointment. Shore Rd (Pelham and Split Rock Golf Course), Pelham Bay Park. 718/885.1461

49 City Island A New England atmosphere persists on this small island that served as a U.S. Coast Guard station in World War II. Attached to mainland New York by only one bridge, this picturesque 230-acre island is four blocks across at its widest point and has the flavor of an island off the coast of Maine, not the Bronx, with marinas (four America's Cup yachts were built here), sea gulls, seafood restaurants, antique shops, and atmosphere. The **New York Sailing School** (697 Bridge Street, 718/885.3103), offers boat rentals and sailing instruction from April through October. The **Northwind Sea Institute** (610 City Island Avenue, 718/885.0701), a nautical museum, traces the history of the island. The park boasts two 18-hole golf courses and horse-back riding along old Indian trails. ♦ Bronx

49 Le Refuge Bed & Breakfast $$ **Pierre Saint-Denis,** proprietor/chef of Midtown Manhattan's extremely popular **Le Refuge** restaurant, has opened this ultra-charming eight-room inn (shown above) in a restored

19th-century sea captain's house. Replete with widow's walk, chamber music concerts, and the best croissants in town, this is the only spot of its kind in the Bronx or New York City. While it's only a half-hour by subway to Midtown Manhattan (and Pierre's must-visit East Side eatery), it will seem light-years away. With a host who's one of Manhattan's premier chefs, you can count on a wonderful breakfast. ♦ 620 City Island Ave. 718/885.2478; fax 212/737.0384

50 Lobster Box ★★$$$ The **Masucchia** family converted a small white house built in 1812 to a restaurant more than 50 years ago, and it has expanded over time to become a local landmark serving up to 2,000 pounds of fresh lobster a week. This is a pleasant outing if you have a hankering for fresh lobster: pick from almost two dozen variations beginning with the simple steamed-and-split (lobsters here are never boiled), or any of the fresh fish and seafood, and watch the fleet of local boats glide by. ♦ Lobster/Seafood ♦ Lunch and dinner. Closed November to late March. 34 City Island Ave (near Rochelle St). 718/885.1952

Staten Island

Geographically distant from the rest of New York, Staten Island seems to be more a spiritual cousin to New Jersey, only a narrow stretch of water away. In fact, Staten Island's political ties to New York City are but a historical accident: The island was ceded to Manhattan as a prize in a sailing contest sponsored by the **Duke of York** in 1687. Before 1964, access was possible only by ferry from Manhattan or by car through New Jersey. In 1964, the **Verrazano-Narrows Bridge** opened, tying Staten Island to Brooklyn. With a new frontier so close at hand, settlers poured over the bridge and changed the rugged face of the island forever. In 1990, tired of being ignored, residents of the "forgotten borough" voted to create a charter commission to provide for the separation of Staten Island from the rest of New York City. In 1993, residents voted two to one in favor of secession. Final approval rests with the state legislature in Albany and **Governor Cuomo.** If they grant independence to Staten Island, it will become the second-largest city in New York.

51 Snug Harbor Cultural Center This 83-acre center for the performing and visual arts—a retirement village for sailors from 1833 until the mid-1970s—is composed of 28 historic buildings, many of which are fine examples of Greek Revival, Beaux Arts, Italianate, and Victorian architecture. Stop by the **Visitors Center** for historical exhibitions and information on current and upcoming events, including indoor and outdoor classical, pop, and jazz concerts. A historical tour is held every Saturday and Sunday at 2PM. ♦ Daily 9AM-5PM. 1000 Richmond Terrace (at Tyson St). 718/448.2500

Within Snug Harbor Cultural Center:

The Newhouse Center for Contemporary Art New and emerging artists not often seen in Manhattan galleries are shown. The Center also hosts an indoor/outdoor sculpture exhibition in the summer. ♦ W-Su noon-5PM. 718/448.2500

Staten Island Children's Museum Hands-on exhibits and related workshops and performances for five to 12 year olds are featured. A recent program gave children the opportunity to study bugs from both the scientist's and the artist's perspective. ♦ Free. Tu-Su noon-5PM; call for extended summer hours. 718/273.2060

 Staten Island Botanical Garden Within are an English perennial garden, an herb and butterfly garden, a White Garden (all blooms in shades of gray and white) patterned after the famous English garden in Sissinghurst, and a greenhouse with a permanent display of tropicals, including the **Neil Vanderbilt Orchid Collection.** It's best to visit from May to October, when the flowers are in bloom. ♦ Free. Daily dawn to dusk. 718/273.8200

51 R.H. Tugs ★$$ Sit on the small outdoor patio and watch the tugboats chug by, or gaze at the twinkling lights of "Joisey" at night. Once an abandoned waterfront shack, this casual and popular restaurant specializes, not surprisingly, in seafood, including its well-known chowder, chunky with shrimp, crab, and fish, and entrées such as simple grilled fish or lobster with fettuccine. But don't discount the delicious barbecued ribs or rib-eye steaks, and try the occasional Caribbean specialties, especially on Thursday night, when a live Caribbean band will put you in the mood. ♦ Seafood/Caribbean/Barbecue ♦ Lunch, dinner, and late-night meals. 1115 Richmond Terrace (at Snug Harbor Rd). 718/447.6369

52 The Alice Austen House This is one of the finest records of turn-of-the-century American life from Alice Austen, a photographer whose work was first discovered in *Life* in 1949. ♦ Suggested donation. Th-Su noon-5PM. 2 Hylan Blvd (at Bay St). 718/816.4506

53 Verrazano-Narrows Bridge Built in 1964 and designed by **Othmar Amman,** this exquisite 4,260-foot minimalist steel ribbon is the world's longest suspension bridge (San Francisco's **Golden Gate** comes in a close second at 4,200 feet). It flies across the entrance to New York Harbor and is especially beautiful when seen from the Atlantic, against the city's skyline. It is named for **Giovanni da Verrazano,** the first European to see Staten Island (1524). The bridge has become familiar as the starting point for the **New York City Marathon** every November. ♦ From Staten Island Expwy, Staten Island to Gowanus Expwy, Brooklyn

54 The Greenbelt Even New Yorkers are amazed when told that the sprawling 843-acre Central Park is not the largest in the city. Measuring in at a remarkable 2,500 acres, Staten Island's Greenbelt offers locals little-known proximity to a variety of landscapes, from shaded woodlands and freshwater swamps to hardwood forests with hiking trails and cross-country skiing in winter. Regular programs, talks, and walking tours are organized by the park service. Call for information and schedules. ♦ Admission. Daily 8AM-5PM. 200 Nevada Ave. 718/667.2165

54 Staten Island Zoo Popular attractions at this zoo, beloved by many for its small (8½ acres) scale, include a re-created tropical rain forest, animal hospital, aquarium, and outstanding reptile collection, which features the country's largest collection of rattlesnakes. A Saturday morning program allows children to feed the animals. ♦ Admission. Daily 10AM-4:45PM. 614 Broadway (between Forest Ave and Clove Rd), Barret Park. 718/442.3100

55 Jacques Marchais Center of Tibetan Art An unexpected outpost of Asian culture and tranquility, this small museum on a hill was founded by the late Jacques Marchais and her husband, **Harry Klauber,** and was also designed by her in 1947. One of the largest private collections of Tibetan art in the Western Hemisphere is shown in two stone buildings resembling a Tibetan temple, along with art of other Asian countries. ♦ Admission. W-Su 1-5PM Apr-Nov; groups by appointment Dec-Mar. 338 Lighthouse Ave (at Windsor Ave), Richmond. 718/987.3478

56 Historic Richmond Town New York City's answer to Williamsburg is a continuing restoration of 29 buildings that show a picture of 17th- through 19th-century village life. Fourteen are open to visitors, including the **Voorlezer House** (1695), the oldest surviving elementary school; the **General Store** (1840); and the **Bennet House** (1839), which is home to the **Museum of Childhood.** There are demonstrations of Early American trades and crafts, and working kitchens with cooking in progress. The **Museum Store** (in the **Historical Museum**) sells reproductions made by village craftspeople. ♦ Admission. W-F 1-5PM Jan-Mar; W-Su 1-5PM Apr-June, Sept-Dec; W-F 10AM-5PM, Sa-Su 1-5PM July-Aug. 441 Clarke Ave (between Richmond and Arthur Kill Rds), Richmond. 718/351.1611

57 The Conference House/Billopp House Built in the 1670s, this was the scene of the only peace conference held to try to prevent the Revolutionary War. **Admiral Lord Howe,** in command of the British forces, hosted the parley on 11 September 1776 for three Continental Congress representatives— **Benjamin Franklin, John Adams,** and **Edward Rutledge.** The house is now a National Historic Landmark with period furnishings and various demonstrations. The rolling lawn is ideal for picnicking. ♦ Nominal admission. W-Su 1-4PM 15 Mar-15 Dec. 7455 Hylan Blvd, Tottenville. 718/984.2086

Bests

Robert T. Buck
Director, The Brooklyn Museum

Brooklyn Bests:

River Café—Classic cuisine—one of New York's outstanding menus combined with an unrivaled view from your table of the Manhattan skyline.

Boerum Hill Cafe—A limited but superb menu, served in perhaps the most beautiful 19th-century atmosphere remaining in New York. Noteworthy is its 30-foot mahogany bar and its steamboat revival carving.

Aunt Sonia's—A large choice of inventive pasta dishes—original combination of New York savvy and California ingredients. Desserts not to be believed.

Tartine & Wine, Inc.—Small "in" spot. Beautiful interior with lace curtains across the glass front. Home-cooked French-style classics with a nice choice of California wines. In fast-changing Park Slope.

Gage & Tollner—Outstanding American cuisine served to generations of happy clients along with a gem of an authentic Diamond Jim Brady interior, sometimes lit with the original gaslight fixtures. One dines surrounded by mahogany and mirrors.

New Prospect Café—Near the Brooklyn Museum, a delightful Art Deco touch on a small storefront yields California nouvelle: delicious dishes and salads with featured European ales, beers, and beverages.

Before the 1850s, immigrants afflicted with diseases were kept on a remote spot on Staten Island. Many local residents became sick and died as a result, and others retaliated by setting fire to the quarantine buildings. This action prompted the state to build Hoffman and Swinburne islands to house the afflicted. The islands are between Staten Island and Brooklyn and date from 1872. They were abandoned in the 1920s following the new immigration laws and serve no purpose today.

Restaurants/Clubs: Red	Hotels: Blue
Shops/ 🌳 Outdoors: Green	Sights/Culture: Black

Index

Restaurants

Only restaurants with star ratings are listed below and at right. All restaurants are listed alphabetically in the main (preceding) index. Always call in advance to ensure a restaurant has not closed, changed its hours, or booked its tables for a private party. The restaurant price ratings are based on the average cost of an entrée for one person, excluding tax and tip.

★★★★ An Extraordinary Experience
★★★ Excellent
★★ Very Good
★ Good

$$$$ Big Bucks ($20 and up)
$$$ Expensive ($15-$20)
$$ Reasonable ($10-$15)
$ The Price Is Right (less than $10)

Hotels

The hotels listed below are grouped according to their price ratings; they are also listed in the main index. The hotel price ratings reflect the base price of a standard room for two people for one night during the peak season.

$$$$ Big Bucks ($250 and up)
$$$ Expensive ($150-$250)
$$ Reasonable ($100-$150)
$ The Price Is Right (less than $100)

$$$$

Features

Bests

Maps

ACCESS® Guides

Order by phone, toll-free: 1-800-331-3761

Name _____ Phone _____

Address _____

City _____ State _____ Zip _____

Please send me the following ACCESS® Guides:

☐ **BARCELONA** ACCESS® $17.00
0-06-277000-4

☐ **BOSTON** ACCESS® $18.50
0-06-277143-4

☐ **BUDGET EUROPE** ACCESS® $18.00
0-06-277120-5

☐ **CAPE COD** ACCESS® $18.00
0-06-277123-X

☐ **CARIBBEAN** ACCESS® $18.50
0-06-277128-0

☐ **CHICAGO** ACCESS® $18.50
0-06-277144-2

☐ **FLORENCE/VENICE/MILAN** ACCESS® $18.50
0-06-277081-0

☐ **HAWAII** ACCESS® $18.50
0-06-277142-6

☐ **LAS VEGAS** ACCESS® $18.50
0-06-277177-9

☐ **LONDON** ACCESS® $18.50
0-06-277129-9

☐ **LOS ANGELES** ACCESS® $18.00
0-06-277131-0

☐ **MEXICO** ACCESS® $18.00
0-06-277127-2

☐ **MIAMI & SOUTH FLORIDA** ACCESS® $18.50
0-06-277178-7

☐ **MONTREAL & QUEBEC** ACCESS® $18.00
0-06-277079-9

☐ **NEW ORLEANS** ACCESS® $18.50
0-06-277176-0

☐ **NEW YORK CITY** ACCESS® $18.00
0-06-277124-8

☐ **NEW YORK CITY RESTAURANT** ACCESS®
$12.00
0-06-277130-2

☐ **ORLANDO & CENTRAL FLORIDA** ACCESS®
$18.50
0-06-277175-2

☐ **PARIS** ACCESS® $18.00
0-06-277132-9

☐ **PHILADELPHIA** ACCESS® $18.00
0-06-277065-9

☐ **ROME** ACCESS® $18.50
0-06-277150-7

☐ **SAN FRANCISCO** ACCESS® $18.00
0-06-277121-3

☐ **SAN FRANCISCO RESTAURANT** ACCESS®
$12.00
0-06-277126-4

☐ **SANTA FE/TAOS/ALBUQUERQUE** ACCESS®
$18.00
0-06-277148-5

☐ **SEATTLE** ACCESS® $18.00
0-06-277149-3

☐ **SKI COUNTRY** ACCESS®
Eastern United States $18.00
0-06-277125-6

☐ **SKI COUNTRY** ACCESS®
Western United States $18.50
0-06-277174-4

☐ **WASHINGTON DC** ACCESS® $18.00
0-06-277077-2

☐ **WINE COUNTRY** ACCESS®
France $18.50
0-06-277151-5

☐ **WINE COUNTRY** ACCESS®
Northern California $18.00
0-06-277122-1

Prices subject to change without notice.

Total for **ACCESS®** Guides:	$
Please add applicable sales tax:	
Add $4.00 for first book S&H, $1.00 per additional book:	
Total payment:	$

☐ Check or Money Order enclosed. Offer valid in the United States only.
Please make payable to HarperCollins*Publishers*.

☐ Charge my credit card ☐ American Express ☐ Visa ☐ MasterCard

Card no. _____ Exp. date _____

Signature _____

Send orders to: HarperCollins*Publishers*
P.O. Box 588
Dunmore, PA 18512-0588

Wherever you go, you need **ACCESS**®

Other Destinations:

- Barcelona
- Boston
- Budget Europe
- Cape Cod, Martha's Vineyard
  & Nantucket
- Caribbean
- Chicago
- Florence/Venice/Milan
- London
- Los Angeles
- Mexico
- Montreal & Quebec City

- New York City
- Paris
- Philadelphia
- Rome
- San Diego
- San Francisco
- Santa Fe/Taos/Albuquerque
- Seattle
- Ski Country Eastern US
- Washington DC
- Wine Country France
- Wine Country N. California

Pack lightly and carry the best travel guides going: ACCESS®. Arranged by neighborhood and featuring color-coded entries, ACCESS® guides are designed to help you explore—not to leave you standing on the corner thumbing madly through an index. Whether you are visiting Miami or Milan, you'll need a sturdy pair of walking shoes and plenty of ACCESS®.